CRICKET

A Modern Anthology

ALSO BY JONATHAN AGNEW

Thanks, Johnners
Aggers' Ashes

CRICKET

A Modern Anthology

Jonathan Agnew

blue door

First published in Great Britain in 2013 by
Blue Door
An imprint of HarperCollins*Publishers*
77–85 Fulham Palace Road,
Hammersmith, London W6 8JB

www.harpercollins.co.uk

This paperback edition 2014

A catalogue record for this book is
available from the British Library

Typeset by PDQ Digital Media Solutions Ltd, Bungay

ISBN: 978-0-00-746655-9

Printed and bound in Great Britain by
Clays Ltd, St Ives plc

MIX
Paper from
responsible sources
FSC C007454
FSC
www.fsc.org

FSC™ is a non-profit international organisation established to promote
the responsible management of the world's forests. Products carrying the
FSC label are independently certified to assure consumers that they come
from forests that are managed to meet the social, economic and
ecological needs of present and future generations,
and other controlled sources.

Find out more about HarperCollins and the environment at
www.harpercollins.co.uk/green

This book is dedicated to the memory of
Christopher Martin-Jenkins, who, through
his skilful broadcasting, prolific writing
and boundless love of the game, was
cricket's greatest friend.

Contents

The Illustrations   xi
Foreword by Rt Hon Sir John Major KG CH   xiv
Preface   xvii

Chapter 1: *The Great Controversies*   **2**

Sir Donald Bradman: *Farewell to Cricket*   42
Duncan Hamilton: *Harold Larwood*   54
Wisden Cricketers' Almanack 1934: *The Bowling
    Controversy – Text of the Cables*   62
    Sydney J. Southerton's Analysis   68
Christopher Douglas: *Jardine, A Spartan Cricketer*   73
Basil D'Oliveira: *The Basil D'Oliveira Affair*   81
Wisden Cricketers' Almanack 2012: *The Obituary*   89
    of Basil D'Oliveira
Sir Derek Birley: *A Social History of English Cricket*   96
David Tossell: *Grovel! The Story and Legacy of*   104
    the Summer of 1976
Paul Nixon: *Keeping Quiet: The Autobiography*   116
Martin Johnson: *Can't Bat, Can't Bowl, Can't Field*   120
Ed Hawkins: *Bookie Gambler Fixer Spy:*   127
    A Journey to the Heart of Cricket's Underworld
Vaibhav Purandare: *Sachin Tendulkar:*   139
    The Definitive Biography
Gideon Haigh: *Sphere of Influence: Writings on*   143
    Cricket and its Discontents
Steve James: *The Plan: How Fletcher and Flower*   146
    Transformed English Cricket

Chapter 2: *The Greatest Test Matches*   **154**

Richie Benaud: *A Tale of Two Tests: With Some*   175
    Thoughts on Captaincy
Ray Robinson: *The Wildest Tests*   185

Denzil Batchelor: *Games of a Lifetime* 205
Rob Steen: *500–1: The Miracle of Headingley '81* 219
Mike Brearley: *The Art of Captaincy* 229

Chapter 3: *The Professional* **238**

Leo McKinstry: *Jack Hobbs: England's* 265
   Greatest Cricketer
Max Davidson: *We'll Get 'Em in Sequins: Manliness,* 268
   Yorkshire Cricket and the Century That
   Changed Everything
John Arlott: *Fred: Portrait of a Fast Bowler* 281
Chris Waters: *Fred Trueman: The Authorised Biography* 289
Amol Rajan: *Twirlymen: The History of Cricket's* 299
   Greatest Spin Bowlers
Geoffrey Boycott: *Boycott On Cricket* 310
Mike Brearley: *The Art of Captaincy* 314
Simon Wilde: *Ian Botham: The Power and the Glory* 331
Phil Tufnell: *The Autobiography: What Now?* 338
Simon Hughes: *A Lot of Hard Yakka* 346
Matthew Hayden: *Standing My Ground* 350

Chapter 4: *Gentlemen and Players* **358**

Geoffrey Moorhouse: *The Best Loved Game* 374
Harry Pearson: *Slipless in Settle: A Slow* 382
   Turn Around Northern Cricket
Harry Thompson: *Penguins Stopped Play* 390
Marcus Berkmann: *Rain Men: The Madness of Cricket* 397
Marcus Berkmann: *Zimmer Men: The Trials and* 404
   Tribulations of the Ageing Cricketer
Michael Simkins: *Fatty Batter: How Cricket* 411
   Saved My Life (Then Ruined It)
R. Chandrasekar: *The Goat, the Sofa and Mr Swami* 418

Chapter 5: *The Pen is Mightier Than* **428**
  the Bat

Sir John Major: *More Than A Game: The Story of* 442
   Cricket's Early Years
R. C. Robertson-Glasgow: *46 Not Out* 449
Sir Neville Cardus: *Days in the Sun* 460
Richie Benaud: *Willow Patterns* 464

John Arlott: *Indian Summer* 472
Timeri N. Murari: *The Taliban Cricket Club* 476
Gideon Haigh: *Sphere of Influence: Writings on* 486
   Cricket and its Discontents
Christopher Martin-Jenkins: *CMJ: A Cricketing Life* 495

Acknowledgements 500
Index 503

The Illustrations

Section 1

The scoreboard at the end of England's first innings of the opening Test, Sydney, December 1932

Harold Larwood bowling to Bill Woodfull during the Fourth Test, Brisbane, February 1933

Basil D'Oliveira batting for England against Australia in the Fifth Test at the Oval, August 1968

Henry Olonga bowling for Zimbabwe against India in the World Cup in England, May 1999

Australia's Jeff Thomson bowling to Tony Greig during the Fourth Test, Sydney, January 1975

Michael Holding of West Indies bowling to Brian Close during the Second Test at Lord's, June 1976

Kerry Packer and Tony Greig outside the High Court in London, September 1977

Cricket under lights at the World Series Grand Final, Sydney, February 1979

Captains Alec Stewart of England and Hansie Cronje of South Africa toss up before the Second Test at Lord's, June 1998

Allan Donald stares down Michael Atherton during the Fourth Test at Trent Bridge, July 1998

The first ever tied Test, Australia v West Indies, Brisbane, December 1960

Mark Boucher celebrates as the scoreboard shows South Africa have overtaken Australia's record ODI score of 434, Johannesburg, March 2006

Ian Botham hooking Geoff Lawson during his innings of 149 not out in the Third Test at Headingley, July 1981

Bob Willis prepares to bowl during Australia's second innings when he took eight for 43 to win the match, Headingley, July 1981

Ian Botham shakes hands with his captain Mike Brearley as England win the Fourth Test at Edgbaston by 29 runs, August 1981

Geoff Miller catches last man Jeff Thomson to win the Fourth Test against Australia by two runs, Melbourne, December 1982

West Indies' Courtney Walsh celebrates a one-run victory against Australia in the Fourth Test, Adelaide, January 1993

Section 2

South African captain Kepler Wessels leads out his team against West Indies in the inaugural Test between the two sides, Barbados, April 1992

Kenny Benjamin dismisses South Africa's top scorer Andrew Hudson for 163, Barbados, April 1992

V. V. S. Laxman and Rahul Dravid leave the field having batted all day for India against Australia in the Second Test at Eden Gardens, March 2001

Harbhajan Singh dismisses Shane Warne to claim a hat-trick in Australia's first innings of the Second Test at Eden Gardens, March 2001

Andrew Flintoff consoles Brett Lee after England had beaten Australia by two runs in the Second Test at Edgbaston, August 2005

Australia's Glenn McGrath is injured during the warm-up before the start of play at Edgbaston, August 2005

Donald Bradman batting for Australia against England in the First Test at Trent Bridge, June 1948

Harold Larwood, who played only twenty-one Tests for England, and none after the Bodyline tour of 1932–3

Donald Bradman's last Test innings at the Oval, August 1948

Trevor Bailey batting for England against Australia during the Fifth Test at the Oval, August 1953

Fred Trueman taking his 300th Test wicket during the Fifth Test against Australia at the Oval, August 1964

Australian captain Richie Benaud bowling during the First Test against England, Brisbane, December 1958

Tony Greig bowling for England against India during the Second Test at Lord's, June 1974

David Steele batting for Northamptonshire, May 1975

Andy Roberts bowling for West Indies during the Second Test against Australia, Perth, December 1975

Ray Illingworth, captain of Leicestershire and previously of England, at the start of the 1974 season

Geoff Boycott scoring his 100th first-class century during the Fourth Test against Australia, Headingley, August 1977

Section 3

Shane Warne bowling England captain Mike Gatting with his first ball in an Ashes Test at Old Trafford, June 1993

Sachin Tendulkar receiving his award for a *Test Match Special* 'champagne moment' from the author during the Second Test at Lord's, June 1996

Muttiah Muralitharan bowling for Sri Lanka against England during the Second Test in Kandy, December 2003

Graeme Swann bowling for England against Sri Lanka during the Second Test at Lord's, June 2011

England captain Douglas Jardine at the crease wearing his trademark Harlequin cap

Wally Hammond of Gloucestershire and England

A poster advertising Len Hutton's benefit match at Scarborough, July 1950

Ted Dexter walking out to bat for Cambridge University, 1958

West Indian cricketers Kenneth Rickards, Frank Worrell, Clyde Walcott, Roy Marshall and Everton Weekes at St Pancras station en route to Australia, September 1951

West Indies fast bowler Charlie Griffith bowling for Burnley in the Lancashire League, August 1964

A game in progress at Belvoir Cricket Club in the evening sunshine

One of many games of cricket played on the vast expanse of open land at the Oval Maidan in Mumbai

Sir Neville Cardus making a typically flamboyant speech

John Arlott bringing his broadcasting career to a close during the Centenary Test between England and Australia at Lord's in 1980

The late Christopher Martin-Jenkins at home in 2008

Foreword

Rt Hon. Sir John Major KG CH

The words 'cricket' and 'Jonathan Agnew' have become synonymous to cricket lovers, and there can be no better guide to the evolution of the modern game.

It is a big story that deserves – and, in these pages, has – a sure guide.

By 1930, although cricket had matured from the country-house pastime of the pre-Grace years, it was still far from the game we know today. Since then, many more countries have entered the Test arena, and the administration of the game has passed into professional hands and away from gifted amateurs. Out-of-date class distinctions on the field have faded away – but only slowly, with reluctance – and the top-class game has become fully professional. New and shorter forms of cricket have emerged to attract millions of new supporters, alongside the grumbling disapproval of traditionalists.

To them, and to most cricket lovers, the spirit of the game – the way in which it is played – has always been at the heart of its charm. It is a rude shock when controversy enters the arena, and far worse when corruption is uncovered.

Jonathan Agnew's story begins with the Ashes series of 1932–3. It was on-field cricket at its most distasteful, as the English fast-bowling attack targeted 'bodyline' bowling at the Australian batsmen instead of their stumps. It was an unscrupulous tactic to curb the mammoth run scoring of Don Bradman. Today, with television tracking every ball, such a tactic would never survive, but 'bodyline' soured a whole series and scarred cricket.

Later, the English cricketing authorities – with an arrogance that, eighty years on, is scarcely believable – ordered Harold Larwood, their fast-bowling spearhead, to apologise. Larwood was entirely right to refuse, saying that he was upholding the instructions of his team captain, Douglas Jardine. But Jardine was a 'gentleman' and Larwood was not – and so it was he who was pilloried. It was, in every way, an ugly and shameful episode.

As a fast bowler, Larwood was one of the heroes that cricket throws up in every generation: their reputation becomes enshrined in the folklore of the game, and lasts long after they have left the field of play. Among the most cherished names, Bradman and Sobers may stand alone on their pedestal, but I fancy Shane Warne might one day join them on it. Most of these great cricketers are a credit to the game.

But not all: some heroes have revealed a dark side and been seduced and corrupted by money. Their names need not be repeated here but match-fixing poses a threat the authorities cannot ignore. Some cricket authorities have reacted vigorously to curtail this evil – but *all* need to do so. The 'Spirit of Cricket' is important to lovers of the game, and where that is flouted, they may turn away in disgust. The extent of corruption induced by betting scams is unknowable but, if it is tolerated by *any* authority, the damage will be acute.

Over recent decades, cricket has been broadcast to a global audience by radio and television. To the avid listener or viewer, the players representing teams on the far side of the world have become as familiar as the stars of their own country. The media coverage is comprehensive, and generally superb.

But cricket is more than a game. For countless millions, it is part of their lives, and given added drama and charm by the skill of the broadcasters. For me, cricket has always been pure pleasure when described by the likes of Rex Alston, John Arlott or Brian Johnston and – more recently – Henry Blofeld, Christopher Martin-Jenkins and the author of this book, Jonathan Agnew – that valuable hybrid of Test cricketer and professional broadcaster. Their sheer love of the game – and the romanticism, sentiment and sheer fun of it that they impart – has woven them into the warp and weft of cricket: it would be sad, indeed, if the contributions of such men were banished from the game.

And, to this observer, that seems a risk. Increasingly, the commentators and summarizers of top-class cricket are former eminent Test players. I welcome their arrival at the microphone because, to this particular cricket lover, they have added an extra dimension of understanding about the game. Their contribution is unique – but I hope it will never be exclusive: a mixture of broadcasters, cricketers and writers may offer the best depiction of the game to listeners and viewers.

In its infancy, cricket spread outwards from England as the British Empire was built. It took root and, as it did so, ceased to be an English game; each country played it in their own distinctive style. As the game spreads further, the focused aggression of the Australians; the Caribbean swagger of the West Indies; the suppleness of the Indians, may yet be joined by the national characteristics of the Afghans and the Chinese. If so, cricket will be the stronger for it.

The question that now arises is – whither cricket? The present growth of the game suggests confidence about its future from the grass roots upwards, with one reservation. The huge appeal of the shorter forms of the game – and the huge money-spinner it has become – means that cricket at the very highest level, five-day Test cricket, must be protected and cherished. It is, to my mind, the finest expression of the game, the peak of its art and, if it were diminished – or even crowded out – by mercenary considerations, then the game itself would surely suffer.

In its long history, cricket has been blessed with great literature: no game has ever attracted so many authors, or so much magnificent writing. In this book, Jonathan Agnew adds to this great canon, and draws on it to illustrate the evolutionary changes of recent decades.

This book is for every lover of cricket who wishes to dig deeper into the history of the game, through the words and sentiments of those who shared – or still share – their passion for it.

March 2013

Preface

Cricket, more than any other sport, has always lent itself to expressive colourful writing alongside intelligent debate – in the sports pages of our daily newspapers, over the broadcasting airwaves, through the pages of *Wisden* dating back to 1864 or, indeed, around the bar in the village pub. Such is the depth and complexity of cricket – spanning its history, politics and characters – that a single, universal view is extremely rare. Even such momentous events as Bodyline, the D'Oliveira affair and World Series Cricket were all strenuously argued about, usually from diametrically opposed positions.

The beauty of assembling an anthology such as this is that those opinions, assessments and descriptions can all be brought together in one place. So this is where we are able to read about and compare the lifestyles and characters of two of England's finest fast bowlers, Harold Larwood and Fred Trueman; savour the deeds of opening batsmen Jack Hobbs and my old friend Geoffrey Boycott; consider first-hand reflections on Bodyline by Sir Donald Bradman; and enjoy a graphic description of the first tied Test between Australia and West Indies by Richie Benaud, who lost his wicket to the second ball of that frantic final over delivered by Wes Hall.

To be given the opportunity to sit, read and select extracts from the works of some of cricket's finest writers and players has been a most rewarding experience. The modern game is so time-consuming – with matches coming thick and fast and increasingly demanding deadlines to hit – that it is difficult sometimes to sit back, take a breath and reflect properly on what has just taken place. However, a book provides the opportunity to include additional information that was not available at the time and that vital element of context, which can only properly be given with the passing of the years. I have frequently found myself surprised as new light is shed on a subject I thought I knew reasonably well. For the first time, for instance, we learn that Basil D'Oliveira was the selectors' third-choice replacement for the injured Tom Cartwright in 1968; he was definitely not rushed into the squad for that ill-fated tour as the South African government believed.

I am delighted that this book has offered me the chance to explore, and now share, some of the most joyful, illuminating and elegant writing ever produced about cricket – without doubt the best sport in the world.

Jonathan Agnew, March 2013

THE GREAT CONTROVERSIES

'I have sacrificed cricket's most coveted job for a cause which I believe could be in the interests of cricket the world over.'

Tony Greig on his transition to Kerry Packer's World Series Cricket

Tearful Batsman (after defying Umpire's ruling). 'All right, I'll go!
But it ain't cricket. They wouldn't do that at Lord's.'

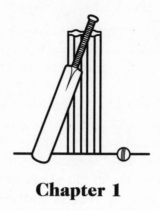

Chapter 1

'I don't want to see you, Mr Warner. There are two teams out there; one is trying to play cricket and the other is not.'

Australian captain Bill Woodfull's disdainful response to the
England manager's suppliant knock on the Australian's
dressing room door during the 1933 Adelaide Test.

G iven that cricket is supposed to stand for everything that is decent and upstanding in the world, it is remarkable how often down the years that the 'sport of gentlemen' has found itself embroiled in bitter controversies and rancour. It is also surprising how these disagreements quickly escalate far beyond the field of play – even in some cases leading to governmental involvement. Surprising, that is, until you consider the framework of international cricket, and how the sport was taken from the United Kingdom to the far-flung corners of the globe in the first place.

For that, we need to travel back to the time to what was supposedly the glorious age of the British Empire. Glorious for Britain, certainly, but not quite so much fun for those who suddenly found themselves conquered ('discovered' in some cases) and ruthlessly exploited as the developing European countries set about expanding their global trade.

Britain was not alone. The Dutch were particularly keen rivals in the seventeenth and eighteenth centuries and evidence of their overseas occupations can be found on the cricket fields of Sri Lanka and South Africa today. Sri Lanka's Burgher people are a Eurasian ethnic group formed by the union of predominantly Dutch settlers and local Sinhalese women. Angelo Mathews, the Sri Lanka vice-captain, is a member of the Burgher community. So too are Graeme Labrooy and the towering Michael Vandort, scorer of two laboured centuries against England in 2006 and 2007, who at six foot five must be the tallest-ever Sri Lankan Test cricketer. Meanwhile, descendants of the first Dutch colonists are regular members of the South Africa cricket team, and there is dedicated television and radio commentary broadcast throughout the Republic in Afrikaans, the guttural language that evolved from Dutch into a daughter language. Ewie Cronje, father of South Africa's disgraced former captain Hansie Cronje, whose Huguenot ancestors took part in the Great Trek away from British rule in the 1830s, is one such specialist commentator.

The French and the Portuguese were also busily establishing overseas trading posts but following the defeat of Napoleonic France in 1815 Britain enjoyed a century of almost unchallenged dominance, to the point that by 1922 almost a quarter of the globe and a fifth of the world's population was ruled by the United Kingdom. (It is worth bearing in mind that this did not include the United States of America, which had successfully fought for its independence by 1783.) Wherever Britain ruled, cricket was played, and all the Test-playing nations – Australia, Bangladesh, India, New Zealand, Pakistan, South Africa, Sri Lanka, West Indies and Zimbabwe – were former colonies within the British Empire. All but Zimbabwe are still associated with the UK through membership of the Commonwealth.

Bloody conflicts were usually Britain's answer to putting down local insurgency, and these have left deep scars in the history of the Empire. Britain was responsible for much of the slave trade that transported Africans in the most ghastly conditions imaginable to the Caribbean to work on the sugar plantations. While African slaves worked in the fields cutting corn, Asians were shipped in from the Indian subcontinent to become the white-collar workers of the time. The resulting division between the two racial groups is responsible for serious antagonism in countries such as Guyana, and Trinidad and Tobago today.

A drive along the potholed roads of Antigua to the little town of Liberta, which lies to the south of the island, is a reminder of those early days, for this is the settlement that was established by the first freed slaves in 1835. Meanwhile, on Barbados, on the main highway from the airport you will encounter the Emancipation Statue, which dramatically portrays a muscle-bound Afro-Caribbean slave stripped to the waist and staring skywards with a broken chain dangling from each wrist. The locals call him Bussa, after a legendary figure in the island's history who helped inspire a revolt against slavery in 1816. Lining the highway is a succession of roundabouts dedicated to notable politicians and great Barbadian cricketers like Sir Garfield Sobers, Sir Everton Weekes and the first black captain of West Indies, Sir Frank Worrell. I wonder if the planners ever intended that this series of roundabouts on such a friendly island should illustrate just how closely the Caribbean's unhappy history is associated with cricket. Little surprise, then, that some opponents of the mighty West Indies sides in the 1970s and 80s believed that seeking revenge for the past lay behind the hostility of the most feared battery of fast bowlers there has ever been – that it was racially motivated, in other words. The West Indian players of the time deny this absolutely, pointing out that they were as driven and aggressive when they played against India and Pakistan, for example, as they were against England or Australia. Geoffrey Boycott, who stood in their way many times as an opening batsman, states categorically that he never heard a racist comment, or felt racially intimidated. Nevertheless, I am sure they gained a lot of motivation from their identity and great pride from being the first predominantly Afro-Caribbean team to sit on top of the world, relishing the new-found respect that came with it.

When the British claimed South Africa from the Dutch in 1806, they discovered a colony that was already established strictly along racial lines. The abolition of slavery in 1834 proved to be the final straw for the Boer settlers, who, in their frustration at British rule, began their migration inland from the Cape on what became known as the Great Trek. They established Afrikaner strongholds, which developed into Boer republics in the Transvaal and Orange Free State, thus setting out the background for the two Boer Wars against the British in the late nineteenth century. During the second (1899–1902) an estimated twenty-eight thousand Boers – many of them women and children – died in appalling conditions in concentration camps set up by the British, whose victory established the Union of South Africa, a dominion of the British Empire. In 1931 it gained its independence from Britain.

With racial segregation already implemented to some degree under colonial rule, independence enabled stricter laws to be imposed by the National Party, culminating in the establishment of *apartheid* in 1948 and the classification of people into four racial groups ('native', 'white', 'coloured' and 'Asian'). Every part of everyday life was affected by apartheid, including cricket. The whites had their own cricket board, the South African Cricket Association (SACA), and only white players could represent South Africa. Non-whites were welcome to watch, but had to do so in segregated parts of the cricket grounds. Despite South Africa's opposition in those days being exclusively from England, Australia and New Zealand (i.e. white), the non-white spectators usually vented their feelings by supporting the visitors. The D'Oliveira affair of 1968 (discussed at length later in this chapter) highlighted the true horror of apartheid to the world. The sporting isolation of South Africa contributed strongly to the dismantling of that abhorrent political system, and cricket played a leading role.

Over the border, in what is now Zimbabwe, the British formed the colony of Southern Rhodesia in 1895. This became simply Rhodesia when the then Prime Minister Ian Smith declared unilateral independence from Britain in 1965. The Republic of Rhodesia was proclaimed in 1970 but was recognized only by its neighbour South Africa until full independence from Britain was gained after years of civil war, known as the Bush War, and Zimbabwe was formed in 1980. Zimbabwe appeared in the 1983 Cricket World Cup, famously beating Australia by 13 runs at Trent Bridge, and played its first Test match in 1992.

The Indian subcontinent was inextricably linked with the British Empire for centuries. Sri Lanka, formerly Ceylon, was ruled by the British from 1815, when once again they ousted the Dutch, and then imported up to a million Tamils from southern India to work in the tea and coffee plantations for which Sri Lanka is famous.

The local Buddhist and Sinhalese population believed that their British rulers showed favouritism towards the Tamil immigrants, creating a schism between the communities. Caused directly by colonialism, this produced a long-running conflict and a civil war lasting twenty-five years that has cost an estimated hundred thousand lives and led to accusations of human-rights abuses by the Sri Lankan government when the Liberation Tigers of Tamil Eelam (LTTE) were apparently wiped out in 2009.

If anyone still harbours any doubts about the domination of the British Empire, then India, which had to be split into three countries, provides the most obvious and richest legacy. Pakistan and Bangladesh (formerly East Pakistan) are the direct results of colonialism, having been formed by the partition of British India on the basis of religious demographics. The plan approved by the British government in 1947 drew lines and frontiers where none previously existed to establish the Islamic state of Pakistan in order to enable the Hindus to live separately from the minority Muslims, and vice versa, if they chose to do so. Pakistan was divided into two, East and West, with the small matter of a thousand miles of Indian mainland between them. Estimates vary as to how many lost their lives as 14.5 million people rushed to relocate in their preferred country, but it is accepted that up to one million perished. Tensions dramatically escalated between the two religions, which had never been so obviously separated before, and such was the hostility and mistrust that relations between India and Pakistan have been plagued ever since. Ownership of Kashmir remains hotly disputed by India and Pakistan, but Bangladesh broke free from Pakistan after the brutal Bangladesh Liberation War in 1971. This conflict produced the highest number of prisoners of war since the Second World War, and an estimated ten million refugees flooded the eastern states of India.

British interest in India began with the traders dealing primarily in tea, cotton, silk and opium who set sail in 1601 to form the East India Company. The Dutch and Portuguese had already established trading posts in Eastern India and hostilities between the three were commonplace, but as Britain gained supremacy against the Europeans – including the French, who were late arrivals in that part of the world – relations with the suppressed locals were often fractious. The best known of the early uprisings occurred in June 1756 when the Nawab of Bengal attacked and took the British fort in Calcutta. Those British who were captured by the Nawab's forces were placed in a dungeon measuring 14 ft by 18 ft, which became known as the Black Hole of Calcutta. In the stifling summer heat, it is claimed 123 of the 146 prisoners died as a result of suffocation, crushing or heat stroke. Major-General Robert Clive attacked the Nawab's camp in February 1757 and the victory that followed resulted in the Nawab surrendering control of Calcutta back to the British. The Battle of Plassey followed in June and produced another victory for Clive over the Nawab, whose troops had failed to protect their gunpowder against the rain and were powerless to fight back. This established British military supremacy in Bengal and finally over Northern India as well, and Clive, by now known as Clive of India, returned to London as a legendary figure – and a very wealthy one too.

One hundred years later there was a mutiny among the sepoys – the Indian members of the British East India Company's army – that quickly spread to most of Northern India, and became known as the Indian Rebellion. The British held out under siege for six months in the city of Lucknow, where more than three thousand men, women and children gathered in the Regency Compound; only one thousand survived. Fifty miles down the road, hundreds more lost their lives in the Siege of Cawnpore (now Kanpur) and the subsequent Bibighar Massacre after an offer of safe passage was reneged upon. I have visited the beautifully maintained Kanpur Memorial Church (originally called All Souls Cathedral), with its many monuments and graves for the British who died there, and recall seeing many headstones bearing the inscription 'murdered by mutineers'.

The uprising, which has also been described as India's First War of Independence, was finally put down in Gwalior the following year, but the rebellion led directly to the dissolution of the East India Company. Back home in London, it was decided that British rule of India had to become much more strictly administered and controlled. The army was reorganized, and the financial system restructured. In 1858, British Crown rule – the British Raj – was established and would last until 1947.

The earliest record of cricket being played anywhere on the subcontinent is of a game played by British sailors in Cambay, near Baroda, in 1721. There is some uncertainty about the precise formation of the Calcutta Cricket and Football Club, but it was certainly in existence in 1792. Following the definitive battle between the British and Tipu Sultan, the Ruler of Mysore, which strengthened the British grip on southern India, another cricket club was founded at Seringapatam in 1799. The spread of cricket throughout the subcontinent had begun.

In those early days, the locals clearly only made up the numbers and there was the feeling that if you played cricket alongside the British, you might receive favourable treatment from them. But as their fascination for cricket developed rapidly, the Indian players also became rather good at it, and were more than capable of holding their own. A game between Madras and Calcutta in 1864 lays claim to being the first first-class match played on the subcontinent, but the most significant development was the founding of the Bombay Presidency Match in 1877, between the European players of the Bombay Gymkhana and the Parsees of the Zoroastrian Cricket Club. This grand occasion was granted first-class status in 1892 and a mark of how Indian cricket had evolved so quickly was the victory that year by the local Parsees over the Europeans. In 1906, the Hindus of Bombay joined the now triangular tournament. In their ranks was the left-arm spinner, Palwankar Baloo, a man whose life story provides a fascinating insight into how the role of cricket was by now expanding in Indian society.

Baloo was born in 1876 into the Dalit population, which according to the Hindu caste system meant that he was one of the lowest of the low, an 'untouchable'. His first job was tending the cricket pitch at a club run by the Parsees in Poona (Pune), where he also bowled occasionally to the members. At the age of 17 he moved to the predominantly European Pune Cricket Club, where he earned four rupees a month rolling the pitch and preparing the practice facilities. Again, he bowled to the members and, encouraged by the captain, J. G. Greig, quickly developed into a fine spinner. However, because of his background, Baloo was never allowed to bat.

When a Hindu club challenged the Europeans to a match, and with Baloo clearly good enough for selection, his lowly status led to several members of the Hindu team refusing to play alongside him. But a compromise was reached. On the field, Baloo was treated as an equal to every other cricketer in the match. However, during the intervals, he was segregated to the extent that while lunch was taken inside the pavilion, Baloo had to sit outside and eat alone.

As time passed, and Baloo's reputation grew, he was permitted to congregate with his team-mates off the field as well as on it, and when an outbreak of the plague encouraged Baloo to move to Bombay in 1896, he played for the Army. Despite further protests from members of the higher castes, Baloo also represented the Hindu Gymkhana Club and played in the famous Presidency matches of 1906 and 1907 between the Europeans and the Hindus, which were comfortably won by the Hindus by 109 runs and 238 runs respectively. These were highly significant victories not merely in cricketing terms, but particularly in the wider political sense, being portrayed in many quarters as a victory for the locals against the colonialists.

Baloo toured England in 1911 and was the outstanding player, taking 114 wickets at an average of 19 each, on what was otherwise an unsuccessful trip for the Indians. Despite regularly playing in what became (in 1912, through the addition of the Muslims) the Bombay Quadrangular tournament between 1912 and 1919, he was never allowed to become captain of the Hindu team, despite mounting pressure for him to do so. He attained the status of vice-captain in 1920 and, in a sign of the times (Mahatma Gandhi's freedom campaign was beginning to gather pace), the captain of the Hindu Gymkhana, M. D. Pai, who, being a Brahmin, was a member of the highest caste, deliberately left the field on frequent occasions, enabling Baloo to lead the team in his absence. This was surely the first time a lowly Dalit was able to command those above his station.

As a footnote, Baloo became politically active in later life, twice losing elections as he continued his personal fight against the segregation of the Indian classes. Although he had become a comparatively influential figure, it is as the very first in India's proud tradition of beguiling spin bowlers that Palwankar Baloo is best remembered.

Kumar Shri Ranjitsinhji enjoyed as different a background from Baloo as it is possible to imagine. An Indian prince who was educated at Cambridge University, Ranji overcame racial taboo to play fifteen Tests for England between 1896 and 1902 before India was admitted to international cricket. He scored 62 and 154 not out on his début against Australia, and he became synonymous with a new range of back-foot, wristy strokes such as the late cut and leg glance. This innovation combined with great flair earned him recognition among the very best batsmen there have ever been. In

1904 he returned to India to reclaim his seat as the Maharaja Jam Sahib of Nawanagar and died there in 1933, the year after India was granted Test status.

It is easy to imagine how a young child reading the history books in a school in any of the countries that were colonized could develop a deep-seated resentment of the British. At the very least, it would be very easy for a skilled orator or motivator to press the right nationalistic buttons and, in the cricketing context, produce a team that desperately wants to put one over its former colonial masters. But there is more to this in that local rivalries and tensions have also been created by colonialism and are played out on cricket fields around the world. This is especially the case whenever India meets Pakistan – fanatical spectators have been known to commit suicide following their team's defeat. And there is nothing that New Zealanders enjoy more than their all-too-rare successes over Australia – although this has more to do with the relative size of the two countries than anything else. It might be argued that these historical rifts have given international cricket matches an extra edge, but it is an unfortunate way of achieving sporting competition. This helps to explain the deep-rooted rivalry that is still keenly felt today. The influence of the British Empire created local conflicts where none had previously existed, and while that has helped to establish the intense rivalry between India and Pakistan, for example, the strong sense of injustice that still lies only fractionally beneath the surface means that nothing motivates England's opponents more than the desire to beat their old colonial master. It is no coincidence, therefore, that most of the really serious incidents in cricket's history have involved England.

While the British colonists were busy acting as cricketing crusaders, taking the game with them all around the world, they were also very keen to ensure that the 'gentlemen's game' was always played to what they believed were their own exacting standards of sportsmanship. Cricket has always been synonymous with fair play, giving rise to that well-known expression: 'It's not cricket.' The requirement of everyone to play within the spirit of the game is enshrined in the Laws of cricket, and there is a very strong emphasis on respecting one's opponents and always accepting the umpire's decision. It was designed to be a genteel and aesthetically pleasing sport, but also one that requires bravery and helps to develop character in its younger participants.

Given the history between the two countries, it is perhaps no surprise that England and Australia became embroiled in cricket's first serious controversy. Test matches between the two always have an extra edge to them, dating back to the very first encounter in 1877, with Australia's past as a former penal colony providing the background to the competitiveness on the field. Usually this is little more than colourful banter, or 'sledging' as the Australians call it, but on the Ashes tour of 1932–3 the hostility was central to the way the Tests were played. That series will forever be known as the Bodyline series.

Cricket matches between Australia and England have been defined by their uncompromising and overtly competitive nature, born out of their shared colonial history and compounded by the wish on the part of most Australians to see themselves viewed as every bit the equal of the mother country. This may have been the historical context, but the seeds of arguably the greatest controversy the game has ever witnessed lay in the vastly differing backgrounds of the two central protagonists: one a patrician Englishman whose philosophy of winning at all costs would shake the game to its very foundations and, in so doing, impact severely on the relations between the two countries; the other an Australian cricketing genius whose achievements while touring England in 1930 meant that finding a strategy to neutralize his sublime run-scoring prowess would be vital if England were to stand any chance of regaining the Ashes.

Douglas Robert Jardine was a son of the British Empire. Born to Scottish parents in Bombay in 1900, cricket was an intrinsic part of his upbringing. His father, Malcom Jardine, had played first-class cricket for Oxford University and Middlesex before becoming a successful barrister in India.

As was typical of the time, at the age of 9, Douglas was sent from India to live with his mother's sister in St Andrews in Scotland from where he was to be educated at boarding schools in England. By the age of 12 he was captaining his school XI to an unbeaten record in his final year. Already the self-belief, some would say an unwillingness to listen to the counsel and advice of others, was showing itself as Jardine repeatedly disagreed with his school cricket coach about his batting method.

While the world descended into the maelstrom of the First World War, a 14-year-old Jardine entered Winchester College, one of

England's oldest and finest public schools. Life at the school was arduous, the prevailing ethos austere, the discipline bordering on the harsh. Sport was an important part of the curriculum, a curriculum designed to prepare the boys for a life of governance and, in many cases, future military duty with every prospect of seeing war first hand. Jardine entered the school with a reputation as a cricketer and soon established himself as an all-round sportsman, playing football, rackets and Winchester College football (a rugby-union-like game with a peculiar set of rules only understood and esteemed by Wykehamists), but it was for cricket that Jardine earned renown. He was in the First XI within three years and remained there until his last year, when he captained the side and topped the batting averages. With him leading the side and scoring 89, Jardine's Winchester College beat Eton College in 1919 – the first time in twelve years Winchester had gained the upper hand. Later in life and after retiring from cricket, Jardine would say that the 89 he scored on a sunny afternoon as his school days came to an end and the world put itself to rights after unimaginable horror was his favourite innings.

Jardine entered Oxford University in late 1919 and won his Blue initially for real tennis. The following year he made his first-class début as an opening batsman, winning his cricketing Blue. In 1921 Jardine encountered an Australian touring side for the first time when Oxford played Warwick Armstrong's side, who had been dominating the season up until that point. Jardine battled to 96 to save the match but was unable to reach his century before the game ended. While contemporary reports suggest the Australians were keen to help Jardine reach the landmark (his 96 not out was the highest score by any player against the Australians so far on the tour), offering some particularly soft bowling, it was not to be. It has been suggested that the request by the Australians to have the game reduced to two days from the planned three in order that they might have a rest day between matches combined with alleged on-field sarcasm by Armstrong directed at Jardine's slow progress sowed the seeds of what would be a lifelong dislike, bordering on hatred, for Australia and Australians by Jardine.

The innings against Australia brought Jardine to the notice of the England selectors and the influential Pelham 'Plum' Warner, and it was thought he might have been selected to play for England in the forthcoming series, but while remaining in contention for a place for some time, he was not selected. Jardine now joined Surrey, replacing the injured Jack Hobbs as opening bat before dropping down the order to number five. What became increasingly clear was that Jardine was a batsman of caution, defensively minded, who came into his own when the pressure to occupy the crease was at a premium.

The following season was largely lost to injury. In 1923, his last year at Oxford, he returned to cricket but was not appointed captain of the side and it has been suggested that his austere unfriendly manner was the reason he was denied the honour, although his absence through injury the previous season may have been a more likely reason. During a match later in the season, Jardine deliberately used his pads to defend his wicket. While within the rules, it was widely seen and reported in the newspapers as being against the spirit of the game. Jardine's biographers have noted that it was this adverse criticism that led to his deep-seated hostility to the press thereafter, something he would retain for the rest of his life.

After Oxford Jardine began to train as a solicitor while playing for Surrey as an amateur. In 1924 he was appointed vice-captain to Percy Fender. As will be discussed elsewhere, captaincy of a county side was the prerogative of the amateurs and although the Surrey side of the day featured Jack Hobbs, still it was Jardine who was seen as the rightful appointee. In the 1927 season Jardine scored 1,002 runs at an average of 91.09 and was named by *Wisden* as one of their five cricketers of the year. By the end of the 1928 season, when he made his Test début against West Indies, selection for the forthcoming winter tour to Australia was seen as a certainty.

Australia's ageing post-war team had broken up in 1926 and England would be facing an inexperienced side led by Jack Ryder. There is no doubt Jardine's first tour of Australia was a success. He began with three consecutive centuries. But already the Australian crowds had begun barracking him for slow scoring and less than agile fielding. Nevertheless, Donald Bradman was full of praise, calling Jardine's third century one of the finest exhibitions of stroke play he had witnessed. The Australian crowds, however, took an active dislike to, of all things, Jardine's choice of headwear.

Oxford University traditionally awarded a Harlequin cap to those who played good cricket. Former Oxford and Cambridge men often wore these caps while batting, in England at least, but it was less usual to wear them while fielding, and, when combined with

Jardine's aloof, angular and unresponsive manner, it inflamed the essentially decent but egalitarian nature of the Australian crowd, whose mood descended from good-natured barracking to outright hostility and abuse. Journalist and Test cricketer Jack Fingleton, who would have an important but disputed role during the Bodyline series, would say afterwards that Jardine had ample opportunity to win over the Australian crowds by the simple gestures of a self-deprecating smile and the odd joke at his own expense. The crowd was knowledgeable and had little doubt about Jardine's capability as a batsman, but Australians like their sportsmen to be human and free of condescension – characteristics far from being evident in Jardine's manner and bearing.

Jardine's good form with the bat continued and his resolute crease-occupying focus played a vital role as England secured victories in the first two Tests. In the Third Test England were left with the difficult task of scoring 332 runs to win on a rain-damaged wicket. In one of their most famous partnerships, Jack Hobbs and Herbert Sutcliffe put on 105. Hobbs had sent a message to the dressing room saying Jardine should be the next man in even though he was due to bat lower down the order. When Hobbs was dismissed Jardine came in and, despite finding batting extremely difficult, saw out the remainder of the day. England went on to take an unlikely win and many commentators said that only Jardine could have coped with the difficult conditions.

In Tasmania Jardine posted his highest first-class score of 214. England won the Fourth Test, Jardine and Hammond putting on the then highest third-wicket partnership in Test history of 262.

Australia won the final Test in Melbourne during which Jardine was used, unsuccessfully, as an opener replacing the injured Sutcliffe. After Jardine had completed his second innings (out for a first-ball duck), he immediately crossed Australia to catch a boat to India for a holiday. This was the era of timeless Tests, and although this was the fifth day, there remained three days of play. Whether his departure was planned or his tolerance of Australia and Australians had finally reached breaking point remains unclear to this day. Nevertheless, the mutual antipathy had been firmly established and would only grow over the next four years, culminating in the events of the 1932–3 series.

The Ashes series of 1928–9 also saw the Test début of a player who would go on to rewrite the record books, find cricketing immortality and unintentionally ensure that forever after Douglas Jardine would be remembered as an unconscionable villain and would-be destroyer of the great game.

When Donald Bradman was two and half years old, his parents moved the family 260 km east from his birthplace, Cootamundra, New South Wales, to the small town of Bowral, where as a schoolboy he would spend countless hours hitting a golf ball with a cricket stump against the curved wall of a water tank, learning to anticipate its unpredictable rebound. By the age of 12 he had scored his first century and at 13 he stepped into the local Bowral team captained by his uncle when they were a player short, scoring 37 and 29 not out in his two innings. He would become a regular for the side, making prodigious scores in local competitions. Bradman's meteoric rise to the heights of the game was under way.

By 1926, an ageing Australian national side was in decline and after England had won the Ashes in the summer, a number of Australia's players retired. Bradman's prolific scoring for Bowral had come to the attention of the New South Wales Cricket Association, who were eager to find new talent. Invited to a practice session in Sydney, Bradman was chosen for the Country Week tournament, where his performances were good enough for an invitation to play grade cricket for St George in Sydney during the 1926–7 season. The following season, at the age of 19, Bradman made his first-class début for NSW, replacing the unfit Archie Jackson at the Adelaide Oval and scoring a century.

In 1928 England would be visiting Australia to defend the Ashes. Against England in early touring matches Bradman scored 87 and 132, both not out, and was picked for the First Test at Brisbane. As is the usual way of things, Euripides had it right when he said, 'Those whom God wishes to destroy, He first makes mad.' In only his tenth first-class match, Bradman's Test début was a salutary lesson as Australia collapsed to 66 all out in their second innings, suffering a defeat by 675 runs – a record defeat that still stands today. Bradman was dropped for the Second Test.

Recalled for Melbourne, he scored 112 in the second innings, becoming the youngest player at the time to make a Test century. By the end of the season Bradman had amassed 1,690 first-class runs, averaging 93.88, and scored his first multiple century in Sheffield Shield cricket (340 not out against Victoria). The following year he would set a new world record for first-class cricket by scoring 452 not out against Queensland at the SCG. The gods of cricket had now changed their minds, shining brightly on their young protégé – and would do so for the next twenty years.

England were favourites to retain the Ashes in 1930, but the true measure of Bradman's genius was yet to register with England's supporters. He scored 236 at Worcester in the opening match and by the end of May had scored 1,000 first-class runs, the first Australian to achieve this feat. He scored a century in the First Test, but Australia lost the game. Then came the Second Test at Lord's. Bradman's contribution of 254 to a first-innings total of 729 ensured a series-levelling win for Australia.

For England things would only get worse as the Third Test at Leeds got under way on a hot day in July. On the first day Bradman scored a century before lunch. He added a second between lunch and tea, and was 309 not out at the close. He remains the only Test player in history to score 300 in a single day. His eventual tally of 334 set another world record. Poor weather saved England's blushes and the match was drawn. The Fourth Test was also a weather-affected draw.

The Fifth and final deciding Test would be played at the Oval. The weather still had its part to play as England posted a first-innings score of 405, taking three rain-interrupted days to get there. Bradman, batting in his customary number three position, added another double century, reaching 232 before being caught behind the stumps by George Duckworth off Harold Larwood. Bradman and Bill Ponsford (110) ensured that Australia had secured a 290-run lead.

However, the conditions and Larwood's fast, short-pitched bowling on a lively rain-affected pitch and Bradman's apparent difficulties were what caught the eye of certain interested spectators. A number of players and journalists thought they detected a distinct unease in Bradman as he struggled with fast, rising deliveries. Nothing could be done with this information now as England were soundly beaten by an innings and surrendered the Ashes.

It was the start of the modern age and Bradman's innings had been caught on moving film. England would have a chance to regain the Ashes over the winter of 1932–3 but to do that they would have to find a way to conquer the greatest batsman the world had ever seen. Maybe the answer lay in the grainy black and white footage?

The story goes that Jardine, on seeing the film, cried out, 'I've got it! He's yellow!' Percy Fender was also in receipt of letters from Australia that described how Australian batsmen were increasingly moving across their stumps towards the off in order to play the ball away to leg. Once the MCC had appointed Jardine captain of the 1932–3 tour to Australia, the possibility that Bradman might be exposed by short-pitched deliveries on the line of the leg stump took hold and a strategy to defeat him, and thus the Australians, was born.

The success of the tactic would rely on England fielding bowlers who could deliver balls with great venom and accuracy. A meeting with Nottinghamshire's captain, Arthur Carr, and his two pacemen, Harold Larwood and Bill Voce, was arranged. Could they repeatedly bowl at leg stump and get the ball to rear up and into the batsman's body? Both agreed they could and felt it might be an effective tactic. A cordon of close fielders would be set on the leg side. The facing batsman would have to choose between ducking, being hit, fending the ball off or executing a hook shot. The last two options are risky with fielders set for catches close to the wicket and deep on the boundary. Fast-pitched balls on the line of leg would also ensure scoring was kept to a minimum.

There was nothing as radical in this as the eventual outcry would suggest. Leg theory had been utilized in the county game and in Australia in previous seasons, although not at the same intensity, and the main criticism it drew was that it always proved an unedifying spectacle for the watching crowds.

Larwood and Voce set about practising Jardine's plan during the remainder of the 1932 season. On 17 September 1932 the MCC team boarded the Orient liner *Orontes* at Tilbury and set sail for the Australian port of Fremantle.

Their arrival in Western Australia was a good-natured affair; they were greeted by a large crowd and the crew of Australian cruiser *Canberra* lined the side and sang 'For They Are Jolly Good Fellows'.

A press conference with the manager of the MCC side, Pelham 'Plum' Warner, was arranged. Warner had led two tours to Australia before the First World War and had a deep respect and liking for the country and its people. In addition to which few men have had such a profound love for the great game and its central ethos of fair play as Warner. On the face of it, he was the ideal spokesman for the team and the perfect team manager. But even now the central issues that would dog the series arose in the press conference.

At the time there was a real danger that the player whom every Australian wanted to see and who was expected to carry all before him would be absent from the series. Bradman was in dispute with the Australian Board of Control after he had entered into a contract with the *Sydney Sun* to write for them during the forthcoming series, a practice the Board of Control had banned all players selected for Test duty from doing. Bradman was adamant that he had signed a contract and was duty-bound to honour it. For a while it looked as if *Hamlet* would be without its prince. Warner refused to comment on that issue but a follow-up question was rather more prescient. Asked about the recent and excessive use of 'bump balls' by Bill Bowes, Warner played it straight back: 'Bowes is a splendid bowler and have not fast bowlers bumped the ball before?'

The first sight Australians had of fast leg theory (the term 'bodyline' was yet to be employed) was during a warm-up game in Melbourne in late November. The England side was led by Jardine's deputy, Bob Wyatt, who deployed the full leg-side tactic for the first time on the tour. Woodfull resorted to unorthodox shotmaking with what looked liked an overhead tennis smash action and England were convinced their tactics were sound, but the crowd's vocal displeasure was a harbinger of what was to follow.

Australia lost badly by ten wickets in the First Test at Sydney. Although Bradman's dispute with the Board of Control had been resolved, he was missing through illness. Larwood roared in, taking ten wickets in the match. Only an innings by Stan McCabe, who stood resolute hooking and pulling with scant regard for his personal safety, salvaged Australia's pride.

The Melbourne Test began with questions about who would captain Australia. Woodfull's captaincy was confirmed only minutes before the game, delaying the toss; it has been suggested that the Board of Control were considering replacing him in the light of his steadfast refusal to retaliate by allowing Australian bowlers to bowl in an intimidatory manner. Vice-captain Richardson had advocated overt retaliation, but Woodfull had immediately responded by saying, 'There is no way I will be influenced to adopt such tactics which bring such discredit to the game.'

In a low-scoring match, Bradman was dismissed on the opening day for a duck (not to a bodyline ball, it should be noted) to the shock and dismay of the Melbourne crowd, while Jardine was openly exultant at his nemesis's demise. However, Bradman would score 103 not out in Australia's second-innings score of 191, ensuring that the Australians beat England handsomely by 111 runs. Many jubilant Australians thought they had found the tactics to overcome the hostility of the English attack, but it would prove to be Bradman's only century of the series and Larwood, in particular, had been badly hampered by a slow pitch (and an injury).

The series moved on to Adelaide, to perhaps the most beautiful cricket ground in the world, which was shortly to witness scenes that would reverberate all the way back to Lord's – and whose aftershocks can, arguably, still be felt today.

On a hot 14 January 1933 a record crowd of nearly fifty-one thousand packed into the ground. It was the second day of the Test and England's innings closed with 341 runs on the board, which represented a good recovery after a particularly poor start.

After Australian opener Jack Fingleton was dismissed by Gubby Allen for a duck, Bradman joined Woodfull at the crease. Larwood had discovered that in the conditions he was able to swing the ball into Woodfull, rather than moving it away, as was usual when he bowled at right-handers. In the third over of the innings, Larwood's sixth ball, short and on the line of middle stump, hit Woodfull over the heart. He staggered away, clutching his chest. The England players gathered around in sympathy, but Jardine's clearly enunciated, 'Well bowled, Harold!' – a remark he later claimed was solely designed to unnerve Bradman – horrified Woodfull and dismayed many who heard it. The spirit of the game was in severe danger of being compromised.

Woodfull recovered and the match resumed. As soon as it was his turn to face Larwood again, there was a break while the field was adjusted. It has remained unclear to this day whether Jardine or Larwood initiated the change, but in any event, the infamous leg-side field was now set. The crowd were deeply antagonized – angrier even than when Woodfull had been hit. They inevitably saw this deliberate use of fast leg theory, against a player who had received such a serious blow, as hitting a man when he was down and viewed it as completely unsportsmanlike. The catcalls and jeering became so pronounced that the England players felt physically threatened and thought the police presence badly insufficient to protect them if the crowd decided to riot and spill onto the playing field.

Larwood soon knocked the bat out of Woodfull's hands and, although clearly unsettled (he would be hit several more times), he would go on to score 22 before falling to Allen. Bradman had departed for just 8. Bill Ponsford had joined his Victoria state captain and would also be repeatedly hit on his back and shoulders as he turned away in an attempt to shield his bat to avoid giving up catches.

Later that day, there occurred the fateful visit by the England manager, Pelham Warner, to the Australians' dressing room, where he was rebuffed by Woodfull with perhaps the most famous quote in cricket: 'I don't want to see you, Mr Warner. There are two teams out there; one is trying to play cricket and the other is not.' Adding, 'This game is too good to be spoilt. It's time some people got out of it.' Warner, it was reported, was physically shaken by the admonishment and was seen hurrying away close to tears.

On the third day, Bert Oldfield was hit a sickening blow on the head that caused a fracture – although, again, the ball was a legitimate non-bodyline delivery that he top-edged. Oldfield later admitted that it was a mistake entirely of his own making; nevertheless, the crowd was yet again incensed.

On the fifth day it would be the ill-thought reaction of the Australian Board of Control – who in deciding to send a cable to the MCC used the injudicious word 'unsportsmanlike' – that would escalate the situation from an unseemly argument about the rights and wrongs of on-field sporting tactics to an all-out diplomatic row that, at its peak, threatened to undermine the relations between what had been the happiest of colonial brotherhoods. (The entire exchange of cables can be read from page 62.)

The match in Adelaide eventually saw Australia needing to score an impossible 532 in their second innings for victory. Bradman, employing entirely unorthodox methods, was eventually bowled for 66, while the ever stoic and brave Woodfull would carry his bat for an unbeaten 73 as wickets fell all around him; Australia were eventually all out for 193, and perhaps the most unpleasant and bitter-tasting Test match came to an inglorious close.

The response of the MCC – who it must be said in their defence had, at the time, no means at their disposal of truly comprehending what was happening on the field of play nor a way of gauging the level of anger in the stands and among Australians in general – was, along with that of the British public, to take considerable umbrage at the term 'unsportsmanlike' (an accusation that went right to the very heart of how Britain's colonial masters, let alone those in charge of the game at the headquarters of cricket, viewed themselves). In short order, a number of high horses were brought in to be climbed upon by the MCC committee members.

Jardine – as one would expect of a true son of the Empire and a man whose deep dislike of all things Australian was already well established – was sufficiently outraged by the temerity of the Australians, of their complaints and the unwarranted accusation of an England team behaving in anything other than a sporting manner, that he, and by extension the rest of the England team, promptly threatened to pull out of the remaining two Tests unless the word 'unsportsmanlike' was withdrawn. In London, the Secretary of State for Dominion Affairs, J. H. Thomas, became embroiled, warning that the present impasse would have a significant impact on trade between the nations. It would take the intervention of Australian Prime Minister Joseph Lyons – who made it clear to the Australian Board of Control just how serious the economic ramifications would be for their young nation if Britain started boycotting Australian goods, something that was being called for back home – for the offending words to be rescinded. The allegation of unsportsmanlike behaviour was withdrawn and the tour would continue.

Jardine, as was to be expected, was unrepentant, and during the remaining two Tests would continue to employ fast leg theory, now routinely described by the media as 'bodyline' (it is widely believed that Melbourne and Sydney journalist Hugh Buggy coined the phrase in a telegraph office). However, slower pitches largely negated its effectiveness and although Australian batsmen contin-ued to be hit, none sustained serious injury. England finished by winning the series 4–1.

Bodyline would still be seen in England in 1933, most notably at Nottinghamshire, who had bodyline's arch-practitioners, Voce and Larwood, on their playing staff. *Wisden* would comment that 'those watching it for the first time must have come to the conclusion that, while strictly within the law, it was not nice.'

In 1934 Australia would tour England with Bill Woodfull once more at the helm. Jardine had retired from international cricket and new captain Bob Wyatt agreed that bodyline tactics would not be used. However, the Australians felt that this was sometimes more honoured in the breach than the observance. In the opening Test at Trent Bridge, Voce bowled fast towards leg in fading light, causing an angered Woodfull to threaten the authorities that, if

Voce repeated the tactic the following day, he and his team would return to London and Australia would not visit England again.

The MCC had hoped that the spirit of the game would prevail and that captains would henceforth ensure that their bowlers understood that the recent MCC resolution citing fast leg theory as being against the spirit of the game would be sufficient to dictate the manner in which the game would be played from now on. Human nature being what it is, a new law was ultimately needed and 'direct attack' bowling was formally outlawed; it would be up to the umpires to identify it and to call a halt when bowlers stepped over the line. Twenty years later, it became illegal to have more than two leg-side fielders behind square of the wicket. Introduced to combat negative bowling at leg stump by spinners and in-swing bowlers, this effectively ruled out bodyline field settings.

If Bodyline gave cricket's administrators an early indication of just how inextricably tangled politics and the noble game can quickly become, an even more serious incident erupted thirty-five years later, this time involving South Africa, whose racist political system was beginning to stir public conscience around the world.

At the centre of this particular drama was Basil D'Oliveira, a South African who was classified by the apartheid regime as 'Cape coloured', or of mixed race, and therefore prohibited from participating in any sport alongside white South Africans. As a youngster he lived for cricket (and football) and used to climb the trees outside the Newlands Cricket Ground in Cape Town to watch the cricket. Through a combination of outrageous talent and a burning desire to succeed, D'Oliveira became captain of the non-white South African cricket team – and also played football for the non-white national team – but he became increasingly frustrated at the political barrier that prevented him from representing his country at the highest level. Left with no alternative, D'Oliveira decided to emigrate to England, helped to no small extent by the cricket writer and broadcaster, John Arlott, to whom D'Oliveira had written in 1958, asking for help in finding a role as a professional in one of England's leagues. This unlikely connection was forged through D'Oliveira listening to Arlott's legendary radio commentary. 'His voice and the words he spoke convinced me he was a nice, compassionate man,' he said.

Arlott managed to secure D'Oliveira a contract for the summer of 1960 with Middleton Cricket Club in the Central Lancashire

League. He subsequently topped the League's batting averages that season, arousing the interest of Worcestershire County Cricket Club, for whom he first appeared in first-class cricket in 1964. Throughout, D'Oliveira maintained that he had been born in 1934, which by most people's reckoning took at least three years off his true age. Indeed, his most likely date of birth was 4 October 1931, but D'Oliveira knew that he would be considered dangerously past his sell-by date had he revealed to Worcestershire that he was approaching 33 when he made his début, rather than 29, and that he would surely have had little chance of making his début for England against West Indies in 1966 had the selectors known he was in his thirty-fifth year. This was just another intriguing subplot in the life of a man whose name will always be linked with the eventual downfall of apartheid.

D'Oliveira's Test career began promisingly, being run out for 27 in his first innings and picking up a couple of wickets with his gentle swing bowling, which was to become surprisingly successful at breaking stubborn partnerships. He scored two half-centuries in his second Test, which England lost, and a battling 88 in his third, at Headingley, where West Indies recorded an even more emphatic victory, this time by an innings and 55 runs, to set up their 3–1 series victory. D'Oliveira's first century for England came the following June in the First Test against India at Headingley. A further 81 not out against Pakistan later that summer helped him to become one of *Wisden's* five cricketers of the year for 1967, and these performances took him to West Indies for the winter tour.

More than five thousand miles away in Pretoria, the South African authorities had been monitoring D'Oliveira's development and knew they had a problem. England, travelling under the auspices of MCC in those days, were due to tour South Africa the following winter and the interior minister, Pieter le Roux, had already warned MCC that D'Oliveira would not be allowed into South Africa if he were chosen in the squad.

In the event, the West Indies tour did not go well for D'Oliveira either on or off the field. He played in all five Tests but passed fifty only once and, on his first tour, it soon became clear to his teammates that Dolly could become quite fiery when he had consumed a drink or two. There were further political developments, too, with the former MCC president Lord Cobham assuring the South Africans that MCC would do everything in its power to ensure that the winter's tour went ahead, and the pressure was ratcheted up a notch when John Vorster, the prime minister of South Africa, warned that the tour would be cancelled if D'Oliveira were selected.

Despite his indifferent form, D'Oliveira was selected for the first Ashes Test of 1968, and although Australia won the match, he top-scored in the second innings with an unbeaten 87. It was when he was replaced by Colin Milburn for the following Test, to make way for a third fast bowler, that the first whiff of suspicion of a possible political intervention was detected. MCC secretary Billy Griffith contacted D'Oliveira and urged him to rule himself out of the South Africa tour. Griffith also suggested, absurdly, that D'Oliveira might make himself available for South Africa instead. In July, with D'Oliveira now out of the England team, MCC approached thirty players to check their availability for the tour – but not D'Oliveira.

Although the Ashes were already lost, England needed to win the Fifth and final Test against Australia to draw the series. Roger Prideaux, who had scored 64 in the first innings of the previous Test at Headingley, was forced out of the match through injury and D'Oliveira was called up. However, he was the only player not to be asked on the eve of the game by Doug Insole, the chairman of selectors, to declare his availability for the tour to South Africa.

The Oval Test of 1968 was a remarkable game of cricket in its own right. England set Australia 352 to win and, just before lunch on the final day, Australia were heading towards defeat at 85 for five when a torrential storm flooded the ground. The sun reappeared shortly afterwards and the groundstaff – helped by volunteers from the crowd who were armed with brooms, buckets and towels – set about drying the outfield. At 4.45, play restarted with only seventy-five minutes remaining.

The captain, Colin Cowdrey, used all his frontline bowlers, but John Inverarity and Barry Jarman could not be shifted. With barely forty minutes before stumps, Cowdrey turned to the great partnership-breaker, D'Oliveira, who duly bowled Jarman in his second over. Derek Underwood, revelling in the rapidly drying conditions, finished the contest by taking the last four Australian wickets in twenty-seven balls with every fielder crouched around the bat.

All of that would surely be enough to make the match memorable. But this game had gained a significance of its own when, in England's vital first innings, D'Oliveira scored 158 from 325 balls. It was not a flawless innings – far from it. In fact he was dropped four times. But this surely was a performance, played under great personal pressure, that demanded selection for the winter tour that followed. However, as we have already established, these were far from normal circumstances.

The selectors convened at eight o'clock on 27 August, the evening the Test finished, and the meeting closed at two o'clock the next morning. Of the five selectors – Insole, Cowdrey, Don Kenyon, Alec Bedser and Peter May – only Kenyon is reported to have supported D'Oliveira's selection. Curiously, the minutes of the meeting went missing and the chairman, Insole, explained D'Oliveira's exclusion by saying that he was regarded as a batsman rather than an all-rounder, and that there were better players in the squad.

These days, with Twitter and other social media, reaction to the news would have been fast and furious. Sporting issues rarely made the front pages back in 1968, when press coverage was rather more sedate and considered, but the Reverend David Sheppard, who played twenty-two Tests for England, stated that the MCC had made a 'dreadful mistake'. This galvanized members of the private club to force a meeting on 6 September and the D'Oliveira affair gripped the nation, with the *News of the World* announcing that they would send D'Oliveira to South Africa to report on the Test series for them.

The next twist of fate involved Tom Cartwright, the softly spoken seam bowler who had been selected for the tour despite having a shoulder injury. He appeared to have proven his fitness by bowling ten overs in a county match for Warwickshire, only to withdraw from the touring squad two days later. D'Oliveira was named as his replacement.

The reaction from South Africa was immediate. Prime Minister Vorster declared that the MCC team had been selected along political lines and that his country would not welcome it. The South Africans pointed to the fact that D'Oliveira had first been considered as a batsman, but then replaced an injured bowler – although, with seven first-class hundreds to his name, Cartwright was more of an all-rounder than purely a bowler. 'The MCC team is not the team of the MCC but of the anti-apartheid movement,' Vorster announced deliberately in his harsh, guttural Afrikaans accent.

What is almost certainly true is that D'Oliveira was not the selectors' first choice as replacement for Cartwright. There was his poor tour report from the previous winter to be considered, and Barry Knight and Ken Higgs were rated ahead of him as bowlers. However, both were unavailable through injury.

A week later, following a meeting at Lord's, the MCC called off the tour, but at a meeting in January 1969 the Club voted in favour of inviting the South Africans to tour England in 1970. That was also abandoned when anti-apartheid protestors first disrupted the England rugby tour by the Springboks in November 1969, then threatened to do the same to the South African cricket tour the following summer. In May 1970, under great pressure from the Labour government, the tour was called off, and so began South Africa's sporting isolation, which was to last until apartheid was dismantled in 1991. Basil D'Oliveira can never have expected to play such a central role in the creation of a new and free South Africa.

Television news coverage had much to do with the success of the anti-apartheid movement in 1969 and 1970. By showing the demonstrations and interviewing key protagonists like future government minister Peter Hain, the general public became much more aware of the political situation in South Africa, even if most of them did not approve of the disruption that was caused to the Springbok rugby tour. Just seven years later, the power of television was to tear cricket apart.

As is always the case with these things, there were a number of separate issues that combined to lead to the formation of World Series Cricket (WSC). The first was the increase in the popularity of television in Australia, where a burgeoning audience was treated to a plethora of imported programmes from the USA. Alarmed at this growing dependency, a campaign called 'TV: Make it Australian' led in 1973 to the imposition of a quota by the government. Crucially, the screening of Australian sport was allowed to be part of that quota, which immediately appealed to the cricket enthusiast Kerry Packer, an Australian media tycoon who, among other interests, owned the commercial television network, Channel Nine. Packer saw the opportunity to break with tradition and broadcast more sport, which up until then had been screened by the Australian Broadcasting Corporation (ABC).

The attitude of the sports administrators at that time was very different from today, in that television was viewed then more as a threat to a live event than as a financial lifeline. It seems crazy now, but with Packer determined to buy the cricket rights at virtually any price, he was throwing money at the Australian Cricket Board, only for his offers to be rejected in favour of the ABC despite the corporation paying considerably less. His final attempt in 1976 was an offer of A$1.5 million over three years, which was eight times the previous contract with the ABC. Again, he was rebuffed.

The third strand was the widespread dissatisfaction of the world's leading cricketers at the level of their pay. Indeed, their salaries were so low and their futures so insecure that persuasion did not even come into it when the offers came to sign up to a concept that was still very much in its embryonic form.

Packer's plan was to enlist Australia's best players and pitch them against a World XI. The matches would be staged in Australia and broadcast on Channel Nine. The former Australia captain, Ian Chappell, was engaged to approach the Australians, while Tony Greig, the captain of England, was recruited in the utmost secrecy by Packer effectively to act as an agent and approach the world's leading players. By May 1977, Packer had clandestinely contracted thirteen of the seventeen members of the Australian cricket team that had just begun its tour of England.

The sensational news was leaked to Australian journalists on 9 May, and the cat was out of the bag. It was hardly surprising that most of the English hostility was aimed at Greig, whose strong South African background only added to the widespread accusation of treachery. Greig was quickly sacked as England captain, but retained his place in the team. The Australians were distracted and divided, and lost the Ashes series 3–0.

At this early stage, Packer still hoped to reach a compromise. He came to England in May to meet the authorities, who had another shock in store when it was revealed that Richie Benaud, the highly respected former Australia captain and television commentator, would be acting as an advisor to Packer. This was not merely an advisory role: Benaud also composed the rules and regulations for WSC. Benaud and Packer met the ICC, cricket's governing body, at Lord's on 23 June to discuss the proposed format of WSC. The meeting appeared to be going well until Packer displayed a rare misunderstanding of the situation by demanding that the ICC award him the rights to broadcast Australian cricket exclusively from 1979. This, of course, was not an ICC responsibility – the domestic television rights had to be negotiated with the ACB – and when this was relayed to him, Packer stormed out of the meeting and made this unequivocal statement: 'Had I got those TV rights I was prepared to withdraw from the scene and leave the running of cricket to the board. I will take no steps now to help anyone. It's every man for himself and the devil take the hindmost.' If the game had any lingering doubts about the seriousness of Packer's intentions, they certainly did not exist any longer.

When the ICC ruled in July that any player taking part in one of Packer's matches would be banned from Test and first-class cricket, war was declared. This was, after all, a direct threat to the players and their ability to earn a living, so when Greig, Mike Procter and John Snow decided to challenge the Test and County Cricket Board (TCCB) in the High Court, Packer put his financial clout behind them. This included audaciously hiring the most expensive QCs in England and paying them a retainer for the duration of the trial to prevent the TCCB from having access to their expertise. In November 1977 Justice Slade backed the players, ruling that any ban on the Packer players by the ICC and TCCB would be an unreasonable restraint of trade. The players knew that they would inevitably be banned from Test cricket, since countries are free to select whom they want, but they would at least now be free to continue to play county cricket.

Packer did not have everything his own way. World Series Cricket was banned from every cricket venue in Australia that had an affiliation with the board. Since poor pitches would make the whole venture look second rate – which was hardly the image Packer wanted to promote on Channel Nine – this was a serious concern. After all, he had now hired some of the fastest bowlers in the world, and the 'Supertests', as they were called, needed to be credible. The solution was drop-in pitches, which were cultivated off-site and then transported to the venue for the match and set in place. This enabled WSC to be played at VFL Park – an Australian rules football stadium in Melbourne's suburbs – and, more unusually, Gloucester Park in Perth, which is a stone's throw from the WACA but is a horse trotting track. Drop-in pitches have become more popular since Packer pioneered the concept, particularly in New Zealand, and they are just one of the many legacies of WSC. Another is the protective equipment that we take for granted these days. Because the early strips were still at an experimental stage, the batsmen were uneasy facing the fast bowlers. When David Hookes had his jaw shattered by a bouncer from Andy Roberts, helmets – which were then more like motorcycle crash helmets – and extra strap-on body protection became essential items in every WSC player's kit bag.

WSC was expanded from its original concept of Australia against the Rest of the World to include the West Indies, who were emerging as the best team in the world with outstanding batsmen like Viv Richards and Clive Lloyd and their fearsome battery of fast bowlers led by Roberts and Michael Holding. The reason was very simple – money. The cash on offer from WSC was more than many West Indian cricketers might have expected to earn from their whole career, and given the status of the team – and Packer's desire to make cricket a more physical, dangerous and therefore more watchable sport – the West Indian fast bowlers were irresistible to him.

The first Supertest was staged at VFL Park on 2 December 1977, featuring WSC Australia versus WSC West Indies. Not surprisingly, not many turned out to watch, but nevertheless, WSC was now up and running.

Packer's plan was for WSC to drive his television audience, and since this naturally peaked in the evening, the solution was simple – to play limited-overs day/night matches under floodlights, with white balls, and in coloured clothing. This was an entirely new concept and one that the authorities mocked. They portrayed the cricketers as playing in pyjamas, and while the choice of coral pink for the West Indies did not go down at all well with the players because of the colour's gay overtones, day/night cricket played on warm evenings under the stars was a genuine innovation, and another of Packer's legacies. Games played under lights might be unsuited for top-class cricket, but slowly, and despite hostile media, crowds warmed to the idea and it clearly had a future.

At this stage, the ACB was winning the battle. Large crowds had turned out to support the traditional and closely fought Test series against India, which Australia won 3–2. Deprived of its best players, the ACB recalled the 41-year-old former captain Bobby Simpson to lead its team of youngsters. Simpson had been retired from the game for ten years but was hugely popular with Australian cricket lovers, who took to the notion that was peddled in the press of this ageing character being recalled to stand up for the proper form of cricket, which was coming under attack from the raucous and thoroughly uncouth WSC.

This image came under fire when Simpson then took his team to the Caribbean in March 1978. West Indies selected all their Packer players and Australia, armed only with Jeff Thomson, took a hammering, although they did manage to win one of the four Tests. Simpson averaged only 22 in the series and was subsequently replaced by Graham Yallop.

The ACB appeared to be winning the early salvos on the home front, at least, in their battle with WSC, but victory would depend on the other cricket boards around the world taking a similarly strong stance. England refused to select its Packer 'rebels' – Tony Greig, Dennis Amiss, Alan Knott, John Snow, Derek Underwood and Bob Woolmer – but the defeat in the High Court meant that they were available to play county cricket. Elsewhere, the WSC situation was widely viewed as being an Australian domestic problem and it soon became clear that no other countries were willing to ban their Packer players. Indeed, the impecunious West Indies board negotiated a WSC tour of the Caribbean for the spring of 1979, and when Packer signed up more young Australians for the second season, which was also to include a senior WSC tour featuring largely recently retired international cricketers, the ACB's position was looking increasingly hopeless.

I was in Melbourne playing club cricket during the second season of WSC and watched a one-day match at VFL Park. Clive Lloyd, captain of the West Indian team, remembered me from a county game the previous summer and invited me into their dressing room to meet Michael Holding, Viv Richards and Andy Roberts. None of them, I can confirm, was best pleased with their outfits. My impression of the live event was that it failed to meet expectation – even of a then 18-year-old cricket fanatic. The floodlighting was poor, the playing area was the wrong shape, and the players were understandably suspicious of the quality of the drop-in pitch. There were very few spectators and the whole thing seemed rather gloomy. However, on television it came across entirely differently, and was very exciting. The floodlights, white balls and coloured clothing all shone on television, and the pitch microphones picked up every word – and there were plenty. WSC traded on being brash and brutal. Gradually sceptical television viewers began to enjoy this new way to watch the best cricketers in the world in a way that had never been possible before. I was changing my mind and began to think it was really thrilling.

The big breakthrough for WSC came in November 1978. Packer persuaded the premier of New South Wales, Neville Wran, to overturn the ban on his using the iconic Sydney Cricket Ground, and 44,377 people turned up to watch the floodlit match between WSC Australia and WSC West Indies. It was a huge success which coincided with the official Australian team losing the First Test to England. That series was to end in a 5–1 defeat for Yallop's men and, as any Australian will tell you, they hate losing. The Supertest final between WSC Australia and WSC World XI was also played at the SCG and attracted a further forty thousand spectators over three days. Just a week later, half that number turned out to watch the Sixth Test between Australia and England. The tide was turning against the ACB, which was also recording alarming financial losses.

So it was with great interest that I attended the annual meeting of the Professional Cricketers' Association at Edgbaston the following April. John Arlott presided over the conference, which coincided with negotiations between the various parties in Australia nearing a critical phase. Greig spoke, and was roundly criticised – publicly at least – but the majority of professionals in the room also hoped that WSC would lead to improved salaries for county cricketers. That was certainly the thrust of Greig's argument.

The announcement of a deal came on 30 May 1979. Not only had Channel Nine won the exclusive rights to broadcast Australian cricket for ten years, but also to promote and market the game. There was a feeling in England that the ACB had sold out – the TCCB had lost a very expensive High Court case, after all – but a solution had to be found. Australia's Packer players were not reselected until the following domestic season, when Greg Chappell was restored as the national captain, and as a sign of a return to normality, Mike Brearley led an England team to Australia to play three Tests. However, it being a shortened series, the TCCB refused to allow the Ashes to be contested – which was just as well, as Australia won every Test – and by refusing to permit its team to wear coloured clothes in the day/night internationals, the English board made itself look positively outdated and reactionary. This delighted the Australians, ensuring that the old rivalry received a much-needed injection of hostility, and after three tumultuous and turbulent years, normal service was resumed.

For a sport that is supposed to abide firmly to a strong moral code of gentlemanly behaviour, cricket has some undeniably dubious origins. By the end of the seventeenth century, gambling was inextricably linked to the sport and there are even suggestions that the emergence of county-based cricket came as a result of gamblers forming their own teams. There are reports of a 'great match' held in Sussex in 1697 being played for a stake of fifty guineas per side. But cricket was not the only sport to attract gamblers, and there is no suggestion of matches in the dim and distant past being 'thrown' or tampered with in any way in return for a pay-off. This was certainly well before there was any spot-fixing or any of the other corrupt activities that have become the scourge of the modern game.

It was in the 1990s that the cricketing rumour mill went into overdrive with claims that international matches were being fixed by players. Perhaps it was purely coincidental that this was also the time of numerous ball-tampering allegations, but it is definitely true to say that cricket's reputation for being a clean and ethical sport was at its lowest ebb. Subsequent investigations and inquiries have confirmed the existence of corruption, fuelled by the massive illegal bookmaking industry in India and Dubai, in particular. The South Africa captain, Hansie Cronje, and his Indian counterpart, Mohammad Azharuddin, became the first high-profile international cricketers to be banned for match-fixing. When the extent of Cronje's involvement unravelled during the subsequent inquiry in Cape Town in 2000, led by Judge King, it became clear that cricket faced a huge problem, and that the integrity of the sport was at stake.

The first claims of match-fixing originated in county cricket. Don Topley, an Essex player, created a storm when he announced that two matches played over a weekend in 1991 between Essex and Lancashire were fixed. The deal, he claimed, was for Essex to lose the Sunday League game in return for Lancashire allowing Essex, who were in the race for the County Championship title, to win the corresponding Championship match. Topley confessed to deliberately bowling poorly in the Sunday League match when he made his allegations in 1994. There was an investigation by the TCCB and, five years later, by the England and Wales Cricket Board (ECB) and the Metropolitan Police, who found insufficient evidence to press charges despite two new witnesses supporting Topley. The inquiry by the ECB was described by some as perfunctory, and it did not appear that many on the county circuit took Topley's claims seriously.

Australian cricket was rocked by the news that two of its favourites, Shane Warne and Mark Waugh, had both been given cash payments by an Indian bookmaker known only as John. Warne received A$5,000 and Waugh A$4,000 in exchange for what the players insist was nothing more than weather and pitch information before matches on their tour of Sri Lanka in 1994–5. An Australian journalist was tipped off that at least one Australian player was being paid by a bookmaker, and the officials were informed. Waugh and Warne admitted their involvement in unsigned handwritten statements, and the ACB chairman, Alan Crompton, fined the players. However, this was kept secret even from fellow members of the board who might have pressed for suspensions to be imposed. Another factor was that Waugh and Warne had both accused Salim Malik, the captain of Pakistan, of attempting to bribe them to lose matches and this information would have damaged their credibility as witnesses in the event of an inquiry.

But the scandal broke immediately before the Adelaide Test between Australia and England in December 1998 when Malcolm Conn, the *Australian* newspaper's cricket correspondent, conducted his own investigation and published for the first time the connection with John, the mystery Indian bookie. In a packed media conference in the Adelaide pavilion, Warne and Waugh admitted to having been 'naive and stupid'. The two players were vilified by the press and public alike, and Waugh received a hostile reception when he walked out to bat on the first day of the Test.

The initial reaction by the ACB does not come as a surprise. It was convenient in the dark decade of the 1990s for the finger of suspicion to point firmly at Pakistan. It is true that most of the rumours about corruption centred on Pakistan's players, and their captain Salim Malik in particular. There appeared to be a determination among the game's authorities to make an example of Malik, who in May 2000 became the first cricketer to be banned for match-fixing.

Malik's fate was determined by Justice Malik Qayyum, a Pakistani judge, who was appointed by the Pakistan Cricket Board to examine allegations of corruption against members of the Pakistan team. In Qayyum's report, Salim Malik was found guilty of match-fixing in Sri Lanka in 1994–5 and attempted match-fixing in Australia in 1994, and banned for life. Ata-ur-Rehman was also banned for life for 'general match-fixing'. Other penalties were imposed on some of the best-known Pakistan cricketers. Wasim Akram was found 'not to be above board' and fined £3,700. Waqar Younis was censured and fined £1,200, as was Inzamam-ul-Haq. The leg-spinner Mushtaq Ahmed, who became England's spin-bowling coach, was fined £3,700. Six years later, Qayyum admitted that he had been lenient on some players, including Wasim Akram, because he had a soft spot for them and was a fan.

The scale of corruption within cricket only surfaced for the first time when the shocking news broke that Hansie Cronje, a man who in South Africa would be ranked only one division below Nelson Mandela in terms of popularity and standing, was suspected of match-fixing. The source was the Delhi police force, which, in April 2000, made public the details of a taped telephone conversation between Cronje and a known bookmaker, Sanjay Chawla. Cronje initially denied the allegations but quickly admitted his guilt in exchange for immunity from prosecution in South Africa. The Indian captain, Mohammad Azharuddin, was also seriously implicated and they both received life bans from the game. During the King Commission of Inquiry, details emerged of Cronje's largely unsuccessful attempts to corrupt a number of his team-mates. Depressingly, these were generally the most vulnerable, either through race or by being on the fringe of selection, and therefore the easiest to influence. Henry Williams, a black pace bowler, testified that he was offered US$15,000 to bowl badly in a one-day international against India, and Herschelle Gibbs, the opening batsman, the same amount to score fewer than 20 runs. As a result of the evidence, both players were fined and suspended by the South African board for six months.

From an English perspective, the most absorbing details to emerge centred on a rain-affected Test match played between South Africa and England at Pretoria in January 2000. At the start of the last day of the final Test, only forty-five overs had been possible throughout the match, and South Africa, in their first innings, were 155 for six. A number of suggestions for making something from nothing had already been dismissed by the administrators. South Africa had already won the series so there was nothing at stake in that regard and, strongly persuaded by Cronje, the England captain, Nasser Hussain, agreed to forfeit England's first innings in exchange for South Africa reaching a pre-agreed total of 250 and forfeiting their second innings in order to set up the prospect of an interesting day's cricket. This went down very well with the thousand or so

England supporters who had made the trip and who were mighty frustrated, and it was hailed from the press and commentary boxes as a great day for cricket. Not everyone agreed, particularly those who had an interest in horse racing. Mike Atherton was a dissenter within the England ranks, while Sir Ian Botham and the journalist Jack Bannister were vociferous in their disapproval behind the scenes. Effectively, the draw – a nailed-on certainty – was suddenly made vulnerable, and this caused alarm in legitimate betting circles where the book had already been closed.

Under the contrived arrangement, England were set 249 to win, which they achieved with just two wickets and five balls remaining, ensuring that the spectators had their entertainment. However, what was known only to Cronje was that, on the evening before the final day, he was approached by a South African bookmaker, Marlon Aronstam, who offered to give 500,000 rand (approximately £33,300) to the charity of Cronje's choice if he declared to make a game of it. When the match was over, Aronstam gave Cronje two payments totalling 50,000 rand (£3,300) and a leather jacket.

Although a large number of South Africans refused point blank to believe a word of the evidence against their national hero, Cronje's fall from grace was dramatic and ultimately tragic. On 1 June 2002, aged 32, he died in a plane crash in mountains near George in South Africa. Inevitably, conspiracy theories flourished in the immediate aftermath, and then again in 2007 when Bob Woolmer – who had been Cronje's coach and confidant – was found dead in his Jamaican hotel room. Woolmer was coach of Pakistan at the time, and his team had just been knocked out of the World Cup at the earliest opportunity as a result of a surprise loss to Ireland. The inquests recorded death by pilot error in Cronje's case, but returned an open verdict in Woolmer's, which left open the possibility that he had been murdered. However, a review of the case by Scotland Yard determined that Woolmer had died of natural causes, most probably a heart attack.

Aware of the damage that was being done to the integrity of the game, the ICC set about tackling the most serious issue the game had ever faced. An anti-corruption unit was set up, which brought in a raft of stringent measures designed to increase awareness among the players and also to make contact with bookmakers more difficult. A zero-tolerance policy was introduced, leaving no one in any doubt that corrupt players would be heavily punished. It was widely accepted, however, that spot-fixing, in particular, would be very difficult to prove. This might involve the number of runs scored by a team during a specified passage of play in a one-day match, or even the outcome of a single delivery. A bowler delivering a wide or no-ball to order is all that is required for bookies to make a killing on the cricket-crazy, illegal betting markets on the Indian subcontinent.

Allegations of match-fixing, in which games were deliberately thrown by the majority of a team, went quiet after Cronje's case because of the increased awareness of administrators, umpires and the media. However, this probably allowed spot-fixing to proliferate as the bookies were forced to change their approach. Cricket had lost its innocence in that the simplest dropped catch, inexplicable run-out or mysteriously slow innings now raises eyebrows. But it is one thing to harbour a suspicion in the commentary box, and quite another to make a serious allegation against a professional cricketer who might be guilty of nothing more than making a mistake.

The tour of England by the Pakistan team in the summer of 2010 provided a significant victory in the battle against corruption, although it took a sting by the Sunday tabloid newspaper the *News of the World* to bring it about. Sharp-eyed commentators working at the Lord's Test – the final match of the summer – were surprised to see Mohammad Amir, the 18-year-old swing bowler, deliver two no-balls. But these were not ordinary no-balls: he overstepped the crease by a remarkable distance, and yet still released the ball, something that was impossible to explain.

It all became clear on the Sunday morning, which was the final day of the match, when the *News of the World* exposed the set-up in which an agent, Mazhar Majeed, was seen accepting £150,000 from the undercover reporter. The deal was that Majeed would arrange for three no-balls to be delivered to order, two by Amir and one by Mohammad Asif. Sure enough, the no-balls were bowled precisely as specified, and the Pakistan captain, Salman Butt, was revealed as the man who had passed the instructions to his bowlers.

The evidence appeared to be conclusive, and this was the verdict of the ICC, which conducted a disciplinary hearing despite the ongoing criminal investigation. All three players were found guilty and, on 5 February 2011, received lengthy bans – Butt for ten years, with five suspended; Asif seven years, with two suspended; and Amir five years. The players maintained their innocence, but in November 2011 were found guilty at Southwark Crown Court of conspiracy to cheat at gambling and conspiracy to receive corrupt payments. Butt was jailed for two and a half years, Asif for one year and Amir for six months. The agent, Majeed, was imprisoned for two years eight months. The case was seen as a watershed moment in the battle that every sport faces against corruption, and it forced Pakistan's authorities finally to take seriously the long-held view that its cricket team was more exposed to corruption than any other.

However, there was a shock in store for followers of county cricket when, in January 2012, a young Essex fast bowler, Mervyn Westfield, pleaded guilty to accepting £6,000 to deliberately under-perform in a match against Durham in 2009. He was imprisoned for four months after alleging in court that he had been persuaded to accept the bribe by the Pakistan and Essex leg-spinner, Danish Kaneria, who had been initially arrested with Westfield. Kaneria was released without charge, and denies Westfield's allegations. However, the case underlines the extent to which corruption has infiltrated the game of cricket and that, potentially, any match tele-vised live to the Indian subcontinent is at risk.

Why is it that cricket has attracted so many controversies over its relatively short life? Racism, corruption, politics – the great game has endured more than its fair share of issues, all of which have threatened its welfare. At least part of the answer must lie in the fact that it is a traditional sport founded upon a strict moral code of fair play and sporting conduct. Any threat to those prin-ciples is big news, and I am quite convinced that cricket crises – particularly of the political variety – make bigger headlines even than football crises because of the game's historical links with the Commonwealth.

It is a fact that cricket has at times played a crucial role in shaping the world in which we live. This is plain to see in the D'Oliveira crisis, which made a nonsense of the often cowardly ambition of many to keep sport separate from politics. Separating the two is almost impos-sible to achieve and, besides, when you consider the dismantling of apartheid, sport – and cricket in particular – made a significant con-tribution. The D'Oliveira affair led directly to the 1977 Gleneagles Agreement in which Commonwealth leaders agreed to boycott all sporting contact with South Africa as part of the international fight against apartheid. Supporters of the rebel cricket tours that broke that agreement will say that the English XI tour in 1990, led by Mike Gatting, played a part in speeding up the end of the reviled political system in South Africa. It did, but not because it was the right thing to do. The ill-timed and insensitive tour was a financial disaster for the South African Cricket Union, coinciding as it did with the unbanning of the African National Congress and Nelson Mandela's release from prison. The tour became a focal point for demonstrators – Gatting famously admitted to hearing a 'few people singing and dancing' outside his hotel – and it quickly became obvious that the tour was unsustainable, and was called off.

Sport and politics are inextricably linked, but the type of sustained pressure that worked against South Africa does not work in every situation. It would not, for example, have made the slightest impression on Robert Mugabe's stranglehold on South Africa's neighbour, Zimbabwe, because sport does not play such a strong part in that country's everyday life. However, an England cricket tour to Zimbabwe in 2003 did allow a precious opportunity for Western journalists – banned at the time by the regime – including myself to enter the country. Once inside, we were able to report on life within the country, from the consequences of rampant inflation to the witnessing of farms being burned to the ground.

It might be everyone's ideal to keep sport and politics as far apart as possible, but not only is that naive, but it also denies sport the opportunity to play its part in civilizing society and improving lives. A number of great South African cricketers had their international careers ruined by the Gleneagles Agreement, and have every reason to be bitter towards the politicians who drove their own country into sporting isolation. Mike Procter, as fine an all-rounder as there has ever been, was restricted to just seven Tests before the curtain came down. 'What's one life,' he asked me, 'compared to the millions who were liberated?'

Determined men will always push the boundaries until their actions expose a frailty in a law, and only then will that loophole be closed. It had been tried in the county game, but without the outright hostility and accuracy of Larwood or the volatile atmosphere of a seething cauldron of a Test arena. And we should remember that an Ashes series was the only series that really mattered to the cricket-watching public in the 1930s. Bowling short with as many men as you wanted on the leg side was a legitimate tactic, but not what cricket was meant to be, or the way cricket should be played. It would take Bodyline for people to see this, and it caused the Laws of the game to be changed to prevent it from ever happening again – quite rightly. Did it work as a tactic against Bradman? England won the series, so the argument goes that it did. Bradman always claimed that it didn't.

The intimidatory bowling of the West Indies in the 1980s was as close to modern bodyline as you can get: the ball whistling past your head at more than ninety miles per hour was extremely nasty. I was a tail-end batsman at the time and did not relish getting out there. Even the top players were unnerved and saw it as a considerable challenge to face up to these great bowlers. But you never heard them complain about it.

The Bodyline story had all the right ingredients: a big, bad fast bowler; a brilliant batsman capable of dominating the series; the unbending patrician figure of Jardine as captain; and a hostile crowd all too ready to find fault with the tourists. Running through the game is the 'spirit' of cricket, something that is considered so central to the wellbeing and future of the game that it is articulated in the preamble to the Laws of Cricket under the heading 'Responsibility of Captains': *The captains are responsible at all times for ensuring that play is conducted within the Spirit of the Game as well as within the Laws.*' This is what holds the game together and I have no doubt Jardine fell short in this regard.

What followed was also a failure of communication, through the purblind inherent conservatism of the MCC and the rash injured pride leading to the intemperate complaints of the

Australians. I have always thought the Australians took the wrong initiative in complaining so much.

Cricket's lawmakers are still getting it wrong: today we have the absurdity of banning runners. It will only take a Test match with twenty thousand in the ground and a team nine down needing ten runs to win. The last batsman has a dodgy hamstring and can't get out to bat so the game abruptly finishes. Is that what it will take for the ICC to realize what a daft rule they've brought in?

DONALD BRADMAN
Body-Line

The last thing I want to do at the close of my career is to revive unpleasant memories. However, I would be failing in my duty if I did not record my impressions of something which very nearly brought about a cessation of Test cricket between England and Australia, especially as I was one of the central figures.

Jardine, who captained England in that series, wrote a book defending his theory. So did Larwood. The defence could have impressed the jury not at all, for body-line is now outlawed.

Of paramount importance is the fact that body-line can no longer be bowled *because the M.C.C. has passed a law which has the effect of prohibiting it*. I make this point very strongly because even today, in parts of England, people think Australia stopped it.

The M.C.C. at first were reluctant to believe the reports emanating from Australia as to the nature of the bowling, called "body-line". They very rightly wanted evidence, and one understands their reluctance to act without it.

Having obtained the evidence they did not hesitate.

Now what exactly was body-line bowling? It was really short-pitched fast bowling directed towards the batsman's body with a supporting leg-side field.

In his book, *Anti-Body-line*, Alan Kippax defines it fairly well in setting out the following objections to that type of bowling:—

1. That a considerable proportion of the deliveries were directed straight at the batsman's body.

2. That many of these deliveries were deliberately pitched short enough to make them fly as high as the batsman's shoulders and head.

3. That an intensive leg-side field was placed, including four and sometimes five men in the short-leg positions, supported by two (occasionally one) in the deep field at long-leg.

Kippax was an Australian batsman, so perhaps it would be more convincing to quote the definition given by an English batsman. This is how Wally Hammond defined it:—

1. Delivered by a speed merchant.

2. Bumped so as to fly high above the wicket.

3. Delivered straight at the batsman.

4. Bowled with a leg-side field of 6 to 8 men.

Of course the protagonists of body-line always claimed that it was leg theory—an entirely fallacious claim.

Warwick Armstrong, Fred Root and others bowled leg theory. Nobody was in the slightest danger therefrom.

With body-line it was different. The risk of actual physical danger to the batsman became his chief consideration.

In order that we may get things in their proper perspective, I feel impelled to quote the remarks of Sir Pelham Warner, who, so far as I know, was the first man to protest in writing against body-line bowling, though at that time the term "body-line" had not been coined.

Writing in the London *Morning Post* of August 22, 1932, of a match between Yorkshire and Surrey at The Oval, he said, "Bowes must alter his tactics. Bowes bowled with five men on the on-side and sent down several very short-pitched balls which repeatedly bounced head-high and more. Now that is not bowling; indeed it is not cricket; and if all the fast bowlers were to adopt his methods M.C.C. would be compelled to step in and penalise the bowler who bowled the ball less than half-way up the pitch."

So Bill Bowes was evidently the first man to use this form of attack in England, and at once it was denounced. It was not leg theory.

Where did body-line originate?

Captain (to bowler). 'Call yourself Larwood, an' goes an' bowls under-'and.' *Bowler.*
'So would Larwood if the only way 'e 'ad ter keep 'is trousers up was by stoopin' darn.'

Jardine in his book is very reticent on the point. He devotes
several pages to details of the evolution of legitimate leg theory
which is really only drawing a red-herring across the track, because,
as I have pointed out, *leg theory is not body-line*.

Learie Constantine in his book *Cricket and I* says:—

"One could read Jardine's book from cover to cover and, if it
were not for the general excitement about body-line bowling,
never discover what the essentials of body-line bowling were."

He is not far out. However, the following points are of interest.

Jardine wrote: "Though I did not take part in the Test Match
against Australia at the Oval in 1930, I have been told on all sides
that Bradman's innings was far from convincing on the leg stump
whilst there was any life in the wicket. I am sorry to disappoint
anyone who has imagined that the leg theory was evolved with the
help of midnight oil and iced towels simply and solely for the purpose
of combating Bradman's effectiveness as a scoring machine. It did,
however, seem a reasonable assumption that a weakness in one of
Australia's premier batsmen might find more than a replica in the
play of a good many of his contemporaries." Larwood, in his book,
was a little bit more direct, for he wrote:—

"Fast leg theory bowling was born in the Test Match at Kennington Oval in August 1930. A spot of rain had fallen. The ball was 'popping'. My great friend, the late Archie Jackson, stood up to me, getting pinked once or twice in the process and he never flinched. With Bradman it was different. It was because of that difference that I determined then and there, that if I was again honoured with an invitation to go to Australia, I would not forget that difference."

Let me first have a word to say *re* Jardine's statement. He quotes a 1930 match as the basis for his idea, but completely refutes his own statement by the following reference to a match in 1932:—

"To our surprise we found an *almost totally unsuspected weakness* on the leg stump in the play of several leading players. This had been particularly apparent in the case of Bradman as early as the second match of the tour, when he came to Perth to play against us."

The thing becomes entirely ludicrous when I tell you that Jardine did not include in his team against us on that occasion any one of his three body-line bowlers, Larwood, Voce or Bowes. Furthermore, I batted twice on a badly rain-affected pitch, scoring 3 and 10.

He must have been amazingly observant to discover such a weakness in those few minutes.

Unfortunately for Jardine, F. R. Foster put the show away when he gave an interview to the press and said: "Before Jardine left England he came frequently to my flat in the St. James and secured from me my leg-theory field placings. I had no hint that these would be used for body-line bowling. I would like all my old friends in Australian cricket to know that I am sorry that my experience and my advice were put to such unworthy uses."

Walter Hammond also made no secret of the development of the theory when he wrote on the subject. According to him "body-line" was born in the grill room of the Piccadilly Hotel, London, where Jardine, Arthur Carr, Voce and Larwood worked out the idea. Hammond claims that P. G. H. Fender had suggested to Jardine that he should adopt these tactics. "Jardine," says Hammond, "spent some days painstakingly analysing all the scoring diagrams which Ferguson, the famous M.C.C. scorer, had made of the Australian batsmen's Test innings." It was after this meeting, according to Hammond, that Jardine went to see F. R. Foster.

From my own talks with members of the M.C.C. Team, I understand this theory was discussed in detail on the way out to Australia, a fact which Jardine does not deny. I think readers will be able to judge what type of bowling it was, and furthermore that I was to be the principal target, with the proviso that success against me would, so Jardine believed, automatically mean success against others.

There is a suggestion by Jardine and Larwood that the theory was justified because of alleged shortcomings disclosed by me in my innings of 232 at The Oval in 1930. The following reports of this match from the press hardly support their case:—

1. "Before lunch at The Oval was a glorious period for Australia today, and provided the most courageous batting I have ever seen. Despite the most difficult wicket, Bradman and Jackson gave the English public an exhibition of versatility, pluck and determination rarely seen on a cricket field.

2. "The dangerous wicket helped the bowlers, who made the ball fly, Larwood being particularly vicious. Frequently the lads, after being hit, writhed in pain, but bruised and battered from head to toe, they carried on. Certainly it was a wonderful display of courage to withstand such a terrific onslaught.

3. "This Bradman is lion-hearted, physically and figuratively. He made a double century despite the whirlwind rib-breaking tactics of Larwood. Don was doubled up with pain when a terrifically fast ball struck him in the chest. Shortly afterwards another Larwood ball crashed onto his fingers. It would be hard to realise the pain he was suffering as he flogged the bowling. It was real cricket courage.

4. The *Daily Mail* comments on "the courage of Bradman and Jackson when facing the fast stuff on a wicket which was distinctly unpleasant after the rain, and when they were hit repeatedly and painfully, but stuck to their task with unflinching determination."

It is worth recording that I scored 98 runs before lunch in that period when the ball was flying on a rain-damaged pitch, and also that I was given out caught behind off Larwood when I did not hit the ball. It swung away slightly as I played at it. Noticing the swing I turned my bat at the last moment, and was amazed when Larwood appealed (he was the only one who did) and more amazed still when the umpire gave me out.

I have a photo of the dismissal. Duckworth is standing with the ball in his gloves, hands in front of his chest. Anyone who has seen Duckworth make a catch will remember how he would throw the ball high in the air, one foot off the ground and emit a war-cry. In this instance he did not appeal. Neither did Hammond at first slip, who is shown in the photo standing upright with hands hung low in front of him.

I am not complaining of the decision. There have been other occasions when I have been out and given not out. My purpose in clarifying the matter is to prevent anyone thinking Larwood and Jardine justified in their claim or that they can support it by saying Larwood obtained my wicket.

Jardine has made lavish use of quotations in his book, and in the preface quotes a long interview given to the *Cape Times* by a Mr. J. H. Hotson. In that interview Mr. Hotson refers to Larwood's habit of reverting to leg theory (after his few opening overs) because he had lost his swing. The inference is clear that such a move was necessary to suit the type of bowling. But it hardly tallies with a photo in Jardine's book showing Bromley (a left-hander) batting to a leg field, and being caught by Verity at short-leg from a shot made purely to prevent the ball hitting him in the face. Larwood goes to great pains in an effort to prove that by 1932 he had developed amazing accuracy and quotes figures to prove it. He cites this not only as a reason for his success, but also as support for the claim that his accuracy precluded any risk to batsmen.

Nobody would dispute his accuracy. That it was newly-acquired is another story.

I imagine accuracy is gauged by runs scored per over. At least that is the basis used by Larwood, for he quotes figures for 1930, 1931 and 1932. They show for 1932: overs bowled 866, runs scored 2,084.

However, a little research revealed that in 1928, four years earlier, he bowled 834 overs for 2,003 runs, and a short mathematical calculation will reveal slightly greater accuracy in 1928 than in 1932.

But a far more important matter is this. If body-line is allowed in first-class cricket, it must be allowed in *all* forms of cricket. One bowler cannot have a monopoly of a theory. For this reason, I again quote Larwood from his book. "If it really was body-line, bowling would be really dangerous to the batsmen."

When the personnel of the English Team to tour Australia in 1932–33 was announced, I foresaw the possibility of trouble because of the abnormal selection in England's team of four fast bowlers.

Body-line was first used against me in a match on the Melbourne Cricket Ground between the M.C.C. and an Australian XI. I reported privately to certain cricket administrators that, in my opinion, there would be serious trouble unless the matter was dealt with quickly. Then after the First Test had been played in Sydney, Dr. E. P. Barbour reviewed the game and made a very strong appeal for the elimination of this new type of bowling. He made the following comment:—

"The deliberate banging of the ball down less than half-way so that it flies up round the batsman's head is not cricket. If continued, and extended to all grades of cricket as they should be if they are fair, the end result of such tactics will be the disappearance from first-class cricket of every champion after he has put up with three or four years of assault and battery. Perhaps a more serious aspect still is the imminent danger to the good fellowship and friendly rivalry that has always been associated with cricket."

Up to this time the cricket administrators had not been sufficiently impressed with the views of players to make any move.

I always visualised the misunderstanding which would arise if exception was taken to body-line bowling at a time when we were being defeated. It was for that reason I again privately, but very forcibly, expressed my views to certain authorities, after the Melbourne Test Match which we won.

Here was the psychological moment, if any action at all was to be taken, to let M.C.C. know Australia's views.

I thought then, and I think now, that Australia's great mistake was in not dispassionately making an effort to clear up misunderstandings when the Tests were one all. It was ultimately done in the heat of battle at a much less appropriate time.

It must be admitted that although the Australian players and most ex-players strongly condemned the new type of bowling at once, this unanimity did not occur so readily amongst cricket officials, many of whom accused our players of squealing. One State Cricket Association had a motion brought before it to the effect that "The Association disassociate itself with the action of the Board in sending the first cable to England." The motion was defeated by only one vote.

The action of the Board of Control and the cables which passed at that time are now history.

The Australian Board appointed a Committee consisting of Messrs. Roger Hartigan, M. A. Noble, W. M. Woodfull and Vic. Richardson to report on what action was required to eliminate such bowling from cricket. The Committee framed a suggested new rule which was duly sent to the M.C.C. for approval, but up to that time the M.C.C. still had no evidence.

When the West Indian Team visited England in 1933, they had two excellent fast bowlers in Martindale and Constantine, who tried out Jardine's theory in the Second Test Match at Manchester. One result was that Hammond "had his chin laid open by one of many short-pitched rising balls" *(Wisden* 1934). Hammond is reported to have said then and there that either this type of bowling must be abolished or he would retire from first-class cricket.

Jack Hobbs made a similar threat after his experience against Bowes in 1932. A humorous sidelight was the reversal of opinion by players when they themselves had to face it.

George Duckworth thought body-line against Australians quite in order. On returning to England in 1933 he gave lectures and said so. That was before Lancashire met Nottingham.

Then it became a different story. Photos were taken of Duckworth's bruises and used as exhibits.

Lancashire broke off diplomatic relations with Notts. and refused to play against them in the County Championship.

Retribution if you like! Fifty years earlier Notts. had declined to play Lancashire because the latter team had amongst its players one whose action Notts. considered unfair.

The M.C.C. took steps to investigate the position, and at a joint meeting of the Advisory County Cricket Committee and the Board of Control of Test matches at home, held at Lord's in November 1933, it was agreed that any form of bowling "which is obviously a direct attack by the bowler upon the batsman" would be an offence against the spirit of the game. It was decided to leave the matter to the captains. This principle was affirmed by the Imperial Cricket Conference in July 1934.

However, this did not suffice, for the same type of bowling still persisted. In November 1934 the M.C.C. issued a communication indicating that "as a result of their own observations and from reports received, the M.C.C. Committee consider that there is evidence that cases of the bowler making a direct attack upon the batsman have on occasions taken place during the last cricket season."

In order to eliminate this type of bowling from the game, the M.C.C. Committee ruled: "That the type of bowling regarded as a direct attack by the bowler upon the batsman, and therefore unfair, consists in persistent and systematic bowling of fast short-pitched balls at the batsman standing clear of his wicket."

I have gone to some length to detail what occurred because I want to establish the all-important point that Australia did not stop body-line bowling. Certainly the original protest came from Australia (if we exclude Sir Pelham Warner's first comment) simply because Australian batsmen were the first ones exposed to its dangers. But immediately the M.C.C. Committee were satisfied that such a type of bowling existed, they acted promptly and firmly to define it and to outline the procedure to be adopted by the umpires to stop it.

Larwood himself was very critical of Australia's attempts to legislate against this type of cricket, and he wrote: "Cricket ought to be eternally grateful that its laws are made by the M.C.C." I hope he is still of the same opinion.

Could Body-line be Mastered?

I doubt if this question can be authoritatively answered.

It was used consistently for only one season against the same players, and nobody mastered it. A batsman who played defensively would certainly get caught by one of the short-leg fieldsmen. To try to hook the ball would result sooner or later in a catch on the boundary. Neither defence nor attack could overcome it for long, unless the batsman was particularly lucky.

Playing the good length balls and dodging the others may sound all right in theory, but it would not work in practice. The batsman doing this must of necessity be hit.

In fact no Australian batsman of any note failed to get hit, some on many occasions. Players naturally began to take the view that there were other sports offering many of the attractions of cricket without the risk of serious injury.

After his retirement from Test cricket, Hammond wrote about body-line, and I greatly admired his forthright condemnation thereof. Remember that Hammond was a member of the English Team which used it, and later became Captain of England. This is what he said:—

"I condemn it absolutely. Body-line is dangerous. I believe that only good luck was responsible for the fact that no one was killed by body-line. I have had to face it, and I would have got out of the game if it had been allowed to persist!

I doubt if there was any answer to such bowling unless grave risks of injury were courted."

In that 1932–3 season I endeavoured to counter body-line by unorthodox methods which involved stepping away to cut the ball to the off, and in my view exposed me to a graver risk of injury than the orthodox type of batting. Whilst not completely successful, I did score over 50 runs in an innings 4 times in 4 Test Matches.

McCabe and Richardson both tried to counter it by orthodox methods. Both were very capable, game players and excellent hookers, yet each of them could only once exceed 50 in an innings in the same four matches. Our comparative figures in those four Tests were:—

	Inns.	Runs	N.O.	H.S.	Average
Bradman	8	396	1	103	56.57
Richardson	8	230	—	83	28.7
McCabe	8	166	—	73	20.7

In many quarters I was the subject of bitter adverse criticism for my methods. Jack Fingleton, a contemporary player, later wrote a book in which he cast very grave reflections on my tactics. It may be well to remind readers that his last 3 Test innings against Jardine's men yielded 1, 0 and 0, whereupon he was dropped from the Australian team. In the same 3 innings I scored 177 runs at an average of 88.5. These figures scarcely give Fingleton any authority to criticise my methods. Apparently I had to make a century every time and also be hit more often than anyone else to satisfy the tastes of some. May I be pardoned for again quoting Constantine, a great batsman, and one of the fast bowlers who used body-line against England at Manchester. He says:—

> "Of all batsmen in the world the last two to whom body-line should ever be bowled are Bradman and McCabe."

Furthermore, he refers to Jardine making a century against it and says that to stand up and play defensive strokes at Lord's or the Oval as he did at Old Trafford would have been quite impossible, and Jardine was over 6 feet in height. How much harder for those of short stature. It wasn't only a question of whether it could be mastered, but rather that fellows would not bother to try—they would not consider it worth the candle.

Undoubtedly body-line was a reaction against the dominance of the bat over the ball, magnified by my own fortuitous 1930 season in England. But it was the wrong remedy. Killing a patient is not the way to cure his disease.

It was also a form of protest against the inadequacy of the L.B.W. law, because bowlers get very exasperated when they beat a batsman only to be deprived of his wicket by his pads.

Body-line certainly did some good in that it caused an alteration in the L.B.W. law (which M.C.C. agreed to at the time).

In my view the L.B.W. alteration, admirable though it was, did not go far enough. Long before the advent of body-line, I was in favour of an alteration to help bowlers. I openly advocated a change in 1933; I again made a strong appeal in an article I wrote in *Wisden* in 1938, and I am still agitating for a further change.

Recently I read an article where the writer was uncharitable enough to contend that my suggestion is related to my retirement. He obviously was poorly informed about my past expressions on the subject.

And there I want to end my references to body-line bowling. It was a passing phase, and I sincerely trust there will never be any need for umpires to contemplate taking action as they are empowered to do.

But I think it is desirable that the facts as detailed herein should be chronicled so that the matter shall be viewed in its proper perspective. The whole thing caused great misgivings and created much feeling. The best way for any reservations in the minds of the English public to be finally swept away is for them fully to understand and appreciate the real facts.

From *Farewell to Cricket, 1950*

To my mind the post-Bodyline administrators badly over-reacted and things should never have escalated the way they did. The Australians, however, saw the great worth of a hard-working man in Harold Larwood and welcomed him back on his retirement when he chose to emigrate with his family to Australia.

This piece is beautifully written, taking the reader right out into the middle during that fateful Adelaide Test. When I was last in Adelaide I spoke with a local historian who pointed out that most of the crowd in 1932 (largely male) would have been wearing heavy tweed suits and, in that temperature, would have been seriously hot and uncomfortable. It would certainly have been part of the reason why the crowd were so quick to anger.

HAROLD LARWOOD

Duncan Hamilton

Adelaide: January 1933

The tipping point of the Bodyline series – the ball that felled Bert Oldfield – wasn't bowled to a Bodyline field either. But it didn't matter. The climate was so fevered that Bill Woodfull, the Australian Board of Control and even those who paid to watch were blind to, and unable to discriminate between, genuine fast bowling and Bodyline – even when Jardine, the auteur of it, didn't deploy a leg-side field. It became impossible for them to distinguish legitimate aggression from the tactic itself. Whatever the strength of the evidence – and however clear that evidence might be – the accused was always going to be Harold Larwood, exposed to a spillage of hate, and the verdict against him was always going to be guilty.

Larwood noticed on his first trip to Australia that one of every three or four balls skimmed off the surface of pitches and that the bounce was unpredictable. 'There was no real need to dig it in,' he said. 'The bounce occurred naturally – especially with the new ball. You never really knew how high it might be.'

Oldfield was on strike when Jardine took the new ball, which he lobbed to Larwood. Oldfield had made 41 impressive runs, frequently pulling Larwood through mid-wicket. The delivery that struck him was short and dropped a foot outside off stump. He decided to step across to hook or pull again, lost sight of it because of the low sightscreen and mistimed his shot. He played blindly and too soon, and got an edge that flew into the right side of his forehead – just below the hairline. The ground began to slide away from him. Oldfield knew immediately that if the ball had struck him on the temple 'it would have been the end for me'. He moved in rapid, short jerky steps from the crease. His legs collapsed beneath him, everything spun – the picket fence, the ground, the faces in the far distance. In confusion and pain, he tried to take his cap off, and then he put it on again. After he had hit Woodfull, Larwood did nothing more than kick the turf at the bowler's end, bringing up a small divot, and then turned his back on the scene, as if he didn't care. This time he dashed up the pitch, his face as white as alabaster. A clammy terror went through him; he feared Oldfield was dead. If the peak of his cap hadn't broken the trajectory of the ball, he might have been. Oldfield was lucky. He suffered a linear fracture of the right frontal bone. 'I'm sorry, Bertie,' said Larwood in blind terror. Oldfield's eyes were flat and blank, like dark windows. 'It's not your fault, Harold,' said Oldfield eventually in a low moan. 'I was trying to hook you for four.' If only Oldfield's reply could have been broadcast at the moment; or if only the crowd could have heard his view that 'criticism of Larwood is unjustified'.

As Oldfield went down under the force of the blow, the Oval swelled with anger, and that anger rolled down and across the pitch as a visceral, shrieking roar that 'frightened' Larwood. The atmosphere turned sulphurous. Crimson faces, with eyes on stalks like cartoon characters, came to the fence and seemed to press against Larwood's own face – even though he was more than 30 yards away from most of them. He could feel the crowd's loathing prickling his skin. There was screaming, and he could see fists clenched into tight balls of hate. 'I felt,' he said, 'as if one false move would bring the crowd down on me.' If one 'idiot' lunged over the fence, he was convinced that thousands would follow and he'd be buried beneath them. He turned to Les Ames, who was equally distressed: 'If they come,' he said, his voice breaking, 'you can take the leg stump for protection. I'll take the middle.'

The police deployed mounted troopers to ensure order. Contemporary reports talked about the threat of riot and physical violence, and all his life Larwood was convinced that view was valid. On the field, he prayed quietly to himself that it wouldn't happen. A jug of water and a towel were brought to bathe Oldfield's bloody, broken head. Woodfull emerged from the picket pavilion gate in a dark suit – his face grim, his stride long, purposeful and bristling, his legs and arms working furiously to get him to his stricken colleague. There's no question that Woodfull's sole concern was the welfare of his wicket keeper. He was a loyal, principled man, and he would have seen it as his duty as captain to be alongside the wounded Oldfield. But the sight of him in such sensitive circumstances – solid and slightly aggressive, like a marching soldier heading for the front line – was inflammatory. Here was Woodfull, who everyone now knew abhorred Bodyline and was sickened by it, emerging as the gallant focus of the opposition to the tourists' tactics; white knight to Jardine's black.

Larwood lay on his side near his bowling mark, tossing the ball up in the air with his right hand, as if casually flicking a coin on a street corner. Waiting for his panicky heart to slow, he began picking at dry stalks of grass and tried to give the impression that the noise – so extreme he could barely think – and the stream of insults didn't worry him. But his stomach was churning, and there was a rough, dry taste in his mouth as he watched Woodfull slowly guide Oldfield off the field.

Larwood got to his feet gradually, as if any sudden movement might provoke the crowd, and the England fieldsmen returned to the same positions for the new batsman, Bill O'Reilly. 'I reckon it took me ten minutes to get in and to shape to the first ball,' remembered O'Reilly. 'I wouldn't have minded if it had taken me twenty minutes.'

Jardine displayed what Larwood called 'cold courage'. He looked unflappable, as if just waiting for a lightning storm to pass. 'I don't know what was going through his mind,' said Larwood, 'but he seemed so calm.' Jardine gestured with a nod of his head to check whether Larwood was composed enough to bowl. As he began his run, the crowd started to count him out in a ghastly shout of 'one, two, three' which ended after ten with the cry 'out, you bastard!' Their words couldn't hurt him. England bowled out the shaken Australians for 222.

On the field, Larwood was so commanding that he created an

illusion. His wide shoulders and stocky build gave the impression of height. Off the field, he could wander into an Australian bar in his suit and tie rather than his whites and no one recognized him. 'I'd go in for a quiet drink and hear them say all sorts of things about me. People who'd just seen me play had no idea that I was standing next to them eavesdropping on their conversation. Most Australians thought I was six foot six.' It explains why at the end of that day's play the flustered policeman who came into the dressing room to escort him out of the ground had to ask: 'Which one is Larwood?' Bill Voce pointed out his friend. 'What have I done wrong?' asked Larwood innocently.

Larwood had been called a 'bastard' so many times that the word had lost its meaning to him. He came out into the jostling knot of swearing, spitting men in suits, who looked ready to string him from a gibbet. The policeman stood close to his shoulder; Voce followed behind to ward off anyone who might lurch at Larwood from behind. 'Bastard ... bastard ... bastard' was all he could hear. Larwood went back to the hotel and stayed in his room.

As the crow flies, just three miles separate the terraced house where Larwood was born and grew up from Lord Byron's ancestral home, Newstead Abbey. Setting aside the geography of Nottinghamshire, the poet and the fast bowler have nothing else in common – except for this: Byron awoke one morning to find that his poetry had made him famous. Larwood awoke, the day after striking Oldfield, to find that his bowling had made him infamous. He sat in the lobby and hid behind his newspaper.

Soon the cables began. The Australian Board of Control was thoughtlessly knee-jerk in its approach and intemperate in its language. It didn't possess sufficient guile to frame an appropriate and subtle policy against Bodyline. It also lacked the cleverness to condemn Jardine strongly without insulting the MCC and the farsightedness to draft a diplomatic plan that might have curtailed the tactics. Rather than resolve the problem, its accusations made it worse. Its first cable to the MCC – sent on 18 January, the penultimate day of the Adelaide Test – fell into the easy trap of relying on the term Bodyline, a word created in the world of journalism rather than cricket, and then of adopting a mildly threatening tone:

Body-line bowling has assumed such proportions as to menace the best interests of the game, making protection of the body by the batsmen the main consideration. This is causing intensely bitter feeling between the players as well as injury. In our opinion it is unsportsmanlike. Unless stopped at once it is likely to upset the friendly relations existing between Australia and England.

The Board of Control made another crass mistake in releasing the telegram as a curt statement to the newspapers at the same time as dispatching it in a huff to Lord's. It appeared in the Stop Press columns in London before arriving at Lord's. The subsequent headlines raised the stakes still higher, and pricked the egos of the MCC committee. In its rush simultaneously to reclaim its dignity, communicate its anger and lash out, the Board of Control failed to grasp two fundamentally important things: from half a world away, the MCC's view of Bodyline was based on accounts in English newspapers, which had been generally positive. If Bodyline was used today, the Test would be live on satellite television. The wickets and major incidents would be seen on an endless loop on news programmes, and played and re-played in slow motion in front of pundits – grizzled ex-pros gathered around a microphone pontificating about it. The newspapers would provide sophisticated graphics of field-placings. The TV cameras would be waiting outside the hospital where Oldfield was taken and the hotel where England were staying. The average-man-in-the-street – in England and Australia – would be canvassed for his views. And Larwood would be pursued for an interview even before leaving the field. He and Bodyline would be in the swirl of 'instant news'.

In 1932–33, newsreel footage could take up to six weeks to arrive from Australia. Bodyline for the MCC was read about rather than viewed. Also, the phrases in the Board's cable, such as 'menace the best interests of the game' – and certainly the use of the word 'unsportsmanlike' – were provocative. At that stage, the MCC saw its duty as supporting its captain and manager. It wasn't fully aware of the sensitivities Bodyline had pricked, the growing resentment among the Australian public, or the passion that had spurred the Board to write the cable in the first place. The MCC slapped the Australians straight across both cheeks. The opening two lines of its cable, which followed after five days of thinking carefully about what to say, were deliberately wounding:

> We, the Marylebone Cricket Club, deplore your cable. We deprecate your opinion that there has been unsportsmanlike play.

The last, very long, line was an exercise in gauntlet-throwing:

> We hope the situation is not now as serious as your cable would seem to indicate, but if it is such as to jeopardize the good relations between England and Australian cricketers and you consider it desirable to cancel remainder of programme we would consent, but with great reluctance.

A week later the rattled and disunited Board of Control sent its reply. The truth came to them belatedly, rather like the descending apple that struck Newton. The Board realized that the MCC's opinion was prejudiced by the fact that it hadn't seen 'the actual play'. It could easily shelter behind the irrefutable point that Bodyline did not contravene cricket's sacred laws; any tawny-coloured copy of *Wisden* proved that too.

The Board finally understood that it needed to act positively rather than negatively. The Australians appointed a committee to report on how Bodyline bowling could be scrubbed cleanly out of the game and added, rather sheepishly, that 'we do not consider it necessary to cancel the remainder of the programme'. For one thing, it would have been financial insanity to have done so. As Larwood made clear: 'Bodyline drew back the crowds.' The Australians did reiterate that Bodyline was 'opposed to the spirit of cricket' – another euphemistic dig at England's supposed lack of sportsmanship – and said that it had become 'unnecessarily dangerous to the players'. The Board missed a trick. It ought to have withdrawn the allegation of 'unsportsmanlike' behaviour, instead of sharpening it. On 2 February, the MCC was able to bite them again – albeit very politely – when it asked: 'May we accept ... that the good sportsmanship of our team is not in question?' Unless it was prepared for the sight of the England players packing their bags and walking up the gangplank on the next boat home, the Board had no option but to concede that Bodyline hadn't been unsporting after all. 'We do not regard the sportsmanship of your team to be in question,' its next cable assured the MCC. It had just performed a Tour de France of back-pedalling.

The accusation of unsportsmanlike play – the worst possible insult because it implied cheating – couldn't be allowed to stand. To have been boneheaded enough to level it in the first place was one thing. To repeat it was more than a slur; it was like the white glove across the face that summoned the recipient to a duel to protect his honour and reputation. The MCC committee was cricket's high society: titled, ennobled through birthright or distinction, mostly educated at Eton or Harrow and Oxbridge, and politically Conservative. If the MCC committee had been a building, then Gaudi would have built it and given it a modernist twist. It was a grand, elaborate, complex-looking construction which included three Viscounts, one Duke, two Earls, four Lords and three Knights. The President was Viscount Lewisham, a former Tory MP and previously Lord Great Chamberlain of England. His father and grandfather were both past Presidents of the MCC; Lord Hawke dominated English and particularly Yorkshire cricket for half a century and served as President during the First World War; Viscount Bridgeman had been Home Secretary and First Lord of the Admiralty during the 1920s; Sir Stanley Jackson was, like Hawke, a distinguished former Yorkshire cricketer – more than 10,000 runs and 500 wickets – as well as an MP, Chairman of the Conservative Party and Governor of Bengal. And so it went on …

This aristocracy, the *Debrett's* of cricket, saw itself as the infallible arbiter of what was and was not cricket. It upheld the values of sporting prowess taught on the lush playing fields of the public schools and had its own clear-eyed view of the proper and correct way to 'play up and play the game'. Even if it hadn't, the players, seething against the term 'unsportsmanlike', would have rebelled unless the Board withdrew its charge against them. As Larwood recalled: 'We felt we were in a false position in having to take the field with the stigma of the Board's term still on us.' Larwood remembered Jardine's anxiety both before and after the cables began. The Australian press whipped up several stories about dissent and squabbling among the England camp, dramatically described as 'being at war with itself'. Maurice Tate was said to have flung beer over Jardine, which Larwood said was untrue. There was supposed to be open hostility towards Jardine's disciplinarian approach, which was only partly true. As Larwood made clear, any 'grievances … were not nearly as serious as was made out' and stemmed not from Bodyline but from the frustration of players unable to force a way into the team. 'There were players who were unhappy,' he said, 'but it was because they couldn't get into the Tests. Australia's an awfully long way to go if you don't get a game.'

At the end of the fifth day of the Adelaide Test, Jardine called a meeting in a private room of the team hotel. There were only two points on the agenda. Should Bodyline/leg theory be abandoned? Should Jardine continue as captain? When Warner was the first to speak, [bowler] Tommy Mitchell told him to sit down and shut up: 'It's got nowt to do with you,' he said. Everyone, however, finally had a say. The players liked the direction and purpose Jardine brought to the series, and the thought of winning the Ashes too. Jardine won his vote of confidence unanimously: 'a vote for England' is how Larwood put it. Bodyline would stay. For him, the ends justified the means. His captain's stiff-upper-lip, win-at-any-cost, grind-the-bastards-down attitude convinced Larwood and others that the Ashes could only be won with Jardine. He was as different as it is possible to be in approach and temperament from the circumspect Woodfull. 'Jardine might have been unpopular with a few of the players,' said Larwood, 'but everybody respected and admired him and many of us liked him.' Asked to define his qualities, Larwood replied simply: 'He was ruthless.'

England made 412 in their second innings and smartly removed the Australians – with Oldfield 'absent hurt' on the scorecard – for 193. In a win by 338 runs, Larwood finished with match figures of seven for 126. 'I was quick there,' he said. 'People just forget it because of what else happened.'

From *Harold Larwood, 2009*

THE BOWLING CONTROVERSY

Text of the cables

During the tour of the M.C.C. team in Australia in 1932–33, exception was taken in that country to the methods adopted by certain of the visiting bowlers, and long correspondence by cable between the M.C.C. and the Australian Board of Control followed. Below will be found, in chronological order, the text of these cables, together with—in proper sequence—a short report of meetings bearing upon the subject.

From Australian Board of Control to M.C.C., Jan. 18, 1933.

"Body-line bowling has assumed such proportions as to menace the best interests of the game, making protection of the body by the batsmen the main consideration.

"This is causing intensely bitter feeling between the players as well as injury. In our opinion it is unsportsmanlike.

"Unless stopped at once it is likely to upset the friendly relations existing between Australia and England."

From M.C.C. to Australian Board of Control, Jan. 23, 1933.

"We, Marylebone Cricket Club, deplore your cable. We deprecate your opinion that there has been unsportsmanlike play. We have fullest confidence in captain, team and managers and are convinced that they would do nothing to infringe either the Laws of Cricket or the spirit of the game. We have no evidence that our confidence has been misplaced. Much as we regret accidents to Woodfull and Oldfield, we understand that in neither case was the bowler to blame. If the Australian Board of Control wish to propose a new Law or Rule, it shall receive our careful consideration in due course.

"We hope the situation is not now as serious as your cable would seem to indicate, but if it is such as to jeopardize the good relations between English and Australian cricketers and you consider it desirable to cancel remainder of programme we would consent, but with great reluctance."

From Australian Board of Control to M.C.C., Jan. 30, 1933.

"We, Australian Board of Control, appreciate your difficulty in dealing with the matter raised in our cable without having seen the actual play. We unanimously regard body-line bowling, as adopted in some of the games in the present tour, as being opposed to the spirit of cricket, and unnecessarily dangerous to the players.

"We are deeply concerned that the ideals of the game shall be protected and have, therefore, appointed a committee to report on the action necessary to eliminate such bowling from Australian cricket as from beginning of the 1933–34 season.

"We will forward a copy of the Committee's recommendations for your consideration, and it is hoped co-operation as to its application to all cricket. We do not consider it necessary to cancel remainder of programme."

The committee appointed consisted of Messrs. R. J. Hartigan (Queensland) representing the Board of Control; W. M. Woodfull, V. Y. Richardson and M. A. Noble.

From M.C.C. to Australian Board of Control, Feb. 2, 1933.

"We, the Committee of the Marylebone Cricket Club note with pleasure that you do not consider it necessary to cancel the remainder of programme, and that you are postponing the whole issue involved until after the present tour is completed. May we accept this as a clear indication that the good sportsmanship of our team is not in question?

"We are sure you will appreciate how impossible it would be to play any Test Match in the spirit we all desire unless both sides were satisfied there was no reflection upon their sportsmanship.

"When your recommendation reaches us it shall receive our most careful consideration and will be submitted to the Imperial Cricket Conference."

From Australian Board of Control to M.C.C., Feb. 8, 1933.

"We do not regard the sportsmanship of your team as being in question.

"Our position was fully considered at the recent meeting in Sydney and is as indicated in our cable of January 30.

"It is the particular class of bowling referred to there in which we consider is not in the best interests of cricket, and in this view we understand we are supported by many eminent English cricketers.

"We join heartily with you in hoping that the remaining Tests will be played with the traditional good feeling."

The Australian Board of Control, meeting on April 21, 1933, considered a proposal submitted to them by the special sub-committee set up to consider the question of "body-line" bowling and cabled M.C.C. asking that body to give the proposal their consideration. The cable read as follows: "Australian Board adopted following addition to Laws of Cricket in Australia, namely:—

"Any ball delivered which, in the opinion of the umpire at the bowler's end is bowled at the batsman with the intent to intimidate or injure him shall be considered unfair and 'No-ball' shall be called. The bowler shall be notified of the reason. If the offence be repeated by the same bowler in the same innings he shall be immediately instructed by the umpire to cease bowling and the over shall be regarded as completed. Such bowler shall not again be permitted to bowl during the course of the innings then in progress."

"Law 48a shall not apply to this Law. Foregoing submitted for your consideration and it is hoped co-operation by application to all cricket."

From M.C.C. to Australian Board of Control, June 12, 1933.

"The M.C.C. Committee have received and carefully considered the cable of the Australian Board of Control of April 28th last. They have also received and considered the reports of the Captain and Managers of the cricket team which visited Australia 1932–1933.

"With regard to the cable of the Australian Board of Control of April 28th last, the Committee presume that the class of bowling to which the proposed new law would apply is that referred to as 'body-line' bowling in the Australian Board of Control's cable of January 18th. The Committee consider that the term 'body-line' bowling is misleading and improper. It has led to much inaccuracy of thought by confusing the short bumping ball, whether directed on the off, middle or leg stump, with what is known as 'leg-theory.'

"The term 'body-line' would appear to imply a direct attack by the bowler on the batsman. The Committee consider that such an implication applied to any English bowling in Australia is improper and incorrect. Such action on the part of any bowler would be an offence against the spirit of the game and would be immediately condemned. The practice of bowling on the leg stump with a field placed on the leg side necessary for such bowling is legitimate, and has been in force for many years. It has generally been referred to as 'leg-theory.' The present habit of batsmen who move in front of their wicket with the object of gliding straight balls to leg tends to give the impression that the bowler is bowling at the batsman, especially in the case of a fast bowler when the batsman mistimes the ball and is hit.

"The new Law recommended by the Australian Board of Control does not appear to the Committee to be practicable. Firstly, it would place an impossible task on the umpire and secondly, it would place in the hands of the umpire a power over the game which would be more than dangerous, and which any umpire might well fear to exercise.

"The Committee have had no reason to give special attention to 'leg-theory' as practised by fast bowlers. They will, however, watch carefully during the present season for anything which might be regarded as unfair or prejudicial to the best interests of the game. They propose to invite opinions and suggestions from County Clubs and Captains at the end of the season, with a view to enabling them to express an opinion on this matter at a Special Meeting of the Imperial Cricket Conference.

"With regard to the reports of the Captain and Managers, the Committee, while deeply appreciative of the private and public hospitality shewn to the English Team, are much concerned with regard to barracking, which is referred to in all the reports, and against which there is unanimous deprecation. Barracking has, unfortunately, always been indulged in by spectators in Australia to a degree quite unknown in this Country. During the late tour, however, it would appear to have exceeded all previous experience, and on occasions to have become thoroughly objectionable. There appears to have been little or no effort on the part of those responsible for the administration of the game in Australia to interfere, or to control this exhibition. This was naturally regarded by members of the team as a serious lack of consideration for them. The Committee are of opinion that cricket played under such conditions is robbed of much of its value as a game, and that unless barracking is stopped, or is greatly moderated in Australia, it is difficult to see how the continuance of representative matches can serve the best interest of the game.

"The Committee regret that these matters have to be dealt with by correspondence and not by personal conference. If at any time duly accredited representatives of Australian Cricket could meet the Committee in conference, such conference would be welcomed by M.C.C."

From Australian Board of Control to M.C.C., Sept. 22, 1933.

"We note that you consider that a form of bowling which amounted to a direct attack by the bowler on the batsman would be against the spirit of the game. We agree with you that Leg-theory Bowling as it has been generally practised for many years is not open to objection. On these matters there does not appear to be any real difference between our respective views.

"We feel that while the type of bowling to which exception was taken in Australia, strictly was not in conflict with the Laws of Cricket, yet its continued practice would not be in the best interests of the game. May we assume that you concur in this point of view and that the teams may thus take the field in 1934 with that knowledge?

"We are giving consideration to the question of barracking and you may rely upon our using our best endeavours to have it controlled in future tours.

"We are most anxious that the cordial relations which have so long existed between English and Australian cricket shall continue."

From M.C.C. to Australian Board of Control, Oct. 9, 1933.

"The M.C.C. Committee appreciate the friendly tone of your cable and they heartily reciprocate your desire for the continuance of cordial relations.

"In their view the difference between us seems to be rather on the question of fact than on any point of interpretation of the Laws of Cricket or of the spirit of the game. They agree and have always agreed that a form of bowling which is obviously a direct attack by the bowler upon the batsman would be an offence against the spirit of the game.

"Your team can certainly take the field with the knowledge and with the full assurance that cricket will be played here in the same spirit as in the past and with the single desire to promote the best interests of the game in both countries.

"The Committee much appreciate your promise to take the question of barracking into consideration with a view to ensuring that it shall be kept within reasonable bounds.

"Your team can rely on a warm welcome from M.C.C., and every effort will be made to make their visit enjoyable."

From Australian Board of Control to M.C.C., Nov. 16, 1933.

"We appreciate the terms of your cablegram of October 9 and assume that such cable is intended to give the assurance asked for in our cablegram of September 22.

"It is on this understanding that we are sending a team in 1934."

A joint meeting of the Advisory County Cricket Committee and the Board of Control of Test Matches at Home, at which the county captains were present, was held at Lord's on Thursday, November 23, 1933, to consider the replies received from the counties to the M.C.C.'s circular letter in regard to fast leg-theory bowling.

A decision was reached that no alteration of the Law was desirable. It was agreed that any form of bowling which is obviously a direct attack by the bowler upon the batsman would be an offence against the spirit of the game.

It was decided to leave the matter to the captains in complete confidence that they would not permit or countenance bowling of such type.

From M.C.C. to Australian Board of Control, Dec. 12, 1933.

"Reference your cable of November 16th, you must please accept our cable of October 9th, which speaks for itself, as final.

"We cannot go beyond the assurance therein given. We shall welcome Australian cricketers who come to play cricket with us next year. If, however, your Board of Control decide that such games should be deferred, we shall regret their decision.

"Please let us know your Board's final decision as soon as possible and in any event before the end of the year."

From Australian Board of Control to M.C.C., Dec. 14, 1933.

"With further reference to your cable of October 9 and your confirmatory cable of December 12 in reply to ours of November 16, we, too, now regard the position finalised. Our team will leave Australia on March 9."

From M.C.C. to Australian Board of Control, Dec. 14, 1933.

"Thank you for your cable. We are very glad to know we may look forward to welcoming the Australians next summer. We shall do all in our power to make their visit enjoyable."

From *Wisden Cricketers' Almanack, 1934*

BY THE EDITOR OF WISDEN CRICKETERS' ALMANACK

Sydney J. Southerton

Had the foregoing cables been the medical history sheets of a person suddenly afflicted by some mental or physical trouble a doctor would have experienced little difficulty in tracing and analysing the disease from its onset to its cure. In like manner cricketers can gather from the cables almost the whole course of the disturbance brought about between the M.C.C. and the Australian Board of Control over the question of fast leg-theory bowling. I have purposely omitted to use the expression "body-line bowling." It may have conveyed to those to whom it was presented at the outset the meaning the inventor of it wished to infer, but to my mind it was an objectionable term, utterly foreign to cricket, and calculated to stir up strife when the obvious aim of everybody should have been directed towards the prevention of any breach.

Happily the controversy is now at an end, and little reason exists, therefore, to flog what we can regard as a "dead horse." But, obviously from the historical point of view, something on the subject must be said. I hope and believe that the ventilation of their grievances by the Australians, and the placatory replies of the M.C.C. will have done much towards imparting a better spirit to Test Matches which of recent years have become battles rather than pleasurable struggles. A false atmosphere has pervaded them. During the last few tours of M.C.C. teams in Australia, and the visits of the Australians to this country one could not fail to detect a subtle change taking place in the conduct of Test Matches—reflected unfortunately in the style of play of the cricketers themselves. The *result* of the contests was given a prominence out of keeping even with the importance of Test Matches, and the true sense of perspective stood in danger of disappearing altogether.

There is no need to enter into some of the reasons for the hostility with which D. R. Jardine in particular and certain of his team were received by the huge crowds in Australia. Animosity existed and was fanned into flame largely by the use of the term "body-line" when Larwood and others met with such success against the leading Australian batsmen. To such an extent had real bitterness grown that the storm burst during the Third Test Match at Adelaide. The dispatch of the petulant cablegram by the Australian Board of Control even placed the completion of the tour in jeopardy. Saner counsels prevailed, and, although tension existed for months afterwards, the M.C.C. for their part never lost their grip of the situation and, what was even more important, refused to be stampeded into any panic legislation. Whatever individual opinions were held at the time the M.C.C. Committee, as a whole, naturally stood by the captain of their Team in Australia. They had heard only one side of the question.

And now, what of this fast leg-theory method of bowling to which not only the Australian players themselves, but a vast majority of the people of Australia took such grave exception? With the dictum of the M.C.C. that any form of bowling which constitutes a direct attack by the bowler on the batsman is contrary to the spirit of the game everyone must unquestionably concur. D. R. Jardine, on his return to England, stated definitely in his book that the bowling against which the Australians demurred was not of this description, and Larwood, the chief exponent of it, said with equal directness that he had never intentionally bowled at a man. On the other hand, there are numerous statements by responsible Australians to the effect that the type of bowling adopted was calculated to intimidate batsmen, pitched as the ball was so short as to cause it to fly shoulder and head high and make batsmen, with the leg-side studded with fieldsmen, use the bat as a protection for their bodies or their heads rather than in defence of the wicket or to make a scoring stroke. Victor Richardson, the South Australian batsman, has said that when he took his ordinary stance at the wicket he found the ball coming on to his body; when he took guard slightly more to the leg-side he still had the ball coming at him; and with a still wider guard the ball continued to follow him. I hold no brief either for Jardine or Larwood or for Richardson, Woodfull or Bradman; but while some of the Australians may have exaggerated the supposed danger of this form of bowling I cling to the opinion that they cannot all be wrong. When the first mutterings of the storm were heard many people in this country were inclined to the belief that the Australians, seeing themselves in danger of losing the rubber, were not taking defeat in the proper spirit always expected from honourable opponents. I will confess that I thought they did not relish what seemed to me at that stage to be a continuous good-length bombardment by our fast bowlers on to their leg-stump. This idea I afterwards found was not quite correct.

There is nothing new in leg-theory bowling. The most notable exponent of it in recent years was Root, of Worcestershire; to go back to just before the War A. Jaques, of Hampshire, often exploited it with success; and to delve deeper into the past an Australian—no less than the famous Spofforth himself—would at times bowl on the leg-stump with an off-break and two fieldsmen close in on the leg-side. Root and Jaques were, however, medium-paced bowlers while Spofforth, even if he had a very destructive fast ball always at command, could not truthfully be classified as a fast bowler consistent in the pace of say Larwood, Knox, Richardson, Lockwood, or Kortright. Moreover, Root, Jaques and Spofforth almost invariably bowled a good length, so that the ball could be played either in a defensive manner or with the idea of turning it to leg, and when the batsman made a mistake in timing or in placing he usually paid the penalty by being caught.

That type of bowling, however, is very different from the kind sent down at top-speed with the ball flying past the shoulders or head of the batsman who has only a split second in which to make up his mind as to whether he will duck, move away, or attempt to play it with the bat high in the air. Against one sort a perfectly legitimate and reasonable stroke could be played without any apprehension of physical damage; against the other it seems to me that by touching the ball in defence of the upper part of his body or his head a batsman would be almost bound to be out. One would not accuse Hammond or Hendren of being slow on their feet, yet Hendren at Lord's on one occasion was not quick enough to get out of the way and received a crashing blow on his head, while last season at Manchester Hammond, in the Test Match against the West Indies, had his chin laid open, and on resuming his innings was caught off a similar kind of ball. We saw in that particular match at Old Trafford what I should conceive to be a somewhat pale—but no less disturbing—imitation of Larwood in Australia, when Martindale and Constantine on the one hand, and Clark, of Northamptonshire, on the other were giving a demonstration of fast leg-theory bowling. Not one of the three had the pace, accuracy of pitch, or deadliness of Larwood, but what they did was sufficient to convince many people with open minds on the subject that it was a noxious form of attack not to be encouraged in any way.

Cricketers whose memories go back to the days of the bad wickets at Lord's, are I think a little too prone to emphasise the fact that W. G. Grace and other famous batsmen of that era were often struck so frequently on the body that after their innings they were covered with bruises, but I should like to suggest that the blows they received were to a large extent caused by good-length balls getting up quickly off the rough turf. I certainly can find no trace in the course of a good deal of research among old reports and comments on these matches that the fast bowlers of those days like Tarrant and Jackson continually dropped the ball short with the idea of making it bounce.

Fast bowlers of all periods have delivered the ball short of a length on occasions—sometimes by accident, and sometimes by intention to keep batsmen on the *qui-vive*—but in modern days some of our bowlers of pace have become obsessed with the idea that it is necessary to do this three or four times in an over. I desire none of my readers to get the impression that I am against fast bowling. Nothing is further from my thoughts. I like to see fast bowling, the faster the better, but I do like to see it of good length and directed at the stumps.

The Australians without any doubt thought that during the last tour they were being bowled at, and small wonder that edging away as some of them unquestionably did they found themselves bowled when, instead of the expected short-pitched "bouncer," occasional good-length straight balls came along and beat them before they were in a proper position to defend their wickets. It is, to say the least, significant that G. O. Allen, whom nobody would place quite in the same class as Larwood, enjoyed many successes and for the most part obtained his wickets by bowling with which we in England are familiar. Surely, with his extra pace, Larwood could have done as well as Allen and so have prevented that bitter ill-feeling which led a good many people in this country to the belief that the winning of The Ashes had been gained at too great a cost to the relations hitherto existing between England and Australia.

For myself, I hope that we shall never see fast leg-theory bowling as used during the last tour in Australia exploited in this country. I think that (1) it is definitely dangerous; (2) it creates ill-feeling between the rival teams; (3) it invites reprisals; (4) it has a bad influence on our great game of cricket; and (5) it eliminates practically all the best strokes in batting. Mainly because it makes cricket a battle instead of a game I deplore its introduction and pray for its abolition, not by any legislative measures, but by the influence which our captains can bring to bear and by avoiding use of the objectionable form of attack take a great part in wiping away a blot. Early last season I heard Mr. Weigall, the Recorder of Gravesend, deliver a great speech at a dinner to the West Indies team, in which in beautifully chosen phrases he exhorted them always to look upon cricket with the idea that the game is of far greater importance than the result. If that lesson is driven home to all our cricketers we shall hear no more of the kind of bowling which so nearly brought about a severance of the cricket relations between England and Australia.

From *Wisden Cricketers' Almanack, 1934*

DOUGLAS JARDINE

Christopher Douglas

In 1939 he was back in the press box again, this time as correspondent to the *Daily Telegraph*. He covered nearly a full season of Championship matches and the first two Tests against the West Indies, and in this period he produced far and away his best cricket writing. The slightly long-winded style had tightened up considerably. He was as generous to the players as ever and even found a kind word or two for the selectors. He seemed to have acquired the greatest of all cricket writers' skills: knowing when to write about something else if the cricket is boring. His reports (lengthy by modern standards) often contained leisurely and entertaining musings on players and matches past and present but he was not given to making unfavourable comparisons with the glories of the past, and he was so modest about his own place in the game's history that when he referred to incidents on, say, the 1928–29 or 1932–33 tours he did so as if he hadn't been there at all.

By the beginning of August 1939 the amount of space devoted to cricket in the *Daily Telegraph* reflected the national preoccupation with the impending hostilities. Jardine ended his description of the Surrey v. Yorkshire match with the words, 'This is the last county match I shall see for some time as I am off to camp with the Territorials.'

Shortly afterwards, he was commissioned into the Royal Berkshire Regiment and went with the British Expeditionary Force to France where he served with distinction. In 1982, this story appeared in *The Observer*: 'He was sent by headquarters in Dunkirk into Belgium to discover why troops there had not made contact. Jardine found them all dead, commandeered a troop carrier and drove himself back through enemy lines.' I have not been able to verify this story but such an act of cold courage would have been quite in keeping with Jardine's character. He was fortunate enough to get back from Dunkirk but, like so many who had been through it, his feet were badly cut about. He volunteered to go back and help to hold Calais but his commanding officer turned him down. They were taking on single men only and not only was Jardine married but his wife had just given birth to their third child.

Over the next few months he was stationed at St Albans as a staff captain and the family rented a house nearby in Harpenden. The British Expeditionary Force was in the process of reorganisation and Jardine's responsibility was arranging transport for troops joining newly formed regiments. Being rather older than his fellow-captains and majors, he made no intimate friendships, but one fellow-officer remembers that he was in no way aloof. In fact, everyone was surprised by his diffidence and shy politeness, which was not at all what they had expected of the terror of Adelaide. He was frequently pressed to discuss the bodyline tour but he refused to be drawn, although he did once remark that, knowing the War Office, his next posting would be as Liaison Officer with the Australian Army.

As it happened, he spent the rest of the war in India – first of all in Quetta and then in Simla, where he was a major in the Central Provisions Directorate. He had a great liking for Simla and its incongruous English architecture, and he loved the historic landscape of the North-West Frontier, which he planned to explore extensively after the war. He became fluent in Hindustani (his daughter remembers that he often used to break into it at home), and he involved himself, albeit rather formally, in the social life of the base. An officer stationed there at the time wrote, 'In the evenings he always wore blue patrols, as ram-rod stiff as a Spy cartoon.' He was perfectly friendly though never intimate. He used to enjoy a game of snooker in the club but would discreetly withdraw when people started to bet on his skill (which was considerable).

He gave a series of lectures to the troops, mainly on cricket and fishing. He even managed to play a few games of cricket, but had little opportunity to show what he could do since the local umpires were as keen to take his wicket as were the bowlers. There was one first-class match however. It was in early 1944 at Bombay and its purpose was to raise money for war charities. Jardine captained a Services XI against an Indian XI led by Mushtaq Ali. Hardstaff and Jardine shared an attractive stand and both players made runs, but the Indian XI won an exciting match with 12 minutes to spare.

It may seem strange that a man with such exceptional gifts of courage and leadership should have been allowed to while away the latter half of the war doling out provisions. It has been stated that he was kept out of things because of bodyline, but this is quite untrue. The explanation, and one is certainly needed, is not so convenient. He had never been a great respecter of authority, or maybe it would be more accurate to say that he was unwilling to submit to the sort of authority for which he had no respect. In the army, his concern for the problems and welfare of those under his command lessened his effectiveness as a leader in the eyes of his superiors. Humanity, the very quality he has been said to have lacked, prevented him from being given more crucial work.

Like many in 1945, he found himself newly demobbed and without prospects. He had hoped to come back to a job in coal mining which had been promised to him, but he found that the job had disappeared and he had to look around for something else. Meanwhile Margaret Jardine had moved the family into an old manor house at Drayton, in Somerset. The move was not altogether successful, Jardine's temperament was not suited to rural tranquility and this, combined with his urgent need to find a job, resulted in another move to Radlett in Hertfordshire. He was then appointed Company Secretary to a firm of paper manufacturers in London, Wiggins Teape.

In 1946 he took part in a perfectly stage-managed centenary match at the Oval. It was not first-class but it was attended with ceremony worthy of a Test match. The sides were Surrey and Old England and the match was played in aid of Surrey's centenary appeal. There was a festival atmosphere with a band playing, the King present and the sun shining. 15,000 people saw Percy Fender lead out his Old England side which included Jardine, Sutcliffe, Hendren, Sandham, Woolley, Tate and Freeman. Surrey batted first and made 248 for 6 declared. Old England very nearly got the runs thanks to substantial innings from Woolley, Hendren and Jardine. Jardine and Hendren put on 108 with Jardine's contribution being 54. 'D. R. Jardine,' said *Wisden*, 'wearing his Oxford Harlequin cap, was as polished as ever in academic skill.'

When he was fielding he cut a lonely figure, according to one person who saw the match. He was positioned on the boundary and chased the ball with stiff-kneed studiousness, not joining in the conversations at the fall of each wicket or in between overs. It was his first major appearance since the outlawing of bodyline, and perhaps he was as nervous about talking to his team-mates as he was about the reception the crowd would give him. Both were cordial enough, it seems, without being overwhelming.

By 1948, a slight change of opinion had taken place. He was not

exonerated exactly, but the need for a scapegoat was not so pressing as before the war. The new attitude was reflected in *Wisden's*
obituary of M. R. Jardine, who died in the early part of 1947:

His son, D. R. Jardine, captained England during the Australian tour of 1932–33 when the Ashes were recovered in the
series of five matches made notable by the 'bodyline' description of specially fast bowling, introduced in a manner since
copied by Australian teams without objection by England or
adverse criticism.

Lindwall and Miller had humbled the 1946–47 English team with
the aid of a liberal sprinkling of short-pitched deliveries. It was not
bodyline but, because the bumper had been used so very sparingly
since 1935, its sudden re-introduction caused a certain amount of
consternation. And when Lindwall and Miller persisted with their
methods in the 1948 series, there were those who feared that things
might be getting out of hand again. The real cause of the trouble
was the usual one: one side had fast bowlers and the other did not.
The English feeling was that the score had at last been settled. The
crime of bodyline had, to a large extent, been expiated and Jardine
was no longer quite the guilty reminder to the nation's cricketing
conscience.

At the end of the 1948 season, he was persuaded to captain an
England XI against Glamorgan, the Champion County, at Cardiff.
His reception from the crowd was warm and enthusiastic. He made
no specially notable contribution to the match and even declined
to go for a win in the final session when it seemed to be there for
the taking. His undeniably slow batting passed almost without a
murmur; those present had the defeat of England in the Tests fresh
in their minds and Jardine's presence was a reminder that when he
was in his prime the Australians were far from invincible.

As had been the case after the First World War, there seemed
little hope of winning the Ashes for quite a few years. An excellent publication called *The Daily Worker Cricket Handbook 1949*,
which one would have expected to have been the least nationalisti-
cally minded, was quite distraught at England's inability to knock
the stuffing out of the Aussies, and bemoaned the absence of men
such as Jardine who had the mettle to put things right. (Just to
please the hard-line readership, though, there was an attack on

MCC snobbism.) He was missed a great deal more than was generally admitted. Indeed, this is still the case. While researching this
book I received letters and listened to testimonies which, while
deprecating the use of bodyline, would frequently finish with the
statement, or variations on it: 'But we could do with a few more
like Douglas now.' And in September 1980 at Lord's I overheard
a senior MCC member saying to his pal, 'Of course, the last *real*
captain we had was Jardine!'

In 1953 he was elected to be the first president of the Umpires
Association. This was a job he thoroughly enjoyed. He had always
been especially interested in umpiring and had the highest respect
for those who undertook it. From 1955 to 1957 he was president
of Oxford University Cricket Club, which might be considered a
somewhat belated honour since he was never elected to captain
the University; he and Lord Harris are the only two Oxonians to
have captained England but not Oxford against Cambridge.

He took up journalism again in 1953 for the *Star* but, whether
because of editorial constraints or for other reasons, his writing
fell some way short of the standard he had set for himself in 1939
on the *Daily Telegraph*. 1953 was the year in which England won
back the Ashes for the first time since Jardine's side had done it in
1933. Jardine had the highest opinion of Hutton's captaincy and
wrote that it was 'a joy to report' his success in that role. Jardine
held different views from Lord Hawke on the subject of professional captains. He had always firmly expressed the view that many
more professionals could with advantage be appointed as captains
and elected to serve on selection committees. Verity, he believed,
would have made a particularly good captain, as would Sutcliffe,
who proved his ability when leading the Players on four occasions.
In fact, if Sutcliffe had accepted the Yorkshire captaincy when it
was supposedly offered to him in 1927, he might well have been
given the England captaincy ahead of Jardine when the time came.

Jardine was moderately successful as a cricket commentator
on the radio. His observations were always perceptive and lucidly
expressed, but his delivery was a little slow for post-war tastes. It
certainly lacked the bite of the modern 'I don't know what's going
on out there' school. He undertook these broadcasting and journalistic engagements more out of a need to earn a living than as
a means of maintaining contact with the first-class game. By now
he had a wife and four children to support. Things weren't quite

as hard as earlier in their marriage when Margaret Jardine had taken to smallholding, but the extra income was useful and Jardine himself contributed short stories to the evening newspapers which brought in a bit more. He tended to worry a good deal about money but defied the constraints of austerity to the extent of running a somewhat decrepit Rolls Royce Phantom II, bought from a chap in Bognor Regis where the family were holidaying.

The family was a very close one and Jardine involved himself more in the children's upbringing than most men of his class were accustomed to do at the time. He read to them, played with them, took them on outings (the circus being a particular favourite), and his daughter also remembers the family sitting round listening to 'The Goon Show', which used to make him cry with laughter. All the children were sent to boarding schools but during the holidays there would be large gatherings of Peats and Jardines either at Hockwold Hall or on the estates that Sir Harry Peat rented in Perthshire. The Peats were a great sporting family; there was a substantial amount of shooting attached to Hockwold Hall and about 25,000 acres went with Crosscraigs House on the south side of Loch Rannoch. The children were all taught to fish, stalk and walk with guns as a matter of course.

To Jardine's great delight, his two eldest daughters, Fianach and Marion, became fond of playing and watching cricket and often went with him to Lord's for the day. His only son, Euan, though, was unable to continue the distinguished cricketing line. Margaret Jardine had come into contact with German measles while carrying him, he was born with a weak heart and suffered from very bad health throughout his childhood. His father was fully aware of the pressure that resulted from having a famous father and a number of contemporaries remember that he was deeply concerned about it.

Jardine was a devoted family man but he was also fond of socialising. They did not entertain much at Radlett and so he tended to do a fair bit of clubbing, lunching and bridge-playing in London. Ian Peebles recalled in *Spinner's Yarn* that 'D.R.J. came to the City at intervals and we saw quite a lot of him. He was a splendid guest with the agreeable habit of particularly addressing his remarks to anyone who seemed shy or left out of the conversation.'

He was chairman of the New South Wales Land Agency, which was a sheep-farming concern. When the company was taken over by the Scottish Australian Company, he was taken onto the board of directors and in 1953 he was asked to travel to Australia on the company's behalf to assess the development possibilities of the property. He hesitated for obvious reasons before undertaking the mission, and he went to the trouble of consulting Jack Fingleton, by now a friend and press box colleague, on the sort of reception he was likely to get. Fingleton tried to explain that Australians do not as a rule bear grudges and that he would be warmly welcomed. With some trepidation Jardine went ahead with the trip and found that Fingleton had been right. There was no pelting with rotten eggs at the airport and he was jovially received, in his own words, 'as an old so-and-so who got away with it'.

A reunion lunch was arranged with Prime Minister Menzies attending, also Larwood, Mailey, Bardsley and Oldfield. Larwood's autobiography includes an account of the occasion, which seems to have been most convivial, with people making jokes about bodyline without any embarrassment. Fingleton remembered that he also gave a talk in the radio series, 'Guest of Honour', which was very well received. Jardine was pleased but puzzled – he could not understand these Australians at all.

Larwood himself had been even more warmly welcomed when, three years earlier, he had emigrated to Australia. Again this had been at Fingleton's instigation. The ex-Prime Minister, Ben Chifley, had personally paid half the Larwood family's hotel bill when they first arrived.

In 1957 Jardine was obliged to make a similar trip, this time to inspect land which he owned in Rhodesia. It was a working holiday and he took with him his second eldest daughter, Marion, for whom the trip was a twenty-first birthday present. While he was there he contracted a disease called tick fever. He did not respond to treatment as well as was expected, but the doctors felt there was no cause for great concern and recommended a long sea voyage back to England.

On his return, he was admitted to the Hospital for Tropical Diseases, where his condition showed no improvement. He was moved to University College Hospital and tests revealed an advanced state of cancer. Deep-ray treatment was administered, but without success. His wife was then told by one of the hospital doctors about a clinic in Switzerland which was having a moderate degree of success against cancer. Jardine agreed to go, although neither he nor his children knew what was wrong with him. The deep-ray treatment had caused him great difficulty with his breathing and he thought that the Swiss mountain air would help.

The couple travelled to Switzerland and he was admitted to the clinic. It was found that he not only had lung cancer but that it had got to the stomach and the brain as well. There was nothing they could do for him beyond giving him pain-killing drugs and on 18 June 1958 he died. His body was cremated and flown home and his ashes were scattered over the top of Cross Craigs mountain in Perthshire.

From *Jardine, A Spartan Cricketer, 1984*

18 JUNE 1934

SHIFTING THE FIELDSMEN

SIR – In order to conciliate the Australians, we are not to allow the bunching of fieldsmen on the leg side by fast bowlers. It therefore seems reasonable that there should be a limit to the closeness by which the Australians may approach the bat when Grimmett or any other slow bowler is bowling.

The batsman knows that the only way to move the fieldsman is to wait for the loose ball and then deliberately take aim, hoping to 'score a bull'. It is not quite cricket, for in the mind of the batsman there is always the irritating feeling that while he does not wish to injure, he must remove the man.

In most cases this unlimited 'in-fielding' amounts to obstruction, and is just as likely to injure a fieldsman as fast bowling to a leg field is likely to injure a batsman.

E.G. Bisseker
London WI

From *Not In My Day, Sir: Cricket Letters*
to the Daily Telegraph, *2011*

While I didn't ever play against D'Oliveira, he was, by my time in the game, the second XI coach at Worcestershire. I would encounter him on several occasions over the years and I remember him holding forth in the changing rooms at New Road, where he was still a huge figure. How was it that this unassuming man could have become such a massive, inadvertent political figure without doing anything other than be selected to represent his adopted country at sport? I think he was just the right person at the right time, who happened to come along and, by being there, helped see the back of the hideous regime in South Africa. His role as a significant catalyst in the anti-apartheid movement is now well documented. The television coverage of the Basil D'Oliveira affair and the 1971 Springbok tour to Australia that encountered so much anti-apartheid hostility meant that the horrors of the system and the vehement protests were brought into people's daily lives. The rest, as they say, is history.

THE BASIL D'OLIVEIRA AFFAIR

Basil D'Oliveira

I held the envelope, staring at it, wondering what was inside but somehow scared to open it. We knew no one in England and I knew of it only as a place where, according to others, I should go to try my luck as a cricketer. Naomi nudged a little closer. She didn't say a word, but I could feel her willing me.... "Go on, open it, it will be all right."

And how right she was! Suddenly the room, already filled with the early morning sunshine, seemed twenty times brighter. After nearly ten years of rumour that I would be going overseas, here was the first real sign. The letter was from John Arlott. Our success on the Kenya tour had convinced him that someone should take the initiative to find out if this chap D'Oliveira did have real potential. He was prepared to do everything he could to get me to England, but first he wanted to hear from me if I was interested.

At any time during the previous ten years I would have dived in off the Cape and started swimming up the West coast. Now I had to stop and think, think for two, and perhaps even for three. Naomi and I had been married three months and we had just begun to suspect that she was pregnant. "Well," she said. "What are you waiting for?" I couldn't say much. I was trying to imagine the consequences of now doing something which for so long had seemed impossible. I heard Naomi say, "You know you've got to go, darling. I'll wait here until…". She didn't finish the sentence. Like me, she couldn't guess what would happen after I had said "Yes".

I dressed and went in search of Benny Bansda, an Indian chum who had been my champion for years. He was head barman in one of Cape Town's biggest hotels, The Grand in Adderley Street. Benny was also a prolific writer on all sporting matters and, after years of campaigning on my behalf, had written the article for *World Sports Magazine* which had finally persuaded John Arlott to write to me.

Benny's first reaction was, "Great! What are you waiting for?" I confessed that my big fear was that I didn't know—had no way of knowing—if I was really good enough. Benny said: "There's only one way to find out." With that he grabbed a piece of paper and he wrote to John Arlott saying that, if any specific job could be found, I would leave right away.

Before I got back home everybody on Signal Hill, it seemed, knew already that I was on my way to England. I learned later that, when John Arlott received my letter, he contacted John Kay of the *Manchester Evening News* and an authority on Lancashire League cricket. John knew that Middleton, for whom he had played, was looking for a new professional and had been negotiating with Wes Hall, the West Indies fast bowler. Wes had provisionally accepted the offer but he insisted that the announcement should be delayed for several months. I gather that Wes was worried he might lose his job and be out of work for six months if it was learned that he was going to take up a League job in England in the spring of 1960.

When the news did leak out that Wes was thinking of going to England, he wrote to Middleton to explain that he could not complete the contract. This coincided with the moment that John Kay received the inquiry from John Arlott. Together, they persuaded Middleton to make me an offer. It was £450 for a year's contract, out of which I had to pay my fare to England, which would cost about £200.

This offer, for which I had waited so long, carried with it its own problems. When I sat down to work out the money matters, I realized that I would have to turn it down because I simply could not afford to travel. I had no money. My parents had none.

I had been earning and contributing to the household expenses. The doctor confirmed that Naomi was expecting our first child and, even if I could have managed to live in England, there wouldn't have been a shilling to send home for Naomi or my parents out of what would have been left of my contract money.

I was about ready to accept it as a dream lost when the coloured lads in Cape Town and all over South Africa threw themselves into a campaign, started by Bansda, to raise the money to send me to England. I think that they, as much as I, felt the honour of an English club coming to them for a professional. Nobody had been asked before and no one had gone before. Coloured clubs all over the country started to arrange special games and collections and white South Africans joined in.

I have never forgotten that, without the help of white South African cricketers—including Peter Van der Merwe who subsequently captained the Springbok Test team—and other first-class players like Jim Pothecary and Dick Westcott, the money which was needed to get me to England might never have been raised. These cricketers played in a side led by Gerald Innes, a former South African tour player who arranged a Sunday match against my own team. This game brought one of the biggest crowds ever seen on the Claremont ground in Cape Town. Together the coloured cricketers and the white cricketers went around with collecting boxes and raised over £150.

I don't know exactly how this match came to be staged or who turned blind eyes, but we knew then—and there has been plenty of evidence since—that the dogma of Mr. Vorster's cabinet is not by any means a true reflection of the wishes of many South African cricketers.

Benny Bansda's campaign eventually raised £450. A word like gratitude seems so inadequate. Every moment I live as a first-class cricketer I owe to all those kind people who spontaneously got together to give me the chance of a new career.

Raising the money to come to England was not the whole problem.

The brief talks with the English county cricketers who had been in South Africa on coaching trips had taught me something about the conditions which existed in England. But now I needed to have it all analysed. Particularly, I needed to know what conditions were like in the League. I had heard that they were different from county cricket but I had no idea in what way.

The man who could best help me was Tom Reddick, who had previously played for Middlesex and Nottinghamshire, and subsequently had been coach to Lancashire. At that time, as I have said, he was coaching in Cape Town. There was probably nobody anywhere in South Africa who knew more about League conditions.

I telephoned him and he said I could go to his house right away. His first words were: "You might just as well know now, lad, you are going into one of the hardest forms of cricket in the world, but I wish you well." He said he would prefer to see me going into county cricket but, if I wanted to try the League, he would give me all the help he could.

First, he told me exactly what a professional had to do. It wouldn't be just playing cricket on Saturdays and lazing around for the rest of the week. It meant working really hard for the club on the ground, helping with the wickets, and coaching the local lads by night.

Four nights each week I visited Tom at his house. I would be waiting for him at six o'clock when he came home and, though he had already devoted a full day to coaching the university students, he would patiently spend hours teaching me everything he could. Not the least important was how he tuned me mentally for the change.

By the time Tom finished with me, my feet were once again firmly on the ground. He warned me that cricket in the Central Lancashire League would not only be vastly different from the cricket which I had been playing, but it would also be different from the first Test match I had seen in Cape Town ten years before, which was indelibly printed on my mind.

For the first time I realised that I would not always be playing on good wickets. I would also have to learn how the conditions of wickets changed with the weather. And I had to learn something about the English weather! Perhaps the most forbidding of all Tom's warnings was that, in the League, I would each week be facing some of the best cricketers in the world, each of whom was in the game to earn a living.

Tom Reddick certainly helped me to come to England. More important, he helped me to stay, especially during the early days when, if I had not had his words to hang on to, I might have given it all up and rushed back home.

Tom gave me something as well. He probably didn't realise it at the time and maybe doesn't now. After our coaching sessions at the back of his house each night he would invite me in for a drink. This was the first time I had ever entered the home of a white man.

I wish he could have been with me in London nine years later, at a function just before Christmas, 1968. In a room glittering with chandeliers, a hundred or more English cricket celebrities sat down to dinner, elegant in their dinner jackets. The occasion was to present a cricket trophy.

As winner of the Lawrence trophy the previous year, I was there to present the silver cup to the new winner, my county captain, Tom Graveney. I also had to make a speech. I sat at the top table between the M C C President, Mr. R. Aird, and Secretary, Mr. S. C. Griffith. I think that, if Tom Reddick had been there, I might have made him feel a little proud and with a glance I could have told him how grateful I was for preparing me for that moment.

John Kay was waiting for me when I arrived at London Airport. He had been in London the previous night to cover a boxing match and had stayed over to meet me and to take me back to Manchester. I had hoped that he or John Arlott would be there, but I was not prepared for the shock when I reached the doors of the aircraft and started to walk down the gangway.

John Arlott had been broadcasting the previous night and had casually mentioned that I would be arriving the next day. As I soon came to learn, a word lightly dropped is enough for the British journalists and photographers who, so far as I have been able to see, keep their readers better informed than is the case anywhere else in the world.

The day was April the First and, if I had been aware of anything, I would have asked myself what sort of fool I was to be taking this step down a gangway into a sea of faces and flashbulbs which made the grey damp morning seem darker.

Someone in uniform handed me a note. It read: "Don't say anything. Meet you inside. John Kay." I thought, "What does he mean? Don't say anything? What had happened? What had gone wrong?" All I could hear was "Mr. D'Oliveira … Mr. D'Oliveira …". Somebody was talking about a television room. Would I go there? They wanted me "on camera". Everyone was staring and I was staring back, hoping to see someone I recognised, someone to hold on to. Normally, there was always someone with me, but here I was on my own. I couldn't turn to anybody for reassurance. I was in another world. A white man's world. There wasn't a black skin in sight. I can't remember a single question I was asked or any answer I gave. I don't even remember the moment when John Kay arrived and introduced himself. The first thing that I recall, after the hiatus of arriving, was sitting in John's car.

We drove to John Arlott's flat. He looked exactly as I had imagined him to be. In South Africa we had often listened to John's broadcasts, and his voice, the way he talked about cricket and the humour which he found in little incidents, gave the impression that he was a warm, friendly person. As I stopped in the doorway waiting for him to say, "Come in," I remember thinking—he looks just like his voice.

Within seconds, he had me chatting like a long-lost friend. I suppose in some ways he *was* that to me, because he had started mentioning me in his newspaper columns and in broadcasts five or six years before.

Although I knew of him as a writer and a broadcaster, I couldn't understand why he needed so many books. The room was lined with them.

John tried to reassure me that I would find everybody anxious to help me settle down and made me promise that, if I had any difficulties with which he could help, I had to get in touch with him right away. He was sure that, with John Kay looking after me, I would be protected from the worst that Lancashire could offer!

John Kay had sent back the hired car which we had used from the airport and we travelled to Middleton by train. Each hour brought a new experience. As I stepped aboard the train, another wave of doubt swept over me. I thought, "Oh my God, not one coloured person on the train! What am I getting into here?"

Although my skin is not noticeably different in colour, I was as conscious of the difference as if I had been a coal-black negro. When you have grown into manhood separated always as black and white, never travelling on the same public transport, eating in the same restaurants, going to the same hotels, being in the same house, sitting at the same table, drinking from the same cup, using the same lavatories, it is not easy to begin to do all these things, without an instinctive mental shying away.

As we had walked along the platform to the train, I was fascinated that everyone doing the lifting and the carrying was a white man. Nowadays coloured immigrants are employed in great numbers on the British public-transport systems. I suppose, even when I arrived, there were coloured people working at the station. But, because I saw white men doing the job which I had previously seen only coloured men do, I would not have noticed any coloured workers, even if they had been there.

John Kay took me into the dining car for a meal and he saw that I was now becoming quite frightened. To have sat down publicly at a table for a meal with a white man would have meant trouble for both of us in South Africa. I was so scared that it was only when John reminded me about it later that I remembered that it had happened.

Indeed, I recollect very little about those first twenty-four hours. I can recall getting off the train. I was wearing a green scarf because of the cold. This was high around my face and I could see very little of what was going on. There were five men waiting for us, all of them Middleton officials. One was George Harwood, the secretary. I was put into a car but I didn't hear what was said or even see what was happening. I heard someone mention a golf club and dinner. All I can really remember of the golf club visit was seeing television for the first time. It was an outside broadcast and the rain was teeming down. I wanted to touch the screen to see if it was wet.

Not until nearly midnight did I arrive at the digs which had been found for me with Mr. and Mrs. Lord, who were to be my "parents" for the next year. They could not have treated me better if I had indeed been their own son. I often look at two photographs—one of my mother and one of Mrs. Lord. Mother is older and her skin is darker, but both are smiling into the camera, both wear glasses and both have the same warm friendly eyes, both the same smile. I can see a likeness, even if others cannot.

That first night Mrs. Lord was worried about me. She was sure that coming from that lovely hot sun into an English night would cause me to freeze to death unless she packed the bed with hot water bottles and blankets and lit every fire in the house. Certainly this was one of those April days in England which would have changed Robert Browning's mind about wanting to be there.

I must have been completely exhausted when I fell into bed that night. That tiredness, plus Mrs. Lord's determination to make me comfortable, sent me to sleep until five o'clock the next afternoon!

The following morning I walked the streets of Middleton and I saw the white man as I never thought him to be. To segregated Africans, the image of a white man is a white shirt, a hat, an umbrella and a smart city suit. For the first time, I saw white men wearing overalls, working in the roads, sweeping the streets, emptying the dustbins and delivering the milk. These were jobs which I had seen only coloured people do.

For a white man to do these things in Africa would be to down-grade him. When I saw the Englishmen at work in Middleton, it gave these jobs a new dignity. Later I realised why. In South Africa the African must sweep the streets, but he cannot then go home, have a bath, put on a suit and go out unchallenged into the world around him.

Having now been away from Africa for nearly ten years, that does not seem a very dramatic thing to say. Indeed, it is the sort of thing others have said for many, many years and some have chosen to say it with aggressiveness and bitterness. This is not the effect I ever want to give. I have been hurt but I do not want revenge.

During the height of the crisis in late 1968 when it was announced that, if I were not going to South Africa as a Test player, I would be sending comments from South Africa on the Test matches, concern was expressed that these might be angled to stimulate more controversy.

Those who voiced such fears had either forgotten or were unaware that, in the years I had been in England, I had revisited South Africa and spent many months there. I had travelled around the country giving lectures and coaching and never once allowed conversation or comments to intrude on things other than cricket. I had also con-tributed fairly frequently a column under my own name in South African newspapers about life in England—life as a cricketer.

Never, with a cough or a comma, had I consciously said or written anything that could be considered racially contentious.

I was grateful to have the chance of a summer alone in England before Naomi came to join me. The life of a professional cricketer is a man's world. Although I missed Naomi very much, being alone did mean that I could be quite single-minded about learning to live in the new world. By the time she joined me, I had more confidence. Perhaps not enough for both of us, but at least it was better than if we had both arrived frightened and confused as I had done.

It was a very slow boat which took me back to South Africa at the end of the 1960 season. I was going back to collect my wife and my child, who was soon to be born, and I was bringing them back to the life which we had always dreamed about and which was indeed as good as the dream itself.

The dream had not been uninterrupted, indeed the first few weeks in Middleton had been more like a nightmare. I was not the only one in that Lancashire town who thought that a ghastly mistake had been made. But, by the end of the month, I had begun to adjust my technique. I recovered from my bad start and finished the season with 930 runs with an average of 48.95 and 71 wickets for an average of 11.72. Middleton had given me a new and better contract and were going to pay my fare and Naomi's back to England the following spring.

From *The Basil D'Oliveira Affair, 1969*

THE OBITUARY OF BASIL D'OLIVEIRA

Wisden Cricketers' Almanack

D'Oliveira, Basil Lewis, CBE, died on November 18, 2011. He was generally thought to have been 80. Basil D'Oliveira was a fine cricketer who, in more normal circumstances, could have played far more than 44 Tests. But the miracle of his life was that he played any at all. His story, and the 1968 crisis known as the D'Oliveira

Affair, had consequences that reverberated far beyond cricket and would define Basil's life. The man himself was not a secular saint or a political campaigner: he was, above all else, a cricketer.

D'Oliveira was born in Cape Town and grew up in the then segregated Coloured area known as Signal Hill. That much is certain; the date is more problematic. When he first arrived in England in 1960, he said he had been born in 1935. According to Pat Murphy, who ghosted Basil's 1980 autobiography *Time to Declare*, he revised that figure twice, first to 1933, then to 1931. *Wisden* adds to the confusion, starting with 1934 then settling on 1931. But in the book D'Oliveira hinted he was even older, and Murphy said he saw a photocopy of a birth certificate saying 1928, making him 37 when he first played for England, 43 when he fended off the Australian attack in 1972, and 83 when he died.

Whatever his age, he was a phenomenon – and he would achieve an honour usually accorded only to all-time greats when, in 2004, it was announced that future Test series between England and South Africa would be for the Basil D'Oliveira Trophy. He grew up in a proud, vibrant and put-upon community with a strong cricket culture that was ignored by South Africa's ruling whites well before the policy of apartheid became enshrined in the 1950s. His father, Lewis, was captain of St Augustine's, one of a stack of clubs who played simultaneously, Indian maidan-style, on the bumpy mats and patchy outfields of nearby Green Point. Basil learned to play in the streets before graduating to his father's team. On days off from his job in a printing works, he soon established a local reputation as both a mighty hitter and a consistent scorer, averaging about nine centuries a season through the 1950s. He was sufficiently dominant to be chosen as captain representing "non-white" South Africa, who scored decisive home-and-away victories against Kenya. The historian André Odendaal said this gives him a better claim than Owen Dunell in 1888–89 to be regarded as South Africa's first captain, since Dunell's team represented a minority of the population. But when MCC toured in 1956–57, D'Oliveira, in his cricketing prime, walked seven miles to Newlands and sat incognito in the segregated area.

At the end of the decade, there was talk of a tour by a West Indian team led by Frank Worrell, but that foundered on the political rocks. D'Oliveira was on the verge of forgetting cricket, and now had other priorities: in January 1960 he married his girlfriend Naomi. Out of the blue, a speculative job application, despairingly written in a series of letters to the commentator John Arlott in England over the previous two years, produced a dramatic reply. Arlott had contacted the Lancashire journalist John Kay, who knew the scene inside out, and Middleton of the Central Lancashire League were suddenly desperate enough to punt on an unknown as their professional. They offered only £450 for a season, feeble even then, especially as the air fare would cost £200. But Naomi, already pregnant with their son Damian, insisted Basil take the chance. A local barman-cum-sportswriter, Benny Bansda, set about raising money, and even some of the white stars played a match to help out. He arrived in Middleton on April 1, 1960 – cold, naive about cricket and the world, teetotal, more fluent in Afrikaans than English – and made only 25 runs in his first five innings. Then he calmed down, relaxed, and scored 930 to top the League averages. A fraction ahead of Radcliffe's pro, one Garry Sobers.

The next year he returned with Naomi and Damian, bought a small house of his own and passed 1,000 runs. He soon became a regular in the televised Sunday Cavalier matches and on tours run by the journalist-entrepreneur Ron Roberts and the coach Alf Gover. Some of these proved racially fraught: Rhodesia had South African-style segregation, less formal but almost as pervasive: Pakistan objected to D'Oliveira's South African passport, which prompted him to apply for a British one. Soon several counties woke up to him, though not the obvious one: the Lancashire eminence Cyril Washbrook wrote him off as "a Saturday afternoon slogger". Tom Graveney took a different view, and in 1964 D'Oliveira moved to Worcester to spend a year qualifying. By the time he made his Championship début, against Essex in 1965, he was, according to the birth certificate, nearly 37. Luckily, he did not waste any more time: he made 106 – followed by 163 out of 289 on a raging turner in the return fixture a week later at Brentwood. The doubters were disappearing. He scored 1,691 runs that summer, and Worcestershire retained the Championship.

By now he had confidence in himself and his method, based on a short backlift and a strong bottom hand; he had traded his old off-spin to bowl swing and cut; he had also, less fortuitously, felt emboldened to drink alcohol. The Establishment were gaining confidence too. In May 1966 D'Oliveira was named in the twelve for the opening Test against West Indies: "HELLO DOLLY!" said the *Daily Mirror* headline, predictably enough. Apart from his age, he was keeping something else quiet: he couldn't throw properly, after a car accident the previous winter. He was made twelfth man for that Test, chosen for the Second and became a star in the Third and Fourth, with three successive half-centuries for a team that was being outclassed, including 88 at Headingley, mostly compiled in a stand of 96 with the tailender Ken Higgs that turned near-extinction for England into a mere innings defeat. His maiden Test century arrived a year later, at Headingley against the weak 1967 Indians. He was an obvious pick now, usually batting No. 5 and often bowling first change, and beginning to build his reputation as a breaker of stands. No one queried his right to tour the West Indies that winter; indeed the speculation questions were starting about the effects of his possible selection for South Africa a year later. As early as April 1967, John Vorster, the South African prime minister, suddenly wavered from hardline apartheid and said racially mixed teams would be accepted "from countries with which we have had traditional sporting ties". The way seemed clear for him to go.

But by now Dollymania had started to fade a fraction. He had a poor tour in the Caribbean, playing in all five Tests but averaging 22 with the bat, 97 with the ball and dropping catches. "Socially, it was a great tour for me," he said in *Time to Declare*. Some felt that was precisely the point – he was now far from teetotal. He did make 87 not out in a shock defeat in the opening Ashes Test of 1968, when England ludicrously picked only three frontline bowlers, then blamed D'Oliveira for not being one of them. Now he was omitted, and remained on the outside, performing patchily for Worcestershire, while England tried and failed to recapture the initiative against a poor Australian side. But all the while the "what-if-he's-picked?" speculation swirled. And then came The Oval: Roger Prideaux withdrew with pleurisy, D'Oliveira came in, and the speculation ceased. He made 158, which helped win the match. He was dropped four times, but he had rediscovered his form, and triumphed. Surely there could be no doubt now? The press thought not: umpire Charlie Elliott thought not: "Oh Christ," he whispered to Basil when the hundred came up. "The cat's among the pigeons now." It certainly was, but not in the way Elliott expected: five days later the tour party was announced, without D'Oliveira.

Quite clearly, all manner of dirty work had been afoot that year. D'Oliveira posed a threat to the credibility of South Africa's policy of rigid racial separation and inequality. What if he came and succeeded? The Vorster government were desperate to avoid this, and sanctioned all kinds of bribes to persuade D'Oliveira to rule himself out, carefully detailed in a 2004 biography by Peter Oborne. MCC, with the former prime minister Sir Alec Douglas-Home high in their counsels, did not want to jeopardise their long and, from their perspective, happy relationship with white South Africa. It is possible to believe that the selectors were leaned on not to pick D'Oliveira by an unholy alliance of Lord's and Pretoria. There was a narrow, rather convoluted, cricketing case to support his omission, based on the fact that there were better specialist batsmen and he was not quite a fully fledged all-rounder. (And he was not young, whatever his real age.) Doug Insole, the chairman of selectors, always maintained this lay behind the decision. There is another explanation, more plausible than either, and supported by well-placed sources: that the selectors remembered the West Indies tour and took that into account, perhaps fearing a disastrous late-night incident. It is notable that the other great socialiser, Colin Milburn, was also left out.

In Cape Town, the South African parliament roared with delight when the news came through. In England, the storm broke over the selectors' heads; MCC became an object of contempt and ridicule. Then, two weeks later, Tom Cartwright, a bowler who batted, pulled out through injury; D'Oliveira, a batsman who bowled, was inserted instead. The cricketing case for this was again elaborate, though perhaps not as elaborate as Cartwright's thinking. He had unusual political awareness for a cricketer (probably more than the chronic appeaser Douglas-Home) and harboured mixed feelings about touring at all; it seems likely he used his twinge as an excuse (see *Wisden 2008*, pages 1552–53). Vorster almost certainly could not have banned D'Oliveira had he been chosen originally. With world revulsion building against apartheid, that would have been too nakedly racist, even for South Africa. But now he had his chance because it looked, not just in South Africa, as if the selectors had caved in to political pressure. The night after D'Oliveira's inclusion, Vorster was speaking (half-drunk, it is said) in the heartland of white supremacy, to members of the Nationalist Party in Bloemfontein. He was able to tell them: "The MCC team as constituted now is not the team of the MCC but the team of the Anti-Apartheid Movement." He got a phenomenal ovation. D'Oliveira would not be allowed in, and MCC had to cancel the tour. Short-term, Vorster had won. But both Vorster and apartheid would be dead before South Africa played cricket against England again, and the sporting isolation created by banning D'Oliveira marked the start of the regime's painfully slow downfall.

Only one man emerged with credit. D'Oliveira made a habit of rising to the major occasions of his life, and he behaved through-out this one with integrity, dignity and implacability. In the years of political strife ahead, he would not let himself be used by either the rigid boycotters or apartheid's apologists: he remained his own man. He played on for England; indeed for the four years after the great rumpus, he did not miss a match (so much for the selectors' original judgment). His performances included perhaps his great-est innings: an unbeaten 114 on a shocking pitch at Dacca in the hastily arranged riot-torn series that replaced the abandoned South African tour. And he continued to play well for Worcestershire until 1979, when he may well have been past 50. He then became county coach for 11 years, forming a notably successful partnership with Phil Neale as captain.

D'Oliveira had always been a good watcher – he worked out how to pick the Australian mystery spinner John Gleeson – and he was a conscientious, tough and effective coach, if stronger on the importance of mental attitude than on the minutiae of technique. And his essential decency shone through in odd ways. The former county secretary Mike Vockins remembered him being saddled with a coaching commitment at a school in Redditch on a snowy day. He was not sure he could make it, so he drove there in the morning to convince himself it was possible, then went back to do the job in the afternoon. Basil also became a proud patriarch. His son Damian played 14 seasons for Worcestershire, and in 2011 his grandson Brett followed them into the team, and also became the fourth gen-eration of D'Oliveiras to play for St Augustine's. By then dementia had overcome Basil, but his family – led by the staunch Naomi – sustained him. And he was revered across the cricket world, most of all, far from Worcester, in the country that once spurned him.

From *Wisden Cricketers' Almanack, 2012*

'I like to think that people are building these West Indians up, because I'm not really sure they're as good as everyone thinks they are. I think people tend to forget it wasn't that long ago they were beaten 5–1 by the Australians and only just managed to keep their heads above water against the Indians just a short time ago as well. Sure, they've got a couple of fast bowlers, but really I don't think we're going to run into anything more sensational than Thomson and Lillee so really I'm not all that worried about them. You must remember that the West Indians, these guys, if they get on top are magnificent cricketers. But if they're down, they grovel, and I intend, with the help of Closey [Brian Close] and a few others, to make them grovel.'

**Tony Greig speaking ahead of the 1976
Test series against the West Indies**

In 1976 I was on the Surrey groundstaff and was present in the pavilion at the end-of-series match that would ultimately complete the West Indians' 3–0 domination of the series. To this day I can remember the amazing atmosphere at the Oval, with the West Indian supporters calling for Greig to grovel, which he duly did. Although Tony was one of my great cricket icons at the time, to see him on the outfield in front of the West Indian supporters on his hands and knees was both funny and sad; it was, however, the right thing for him to do. Tony was a great showman and if anyone was actually going to get down and grovel in front of thousands of people, then it would be Tony. Having spoken to him on many occasions about it since, I know that he regretted making that comment and admitted it was a stupid thing to say. He knew the moment the words were out of his mouth it was a mistake, but he was frustrated at the time by the interviewer, who he felt, if not exactly belittling England, was not giving them the credit they were due going into the series. Of course it would all come back horribly to haunt him.

WORLD SERIES CRICKET

Sir Derek Birley

By 1975 England had ceased to be the unquestioned leaders in world cricket. It was no longer politically correct to talk about the British Commonwealth and by the same token the International Cricket Conference was somewhat less Anglocentric than of yore. But tradition and prestige still counted for a good deal. MCC might by then be more shadow than substance, but the club still owned what was probably the finest cricket ground in the world. Lord's was still the place for the great international occasion. It was the obvious place for the Prudential Cup, the first international limited-over tournament, later known as the World Cup. The takings, despite England's mediocre showing, came to £200,000 and the final between West Indies and Australia was watched by 26,000 people and took a record £66,000.

Australia stayed on after the Cup for the resumption of the bouncer war. Obliged to discard the shell-shocked batsmen of the previous winter, England had to look for coarser-grained but tougher customers. They discovered the kind of hero so beloved of tradition as to be part of the national self-image – the quiet, unassuming chap who stands up to the bully. This was David Steele, a thirty-four-year-old from unfashionable Northamptonshire whose grey hair made him look even more venerable, and who wore glasses. Having long given up hope of being picked for England he found himself having to go in to stop the rot against Lillee and Thomson.

Steele recalled the scene as he walked out at Lord's:

People were looking at me. I could hear them muttering, 'Who's this grey old bugger?' as I walked past. Tommo stood with his hands on his hips. I said, 'Good morning, Tommo.' He said, 'Bloody hell, who've we got here, Groucho Marx?'

Scorning thigh pads and chest-protectors – just a towel or two stuffed in his clothes – Steele made 50 and went on to have a splendid series. That England staved off total disaster that summer also owed much to the courage of John Edrich and the wicket-keeper Alan Knott, and, not least, to the aggressive approach of Tony Greig, who replaced the nice-mannered but ineffectual Scot, Mike Denness, after the first Test.

Denness himself was an emollient successor to Illingworth, whereas Greig, born in South Africa of expatriate parents, represented the return swing of the pendulum. Greig's appointment aroused dismay amongst English nationalists. This was not generally for his specifically South African connections, which only troubled a handful of liberals. The TCCB's deep regret at having to cancel the planned 1976–7 tour of South Africa, on account of the Commonwealth leaders' Gleneagles agreement which excluded South Africa from sporting contests, was probably shared by most cricketers.

The purists' concern was that Greig, though captain of Sussex, was a carpetbagger, not normally resident in England. That winter, *Wisden* noted, he had played cricket for Waverley, a Sydney club, for a fee of some £12,000. And when Greig subsequently fell from grace, accused of disloyalty, John Woodcock, the eminent cricket correspondent of *The Times*, explained to his readers:

> What has to be remembered, of course, is that he is an Englishman, not by birth or upbringing, but only by adoption. It is not the same thing as being English through and through.

Greig's other disadvantages as an England captain – his gamesmanship, his mastery of the art of needling opponents, his violent mood swings, impetuosity and so forth – were presumably also attributable to his insufficient Englishness. However, some, in the summer of 1976, were convinced that his declared intention to make the touring West Indians 'grovel' was attributable specifically to his South African background. Certainly the remark enraged the touring captain, Clive Lloyd, and gave added spice to the bowling, as forty-five-year-old Brian Close and thirty-nine-year-old John Edrich joined Steele in the firing line, and Greig confessed himself frightened for the first time in his life. But it was all astonishingly good for business and the TCCB found themselves with a total of £950,000 to share out at the season's end from their various enterprises. This was an increase even in real terms, a qualification that everyone had to get used to making in those ultra-inflationary times.

Greig, meanwhile, who so far had not won a match as captain, found welcome relief on the tour of India with its slow bowling traditions. *Wisden* cooed with satisfaction over England's victory and Greig's inspired and inspiring leadership. It was also pleased that the Cricket Council had dealt so promptly and conclusively with the accusation that England's bowlers, Willis and Lever, had been guilty of ball-tampering. They had adopted the unusual practice of sticking gauze strips to their foreheads with vaseline, purportedly to keep the sweat from running into their eyes, but the Indian captain, Bishen Bedi, had complained that they were in fact using the sticky substance to keep the shine on the ball. The Cricket Council, after telephoning the England captain and manager, utterly refuted the foul allegation.

That winter's tour was, however, to be remembered chiefly for the Centenary Test match, commemorating the anniversary of the first match played on level terms between English and Australian players. More precisely it was remembered for the subsequent discovery that Greig, the England captain, had used the intervals of play to recruit members of his team to the service of Kerry Packer, son of an Australian media tycoon. Packer had tried to negotiate with the Australian Board of Control for the right to televise matches exclusively on his commercial Channel 9, and when they peremptorily refused had decided to run his own international contests, hiring all the teams.

Greig's sorties on Packer's behalf were conducted in great secrecy, and no one at Lord's had any inkling of what was in store. All the talk was of the great news that a sponsor had been found for the county championship: Schweppes were offering £360,000 for three years, a generous sum considering the limited amount of television coverage that could be expected. Even when in April rumours began to circulate that a number of South Africans had signed to play for Packer in an eight-week series in various parts of the world, no one thought much about it. The Australian tourists arrived on schedule, armed with contracts newly negotiated with the ABC (£12,000 a man and a pension scheme, the word was), and old-stagers shook their heads at what things were coming to. Then Packer announced that he had signed thirty-five Test players, including thirteen Australian tourists and four current English players, Greig, Knott, Snow and Underwood.

The TCCB's response was to relieve Greig of the captaincy, because of the breach of trust, and to call a meeting of the International Cricket Conference (formerly the Imperial Cricket Conference, adapted to accommodate loose cannons like South Africa and Pakistan), where it was agreed that no action be taken for the immediate series, but that afterwards five conditions be imposed on players who contracted to play for Packer. These conditions were not wildly unreasonable, but were paternalistic in the best MCC traditions. However, this soon became academic, for when the ICC met Packer he insisted on his original demand of exclusive television rights, the ABC saw this as blackmail and refused, the ICC stood by them and the trial of strength resumed.

Packer signed another dozen or more players, including two current English Test men, Dennis Amiss and Bob Woolmer, to play what he called 'Super-cricket' and what the establishment referred to as a 'circus'. This was a conscious attempt to relate the Packer scheme to Old Clarke and the All-England XI, which was a horror story told in the best circles about a dastardly plot to wrest the game from MCC's lawful grasp. In 1866 the happy ending had come when MCC had laid down the conditions on which they would engage the rebels for future matches. In 1977, when the TCCB and ICC tried to do the same, they found themselves in court answering an application for an injunction and damages from the Packer organisation and three of their contracted players, headed by the infamous Greig. Furthermore, they lost the case with costs, some quarter of a million pounds. As a *Guardian* leader put it, 'Mr Kerry Packer may be a bounder and a cad. But he is a legal bounder and a High-Court-sanctified cad.'

To rub salt in establishment wounds, Richie Benaud, who emerged as the brains behind Packer's scheme, announced that it would not be played under MCC laws, which he had the temerity to call mere 'rules', and preparations gleefully began for World Series Cricket (WSC). Furthermore, it was evident that some counties were more concerned to retain the crowd-pulling power of their overseas players than to uphold TCCB dignity. Sussex expressed relief that they were not to be deprived of the services of Greig, Snow and Imran Khan, the Pakistani star. Gloucestershire's treasurer likewise declared himself 'ticked pink' that Mike Procter and Zaheer Abbas would be staying. The Hampshire captain, R. M. C. Gilliat, of Charterhouse and Oxford University, said it was 'good news for Hampshire cricket'. There was, of course, much huffing and puffing from choleric upholders of tradition, but as the TCCB made no move to appeal against the judgment there was little they could do but seethe.

Loyalist indignation was further aroused when Sussex declined to follow England's lead, and renewed Greig's captaincy for the 1978 season. (Nottinghamshire proposed and Lancashire seconded a motion to expel Sussex from the championship.) Kent followed a more politically correct line when they removed Asif Iqbal as captain, but they were careful not to try to dispense with his services as a player. All but the fiercest accepted that the counties had little choice but to honour existing contracts with the 'rebels' (though it was assumed that it would be a different story a year later: the judgment had said nothing about renewing contracts). Warwickshire took a similar line. Stiff upper lips were *de rigueur* and crossed fingers were hidden under board-room tables.

Two things saved the bacon, if not entirely the face, of official-dom. First, World Series Cricket was not the immediate runaway success Packer had predicted, for although it attracted television audiences of a sort, and floodlit matches were a great novelty, the jazzed-up proceedings did not seem to stir up any great concern for who won or lost. Second, the assault on the citadel had led to some rallying round amongst lovers of the authorised version. The TCCB landed £1 million sponsorship from Cornhill Insurance for the Test matches. Fees went up from £3,000 to £5,000 (plus winning bonuses) for tours and from £200 to £1,000 for each home match. Players were thus given pause before they rushed to sign for Packer, and some English players of a certain age or temperament saw this as an opportunity to thin the ranks of overseas players on the county scene, which they now dominated. Personal ambitions and old feuds came into play.

World Series Cricket put a further twist in the ravelled skein of Geoffrey Boycott's fortunes. Not everyone was as pleased as *Wisden* with the choice of Mike Brearley, the Middlesex captain, to replace the alien Greig. Sceptics who thought his batting below standard also pointed out that he had not spoken out against the Packer 'circus', and hinted darkly that the only reason he hadn't actually joined them was because he wasn't good enough to be made an offer: Boycott, by contrast, had been amongst the first to be invited but had ostentatiously refused. Instead he had offered his services to England in her hour of need, and had scored his hundredth century on his home ground, as England took advan-tage of Australia's greater disarray to put it across them in that summer's Tests.

The Cricketers' Association had members on both sides of the argument – which essentially was whether Packer's intervention was likely to benefit all cricketers or would merely further widen the gap between the stars' pay and that of the rest. At the time the basic pay of the 150 or so capped English players averaged about £2,600 a season, rising to perhaps £3,000 with bonuses. Test players averaged nearer £5,000, which was the normal minimum for overseas stars, some of whom commanded £10,000 or more, and the immediate effect of World Series Cricket was to increase the disparities. Boycott further developed his role as champion of the loyalist cause in Pakistan in the winter of 1977–8. When the Pakistan Board of Control lost their nerve and proposed to select three Packer players, Boycott, as acting captain, led a dressing-room revolt.

This, without helping intra-ICC relations, was a setback to the rebels' hopes of breaking up the fragile alliance. Greig vented his spleen in the *Sydney Sun*, claiming that Boycott had had a special reason to fear the return of the Pakistan rebels – the pace of Imran Khan. Greig was suspended by the TCCB for breaking his contract and Sussex dolefully dismissed him as captain and 'allowed him to go' during the year. As ICC's united front began to crumble under pressure from West Indies and Pakistan, neither of whom could afford to adopt high moral principles, discussions began with WSC, who were going to greater and greater lengths to try to drum up interest, notably fast bowling of such ferocity that helmets ceased to be regarded as wimpish. 'Roller-ball cricket', traditionalists called it.

Neither side was yet ready to concede, but cynics were already predicting that money would have the last word. When John Arlott, president of the Cricketers' Association, reported in August that ICC had made a 'considerable advance towards accommodation' with Packer, the writing was already on the wall. Kent announced that they would re-sign their Packer players for 1979 on the grounds that if they didn't other counties would. And when Warwickshire announced shortly afterwards that, in view of a letter from the other players, they did not propose to renew Dennis Amiss's contract, it caused a great furore amongst the members, for Amiss had had his best season ever for the club: 'Why should we suffer when Kent don't intend to?' the dissidents asked. But when they asked for a special meeting, arranged for late September, Amiss himself asked for it to be called off, advised, apparently, by the Cricketers' Association, who were confident that a settlement would be reached during the winter.

Little more needs to be said about this ignoble episode in the affairs of the noble game as the saga lurched towards the inevitable surrender by the ICC. English disapproval of Packer was alloyed somewhat at the outset by the fact that his impact was greatest in Australia, whose Test teams dwindled into insignificance as a result. Conversely, though the Australian Board made war-like noises, the Australian public made it clear that, while not everyone liked the frenetic WSC approach, they certainly were not going to pay to see their reserves trampled on by the Poms. The

English public, meanwhile, became relaxed enough in their unaccustomed supremacy over the old enemy to indulge in a nostalgic North v. South, Gentlemen v. Players debate about the claims of Boycott and Brearley to the captaincy. One side followed the lead of John Woodcock of *The Times*, who backed the Middlesex captain despite an average of under 20 in his previous twelve Test matches – 'because England are at ease under Brearley and play the better for being so'. A diametrically opposed minority view was expressed by Albert Hunt, a Bradford contributor to *New Society*: the north-country 'professional' Boycott, having swallowed his pride and gone out to tour Australia under Brearley, had been unchivalrously denied the opportunity to practise at a crucial stage in the tour by the Cambridge 'amateurs' Brearley and the manager, Doug Insole.

This unique reversal of roles may indeed have affected Boycott's performances. So also may his dismissal as Yorkshire's captain two days after the death of his beloved mother and a couple of weeks before the tour began. Boycott himself even blamed his personal troubles for his deplorable outburst against one of the umpires, whom he called a cheat when he gave him out. Anyway Boycott was glad to get the tour over and returned home, intent on pressing hard for a ban on Packer players at the Cricketers' Association meeting in April 1979. This was expected to be a stormy affair, but it turned out to be an anti-climax, for the members were advised to take no decisions but to await developments. By the end of the month it was all over: the Australian Board had done a deal, conceding Packer's exclusive television rights, and the wind went out of loyalist sails with a rush.

From *A Social History of English Cricket, 1999*

TONY GREIG

David Tossell

Grovel!

By the final Saturday of the series, with the temperature topping out at 82 degrees, the great British drought was biting so badly that the Queen had ordered her gardeners to stop watering the grounds at all Royal households. Industry bosses called on the public to use less water, leaving more for factories. Martin Trowbridge of the Chemical Industries Association said, 'Jobs are at stake. Is it better to have a well-watered flower bed or a pay packet?'

Such concerns were far from the minds of a cheerful crowd, some of whom took time to settle into their seats behind the bowler's arm. Once they had, Daniel sent the first ball of the day down the leg side for four byes. The first four off the bat was all-run after Amiss clipped Daniel through mid-on. Woolmer again started carefully, but in Holding's second over he shuffled across his crease and was beaten by speed, giving Dickie Bird an easy lbw decision.

Amiss drove well and played confidently off his legs, recalling that 'they were bowling at leg stump and feeding me'. One square cut looked a little edgy and Holding, generating fearsome pace through the air and off the most docile of wickets, had him groping outside off stump. But then Amiss whipped the ball past leg slip to move to 52.

David Steele remembers, 'I had been in about a quarter of an hour when I went down to Dennis and he said, "How am I doing?" I said, "What do you mean, how are you doing? You have got 70 on the board. How am I doing?" He said, "Oh, you are all right." He had no confidence in himself. He was a man of theory, a man of doubt, but a wonderful player. He was a lovely timer of the ball and when he got in he kept going. He got big scores. With that big step to the off side, he just flicked everything.'

Amiss and Steele offered an interesting contrast in styles. In comparison to Amiss's back-foot shuffle, Steele continued to commit to the front foot, leaving him vulnerable when Holding moved the ball away. Steele punished a couple of loose deliveries off the experimental spin of Roy Fredericks and England, having made good progress throughout the morning, took lunch at 137 for 1.

Confident in his new technique, Amiss, 80 at lunch, felt clear-headed. Instead of the lethargic thoughts he'd harboured at Lord's, here he occupied the time during Holding's extended approach to the wicket by reinforcing his action plan. 'You talk to yourself. You say, "Keep your head still, watch the ball, watch the ball, watch the hand." You are just devising in your mind what you are going to play. Is it swinging, is it bouncing? Once you have got used to the bounce and pace of the wicket it helps you to mentally prepare for any shot. If you have fast bowlers coming at you from both ends you have not got much time to switch off. You are always under pressure and you have no time to get away from it. You do go through periods when facing fast bowlers can get on top of you, but the better batsmen come through it. I felt mentally strong and my technique was working.'

Steele began the afternoon by helping a climbing ball from Holding over backward point, repeating the shot next ball. It moved him to 44, but Holding, having switched to the Vauxhall End, pinned him lbw with a ball that broke back. New batsman Chris Balderstone was soon treading Steele's path back to the pavilion. Holding twice struck him on the pads and induced a rash shot outside the off stump, before putting him out of his misery with a yorker that brushed the inside edge before dismantling the stumps.

Amiss was undeterred, twice dispatching Roberts through mid-wicket with a circular flourish of the bat. On 96, and after 209 minutes' batting, he stood one stroke from a century that would complete his courageous return from the precipice of his Test career. He stabbed at a Holding half-volley and the ball shot past the bowler for four. It was one of England's feel-good moments in a summer that had offered precious few. Recognising the journey Amiss had undertaken since they had seen him in distress at Lord's three months earlier, the West Indies players joined the crowd in applause. A few fans bounded out to offer personal congratulation, one of them handing Amiss a ten-pound note, which was given to umpire Bird for safe-keeping. 'It was a good feeling,' says Amiss. 'I have always thought that the 262 at Sabina Park was the better innings, but there was more pressure on me at The Oval. My international career and my ability against fast bowling were at stake.'

Amiss was never one to consider that the job had been done once he had three figures against his name. Of the eleven Test centuries he would make in his career, eight ended in scores of more than 150. On such a good wicket he was determined to continue batting. 'An old coach of mine used to say to me, "Den, if you get a hundred, get another – because it makes up for all the noughts and ones. That is the way my confidence was. If I got a hundred I often got 150-plus. Also, I tell these lads now at Warwickshire, that if you get a hundred then you can really learn all about your technique and batting. You are seeing the ball early and that is when you learn shots you never thought you had.'

Settling in again, Amiss escaped when he was caught by Murray off a Daniel no-ball. Then Peter Willey slashed hard and was dropped at first slip, Daniel again the unlucky bowler. Amiss responded by caressing Holder twice past backward square leg and driving square to take the score beyond 200. Richards and Fredericks, bowling in tandem either side of tea, served up enough bad balls to allow Amiss to move relentlessly past 150. Willey, never showing the fluency he had exhibited in the fourth Test, had contributed 33 to a 128-run stand when he got an inside edge to King and saw the ball fly off his pad to Fredericks at gully. Clearly not believing that contact had been made by his bat, Willey departed in despond.

Greig was greeted by an ovation to rival that of Amiss's century, much of it directed ironically by the West Indies fans. To add to the drama, the new ball became available almost immediately and Roberts and Holding rejoined the attack. Greig hurled himself into cover-driven fours off both bowlers and Amiss had to jerk away from a rearing Roberts delivery before waiting on a back-foot drive to raise the 300.

'They had been bowling at about 85 miles an hour, with one bouncer an over,' Amiss explains. 'That was fine and we were picking up ones and twos. But as soon as Greig came to the wicket he was all, "Come on, let's get this fired up. We are going to smash these buggers out of sight." I was saying, "Look, it's nice out here, don't upset them." Now, because it was Greig batting, suddenly it was 95 miles an hour and three bouncers an over.'

Amiss's concerns were quickly resolved. The Oval erupted as Holding pitched on a full length and Greig, playing slightly across the line as he fell towards the off side, was bowled middle and leg. 'It was the first time I have ever been pleased to see the England captain get his leg stump knocked out of the ground,' laughs Amiss.

There was no containing the elation of the West Indies fans, who raced to the square from their places around the boundary. One fan even offered Greig a copy of 'Who's Grovelling Now', a record that had recently been released by reggae artist Ezeike. 'Everyone had a copy,' recalls Trevor Nelson. 'I remember learning all the words from my dad.' Neither police nor ground-staff were able to clear the field of spectators who seemed reluctant to leave even after Greig was long gone. Alley and Bird took the players to the pavilion in response to what commentator Richie Benaud was calling 'one of the lousiest crowd performances I have ever seen'. He suggested that the authorities should 'should stick those fellows in jail and fine them'. After a nine-minute delay, the last few balls of the day were completed, with night-watchman Underwood at the crease and Amiss on 176 not out from a score of 304 for 5.

As far as anyone could remember, the pitch invasion represented the first time a Test match in England had been halted by the crowd. There had been 80 policemen on duty and Surrey secretary Warren Sillitoe estimated it would take 200 to ring the entire boundary effectively. The priority, he said, was to protect sensitive areas, such as the square and the entrance to the pavilion. Meanwhile, groundsman Harry Brind said that he had been concerned about such disturbances and had taken the precaution of using an old set of stumps. The *Daily Mail*'s Alex Bannister suggested, 'The West Indians must be made to understand that if they want to watch, they must abide by English codes of cricket behaviour.' A warning was issued that anyone encroaching on the playing surface would be removed from the ground.

By the time the fourth day began on yet another glorious morning, the first 100 standpipes had now appeared in Devon, where many households were without their regular water supply. The new Drought Act was to be enforced in the area, making it illegal to wash cars and fill paddling pools. The worst drought in 250 years was causing increasing numbers of forest fires and forcing Dorset firemen to have holidays cancelled. While the summer sun had at first been thought to offer an advantage to the players from the Caribbean, Clive Lloyd suggests, 'It led to a string of slow, ideal batting pitches which really were no good for our fast bowlers.'

On this slow Oval wicket, the draw still appeared the mostly likely result, especially when Amiss picked up where he had left off on Saturday. Bowling round the wicket, Holding and Roberts were both clipped uppishly behind square for four. Amiss leaned into Roberts's slower ball, before Holding, abandoning his early-morning tactic, was driven airily through the covers, taking Amiss to 199. Two balls later, Holding over-pitched and Amiss flicked over Greenidge at square leg to complete the second double-century of his Test career. The first had been a match-saving effort in the West Indies and if Amiss could find someone to stick around with him, maybe he could give a repeat performance.

Underwood's stay at the wicket had already ended, losing his off stump in Holding's third over of the day, giving the bowler his second five-wicket haul of the series. Knott was the ideal character for a rearguard action, turning Roberts over the fast outfield for four and causing Daniel, who had been warming up to replace Holding, to pull up with a hamstring injury as he gave chase. The partnership England needed, however, failed to materialise when Amiss finally fell victim to his new strategy. His right foot was frozen a long stride outside off stump as Holding's delivery brushed lightly against the pad on its way to the stumps. With 203 to his name, including 28 fours, Amiss could feel that his method had paid its way.

'It was a great innings by Dennis, a one-off,' says Mike Selvey. 'He had worked towards that ever since he'd got hit and I know how hard he had worked. He had a reputation of not liking quick bowling, but it was just that he didn't play the bouncer that well. He wasn't a scared batsman. His technique involved standing right over onto off stump but he was absolutely monumental through the leg side anyway. He would clip the ball away for hour upon hour.'

According to Derek Underwood, 'I can't recall a greater come-back innings throughout my career. If anyone gave a V-sign to the selectors, Dennis did it on that occasion.'

Amiss would tour once more with England, but within a year – with Australia again the visitors – he would be out of Test cricket. This innings, however, had ensured a much kinder epitaph for his career. 'It helped me to go out of the game on a better note,' he admits. 'It was nice to have done it.'

Knott was in one of his creative moods, timing drives either side of the wicket against Holder and King, whose strengthening of his leg-side field simply persuaded Knott to go the other way. Geoff Miller's first Test boundary had been nudged through the slips and when he aimed an expansive back-foot drive against Holder he lost his stumps – just as Dickie Bird's cry of 'no-ball' was reaching his end of the wicket. A neat drive off Holder helped Miller settle before Knott turned the final ball of the morning off his toes to reach 45 out of 401 for 7.

The gathering afternoon clouds looked like symbols of England's fate when Knott was rapped on the pads by Roberts and Miller was beaten by Roberts and Holding. Both batsmen survived. Knott hit Roberts through mid-wicket and then pushed a single to complete his fifty. The next ball Knott faced, from Holding, was short of a length and, getting in position to force through the off side, he edged into his stumps off the inside of an angled bat.

Selvey found the ring of close fielders reinforced by an extra gully, short leg and silly point, but he saved them a job by chopping his first ball against the stumps in the identical manner to Knott. It gave Holding his eighth wicket, none of them having required any assistance from a fielder. His father, Ralph, watching his son in England for the first time, claimed, 'He always bowled straight, even when he was at school.'

Holding's hopes of capping his remarkable performance with a hat-trick disappeared with a sloppy delivery down the leg side. Miller, left with the task of getting England closer to the follow-on target, drove Roberts off the back foot and was quickly into position for another boundary. But then he mistimed a pull to Bernard Julien, the substitute fielder, at mid-on to end a promising début innings of 36, leaving England 435 all out.

With a lead of 252, Lloyd – his bowlers depleted by Daniel's injury and with almost 130 overs in their legs – decided not to enforce the follow-on. The West Indies openers, their gameplan to slog as many runs as quickly as possible, came out to bat with 55 minutes remaining before tea. The West Indies fans greeted them excitedly and were rewarded by seeing Greenidge, having been brushed on either the glove or arm by a Bob Willis lifter, hit three fours in the first over. The first was an effortless hook; then Greenidge thrashed a cover drive and, with extravagant back-lift, hoisted Willis over mid-wicket. Two more short balls disappeared to the boundary in Willis's next over. To see the supposed saviour of England's fast bowling being dealt with so callously so soon after Holding's brilliance brought the home side's predicament even more sharply into focus. The subsequent comment of former Australian batsman David Hookes that 'Bob was a fucking off-spinner compared to Michael' could easily have had its roots at The Oval.

Roy Fredericks showed Selvey the perils of bowling even slightly short before Greenidge lifted Greig over extra cover to give the West Indies 66 runs off 13 overs at tea. Fredericks's steady accumulation was less brutal than that of his partner but resulted in him reaching his half-century first when he drove Selvey for two fours in an over. Greenidge cut and swept Underwood as the boundaries came in a cluster and the score reached 150 in two minutes short of two hours. Greenidge took one long stride to meet Willis with a towering drive into the pavilion for six, the start of his sequence of 22 runs off 11 balls. Shortly before six o'clock, at the end of the 32nd over and with both batsmen in the mid-80s, Lloyd waved his men back to the pavilion. A score of 182 for 0 had produced a lead of 434.

The two-hour passage of play had underlined once again the difference in talent and effectiveness of the two teams. Greig, meanwhile, understood what it meant for him personally in the light of his comments at the start of the summer. Never one to hide from his critics or deflect the glare of attention, he gave the cheering West Indian fans what they wanted. As the England players left the arena, he walked towards the open stands on the Harleyford Road side of the ground and dropped to the grass. Smiling in the direction of the crowd, he crawled on hands and knees, an attempt to make his peace with the West Indians. Over the delighted din, Tony Cozier told BBC Radio listeners, 'For three or four paces he has, in his own words, grovelled.'

Greig would explain, 'It was just a bit of fun. I was walking on my knees. I realise I made a mistake in using that word at the start of the series and they haven't let me forget it.'

Clyde Walcott described Greig's antics as 'a delightful way to end a happy and rewarding series', although the action wasn't quite finished. Lloyd's declaration left England with 20 minutes at the crease before stumps. Curiously, Lawrence Rowe remembers the West Indian bowlers having urged Lloyd not to end the West Indies' innings. He recalled Lloyd being urged, 'Don't declare, Skip, because we can't get these people out on this wicket.' According to Rowe, Lloyd argued, 'If we bat out the day, we are just going to kill the cricket. We have to declare.'

It seems an unlikely scenario. The wicket might have been flat and the evening sun warm, but England's batsmen knew that, against Holding and Roberts, a lead of 435 with one day and a few minutes left was far beyond their abilities. This was not an era when 400 runs in a day's Test cricket was considered achievable, especially when teams could slow the over rate with impunity. It is hard, therefore, to believe that there was reluctance on the West Indies' part to get at them – although the five overs bowled before the close do lend more credence to Rowe's memory.

Holding fired the first ball of the innings down the leg side for four byes and continued to bowl waywardly. Woolmer steered Roberts behind square with a late drive, flicked a full toss off his toes and worked a short delivery to fine leg for three successive boundaries. Amiss executed a firm off-drive and, after suffering a painful blow on the left arm, glanced the last ball of the day to fine leg. Any chance Roberts had of an interception was wrecked by the young fans who ran towards the square. 'That's ridiculous,' spat Benaud. England had scored 43 without loss. Even if no one dared to hope for the impossible, English optimism at least extended to thoughts of a draw.

The final day was prefaced by something of a diplomatic foul-up following the conclusion of Monday's action. Only an apologetic Alan Knott and Derek Underwood of the England players turned up at the Surrey Tavern for a reception to present the Wisden Trophy to the West Indies team in recognition of their victory in the series. *Wisden* editor Norman Preston told reporters that he had given the England squad's letter of invitation to Alec Bedser four days earlier, but was told that the letter had been left in the committee room at The Oval and was discovered only a short time before the event.

England's batsmen could have done without anything else occurring to stir up the West Indies bowlers when, maybe, they might have been content to coast through the final day of the series on a feather-bed pitch. Even Holding initially seemed a little lethargic, but he still got the ball to lift enough for Amiss, hanging out his bat, to edge to Greenidge. The first wicket was down for 49.

Woolmer had played a big innings on this ground to save the Test against Australia a year earlier and one of the most disappointing aspects of the summer was the fact that he had not built on the promise he had shown in that game and in his first innings of this series. A well-timed drive through mid-wicket took his score to 30 and the prospect of a full day's batting lay ahead. But, for the second time in the match, indecisive foot movement was his undoing as he nudged at Holding and presented a thin edge to Murray.

Balderstone's second ball from Holding, working up towards full speed, was a leg-stump yorker, striking him on the foot. Then an ugly stab outside off stump was lucky not to produce an edge. Balderstone endured 25 minutes of scoreless purgatory before Holding's yorker flattened his off stump. A miserable pair for Balderstone, of whom Selvey says, 'He was just out of his depth against that lot.'

Steele had taken almost half an hour before poking Holding round the corner for a boundary and had edged the Jamaican just short of the slips. With the third wicket down at 64, he wore a more determined look than ever, surviving an lbw appeal against Holder before marching into a productive off-drive. Willey, though, could not survive Holder's second over when he cut hard and edged a low catch to Greenidge.

For the final time in the series, here came Greig. He milked the moment, halting a few paces onto the grass and standing to attention while he enjoyed the catcalls of the West Indian followers. He pushed a single off his third ball, enabling him to keep the strike. In raced Holding and, almost too fast for the eye to see, removed the leg stump with yet another yorker. It was an even more resounding exclamation mark to the series than Richards's batting earlier in the game. Greig's feet had not even had the chance to move before his stumps were demolished, the fifth time he had been clean bowled by such a delivery in the series; the fourth in his last five innings. But more than the facts and figures, the dismissal would endure as one of the iconic images of the series. Holding leapt skywards, teammates whirled around, hugging him, pausing only to wave away the fans who once again were rushing the field. Greig, his form at Headingley seemingly a long way in the past, made his weary way off the field.

Knott joined Steele at 78 for 5 and the pair lasted an hour and a half before lunch, adding 50 to the total. Knott was as dogged and defiant as he'd been in his previous two innings, stubborn defence mixed with impish attack and a bit of luck. The bowling of Richards, Fredericks, King and Lloyd offered a restful aperitif before the meal break, which was taken with Knott on 28 and Steele, who had not scored for half an hour, 31. But it was back to reality when Holding returned in the afternoon, the ball twice smacking into Knott's pads. Steele failed to get fully behind the ball and King made a valiant, but unsuccessful, effort to take a low catch at slip. The score had moved to

148 when Holder, achieving a little away swing and extracting bounce, was rewarded by the sight of Steele edging to Murray for 42. It was an inconclusive end to the series for Steele, whose two scores in the 40s represented a partial return to form but would not be enough to ensure him of a place on England's winter tour. Holder had his 15th wicket in four Tests, a solid performance by a man whose steadfast bowling was often overshadowed by his more eye-catching colleagues.

Miller took 32 minutes to score the first run of a knock that would build on the promise of the first innings, but then settled in against the spin of Richards and Fredericks. Knott squeezed runs to all parts of the field and completed a fifty by turning Holder to long leg for three. With 50 minutes plus 20 overs left, a flicker of hope for survival began to play in the minds of the England followers – only for part-time spinner Richards to bowl Miller with a quicker ball that beat his back-foot shot and flicked the pads. With only three tail-enders to bat, the game was up.

Holding came back to administer the last rites. His fourth ball moved a little off the seam and took out Knott's off stump; 196 for 8. With that wicket, Holding, who had not even warmed up enough to remove his sleeveless sweater, had become the first West Indian to take 13 wickets in a Test match. Roberts, meanwhile, was still waiting for his first. At last he got it when Lloyd took a brilliant diving catch just off the ground in the gully to remove Underwood. Roberts danced in relief.

Holding raced in from the Vauxhall End one final time. A fast yorker beat Willis's defensive effort and hit him on the foot; an easy lbw decision. At 4.20 pm, the series was over. Holding's return in the second innings was 6 for 57, giving him an astonishing 14 for 149 in the match. The figures are impressive enough, but even more so for having been achieved on such an unhelpful wicket.

Holding's recollection of his performance is 'just running in and bowling fast', crediting the naivety of youth for his success. 'It was such a flat pitch that if I had been more experienced I would have said, "This is not working. It is not worth all this hard work and strain on my body." When you are young and excited you just run in fast and do what you do.'

Willis notes, 'Having bowled on the pitch, I know that there was nothing there to help the pace bowlers. But Michael managed to make it seem perfect for speed.'

It was this match that confirmed Holding's arrival in the very top bracket of fast bowlers, where he had only Roberts, Lillee and Thomson for company. It had been a spectacularly brief journey, gathering momentum after a promising, if stuttering, start in Australia, where his figures had not quite matched his potential. 'If I had been English that would have been it for me,' he said, recognising the West Indies' selectors' faith in him – although it seems unlikely that even England's management could have resisted such a phenomenon, however unproven, at a time when any moderate fast bowler with one good leg stood a chance of selection.

Holding's captain, Lloyd, called his performance 'the finest fast bowling I have ever witnessed in Test cricket. For sustained speed and accuracy, it would be impossible to improve on Holding's performance.'

Selvey, one of those who suffered at Holding's hands, also watched in awe. 'In later years, it would have been the perfect wicket for Waqar Younis or Wasim Akram to come on and take five for something with reverse-swing yorkers. But no one knew about reverse swing back then. What he did was bowl very fast, very straight and very full. To put it into context, look at the figures of all the other pace bowlers in the match.'

With the crowd still thronging around the pavilion following the post-match formalities, fast bowling was the dominant topic as BBC front man Peter West sat on the balcony with Lloyd and Greig. Dressed in civvies – not a sponsor logo in sight – the two captains were invited to dissect a series in which, West declared, 'England have taken a hammering.' Greig, in no position to disagree, said, 'They have given us a hiding.'

After an exchange of pleasantries, in which Greig said he would love to see the new West Indies team take on Australia and Lloyd praised the quality of the young English players he had seen around the country, West asked Greig what England had taken out of the series. 'I don't think we have come out of this series with too much,' he replied with typical frankness. 'It has been tremendous to be part of this series because people have seen tremendous cricket. I think what we have realised more than anything is that we have to start building up a new side. The big thing is to pick the right youngsters. Chaps have got to come and go before we find the right combination. But the most important thing is that in Test cricket these days you have to have quick bowlers, and until such time as we can find those quick bowlers we are going to struggle a bit.'

As a defiantly-smiling Greig offered that final postscript to the BBC's coverage, it was impossible to fight back images of the broadcast that had heralded a memorable Test series. Here was Greig once again sat high on a pavilion, greensward stretching behind him. Hundreds more fleeting snapshots of the summer had passed in and out of consciousness since his delivery of the comment by which the England–West Indies contest would forever be identified. But however many England players had been and gone, swept up and spat out by the slipstream of Holding, Roberts and Daniel, Greig's choice of the word 'grovel' had danced enduringly through the summer, taunting its speaker like a mischievous sprite. It had provided an ongoing soap-opera backdrop to the action right up to the closing scene: that symbolic final destruction of Greig's stumps. A new entry had been etched permanently into cricket's lexicon.

From *Grovel! The Story and Legacy of the Summer of 1976*, 2007

I couldn't believe it at the time and still struggle with it now when I think about it. I was driving up the motorway on my way to Aintree for the Grand National in 2000 when the phone rang. It was the BBC sports desk saying a story was coming in over the wires that the Indian police had irrefutable evidence of South Africa's Hansie Cronje being caught up in match-fixing. I dismissed it out of hand as I simply didn't believe it. In any case I was going abroad the following day and would be unavailable for comment. When I got back to the UK a week later, it seemed like the world had gone mad.

Later I attended the King Commission in Cape Town and watched as Hansie's dad, Ewie Cronje, sat shaking his head in utter and profoundly sad disbelief.

I had met Hansie on several occasions and he had always been the epitome of politeness; I had played cricket with Gordon Parsons at Leicestershire, and Gordon had gone on to marry Hansie's sister, so I felt I had a slight connection with him. Next I remember commentating at Edgbaston when *Test Match Special* producer Peter Baxter handed me a note saying Cronje had died in a plane crash. I felt a deep well of sadness for a man who should have been a transcending figure that his rejuvenated nation could continue to look up to for decades. What a tragedy.

HANSIE CRONJE

Paul Nixon

Not that it was all misery that year. At Leicestershire we had a new overseas player with a formidable reputation. Having recently been appointed South Africa's captain, we knew we were getting a first-class operator in Hansie Cronje but we didn't realise how much of an example he would prove to be. As with Phil Simmons, our recruitment of Hansie was another departure from the habit of

going all-out for big West Indian fast bowlers, who were often incon-
sistent, frequently got injured and didn't always work wonders on
flat pitches. Hansie was a different specimen altogether – he was a
high-class batsman, an amazing player of spin, and a tactical genius
in any given situation.

He appeared as disciplined a sportsman and as decent a man
as you could wish to meet, but it was his approach to fitness
that impressed me the most. I had always been regarded as the
fitness king at Leicestershire, but Hansie offered serious competition for the crown. He had apparently trained with Zola Budd, the
Olympic middle-distance athlete, in South Africa, and his appetite
for running was clear as soon as he arrived at Grace Road. Every
evening, after a day's play, he would pull on his trainers, sprint
around the boundary edge from one sightscreen to another, walk
to the next, and then sprint again. He would repeat this gruelling
routine six times, while the rest of the players were nursing their
aches and pains in the dressing room.

I loved the challenge of testing myself against Hansie. We competed against each other every day and pushed ourselves to the
absolute limit. As much as anything, it gave me something new
to tackle instead of just moping around after the broken thumb
episode, but I still only got the better of him once, when we went
for a 5-mile run and followed it with a series of bunny-hops – a
routine which rendered his legs so stiff the next day that he had
to pull out of our next Sunday League game. Otherwise, he was a
physical machine who brought a new intensity to our training and
nets and never flagged. Around the club, he commanded natural
authority with his 1,300 Championship runs, his mastery of run-
chases, and his helpful attitude towards the younger batsmen.

He was the perfect man to have around, really – in a few short
months he had got me feeling better about life – and it seemed
innocuous when the jokes started flying around about his legendary
love of money. As quickly as he earned admiration for his approach
to cricket, Hansie attracted a reputation as the tightest man at
the club. Early into his stay he latched onto Gordon Parsons, his
brother-in-law (Gordon was married to Hansie's sister, Hester) and
began heading to his house every night for dinner. This, we concluded, was mainly because he was too stingy to buy his own food.
We hammered him relentlessly, branding him Scrooge, but this
never seemed to bother him, apart from one memorable occasion.

Hansie was very well-paid, drove a sponsored BMW and had all the trappings, but was notorious for never buying a drink. And so, before a game in London against Middlesex, we resolved to stitch him up. Prior to the trip, a few of us devised a rule whereby the first person who reached the hotel bar would have to get the first round in. This information was then shared with the rest of the team, with only one man left in the dark. We finally informed Hansie of the new directive seconds before we rocked up to our expensive London base, and as we walked into the foyer we surrounded him, shoved him to the front of the group and threatened to pile on him and remove his clothes if he didn't break the habit of a lifetime.

'Ah, no, come on guys …'

He pleaded and protested, but eventually gave in and the resulting round relieved him of about £200. Judging by his expression, he would have preferred to have handed over one of his limbs than the money.

Joking apart, he was as sharp as a tack when it came to financial matters. Whenever he was dismissed in a game, he would briefly disappear into the dressing room, to get his frustrations out of his system, and would then reappear on the balcony with some paperwork, or a laptop. He was doing his accountancy qualifications, he explained – another string to his impressive bow. The only time I saw a different side to him, in all honesty, was when he invited me on his stag do in Bloemfontein during one of Leicestershire's pre-season trips to South Africa. Many of the details are vague but one image is clear: Hansie, chained to a bar stool, talking nonsense and the great man well and truly away with the fairies.

For some reason, probably because I was somehow more sober than the others, it fell to me to take him back to his house at the end of the night. This was an experience in itself, for Hansie's residence was a huge, lavish place the size of a hotel. Its front gate was operated by remote control and it took me ages to figure out which buttons to press in order to gain entry. Finally, after ten minutes of garage doors flying up and down, and lights coming on and off, the gate at last flew open.

Once inside, I somehow had to get Hansie into a prone position, where he would hopefully sink into a quick and safe sleep. Again, easier said than done. As he entered the house, he swiftly careered into the dining room, bashing against furniture and then veering shambolically towards a table. On the table stood a big, shiny trophy – his international player of the year award – and it was about to hit the floor.

I lunged in front of Hansie and grabbed the silverware just in time. I put it somewhere safe and then returned to the job at hand. Eventually I brought Cronje under control, directed him through to his lounge and helped him down onto the sofa. I whipped a bin out of the kitchen, placed it next to his head, and departed to the sound of a country's greatest sporting icon throwing up.

If you had told me then that this would be the last time I would see Hansie Cronje in the flesh, and that a few years later I would be watching the news and learning about his involvement in one of cricket's most appalling match-fixing scandals, with his eyes no longer sparkling as they used to, but sunken and hollow in a televised courtroom scene, I wouldn't have believed you. If you had then predicted I would wake up a couple of years further on to reports of his death in a plane crash in the Outeniqua Mountains, I would have chased you out of town. Not just because he hated flying and always preferred to drive from Bloemfontein to Cape Town for two days rather than make the trip by plane, but because of who and what he was.

Back then, he just seemed like the rest of us at Leicestershire during those mainly exciting, formative times – so young, so fit, so full of vitality, so skilful, so hungry, and ... well, just so bloody *good*.

From *Keeping Quiet: The Autobiography*, 2012

The Mike Atherton dirt-in-the-pocket affair at Lord's during the 1994 England v South Africa Test is destined to go down in cricket history as one of the more bizarre examples in the exercise of sporting justice. What is the difference between using common-or-garden dirt a) straight from the pocket or b) straight from the ground, in order to dry fingers or ball? Absolutely none at all, the authorities decided – innocent on both counts. But context is everything. With the media now ready to pounce on any new allegation of cheating in the game after the marked increase in on-field controversy, being innocent has to be accompanied by talking innocent. This incident remains the most awkward I have ever had to report on. In hindsight, Martin Johnson is correct to state that I was wrong to describe Michael Atherton as a personal friend because it was irrelevant at the time. But I am glad that we remain so today.

MICHAEL ATHERTON

Martin Johnson

Lord's

First Test, 4th Day

South Africa won by 356 runs

A furore that has muddied reputations

England's performance off the field yesterday was not conspicuously better than their performance on it. Their captain denied doing anything illegal, his denial was accepted by his chairman of selectors, and the same chairman of selectors, Raymond Illingworth, then fined him £2,000. The cynical answer is that Illingworth's fine was meant to achieve two things, both of which are doomed to failure. Firstly, to appease the Pakistanis (who still believe the allegations of ball-tampering made against them in 1992 to be an English imperialist plot) and secondly to appease the Press.

'The matter has been dealt with and is now closed,' Illingworth said. In fact, within five minutes it was announced that Peter Burge, the International Cricket Council match referee, will be issuing his own statement this afternoon. The oddest part of this whole business is that Atherton had two opportunities to answer the most relevant question of all. 'Did Burge at any time on Saturday night ask you whether you had anything in your pocket?' Atherton replied, both times: 'That conversation remains a private one between me and Mr Burge.' If, however, Burge did not ask this question, it hardly places him in the Perry Mason class of cross-examination. If, on the other hand, Burge did ask him, then people are perhaps entitled to construe Atherton's omission to mention the dirt (as opposed to the reply given that he was merely drying his hands inside his pocket) as information he did not wish Burge to be aware of.

Professional cricket is now in an era when Denis Compton wouldn't dare plaster his hair with Brylcreem, and the subject is so sensitive that Atherton is at least guilty of being unwittingly unintelligent. And Atherton is as intelligent a bloke to have captained England since Mike Brearley. Atherton says he is not a cheat, and anyone who knows him believes him to be a man of his word. However, it is well known that professional cricketers cheat, and that tampering with the ball is the best known example. In days gone by, there were bowlers around with finger-nails that could open a can of baked beans, never mind lift a seam, although umpiring (and television) scrutiny is now such that it is the outfielders, rather than the bowlers, who mostly do the dirty work. One of the most popular methods, and one which Atherton doubtless felt he was suspected of, is to carry a stick of lip salve inside the trouser pocket for polishing purposes. These come in a variety of flavours, and one former Test bowler said that when a batsman 'sniffed the leather', as West Indian quickies are fond of saying, he was as likely to be overcome by an aroma of peppermint or raspberry as fright.

Atherton was convinced enough of his innocence to offer his trousers (deemed to be unnecessary) and he said to a former team-mate on Saturday night: 'If anyone wants to accuse me of cheating, I'll be a rich man.'

'Who's winning?'
'No one ain't–she won't come out!'

Media pressure puts the squeeze on Atherton

Somewhere in England, a long way from his Didsbury flat, and possibly wearing a false beard and dark glasses, Michael Atherton is contemplating his future as England's cricket captain. Does he soldier on, as his chairman of selectors has invited him to, or does he take the cyanide capsule urged upon him – as is usually the case at times like these – by an increasingly insistent media?

If Atherton was close to a radio set yesterday, he would have discovered that the most trenchant voice urging him to hand in his badge belongs to Jonathan Agnew, the BBC cricket correspondent. Agnew also expressed similar views in a newspaper column, citing pictures '... clearly showing Atherton rubbing dirt into the ball' (i.e. illegal tampering) and describing his position, as a result, as 'untenable'. Agnew has also prefixed his comments by describing Atherton as a 'personal friend', which may be news to Atherton, and in any event is totally superfluous unless intended to convey to his audience that his comments thus carry more weight and gravitas than would be the case if Atherton thought he was a total plonker.

However, as the England captain has denied cheating, Agnew is basically describing him as a liar and a cheat. If this piece of mud sticks, particularly through the medium of the BBC, it really would make Atherton's position untenable, and unless he replies to it, either personally or through his lawyers, the effect may be as if Agnew has proved the case against him. However, the point that needs to be made this morning is that the only conviction for an illegal act (as opposed to a stupid one) has been made by the media. Peter Burge, the International Cricket Council referee, has cleared Atherton of infringing Law 42 (unfair play), so have two umpires, so has Raymond Illingworth, and so – by declining to get involved – has the South African cricket team.

However, the reason that Atherton will be considering his position at the moment, wherever he might be, is the sheer weight of media pressure. These sort of things are rarely allowed to die, and inevitable [listener] phone-ins are now adding to the hype. Yesterday, the Test and County Cricket Board hierarchy were grouping themselves firmly behind their man. Ossie Wheatley, the chairman of the TCCB's cricket committee, said: 'If someone does something thoughtless it should not destroy a promising career as this seems to be in danger of doing. We have had England captains pushed too far by the media before. I hope that doesn't happen to Michael because he's a fine captain and a fine man.'

Atherton has been silly in the things he has left unsaid, and not just in not coming clean about the dirt earlier than he did. For some reason, he also failed to say at the press conference that he used to carry dirt in his pocket when he bowled leg spin for Lancashire, when a dodgy back made it painful for him to bend over and dry fingers in the conventional manner. Had he done so, it would at least have made the unusual act of carrying some around in his pocket seem slightly less odd.

Atherton to fight on as England's captain

The drowning man finally re-surfaced in Manchester yesterday and announced his intention not only to clamber back on board, but also to return to the bridge as captain of the ship.

Atherton reiterated his claim that he used dirt on his fingers during the Lord's Test solely to keep one side of the ball dry, and if his palms were sweating in front of the cameras yesterday, he refrained from dipping his hand into his trouser pocket. When the cameras caught him doing this at Lord's, he said, '... it was not with the intention of altering the ball in any way.' Atherton, flanked by two Lancashire committee members, read from a prepared statement before fielding a battery of questions. The one regret he had, he wrote and said, was in not telling the International Cricket Council match referee Peter Burge, 'straight away' that he had dirt in his pocket. 'I should have come clean straight away,' Atherton said.

So why didn't he? 'I was concerned, as I said last week, about misrepresentation. However, I am totally regretful and I've duly been punished, both by a fine and by the weight of public and media scrutiny. We all make mistakes in life, but I am not dishonest. I even took my trousers into the initial meeting with Peter Burge and offered them for inspection. He asked me if I had any resin in my pocket. I said no. He asked me if I had any other substance in my pocket. I said no. This was obviously my mistake. I was thinking of things like Vaseline and lip salve and I confirmed to Mr Burge that there was absolutely no artificial substance of any kind in my pocket.'

Atherton revealed that he had been away for three days in Cheshire and the Lake District – deliberately avoiding newspapers, radio and television – and that his objective had been to clear his head and not come to any hasty decision over whether to resign. Had he seriously thought about resignation during that period? 'Yes,' Atherton replied. However, he decided to carry on firstly after making a telephone call to his chairman of selectors, Raymond Illingworth, who reconfirmed his earlier public support. 'Had he thought otherwise, I would have resigned,' Atherton said. 'The only reason for going then would have been to bow to the press and media clamour, and if I felt I was unable to do my job properly in the next Test match at Headingley.

Atherton confirmed (as he should have done last weekend) that he used to use dirt in his pocket to dry the ball when he bowled his leg-spinners. 'I never attempted to disguise my actions at Lord's and if you look at other spinners – Ian Salisbury in particular – they are forever rubbing their hands in the dirt to keep them dry and maintain their grip. There is nothing in the rules to say I can't carry dirt in my pocket and I was very open about what I was doing at Lord's. However, if it's hot and sticky at Headingley then I'll be rubbing my hands on the ground to keep them dry.'

The Oval

Third Test, 4th Day

England won by eight wickets

Television pictures revealed Atherton's dirt-in-the-pocket, and TV close-ups are becoming the prime source of evidence used by match referees to judge on a range of misdemeanours, including the minutiae of body language. Only two Tests after his Lord's scrape, Atherton was back in hot water, fined for examining his bat after being given out lbw for 0.

England find the steel for re-building

It is rather ironic that at the precise moment England are discovering the strand of steel required to compete with Australia this winter, the International Cricket Council has apparently decided that Test cricket is actually some kind of recreational parlour game, and that anyone not immediately kissing the umpire on both cheeks after being adjudged lbw to a ball that would not have struck another set of stumps, should be required to bend over and hand over all their pocket money. In fact, if England have discovered an Australian-style aggression, and someone like Burge is in charge this winter, there will be so many suspensions that the final Test might boil down to a single-wicket competition.

Perhaps the biggest talking point of the entire summer is the way that television cameras are now influencing Test cricket to a hitherto unparalleled degree. Previously, the close-up shot was only a worry to the spectator who has phoned in sick for a day off work, or is forgetfully nibbling an ear lobe attached to someone other than his wife. Nowadays, though, a cricketer only has to sneeze for the ref to launch a fierce investigation as to whether he has anything more sinister up his nose than traces of Vick's Sinex.

The evidence for Burge's swingeing fine on Atherton being vindictive is hardly weakened by the fact that the most obvious display of dissent of all came from DeFreitas on the opening day, when an lbw appeal was turned down. Furthermore, having fined Atherton, Burge then had no option when Fanie de Villiers's reaction to something similar was the rough equivalent of Steve Davis scratching his head after the referee had replaced his ball for a deliberate miss. In fact, ever since the dirt-in-the-pocket business at Lord's, clarity of judgement appears to have come a nasty cropper. If Atherton was a bit silly to stare at his bat, can someone tell me who on earth at the BBC decided that Allan Lamb was the man to interview (and call for Atherton's resignation)? Allan Lamb? Ye Gods. Apart from credentials extending to losing all three Tests in which he captained England, and being notoriously opinionated, Lamb had as much relevance to the argument as the Queen of Sheba, or Jonathan Agnew's mum.

When he was appointed last September, Atherton would have sold his house for the job. Now, with all these fines, he may have to, and the sparkle in his eyes 11 months ago has now been replaced by a dull, glazed look, like a three-day-old mackerel on the fishmonger's slab. As for Atherton's latest punishment, Illingworth says: 'If football's Premiership was run on the same lines, there would be no one left on the field by half-time. We have got to allow a bit of what happens in the split second after a dismissal. We don't want all the aggression taken out of what is an emotional game.'

From *Can't Bat, Can't Bowl, Can't Field, 1997*

How can you possibly fix a World Cup semifinal between Pakistan and India? This would be a match that the whole of the cricketing world would be watching. And with the countries' prime ministers, Manmohan Singh and Yousuf Raza Gilani, sitting together, the 2011 match played in the Punjab Cricket Association Stadium in Mohali – less than 200 miles from the border with Pakistan – would be both politically sensitive and as high-profile as it gets.

And yet Ed Hawkins claims in his book he received in advance a 'script' of how the match would play out. Since the script stated that Pakistan would bat first, I have to query whether Hawkins believes the toss was fixed. Surely if two of cricket's greatest sides are going to collude in throwing a World Cup semifinal, you would expect the outcome not to be entirely reliant on the 50:50 toss of a coin.

Nevertheless, there is a lot to be assimilated and understood about the way Indian bookmakers have inveigled themselves into the game. I have had bookmakers follow me on Twitter and when I can identify them I have managed to block them, but theirs is an invidious encroachment.

This is a book the ICC has to read. Any and all information to do with match-fixing has to be taken on board and analysed or another scandal will engulf the game when we least need it.

BOOKIE

Ed Hawkins

Vinay does not fit the stereotype of the Indian bookmaker. He does not emerge from the shadows and, instead of skulking through the lobby doors of a hotel in Bhopal, he bounds in. His smile is broad and genuine, his handshake warm.

'Great to meet you,' he says. 'How are you enjoying it here?'

This is not what one expects when meeting someone from one of the largest criminal fraternities in India. There are estimated to be up to 100,000 bookmakers in the country. Enemies of the state and the supposed scourge of international and domestic cricket, their modus operandi is, reportedly, violence and intimidation.

Certainly I had been gripped by apprehension. Taking an early-morning flight from Delhi to Bhopal, the capital of Madhya Pradesh, the state known as the Heart of India, it had gnawed away that I was travelling into the unknown. Apart from Twitter messages, emails and the odd phone call to Vinay, when both of us found it difficult to comprehend what the other was trying to say, I had no idea who he really was. I could not even be sure that he was a book-maker, let alone trust him.

My mood had not been helped by advice from Murali Krishnan, the investigative journalist from Delhi. When I told him of my plans, his face creased with concern. 'Be smart. Couple of friends of mine had a beer, slipped a tablet, drugged and robbed. So trust your instincts. Don't take any shit.'

After checking in at 8am, I lay on my bed and fretted over whether I had been horribly naive. My cellphone was ringing con-stantly. It was Vinay, wanting to know where I was staying. Having finally summoned some courage, I told him and then waited ner-vously in the lobby with the strains of pan-pipe music only adding to the unease. So you can see it was a relief to be welcomed in such a bright, genuine manner.

Vinay, wearing an Armani shirt and expensive-looking sunglasses resting on the top of his black hair, chuckled at his reputation. 'My dad didn't want me to become a bookie,' he says. 'He was upset. But that's because it's illegal here, not because I'm beating up persons or fixing matches. Bookmaking is a good business. Shadowy? No, it is quite clear. I would say it is the fairest thing.'

I ask him whether, as per his invitation, he has the time to explain exactly how the bookmaking industry works. He flinches. 'Of course,' he says, before lowering his voice. 'But not here. We could get in trouble if people overheard, so we can go somewhere private.'

In the lift to my hotel room, Vinay explains how he became a bookmaker: 'I had a friend, he was a bookie. I used to go to his shop when I was at school. I was 21. At that time in India everyone doesn't know the computers. I was OK at computers. He asked me to help with his computer. There was a software problem. I repaired that.

'After that he asked me whether I could design a software for him for his bookmaking. My father did not like this. He didn't want me to become a bookie. He said it was illegal. He was in the service industry, a sales manager. Cement industries. He said, "You can't do that." My friend approached my father and said, "I'm not making him a bookie, I am just learning computers from him." My father says, "OK, for 15 days, OK?" "It will not even take 15 days," my friend told him. But those 15 days are still going!

'After that we became partners. But we had a big loss. You see, other bookies took some of our bets because we don't have all that money. Sometimes bookies share bets. This bookie took 35 per cent of one of our bets, but he didn't pay us back, so we didn't have the money for our customers. But we had to keep our reputation in the market. We have to pay. We have to pay from our home. After that I started my own business. I started with just 100 rupees. I had five customers. Only five. Then it rose to 135. Up, up, up.'

While setting up his laptop and juggling two mobile phones – he changes his number every three weeks to avoid detection by police – Vinay explains how he makes 50 lakhs (about £60,000) a year from his bookmaking business, which has more than 200 customers. The average wager is one lakh (£1,200). He takes customers only on recommendation. This is uniform with the rest of the Indian industry, he tells me.

'You see, you wouldn't find it easy to get an account with a bookmaker because you don't know a local person. I don't know you, so I don't give you a credit account. Almost all of the accounts are credit accounts. It is all based on trust that the punter can pay and the bookmaker can pay, whoever wins. Maybe for you or someone new, we would take a cash advance and then, once you are trusted, we can give you a credit account.

'It works the same way when I have to pay my customers their winning monies. They have to trust me. If they do not trust me I have no business. This is the same throughout India. We all get along. Nicely, nicely. No rowing, no fighting.'

I allow myself a wry smile at an industry, maligned for malevolence and mistrust, apparently operating with honesty and integrity.

'You are surprised?' laughs Vinay. 'This is business. The customer comes first.'

Vinay has four offices dotted around the region, each with two people recording and writing down the wagers next to the name of the customer, who might use a nickname like 'K-Man' or 'Indian'. There are no betting slips. Each bet is struck via cellphone. 'Everything is recorded so there can be no dispute. We can play the bet back to the customer and we can show them in black and white. Dispute is very unusual, though.'

Once a customer is accepted, he will be given a number to call a telephone commentary service. A voice continuously relays the odds. This is called the bhao line.

'So we can have a room with 120 mobile phones all set up,' Vinay says. 'They are each capable of conference calling, and 600 customers are connected to one phone. So you can see how it spreads across the country with similar bookmaker operations around the country – 600 times 600, times 600, and so on and so forth.

'These phones are all connected to the bhao line. This is a man who is sitting in the same room as the mobile phones that are linked to his microphone, where he continuously reads out the live match odds. When the match starts [the first one-day international between India and England in Hyderabad on 14 October] we can listen and you will hear for yourself.'

Customers are paid the next day, without fail, using the hawala system.

'No bank transfers because we don't pay tax,' Vinay says.

The hawala system is glued by trust. That word again. It is a simple system. Money is transferred via a network of hawala brokers, often family members, or hawaladars. But the money does not, in fact, go anywhere, either physically or electronically, and the system can be defined by the term: money transfer without money movement. A customer will approach a hawala broker in one city and give a sum of money to be transferred to a recipient in another city. The hawala broker calls another hawala broker in the recipient's city, gives instructions of the funds and promises to settle the debt at a later date. All parties are given a code or password and at the start and end of the process, the broker charges a small fee. All money is paid out from the same pool that they take in.

'Ya, we use hawala,' Vinay says. 'The customer has to pay 300 rupees [£3–£4] per lakh [£1,200] for each cash transaction if they win. This is payable to me, the bookie.'

I ask Vinay how 'big' a bookmaker he is in the market. 'Oh, I am first-tier bookmaker. Do you have a pen and paper and I will explain?' The hotel stationery and complimentary pencil are pressed into action. Vinay starts to draw a family tree-style diagram. At the top he writes 'syndicate' followed by tentacles reaching out below to five 'first-tier bookmakers'. Below them are the second-tier bookmakers, followed by the third tier and so on. They are ranked by the number of customers they have. At the bottom are the customers.

'This second tier is a chain of about 50,000 bookies,' he says. 'The betting syndicate is a group who want to take big bets from all over India. They open up their prices, they tell the world what their prices are and the world bets on their prices. It means they are uniform. They post the prices and after that they put their prices up or down on the amount of money they get. If they get money on India they decrease the price.

'When the betting syndicate opens the prices to the general public, they want to bet. It means the betting syndicate are saying to them: "What would you say?" The general public does not know what the prices should be. He doesn't know whether it is a good price to back or lay, so he puts his money down.'

'Who is at the top of the syndicate?' I ask him.

'They are in Mumbai,' he says. 'All of them. At present. But when the matches start, they go to different parts of the country because in Mumbai at the moment they are very strict. The police. It is very risky. They don't want any trouble. We have to use Blackberry Messenger to communicate with each other because the police might intercept. I'm worried sitting here now with you. Mobile phones, laptop, cricket on television. This does not look good if the police knock on your door.

'The syndicate won't meet you. They won't trust you. Because I am outside, I can see you here. Jayanti Malad and Shobhan Kalachowki are syndicate heads. They will pick up my call within a single ring, but if you call them they won't.'

Vinay's anxiety over the police is not without foundation. At the time Malad, who Vinay describes as 'Delhi's biggest bookie', is 'on the run' after two of his associates were arrested for accepting bets on the Champions League Twenty20 tournament, which was won by Mumbai Indians. They were Indore-based bookies operating from a rented flat in Andheri, a surburb of Mumbai. Police confiscated 2.5 lakhs (£3,000), laptops, 20 SIM cards, mobile phones and voice recorders.

'Jayanti has been absconding since the arrest of his two associ-ates. We have intensified our search for him,' said a crime branch officer.

Malad's real name is Jayanti Shah, but the best-known Indian bookmakers remove their surname in favour of the town or suburb from which they operate. Shobhan Mehta, for example, is known as Shoban Kalachowki, a suburb of north-central Mumbai. Vinay is not yet notorious enough for a surname change.

'You have to understand that bookmaking in India is based on a tiered system, like arms reaching out, far and wide. It is like a food chain. The syndicate could be based in Dubai, London or New York. They set the odds and the rest follow. Every bookie is connected. I show you.'

Vinay's laptop whirs into life. He logs on to a website called unicel in, which allows him to send hundreds of SMS messages at a time. 'You see, I put the odds in here for the markets and then I send them to all the bookmakers. They send them on to other book-makers. And so on. This is how the customers get the odds, you see, all the way from the top of the syndicate. This is a very important part of how we work … I will include your phone when I send this.'

Seconds later my phone beeps and I have the odds for three markets in front of me. India are 86–89 favourites to win today's first one-day international against England in Hyderabad, the 'lunch favourite' is priced at 45–47 and 'lambi' at 276–280. These are what are known as 'forward bets', markets which close as soon as the match starts. In traditional bookmaking parlance they are known as ante-post wagers because they are not updated ball by ball. The live match betting, which is updated, is the second type of market and will include a new set of match odds, lambi and brackets.

'Lambi' is the term used for innings runs. The quote of 276–280 is not odds, but a spread on the number of runs that will be scored. Both teams are quoted and punters have the option to go over or under the runs quote: 'I think India will score less than 276' or 'I think India will score more than 280'. Brackets, which are only avail-able when the match is underway, are the amount of runs scored in ten-over segments and are an estimation on the number of runs scored. Again, gamblers are betting on whether the team will score more or fewer than the spread given by the bookmaker. The odds for these over or under markets are 9–10 (bet £10 to win £9).

'If a customer wants to bet on a market he uses one of two words:

"lagana" or "khana". If he thinks India will win, he phones up and says, "86 lagana India". If he thinks England will win he says, "86 khana India",' Vinay says. 'Lagana' means back [to bet on a team to win] and 'khana' means to lay [to bet against an outcome]. It translates as 'to eat'.

'The lunch favourite is offered as a forward bet, or pre-match bet, so it is not available when the match is in play. It allows the customer to be betting on whichever side is favourite at the lunch break in a Test match or at the innings break in a one-day international.

'It doesn't matter who the team is, England or India. That is your team.

'The forward market we close just before the toss because of the weather and team news. They have big impact on our odds. So earlier today my friend who is at the stadium in Hyderabad called me and said: "It is overcast." So we have to adjust our prices because that favours the England bowlers. Team news is very important. If a player like Kevin Pietersen is not playing, that can have very huge impact on the odds. You see why bookmakers in India love to get their hands on information? They can make money from that.

'But for now the match odds are 86–89 India favourites. If a customer bets, say 15 lakh [£18,000] on India at 86, it means that our liabilities are 0.86 multiplied by 15 lakh.'

It is worth noting the difference between the Indian and the UK markets in terms of the format of the odds offered. The Indian market uses a decimal system, which is favoured because almost all customer accounts are credit accounts. The formula is: stake x decimal odds = payout. In the UK, bookmakers still use the traditional fractional odds and in this regard are rather stuck in their ways. Fractional odds go back centuries, as proved by Shakespeare, who wrote in *Henry IV*, 'If we wrought our life 'twas ten to one.' Fractional odds quote the net total that will be paid out to the bettor should they win, relative to their stake. For example odds of 5–1 imply that the bettor stands to make £100 on a bet of £20. If the odds are 1–5 the bettor will make £4 from a £20 stake.

The match odds, lambi, brackets and lunch favourite are the only four markets that the structured Indian system operates. 'We don't take these fancy bets on which bowler will open the bowling, number of runs off an over, the toss,' Vinay says. 'There are some very small bookmakers who might, but the bets are restricted to 25,000 Indian rupees [£306]. Very small time, very small time.'

This explodes the first myth about the Indian system, which although vast and unregulated in terms of legality, does not tolerate chaos. The notion that one can approach an Indian bookmaker and ask to place a wager on a weird or wonderful event occurring during a match is farcical, according to Vinay. It is systematic and methodical, making a mockery of reports one might have read about the number of markets available. I asked whether any specific bets might be available: such as the outcome of the toss at the beginning of a match, the end from which the fielding captain elects to bowl, a set number of wides, players being placed in unfamiliar fielding positions, individual batsmen scoring fewer runs than their opposite numbers who batted first, batsmen being out at a specific point in their innings or the timing of a declaration.

'None of these,' Vinay says.

'What about the number of no-balls?' I ask.

'Ah, I see why you are asking,' Vinay says. 'The Pakistan spot-fixing trial in London. No. Nobody is making money on that. There is no such market. The match odds, brackets, lambi, lunch favourite – these are the only markets across India. Sometimes there is a market for there to be a completed match because of the weather. But we don't take all these fancy bets that people say.

'I don't know of this Majeed [Mazhar Majeed, the fixer convicted in the spot-fixing trial at Southwark],' he said. 'There are much smarter ways to manipulate betting. Look, I'll show you.'

He logs on to Betfair, the betting exchange. Set up in 2000, it is a person-to-person exchange that allows customers to choose their own odds, just like people on the stock market choose the price at which they want to buy and sell shares. Betfair matches all the bets. On average, Betfair attracts about £15 million for an England one-day international. The money comes from gamblers logging on from their laptops all over the world. Vinay opens up a new window to send via SMS the updated odds to bookmakers across the country after it is announced that India have won the toss and will bat first. He prices India at 85 (5–6 in traditional fractional odds).

Vinay is acting as the syndicate, who normally decide what the betting odds should be, and has been all morning, I notice. 'I thought you were a first-tier bookie?'

'Ya, but sometimes we set the odds. Sometimes we see that we are capable of managing the market. For example, if we are earning from last six months continually, we are getting a huge amount of money. We are the kings. Those bookmakers will follow us. It is all linked. Directly or indirectly, all bookies are linked.

'Now watch how I move the Betfair market,' he says. 'I have sent the odds to all the bookmakers and soon Betfair will have our odds showing. It is currently India 1.95 [20–21]. Watch how they become 1.85 [the Betfair market includes the 1. because it requires a stake] in line with our odds … wait, you'll see here how it works … we want to get India short because it will be difficult to chase at Hyderabad … there, you see, India 1.85 now on Betfair.

'Indian bookmakers move the Betfair market up and down as we get the odds. If there are only three-figure sums available on Betfair, the India market is not present. It is when you see four- or five-figure sums.'

Vinay is referring to the amount of money available to bet on the match odds market on Betfair. Gamblers are given the opportunity to back or lay the two teams (and a draw if it is a Test match) on the exchange and there is a limited sum of money available to do so on each set of odds. For example, one might want to back England at 2.00 (even money) on Betfair, but there is only £500 to do so. Vinay is suggesting that is not Indian money. Only when one sees greater sums, or liquidity as Betfair calls it, are the illegal bookies pumping in their cash.

With the match about to start, Vinay's two mobile phones are competing for attention.

'Bookies,' he says, as he ends one call and prepares to answer another. 'They want to know about any information my man in Hyderabad has.'

Vinay's speech is in rapid-fire mode, rattling off instructions and advice in Hindi, each conversation ending with a soothing 'theek-hai, theek-hai' (OK, OK) before he has to send more odds via SMS. One telephone call is from a gambler in New Zealand, who Vinay says is one of my followers on Twitter. He passes over the phone and we talk about England's prospects in the match and the series. Neither of us is able to give a ringing endorsement against the more experienced home team.

India have made a slow start in the game, however, and Vinay is watching the odds on Betfair carefully. At 17 for no wicket off three overs, their odds are beginning to drift, suggesting gamblers were expecting India to score runs more quickly. On the fifth ball of the fourth over, Parthiv Patel, the India opening batsman, is run out when he is guilty of backing up too far at the non-striker's end as the angular reach of England's fast bowler Steven Finn deflects the ball on to the stumps. India's odds lengthen further to 2.02, although, noticeably, there are only three-figure sums available to bet with. The Indian money is not present.

'We don't want that,' Vinay says. 'We want India shorter than that. Here,' he says, nudging the computer towards me, '… send out the odds so we can get India's price shorter.' He instructs me where to type in the 'message' to send to bookmakers and prices India at 80. I press 'send'. A few seconds later, the 2.02 on India is no more and thousands are available to bet on the home team at … 1.80.

'We move the market,' Vinay reiterates. 'We cannot lose when we are able to change the odds to what we want them to be.'

How can they lose, indeed? Forget arbitrary estimates about the number of bookmakers in India and the volumes of money they generate. This, in a hotel room in Bhopal, is the illegal market in all its powerful and unrelenting glory.

The ability to move a global betting market – and Betfair is exactly that, with customers from Palestine to Panama – is a trick of the gambling gods. At the click of their fingers or of a computer mouse, the Indian bookmaker dictates to the rest of the world. It is not a delicate alchemy, it would appear. It is not done with smoke and mirrors. It is sheer weight of money. A controlled landslide.

At the very least the tentacles, or 'arms' as Vinay describes them, manoeuvre odds in their favour so to allow them to 'hedge their bets'. Profit is guaranteed and can be generated almost at will. By playing the odds much like a trader might the stock market, the bookmaker renders the bets he has struck with his customers largely irrelevant. The broker will aim to buy low and sell high (or vice versa); the bookmaker will do the same. For example, a bookie may have accepted a wager from any Tom, Dick or Hari of £10 on England to win at even money. This has the potential to cost the bookie £10. However, when England's odds during the game drift to 6–4 (greater than even money) either by momentum siding with the opposition or Vinay sitting in a hotel room in Bhopal manipulating the market, the bookie can lay off or, to continue the stock market analogy, 'sell high'. The original bet struck risks him £10. By placing a wager on England at greater odds of 6–4 for £10 he wins £15; £15 minus £10 is guaranteed profit of £5. Now consider the potential when four or five figures are involved.

This talent to move markets is at its most interesting, and potent, in the context of spot-fixing, particularly the 'script' for the India versus Pakistan World Cup semi-final. In this example, bookies could have been able to manipulate the odds they were offering their customers and doing the same on the betting exchanges. While the bookies were betting with their eyes open, the rest were blindfolded.

A professional gambler will often pontificate about how, when it comes to betting on sport, timing is everything. To be a successful gambler, bets need to be placed before a match- or game-altering incident occurs: a break in serve in a Wimbledon semi-final, a sending-off in the local derby, a wicket in a World Cup semi-final. Mere mortals can only guess when such events will occur, events that guarantee a seismic shift in odds. The bookie or fixer knows. It is written down in front of him. The 'script' is, literally, a licence to print money.

When told of 'the script' for the India versus Pakistan World Cup semi-final, Vinay nods sagely and talks about the money that can be made from fluctuating odds. Frustratingly, however, he does not know the men behind the fix.

'Ya. We heard about that game. But I didn't know the details that you did. We just heard a lot of talk that India would win the game so we priced them very, very short in the odds. People bet on them, but because the game was close for periods we were able to use the Betfair to manage our positions. Not a problem for us.

'I hear about matches, though. A bookmaker friend phones me and says: "Don't sit in this game, it's fixed." So I phone 30 bookies and say this. My business partner refuses to sit in games with Pakistan because he doesn't trust them. He worries the fix is on. It is more punters who try to fix things now. They know the players and ask for favours. But this is the life. People say: "Legalise betting in India and fixing will stop." We are ready to pay tax. I'm tired of paying off the police. But it will not stop fixing. Never. Everyone wants to make money.'

This manipulation of odds may have led to the erroneous belief that Indian bookmakers offer a wealth of markets to bet on. If a fixer has approached a player to bowl a no-ball in a one-day inter-national, it is assumed that he is doing so in order to place a bet on that event occurring at that particular time. But according to Vinay this is not possible. Instead, a no-ball in a limited-overs match, particularly a Twenty20 match where a free hit is an extra punishment – a reliable source of extra runs to a team's total – can be considered an event which moves the odds enough to generate profit. Indeed any of the 'phantom markets' about which I asked Vinay earlier – the outcome of the toss at the beginning of a match, players being placed in unfamiliar fielding positions, batsmen being out at a specific point in their innings and the timing of a declaration – would allow a bookmaker, punter or fixer with prior knowledge to manipulate the odds.

'You have it exactly right,' Vinay, triumphantly, says. 'You know, so much money could have been made from that India–Pakistan game by bookies moving their odds just before a wicket fell. What is that saying? Information is power? No. Information is money. All information we can make money out of.'

Vinay's phone rings again. It is his wife reminding him to pick up his son.

'Oh, I am sorry, I must go. My son, he is two, and he is always hiding my phone. He is very naughty. Come to lunch tomorrow at my home and we can talk more of this fixing. I'll send a car.'

From *Bookie Gambler Fixer Spy: A Journey to the Heart of Cricket's Underworld*, 2012

I have been to the maidan in Mumbai many times. Looming over it, the Victoria Terminus (Chhatrapati Shivaji Terminus) – a 'preposterous medley of shapes and designs' as Geoffrey Moorhouse once described it – stands as a monument to the Raj.

On the maidan you see a multitude of games of cricket going on; it feels chaotic – how is it organized, how does it all happen? Only in India, you think to yourself. Somehow, amid this tumult of joyous cricket, a young player emerged who would go on to become one of the greatest batsmen ever to grace the game.

Sachin Tendulkar is a charming man beyond even film-star status in India, yet, in my experience, he still has time for everyone. His tolerance and graciousness was put to the test at Lord's a few years ago when I tried to present him with a magnum of champagne for the *Test Match Special* champagne moment. The then Secretary of the MCC, Roger Knight, asked the BBC not to photograph the presentation in front of the pavilion as the members 'didn't like it'. As I turned to Sachin to apologize, he immediately volunteered to walk the hundred or so yards to the Nursery End for the photograph, carrying all his kit as he had just finished in the nets. The clock was ticking down to the start of play, so we had to walk pretty quickly, then, after the presentation, he had to jog back to the pavilion.

Sachin Tendulkar is the complete batsman whose combination of grace, timing, perfect footwork and a wide array of shots makes him the player of our time. I have no doubt that in many years to come cricket lovers throughout the world will be saying that they were lucky to see him play.

SACHIN TENDULKAR

Vaibhav Purandare

On the first day of the Mohali Test, India were bowled out for 83 runs. It was an awful crashout, and Tendulkar, marking a new beginning as captain in Tests, batted with indecisive apprehension for 18.

Some pride however was restored when the team batted for the second time. India not only wiped out the deficit of 132, but also went on to notch up 505/3 before declaring. Rahul Dravid and Tendulkar got a hundred each, though the captain's was far from an authoritative knock. Creditably, New Zealand batted out 135 overs to force a draw when the advantage clearly lay with the home team. India, however, did not get too much blame, it was rather commended for staging a fightback after the first innings ruin. In the second Test at Kanpur, it won praise after its spinners fashioned an easy victory. In the third Test at Ahmedabad, played from 29 October to 2 November, there was confusion and a controversy that found its way into the CBI probe into match-fixing.

Before the onset of the match-fixing affair, however, Sachin Tendulkar settled one conundrum concerning his Test career. Why couldn't he get a double hundred in Tests? It was a question that had baffled many. The settled-for answer was that he lacked the patience and single-mindedness needed for such a knock. He had not done much to rubbish this charge, and even his first double ton in first-class cricket, against the Australians at Mumbai, had come in 1998, nine years after his Test début. At Ahmedabad, as India batted first, he got his first double ton in Test cricket and erased those doubts. For him, the 217 was mentally a major push, because it was after five years that he had outdone his highest Test score of 179 and reached the elusive figure of 200, that too at a time when he needed a feel-good factor about his batting after recovering from an injury. It was an extraordinary coincidence that he had got the big score on the same ground where two towering lights of Indian cricket, Sunil Gavaskar and Kapil Dev, had got world-record-setting career landmarks. Gavaskar had played a delicate little late-cut here to get his 10,000th run in Test cricket, and Kapil Dev had bettered Sir Richard Hadlee's record for the highest number of Test wickets.

After declaring at 583/7, India dismissed the Kiwis for 308. A large part of the fourth day remained when the New Zealand innings folded, so India was expected to press the follow-on. Surprisingly, the Indians batted again and declared only after they were 148/5. New Zealand then batted ninety-five overs, lost merely two wickets and saved the Test.

Tendulkar's decision not to enforce the follow-on was strongly criticised from all quarters. It was variously called bewildering, boring and dreadfully defensive. The Indians of course felt it had robbed their team of a victory, but even former New Zealand greats said they were upset by the sheer defensiveness of the act. The Indian captain defended his move saying his four specialist bowlers had been utterly exhausted by bowling a full ten hours in the New Zealand first innings and had asked for some rest. The heat was oppressive at over forty degrees Celsius, he said, the bowlers had already bowled 140 overs, and to ask them to bowl another 160 (the total number of overs that could be bowled at that stage) was to run the risk of some of them collapsing.

However, the spearhead of the Indian attack, Javagal Srinath, had gone out to bat in the second innings and had spent half-an-hour in the sweltering sun before the declaration was made.

When the match-fixing scandal hit the cricket world full in its face in 2000, it was inevitable that this refusal to enforce a follow-on should come under the scanner of the authorities. By that time, allegations of match-fixing against Kapil Dev had also created a sensation in India, so the actions of the Indian coach became part of the CBI investigations into Indian cricket's darkest chapter, and both he and Sachin were questioned. While Kapil, along with many other cricketers like main accuser Manoj Prabhakar (who later became one of the main accused), Azharuddin, Ajit Wadekar, Nayan Mongia and Ajay Jadeja were questioned at the CBI headquarters in Delhi, Tendulkar was questioned at his Mumbai residence. That was because the media presence at the CBI office was strong throughout the months of the many depositions. If Sachin were to turn up, things would have become unmanageable.

The CBI cleared both Kapil and Tendulkar of any wrongdoing. So did the then CBI joint director, K. Madhavan, who after CBI's submission of its own report was appointed by the BCCI to investigate matters on its behalf. Madhavan questioned Tendulkar in June 2001 but clarified that he had been 'examined as a witness only'.

Kapil Dev, the coach of the Indian team at the time, said the decision of not enforcing a follow-on in Ahmedabad was taken in consultation with the captain, vice-captain and other senior players. The CBI report recorded his statement as follows:

One day prior to the decision, there was absolutely no doubt in his mind that the follow-on should be enforced. At the end of play on the third day, the team did not meet to work out a strategy for the next day. Somewhere during lunchtime on the fourth day the bowlers, especially Srinath, complained that they were very tired and India should bat again and score quick runs and make New Zealand bat thereafter.

On being told that the bookies in Delhi allegedly knew about the decision not to give a follow-on on the night of 31 October 1999, Kapil stated that no decision to this effect was taken on that day and hence it was very surprising. On being asked whether somebody could have subconsciously influenced this decision on the next day, he stated that it could not be ruled out.

The investigating agency, CBI, heard Sachin out as well:

Sachin Tendulkar, former Indian captain when asked about the India–New Zealand Test at Ahmedabad in 1999, stated that by the end of the third day's play when New Zealand had lost around six wickets, he had thought to himself that he would enforce the follow-on the next day. However, the New Zealand innings dragged on till after lunch the next day and by then he, coach Kapil Dev, Anil Kumble and Ajay Jadeja decided that the follow-on would not be enforced since the bowlers, especially Srinath, had insisted that they were very tired. Therefore, it was a collective decision not to enforce the follow-on. On being asked whether anybody could have influenced this decision since the bookies in Delhi allegedly knew one day in advance that a follow-on will not be enforced, he accepted that it was possible.

As for the one-day series against the Kiwis, India achieved a favourable though not a completely convincing 3–2 result. Meanwhile Sachin, post his injury and the Test double hundred, secured yet another record – 186 not out, the highest score by an Indian in ODIs – in the second fixture at Hyderabad. Here, as in the World Cup game against Kenya, Rahul Dravid stood alongside him, and the two had the highest ever partnership (331) in one-day cricket. Both stepped up the gear nicely after they had crossed their hundreds, and if Dravid played some classically correct drives, Sachin was all innovation. It was as if, between them, they were exploring the full range of batsmanship. The most accurate of yorkers became useless as Tendulkar got his left leg out of trouble and kept thwacking on the leg-side; some balls on the off and middle were hit behind square leg for four, and at one point, four full tosses from Chris Drum were directed to four different parts of the ground.

On the whole, however, New Zealand had not proved as easily beatable on the dry and flat Indian surfaces as they had looked to be. India was scheduled to leave soon for Australia, for three Tests and a triangular one-day series. How would Steve Waugh's Aussies be on their own fast tracks? They were on a roll in any case. After their World Cup triumph, they had crushed New Zealand and Zimbabwe and, just before the Indians arrived, they had completed a 3–0 clean sweep against Pakistan.

From *Sachin Tendulkar: The Definitive Biography, 2008*

SPOT-FIXING

Gideon Haigh

Now What?

In 1936–7, Australia, led by Donald Bradman, staged one of cricket's greatest comebacks, fighting back from a 0–2 deficit to overcome England 3–2. There was joy – and some scepticism. Bradman's father put it to him that the first two Tests *must* have been rigged, to guarantee interest in the last three. 'I told him you can't rig a game of cricket,' Bradman recalled, 'but I can't say I convinced him.'

Pace the Don, his father was right. You *can* rig a game of cricket, lucratively, and you need attempt nothing so ambitious as meddling with the result: reach a score at a pre-determined point, yield a certain number of runs in a spell of bowling, and you can take a cut when others clean up.

Cricket is particularly susceptible to manipulation. Its myriad variables and long duration make for plentiful betting opportunites.

It is most popular in Asia where gambling is either very restricted or illegal, beyond the reach of supervision and regulation. It has grown rich comparatively quickly – in the last generation – so that its attitudes and institutional structures have struggled to adapt.

In India, cricket's candy mountain, the attitude to corruption is cavalier, even light-hearted. Indian cricketers, it is argued, are so extravagantly rewarded that they would do nothing to endanger their careers. Yet being rich beyond the dreams of avarice did nothing to stop Wall Street financiers driving the world's economy into a ditch. Money does not lead naturally to a state of satiety; more often it instils a yen for more.

Attitudes to fitting reward, moreover, have been debauched by the advent of Twenty20 leagues, which make overnight millionaires of ordinary players who happen to hit a long ball even if they have no other faculty. Cricket, then, is becoming a decidedly unequal society, of haves with a sense of entitlement, and have-nots with a sense of grievance. You could not engineer an environment more conducive to corruption if you tried.

In the last decade, cricket has gotten extremely lucky twice. Indian police tapping a gangster's phone overheard his conversations with Hansie Cronje; a British tabloid caught an intermediary selling the services of Salman Butt, Mohammad Amir and Mohammad Asif. Cricket's authorities can derive no satisfaction from these isolated prosecutions, which they themselves did nothing to initiate. The game will languish under the pall of corruption a while yet – and, frankly, it deserves to.

Sydney Morning Herald, March 2011

From *Sphere of Influence: Writings on Cricket and its Discontents, 2011*

In an ideal world people would rather not see politics mixed up with sport, but sometimes the issue is so overriding that only a sporting protest will bring it the attention it so desperately deserves – as was the case at the Harare Sports Club, Zimbabwe, in 2003 during the World Cup. With Robert Mugabe's residence next door to the ground, here were a white man and a black man publicly mourning the death of democracy in their country. Both players had to leave Zimbabwe shortly afterwards.

On a lighter note, I have learned that you should never follow Henry Olonga when you are both speaking at the same function. On the last occasion we were due to speak together, Henry said he would quite like to go first. Thirty minutes later, when he announced to the audience that he would like to finish by singing 'Nessun Dorma', my heart sank. Sure enough, opera-trained Olonga brought the house down – and with a final flourish declared, 'Over to you, Aggers.' I could hear Henry's *sub voce* parenthesis in my head as I looked down at my notes: 'Now follow that . . .'

I have huge respect for Andy Flower who is a shrewd, calculating sort of person who never says a word without thinking about it first. He was a wonderful cricketer who was number one batsman in the world while keeping wicket for Zimbabwe, which tells you all you need to know about him as a player. Now an excellent coach, he is a hard man in the right way: people know where he stands with them and they know where they stand with him. The Kevin Pietersen row was an interesting test of his resolution; we shouldn't be surprised that Andy gave no ground and wasn't prepared to make an exception – even for a truly great player.

ANDY FLOWER AND HENRY OLONGA

Steve James

'Don't Come To Zimbabwe Or Your Players Will Be Living In Fear For The Rest Of Your Lives.'

It was dated 6 January 2003. The letter was post-marked London, sent to the ECB and received by Lamb [Tim Lamb, then chief executive officer of the ECB] on 20 January. He had been concealing it for nearly three weeks. 'What was the point of worrying the players? We didn't want to let it out too early,' explains Lamb, none too convincingly. 'There were one or two sensitive souls with young families, and it didn't seem sensible to share it.'

Now it did, though. Security was the only reason England could give for not going to Zimbabwe. Not that Lamb believed the threat for one minute. 'I never took that threat seriously,' he says. 'Maybe I should have burned it and put it in the bin. Why didn't I just shred that bloody letter, because I knew it was a hoax?'

Into this mess had stepped [David] Morgan, newly appointed as ECB chairman. As a Welshman, Morgan will probably appreciate the analogy that it was like a hospital pass as first touch on début for an international rugby fly-half. But Morgan managed to avoid the oncoming forwards pretty well. That is because naturally he seeks to avoid confrontation. Diplomacy and conciliation are his constant allies. They were good friends to him here. Without Morgan the consequences of this situation don't bear thinking about.

Call me biased, if you like, as Morgan was, of course, chairman of Glamorgan before he went on to become ECB chairman and then ICC president, but I will refer you to my father on this matter. He is an exceptional judge of character and he reckons that the two best people he has ever met in cricket are Morgan and Geraint Jones, whose first season playing cricket in England was at my own Lydney CC. The club had a habit for a number of years of employing professionals from Australia (or rather putting them up wherever they could and finding them some part-time work) and for a while Jones stayed with my parents. Jones was the only player about whom my father, as president of the club, felt moved to write a letter (to Jones's father) to pay a compliment on his behaviour and attitude.

Morgan took control. 'In the early stages all the meetings were chaired by officials of the PCA – by Richard Bevan with his lawyer – but I decided that I would chair all further meetings,' he says. 'I felt sure that if it was safe and secure for the team they should go. I interviewed players one-to-one on the importance of the match taking place. But I was persuaded by Nasser [Hussain] that I should not insist on one or two of the younger players coming in one-on-one, so I spoke to them as a group of three. I remember Ronnie Irani standing out as somebody who really wanted to go and play. He set a great example. He was a substantial figure in all of this.'

England also had some visitors to their Cullinan Hotel. Secret visitors, smuggled in. The first was a member of Zimbabwe's opposition party, the MDC (Movement for Democratic Change). For a long time afterwards his name was not revealed ('he must remain anonymous for his own safety,' said Hussain). But it has since emerged that it was David Coltart, now Zimbabwe's Minister of Education, Sport, Arts and Culture. He spoke to Fletcher and Hussain about the fact that he was working with two of Zimbabwe's players, Andy Flower and Henry Olonga, on making some sort of protest at the death of democracy in their country and wondered whether England might do the same if they were to play in Zimbabwe. He then led Fletcher and Hussain into another room of the hotel, and standing there were Flower and Olonga. Two England coaches, present and future! What irony. Not that the situation was laced with it then. Rather it was fear that pervaded the room, as Flower and Olonga outlined their plans. 'There go two incredibly brave people,' said Fletcher solemnly to Hussain as the pair left the room.

The idea to make such a stand had been first suggested to Flower by a chap called Nigel Hough, although Coltart's influence should never be underestimated. 'He [Flower] rates Coltart as a human being,' says Alistair Campbell, the former Zimbabwe captain. 'He rates him as one of the bravest okes he knows in fact.' 'Oke' is South African slang for bloke, if you're wondering.

Like Coltart's, Hough's was a name that had remained anonymous for a long time, indeed until Olonga revealed it in his autobiography *Blood, Sweat and Treason*, although he spelt his surname 'Huff', which may or may not have been some kind of cover-up. Flower has been careful never to mention Hough's name in public.

I knew Hough from my time playing cricket in Zimbabwe. He

was a decent batsman, who occasionally bowled some leg-spin. I recall him scoring a double-hundred against the touring Durham county side for a Manicaland Select XI in 1992. I also recall him having an eccentric sense of humour. He was always saying something on the field. And for some reason I remember him once saying, 'Come on, boys, let's be alert.' There was a silence as his team-mates looked at him, as if to say 'Come on, you can do better than that'. And then Hough said, 'Yes, Manicaland needs lots of Lerts today.' Bizarre.

Hough is better known for him and his white family being the subjects of Christina Lamb's excellent book *House of Stone*, the true story of their terrible troubles during Mugabe's land redistribution policies and especially of their complicated relationship with their black maid, Aqui.

I'll allow Flower to take up the protest story, as related in a subsequent interview with the *Guardian*:

About a month before the World Cup started in South Africa I met a friend with whom I'd played Zimbabwean cricket. He'd just been thrown off his farm at the dead of night. He had lost this magnificent farm where he'd employed hundreds of people and had set up a school and clinic. He said, 'We'll take a drive and I'll show you what's happened to this once thriving community.' And he took me around and it was very sad to see. He was quite religious and he said, 'I believe you guys have an obligation to bring this to the world's attention.'

On the same day I opened a newspaper – it was the only independent paper at the time and was constantly harried by the Government. On the inside page was an article about an MP who had been arrested and tortured in police custody. It was a tiny article, hardly any space at all. And suddenly I was struck, as if for the first time, by the sheer horror of living in a nation where torture is so widespread it does not even make front page news.

He [Hough] wanted us to boycott the World Cup but I wasn't comfortable with that. We came up with a different plan. It changed my life because it was, I guess, a little scary. But once the principle had been planted in my mind, and I planted it in Henry's mind, there was no other way to go. Without sounding pious we knew it was the right thing to do. We had to do it, regardless of the consequences. I've never been able to go back to Zimbabwe – and neither has Henry. The sacrifice he made was huge.

I'll be honest and say that I was surprised when I heard Flower and Olonga were doing something together. They were not close. Flower, so I reckoned, was not alone among the Zimbabwean team in considering Olonga a little soft. Olonga seemed to succumb rather too easily to niggling injuries. If there was one thing I had learnt during my time in Zimbabwe it was that Flower, like Fletcher, abhorred any sign of softness in a sportsperson.

When Flower first asked to speak to Olonga, the black fast bowler was surprised too. 'I couldn't figure out why this guy who hadn't been prepared to give me the time of day for so long would want to talk to me now,' Olonga wrote.

'I wouldn't say Andy was my best friend, but he was my captain for years and I respected him as a player,' said Olonga later. 'How he knew I had the aptitude to make this protest, I don't know. He needed a black person, and a black person with some influence. I certainly had that: I'd sung a song and people loved it, I was the first black player to play for Zimbabwe, and if I said something it had some weight. Andy is world class, I'm not, but we'd got a combination of sport and music – Posh and Becks, if you like.'

Flower's brother Grant wanted to be part of it too. 'I asked if I could be involved,' Grant admits now, 'but they said they'd rather not. They wanted one white and one black guy and did not want it to be seen as a racist thing. None of the other black guys would have done it. One other white player, Brian Murphy, showed some interest, but no one else really knew about it.'

Indeed they didn't. It was all very secretive. It had to be. And it was not a case of Olonga being persuaded to do something he didn't want to do. He too felt strongly about the mess into which his country had descended. He made up his own mind. 'My motivation was that, two years ago, I had been handed a dossier of human rights abuses that occurred in Zimbabwe, notably the early 1980s Matabeleland massacres,' he said. 'Up to that point, I'd thought Robert Mugabe was a very fair, true, honest president.'

He and Flower thought long and hard about how they could best make a stand before coming up with the idea of a black armband protest at their first World Cup match, against Namibia in Harare on 10 February, accompanied by a statement detailing their feelings. Coltart, a lawyer by trade, helped them draw it up.

An English journalist, Geoff Dean of *The Times*, was involved too. 'Andy took me aside at nets the day before the game,' recalls Dean, 'and asked if I could do him a favour. I said, "Sure. What is it?" He said he couldn't tell me. I just laughed. But he said that if I was willing to do it, I should wait outside the entrance to the Harare Sports Club half an hour before the game was due to start the next day, and there someone whom I would know would meet me. It was all very cloak and dagger!'

The following morning Flower put about fifty pieces of paper into his cricket case. On each was printed the following statement:

Issued 9.30 a.m. February 10, 2003, at the start of Zimbabwe's opening World Cup match against Namibia.

It is a great honour for us to take the field today to play for Zimbabwe in the World Cup. We feel privileged and proud to have been able to represent our country. We are however deeply distressed about what is taking place in Zimbabwe in the midst of the World Cup and do not feel that we can take the field without indicating our feelings in a dignified manner and in keeping with the spirit of cricket.

We cannot in good conscience take to the field and ignore the fact that millions of our compatriots are starving, unemployed and oppressed. We are aware that hundreds of thousands of Zimbabweans may even die in the coming months through a combination of starvation, poverty and Aids. We are aware that many people have been unjustly imprisoned and tortured simply for expressing their opinions about what is happening in the country. We have heard a torrent of racist hate speech directed at minority groups. We are aware that thousands of Zimbabweans are routinely denied their right to freedom of expression. We are aware that people have been murdered, raped, beaten and had their homes destroyed because of their beliefs and that many of those responsible have not been prosecuted. We are also aware that many patriotic Zimbabweans oppose us even playing in the WC because of what is happening.

It is impossible to ignore what is happening in Zimbabwe. Although we are just professional cricketers, we do have a conscience and feelings. We believe that if we remain silent that will be taken as a sign that either we do not care or we condone what is happening in Zimbabwe. We believe that it is important to stand up for what is right.

We have struggled to think of an action that would be appropriate and that would not demean the game we love so much. We have decided that we should act alone without other members of the team being involved because our decision is deeply personal and we did not want to use our senior status to unfairly influence more junior members of the squad. We would like to stress that we greatly respect the ICC and are grateful for all the hard work it has done in bringing the World Cup to Zimbabwe.

In all the circumstances we have decided that we will each wear a black armband for the duration of the World Cup. In doing so we are mourning the death of democracy in our beloved Zimbabwe. In doing so we are making a silent plea to those responsible to stop the abuse of human rights in Zimbabwe. In doing so we pray that our small action may help to restore sanity and dignity to our Nation.

Andrew Flower – Henry Olonga

Once inside the ground, Flower met his father Bill. He was the man Dean would know. Dean had known the Flowers and most of the other Zimbabwean cricketers for some time, having covered their inaugural Test series against India in 1992 and having played some cricket in Zimbabwe on various tours. 'The instruction I was given was to distribute these statements to everyone in the media present that day,' says Dean, who still has a couple of the statements at home as mementos. 'I read it and straight away knew it was going to be dynamite.'

So it was. And that was just within the Zimbabwe Cricket Union. Coach Geoff Marsh, team manager Babu Meman and CEO Vince Hogg were all shocked, pleading with Flower and Olonga not to go through with their protest. But, as the pair emphasized, it was too late. The world already knew.

Flower has obviously gone on to achieve greater fame, but for Olonga it was his defining moment. 'Did I change the world?' he asked later. 'Probably not. Did I change Zimbabwe? Probably not – but I played my part. And if I hadn't embraced the moment, I could have been a nobody, had a mediocre World Cup, and no one would have remembered. Now I'm remembered as the guy who wore a black armband.'

Not that Olonga was particularly prepared. Flower had always planned to retire from international cricket after this event, and leave Zimbabwe to play in England for Essex (and in Australia, although his stint with South Australia lasted only one of its three intended years). Olonga thought maybe he could still live in Zimbabwe. As the days passed after his protest that looked more and more unlikely. There was a vicious campaign against him in the local press and he was followed by state security agents. A few days before Zimbabwe's last qualifying match against Pakistan in Bulawayo, he knew for certain he couldn't stay. His father had received a message from someone high up in the secret police: 'Tell your son to get out of Zimbabwe now!'

Had Zimbabwe lost to Pakistan in Bulawayo they would have been out of the World Cup and Olonga would not have had a ready-made escape route. As it was, it rained, allowing Zimbabwe to progress to the Super Sixes in South Africa. 'I believe in God, and in a way I believe God sent the rain that day,' said Olonga.

That Pakistan match was on 4 March, so there had been nearly a month since the protest, time enough for Flower's father Bill to confirm that it was time to leave. 'We had been planning a with-drawal for a few years,' he says. 'The signs had been there. Then Andrew visited us one day and explained what he was going to do. One thing I was adamant about was that he should not boycott the World Cup, as Nigel Hough would have liked to have seen. But after the protest, we definitely had our phone tapped. Several times we picked up the phone to dial and we could hear them chattering at their listening posts. We always felt someone was listening in. Then when we went down to Bulawayo to watch the matches down there, we stayed with my sister-in-law and she got a phone message from an anonymous African to say something along the lines of "You are part of the Flower family and you'd better watch your back!" Then when we were watching one of the games, some Africans dressed in sharp suits came and sat either side of me and Jean [his wife]. They knew nothing about cricket and were trying to pick up what we were saying. They were from the CIA [Zimbabwe's version of the Central Intelligence Agency]. We drove back to Harare after that last match against Pakistan and packed up Andy's household with Becky [his wife], and then we all left together.'

Andy Flower still owns that house in Harare. Indeed he went back there after the World Cup had finished, much to the consternation of family and friends. 'What could they do?' he asked me later. 'Kill me?' Well, yes, they could have done.

The last I heard his house was being rented by Chris Harris, the former New Zealand all-rounder, who was out in Zimbabwe coaching the national Under 19 side and playing in the domestic Twenty20 competition. Surprise, surprise, Zimbabwe Cricket (as the ZCU became in 2004) was a little slow in paying the rent for Harris.

From *The Plan: How Fletcher and Flower*
Transformed English Cricket, 2012

THE 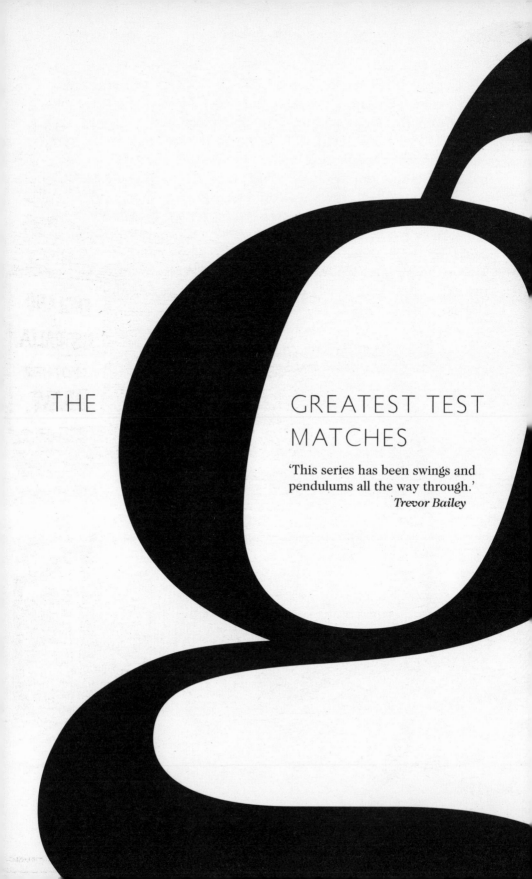 GREATEST TEST
MATCHES

'This series has been swings and
pendulums all the way through.'
Trevor Bailey

Disgusted Miner. 'Why don't they work longer hours?'

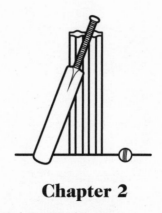

Chapter 2

'If the tension here was a block of Cheddar cheese, you could cut it with a knife.'

Henry Blofeld

Playing any sport at the highest level is all about striving to be the best. Not many of us actually get there and reach the pinnacle, but when professional sport, with all of its inherent unpredictability and so many critical moments decided by sheer chance, pays the bills and puts food on the table, nothing less than aiming for the very top will do. There is just about enough room somewhere in whatever part of the body it is that makes an athlete tick to squeeze in love of the game as an additional motivating factor, but to be a successful sportsperson you need much more than just sentiment to drive you over the line before the others. Full-on commitment, constant dedication and raw talent plus a good deal of luck all have a part to play in determining the course of a professional sporting career and in determining its ultimate success. Then, bright-eyed and bursting with ambition, the younger, fitter and stronger athletes of the next generation muscle their way in and bring the curtain down on the old lags still occupying the crease.

Attempting to compare and analyse the skills of different cricketers through the ages is as fascinating as it is futile. How on earth can you realistically set up W. G. Grace alongside Graham Gooch and decide who was the better batsman? Or compare Fred Spofforth with Michael Holding? Or, indeed, contrast the manner in which a Test match was played by Don Bradman in 1948 with one played by Sachin Tendulkar today? The modern game places a whole set of different demands on the body even if the essential talent and skills required by great players are not so very different.

Oops! There I go – I have used the dreaded 'g' word. 'Great' is impossible to define satisfactorily, and grossly overused by people like me when 'good' or 'very good' does not seem quite sufficient. I will bet that we have seen many more 'great games' and 'great performances' by 'great sportsmen and -women' in recent years simply because excitable commentators and headline-seeking writers have told us so, rather than reserving that most exceptional of accolades for only the truly outstanding.

To coincide with the 2,000th Test match ever played, the inevitable question of which of those 2,000 might be considered the greatest of them all taxed the minds of the great and the good throughout the cricketing world. There was a minor irritation in that, in the view of many, the 2,000th Test – played at Lord's in 2011 – was only really the 1,999th because the ICC's one-off match between Australia and a World XI at Sydney in 2005 had been artificially elevated to Test status. The game was designed to be the culmination of Australia's celebrations of being crowned the number one Test team in the world according to the ICC's ranking system, but still should never have been classified as a Test. A Test match is a game between two full members of the ICC – between two countries, in other words – with all the patriotism, rivalry, passion and pride that only such a contest can produce. It was an exhibition match and nothing more, but in order to beef it up, to make it an easier sell for television and, presumably, to lure the players from both teams into taking part, the ICC stubbornly refused all approaches to abandon the decision to award it Test status. Their refusal to change their minds resulted in the thoroughly unsatisfactory situation that there are now effectively two sets of Test records: those that include that game and those that do not. One day, hopefully, common sense will prevail and the ICC game (played over six days, incidentally, rather than five) will be classed in its rightful place alongside those played between England and the Rest of the World in 1970. Mind you, perhaps it is appropriate that a debate over something as thorny and divisive as selecting the greatest Test of all time should have as a starting point the question of what actually constitutes a Test match.

Almost as many words have been written in the attempt to define the essential criteria for judging the greatest Test of all time as have been used to describe the actual matches. Most commentators are agreed that a close, nail-biting finish is important, although not critical – a resounding victory against all odds can be equally worthy if not quite so dramatic. A great Test requires a superb individual performance or two, especially in adverse conditions or circumstances, and the fluctuating fortunes of both teams that lend Test cricket its unique ebb and flow over five days. It also helps if your own team wins, because, however great a Test might have been, it is forever tinged with disappointment if your lot have come second. The significance of a result might also be a factor. It could be the first victory imposed by one team against the other, such as the win by West Indies over England in 1950, which put West Indies cricket on the map, or a result completely against the odds, such as New Zealand beating West Indies in 1979–80 or Zimbabwe defeating Pakistan in 1994–95. One thing is certain – that a mountain of runs scored does not usually make for a great Test match. It would definitely have been noteworthy had Sri Lanka managed to score the 48 more runs they required to reach 1,000 against India in Colombo in 1997, but time ran out and they declared at the end of the final day on 952 for six in order to spare the commentators and any surviving spectators from further punishment. India had scored 537 for eight in their first innings. Loads of runs, maybe, but the game itself was an absolute stinker.

Of course, the same cannot be said for one-day cricket. Lots of runs and a full house who are beyond tense, gripping the edge of their seats, are both essential components of a great limited-overs one-day international, which surely makes the Fifth ODI between South Africa and Australia at Johannesburg in March 2006 an unassailable leading candidate for the best one-dayer ever. Chasing a record-breaking and seemingly impossible target of 435 to win, South Africa reached their target with just one wicket and one ball to spare. We surely all remember where we were that day – in my case, in a shambolic hotel in Chandigarh, India, from where I watched the match in a rising crescendo of utter disbelief.

That deals with the greatest one-day match at a stroke, but positioning the greatest Tests into a widely accepted top-ten-style list upon which we can all agree will be much less straightforward.

It is likely the first time that media coverage of a Test match in England brought the country to a halt was in 1963, when England and West Indies played out a nail-biting draw at Lord's. Televised cricket at the time was still watched only by a minority, but the dramatic commentary supplied by BBC Radio's *Test Match Special* of Colin Cowdrey walking out to bat with his broken left wrist in plaster gripped the nation. England were nine wickets down, needing six runs to win with two balls of the match remaining. Wes Hall, the great fast bowler who had broken Cowdrey's wrist earlier in the second innings, fired down the last two deliveries, which were survived by David Allen. Thanks to the power of radio and Cowdrey's bravery, a legion of new fans were introduced to the thrill of Test cricket. A lesser-known fact about that Test was that the first three deliveries of the game, bowled by Fred Trueman to Conrad Hunte, were all despatched for four. In later years Fred was surprisingly reluctant to mention it!

Cowdrey's courage was surpassed twenty-one years later in 1984 by England's Paul Terry, who, unlike Cowdrey, actually had to take strike against the West Indies, who possessed the most feared bowling attack in the world. Terry's left arm had earlier been fractured by Winston Davis; by returning to the crease, he enabled Allan Lamb to score the two runs he needed for a century. But unlike Cowdrey's, Terry's bravery had no impact whatsoever on the outcome of the match, and Lord's 1963 will always feature high in the list of tense finishes in Test cricket.

One of the most memorable 'timeless' Tests stood for many years as the finest example of a team winning from a long way behind. It was December 1894 when Australia and England met for the First Test in Sydney and, having chosen to bat first, Australia were quickly reduced to 21 for three, all bowled by the finest fast bowler of the time, Tom Richardson. But led by George Giffen, who scored 161, Australia's middle order rallied with Frank Iredale making 81 and Syd Gregory 201 in only 243 minutes. An entertaining first day ended with 346 runs having been scored for the loss of five wickets and when Gregory raised the Australian total to 586 – not least by adding 154 for the ninth wicket with the captain Jack Blackham – he was treated to a collection from the crowd, which gathered the princely sum of £103, worth approximately £8,000 in today's terms.

Needing 387 to avoid following on, England lost wickets on a regular basis, slipping to 155 for five and 252 for eight before being bowled out for 325. There was a rest day at least, but by the time England were finally dismissed for 437 in the second innings, thanks to Albert Ward's 117, Australia had been in the field from Saturday until Wednesday. Giffen bowled 118 overs of medium-paced cutters in the two innings for his eight wickets, and Australia had virtually all the time in the world to score 177 to win the Test.

At the close of play on the fifth day, Australia had reached 113 for two and were well on their way to victory until it rained overnight on the uncovered pitch. Legend has it that Bobby Peel, the distinguished Yorkshire left-arm spinner, slept through the storm – unlike the anxious Blackham – and was astonished when he saw the pitch, which, by next morning, was drying under the hot sun.

'Gie me t'ball,' he urged the England skipper, Mr Andrew Stoddart, and with Johnny Briggs, Peel proceeded to take the last eight Australian wickets for 53 to give England victory by just ten runs. Until Headingley 1981, this match stood as the only example of a team winning having followed on.

At Melbourne in December 1982, England's winning margin was a mere three runs. It was a classic, fluctuating Test match with all four innings totalling within ten runs of each other and Australia almost pulling off a last-gasp effort to snatch an unlikely victory.

England's first-innings 284 was built around 89 by Chris Tavaré and 83 by Allan Lamb. Three Australians – Kim Hughes, David Hookes and Rodney Marsh – passed 50, but their total only surpassed that of England by three. Graeme Fowler made 65 in England's second innings of 294 – the highest total of the match – which coincided with close of play on the third day. Set 292 to win, Australia looked to be well placed on 171 for three when Hughes, who had seemingly got set but had failed to press on, was caught by Bob Taylor off Geoff Miller for 48. This brought a hopelessly out-of-form Allan Border to the crease. His previous fifteen Test innings had yielded only 245 runs at an average of just over 16, and when Norman Cowans produced his most devastating spell in Test cricket, removing Hookes,

Marsh, Bruce Yardley and Rodney Hogg, to reduce Australia to 218 for nine, an England victory appeared to be a formality.

When the last batsman, Jeff Thomson, joined Border, England's captain, Bob Willis, changed his tactics. Rather than attack Border he set a deep field, which enabled Border to take a single whenever he chose. Willis was effectively targeting Thomson and by so doing lifted the pressure from Border's shoulders. By close of play on the fourth day the last-wicket pair had added 37 precious runs, leaving exactly the same number to be scored on the final day for Australia to regain the Ashes, which they had lost in 1977.

Entry for the spectators was free, and 18,000 turned up in the hope of seeing Australia win the prized urn. To everyone's surprise, Willis continued with his controversial tactic, even when England took the new ball. Border's confidence grew, and 'Thommo' was certainly no mug with the bat. Every run was cheered to the rafters by the partisan Australian crowd and England could have been forgiven for thinking the game was lost. With just four runs required for an Australian victory, Ian Botham – who else? – produced a delivery that was short and wide of the off stump. Ordinarily, it would have been no match-winner, but on this occasion Thomson edged it to second slip. Not a difficult catch by any means, particularly to a slip fielder as consistent as Tavaré, but he succeeded only in parrying the ball behind him. Quick as a flash, Miller, at first slip, took two strides to his right and caught the rebound with the ball some 18 inches from the grass. It was a heartbreaking moment for Thomson, who had batted for more than two hours with Border, whose 62 not out had taken the best part of four hours. During their partnership of 70, the pair declined to take 29 comfortable singles that would easily have won Australia the match. No doubt, Willis would point to that statistic in support of his theory while others will argue that Border's confidence was allowed to return in the absence of pressure. In the following Test at Sydney – the last of the series – Border scored 89 and 83, which helped Australia earn the draw that meant they had regained the Ashes.

At Edgbaston during the summer of 2005, England's margin of victory in the Second Test was even slimmer – just two runs – following a similar partnership between Australia's last pair. On this occasion, however, there was no senior batsman to hold the number eleven's hand; the task of scoring the last 62 runs was left to the fast bowlers Brett Lee and Michael Kasprowicz, who came breathtakingly close to seizing a remarkable victory only to be denied by a dramatic diving catch by the wicketkeeper, Geraint Jones.

This was an extraordinary match in many ways, the best I have seen in the flesh, and has many good reasons to be considered one of the greatest Tests ever played. It came hard on the heels of the First Test at Lord's that the apparently unbeatable Australians had won comfortably within four days. Having won the Ashes in 1989, and held on to them with an iron grip ever since, Australia's performance now appeared to make a mockery of the heightened confidence in the England camp. But after a week of soul-searching, and contrary to most advice freely given by the media, the selectors chose the same team for Edgbaston with the simple instruction to play better.

I recall sitting in a traffic jam outside the ground when first reports filtered out of a bizarre accident involving Glenn McGrath – who had taken nine wickets at Lord's – and a tennis ball during the early pre-game warm-up. McGrath hobbled from the field, and was clearly out of the match with damaged ankle ligaments, but the loss of his main strike bowler did not deter Australia's captain Ricky Ponting from putting England in to bat. It was a cloudy morning and the pitch had been under water beforehand, but the row that could be heard emanating from the Australian dressing room on Ponting's return after the toss suggested his decision was not universally popular.

We will never know whether it was McGrath's absence, a rousing team talk or just the determination to make amends for Lord's, but England's batsmen came out like men possessed. The openers, Marcus Trescothick and Andrew Strauss, set about the Australian attack, putting together a stand of 112 in only twenty-five overs that set up the continuing assault by Kevin Pietersen, whose 71 came from seventy-six deliveries, and Andrew Flintoff, who struck five sixes in his sixty-two-ball 68. The Australians conceded more than five runs per over – more than they had conceded on the first day of a Test since 1938 – as England posted a remarkable 407 all out in fewer than eighty overs.

They were batting again before the close of the second day having bowled Australia out for 308, with Flintoff and Ashley Giles taking three wickets each. Matthew Hoggard had struck a hammer blow when Matthew Hayden drove his first ball to Strauss at cover, and although Australia's top order all got in, wickets fell regularly to give England their lead of 99. Strauss was bowled by a massive leg break by

Warne, who, on the third day, bowled unchanged from the City End. England were struggling at 31 for four – which included the night-watchman, Hoggard – and for the second time in the game Flintoff strode out to snatch the initiative. This time he hit four more sixes in his 73, which came from eighty-six balls, and he was the last man out after an entertaining and, as it turned out, crucial last-wicket stand of 51 with Simon Jones. This left Australia forty-four overs to bat in the day, and by the close they seemed destined for defeat on 175 for eight, still needing a further 105, with Steve Harmison landing a killer blow by bowling Michael Clarke with a brilliantly disguised slower ball to end the proceedings.

With England needing only two wickets to win, some spectators might have been forgiven for choosing not to bother with the trip to Edgbaston for the fourth day. But cricket-lovers all, they came in their thousands, and what a morning they had. Warne batted with typical belligerence to score 42, but trod on his stumps as Flintoff drove him onto the back foot, and when Kasprowicz joined Lee, the crowd was ready to celebrate.

But England's pacemen bowled too short. They inflicted a bruise or two, but were wayward as well, and slowly but surely the brave tailenders inched towards their target. The crowd at first fell silent, then roared its disapproval when, with only 15 to go, Kasprowicz sent the ball flying to Simon Jones at third man. It was not an easy chance and, diving forwards, the fast bowler put the catch down. There now seemed to be an inevitability about the outcome, and everyone in the ground felt it to the extent that, in the *Test Match Special* radio box, we observed tradition by ushering the Australian commentator Jim Maxwell to the microphone to deliver the *coup de grâce*.

With Australia needing just three to win, Harmison let another short ball go down the leg side but this time Kasprowicz offered a tentatively prodding bat. As he began, involuntarily, to take his hand from the bat handle, the ball flicked the glove and was caught by the tumbling Geraint Jones. The primeval roar from the crowd in the Hollies Stand remains the most rousing and forceful I have ever heard at a cricket match.

Flintoff, the man of the match, crouched beside Lee, who had slumped in devastated fashion to his knees at the non-striker's end, and wrapped a consoling arm around the Australian's shoulders. It remains an iconic image of Ashes cricket played in its true spirit, and the match itself did wonders for Test cricket as a whole. Had

Australia won, they would almost certainly have retained the Ashes for an eighth consecutive time. Instead, we were treated to one of the most memorable summers of cricket there has ever been.

An erroneous umpiring decision appeared to deny Australia another fiercely fought contest, this time against West Indies in Adelaide in 1992–3, with the margin on this occasion being a solitary run. It was a low-scoring Test – unusually so for Adelaide – and Australia needed to score 186 to win in the final innings and, with it, lift the Frank Worrell Trophy. When they were reduced to 102 for eight, it seemed most likely that the West Indian attack of Courtney Walsh, Curtly Ambrose, Ian Bishop and Kenny Benjamin would simply mop up the residue and complete a comfortable victory. But Justin Langer, batting at number three in his first Test, teamed up with Tim May to add 42 for the ninth wicket. Australia inched towards their target, television viewing figures soared and thousands of spectators swarmed out of the city, over the River Torrens and into the Adelaide Oval to savour the drama.

With 42 more needed, Langer edged Bishop to the wicketkeeper, David Murray, bringing in the fast bowler Craig McDermott to join May. Confronted by a barrage of hostile fast bowling, the last pair fended the ball away and picked up runs wherever they could along the way. With Australia needing just two runs to win, the crowd grew increasingly belligerent, singing 'Waltzing Matilda', as Walsh steamed in and with a last-gasp effort hurled down another lifting delivery to McDermott.

The ball definitely hit something – there was a noise as it flew past McDermott at shoulder height – but umpire Hair's view was obscured because McDermott was attempting to take his bat and gloves out of harm's way. Replays show the ball clearly hitting high on the grille of the batsman's helmet with his gloves only at chest height and the bat also some distance from the ball. But Hair upheld the frantic appeal – accompanied by premature celebrations of the West Indian fielders – and the crowd fell completely silent. To be fair to the Australia camp, no criticism was made of Hair's decision and its impact on the outcome of the game, but the replay is available on YouTube for all to see.

This was definitely a classic Test, and not just because of the narrowness of the margin. There was the drama of 22-year-old Langer displaying on his début the bravery and resolve with which he became synonymous (he was forced to replace his helmet after it was split by a bouncer from Bishop) and of David Boon returning to the crease having been forced to retire hurt with an injured elbow. There was drama of a different sort with the last six West Indian second-innings wickets collapsing for just 22 in nine overs of spin bowling, May eclipsing Warne with figures of five for 9. Finally, there was the controversy of a crucial umpiring error that cruelly snatched victory from the Australians at the last moment. It was, indeed, a fiercely competitive and dramatic Test, a match that definitely deserves to be considered among the very best.

Clearly for the ultimate in tight and, surely, chaotic finishes you cannot beat a tie – that is to say when the last team to bat loses its last wicket with the scores level. It is a rare phenomenon with only two instances in the history of Test cricket, and Australia have the distinction of being involved in both of them. The brilliant black-and-white photograph of the defining moment at Brisbane on 14 December 1960 must be etched on the memory of every cricket enthusiast. There is Joe Solomon, in mid-stride with his left knee impossibly high, appealing for the run-out having hit the wicket direct. The batsman, Ian Meckiff, is striving to reach his ground at the far end with his left arm and bat at full stretch while his partner, Lindsay Kline, glances anxiously behind him. There is sawdust everywhere, and deep foot holes made by the great fast bowler, Wes Hall, who had been hurling the ball down in the course of a spell that had transformed the game. The successful run-out of Meckiff, which secured the tie, was the third wicket to fall in the final over of the game and the third run-out in the space of four runs. What a frantic climax it must have been!

Two high-scoring first innings saw West Indies make 453, having been 65 for three, with Garfield Sobers hitting 132 in less than three hours. Australia replied with 505 thanks to Norm O'Neill's 181 to establish a lead of 52. West Indies mustered 284 in their second innings to set Australia 231 to win and take the First Test. At 92 for six, with the rampant Hall taking four wickets, they seemed dead and buried, but a stand between Alan Davidson and Richie Benaud appeared to make the game safe. This was certainly the view of the leading ABC radio commentator of the time, Alan McGilvray, who opted for an early flight to Sydney. Picked up at the airport by his wife, he asked if, indeed, the game had been drawn. 'Yes,' she replied. 'But I think they actually called it a tie!' McGilvray had to re-record the commentary of the final over in a studio at a later date.

Playing increasingly expansively, Davidson and Benaud added 134 to take the score to 226 for six – within seven runs of victory – when, with time ticking away, Davidson was run out by Solomon, who hit the stumps from mid-wicket. Wally Grout took a single from the last ball, leaving Australia to score six from Hall's final over with three wickets in hand. Remember, they were eight-ball overs in Australia in those days, so it should have been a cakewalk.

Australia scrambled a single from the first ball, but Benaud had a swipe and was caught behind off the second for 52. The third was a dot ball and they ran a scampered bye to the wicketkeeper off the fourth. Four to win from four deliveries. Wally Grout hit the fifth ball high into the air, but Hall himself dropped the catch and the batsmen took a single. Three to win. Meckiff flicked the sixth ball into the leg side and there appeared to be three or possibly even four runs on offer – certainly sufficient to win the game. But Conrad Hunte fielded superbly to prevent the ball hitting the rope and ran Grout out by a foot as he tried to complete the third run. So, with one to win from two balls and the last pair together, Hall charged up to bowl at the number eleven, Kline, who prodded the ball to mid-wicket. Meckiff set off for the run, but was scuppered by Solomon, who, for the second time, hit the wicket with a direct throw.

Would we see a Test played quite like that these days? Australia certainly threw caution to the wind, especially when you consider this was the first Test of the series. It is a match, and a last over in particular, to remember when often lazy comparisons are made of the standard of modern-day fielding with that of earlier generations. The West Indies were red-hot under pressure on that day in December 1960.

Twenty-six years later in Madras (later renamed Chennai) 30,000 spectators watched a nerve-jangling finish to a Test that both India and Australia should have won but which instead finished in a tie. Rare as a tie is, it is a fact that had India scored just one more run, the match would have been one of those almost-as-rare Tests ending in defeat for the first team to bat and declare its first innings closed. For the Indian supporters, much of the interest would have been centred on the remarkable landmark reached by Sunil Gavaskar, who became the first cricketer to appear in 100 consecutive Tests. But he scored only eight in India's first innings, having fielded for more than 170 overs while Australia painstakingly racked up 574 for seven. Boon scored 122 and Border 106, but the highlight was Dean Jones's 210. He batted for nearly eight and a half hours in searing heat and sapping humidity, which induced bouts of sickness and crippling leg cramps, to achieve his maiden Test century and the highest score by an Australian in India.

Finally, India's first innings got under way on the third morning and by the close they faced the real prospect of following on at 270 for seven. At 330 for eight, with 45 still needed to avoid that ignominy, it was left to the captain Kapil Dev to take charge. Having added 85 with Chetan Sharma, Kapil opened his shoulders to score 119 from 138 balls. While he saved the immediate crisis, the fact was that when he was the last man out, Australia's lead stood at a commanding 177. The visitors batted for just forty-nine overs in their second innings before Border declared for the second time in the game to set India 348 to win in a minimum of eighty-seven overs. Gavaskar and Kris Srikkanth put on 55 for the first wicket, and although Gavaskar and Mohinder Amarnath batted patiently, they added 103, opening up the real possibility of an unlikely Indian victory. At tea, India needed 158 more runs in thirty overs with Gavaskar well set, and at the start of the final twenty overs, India had to score 118 to win with seven wickets in hand. As had been the case at Brisbane in 1960, the batting team were seemingly in command.

It takes only one wicket to change the situation, however, and – having batted for more than four hours for 90 – Gavaskar mistimed a cover drive off the slow left-arm spinner, Ray Bright, and gave a catch to Jones. Mohammad Azharuddin made a quick 42 out of a stand of 47 with Chandra Pandit, who was sixth out with 57 still required.

With Ravi Shastri sensibly mixing defence with attack, India's target came down to just 18 runs required from 30 balls, but Bright struck twice in an over when Sharma was caught on the boundary and Kiran More was lbw for a duck. Suddenly Australia were two wickets from victory. Shivlal Yadav hit Greg Matthews for six, but was bowled by Bright to leave India needing four runs and Australia one wicket from the remaining eight balls. Maninder Singh carefully blocked the last two balls from Bright, so leaving Shastri to face Matthews, who started the final over of the Test.

Shastri defended the first ball and picked up two runs from a mishit into the leg side from the second. Shastri pushed the third ball into a gap at mid-wicket, and the batsmen completed the single that levelled the scores and eliminated Australia's hopes of winning, so with three balls remaining the possible outcomes were either an India victory, a draw or a tie. Maninder awkwardly survived the fourth ball, but was lbw to the next to give Matthews his tenth wicket of the game, and cricket only its second tie in Test history.

I was lucky enough to witness one of the most dramatic final days of Test cricket there can ever have been when, in April 1992, the West Indies turned the tables on South Africa to win the first Test played between the two countries. Politics was never far from the surface during this time of South Africa's return to international sport, and it also happened as the first distant ringing of alarm bells could be heard about the future of West Indies cricket. Viv Richards had, by now, retired, and this was Richie Richardson's first Test as captain.

In fact, this match was the subject of a boycott by the majority of the Barbados cricket-loving public over the non-selection of Barbadian pace bowler Anderson Cummins. 'No Cummins, no goins' was the slogan that rang out around the Kensington Oval, but while Cummins was a reasonable performer, the real cause of local unhappiness was that there was not a single Barbadian in the team – something, until now, unheard of in West Indies cricket.

Batting was never going to be easy on an uneven pitch, and South Africa were indebted to a painstaking first-innings century from Andrew Hudson, who batted for more than eight and a half hours for 163 – nearly half of South Africa's 345. His defiance gave South Africa a lead of 83 and although Brian Lara scored 64 and Jimmy Adams 79 West Indies could only set South Africa 201 to win. Hudson was taken at slip by Lara from Ambrose's second ball, but although Mark Rushmere was bowled for three, at the close of the fourth day South Africa were well placed on 122 for two, needing 80 to win and with Kepler Wessels and Peter Kirsten on 74 and 36 respectively.

Then someone in the South Africa camp made the disastrous decision overnight to issue a press release. Not only did this statement presume South Africa would win the game the following day, but it also commented on the state of West Indian cricket, suggesting that the South Africans were confident that things were not as bad as they seemed and all would be well in the end. Even by the clumsy standards of the South African public relations machine at the time, this was astonishing.

Whether it was this statement that fired up West Indies or, quite possibly, an early example of South Africa choking under pressure, we will never know, but Walsh roared in like a man possessed to grab four for 8 as South Africa's last eight wickets fell for 26. Sadly there were fewer than 500 spectators in the ground to witness this remarkable victory and to see Richie Richardson lead his new team around Kensington in a lap of honour. It was a stirring sight, but my own personal memory of an incredible morning was of then having to snatch an interview with the elated Richardson in the gents' toilet.

If this match was a marvellously entertaining example of a dramatic turnaround in the fortunes of a Test match, it is nevertheless put in the shade by the following two Tests, both great matches that will always vie for the top spot in this particular debate. If you are an England supporter, I imagine you would vote for the match that has simply become known as 'Headingley '81'; if you follow India, you will probably champion the remarkable Test in Kolkata in March 2001. I am not sure which of the two an Australian would vote for, since they were the losers on both occasions, but one man – Peter Willey – can lay claim to the unique position of having been on the field of play for both Tests – as a player at Headingley (the first of his nineteen Tests in which he was on the winning side) and as standing umpire at Kolkata. He has subsequently told me which match he considers the best of all time, and I will deliver his verdict later in the chapter.

Let us start at Headingley and the Third Test of the 1981 series against Australia – for reasons of chronology if nothing else. Under Botham's captaincy, England had recently returned from a poor series in West Indies, which they had lost 2–0. As the teams convened at Leeds, England were already 1–0 down in the Ashes having lost the First Test at Trent Bridge, this despite securing a slim first-innings lead. Botham had top-scored in England's second innings with 33 out of 125 all out, but he bagged a pair in the Second Test at Lord's, where the MCC members gave him an unforgettably cool reception as he returned to the pavilion. Such was its impact that Botham refused to acknowledge the MCC members for the rest of his career, and he officially resigned as captain shortly afterwards, although the chairman of selectors at the time, Sir Alec Bedser, announced that Botham would have been sacked anyway.

The captaincy was returned to Mike Brearley, who had previously given way to Botham, losing his England place in the process. The England cricket public were desperate for a quick improvement in the team's performance, but surely not even the most patriotic and committed England supporter would have been dreaming of what was to follow: England ultimately winning three of the remaining four Tests to take the Ashes 3–1, a performance inspired and illuminated by the majesty and sheer brilliance of Botham's on-field heroics, which at times bordered on the fictional. Much of the credit for Botham's apotheosis – and the mesmeric performance by Bob Willis at Headingley – is credited to Brearley, who subsequently became a psychoanalyst and whose man-management skills are widely held to have been responsible for the rejuvenation of Botham's flagging career.

However, for much of the Headingley Test, it appeared that not a great deal had changed. Australia won the toss and batted for most of the first two days, scoring 401 for nine. Botham found himself amongst the wickets, taking six for 95, but England were under the cosh, particularly when Gooch was out in the first over of the third morning, and Boycott and Brearley were both dismissed before lunch. Botham reached his first half-century since becoming captain thirteen Tests earlier, but England were rolled over after tea for just 174. With a lead of 227, and England's woeful batting looking bereft of confidence, it was no surprise that the Australian captain, Kim Hughes, should enforce the follow-on. Gooch was dismissed by Dennis Lillee in the first over to leave England still 221 behind at the close with nine wickets left.

Leeds is close to Botham country and, Sunday being a rest day in those days, the former captain threw one of the mid-Test and generous parties for which he is well known and indeed much admired. The feeling at the party was that England were destined to lose heavily on Monday, so the players took the opportunity to enjoy themselves well away from the savaging they were on the receiving end of from the Sunday newspapers. This generally disparaging view of England was held by many, including the bookmaker Ladbrokes, who were now offering odds of 500–1 on an England win.

One interested punter was the driver of the Australian team bus, who alerted Rod Marsh and Dennis Lillee to these remarkable odds when the players returned to Headingley on Monday morning. Simply because these odds in a two-horse race were so blatantly ridiculous, the Australians handed over £15 with which the driver disappeared into the bookmaker's tent. The England team, meanwhile, arrived at the ground having checked out of the team hotel a day early in the depressed certainty they would lose on the fourth day. By midafternoon, when they were 135 for seven, still 92 runs adrift and facing an innings defeat, their pessimism seemed well judged.

Oh, to have been a spectator at Headingley that day; to have experienced at first hand the astonishing events that would unfold over the next eighty minutes when Botham and England's number nine, Graham Dilley (who had been instructed by Botham simply to 'enjoy himself'), launched their ferocious counterattack. They added 117, which was only seven short of the record for the eighth wicket, and the Australian fielders were scattered all over Headingley. Botham's massive hitting was the main feature, but Dilley also hit the ball cleanly to score 56 from 75 balls before being bowled by Alderman. Chris Old continued where Dilley had left off, striking six fours in his 29 while Botham continued his rampage at the other end, and at the close of play England were 124 runs ahead with Botham on 145 not out and one wicket left to fall.

Willis did not last long on the final morning, leaving Botham undefeated on 149 from 148 balls, including 27 fours and a six, which set Australia 130 to win. At 56 for one, and England's attack not looking threatening, Brearley decided to switch Willis to the Kirkstall Lane End, which was downhill and with the wind at his back. It was curious that Willis had not started the innings from that end anyway, with reports suggesting that Brearley had denied him the new ball and the favourable conditions quite deliberately in order to anger his big fast bowler.

Almost immediately, Willis removed Trevor Chappell with a delivery that climbed nastily from a good length, and the now-famous rout was under way. Willis appeared to be in a trance, showing little emotion but absolute concentration as he pounded in relentlessly. There were some excellent catches in the field, notably Dilley's splendid effort at fine leg to dismiss Marsh and Gatting's tumbling catch running in from mid-on, which ended a dangerous stand of 35 in four overs between Lillee and Ray Bright. One run later, Willis shattered Bright's stumps to finish with eight for 43 as Australia's last nine wickets tumbled for 55 and surely the greatest Test of the time, at least, was completed with England's triumphant players pursued from the field by hundreds of disbelieving and very happy spectators.

Headingley '81 was only the second Test in history to be won by a team that had followed on. Twenty years later, Peter Willey, who had scored 33 in England's second innings, officiated in a Test that he considers to be the even better match. The Second Test between India and Australia, played at Kolkata's Eden Gardens in March 2001, was the third such Test. At first glance, there is nothing exceptional about the winning margin of India's victory – 171 runs compared with only 18 runs at Headingley – but, as is usually the case with Test cricket, the result is only a small part of the story.

This was a tour by the great Australian team led by Steve Waugh, who had vowed to defeat India on their home soil for the first time in more than thirty years. It was the second Test in a three-match series, Australia having already won the first, to extend their record run of consecutive victories to sixteen. When Waugh himself scored 110 out of Australia's first-innings total of 445, the captain could already feel one hand tightening its grip on the Border–Gavaskar Trophy. He had to work for his runs because Australia lost seven wickets for 76 – including a hat-trick by Harbhajan Singh, who took seven for 123 – and he relied upon determined assistance from Jason Gillespie (46) – with whom Waugh added 133 – and Glenn McGrath (21 not out).

When India had been bundled out on the third morning for just 171 in fifty-eight overs, with McGrath taking four for 18, Waugh had no hesitation in enforcing the follow-on. The prized wicket of Sachin Tendulkar was claimed by Gillespie with India wobbling on 115 for three – still 159 runs short of making Australia bat again – but with V. V. S. Laxman batting determinedly at the other end, having been promoted from number six to three following his positive first-innings score of 59 and concerns about Dravid's form. It was to prove an inspired decision by the captain Sourav Ganguly, with whom Laxman now added 117 for the fourth wicket.

India were still in negative territory when Rahul Dravid, batting at number six, joined Laxman. They batted together for 104 overs, including the whole of the fourth day, on which they added 335. Their record partnership extended to 376 and when Laxman was eventually dismissed for India's highest Test score of 281 he had batted for ten and a half hours and struck forty-four boundaries. Dravid fell for 180 and Ganguly was able to declare on 657 for seven, which left Australia an impossible 384 to win or seventy-five overs to survive in order to protect their 1–0 lead.

Matthew Hayden and Michael Slater survived until the twenty-fourth over, when Harbhajan took the first of his six wickets, and when he removed Langer for 28, Australia were 106 for two in the twenty-eighth over. Hayden was lbw to Tendulkar for 67, but only Steve Waugh offered any resistance thereafter as the spinners, supported by attacking and vociferous fields, steadily worked their way through the Australian batting order. After Adam Gilchrist had departed for a king pair, McGrath and Kasprowicz did all they could, holding on for ten overs, before McGrath was trapped lbw by Harbhajan to secure India's remarkable victory.

To be considered a truly great Test match, the game clearly requires that classic ebb and flow that makes Test cricket unique. The match needs to be unpredictable, a game of twists and turns driven by key individual performances (an audacious innings, an inspired spell of bowling, a blinding catch or a run-out that breaks an otherwise impregnable partnership) building into a narrative capable of passing into cricketing folklore – the 'I remember where I was when ...' factor. From a personal perspective, I am also certain it helps to have been there, or at least to have watched the match on television or listened to it on the radio. That way, you have lived the game, and experienced its tension for yourself.

I am incredibly lucky to be able to enjoy the thrill of Test cricket as part of my working life. To describe the drama and excitement to those who cannot be at the ground is a great pleasure as well as a privilege, and I am constantly reminded of lying in bed as a child and listening to the commentary crackling into my earpiece throughout the night from some distant part of the world. Every day of every game is different, and I turn up for work in the morning not knowing what might happen over the next seven hours or so.

Choosing just one from the more than 250 Tests matches I have seen is difficult, but the Edgbaston Test of 2005 stands out as my favourite. I will never forget the wall of sound that exploded from the Hollies Stand and rolled across the ground at the fall of the final wicket and it still makes the hair stand up on the back of my neck whenever I hear a recording of Jim Maxwell's brilliant commentary. Like everyone else, we in the *Test Match Special* box had given up and assumed that Australia would win, which is why Jim had been ushered to the microphone in *TMS*'s time-honoured tradition of having the winning team's compatriot report the final overs.

Classic Tests are pure theatre, and Edgbaston 2005 had everything – including the happy ending that set up the most memorable Ashes series ever.

Richie Benaud is one of my broadcasting heroes. I first heard him as a commentator – along with Peter West and Jim Laker – on my black-and-white television set as a young boy. He has always been so precise and measured in his approach that people think he is hugely careful on air, but that's far from being the case as he can be quite outspoken, passionate even, about the game he loves. The greatness of Richie's broadcasting lies in his ability to choose the perfect words, or sometimes a single word, to describe what he sees and, equally importantly, to know exactly when to deliver them; his timing is impeccable.

Over the years I have found him brilliant to work with. From the first time we met he demonstrated considerable patience and kindness towards a young upstart. In fact he rescued me during the 1999 World Cup.

By 1999, the BBC had lost the television rights for home series Test matches (to Sky and Channel 4), but had the broadcast rights for the World Cup, which was being staged primarily in England. The BBC's stable of cricket commentators and pundits had moved on, except for Richie. In desperation, the BBC asked me to present the series and, after one day's training with Peter Purves, off I went.

From the start I couldn't handle the countdown in my earpiece. My timing on radio is fine as everything is done by stopwatch, but to hear that horrible robotic voice relentlessly counting down each second from the sixty-second mark was utterly disorientating. The first few times on air I messed it up. Richie came to my rescue and we agreed that as soon as the countdown started I would ask him a question. He would talk for exactly fifty-three seconds to the seven-second mark, and then I would sign off. Richie was a great shoulder to lean on and it got me through my television baptism (with mixed success and reviews, it has to be said).

TIED TEST

Richie Benaud

One Brisbane morning is much like any other and there was nothing unusual about this morning, nothing that shouted, "This is different—this is the day to remember." Breakfast at the excellent Lennon's Hotel in the heart of the city tasted the same; the *Courier Mail* discussed the chances of both sides and slanted a little to my own assessment, that as the game stood at the moment Australia had the edge.

I picked up a couple of the team at the lift and as usual there was a big crowd in the foyer of the hotel. An even bigger one waited on the footpath outside, hoping to catch a glimpse of the West Indians who had set the Gabba alight in this Test, and the Australians who were to do battle with them in the coming hours. There was a general air of excitement among the watchers as the players got into the cabs for the drive to the ground. For the players themselves the excitement was there also; in addition there was that tight feeling in the pit of the stomach that seems to be present whenever a Test match is played, and makes one apt to be a trifle short with the spectator who wants to talk.

I made a bad start at the ground. When I walked through the gate and along the side of the pavilion to the dressing rooms I could see white flowers dotting the turf; clover flowers. It was obvious that the ground hadn't been mown this morning.

I ask for a mowing but the curator tells me there was a heavy shower just after seven o'clock and he hasn't been able to get the mower on the ground ... now he hasn't time to do it. Short of getting the mower and doing it myself it seems that the grass will not be mown today. I don't s'pose it matters a great deal really, we'll only have a bit over 200 to make.

So I thought at the time—but how wrong can one be?

It was a dismal morning for Australia. With only one run on the board, Simpson was caught at short-leg off Hall. The fast bowler landed the ball short and for some reason Bobby went to duck instead of swaying away from it as he had been doing. When he changed his mind, and tried to play a stroke, it was far too late. All he could do was push the ball weakly to short-leg. Harvey made five before he was out to an absolutely brilliant catch by Sobers at slip, and we were 2 for 7 … bad but not irretrievable, for the next man in was O'Neill.

Just two years before I had seen this brilliant player massacre the MCC attack on the last day of the first Test to give victory to Australia. Now Norm was in fine touch again, for his near double-century in the first innings had given him confidence, so I settled down to watch him take this West Indies attack apart.

"Have a look and then thrash them!" was the only advice I offered as he went out. But he just couldn't do it this time, and neither could Col McDonald, who battled till lunch-time for a handful of runs.

Hall called the tune for almost the whole of this pre-lunch session, and the West Indies were completely on top. We had taken over an hour for less than thirty runs and from lunch we had to score at the rate of nearly 50 runs per 100 balls to win the game. But we had eight wickets left, and I thought we still had the chance of victory in the remaining two sessions.

Lunch nowadays at the Brisbane Cricket Ground is a pleasant affair. Unless of course you happen to be one of the not out batsmen who "just don't feel like food", or the captain of the side who spends most of the time preoccupied, calculating runs per minute and runs per over.

The batsmen come off the field weary from concentrating and sweaty from the steamy tropical heat that had brought the early morning showers.

"What about it, Benordy?" O'Neill wanted to know. "What do you reckon about the scoring?"

"We're going much too slow," was McDonald's comment. "Sorry, but they're bowling pretty well out there."

"I know they're bowling well," I said, "but we'll have to step it up a bit if we want to get there …" and mentally realised that it was very easy to say that but not quite so easy to carry it out against Hall with his pace and length of run.

"Just see what you can do and watch the short ones … we want to win this one," was all I said as Norm and Colin went out to resume after lunch.

Cricket spectator (during dull game). 'An' they call this cricket!
Blimey, they're only *playing* at cricket!'

Immediately they went berserk against the big Barbadian, and took 28 from four of his overs. The main run-getting came from O'Neill, who took three fours and a three from him.

But O'Neill and McDonald were suddenly dismissed within a few balls of each other, the former in trying to cut Hall and the latter bowled by Worrell. Favell made only seven before being caught off Hall (a little unluckily, for he tried to hook and the ball flew from glove to short-leg).

We were 5 for 57 and most of the afternoon left to play. The situation didn't look too good.

Mackay and Davidson added 35 of which "Slasher" made 28 in pretty good style, too, before he tried to drive Ramadhin's leg-break and was bowled. I passed him on the way out, and he managed a wry grin as he said: "Sorry—she turned a bit." Now the only names left on the scoreboard were Davidson and Benaud—the two batsmen in—Grout, Meckiff and Kline. Five names between defeat and victory for Australia and mine was one of them.

It's a lonely feeling to walk on to a Test arena to do battle with eleven players from another country. Lonely as you walk to the centre with the thousands of eyes focused on you from the stands— the twenty-two eyes of the opposition fixed on you as you near the stumps. Lonely … exciting … and challenging for both the batsman himself and the opposition. I hadn't made many runs lately but if ever they were to come along, today would be the best time I could possibly imagine.

> *Ram's bowling and Val's on the other end, I thought. They're very good ... but not as good as they used to be, although the little fellow has probably got his tail up from bowling "Slash" ... forget it and concentrate ... concentrate ... concentrate. Don't do anything silly ... but keep your head down and concentrate. You can bat better than any of these jokers can bowl ... but concentrate!*

You feel better once you're right out in the centre and not many of the thousands watching anxiously would guess that you're nervous all the same. Perhaps a little quiver of the bat as you ask for leg stump and the urge to shuffle the feet a little before facing up to the first ball, but apart from that you're O.K. Just that empty feeling in the pit of the stomach as Ram gives that little skip before his flurry of shirt sends the ball on its way.

The first one hit the middle of the bat but the second produced a cry of anguish as it skirted to top of middle and off and flashed past Alexander for wonderful runs—byes. Davo at the other end was steady as a rock but took his chance to capture five runs from Valentine's next over. I'd got the strike again and was still on nought ... never had a half-volley looked so good and I smashed it away to the cover fence as the clock showed tea-time.

There were 92 runs on the board ... and 6 wickets down ...

I sat with Davidson at tea in the players' section and we were joined by Sir Donald Bradman who was obviously enjoying himself. He said what a wonderful game it had been over the four days and that today was building up to a great last session.

Then he added: "What are you going for, Richie—a win or a draw?"

"We're going for a win, of course," I replied.

His answer was a direct "I'm very pleased to hear it."

Later I realised what a good thing it was that the Chairman of Selectors had spoken as he did at the team meeting I mentioned earlier, that he was obviously completely against any ideas of playing for a soulless draw ... but there was little chance to think of that at the time.

With Davidson, I had to concentrate on trying to get the 123 runs still needed in even time if we were to win. As we walked back on to the field neither "Davo" nor myself had any knowledge that we were to play a part in one of the most fantastic cricket sessions of all time.

Davidson had already performed heroically in the match ... eleven wickets for 222 runs from 55 overs and a near half-century when we batted in the first innings. Now as we followed the perky Kanhai and quiet little Joe Solomon on to the field he was needed again. What will happen when he's not around to bat, bowl and field for Australia brings a furrow to my brow ... but on December 14, 1960 he looked as dependable as ever as he strode to the wicket, his shoulders thrown back, and bat tapping the turf as he went. He didn't say much ... we'd already discussed the plans of taking short singles and thrashing at anything loose ... and then more and more short singles.

They'll crack, if only we can get the pressure on them. Pressure and more and more pressure and they must crack ... they've done it so often before.

But although this was the same team as they'd had before, they had a leader this time ... a great player in his own right, a shrewd tactician and a man who had the respect and liking of his side ... and of the opposition, too. A great cricketer this Worrell ... a great cricketer in every sense of the word. A quiet man with a sense of humour, and a throaty laugh, the sort of man one cannot imagine falling into panic.

The play immediately after tea went magnificently with short singles coming apace and the occasional four keeping the scoring rate about a run a minute. We added fifty in around even time, with ones turned into twos and half runs turned into quick singles. Davidson played two hooks from Hall that I can still see as if they were happening now. The second hit the ground a foot or two inside the fence and was a glorious stroke. Despite all this, however, we still had to push the scoring rate along to keep up with the one a minute needed for victory. Worrell changed his bowlers and put Hall in cotton wool for the new ball. Sobers, Valentine, Worrell, and Ramadhin all bowled but with little impression and gradually the game was tilting our way.

There was great tension around the ground. Not out in the centre where the players remained cool, keeping the simmering excitement of the game within bounds, but in the crowd there was a frenzy that I hadn't seen before at a cricket ground. Spectators hushed to the delivery of each ball and then would come the shaking burst of excitement—or a long sigh if nothing happened.

The new ball had the crowd simmering ... they had expected it, but now that it was here, it was a new device to put them on the edge of their seats. In the dressing rooms players who would think nothing of being in a similar situation to the players if on the field, were shaking like schoolboys at their first match ... and twenty minutes later I was suffering the same emotion ... but out in the centre it was all so different.

Come on now concentrate, I thought. Wes has got the new ball ... but don't worry about it ... just play it like the old one. You've got twenty-seven to make in half an hour ... so just get your head down ... this'd be a hell of a game to win after being in such trouble.

Worrell also had a pretty good grip of the game in the middle. During this tense period when lesser men and skippers would have panicked, he ruled with an iron hand.

"Relax, fellas and concentrate ... come on now, concentrate," he would exhort.

Joe Solomon was to achieve a moment of some fame in the second Test in Melbourne when he was given out through his cap dropping on the wicket, and 67,000 spectators rose to his defence ... but his real fame came a few weeks earlier on this beautiful Brisbane afternoon.

The clock above the scoreboard showed ten to six and Australia needed nine runs ... just nine runs. Sobers bowled a ball down the leg stump and a little push to the onside made it eight runs to go ...

Solomon was a bit slow getting to it—watch for another one there, Alan.

A single to Davidson and I had the strike again. The ball pitched down the line of the leg stump ... again I pushed it wide of Solomon at forward square-leg and called for "One". But this time Solomon was on to it in a flash and in the same action threw from side-on to the stumps. The bails were scattered as Davidson vainly tried to make his ground at Alexander's end. The West Indians were jubilant. But I was far from jubilant. It was a bad call ... a dangerous call. Even if Solomon hadn't hit the stumps Davidson would have been out by a yard with Alexander crouching for the return.

It was tragic but it had happened and I did some harsh thinking ...

Come on now, concentrate ... don't let's have any more run outs.

Grout came in, played two balls and took a quick single off the second-last ball of Sobers's over ... the second-last over of the day and of the match. Try as I might I couldn't get the last one away to take strike to Hall's last over and Wally was left with the job at the bottom end.

Hall took the ball in his hand and slowly paced back to his mark. The mark was a long, long way from the batsman, nearly out to the sightscreen and just before he turned for his run-up the players in the dressing room and on the patio in front of the room had a much better view of him than the crouching batsman. He's a tall man, almost ebony in colour, with flashing white teeth that light his face when he smiles. He has broad shoulders, and a lithe bouncing run to the wicket, gathering himself in as the popping crease approaches, to explode in what seems a flurry of arms and legs as he hurtles the ball at the opposing batsman. He likes an occasional drink and singing calypsos ... but he dislikes batsmen.

As he walked back to the mark there were four minutes to go—this was definitely the last over.

Grout had the strike in this last over of the most memorable of cricket matches, and waiting in the pavilion were bowlers Meckiff and Kline, waiting in case they were needed to make the last six runs for victory from those eight balls from Hall.

Meckiff had spent the early part of the innings at the back of the dressing room, but as the score mounted he and Kline either sat on the edge of their chairs or paced up and down near the windows, to watch the game. Grout had prefaced his arrival at the crease by some nervous chain-smoking, and when Davidson was dismissed had searched desperately for his batting gloves ... only to find he was sitting on them! Now he was facing the first ball of this last vital over from "Big Wes".

I watched, every nerve tense …

Just push a single, Wal … anywhere will do … Get an edge … off the pads … anything … but we must have a single so I can have the strike.

We got it, too, but in a painful way. Wally was struck in the solar plexus, a crippling blow, and the ball fell at his feet. It had hardly hit the ground before I was on my way without calling. Wally saw me coming and made off down the pitch holding his stomach … an agonising single to be sure.

Five to win and seven balls to go … I thought. One four will do it just one four … concentrate … concentrate.

Next ball … it was a bumper. Surely no one in his right mind would bowl a bumper at that stage of the match … but it was a bumper delivered with every bit of speed and power the big fella could muster. I tried to hook … trying for the four runs that would have all but won the game. The only result was a sharp touch on the gloves and Gerry Alexander's victory shout as he caught me.

Have you ever tried so hard to do something … concentrated so desperately that everything else was pushed out from your mind … and then seen it disappear in a fraction of a second? Then you'll have some idea of how I felt as I passed Grout at the other end and said: "All yours, Wal …"

He merely lifted his eyes and muttered, "Thanks very much!"

Now it was five to win—and six balls left.

Meckiff played the first ball and missed the second and the batsmen scampered for a single as the ball went through to Alexander. A bye … brilliant thinking from Grout … and near heart-failure for the spectators as Hall grabbed the return and hurled it at the stumps at the bowler's end. Valentine just managed to get behind the ball and save it from four overthrows. This was almost too much for me. I leaned across to Jackie Hendriks and whispered: "What's wrong with Wes, Jackie? He can throw much harder than that."

Grout had the strike now, and someone near me muttered:

"Please bowl another bouncer, Wes ..." Wally is one of the best hookers in Australia and we needed only four to win.

Evidently Grout also expected a bouncer for he got into position to hook only to find the ball was of good length. He misjudged his shot and it skewed off the top edge straight to Kanhai at backward square-leg.

Kanhai set himself under it as the Australian players watched. But in a flash Wes changed direction and was hurtling towards the now dropping ball. It was a nerve-racking sight, even for the Australians who didn't have time to realise the implications of Hall's charge.

Someone gasped: "Wes! No Wes!" Too late! Next moment the ball was whisked away from Kanhai's steady hands and fell to the ground.

The dressing room patio was sheer chaos. All restraint disappeared and players shouted and assured one another that this was the end ... they couldn't take any more.

Just three runs needed—only three more. Meckiff trusted to a five-iron shot from the next ball, hitting "outside in" and the ball flew to the mid-wicket boundary.

Watching from the patio we lost the ball in the setting sun but the batsmen were scampering up and down the wicket, determined to get the three runs needed for victory in case the ball didn't hit the fence. It didn't ... the ball stopped a foot or so short of the boundary—a curse on that uncut clover!—and was picked up by Conrad Hunte.

Of all the minor miracles that took place on this day I give pride of place to this one. Hunte was about eighty yards from the stumps when he picked up, turned and threw in the one action. I couldn't see the ball ... all I could see was the blurred throwing action to my right and the batsmen turning for three. For Grout to be run out the ball had to go directly to Alexander ... not to the right or left but directly to him ... thrown on the turn and from eighty yards. It was a magnificent throw and as Alexander swept the bails from the stumps Grout was hurling himself towards the crease ... but still a foot out of his ground.

The game was tied, with two balls to go! One run to win ... and last man Kline joined Meckiff.

Hall bounded in to bowl the second last ball of the match to Kline. He knew he must be deadly accurate ... the only way to prevent the batsman getting the run that would mean victory for Australia was to bowl at the stumps ... to spreadeagle them if possible.

There was not much sound on the ground at that moment, and even less as Hall let the ball go. It pitched in line with the middle and leg stumps and Kline played it with the full face of the bat to forward square-leg.

The crowd screamed as the two batsmen set off on the winning run. They crossed as Joe Solomon was just about to gather it in both hands ... he picked up as Meckiff got to within about six yards of the safety of the crease. Solomon the quiet one ... good and dependable ... the sort of man for a crisis. Was there ever a more crisis-like moment in a game of cricket than this?

There surely could never have been a better throw. The ball hit the stumps from the side on with Meckiff scrambling desperately for the crease. Umpire Hoy's finger shot to the sky and there came a tremendous roar from a crowd of four thousand ... who sounded like twenty times that number ... greeting the end of the game. A TIE ... the first in Test history.

From A Tale of Two Tests: With Some
Thoughts on Captaincy, 1962

John Snow was one of England's finest fast bowlers who on retirement from the game established a successful travel agency. While he was great company on tour, I am astonished he never got me lost because he would write down my various travel instructions and changes to itinerary on little scraps of paper in writing so tiny that it's a miracle he could ever read it. If you speak to Ian Chappell or Keith Stackpole, both good gutsy Australian batsmen, they will say he was the one they were worried about in the England bowling line-up – he was always nipping the ball both ways off the seam at a deceptive pace. As a boy I would sit transfixed watching him on television. I don't think I have ever seen anyone bowl like John with his loping, deceptive run-up that would transform into a sideways, classical action. Whenever an Ashes series comes up, you can be sure that among cricketers Snowy's name won't be far away.

JOHN SNOW

Ray Robinson

Bouncers and Beer Cans

I CAN think of no better term for a shooter than the meanest ball on earth, and that's not metaphorically speaking. Yet the lowest shooters are nothing like so contentious as bouncers that sometimes bruise ribs, raise lumps, gash scalps and leave sickly expressions on the faces of hitherto brave men. Since the dust died slowly down after the Battle of Adelaide in 1933 bumpers have not provoked such a disagreeable scene as Sydney saw in February 1971 – incidents that will be discussed long after much eventful cricket in the game is forgotten.

Last of six Tests played in Australia by Ray Illingworth's victorious Englishmen, this match brought to boil-over point an issue that had been simmering and sputtering through almost three months since John Snow's first bouncer to Ian Chappell in Adelaide and Alan Thomson's first to Colin Cowdrey in Melbourne. Episode Six became by far the most dramatic of the series, a Test that had everything except a century. It was marked, and marred, by a bouncer stunning a tailender, an international captain angrily disputing an umpire's ruling in midfield, a drunken onlooker grabbing the shirt of a bowler fielding on the boundary and the first team walk-off in Test history, after incensed barrackers threw empty beercans and a few bottles on to stretches of the outfield.

Few individual bowlers or batsmen have ever dominated a series as Snow did this one. Without being the biggest man on the field – Bob Willis stands 6 feet 5½ inches – Snow was like a swordfish among salmon; to most of Australia's batsmen a more apt simile might be like a piranha among perch, ready to tear strips off their already-wan confidence. His quick bowling allowed batsmen's nerves no chance to recover from stresses imposed by Mike Procter's hostility in South Africa. To mix a meteorological metaphor, something short of a hail of bumpers left Australia's batting snow-bound.

Dark sideburns descend from this handsome and headstrong bowler's wavy hair. Semi-stovepipe pants show a couple of inches of sock above his boots; they look like trousers tailored for a smaller man. John is the only fast bowler who can turn a poetic phrase as well as seam the ball either way off the track or make it prance towards a batsman's chin. His well-muscled back and broad shoulders combine in convulsive effort – recalling his boyhood hero Keith Miller – often making the ball get up as nobody else in this series could. Willing to go to almost any length to get Australian wickets, the 29-year-old bowler preferred to be short of a length on hard strips, finding that, unlike English tracks, they helped bounce much more than seaming. I've seen a lot worse verse than Snow's. In his *Contrasts* one poem ends:

> On the treadmill rolls
> As the body mindless bowls
> Down paths
> And the wheel which turns
> Is turning much faster than before.

Some of his poetry takes a little longer to sink in than his bouncer; no batsman likes to feel that sinking in, and they tend to remember it longer than anything he puts to metre. Like many another successful speedman in international cricket, he has a healthy splash of brimstone in his bloodstream.

John Snow is a powderkeg of a bowler with a short fuse – a fuse no longer than a man's tongue, if that man is an umpire. Three times in earlier Tests he had been cautioned, by two umpires. In the second innings in Perth when Lou Rowan asked him to 'Watch it,' he asked brusquely: 'What for?' and was told he was dropping too many balls too short in line with the batsman (Bill Lawry). Soon afterward persistent bumpers made Ian Redpath sway back direfully and the umpire repeated the warning. The fast bowler sent along an irreproachable ball then flung the next down half-way. It reared over the six-foot Victorian's head and Snow said emphatically: 'That's what I call a bouncer!' With the second Perth warning, Rowan notified the captain – the second step Law 46 specifies toward ordering an offending bowler off for the innings. When Illingworth contended: 'They're not bouncers,' the umpire was heard to reply: 'Somebody's bowling them from this end and it's not me.'

Even on such a busy tour I doubt whether England's skipper forgot his first Melbourne appearance against Victoria having been greeted with three short-pitched balls in Thomson's first four balls to him. The second struck Illy's shoulder and the third bouncer brought a caution from umpire Bob Figgis. Victorian captain Lawry came from mid-off to ask the umpire why.

Far from being too strict, I thought some of the umpiring permissive rather than punctilious at times, allowing intimidatory bowling by Snow and Thomson to pass without visible check. The point demanded discussion when several overs of the Melbourne Test contained four or more bouncers, including the first over of the match to Keith Stackpole. Standing in a Test for the first time, Max O'Connell seemed unwilling to project himself into mid-picture in his opening minutes as an international umpire by warning the year's outstanding bowler.

BBC broadcaster Brian Johnston asked ex-captain Lindsay Hassett how many bumpers in an eight-ball over should an umpire allow. Hassett: 'As a batsman I'd say two. A bowler might consider he could get away with three. Four in an over would have to be questioned.' Two an over was the limit set by Trinidad umpires after excesses early in England's 1960 series in the West Indies. Using arithmetic as the test whether bowling is intimidatory has never seemed the answer to me but a bowler warned after three bumpers in an over can hardly complain that justice does not appear to have been done.

With each of four bouncers to Brian Luckhurst's end in Melbourne, Thomson's long-range follow-through to the off side resulted in his return trek to starting-point taking him around the Cape, meaning nearer extra-cover than the bowler's umpire, Rowan. Watching through binoculars I wondered would the umpire walk across to intercept 'Froggy' with an admonition. I saw no sign of this, nor anything being said to the bowler when a fifth bouncer, second ball of his next over, struck the ducking Luckhurst near a shoulder-blade. According to the grapevine – not always as reliable as the Central Intelligence Agency – Alan's cheerful expression changed when he 'got the message'. If so, the Englishmen were unaware of this when four bumpers to Doug Walters in Snow's fourth over in the second innings caused O'Connell to say: 'That's enough!' Nettled, Snow hurled down a fifth short ball but it failed to bounce much more than bail-high. Running from point, Illingworth protested to O'Connell about Snow being warned for fewer bouncers than he said Thomson had let fly in one over in the first innings.

Never encouraged, reporters' questioning of umpires has brought to light some inconsistency of opinion and one relevant fact: some umpires disregard fliers that sail wide of a batsman – a distinction too refined to comfort a man aware that he has been spared only by inaccuracy and that the next bumper may be right on the button. I'd think that is how Luckhurst and Cowdrey felt more than once. For Colin, no doubt it stirred painful memories of his call for padded vests in the West Indies.

Batting eighth in the Melbourne Test, Snow ducked under a couple of bouncers from Thomson; none of the watching fieldsmen raised a smile. When the pair met at an Adelaide reception John ran a finger along Froggy's sandy hair and laconically asked where he'd like it parted.

As the teams were named for the final Test the prevailing impression was that England had missed a chance to be two up through failure to order a follow-on in Adelaide when Australian morale had sunk below seagull level. That reprieve failed to save Lawry's neck from the selectors' block which had been awaiting it for weeks. Next, a fractured left forearm denied England the stable batting of Geoffrey Boycott, heaviest scorer of the series.

Winning his first toss as Australia's captain Ian Chappell, who had never put any opposing side in, sent England in to bat on a pitch prepared in Sydney's wettest summer in 16 years. The 27-year-old skipper followed this up by giving his bowlers the most attacking fields of the series, at times resembling the Benaud touch.

Chappell's fast bowlers, Dennis Lillee and left-hander Tony Dell had difficulty directing the glossy ball along compelling lines, especially the newcomer, Dell, so nervous that he confessed he was unable to see the batsman's stumps for a while. On legs solid as an Epstein statue's, the 6 feet 4½ inch Queenslander scarcely looks a Nureyev in his run-up but uses his height, backed by 16½ stone, to make the ball lift nastily from a fresh track. When Gregory Chappell's sharp catch at third slip helped Dell to his first Test victim, John Edrich (30), the fields-men's joy showed how highly they valued the wicket of the stocky left-hander, whose batting is made up of equal parts of skill and sang-froid. In making 33 Keith Fletcher twice could not avoid blows on the left arm and chest, and Dell bruised D'Oliveira on the body before his in-dipper flicked from Basil's bat into the stumps.

Under the general applause greeting Illingworth I was surprised to hear an undertone of boos, like a rumble of far-away thunder while the sun shines overhead. Nothing in the captain's play in Australia warranted such sour incivility from a minority of dubious mental age. Throughout he had impressed me as a practical skipper, a man among men. His team respected his deeper knowledge of the game, his efficiency as a tactician, his Yorkshire fibre. They had the fullest faith in his judgment. No generation gap here, though Illy was 38 and his cream trousers were unfashionably wide. There was room, too, for belief that his captaincy qualities were most evident when England fielded: wisdom in judging which bowler would get most out of the wicket and bring the worst out of each batsman, also where to place fieldsmen for likely catches without forgetting economy. I could only attribute the surly undertone of boos to what Sydneysiders had seen on television of bouncers harrying O'Keeffe in the Melbourne Test, low daily quotas of balls by England's bowlers (average only 98 balls an hour) and a tendency to blame his side for dull stretches in earlier Tests. I believe Illy was well aware of drawbacks in his team's play but where is the Test captain who would risk upsetting his bowlers in mid-series by pressing them to break time-taking habits acquired over years?

An alert infielder, he held every catch he could reach and as batsman he showed more interest than most of his specialists in trying to keep the scoring rate from dozing off. As forward shots sprout as rarely from his play as papaws in Pudsey he puts his faith in hooks, sweeps, square-cuts and back-foot forces through the covers; they did not let him down in Australia. This time four were out for only 69 yet, except for brushing his forelock with his left glove, Illy showed no concern. The best and squarest hooker in the side, he was the only one of England's first six batsmen to break up the close fields with which Chappell kept pressure on for 37 overs – nearly half the innings.

Knott was the only partner who lasted long with his captain, and England had lost six for 145 when the 66th over entitled the Australians to a new ball. Orthodox captaincy would have called for it instantly, and Chappell discussed this with vice-captain Redpath as they walked to the other end, but the new skipper thought spinners Kerry O'Keeffe and Terry Jenner were bowling well enough to deserve longer tenure of the creases. Within 11 appreciative overs the pair spun the innings to an end. Jenner rattled the stumps three times in his last four overs, twice with legbreaks and once with a wrong'un that removed Illy, whose 42, top score, contained six well-hit boundary shots.

For the first time in his life O'Keeffe found his mixed spin supported by a close three-man legtrap, in addition to his captain at slip waiting for an edged legbreak. The deployment rewarded the lean and keen young bowler's quick-armed spin with his first Test wickets: Stackpole's fleshy but swift hands caught Fletcher and Knott at leg-gully and Jenner held Lever at silly mid-on (none was as near as Brian Close stands, tempting extinction, when O'Keeffe bowls for Somerset).

In his breakaway from routine tactics Chappell made much less call on four seam bowlers: brother Greg's medium-pace quota shrank to three overs in the match instead of about 20. Sharing 40 overs this day, the two spinners were entrusted with both ends for 24 consecutive overs, causing onlookers with bygone haircuts to think back to O'Reilly and Grimmett. In an hour after tea the pair provided 144 balls of cricket – 18 overs here, the equivalent of 24 overs in England. Stimulating more verve in his players' response, the new leader achieved the triple distinction of dismissing England in less than a day for their lowest total of the series – all done with 150 fewer balls than it had taken to end any English innings in the preceding Tests. Among ex-skippers who praised this captaincy was the latest recruit to their ranks, Lawry, who said Ian did everything right. I met only one man who qualified this, ex-bowler Bill Hunt who thought it would have been wiser not to try too hard to get the last couple of wickets until nearer the day's end, in the belief that the track would be easier for batting next day.

With only 184 on the board the bowlers knew England was heading for defeat unless they could do something drastic. Snow sounded the tocsin by bumping the first and seventh balls of the innings to crew-cut Ken Eastwood, replacing the deposed Lawry as left-handed opening partner for Stackpole. The newcomer fell to Peter Lever for five when wicketkeeper Alan Knott reached a low legside snick.

Snow turned Australian concern to consternation with a superb over – his best of the series, I'd say – to get rid of the bravest of batsmen, Stackpole, the man whom England most needed to prevent settling in. Following up a blow in the hip region (no bumper) John seamed a couple of balls away from the off stump so sharply that Keith walked along the pitch to give the spot pacifying taps. With outgoers on his mind, Stackpole was left standing by a perfectly pitched incutter that clipped the outside of the off peg as it ripped through. Both openers gone for 13! Rather than send another nightwatchman in, Chappell came in himself with two minutes to go – an action reminding me of the captaincy of his dauntless grandfather, Victor Richardson.

Saturday was election day in New South Wales, but the Test topped the poll, judging by the number of voters carrying transistors tuned to the cricket. In the first hour, calling of two front-foot no-balls scarcely mollified Snow. After the second call he walked sternly to the crease and stared at the ground almost as intently as a Queensland backtracker. In one such dialogue earlier Snow had asked: 'Where's the footprint?' and the umpire replied: 'I don't need a footprint to tell me where I saw your boot land.'

As catcher and third paceman, Willis, tall as Chips Rafferty, drove a wedge into Australia's batting. Rod Marsh's leg shot off

Lever looked to be worth four runs until Willis's exceptional reach and lunging experience as Corinthian Casuals' goalie, enabled him to intercept a catch, otherwise non-existent. Chappell tried to drive a well-up ball with which Bob sent his off stump cartwheeling. Puzzled, Ian asked his partner had he unknowingly played across the ball. Four down for 66 made Australia's position precarious.

After lunch England's quick bowlers put plenty of fire into an attempt to break Redpath and Walters' fifth-wicket stand. Squatting under three bouncers in two overs from Lever did nothing to brace Walters' nerve for facing Snow's greater menace from the other end. Seeing Doug backing away, yet still aiming desperate square-cuts at flying balls, Snow pressed his thrustful attack, unsparingly, as if he wanted to drive Walters not only from the wicket but off the continental shelf. His last bumper to Doug was nearer a quarter-pitcher than a half-pitcher. It was the shortest ball I ever saw John bowl. Yet fortune favoured the at-bay batsmen so much that 18 agitated runs came off two overs, causing Illy to spell his most dangerous bowler half an hour after lunch.

Whenever Snow chased a shot near the boundary a rumble of boos beneath the applause for the shot suggested that had some onlookers been umpiring he would have been warned for intimidation.

Cutting boldly on a track still aiding bowlers, Walters gave chances off Underwood at 16 and Willis at 27. The Englishmen found him harder to catch than Ronald Biggs. At 41 a foozled drive at Underwood coiled from Doug's boot toward silly-point. Knott's simultaneous pounce and backward flick to the stumps – do his heels have radar? – were like magic. Television playbacks proved that this close decision should have gone Alan's way, but a run later he stumped the venturesome Walters off the same bowler.

Redpath, bouncer-harassed yet persevering stoically, drove well in reaching the first 50 of the Test. Willis, Underwood and Illingworth's accuracy limited him to eight runs in the next 45 minutes, amid an ungrateful tincan chorus – barrackers' clanking disapproval of slow scoring by foe or friend. After Derek caught Redpath's drive and Knott snapped up O'Keeffe off Illy at 178 the last recognised batsman, Greg Chappell, put Australia ahead of England's 184 with only three bowlers left to help him.

Sensation was waiting in the wings when, after 2½ hours at grass, Snow was recalled for the 66th over. He took a new ball for the third delivery and completed the over with a legside bumper to Chappell.

Bouncers had become so frequent in the series that less notice was being taken of them than in most Test rubbers I have watched – except by batsmen, among whom familiarity never breeds contempt. Partly, I suppose, because Tom Brooks is an old fast bowler, much of the umpiring was more lenient than in 1961 when four in one over and three in another caused Colin Egar to intervene twice as Wesley Hall bowled to McDonald and Simpson in Melbourne. In Sydney's January Test, 1971, a Snow bumper caused the ninth man, McKenzie, to retire with his mouth bleeding. In the next Test one of several bouncers to the eighth man, O'Keeffe, bruised his chest.

Now in the final Test in Sydney live television showed millions of viewers in Australian cities that three balls in Snow's second over with this new ball were to the ninth man, Jenner. As the first rose toward his ribs Jenner gingerly fended it away with his bat. It ran around the corner for a single, giving Chappell the strike for four balls. Facing Snow again for the sixth ball, Jenner unhappily squirmed out of its way as it reared. Had he stood still, it would have struck him near the left armpit. The over count so far to Jenner: two short-pitched balls, at least one of which an umpire could have classed as intimidatory.

To follow up Jenner's apprehensive wriggle from the sixth ball Snow's field-setting was changed by bringing Willis from mid-off across to the on side. This made four leg-trap fieldsmen: deep-leg (Underwood), leg-gully (Hampshire), close short-leg (Illingworth) and mid-on (Willis). Stepping back, Jenner stared at the reshuffle like a bird transfixed by a snake's mesmerism. Like every cricketer watching, he recognised the field adjustment as preparation for catching a mishit off a bouncer to come. It came. Banged down short, it cut in as it reared toward Jenner's collarbone. As he tried to duck beneath it, the ball struck the left side of his head near the back and rebounded toward cover.

Jenner's collapse on the pitch brought a thunderous hoot from the keyed-up crowd. The outburst reflected a similar sense of outrage to that felt much less demonstratively at Trent Bridge in 1966 when a ball from massive West Indian fast bowler Charlie Griffith struck England's last man, Underwood, on the mouth. The bowler's captain, Sobers, looked upset but waited until they were back in the room before telling Griffith he should apologise. The bowler did so in writing. Disgusted viewers wrote letters to editors. In being spared severe injury Derek was more fortunate than another tailender, Tony Lock, whose left arm was broken at Perth in 1963 by a bumper from Peter Pollock, then at his fastest.

I had been sorry to see Snow, a top-class cricketer, master of the compelling art of quick bowling, add his name to those who have misinterpreted their craft by breaking the once-honoured unwritten law against bouncing the cricket ball at unskilful tailenders. When Alec Bedser, promoted from the lower division to nightwatchman at Leeds in 1948, was hard to shift next day, an exasperated fast bowler, Ray Lindwall, let fly a bouncer which struck Alec on the chest. That night Bill O'Reilly, who was Lindwall's club captain in Sydney, quietly told Ray: 'I hope I never see you bowl another bumper at a bowler.' Trying to duck under bumpers from Freddie Trueman at Edgbaston and the Oval in 1958 New Zealanders Noel Harford and John Sparling retired hurt by blows on the head. England's ex-captain Sir Leonard Hutton commented: 'I do not like to see bouncers bowled at any except the very top-class batsmen – batsmen with the skill and experience to look after themselves in the face of such an attack.' Harford was in the upper half of New Zealand's batting order and Sparling went in eighth. From what I have seen and heard at Test grounds in six countries the principles expressed by O'Reilly and Hutton are much closer to most cricket-goers and players' concepts of fair play than opinions attempting to justify a bullring outlook. Where else more so than in Sydney, the city where selector Edmund Dwyer first proposed in 1952 deleting the words 'standing clear of his wicket' from Law 46, forbidding intimidation of a batsman by persistent and systematic short-pitched balls?

From close-leg, five yards away, Illingworth was first to the stunned Jenner. Hooting and abusive shouts from the Hill continued as the pallid tailender was lifted to his feet. Willis carried the dropped bat as masseur David McErlane and Lever helped Terry walk unsteadily off, blood oozing through his hair.

As Snow turned to walk back for his run-up to bowl to the tenth man, Lillee, umpire Rowan called: 'Before you go, John ...', seemingly intending to caution him. Snow gave no heed. Nearby players heard the umpire call more loudly: 'Just a minute, John!' The bowler walked on with a muttered remark. Rowan: 'I am not impressed by your performance and am giving you a first warning.' He turned to signal with one finger to square-leg umpire Brooks.

The bowler whirled around, objecting loudly: 'That's the first bouncer I've bowled this over – your blokes have been bowling seven an over.' Illingworth hurried down to support him, looking rather like the Khmer god whose glance could set objects on fire. 'What's going on?' he asked. Rowan, a detective sergeant by occupation, repeated: 'I'm giving the bowler a first warning.'

Holding up one finger Illingworth contended it was unfair to warn a man for bowling 'one bouncer in the over.' In the heat of the moment language more likely to be heard in locker-rooms than libraries burst from the warned bowler and the worried skipper hotly taking his part. Not the sort of words that figure in the Sussex sonneteer's poetry, though fairly easy to rhyme with a simple cricket term or two. It was a frustrating moment. No wonder Britain was accelerating moves to enter the Common Market!

Caught between two fires – Snow was baying toward his left ear and the captain toward his right – umpire Rowan waved a hand as if to indicate that this confrontation must now cease. 'Get on with the game!' he said. 'Push off!' They did, after Illingworth turned back and, jerking his thumb toward the pavilion, said: 'We'll see who has the last word on this when we get out there.'

By word and gesture Illingworth had shown he did not class either of the two preceding balls to Jenner as a bouncer. A number of onlookers thought otherwise. Definitions vary. A prison that New York calls a Correction Facility still looks like a jail to most people. In cricket, a thudding bouncer can hardly be mistaken for a length ball, and *vice-versa*, but when a borderline ball pitches the game suffers if the opinion of the man appointed to judge is not accepted. Spectators were astonished to see an umpire's decision being disputed by a captain from the country that taught the world how to play. King Arthur wouldn't have done it. It was the one action on the tour that Illingworth regretted, as he told *Sunday Express* readers later.

Why should a seasoned, level-headed Yorkshireman blow his cone? Only by travelling with Test teams can you appreciate the countless pressures on a captain's mind through most of his waking hours for several months on end. Illingworth's quota of these was more trying because all except four of his side had suffered injuries. A breakdown of his swiftest bowler, Alan Ward, upset his main strategy. His surest batsman, Boycott, was disabled, left arm in a sling. Illy was the first skipper to cope with six Tests in a series, and a New Year washout resulted in his bowlers having to saddle up for three Tests in the last four weeks. He felt it unfair that the other side's shortest-pitching bowler had, seemingly, escaped warnings of the sort two umpires had given England's fastest bowler. If two repeat warnings this time cost him his main bowler for the rest of the innings and enabled the Australians to square the rubber, he would never hear the end of having let them off the hook in Adelaide by not ordering a follow-on. Though I believe he acted there as his bowlers wished, the blame for letting the Ashes slip would settle on him. This outline is not given in an attempt to justify the inexcusable but I think the culmination of all these factors explains why Illingworth slipped his trolley.

Instead of the on-target bouncer and its hot-worded sequel monopolising weekend headlines they were supplanted by a sensation in which the crowd's hooligan fringe got into the act.

As Snow ran up to deliver the last ball of the dramatic over to the tenth man, Lillee, a crescendo of hoots from many parts of the Hill showed the crowd's wrath at a bumper having knocked down a tailender. There is no way of estimating how many of the 29,684 present joined in, but the hooting was much more impassioned and widespread than earlier Sydney booing of bumpers, such as Miller to Hutton, Lindwall to Compton and Weekes, Hall to Harvey, Loxton to various batsmen.

While the Englishmen had drinks near midfield a dozen cans were thrown from the rowdy lesser Hill at the north-east corner into the vacant outfield, presumably in resentment at the felling of Jenner. Calling to Snow not to go there to field, Illingworth sat down while a ground attendant tossed the cans into a gutter at the foot of the fence. 'Better go to third man,' Illy advised. Snow: 'No, I'll go down.'

As Snow walked to field at deep-leg an indistinguishable tirade of taunts greeted him. He responded in kind, and gesticulated an invitation to anyone who wanted to make something of it. Instead of stopping at his usual spot about eight yards from the excited corner he went close to the fence. Youths and boys leaned across to shake his hand or pat his shoulder. 'Thanks mate, thanks mate!' he repeated to each hero-worshipper. A middle-aged drunk in an orange shirt and white towel hat thrust out a hand but, instead of patting, grabbed his shirt and dragged him against the pickets. 'What the hell do you think you're doing?' exclaimed Snow. The man would not let go until neighbours hauled him over backwards, aided by a shove from the poet-bowler's right palm. (Asked had the grabber said anything, John said: 'He couldn't speak – he was stoned').

As Snow walked about 15 yards in from the boundary a second wave of cans landed around the stretch of outfield in front of the lesser Hill. Most of them, yards from Snow, appeared to be a renewal of a distorted form of protest but one skidded past John a couple of feet from his right boot. Snow pointed to the cans – there were then six at his end – but nobody could tell whether more would follow and be aimed at him. In case he might need help, Willis loyally ran to join him, only to undo the effect by shouting at the crowd. More cans followed.

Running from midfield toward the pair, their captain kicked a couple of cans toward the gutter and pulled Snow further away. Then he waved an arm to his fieldsmen and, forgetting the umpires, led his team off, apparently feeling his move necessary as a skipper's duty to safeguard his players. (We were not aware until his later statement that a couple of bottles had flown past his and Snow's heads.)

Sitting side by side broadcasting, ex-captains Benaud and Lawry had made a small diversionary bet on the match. Illingworth's disappearance through the gate reminded Lawry of this. Turning to Richie, he said: 'It's a forfeit. Pay up, Benordy!'

The batsmen stayed at the wicket. Lillee, playing his second Test, walked along to Chappell and asked: 'What do we do now?' Greg: 'We stay here until we are told to do something different.'

The umpires walked to the Englishmen's room, where Rowan asked: 'What's going on, Mr Illingworth? Is your team coming back on the field or are you forfeiting the match?'

The captain replied that he had a duty to safeguard his players and said the ground should be cleared.

At the other end a few youths from the main Hill were helping ground staff throw cans into the boundary gutter at 5.10 p.m. when secretary Alan Barnes broadcast through amplifiers: 'The ground will be cleared and the players will return. Clear the field and play will go on!' Mixed boos from the Hill and applause from the reserve greeted that, and were repeated when Illingworth led his team back from a seven-minute sit-in.

Looking on was Colin Egar, who had held the confidence of

skippers from four countries before he ceased umpiring in 1970. Asked what he would have done had he been umpiring the Test, Egar replied: 'I'd have been out there getting the outfield cleared while Rowan was in England's room telling them to play or forfeit.'

When Lever bowled the next over Willis was fielding 15 yards in front of the shirt-grabbing spot, Illy having switched Snow to third-man in front of the members' pavilion. As Snow walked 30 paces to begin the following over applause dominated the noises, as if the bulk of the crowd wished to dissociate themselves from the yahoos' can-throwing. (In all, 40 cans and a few bottles were found in the boundary gutters; more than one-third of them were soft-drink cans, causing ground manager Keith Sharp to conclude that boys formed at least one in three of the throwers.)

We heard some booing as Snow ran up but it petered out with the first ball. After this over, his third with the new ball, his end was taken over by Willis. When a shortish ball from Bob struck Lillee in the stomach, doubling him up, some token boos and catcalls came from the still-fuming Hill. Hundreds had left but I should say 20,000 stayed to watch. Greg Chappell was worth watching. It would take more than bouncer incidents, a can-throwing distur-bance and a team walk-off to put this 22-year-old cricketer off his game. By Saturday night he had steered Australia to a lead of 51 with three wickets yet to fall.

I learned later that just before the shirt-grab police at the ground were alerted by their chief, Commissioner Norman Allan, who was watching ABC television in his suburban home at Balgowlah and listening to comments by Norman May and Frank Tyson. In reply to my questions Commissioner Allan said: 'A few minutes after the injured batsman fell, the screen showed Snow walking towards the fence, where he was being vigorously booed. Sensing that there would be trouble, I spoke on my hot line to Metropolitan Superintendent Ernest Lynch, in charge at the ground. I said it would be advisable to place police inside the fence in that area, as the crowd was simmering. Police reported there had been a mêlée there a few minutes earlier and they arrested two men for unseemly conduct. Snow, angered by boos and taunts, answered them pro-vocatively. This was indiscreet, of course, but understandable.

'Superintendent Lynch gave the order but before police could be posted inside the fence Snow's shirt was grabbed. After that, nine men were arrested and charged with unseemly conduct, unseemly

language or offensive behaviour. No one was charged with assaulting Snow, who laid no charges. When police lined inside the fence
the crowd kept its emotions under control and there were no more
ugly incidents.'

Noticing that Jenner was recovering from shock, Dr A. B. Corrican
asked him: 'Do you think you will feel up to batting again, if needed
this evening? If so, I'll have to stitch your head.' He did so and
players helped buckle Jenner's pads on again.

Immediately after the dazed batsman was helped off the field
vice-captain Colin Cowdrey came to see whether the injury was
serious and to express sympathy. Before leaving at the day's end
for their motel Snow accompanied manager David Clark to the
Australians' room. Snow expressed no regret but asked Jenner:
'How are you?' He brushed his hand across Terry's hair, as if to
indicate a glancing blow. Jenner's dark hair was matted with con-
gealed blood at the back and the doctor had warned him not to let
water touch the wound area.

One report in London suggested that if this amount of beer cans
justified a retreat there are some parts of the world where no cricket
would be played at all. Before Sunday's play, however Illingworth
told reporters: 'John Snow was in physical danger. That's why we
walked off. Bottles as well as cans had been thrown in his direction. I
have seen people hit by bottles and it makes a bloody mess of them.
At Port of Spain in 1960 we sat on the ground while bottles were
being thrown. They kept on throwing and in the end play was called
off. By leaving the field yesterday we settled the whole thing in five to
10 minutes. It could have gone on indefinitely if we had not gone off.'

Nobody could disprove that opinion, though it was the opposite
of the stand by another Yorkshireman, Hutton, at Georgetown 17
years earlier. In his snap decision to quit the field Illingworth ran
the risk of antagonising more of the crowd than the splinter-group
of can-throwing louts who, if any were trying to hit Snow, should
have been disgusted with their marksmanship as well as ashamed
of their larrikinism. As nothing marred the 45 minutes of play after
the Englishmen reappeared, Ray could feel he had not misjudged
the situation. His mail supported this view: more than 100 letters
expressed regret for the disturbance and did not blame him for the
walk-off.

In a letter addressed to the Australian Board of Control Illingworth
restated his midfield contention and added: 'The short-pitched ball

is a legitimate part of a fast bowler's armoury and, in my opinion, to warn Snow on one such ball was unfair tactics. In my opinion this warning was one of the major factors which caused the subsequent crowd disturbance which in turn led to my having taken England off the field'. The letter was never delivered but each captain filled in a routine report after the match on forms provided by the Board.

Pressmen who tried to interview Rowan had to be content with a cryptic typewritten statement: 'Because of my love of cricket and my respect for the greatest majority of people closely associated with it I have no comment to make. I will not join the group at any wailing wall'. (At the Board's request, however, Rowan supplied a report on the incidents. A copy of this was among information considered by the Cricket Council at Lord's before the warning that players dissenting from umpires' decisions would in future be penalised.)

Applause was the only sound heard as the Englishmen entered the field on Sunday, the third day. A different attendant had charge of the Main Hill sightscreen as the man on duty on Saturday had been too upset by the disturbance to resume duty at that post.

Bowling from umpire Brooks' end, because of a change of wind, Snow kept the ball up to a length. Nothing more startling occurred in his three overs than an appeal for leg-before-wicket against Jenner, who had returned to the wicket after Knott caught Lillee off Willis. As the appeal was being easily answered, one watching cricketer caused a ripple of mirth by asking: 'How could he be lbw when he was so far away to leg?' Lasting 32 more balls Jenner added 22 runs before Lever bowled him off his thigh for 30. Taking risks as he ran out of partners Chappell (65) had his exposed leg stump hit – Willis's third victim.

England's second innings began 80 runs behind but Luckhurst's dread of a second 0 was not allowed to cramp his style. He played the bowling on its merits – and as if it had few merits – in making 40 of England's first 60. Mulberry stains from the new ball covered much of his blade while Edrich's bat looked unspotted. Between overs Luckhurst apologised for having so much of the strike. The left-hander's characteristic response: 'Don't worry. You carry on. I'll watch.' After a half-smothered yorker wriggled past the leg peg Brian lowered his bat crossways along the ground to show how he would deal with any more like that one. Flashes from halfway up the Hill caused police to explore the slope for a mirror or shiny lunch tin, without locating the unsporting or negligent culprit. Confident square-cuts helped Luckhurst make 59 of the first 94, putting England 14 ahead before his sweep at O'Keeffe's legbreak gave Lillee a long run for a well-judged catch. Fast bowlers are among the best fielders these days, as Snow, Willis and Lever had shown.

Few people knew what to expect when Chappell handed Eastwood the ball before tea. Ken turned out to be a left-hand wrist-spinner with a penchant for full-tosses. Two minutes before the interval Keith Fletcher (20) tried to place one of these too carefully, Stackpole held the third of his four catches and Chappell's hunch almost earned him a halo. Compelling Edrich (57) to defend against one near the off stick, O'Keeffe saw an edged wrong'un pop in and out of the falling captain's hands as Chappell slewed his body under it in case his second clutch failed.

When not finding gaps, John Hampshire was stinging cover fieldsmen's hands. Attempting another murderous sweep against O'Keeffe he skied the ball over untenanted ground behind the wicket. When Ian Chappell began racing outward from slip with his back to the wicket it looked a forlorn chance until a delighted yell from the crowd he was facing told of his ankle-high capture of a catch almost as difficult to judge as it was hard to overtake.

Only 85 ahead with four of the best gone – that was the tight corner for England when Illingworth joined Basil D'Oliveira, who in so many Tests for his adopted country has been a cool man in hot spots. Basil's bat of yellower willow looks more natural than the other bleached blades and it suits the play of a batsman observing natural laws rather than cranial theories.

Once as O'Keeffe was running in Illy twisted away from his wicket to look at the leg fielders' positions. A minority of the previous day's hooters started to rumble, inexplicably, and a dozen clots began rapping cans together, irritatingly. Next time Redpath's short-leg position was altered umpire Brooks stood in the bowler's path until all was settled. He also motioned close fielders a few paces back if their shadows fell on the pitch. Recall of Dell and Lillee with a new ball for the last half-hour pained both batsmen, as the towering Queenslander struck Dolly three times on the thigh and waist and a blow on Illy's left knee made the skipper finish the day limping.

While the cricketers relaxed on their rest day, Monday, and

Bernard Thomas used physiotherapy on the captain's leg, a Central Court magistrate began fining 13 men a total of $700 when they pleaded guilty to offensive behaviour, resistance to arrest or unseemly words. Nearly all between 25 and 18, they included labourers, clerks, students, firemen, a glazier and welder who admitted having thrown two stubby bottles. The magistrate said people were entitled to go to cricket without being subjected to the menace of flying beercans from men acting like hoodlums. The shirt-grabber was not apprehended but one labourer's offensive behaviour consisted of running across the field to shake Greg Chappell's hand at 50; he told the court he was carried away.

Illingworth did not need a runner on Tuesday but he added only four to reach 29 before Lillee hit his left boot. Of 10 appeals for lbw or bat-pad catches in England's innings this was the only one the umpires upheld. D'Oliveira's timely 47 helped the total grow by 93 before Chappell dived to a low snick off Lillee's outswinger, the captain's third catch among the first six wickets. Unable to prevent the last four men from adding 51 to make England 302, the Australians found themselves needing 223 to win. Use of only a light hand-roller was due to their thoughts about the state of the track.

Before a run came luckless Eastwood was yorked by Snow who after his second over was the victim of misadventure at the same spot as Saturday's exploits. Against the background of a high stand he misjudged a hook by Stackpole off Lever which would have been catchable had he stood with his back to the fence. Moving forward, John wheeled around too late and, as the ball went over, his outflung right hand jammed between picket-tops. Teeth bared in a sardonic grin of pain, he hurried off holding his torn and dislocated little finger, with a bone protruding. Under general anaesthetic in hospital the finger was repaired and bandaged.

Addition of his outstanding bowler to England's casualty list must have made Illingworth feel like the commanding officer of the Light Brigade at Balaklava. However he and his men felt, they pushed on purposefully with the job of winning the battle. In Lever's third over a model outswinger found an edge and Chappell walked as soon as he saw the ball lodge in Knott's gloves. Placed exactly the right depth down the gully, Dolly held Walters' slash off Willis. With four out for 82 by the 25th over, only two men could lift Australia away from impending defeat, Stackpole and the younger Chappell.

Hooking Dolly, Keith became the only man in the series to be credited with two sixes in a Test but he was steadied by Illingworth who had Redpath smartly caught at leg-gully. In his gentle, wide-trousers jogtrot of eight steps Illy looks innocent as a backyard trundler in slippers, but not to batsmen who have to cope with his on-the-dot length and line plus deceptive drift that sways some balls outward when inward turn is expected. From over the wicket he spun offbreaks into the pads of Stackpole and Chappell, but, unlike Knott, uttered no appeal, simply tilting his head across to calculate whether the ball could have hit the stumps. When Stackpole, attempting a sweep, was bowled behind his meaty legs for 67, top score, eight fieldsmen crowded to pat the broad back of the skipper whose guile had removed the biggest obstacle to an English victory.

As Knott missed a legside chance to stump Marsh an incredulous gasp around the ground was a tacit tribute to the finest wicketkeeping by any visitor Australians have seen in my time. This let-off was the gloved genius's only real error in coping with 8,000 balls in the series. (In all the Englishmen turfed 20 chances and the Australians 23.)

For the first time in the rubber here was a pitch on which Illingworth really liked bowling, even with a sore knee. For two-thirds of the innings he held control into the breeze, in one stretch bowling 11 overs straight. On the fifth morning Greg Chappell, 30, aware that quick runs from him were the only hope, advanced to drive the off-spinner but a drifter curved past him. The stumping brought Knott his 24th wicket – a record for any series in Australia – and Illingworth rested with three wickets for 39. The skipper's 160 balls allowed only 18 scoring shots, 10 of them singles. In the last overs Dell averted a hat trick by D'Oliveira before Underwood ended the innings at 160.

Sportsmen have been known to get up from the floor to win but this is the first time a whole team has quit the scene and returned to carry off the match. Victors by 62 runs, the Englishmen swarmed around their captain and hoisted him on to Hampshire and Edrich's shoulders. Triumphantly they carried off the first skipper for 38 years to have wrenched the Ashes from Australia's grasp Down Under and the only one not to have allowed the Australians one win in a rubber since the 30-hour time limit began there in 1946. Australia's captain and the New South Wales cricket president, Alan Davidson, acknowledged the Englishmen's superiority and congratulated them on fighting back so convincingly after the loss of star players.

Two of these, Snow and Boycott, each had an arm in a sling as they accepted presentations on the field in front of the pavilion. If cricket had judo-style gradings the Black Belt for fast bowlers would surely have been bestowed on Snow. John was so clearly the Man of the Series that I think this award would have been endorsed by any public opinion poll, including those who normally answer 'Don't know'.

From *The Wildest Tests, 1972*

I was one of *Wisden*'s five cricketers of the year in 1988 and was sat with Gubby Allen at the celebratory dinner. I found him an absolutely fascinating man and by the time dinner was over we had come to the conclusion that we were similar bowlers who essentially pitched it up and swung it. It seemed to me that he was always feared at Lord's, and not much revered either; a difficult individual who still wanted to rule the MCC with a rod of iron – even though he wasn't ruling anything much any more. I remained rather fond of him after that dinner and, in fact, he signed my own copy of *Wisden* that year.

GUBBY ALLEN

Denzil Batchelor

The Brisbane Miracle

I am a Selector. It is true that, up to now, I have been overlooked by what dyspeptics in the press-box like to call the Moguls of the M.C.C. when it comes to picking teams to play Australia or the West Indies. Indeed, I am never even invited to nominate eleven Gentlemen to challenge the Players in what I am given to understand is an obsolete engagement, despite the fact that it seems to produce more thrilling cricket and tighter finishes than most other fixtures one manages to see. But I am a Selector, all the same. In the long winter evenings I choose World Elevens to play against Mars. My system is simple. I pick my men *at their best*. They never suffer from lack of form. I know that if they have *ever* fielded smartly at slip they can be trusted to be in top form in that position on the field of Mars, even though they are generally hidden away at mid-on.

With this reassurance behind me, I am free to select men who, at their very best, are pre-eminent as bats, bowlers, or all-rounders. On this principle, it is, you may be surprised to learn, very hard to exclude G. O. Allen from the *corps d'élite* presently booked to play against Mars some fifteen years ago (for, with Dunne giving me moral support, there has never been any difficulty about regrouping past and future in the interests of a good game).

You see, G. O. Allen was such a very various player. Write him off as a magnificent fast bowler, and he bobbed up and hit a hundred in a Test Match; or a 68 against Australia on a breaking wicket, one of the finest fighting innings I ever saw in my life. One thing at least you could have good hopes of: if "Gubby" Allen was succeeding as batsman, or bowler, or as both, he was likely to be playing more than his part as a fieldsman near the wicket.

"Gubby"—he is called Gubby by all from nodding acquaintances to intimates, but Obby by his family—began life as an Australian. At six he reformed; and came to England to be educated. There is a story, possibly apocryphal, of an early single-wicket game in an English garden. Gubby is said to have batted faultlessly for an hour, whereupon the grown-ups prevailed upon him, with difficulty, to declare. He then bowled down his opponent's wicket first ball—and went on with his innings.

You will find him opening the Eton batting in 1919; because of a back injury which troubled him until the end of his 'Varsity days, you will not find his name in the side's bowling averages at all. Against Harrow he went in first and was run out in the first innings by his great friend, Hill-Wood, before he had even taken guard. In the second innings he scored an elegant and forceful 69 not out. It was due to Allen's batting as much as to Hill-Wood's bowling that Eton won the match, with Harrow crumpling up to score but 41 on the last day.

Then came two years in the University team. If he did little in the 'Varsity match of 1923 owing to the recurrence of his injury, in the previous year he did more than anyone to win the game for Cambridge. He took 5 for 60 in the first innings; 4 for 18 in the second: and among those in the routed Oxford side were R. H. Bettington, B. H. Lyon, L. P. Hedges and G. T. S. Stevens. The long and imposing career in first-class cricket was well launched. Allen was to tour South America in 1926, and captain our ill-fated team in the West Indies in '47–'48; and in between to figure as a member of Test teams and of the side which visited Australia in '32–'33, and as leader of the '36–'37 side down under. In addition, of course, he was to head the attack for Middlesex for many seasons. The most marvellous bowling performance of his career—it had a great deal to do with his selection against Mars—was achieved for his county. On a well-behaved pitch at Lord's in 1929 he got out every Lancashire batsman in the first innings. Ten wickets for a trifle of forty runs—and eight of them clean bowled. Among his victims on that red-letter day were Hallows, Watson, Ernest Tyldesley (who made a masterful century), Iddon and Hopwood. The first two, at least, on that imposing list were the sort of batsmen whose stumps you hardly ever hoped to hit, so impregnable was their defence.

If you had watched Allen bowling then, you would have remarked the special features of his excellence. He seemed to me to have a shorter, and thus less tiring, run to the wicket than most fast bowlers; to reach the crease in top gear; to wheel up and over releasing the ball in a natural swing, without the intrusion of any action which could take pace off delivery; and to straighten up neatly and quickly to conjure himself from bowler to fieldsman. A trim, an economic action—a fast bowler from whose technique all the inessentials had been shorn away. Only in the actual split second of delivery was Allen possessed by that demon of combativeness that obsessed other faster bowlers, including Larwood, from the moment they turned to begin their long rush to the wicket. A whippet, rather than a greyhound. A pocket Hercules—that was Gubby.

Such was the bowler, shortish, slim, good-looking, and seeming to be younger than his years: an Etonian at Cambridge; an undergraduate in appearance when picked at twenty-eight for his first Test against Australia in 1930. Against New Zealand at Lord's he was chosen, you understand, like A. J. Raffles before him, "as a bowler man"; but—again like Raffles in that fine story *A Bad Night*—it was with his batting that he won immortality. He went in ninth, after we looked like being led on the first innings by a New Zealand who had managed to scrape 224. At the other end was Ames, heroic in scale, cool, ox-eyed and confident. The two of them lost no time in taking the bowling by the scruff of its neck and shaking the life out of it. When at last they were parted, two and a half hours later, they had added 246 runs; a Test Match record. Allen's contribution to the innings was a score of 122, bristling with fours and sixes. He gave no chance and dazzlingly drove Cromb, Blunt and Merritt to every corner of the thunderously cheering ground.

So to the Second Test at the Oval, where, after England had declared with 416 on the board and four men out, Allen was the chief instrument in shooting out a team, which lacked the support of Dempster, for fewer than they needed to save the follow-on;

and the match. On a wicket which was expected to help the spin bowlers, Allen was not called on till third change. Then he clean bowled both the opening batsmen, and with the help of Ames who held three catches for him, finished with an analysis of 5 wickets for 14 runs for the innings. What an opening season in Test cricket! If he could have kept it up there would be no argument as to who was the greatest all-rounder between the wars.

After this marvellous initiation, Allen was to have famous days in the biggest cricket; and if they were rarer, they were certainly of more serious importance. He captained England against the Indian team that visited us in 1936, took more wickets than anyone else in the Test Matches, and virtually won the low-scoring game at Lord's by taking 10 for 78 in the two innings. In this game not even Merchant could oppose a confident bat to his spitfire attack.

At the very end of his career it fell to him to captain the weak touring England side in the games against a West Indies team suddenly enriched to the multi-millionaire class by the arrival on the scene of Worrell, Weekes and others. Allen could do little to stem the avalanche of disaster emptied upon his team; but at the age of forty-five he batted and bowled better than many a young player upon whose future our hopes were firmly fixed.

So much for the embroideries; the main theme was, of course, the cricket he played for England against the land of his birth. In all, he appeared in a dozen Tests against Australia; and repeatedly did well in them, rarely as intended. For example, in his very first Test, the Lord's game of 1930, it was hoped that his fast bowling would unsettle Bradman early in his innings. But Bradman stuck around and made 254; and Allen's bowling analysis was a record of failure. Nevertheless in the second innings, when our need was most desperate, he reached his greatest heights as a batsman. When he came in, fifth wicket down, defeat by an innings seemed certain. Chapman, slashing whirlwind drives all round the outfield, and Allen, cutting Wall like a nineteenth-century master and driving Grimmett imperiously, added 126 runs; and for an hour made us see a lost cause in the rosy light of optimism. When Grimmett at last whipped a ball past Allen's broad blade, the game was lost: he was as important a bastion in our defence as that. But 57 runs for a side struggling against defeat was not enough to earn him an invitation to Lord's, Manchester or the Oval. England lost the Ashes without further help from G. O. Allen.

He reappeared in D. R. Jardine's team which won as many Test Matches as any touring side England has ever sent to Australia. Allen was, I should say, much less fast than Larwood during that tour; but a little faster than Voce. Unlike Larwood, he did not bowl to a packed on-side field. Unlike Voce, he did not bowl bumpers which must have intimidated many a highly strung if mahogany-faced Cornstalk. He came up from square leg to bowl as first change, and gave the batsmen little peace with well pitched-up tearaway stuff directed at the stumps. In the First Test, possibly in the ecstasy of relaxation that they no longer had the main assault opposed to them, Australian batsmen hit him with abandon; but at Melbourne he took four fine wickets cheaply enough; at Adelaide he was the bowler of the match; and at Brisbane, with the help of some good slip fielding, he did as much as anyone except Larwood and Paynter to turn a close game England's way.

He did not, during this tour, have any major successes with the bat but in the low-scoring Melbourne Test he scattered the attacking field, clustering in the shadow of the bat, before dying a hero's death in the attempt to hit O'Reilly off his length. In the final Test, he alone gave body to the second half of the English batting—which but for him was all tail.

After that there were appearances in 1934 against Woodfull's team at Manchester and the Oval. During that summer he was never a really fit man, owing to an operation he had in the middle of March. In the first game he was picked as a bowler, sent in ninth, helped Verity to add 95 runs off Wall, Grimmett and O'Reilly, and was finally bowled for 61 by an innocuous ball from McCabe. In the final game he made adequate scores by our pitiful standard, and, while taking wickets, was no worse bludgeoned and bastinadoed by Bradman and Ponsford than any of the rest of our so-called attack.

And so to Australia, as captain of the team that sailed in 1936 to try to win the Ashes and at the same time endear itself to an Australian public still smarting from the last invasion. It wasn't, to be frank, the strongest team ever to sail from England. It lacked Sutcliffe, Paynter and Bowes; the first named, in particular, to be needed before the tour was over. The side was short of a senior batsman to support Hammond and Leyland. As things were, the batting was the most untrustworthy feature of the team: a queer thing when you reflect that there were men like Ames and Hardstaff, Barnett and Wyatt in the side, besides our two giants.

Whatever the Australian press may have thought of the team while still invested with mystery on the high seas, when its weaknesses were exposed as early as Melbourne, it made up its mind to be tolerant to the point of generosity. It was clear that a side which couldn't hold its own with State sides was not worth being ungenerous about. At Adelaide, Ward had reduced the batting to baffled ineptitude: he might have been Merlin, or he might have been Grimmett. At Sydney, Mudge and Chipperfield set men groping blindly who had spent the summer playing Freeman as if with a broomstick. So far, so bad: but worse was to follow. In Brisbane, the Queensland player Allen emitted a battery of sluggish donkey-drops which routed the England batsmen like so much mortar fire.

By the time the First Test was reached you could have written your own ticket about Allen's chances in that game. No objective Australian cricket writer (assuming for the moment such a prodigy to have been possible) would admit that England had the bowling to cope with Bradman, McCabe, swart "Jack" Badcock, Robinson and Fingleton. As for the bowling, well, McCormick was going to prove himself another Larwood during this tour; Sievers had staggered humanity in a match at Melbourne; Ward's gigantic leg-break had displaced Grimmett from the Australian attack—and there was also O'Reilly. You couldn't expect a hard-fought match under equal conditions.

It is possible that only journalists are self-hypnotized by the predictions they naïvely pronounce as the result of a myopic study of form. *Because* a side has done very badly before a Test Match, it cannot be taken as certain that they will do badly in the big game. *Because* batsmen have been getting out to leg-breaker X is a very good reason for supposing that in the critical contest they will get out to fast bowler Y; and X will return an analysis of 0 for 147. Certainly the unanimous prophecies of disaster cast forth by the Australian press left Allen in a condition untroubled by hope. All he had to do was pick a team and play a game of cricket—he had nothing to lose, for he had obviously lost already.

The first thing was to pick a team. The selectors met round the dinner-table: R. W. V. Robins, Hammond, Leyland, Ames and Allen himself. Generally the question on such occasions is—who can be left out? Somebody suggests McChampion, and the murmur goes round, "You *can't* leave *him* out"; but after a good many others as illustrious have been greeted with similar acclaim, McChampion finds himself twelfth man in tomorrow's *Times*. This time there were no murmurs of "You *can't* leave him out." The only question was, whom could you possibly put *in*? Somebody suggested Arthur Fagg. Now Fagg, a beautiful player, was manifestly out of touch; and the immediate reaction to his name was the scornful comment: "Fagg! Pick him, and I'll tell you what you'll get from him—thirty-one runs in the match."

Damning enough, you'd have thought; but Allen burst in with: "Do you think so—do you *really* think he'll make thirty-one runs? Let's pick him at once!"

So Fagg was picked—to score four in the first innings, and 27 in the second.

Then there arose the question of the opening pair of bowlers. With the batting as faltering as it was, there remained room for only two of the three fast bowlers on the strength. Allen was one of those two. Who was to be the other: Farnes or Voce? Four voices immediately spoke up for Farnes. Allen alone championed Voce. But why? *Why*? Farnes was the obvious man, the arrowy Farnes with the fine flash off the wicket. Not Voce—a shadow of Larwood's famous partner of four years earlier. Then Allen put his point. At that stage in his career, Fames was a sensitive soul who was apt to become erratic if someone got after him. "I myself am another of the same type," he added, "and two of us would be one too many." The point was chewed on. Then Walter Robins nodded. He was convinced, he said; and one after another the remaining selectors were won round.

At last the team was chosen to take the field on a blazing December day on the khaki Woolloongabba ground relieved by a patch of purple bougainvillaea on a small house opposite the press-box and the Queensland flag hanging limply on a sweating flag-pole. I am not likely to forget the opening of this melodramatic match, the first Test I ever reported. I had settled myself in my seat with every hope of sitting in quaking inaction till the lunch interval. The *Sydney Morning Herald* expected nothing from me until six p.m., by which time the score, in this timeless Test, would probably stand at 105 for 4 wickets, and I should have a good enough lunch to be able to cope with the situation. There would be nothing to worry about for a couple of hours. The protagonists would just be sparring for an opening, like ... like, and as my mind groped about for a comparison, McCormick bowled the first ball of the match,

Worthington scooped the ignoble long-hop above his head—and Oldfield dived forward to clasp his eager gloves over the catch. Yes ... that was it: the protagonists sparring for an opening like— *Carpentier and Beckett.*

Well, I was shocked out of my nervousness now. I sharpened an expectant pencil; the while Barnett jauntily cut the fast bowler off his stumps to the boundary. Yes, there was my pencil—it had a point to it at last. And just in time too; for there went Fagg, flicking a leg-glide that the wicket-keeper floated out to skim clear of the grass with the speed and grace of a seagull taking a flying-fish above the foam.

Two gone for a handful: and here came Hammond. The Old Master advancing on the wicket, invincible, unperturbed. The rest of our wickets might tumble like ninepins, but Hammond would tower above the tempest, an unbowed oak. The Old Guard, the centurion of the Tenth Legion, was divinely ordained to score 200 hall-marked runs on an occasion of this sort. How often with Chapman's team had the game been swung England's way by that impregnable defence, gradually giving way to majestic cover-drives and gracefully sturdy cuts through the helpless slips. And here Hammond stood, taking guard, the Oxford blue sky above him; around him Brisbane in its shirt-sleeves, with crumpled and knotted handkerchiefs shielding sweating scalps and napes. He conveyed the sense of calm dominance of a British battleship flying the Admiral's pennant in some potty little foreign port which had the impertinence to imagine itself to be in a state of unrest. Up tore that gangling anarchist, the young McCormick. Round he wheeled at the wicket, and down came his bomb. And Hammond—invincible Hammond—poked his bat gently forward, lobbing the ball in the hands of an incredulous silly mid-on. The battleship was sunk without trace: there was but a bubble left, and that appeared on the scoreboard. Anarchy had triumphed. Three out for twenty runs.

Australia's triumph was short-lived. McCormick, who had taken all three wickets and who was bowling with peerless aggressiveness, suddenly was seen to limp off the field. A wrenched leg muscle was to cost his side dear: for he, and he alone, could consolidate this early advantage, could push home the little collapse into a full-scale rout.

And as McCormick, the Demon King, departed, the spotlight settled on the forces of law and order—or were they the broker's men? Barnett and Leyland endured in their vastly different ways. To me, Barnett always appeared out of place in timeless Test cricket. When he strode out to the wicket (and he *did* stride, as Hammond marched and Leyland waddled), cheerfulness kept breaking in. There he went now, lashing out with his niblick to loft Frank Ward into the crowd for six. Barnett could be as Elizabethan as he chose, but Leyland remained sternly Roman. His defence was on the lines of a very old hand who isn't going to be hustled into committing himself by the most nosy cross-examination. O'Reilly plugged away, never losing his length, never allowing relaxation to his attacking field, crouched around the crease and straightening themselves like a drill squad after every ball. At the other end was Ward. His leg-break wriggled across the wicket, hissingly quick as a rattlesnake; but he lacked Grimmett's subtlety.

Against them, Barnett throve and bloomed: and stolid Leyland stood fast. Now and then a shorter ball would be thumped through the outfield; now and then a ball wide of the leg stump would be whisked around the corner with a deft application of those deceptively fine-sprung wrists. His runs stole up on tip-toe, till he had put behind him the most priceless if the least glittering of all his Test Match centuries. It was better than a captain's innings: it was the innings of a senior pro.

The partnership, by the standard of this game grandiose indeed, survived until all thoughts of a nightmare collapse were effectively banished. And when Barnett had flicked the ball into Oldfield's gloves and Ward had spun a big break under Leyland's imperceptibly raised bat, the rest of the side showed form it had never reached in the games against the States. Hardstaff, academic rather than classical, made run-getting look hard, but stubbornly stayed on to prove that it was not impossible. Robins made light of all the rules and hit impudently all round the wicket. Occasionally the strokes went one way, the ball another. Finally Allen batted like a captain who has gained squatting rights and doesn't propose to lose them for less than a writ of eviction.

O'Reilly's unflagging bowling never gave any batsman on the side an over's tranquillity. With McCormick out of the battle-line, half the attack fell on to his broad shoulders. He became opening bowler and first change, and revelled in both rôles. Ward was disappointing after his brilliant success at Adelaide, and neither Sievers nor Chipperfield looked like a Test Match bowler at all.

The Australian fielding had the galvanized alertness that distinguishes it from all other fielding; it is like first-class ballet in contrast with the dancing troupe recruited for the end of term entertainment at the local Academy for the Daughters of Gentlewomen.

The second day was largely given up to Australia's reply. The side should have built up a lead but the batsmen lacked nerve and courage, and the English bowling was quick to take advantage of the tentativeness of their performance. Thick-set "Jack" Badcock, whose bat always seemed to me only less heavy than Ponsford's gigantic timber, hooked once too often at Allen before his falcon's eye was in. His leg stump measured its length against the ground, like the victim of a firing-squad.

And then came Bradman.

For once he advanced to the wicket in quick-step, like a relieving unit of Light Infantrymen. He gave beady glances to the leg boundary where Leyland chewed a meditative blade of grass; to Voce, Verity and Hammond in the slips; and to Joe Hardstaff, handsome as a wax figure in Messrs. Lillywhite's sportswear department, at cover-point. Then, still in quick-time, he went to work. He drove Allen surely, perhaps cocksurely; he cut a short ball past third man with leisurely, disdainful brilliance, like a conjurer explaining his tricks at the school treat. Verity slowed him down with a series of overs which had the testing subtlety of so many Brains Trusts; and perhaps in a moment of relief at no longer having to face this ruthless cross-examiner, Bradman flicked at a tearaway out-swinger from Voce, and Worthington swung round as if by reflex action to adhere to the catch.

The crowd, which had cheered Bradman all the way to the middle, now fell strangely silent. *Was visions about?* Was the side about to fold itself up like a beaten team, now that the champion was gone? Not, every man told his neighbour, while "Napper" McCabe and Jack Fingleton enjoyed rude health. McCabe rollicked like a tar on leave. He was man enough to play a pugnacious straight drive off his back foot that was already a red blur when Voce dived for it in vain. He made fierce sweeps to leg off Robins, rolling them down as if getting the stiffness out of his shoulders at the first net of the season.

And while McCabe blazed with pyrotechnic brilliance, the small flickering flame of Fingleton's genius burned on unquenchable. A gust from Allen would blow it one way, the strong streaming current of Voce's attack would waft it the other, but the little flame lifted its head and burned on. His defence, owing little to footwork, much to keenness of eyesight, was unruffled by change of pace or by the crowding in of the vultures of a belligerent field. The runs were apt to come off the two edges of his bat, but they came. Now and then they trickled or streaked through the slips; now and then there was a pat to long leg; now and then a notable off-drive sprang away from his bat. There were no chances; and only Voce, bowling like a war-horse that has sniffed powder, kept the batsman at bay. But in the end, Voce grew tired, and had to be taken off at a time when a new ball became due. He was not done with before he had forced McCabe to mis-hit him into Barnett's hands; and after that, Verity sent a quick spinner under Fingleton's bat into his stumps.

Thereupon the side crumpled up as if white ants had penetrated to its foundations. R. Robinson, reputed to be a finer stroke-player than Bradman himself, havered against Voce and was comfortably pouched by Hammond at slip. At the innings' end the batsmen found no defence against the fast bowlers. The last seven batsmen made but 27 runs between them. On figures you would have thought that Voce had looked a better bowler than O'Reilly had been, which is only one more proof of the untrustworthiness of "those damned dots".

The incredible statistical fact that it did not take a statistician to appreciate was that England—the side that didn't equal a top State team—was leading Australia by 124 runs on the first innings. The second half of the game began with the crowd prepared for anything.

The wicket was breaking up. It wasn't (and indeed I don't think it ever became) a really malevolent wicket, but the breaks of Frank Ward came off the pitch with an extra flip now, and spun across with greater zest than in the first act of the tragicomedy. The English batting was, by turns, sombrely defiant and hopefully madcap. Ward had Hammond in difficulties from the first. The great batsman never relaxed his concentration, but ball by ball he found himself forced back on to his citadel, and finally—with the air of a chess player who resigns rather than face the indignity of being check-mated—he actually retreated into his stumps.

Leyland faced the problem in a different mood. He began by covering up behind pads that almost hid him from the umpire; then, when he had laid the foundations of a grand defensive innings, he stepped forth recklessly and started to hit against the break. There was only one end to such behaviour, and Leyland suffered it.

Five batsmen were gone for 122 when Allen came in with the destiny of the game in his hands. If he failed now, the side would be out for 150; Australia's morale would be high; a good start might be made to their second innings overnight and England stood to lose the match after all. But Allen did not fail. He wasn't afraid of the widest leg-breaker in Christendom, and he wasn't afraid to use his own feet in a good cause. He jumped down the wicket and flayed Ward into a deserted out-field. The next ball had a subtle variation of flight; but Allen was quick enough to play a chopping defensive stroke and scramble back to his crease in time. He managed to make O'Reilly look like a bowler whose obvious mission was merely to keep the runs down. He punished Chipperfield severely for his presumption in bowling in a Test Match.

The senior batsmen had all the advantages that experience and polished technique can provide; but Allen had something more— the passionate determination to hold his end up, and to hit up runs until they got him out. You have seen a newcomer to a school team play that sort of cricket, and win the match, a place in the side, and the respect of everyone from the Head downwards for a newly revealed strength of character. Well, this was just that sort of human achievement, with the moral obstacles increased tenfold by the importance of the occasion and the determination of the skilful opposition. The hard-driving innings of 68 was a greater achievement than Hammond's double century at Sydney in the following match; and *that* was a match-winning innings if ever there was one.

Nevertheless when Sievers polished off the English tail there were not wanting experts in the press-box who were ready to explain to you that Australia would make the 381 needed for victory, the England team being so sadly deficient in spinners.

I remember a Lynn-Walls farce set in a haunted house where the intrepid heroes set out to restore peace and quiet with a duck-gun, though one of them remarks dubiously, "Personally, I don't think this trouble is caused by ducks." In the last innings of this match spin-bowlers were to prove as unnecessary a piece of artillery as that duck-gun.

The innings began in a twilight even a Celtic poet would have boggled at. Why Fingleton and Badcock consented to bat under such conditions I cannot conceive: I know full well what Sidney

Barnes would have done about it. Against Allen and Voce, the Australian opening pair, who must have played by ear, were at once seen to be helplessly out of touch. They got through Allen's first over somehow, but Fingleton's defensive spar at Voce's first ball appeared from the press-box to coincide with the crash of his leg stump. That was that. A few minutes later the players found their way back to the pavilion.

There was a storm in the night, and brilliant sun next morning: yet the wicket, though presenting real difficulty, was less than the gluepot Melbourne would have greeted us with. Allen bowled the first over and he did so only because Voce had finished off the previous day's play, and wanted to be switched to the other end. His kind captain having self-sacrificingly put himself on as stand-in for one over, sent his first ball whipping up past the batsman's chin; while his second veered away from the off stump, found the edge of Badcock's bat, and came to rest between Fagg's palms at slip.

Once again, Bradman!

Wasn't it his turn to save his side on a rain-affected pitch? All of us invariably said that he couldn't do it on this sort of wicket; all of us except Hedley Verity. Hedley used to vow that Bradman *could* bat under these conditions, and here was Don's chance to prove that Hedley was right. But from his nerveless bat came a feeble flicker and the ball rose in a gentle parabola to slip again: this time to Fagg's unfaltering right hand.

Three out; and each man for a duck.

If you had been stricken blind at that moment you could have described the sort of innings McCabe was bound to play in the circumstances. He came out with Napoleonic chin up, and with a glint of defiance in his eye. There came a hectoring hook, and—while Leyland tossed the ball up as cheerfully as if it were a Westminster School pancake—he came in out of the nightmare from which he could soon hope to wake.

Incredible to learn, fifteen years later, that Gubby had only bowled that opening over on the last day to enable Voce to change ends! And that he had only bowled a *second* over because he had got two wickets in the first. And only when a wicket fell in that over too did he decide to keep himself on. It was a wise decision. With the great gone, there came a cheerful innings from Chipperfield, and from Oldfield a few text-book strokes (like suitably pious last words from a public figure); and Allen and Voce brought the innings to a close.

The team that had no chance at all, the team that you could write your own ticket about, had won by 322 runs. Never again consult the form book when deciding who is to win a cricket match! And never again suggest to me that Australians (of that era at least) know as much as a respectable northern county side about batting on a rain-damaged wicket.

As the Englishmen return to the pavilion, Hammond and Ames gently shepherd Allen and Voce to the front to receive the applause that an upstanding pavilion tenders them. The rain had helped, but these two men (not forgetting that dogged century of Leyland's) had won the match for England. And, if one hero must be exalted above the other, Allen is the man of the match. The second innings of both sides had been dominated by him. His 68 on an uneasy wicket was the one attacking innings played for England; and the two overs he bowled as a stand-in, ridding us as they did of Badcock, Bradman and McCabe, clinched the game for his dazed and revitalized team.

From *Games of a Lifetime, 1953*

Placing that 500–1 bet on an England win when they were following on at Headingley in 1981 has haunted Rod Marsh and Dennis Lillee ever since. The asinine debate that followed about match-fixing and whether it was done to throw the game has been a ludicrous waste of everyone's time. I know both of them well and the thought of either of them involving themselves, intentionally or otherwise, in any sort of underhand business is ridiculous. This was not, even remotely, about match-fixing and yet there are people who still insist on harking back to it. The simple truth is that both of them liked a punt and on seeing the odds (which were never meant to be taken seriously) they couldn't resist it. The story of those magical days at Headingley is extraordinary enough as it is without trotting out ridiculous conspiracy theories; the saga of the bet was just a (small) part of what was one of the most remarkable matches in the history of the game. Marsh and Lillee are as straight as a die and deserve better. That is why I have chosen this piece.

ROD MARSH AND DENNIS LILLEE

Rob Steen

The bet

*'I don't bet on cricket. Is somebody
having a go just because we lost?'*

The statement was clear enough. Dennis Lillee was letting it be known in typically forthright fashion that no way would he have a plunge on the game. Only trouble was, he had and a lot of people knew it.

Two days after England's win at Headingley, the *Sun* splashed the story on its front page: 'Mystery of Aussie Bets Coup'. Next to photographs of Kim Hughes and Lillee, the story ran: 'Two Australian cricket stars allegedly netted £7500 between them yesterday by backing England to win the Headingley Test. The two players made their bets on Saturday when Ladbrokes offered 500–1 odds against an England victory. One put £10 on an Australian defeat and another put on £5.'

Australian manager Fred Bennett was quoted saying: 'I spoke to the entire team about it. It was emphatically denied by all the players. There is no law about betting in cricket. But I would certainly be concerned if this had been done because of the damage it could do to the image of the game.'

Unfortunately, a few column inches above he was contradicted by a Hughes quote which ran: 'Two of the lads gambled – not because they want to bet against their team, but because the odds were too good to miss.'

Lillee's angry denial followed. The Aussie fast bowler was to keep schtum about the bet until his retirement a few years later. His admission in a book that he had taken up the 500–1 odds greatly upset the other punter – his long-time mate Rod Marsh, who had hoped the allegations would be quietly forgotten. Twenty years later, he's still having to talk about it.

That a £15 bet would still be discussed in the next millennium would have seemed ridiculous to Marsh, Lillee and their team-mates back in 1981. But when they arrived at Headingley on the Tuesday before the match, Australian eyes would have been eagerly scanning the ground for the Ladbrokes marquee.

With betting unknown on Australian cricket grounds, many of the touring press and players were drawn to the red candy-striped tent like bees to a honeypot. Most money went on the horses of course, but a favourite bet with the press was on Marsh to be highest scorer with some attractive odds set by former Kent and England wicketkeeper Godfrey Evans and Ladbrokes director Ron Pollard. Marsh told the newspaper boys they would get lucky soon, but was never able to deliver.

'It's part of the tradition of the Headingley game to have a Ladbrokes tent between the Western Terrace and the main stand,' says Yorkshire CCC secretary David Ryder. 'It's principally to take betting on the racing, the cricket's just an extra.'

It was late on the Saturday of the Headingley Test, after play had been halted for bad light, that the 500–1 odds were first posted – and not during the Monday lunch or tea break as is often claimed. 'We were absolutely certain we could not lose after England had to follow on. After all, no team has won from that situation since 1894,' Pollard told the *Sun*. Ladbrokes eventually paid out winnings of £40,000 on bets totalling just £25,000.

The odds set, they were chalked up on the blackboard outside the Ladbrokes tent. 'Somebody told the electronic scoreboard operator,' remembers Ryder, 'and he decided to put it up – to give everyone a laugh I suppose, a bit of black humour.'

Australian squad member Dirk Wellham saw the odds flash up. 'I can remember the whizzbang electronic scoreboard's tongue-in-cheek offering of 500–1 against England. I can even recall the crowd's spontaneous murmur of amusement at the sight of the board's message on that murky afternoon.

'As the light continued to fade and it was more certain that play would be over for the day, we relaxed in the first-floor dressing room, hearing the crowd meandering about below, muttering unhappily about the plight of English cricket.

'The black scoreboard stared at us from the opposite side of the field. In the brand new bright yellow dots, the Ladbrokes odds on the result of the Test were dramatically revealed for all who cared to revel in the plight of the English.'

Wellham claims that the cricketers from Western Australia, particularly Lillee, Marsh and Hughes – who were 'not so enthused by the conservative approach of those from the hypocritically corrupt eastern states' – found the 500–1 odds very interesting indeed. 'The odds were openly discussed in a light-hearted tone, as cricketers do when they are in England, touring, waiting for the weather to clear. It was just a joke, some relief at the end of a satisfying conclusion to a good day's toil. No one took the comments seriously. It was just a joke at England's expense.'

The timing of what happened next is not clear. It is possible – as suggested by the report in the *Sun* – that the Lillee/Marsh bet was placed during the brief resumption of play at 5 o'clock on the Saturday evening with England 0–1 in their second innings. However, Lillee himself and some of his team-mates seem to remember it happening on the Monday lunchtime with England still 149 runs behind and only six wickets left. Others claim the punt took place at tea, with Botham warming up but England dead and buried at 176–7. Speaking in 2000, Lillee claims to have 'sat down and thought about it' before placing the bet.

Many recall, as you have read, seeing the 500–1 being displayed on the scoreboard during Monday and believe that bets were still being taken by Ladbrokes at those odds. However, on *Test Match Special* Henry Blofeld began that morning's commentary by suggesting the odds against an England victory had been revised down to 200–1. What is clear is that Lillee concluded that he could not pass up 'the chance of a lifetime', even one supplied by 'such stupid odds'. Lillee declared that he was going to bet £50 of the team fund on England to win at 500–1. Marsh snatched the money away. The other players laughed, told Lillee he was mad and suggested he put the money behind the bar during the inevitable Aussie victory celebrations.

According to Allan Border that was the final straw for Lillee. He said that he was going to bet £10 of his own money and the rest could do as they liked. 'It was an instinctive and impulsive reaction – he couldn't resist it,' claims ex-*Daily Star* writer and close friend Ted Corbett. 'Dennis thrills at all forms of sport and loves a bet. Probably his best friend in England is Charles Benson, the *Daily Express* horse racing tipster.'

As it became obvious that Lillee was serious there was some half-hearted fumbling in pockets. 'Lots of guys threw in their small change,' remembers Peter Philpott. 'I think I threw in a couple of bob myself. Everyone was killing themselves laughing.'

'I actually looked in the pockets of my trousers hanging on the peg behind me in the search of money,' recalls Geoff Lawson, 'but I came up empty and my wallet was locked away in the valuables bag. As a poor uni student I could have paid my fees and rent for the rest of the year had I found some loose change.'

Ray Bright too resisted the urge to chip in. 'Initially I was going to bet £2,' he says, 'but I thought about the lager I could buy instead and left it.'

John Dyson was more adamant. 'Dennis said, "Have a quid on it." I said I didn't want to waste the money and didn't think any more about it.'

Lillee was keenest of all that his mate Marsh should join him in the bet. 'Have a fiver on it, Bacchus, just to be with me,' he pleaded, but Marsh was having none of it.

Then came the question of who should place the bet. Lillee handed over his tenner – he did not bother with the loose change – to the Australian coach driver Peter Tribe. Tribe, or 'Geezer', as most of the Aussies called him, was a streetwise guy. He soon became an integral part of the squad and the person they turned to when they needed a favour.

Play then restarted and the Aussies returned to the field. Just as they were walking out to the middle, Marsh spotted Tribe walking round the boundary towards the Ladbrokes tent and changed his mind. 'Geezer,' he shouted and raised five fingers to indicate his stake. Tribe shook his head, as if to tell Marsh not to waste his money, and continued on. 'Geezer,' shouted Marsh again and then, as Tribe turned around, he waved his five fingers a second time before clenching his hand into a fist in mock anger to suggest what would happen if the bet was not placed.

Tribe nodded and set off, but again he thought how ridiculous the whole idea was and headed back to the dressing room, planning to return Lillee's money. Nearly there, he changed his mind for the last time. 'I've heard of these things happening, so I'd better not take the risk,' he thought, and turned around for the final time.

A man who knows both Australian punters well on and off the field, David Gower, is not surprised that Marsh eventually caved in to temptation:

'Marsh and Lillee would have a punt on the Martians landing if they had got [those] odds. They've had a few bets on horses that barely answered to the description.'

In fact, Ladbrokes had just offered an American woman 500–1 against aliens landing on Earth.

When they got back to the dressing room, the two Australians received confirmation that their bet had been placed. 'Lillee was standing at the top of the stairs,' remembers Headingley grounds-man Keith Boyce. 'He was grinning and holding up both hands, fingers outstretched. Marsh was at the bottom, nodding and holding up one hand.'

But while Lillee and Marsh had got their money down, one England player had failed in his attempt. Bob Taylor was the unlucky man. 'During the Monday lunch break I was in the players' dining room with Mike Gatting and physio Bernard Thomas. Gatting, who was just out, was sulking [he was less than happy with his lbw decision]. Most of the Aussies were there as well. I was sat with my back to the ground, facing the Aussies' table. All of a sudden, the Aussies started laughing and pointing towards the ground. I turned round to see the scoreboard showing the 500–1 odds against us. I got my head down again but they kept pointing – I thought they'd mistakenly added a nought.

'I turned to Gatt and said: "See that? Good odds for a two-horse race, eh?" I asked him if he wanted a bet but he was too fed up. I nipped upstairs to the dressing room to get some cash. I offered the information about the odds to the other England lads, but they were too disappointed with their efforts to bother. That didn't put me off and I rushed downstairs to get the bet placed. As I walked out of the door, I ran into a swarm of children. There always seems to be more autograph-hunters at Headingley than at any other ground and I was besieged right away. I signed a few and yet the swarm began to increase. By this time the resumption of play was just ten minutes away and I still had to get to the other side of the ground. Yet I couldn't get away and was conscious that, if I walked away, I would get the usual subtle Yorkshire reaction of, "Hey, bighead, David Bairstow always signs, you know!" I was next but one man in and had to be padded up as the players walked out, so I had to give up and sign the rest of the autographs. I thought no more of it until the following afternoon when Australia's last pair were at the wicket. Then I turned around and, for the first time that day, my concentration was broken by the sight of the Ladbrokes marquee. I thought, "I could've won £1000". The irony was that those kids probably had my autograph many times over.'

Again, although Taylor remembers the events happening on Monday, they could have taken place on Saturday. Gatting was out in controversial circumstance on that day as well, with not everyone agreeing with the umpire that the ball hit his bat after colliding with his pad. Taylor was also the team's designated nightwatchman and therefore would have to be padded up as Brearley and Boycott returned to the crease.

Two other equally distinguished cricketers also believe they lost out on making a killing. 'Ted Dexter and I were in the habit of checking the racehorse fields each morning,' remembers Richie Benaud, 'and then leaving a note for Godfrey Evans when he came upstairs to the commentary box, as he did every day of a match, with a couple of Ladbrokes' pink slips. Ted and I decided that whichever of us was not on TV first would take the 500–1 on the fourth morning for a tenner each, just for the sake of not allowing something to run unbacked at that price in a two-horse race.' Unfortunately for Dexter and Benaud, Evans and Pollard had already left Headingley, thinking the match would finish that day. 'It was a good lesson for me never to bet on anything that can talk,' Benaud concludes.

News of the Lillee/Marsh bet began to leak out almost straight away. 'I was talking to Denis Compton,' says Frank Crook, then reporting for the Australian *Sun*, 'and he said he had heard a whisper that a couple of players had taken the 500–1 odds.'

Word reached the England dressing room, though Graham Dilley for one was not impressed: 'I remember thinking, "what a waste of money that is".' Gower, however, reckons that such experienced, if compulsive, punters knew, or thought they knew, that they were throwing their money away. 'As the England team at the time bore more resemblance to a donkey than a racehorse, they could scarcely have imagined that they would collect.'

The story reached the press the day after the match. 'I was driving home from Leeds when the sports editor called to say they'd had a tip-off that two Aussie cricketers had taken the 500–1 odds,' remembers Steve Whiting, then the cricket correspondent for the London *Sun*. 'Some guy in the Ladbrokes tent had heard Tribe laying the bet for Lillee. I spoke to Hughes and he confirmed the story.' Whiting then told Crook that he had the bet story and that it was going to run the next day. Crook had until 10 p.m. on the Wednesday to file a story of his own. As often happens on cricket tours when a big story breaks, the touring press gathered in a hotel room to talk it over. But to Crook's surprise, some of his colleagues thought there was nothing to talk about. 'I was astonished,' remembers Crook. 'I said: "If I file this story it'll be page one." And one bloke said: "Page One!? It won't even get a run at all." Then a guy from one of the Melbourne papers got a call from his sports editor asking him about the story and he said: "There's nothing in it, I'll give you a few paragraphs." By this time it's about 9.40. I excuse myself and go and write the story. Of course it's page one the next day.'

Brian Mossop, who was working for the *Sydney Morning Herald*, explains why most of the Aussie press corps did not share Crook's enthusiasm for the story. 'We thought it was a bit of a joke. Even after the story had appeared in the London *Sun*, we found it hard to take seriously. You just didn't think about bookies and betting then. Even the tour books didn't make much of it. We were pretty dismissive of the whole affair.'

So what happened to the Australian winnings? Lillee had won £5000 and Marsh £2500, which was a lot of money in 1981. If they'd wished, their cash could have bought Marsh a new Fiesta Popular, while Lillee could have had the latest Ford Capri shipped back to Perth. Back in the Antipodes, the money might even have bought a house.

Dirk Wellham remembers talk of Lillee giving some of his winnings to charity. Graham Yallop confirms that it did not go into the team fund, though the two West Australians were not allowed to be anything other than generous when it came to keeping their teammates' throats well-lubricated. It was this expected largesse which Crook thinks might explain why the defeated Australians, once they got back to the hotel, 'were in high spirits, with everybody chortling and laughing'. Interviewed by the BBC for its *Clash of the Titans* programme, Terry Alderman recollects that, in the gloom of defeat, 'things perked up' once the Aussies remembered the bet.

The next day Crook gave Alderman and a 'chirpy' Kim Hughes a lift to Edinburgh. 'What's the go on the betting?' asked Crook, only for Hughes to dismiss the story and claim that journalists had made up quotes from the Aussie players and management.

Lillee himself was treating the revelations very lightly. 'He revelled in the controversy, he didn't think he had done anything wrong,' remembers Corbett. 'His biggest concern was taking such a large sum of money out of the country.'

Geezer went to collect Lillee's and Marsh's winnings when the tourists played against Worcestershire just before the fourth Test – delivering it to the tourists' dressing room. The bus driver became one of the biggest beneficiaries of the bet. Marsh and Lillee used some of their winnings to buy Geezer a set of golf clubs. Later they flew him and his wife out to West Australia for a holiday.

So is there any possibility that the bet influenced Marsh and Lillee's efforts in the match? Few connected with the game think so. The *SMH*'s Mossop has an unshakeable belief in the two Aussie legends: 'A lot of people say that Lillee and Marsh played some part in the defeat because of the bet. I'll never believe that because I know they loved nothing better than beating the Poms.' Graeme Wood is more succinct, but just as sure. 'It was a bit of a joke that backfired, but it certainly didn't affect their performance,' he insists.

Others had doubts. Dilley, who was hardly in the most positive frame of mind, admits: 'I can remember wondering about the result and being typically English in not totally believing we'd won entirely through our own efforts. The bet just put an element of doubt in my mind, even though I knew nothing dodgy had happened.'

Certainly, you would be wise not to suggest anything 'dodgy' to Dennis Lillee's face. A few years later he claimed: 'I'd flatten anyone who ever suggested I threw a game. I have a completely clear conscience over the betting incident. I believe my integrity as far as playing to win every game I've played is unquestioned. I didn't regard it as betting against my team or my country. At no stage did any of the other players think there was anything wrong with taking the odds and betting against Australia, just that it would be stupid to throw the money away. I just thought odds of 500–1 were ridiculous for a two-horse race. I was prepared to risk £50 on the off-chance that I might get £25,000. The thing that irks me is that it was by no means the first time players had bet on the other team. I certainly wasn't the first, although I was the first to be crucified for it. I'd planned to have £50 on England. That I got cold feet about virtually throwing big money away and only made it a £10 wager is still a matter of regret to me. At the time we realised we'd won the money we felt a bit bad about it, but what could you do?'

Fifteen years later his views had not changed. In 2000 he told the *West Australian* newspaper: 'I have never lost a moment's sleep over it. You'd have to be very naïve to think anyone who knew what the result of a match was going to be would only bet £10 on it. If you knew the result you'd put your house on it.'

Marsh has always been much more tight-lipped about the bet. But, as head coach of Australia's ultra-successful Cricket Academy, he has had a hard time avoiding the subject. After lecturing his young charges on the dangers of match-fixing, he told the press: 'I have no conscience about that [the '81 bet], I have no problems about talking to anyone about that. That's something that happened, that's a fact of life. I had a five quid bet. I mean, big deal. Most Australians have done that.'

Few doubt Lillee's and Marsh's denials that the bet affected their performance, but Corbett believes the game's players, officials and fans were not, in any case, keen to think the unthinkable. 'So many people's perceptions of what's exciting, captivating and unpredictable about cricket stem from that game,' he says. 'That's why Lillee and Marsh got off lightly. It would be like finding that the Germans at Dunkirk didn't have any bullets. It would have destroyed the legend.'

It was almost exactly 16 years before Ladbrokes again offered 500–1 odds against an England victory. By a huge coincidence, their opponents were again Australia and the venue Headingley. England batted first and made 172, two fewer than in the '81 first innings. Australia again declared with nine wickets down, but this time added exactly 100 to their '81 score. England went in again, 329 runs behind and the 500–1 odds were posted. Nasser Hussain and John Crawley attempted a Botham/Dilley, adding 133 for the fifth wicket, but once their partnership was broken England crumbled to lose by an innings and 61 runs. Had any of the Australians fancied a punt they would have been taking a big risk. In the wake of the Lillee/Marsh bet a new clause was added to the contracts of all Australian players. It read: 'The player undertakes that he will not directly or indirectly bet on any match or series of matches in which he takes part.'

All bets, or so we thought, were off.

From *500–1: The Miracle of Headingley '81*, 2007

In 1981 Mike Brearley made a huge impact on English cricket. English cricket was in a mess: there had been the disastrous tour to the Caribbean; the debacle of Ian Botham's tenure as captain; and the Lord's Test against the Australians in which Botham had been dismissed for a pair and greeted in stony silence by MCC members as he passed through the pavilion. It had become clear that someone new would have to come in to lead the team. The challenge for a new captain would be to get the best out of an undroppable Botham, and Mike Brearley was the man to do it. Recalled to the side, Brearley was a man and a captain whom Botham respected: a great thinker about the game with a profound ability to understand the disparate personalities in the side and superb man-management skills. Australian fast bowler Rodney Hogg described Brearley as having a 'degree in people'. The extraordinary summer of cricket that was to follow has gone down in history and was, in large measure, due to Brearley's captaincy.

BOTHAM AND WILLIS

Mike Brearley

The captain may also have to pay attention to the role that a certain player has in a team. Roles may be restrictive or enabling. For instance, Willis had, in 1981, been the spearhead of England's attack for a decade. But during the previous two years there were periods when his ability to bowl fast appeared to be waning. At the same time, Graham Dilley had been emerging as a genuinely fast bowler, but he was still raw and had, in Willis's words, to be mothered and used mainly in short spells. Moreover, in 1980 and 1981 Ian Botham could be depended on less to bowl reliably and aggressively for long periods.

All these factors meant that, in the early part of the 1981 season, Bob was called upon to bowl more overs in a day than before. It was impossible for him to keep going flat out throughout. He had there-fore begun to aim more for accuracy than for speed. His role in the attack had gradually, and without explicit recognition, changed from that of the front-line strike bowler to being – partially at least – a stock bowler.

In the first innings of the Headingley Test Bob had bowled pretty well, but without taking a wicket. He had not reached maximum pace, partly for the reasons already mentioned, partly too because he was anxious about even more no-balls if he aimed for that final edge of speed. On the evening before the last day, when Botham's prodigious innings had given us an outside chance, we talked in the bar. Willis himself made the crucial suggestion that in the first innings we had been too concerned to bowl a good length and let the pitch 'do' the rest. Shouldn't we, and he in particular, bowl faster and straighter? I agreed. Graham Gooch underlined the point. 'Even Gatt is harder to bat against when he really runs in,' he said. I told Bob to forget about no-balls, the thought of which had made him hold back. On a pitch with such uneven bounce the harder the ball hits it the more devastating its variations will be. Moreover, bowling on the next day would be an all-or-nothing affair, a huge effort without thought of conservation of energy.

We were, in effect, restoring Bob's old role to him. The effect was spectacular – eight wickets for 43 runs, and a nailbiting win by 19 runs.

I should like to end this chapter by looking at this final, dramatic innings from my own point of view, as captain, to indicate the sorts of consideration that entered into my decisions.

The first question was, who should open the bowling? We had four seamers for the match, and in the first innings I had started with Willis and Old. Willis and Dilley had both preferred to come up the hill from the Football Stand End, with the wind slightly behind them, while Old and Botham wanted the other end. Such an amiable division is rare; as the match went on, and the wind veered, there was a time when all four were keen to bowl from the Kirkstall Lane End. At times a captain has to point out to his bowlers that someone has to bowl the other end, and that batsmen cannot choose theirs: but hills and winds do make a considerable difference. Running downhill, a bowler is liable to bowl no-balls, over-pitch and generally lose control. Running up the hill, on the other hand, a bowler may find himself under-pitching, straining to get to the crease and, especially if the wind too is against him, he may lose his fire.

By the last day of the match the wind and the bowlers' preferences were again as they had been on the first, but I chose to open with Dilley and Botham. I felt Dilley's batting (he had scored a brave 56) had lent him confidence. He had a high wicket-taking rate with the new ball. I also thought that if the match became tense it would be impossible to expect him to bowl his first spell when we had few runs to play with. I would give him two or three overs in which to click; if he didn't, I would bring Willis on early. The other choice was also influenced by what had happened so far. Botham's bowling, like his batting, had been transformed. If anyone could create a miracle it was he. As he took off his pads, undefeated on 149, I reminded him of our conversation before the match in which I had commiserated with him for the way in which he had been harassed and pursued by the media. I had added, half-joking, that he would probably score a century and take twelve wickets in the match! Now, almost a week later, I mentioned that he still owed us six wickets.

Well before we went on to the field, I told all four fast bowlers who would be starting. I made a brief exhortatory speech to the team before we went out. 'More aggression, more liveliness, more encouragement for the bowlers,' I said. '*They're* the ones who are nervous now.' I think I also said then what I had said at the end of the first day's play, when Australia were 210–3: 'On this pitch, a side could be bowled out for 90.'

Botham's first ball was a long-hop, his second a half-volley, and Graeme Wood hit both for four. In the third over, we had a stroke of luck; Wood misjudged a half-volley from Botham and edged to Taylor. Despite these three bad balls, Botham was bowling well, but without sharp movement or real pace. I was more worried about Dilley. His first two overs went for 11 runs. I decided to take him off. Moreover, he told me he was feeling a thigh strain. I sent him off to have Bernard Thomas, the team's physiotherapist, look at it. He was soon back on the field, strapped up, with the message that he could bowl through the injury if needed.

For the sixth over I gave the ball to Willis. He said, 'Faster and straighter, right?' I nodded. At once he bowled well, coming up the hill as he wished.

The wind should have helped Botham's outswing; in fact, the

ball was swinging little in the bright sunshine. Trevor Chappell and John Dyson struggled on, beaten from time to time, but nudging runs here and there. As we had decided before the innings began, we kept a third man and a fine-leg to stop the edges and deflections from going for too many runs over the fast outfield.

After he had bowled five overs, Willis said to me, 'Give me a go at the other end.' I had just replaced Botham with Old at that other end, hoping, probably vainly, that he might be able to swing the ball out. My reaction, playing for time, was, 'You mean you've had enough of coming uphill into the wind?' This acknowledged Bob's problem (the wind had again veered slightly) without committing myself. The response probably also expressed irritation that he should suddenly prefer the other end and thereby make my plans less clear-cut. Willis replied, grumpily, 'Okay, I'll carry on here then.'

During the next over, Old's second, I put Bob's question to Bob Taylor and Botham. They favoured giving Willis the choice of ends. Ian said, 'He's looked our most dangerous bowler.' I agreed. We must give Willis his head. I indicated as much by signalling to him down at fine-leg.

Someone had to bowl the next over from the Grandstand End. I was not keen to try Dilley again, as I feared that he might be expensive. Botham was a possibility, but he had not looked penetrative. Old was the more likely bet to bowl with Willis, but he could not bowl two consecutive overs. I decided to put Peter Willey on. Not only for want of anyone better: he had turned his off-breaks even on the first day, so he was bound to find some assistance from the pitch on the fifth. I felt, too, that neither Dyson nor Chappell would go on to the attack against him. Anxious about taking undue risks, they might give a catch to a close fielder, and even if not, two or three overs should not prove costly. This was almost certainly the last chance to see if Willey's spin looked capable of making a decisive contribution. (I still felt that we might miss John Emburey after all, whose omission from the twelve had been a difficult decision: but selection is not the issue at this stage in the book, nor was it a factor at this point in the match, so I will leave it until later.)

Willey bowled three overs. They did not look particularly dangerous, though the ball did turn. At least they cost only four runs. After them I reverted, with conviction, to Old.

Our Fast Bowler. 'Ain't you going to take off your glasses?'

Meanwhile, Bob was steaming in downhill. We reminded him not to worry about no-balls and encouraged him to keep harrying the batsmen as he was doing. At last his – and our – luck changed. First Willis bowled a perfect bouncer at Chappell who, hurriedly protecting his face, could only lob the ball up for Taylor to catch. Next over, Old twice hit Dyson painful blows on the hand as he pushed tentatively forward. There was nothing tentative about the bowling or the fielding now. Old, too, was bowling with more aggression than earlier in the match, and his contribution as the accurate, mean foil to Willis proved invaluable. Until Bright took 10 off his last over with a couple of slogs to leg he was hit for only 11 runs in the eight overs he bowled.

Willis summoned up all his energy for his last over before lunch. In four balls he took two wickets – those of Kim Hughes and Yallop. Once Hughes had gone, with the score 58–3, we knew we had a real chance. We roused Bob still further: he must surely fancy getting Yallop out this time. Yallop lasted just three balls, beautifully caught by Gatting at short-leg off a nasty, kicking delivery.

The score was 58–4. We lunched – in the dressing-room, at such a crucial stage – knowing that the odds must have come down from 500–1 to about 6–4.

We spent some time trying to predict how the remaining batsmen would play. Rod Marsh might well 'have a go'. In the first innings of the first Test, at Nottingham, on a similar pitch, he had slogged a quick 19 before being caught off a skier at long-leg. Geoff Lawson and Lillee too might have a swing (if we got down to them) especially if we pitched the ball up. Dyson, Allan Border, and Bright would probably 'graft' – that is, fight it out by orthodox batting. One thing was clear: we must keep running at them, and attacking.

It was also clear that, unless there was an unpredictable change, I should rely on Willis to bowl until the death from the top – Kirkstall Lane – end. There was also no difficulty in deciding to continue with Old, especially as Border was the next batsman; Old has always fancied left-handers.

In the event he soon bowled Border, for a duck, and Willis dismissed Dyson and Marsh in quick succession, the latter falling to another fine catch, this time by Dilley, a few feet in from the boundary at fine-leg: 74–7. Between overs Bob came up to tell me that umpire David Evans had told him not to bowl bouncers at Lawson. I was surprised. Lawson is a more than competent batsman – except against the bouncer. 'Forget it,' I retorted to Bob. 'But don't bother with an out-and-out bouncer at first; just short of length, rib-height.' Next over, with his very first ball at Lawson, Bob had him caught behind: 75–8.

Willis had taken six wickets in six overs, after bowling thirty-seven overs in the match without a single wicket. In fifty-eight minutes seven wickets had fallen for 19 runs, on a pitch playing little worse than in the first innings, when the same batsmen had amassed 401–9.

This extraordinary match still had an unnerving twist or two in its tail, and some awkward captaincy problems calling for quick decisions. Australia may have been 75–8; but they still needed only 55 to win. In four overs Lillee and Bright added 35. I have already mentioned Willis's block against bowling at his best to Lillee. Lillee is no mug with the bat, capable of shrewd improvisations as well as a resolute correctness. We soon saw that he had settled for unorthodoxy – a policy that was entirely justified by the conditions.

As soon as Willis dropped short Lillee stepped back and poked the ball high over me at first slip for four. I decided that we had to guard against that shot, so I took Gooch from third slip and put him at deep fly slip, behind second slip. Again Lillee made room to cut, this time beating Dilley at wide third-man: another four. Immediately Willis was forced to switch either his length or his line, or both. So Lillee deftly moved the other way, towards off-stump, and clipped the ball away to backward square-leg for three more runs. When he cut another four, and Bright connected with two solid, though risky blows to leg off Old we were suddenly back on the defensive, on the brink of defeat. This was the point at which Gatting helped us to dismiss Lillee. At this stage we could afford only two close catchers, both at slip. We had been forced to have two third-men, as well as a backward point and an extra-cover. And short-leg had gone back to backward square-leg, saving one. Now Lillee tried to play more conventionally – again a reasonable approach, as we had so few close fielders. He may have changed his mind when he saw the ball well pitched up, and decided too late to drive it.

Terry Alderman, the last man in, really is a moderate batsman. I was not in favour of wasting bouncers on him. But Bright had the strike, at the end of Willis's over. I took Old off and brought Botham back. This too seemed a straightforward decision. However well Old had bowled Bright had obviously got used to his action and had picked him up all too easily: a change was essential. Australia still needed 20 runs, so I decided to allow Bright a single at the beginning of the over, if he chose to take it. We could then bowl at Alderman. Bright accepted the single. I discussed fields with Ian. We agreed that we needed a mid-off, as Alderman's lunge forward might give him runs in this direction. We also needed a square-leg, rather than a short-leg, to cut off thick edges or nudges on the leg-side. We were left with only three close fielders. Two should be at slip. I was not sure if we could afford a third slip, as there would then be a wide open space backward of cover. I asked Botham which he preferred, third slip or gully. He wanted the extra slip; he was right. Agonisingly, two sharp chances went to Old in exactly that position, and he missed both. Perhaps it was as well that it was a Yorkshireman standing at third slip at that moment.

But a few moments later it was all over. Appropriately, Willis finished the match in a perfect, most emphatic way, clean bowling Bright middle - stump with a yorker. Australia were all out for 'Nelson' – 111. It was only the second time in Test history, and the first this century, that a side had won after following on.

From *The Art of Captaincy, 1985*

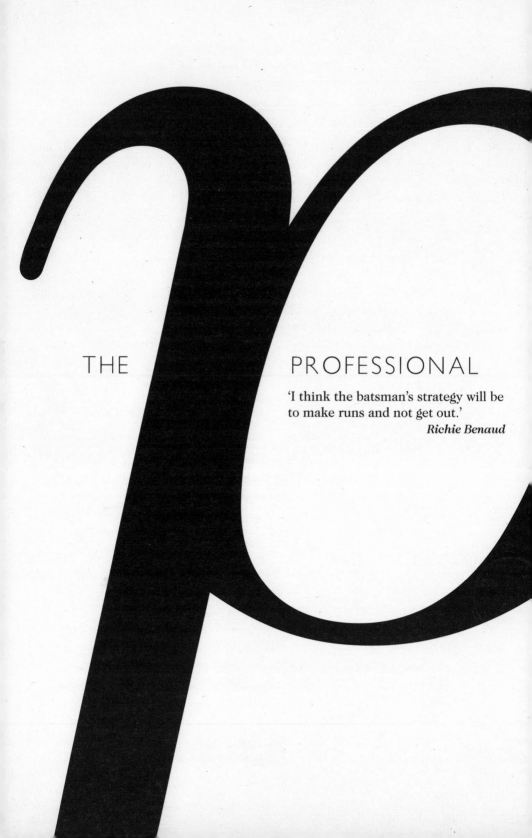

THE PROFESSIONAL

'I think the batsman's strategy will be to make runs and not get out.'

Richie Benaud

England on their way to winning the opening Test of the Bodyline tour of 1932–3 in Sydney by ten wickets. With Don Bradman missing due to illness, only a heroic innings of 187 not out by Stan McCabe in Australia's first innings countered the English use of 'fast leg theory'.

Australian batsman Bill Woodfull ducks a bouncer from Harold Larwood during the Fourth Test at Brisbane. With as many as six close catchers on the leg side, the controversial tactics may have worked but victory came at the expense of Anglo-Australian relations, which were seriously damaged for many years thereafter.

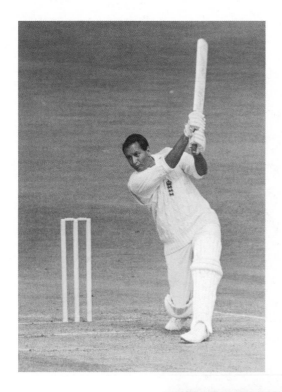

Basil D'Oliveira was a graceful all-rounder who represented England because he was barred from playing first-class cricket in his home country. He will be remembered not so much for the quality of his cricket but for the role he played in dismantling the hated apartheid regime in South Africa.

The dashing Henry Olonga was the first black cricketer to play for his country. His international career ended abruptly when he and his colleague Andy Flower, now England coach, were banned for life after they wore black armbands during the 2003 World Cup as a silent protest to 'mourn the death of democracy' in Zimbabwe.

Jeff Thomson was arguably one of the fastest bowlers who ever played. On the rock-hard Australian pitches of the time against batsmen who weren't wearing helmets, he was lethal. England captain Tony Greig gets a couple of runs off the bat handle during the Fourth Test in Sydney, 1975.

England captain Tony Greig had rashly promised to make the West Indian side 'grovel' ahead of the 1976 series. The result was a 3–0 pasting for the home team. Michael Holding gives England batsman Brian Close a bit of 'chin music' at Lord's. A steady succession of West Indian fast bowlers eventually led to a change in the Laws about the number of bouncers allowed per over.

Tony Greig (right) was Kerry Packer's recruiter in chief for the formation of World Series Cricket, which challenged the sport's establishment between 1977 and 1979. It took a High Court hearing in September 1977 to loosen the authorities' hold over the game. One of the beneficial effects it had was to ensure greater financial rewards for cricket as a whole.

'Pyjama cricket' as it was known at the time took a little while to catch on. The introduction of coloured clothing, night cricket and restricted field placings ultimately paved the way for the modern equivalent that is Twenty20.

Alec Stewart and Hansie Cronje toss up before the Second Test at Lord's in 1998. The South African captain's subsequent disgrace over match-fixing has cast doubt over some of the matches he played in, although there is no evidence this was one of them as South Africa won comfortably by ten wickets.

In 1998, Allan Donald of South Africa was the world's fastest bowler and he was convinced – as were most people in the ground – that Michael Atherton had nicked a catch to the keeper the ball before. Atherton was unmoved and went on to help England win the Fourth Test at Trent Bridge and ultimately take the series.

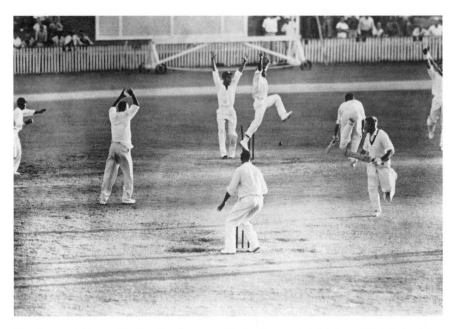

The frozen tableau signifies the first ever tie in Test match history. West Indies' Joe Solomon (out of shot) throws down the stumps from cover point and runs out Australia's Ian Meckiff by inches with just one ball of the final over from Wes Hall remaining.

If there is some dispute about the greatest Test match of all time, there is no debate about the greatest one-day match. Mark Boucher celebrates as South Africa chase down Australia's world-record score of 434 at the Wanderers Stadium in 2006. I was watching the match with increasing disbelief in a run-down hotel in Chandigarh, India.

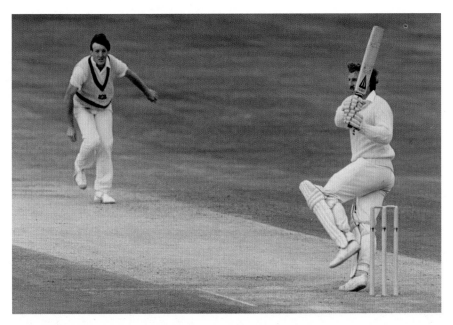

The 1981 Ashes was arguably the greatest Test series of all time. After stepping down as captain following defeat at Lord's, Ian Botham returned to form with a vengeance. He hooks Geoff Lawson to the boundary on the way to a match-winning innings of 149 not out at Headingley.

Australia still only needed 130 runs to win but wilted in the face of an inspired spell of fast bowling by Bob Willis, who took eight for 43. It was only the second time in Test history that a side following on had won.

The 1981 series went down in history as 'Botham's Ashes' but Mike Brearley's astute captaincy and man management had a lot to do with England's recovery and ultimate success against Australia.

The very next Ashes series produced another cliffhanger, this time in Melbourne. After putting on 70 runs for the final wicket with skipper Allan Border, Jeff Thomson falls to Ian Botham just three runs short of victory, caught on the rebound by Geoff Miller at second slip.

Australia again end up second best in a tight finish, this time against West Indies in 1993. Courtney Walsh celebrates a one-run victory in the Fourth Test in Adelaide as he dismisses Craig McDermott – controversially as it later transpired – following another brave last-wicket stand of 40 with fellow tailender Tim May that had taken Australia to the brink of victory.

Kepler Wessels leads out the South African team in Barbados for the one-off Test against West Indies in April 1992. It was South Africa's first Test match since their return to the sport following their suspension in 1970, and the first official Test match between the two teams.

Kenny Benjamin dismisses potential match-winner Andrew Hudson for 163 in the first innings. The stands were largely empty in protest at local favourite Anderson Cummins being left out. 'No Cummins, No Goins' was the memorable slogan that accompanied the boycott. Sadly, barely 500 people were in the ground to witness an astonishing West Indies victory as they bowled South Africa out for 148 on the final day.

V. V. S. Laxman and Rahul Dravid leave the field at Eden Gardens, having batted all day in the Second Test against Australia in 2001. Laxman's innings of 281 denied the visitors a world-record eighteenth Test victory in a row and Steve Waugh the prize he most wanted – a series win in India.

Harbhajan Singh becomes the first Indian bowler to record a Test hat-trick as he dismisses Shane Warne on the first day. He went on to take thirteen wickets in the match and sealed a remarkable turnaround that had been initiated by Laxman's marathon innings.

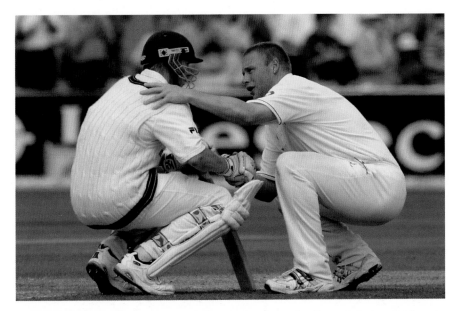

Andrew Flintoff consoles Brett Lee after England win the Second Test at Edgbaston in the 2005 Ashes series by just two runs. Lee remained undefeated on 43, having put on 59 for the last wicket with Michael Kasprowicz. It was the closest winning margin in Ashes history. Flintoff's gesture has itself become iconic.

Before play had even started, Glenn McGrath, the spearhead of Australia's attack whose nine wickets had helped Australia win the opening Test at Lord's, was injured in a freak accident during the warm-up. It was to have a decisive effect on the outcome of the series and helped England regain the Ashes after sixteen years of hurt.

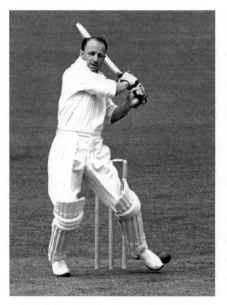

There are few statistics in sport that you can say will never be eclipsed. Sir Donald Bradman's Test average of 99.94 is surely one of those. He dominated the game for a period of twenty years, accumulating runs at an astonishing rate. Without doubt, he is the greatest cricketer who ever lived – how I would have loved to have seen him play.

Harold Larwood had a classical fast bowler's action. He never played another Test after the Bodyline series but, despite the almost universal opprobrium he received afterwards, he was welcomed back to Australia when he emigrated there in 1950.

The England players, led by captain Norman Yardley, applaud Bradman at the start of what turns out to be his final Test innings at the Oval in 1948. History records that he was bowled second ball by Eric Hollies for a duck and ended his Test career four runs short of recording a three-figure average.

Trevor Bailey may have been an obdurate, defensive batsman at times but he was the leading all-rounder of his generation, achieving the double of 1,000 runs and 100 wickets in a season on eight occasions. He was a brilliantly concise and humorous fellow pundit for twenty-five years on *Test Match Special*.

Colin Cowdrey catches batsman Neil Hawke at first slip in the Fifth Test against Australia at the Oval in 1964 and Fred Trueman has his 300th Test wicket, the first Test bowler to achieve this landmark. Fred may have missed as many as fifty Tests during his England career due to frequent clashes with authority. He was another marvellous stalwart of *Test Match Special*, even if he never knew what was 'going off out there'.

In terms of reading the game, there has never been a better player turned broadcaster than Richie Benaud. He was a fine leg-spin bowler, and captained a successful Australian side with distinction on twenty-eight occasions, regularly playing alongside Alan Davidson as one of two bowling all-rounders.

'It is often forgotten that Tony Greig was a highly versatile cricketer, bowling both medium pace and finger spin. He famously bowled West Indies out twice in Port of Spain in 1974, taking thirteen wickets in the match and enabling England to square the series.

David Steele was someone I admired immensely. I watched him make his Test début in 1975 at the age of 33, and face down Lillee and Thomson, bravery that earned him the Sports Personality of the Year award that year and the soubriquet 'the bank clerk who went to war'. He showed me what could be achieved through sheer hard work and dedication.

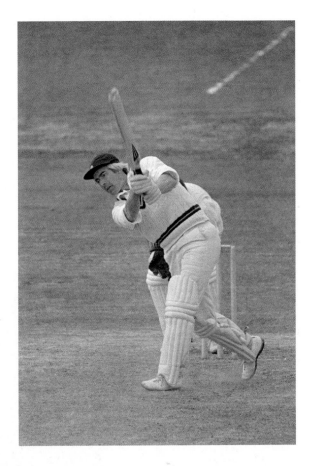

When Andy Roberts arrived at Leicestershire in 1983, I knew it would limit my chances of making a regular spot in the first team. However, I learned a huge amount just by watching him in the nets and before long, I became his regular opening partner. As his sometimes passenger, I can confirm he drove every bit as fast as he bowled!

Left: Ray Illingworth was my first club captain at Leicestershire and a master tactician who was always thinking about how he could get one over on the opposition. He was the last player to have taken 2,000 wickets and scored 20,000 runs in first-class cricket and was one of England's most successful captains.

Below: Geoffrey Boycott on-drives Greg Chappell to the boundary and reaches his 100th first-class century in front of his home crowd at Headingley in the Fourth Test against Australia in 1977. Age will not have diminished his memory of that special moment.

It has been described as 'the ball of the century'. A young Shane Warne bamboozles England captain Mike Gatting with his first ball in an Ashes Test at Old Trafford in 1993. He went on take 195 English wickets, a record in Ashes history.

A youthful Sachin Tendulkar receives his *Test Match Special* 'champagne moment' from Jonathan Agnew at Lord's in 1996. In India, he is mobbed everywhere he goes and, as with Bradman before him, cricket lovers will travel from far and wide to see him bat. In 2012, he became the first batsman to score 100 international centuries.

Sri Lanka's Muttiah Muralitharan took over from Shane Warne as Test cricket's leading wicket-taker and registered his 800th victim with his final ball in Test cricket in 2010. His unorthodoxy led to many questioning the legality of his action. What is beyond doubt is that his record will take some beating.

England's spin king Graeme Swann was a key player in getting England to the top of the Test rankings in 2011, a year in which he was the most highly rated spin bowler in both formats of the game. He is an attacking bowler who can also give his captain control by tying down an end.

Douglas Jardine, the England captain at the centre of the Bodyline storm, displays a typically patrician demeanour as he poses at the crease in his Harlequin cap, which he insisted on wearing throughout the tour, much to the annoyance of the Australian crowds.

Wally Hammond began his career as a professional but became an amateur partly so that he could captain his country. As a result, he is the only person to captain both Gentlemen and Players. His total of 22 Test centuries remained an English record until overtaken by Alastair Cook in 2012.

The awarding of a benefit by your county was very important financially, even for England players. Len Hutton's in 1950 raised the princely sum of £9,713. Traditionally, the Yorkshire Committee invested two-thirds of the money raised. Hutton didn't receive the full amount until 1972.

LEN HUTTON'S BENEFIT MATCH

SCARBOROUGH
v.
BECKETT CUP CRICKET LEAGUE XI
ON

Scarborough Cricket Ground
(North Marine Road)

Thursday & Friday, 13 & 14 July, 1950.

Wickets Pitched 6-30 p.m.

Admission : 6d. each night.

Match Tickets : 1/- each,
obtainable from your Club Secretary.

ALFRED RUTHERFORD,
Local Secretary.

Ted Dexter was the last amateur to captain the Gentlemen in 1962 in a match that coincidently ensured his selection for MCC's tour of Australia that coming winter. His opposing captain, Fred Trueman, thought the Gentlemen v Players fixtures 'a ludicrous business' and they were mercifully consigned to history the following season.

Frank Worrell, Clyde Walcott and Everton Weekes – known collectively as the 'three Ws' – were hugely popular cricketers both at home and abroad. They are seen here with team-mates Kenneth Rickards and Roy Marshall at St Pancras station as they make their way to Australia in 1951. Worrell went on to become the first black captain of the West Indies and a Jamaican senator but his life was cut short by leukaemia at the age of 42.

The Lancashire League was a valuable nursery for overseas Test players. West Indian pace bowler Charlie Griffith was Burnley's professional in 1964, the same year he was voted a *Wisden* Cricketer of the Year. He helped them win the championship, taking 144 wickets at the parsimonious average of 5.20.

Sun-dappled and slow-moving long summer afternoons with white-clad figures in the middle distance form the quintessential image of club cricket. This wonderful photograph of a late evening game at the Belvoir Cricket Club in Knipton – my local club – was taken by Laurence Griffiths for his book *From the Boundary's Edge*.

Arguably, in India cricket occupies its very heart and soul. Visit Mumbai and you will see cricket of every level being played at the Oval Maidan, a large area of recreational land in the city centre given over to the residents' association. The games take place against a magnificent Victorian architectural backdrop.

Sir Neville Cardus, as a correspondent of the *Manchester Guardian* in the 1920s and 1930s, transformed writing on cricket from dutiful unanalytic match reports to a level of insightful criticism that has set the standard for all subsequent intelligent reportage of the game. From humble beginnings, and largely self-educated, he was assured of his place as one the very greatest writers on the sport.

John Arlott was an absolute natural as a broadcaster. Whether on TV, on radio or in print, he described cricket with a lyricism and insight few have matched since. This photograph shows John during the last moments of his broadcasting career at the 1980 Centenary Test at Lord's. He inspired me, and many others, to follow in his broadcasting footsteps, but will always remain *primus inter pares*.

Christopher Martin-Jenkins, affectionately known in the pressbox as 'the Major', was *Test Match Special*'s longest-serving commentator. No one had a greater love of the game or a deeper knowledge of it. He gave so much to cricket, and cricket will be so much the poorer without him.

HOW FAST BOWLERS ARE MADE.

Captain (to hurricane perfomer), 'Of course I should hate you to hurt anybody, Charlie, but I thought you might like to know that this fella coming in is something to do with income-tax.'

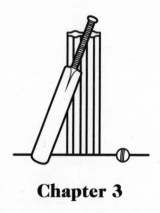

Chapter 3

'*He's been at Cambridge. He's never really gone out to work and earned a living in his life. It's pretty hard going for him.*'

Raymond Illingworth, chairman of the selectors, on Michael
Atherton's shortcomings as England captain, 1995.

Achieving the ultimate ambition of playing your favourite sport for a living is a privilege reserved only for the very fortunate. Every individual whose dream actually does come true leaves in his wake a trail of disappointment and volumes of bad-luck stories. The roadside to the very top is littered with casualties: those who were simply not good enough to start with; some who were genuinely talented but lacked that crucial percentage point to get them over the line; and others who came perilously close to making the big time, only for bad luck or injury to deal a cruel blow at the defining moment. It is not an easy path, and every professional sportsperson can look back at that stroke of luck they needed to propel them to the top. It might be the right coach being there at the right time, or having an especially good game when the talent spotter was in attendance. It could be little more than the rain staying away when it mattered, or possibly a timely injury to someone else that gave you the opportunity that was subsequently seized. Even the very best have benefited from an element of luck that enabled them to go on to experience the remarkable and fulfilling world of professional sport.

My lucky break lay in the solid and trustworthy reputation of Maurice Hallam, the former Leicestershire County Cricket Club captain and stalwart of the club, who had become my coach at Uppingham School. On every occasion that the secretary/manager of Leicestershire, Mike Turner, made the journey to watch me play with a view to signing me up as an 18-year-old professional, the heavens opened. The third time it happened, Mike gave up and, on Maurice's word, offered me a contract. It could so easily have turned out very differently.

To develop the deep and abiding love for a particular sport that is so necessary to supply the inspiration and constant motivation for all the hard work that is needed to ultimately take you to the top is the opportunity, at a young age, to discover heroes, the individuals at the top of their game whose successes you celebrate and whose failures and disappointments you share every bit as keenly as the sportsman himself. The importance of professional sportsmen and -women acting as role models for the younger generation cannot be overestimated. It is one of the responsibilities of being in the limelight that every top sportsperson should fully understand and embrace. Sadly that is not always the case.

My early heroes are those I watched on television, back in the good old days when cricket was free-to-air on terrestrial TV and available for everyone to watch live. While the enormous sums of money generated by the sale of satellite television rights help significantly to fund the game at all levels, and has played its part in creating a successful England team, it has to be a real concern that restricted access to live coverage will bite the game hard in the end. Viewing figures for the 2005 Ashes series, shown on free-to-air Channel 4 in the United Kingdom, averaged just under three million, with 7.2 million tuning in to watch the high drama unfold at the Oval in the final hour as England sealed their victory. Four years later, viewing figures for satellite pay-for-view coverage of an equally enthralling Ashes series averaged under a million. How can you fall in love with a game, and its players, that you cannot see?

As a very young boy I spent days in our darkened sitting room at home watching Test matches in their entirety. This was in the late 1960s and early 1970s, when Test cricket was arguably at its most tedious. The role of opening batsmen was to blunt the new ball, and run-scoring, in the first session of play, was very much of secondary importance. However, this didn't seem to matter to the spectator, either in his or her armchair or at the sun-dappled or rain-sodden ground. This was the way cricket was played then, before one-day cricket had influenced the tempo of the game and increased the expectation that the batsmen would get on with it a bit. We all had great admiration for the concentration of Geoffrey Boycott and John Edrich, even when they made India's new-ball attack of Abid Ali and Eknath Solkar appear positively threatening. John Edrich, to be fair, usually played more shots than Boycott. He scored 310 not out against New Zealand at Headingley in 1965 with 77 per cent of his runs coming in boundaries, although it has never been lost on Boycott that Edrich was only playing that day because he, Geoffrey, was ill.

Watching the action on the television at an early age was vitally important. It was how I acquired the beginnings of an understanding of the strategy of the game, and learned to judge and admire the technique of many fine players. I enjoyed the commentary, too, of Richie Benaud, Jim Laker and, of course, the inimitable Brian Johnston. But it was through trying to emulate the players we watched in the garden afterwards with my brother, Chris, that really inspired in me a passion for the game. I would bowl like John Snow (I wish) or Geoff Arnold and loved trying to repeat Tony Greig's jerky action. Then it was time for some spin, courtesy of Ray Illingworth, complete with the tongue sticking out. These heroes made such an impression on me as a 10-year-old that I could still repeat their run-ups and actions today, and it was around that age that I knew I wanted to be a professional cricketer.

My ambition was eventually encouraged to a large degree through the influence of the first three professional cricketers I encountered. Ken Taylor, of Yorkshire and England, was coach at my prep school, Taverham Hall. Now living in Norfolk and a highly accomplished artist, Ken was very gentle and kind. Although I could not have appreciated it at the time, Ken was a fine example of how different characters mould a team and how important that diversity is to its success as well as contributing to the wellbeing of any county dressing room. He must have been easily the quietest member of the great Yorkshire side that won seven championships between 1959 and 1968, that contained extrovert and outspoken characters like Fred Trueman, Brian Close and Ray Illingworth. Had he been more forceful, Ken might have played more than his three Tests, but his mild temperament made him ideally suited to coaching young schoolboys.

Les Berry was coach at Uppingham School before Maurice Hallam, and was also from Leicestershire. Les Berry's prolific career was interrupted by the Second World War, otherwise he would have played for England in all likelihood. No one scored more runs for Leicestershire than Les, a slightly portly and kindly man who, in his early seventies, was still bowling very slowly in the nets at the school. Les was the sort of coach who would prefer to have a quiet word in your ear, rather than anything too demonstrative, and this he would do from halfway down the net, always with his battered old Leicestershire cap set at a slightly jaunty angle. He and Ken followed a typical career path in those days – play county cricket for years, then become a professional coach at a public school.

Another alternative for a retired old pro was to run your own coaching school, which is what Alf Gover, of Surrey and England, chose to do. His famous establishment was located above a garage in Wandsworth, London, and was home to a number of former cricketers who, it seemed, had been unsuccessful in finding anything else to do outside the game. To this day, that remains one of the perils of the professional's lot. John McMahon, an Australia-born county cricketer with Surrey and Somerset, fell into this category (though I am not sure the stories about his bunking down in Alf's bar were ever verified) and he took me under his wing when, in 1976, my dad took me to the Gover Cricket School for three days for my sixteenth-birthday present. John was a left-arm spinner, but I was determined to bowl fast, and it did not take long for Alf to take a personal interest and assume responsibility for me. Alf was 68 at the time, a legendary fast bowler who had toured India before the Second World War. It was on that trip that, having unleashed one delivery from his very long approach, Alf simply kept running with great urgency straight off the ground and into the pavilion, where he sought comfort in the dressing-room toilet. 'Longest follow-through in Test cricket, old boy!' he observed as we ambled the length of the net to pick up the balls that I had propelled at an unprotected wicket. Alf still bowled, but with a very loud grunt and an arm as low as a discus thrower's. In the adjoining net I recall seeing the actor and loyal Lord's Taverner Brian Rix turning his arm over in preparation for another season of charity cricket.

Thus far, my journey to becoming a professional player had been entirely straightforward. I bowled fast for my age, was naturally lean and fit, and had yet to encounter any serious obstacles along the way. Things were about to become more serious because, at the end of my three-day visit, Alf told my father that he wanted me to attend pre-season nets at the Oval with the hope that I might be taken on by Surrey during the summer holidays. Naturally Dad agreed and a date was fixed.

For a Lincolnshire poultry farmer and his 16-year-old son, the Kennington Oval was a forbidding place. Neither of us had been there before, and I have to say it was not exactly welcoming. It just seemed big, empty and soulless. Arthur McIntyre, the Surrey wicketkeeper during the club's golden age in the 1950s, was beginning his final season as club coach and after I bowled in the nets to, among others, England batsman Graham Roope, he invited us up to his office on the first floor of the pavilion for a chat. It was all terribly formal, with Arthur wearing his brown blazer; in fact everything was strict. The atmosphere in the nets was not one of people enjoying themselves. To reach the nets, you had to walk all the way round the vast square rather than take the direct route from one end of the ground to the other (you still do, in fact), and, as I discovered after I accepted Arthur's generous offer to come down at the end of term for £20 per week (which did not include either board and lodging or daily travel expenses), the old-fashioned and deeply entrenched hierarchy made the experience unpleasant for young enthusiastic hopefuls like me and my peers Monte Lynch and David Thomas. I am not suggesting we were bullied by members of the first team, which included players like John Edrich, Geoff Arnold, Robin Jackman and Intikhab Alam, but junior pros were kept very much at arm's length, and viewed with a surprising degree of hostility – as if we were a serious and immediate career threat. John and Robin have since become good friends and would probably say that my reaction at the time was that of a naive young country boy, straight out of a public-school boarding house. But it was not very agreeable, and quickly shattered my illusion about what life as a professional cricketer should be. It became even worse when, the following year, Fred Titmus became head coach.

To his peers, Fred seemed to be very popular and quick with the one-liners. Essentially, though, he was a quiet man who was quite deaf in one ear, an attribute that made communication more than a little tricky. Titmus was undoubtedly one of England's finest off-spin bowlers. Despite his losing four toes in a horrific boating accident in Barbados during England's 1967–8 tour of West Indies, his first-class career with neighbouring Middlesex spanned five decades, and his ability to bat anywhere in the order should have made him an ideal coach.

Unfortunately, his attitude to the young players at the Oval was one of complete indifference, coupled with an unwavering opinion that we should be seen and never heard. It was while I was struggling with a no-ball problem during a second-eleven match on one of Surrey's out-grounds in 1977 that I approached Titmus for help. 'Go in the nets and sort it out yourself,' was his gruff response, without averting his attention from the fruit machine that he was playing in the clubhouse bar. This was typical of the attitude of that time at the Oval – and probably elsewhere on the county circuit as well. Such was the determination of the senior players to cling on to their places in the first team – and therefore protect their careers – that they gave the youngsters absolutely nothing in the way of help or encouragement. On twelfth-man duty, we were expected to pour the orange squash for every returning batsman and then keep well out of the way. No doubt this was how that generation of Surrey first-team players had been treated on their way through the ranks, and the generation before them, too. But Titmus was supposed to be the coach, and the overall experience, though illuminating and toughening, was a disagreeable one. So when Mike Turner, chief executive of Leicestershire, offered me the chance to switch counties, I jumped at the opportunity.

The atmosphere at Grace Road was a breath of fresh air. The club captain, Ray Illingworth, was every bit as old-school as the Surrey pros, but here was a man who clearly enjoyed passing on his vast wealth of cricket experience. I discovered that just sitting in the same dressing room as Illy made the game of cricket open up in a way I had never appreciated before. As a perpetual on-field and dressing-room chunterer, one of Illy's endearing qualities was his ability to repeatedly come up with the most outrageous excuses to explain his own batting failures. While Leicester were in the field, he used to think out loud, running his ideas past senior players like Brian Davison and Chris Balderstone, and was always entirely focused on the game as if he was waiting for the moment to pounce. Illy was, quite simply, brilliant at manoeuvring the game.

Now aged 18, this was all a giant leap for me from the schoolboy unsophisticated cricketing world of silly mid-ons and silly mid-offs. Lonsdale Skinner – the delightful Guyanese wicketkeeper who was regularly in Surrey's second eleven during my short stint at the county – would often shout as I approached the start of my run-up, 'Give him some widff, Spiro! Give him some widff!' But in truth, I never understood what he meant. Tactically I was understandably very naive and now here I was playing in the same team as the man widely recognized as one of the most astute captains in the history of the game. Somehow Illingworth always made the opposition batsmen feel as if Leicestershire were fielding fifteen players, so precise were his run-stopping field placings.

That day, Illy brought himself on to bowl in my first County Championship match, against Lancashire, and from mid-off I could clearly hear him set his field for the towering and mightily destructive West Indian batsman, Clive Lloyd.

'Come on, Baldy,' he shouted to Chris Balderstone, who was out on the boundary at deep square leg. 'It's a slow pitch, I'm bowling uphill and into the wind. You should be ten yards squarer.' Balderstone moved as directed, and when Lloyd duly played a sweep shot, the ball sailed directly into Baldy's midriff. He did not have to move an inch. Was it simply a fluke, or a tactical masterstroke? Who knows? But my jaw hit the ground in amazement.

Life as a young professional in the late 1970s was hard work, with a great deal of net practice, and was very competitive. The ambition of the entire playing staff of twenty-two was to play in the first team and, clearly, that was not possible. Inevitably there would be a disgruntled senior player or two who found themselves playing in the second team, or 'the Stiffs', as it was known; and the quality of second-team cricket was all the better for their presence. Ken Shuttleworth and Alan Ward were in that position in my early years at Leicestershire, and they also resided in the same bed-and-breakfast establishment as I did on Grace Road. Run by an eccentric Yugoslav called Raddi, the Wyvernhoe was, fittingly perhaps, eventually converted into an old people's home.

Those two fine fast bowlers, who had both played for England in their time, were now past their best and resigned to limited first-team appearances, but in contrast to my experience at Surrey, Shuttleworth was a great help. He would certainly have viewed me as a threat to his diminishing career prospects, but he never once showed it. 'Shut' was a great character, with a dry, acerbic wit, and he became very proud of his paternal influence on the youngsters in the second eleven.

I suspect every youngster's early appearances in first-class cricket were a bewildering experience; mine certainly were – a sharp learning curve when, thanks to others' injuries, I was propelled into the first team barely a month after leaving school. To suddenly be bowling at top-class batsmen like Clive Lloyd, Allan Lamb, Derek Randall and Clive Rice was a nerve-shredding business, but now I was sitting in the dressing room waiting to face up to West Indian fast bowler Colin Croft, New Zealand great Richard Hadlee and Pakistan's opening bowler Sarfraz Nawaz. I was, frankly, terrified, my stomach churning. The speed of the ball would be bad enough, but the prospect of having to face these giants of the game wearing schoolboy pads and gloves that were not remotely suitable for first-class cricket was enough to turn my legs to jelly. As things turned out, I was fortunate not to actually face any of these tyros and my batting experience in my first four outings before the end of the season was confined to a brief 1 not out against Nottinghamshire which, I recall, was scored off the Indian left-arm spinner Dilip Doshi.

Personally speaking, everything was on the up and up. I took three wickets (Geoff Cook, David Steele and Allan Lamb) in the first innings against Northamptonshire in the penultimate game of the season and Illingworth was happy to give me the new ball. As the season drew to a close, however, I became aware of another of the less pleasant aspects of professional sport: it came in the form of a letter informing the unlucky recipient that his services would not be required by the club the following summer. In reality it meant that in approximately three weeks' time he would be out of work. I am quite sure that Mike Turner took no pleasure in delivering the bad news, but in the run-in to the last weeks of the season it cast a deeply unsettling atmosphere in the dressing room. Tension would mount in the days leading up to the committee meeting that would determine all our fates, and there was always an angry atmosphere and negative attitude towards the club when players were sacked. I remember how sad I felt for Alan Ward when he received his bad news at the end of that 1978 season. These things are generally managed much better today.

Another issue was winter employment. There were no twelve-month contracts in those days; you simply picked up your P45 (the British government's form entitled 'Details of employee leaving work') from the assistant secretary after the last game of the season. He would wish us a Happy Christmas and, with a cheery 'see you next April', that would be that. Looking back now, it seems remarkable that professional cricketers were expected to lead quite such a financially unsustainable life, bearing in mind that the money you earned on the county circuit in the summer was nowhere near enough to get you through the winter. Imagine what it was like with a wife and a couple of children to support. In the days before central contracts and year-long employment by the counties, it was this perpetual uncertainty, and the need to find work, that eventually took me to Radio Leicester's door, early retirement from professional cricket and a new career in journalism.

Fortunately, my first close season as a professional was taken care of by a wonderful sponsorship arrangement with Whitbread, the brewers. It took the form of a scholarship to Australia for the whole winter, and would include playing top-class grade cricket in Melbourne. On landing, I was picked up at the airport by legendary retired England fast bowler Frank 'Typhoon' Tyson.

Like another English fast bowler, Harold Larwood, Frank had been welcomed to Australia when he moved there after his playing days were over. This despite having blown away the Aussie batsmen in a spell of fast bowling at the Melbourne Cricket Ground in the 1954–5 Ashes series that is still talked about in reverential terms today, when Frank had taken seven for 27 in a furious spell to skittle Australia. Now he was the coach of Victoria. He was also still, as I discovered when I moved into his house, very competitive, especially after a surprisingly small amount of beer. 'Reckon you're fast, then?' he would suddenly announce, putting down his can and grabbing a tennis ball, which he would then proceed to hurl quickly and comically all around his back garden until it vanished into a hedge.

Frank was great. He dispatched me all over Victoria to coach in small towns and rural communities. I was still only 18, and this was the opening-up of a whole new world for me. At the weekends I played for Essendon in north Melbourne and experienced at first hand the strength and competitiveness of club cricket in Australia. This was followed by a tour of Australia with Young England, although this ended prematurely when I injured my back. And so I returned to Leicester for the beginning of the 1979 season, my first as a full-time professional cricketer.

Now was my first taste of pre-season training – a period of three weeks or so in which we had to work off all our winter excesses and transform ourselves into well-honed professional sportsmen ready for the arduous season ahead. Today, watching the current England team go about their fitness training makes our erstwhile efforts seem utterly laughable. We would jog along the canal bank from Grace Road to the Leicester Polytechnic, as the De Montfort University was called in those days – a distance of no more than two miles. This was followed by some light gym work, a game of basket-ball or badminton, before jogging back along the canal bank and into The Cricketers pub for lunch, where we would eat a cheese roll or two, and some – notably fast bowler Les Taylor and the hard-hitting batsman Brian Davison – would have a pint of beer before spending the afternoon in the nets. The emphasis was very much on becoming fit for playing cricket, which meant bowling longer spells in the nets than they do nowadays, and it seemed to work for us. Certainly I was worn out every evening as I shared dinner – almost always pork chops – with Ken in the Wyvernhoe. Attitudes to physical fitness and nutrition have changed markedly since those days and most county cricketers, thanks in part to more lucrative year-round contracts, work on their fitness throughout the winter months.

In another rite of passage, I attended my first players' meeting, which was held in the first-team dressing room. Raymond Illingworth had retired as captain at the end of the 1978 season and the new incumbent, Ken Higgs, was in the chair. He routinely addressed everyone as 'kid' and although he could be something of a rough diamond on the field, Higgy was in fact a dear man who was to become the club coach, and was hugely respected and loved by my peers. He was not a great communicator and was happy to let the ball do the talking. He was once dragged out of retirement at the age of 49 because his young charges were all injured, and took five for 22 against Yorkshire. I have never seen a more natural away-swing bowler than Ken Higgs.

There were a number of topics of conversation at the team meeting. The first was the amount of money each player would receive for securing bonus points in the County Championship. It was peanuts, really, and throughout my career the rallying cry would be heard on the field: 'Come on, lads. One more wicket for a bag of chips!'

The car list, I discovered during the course of the meeting, was a tremendous perk for the top five ranking players in the first team. It meant that you had to drive one or two team members to and from an away fixture in your own car, but the expenses on offer that went straight into your pocket seemed to make it an attractive arrangement. It was also a good way of getting to know more about your team-mates, and since pairings were usually based on geo-graphic convenience, the driver/navigator combinations became a regular thing. David Gower was always a good catch on the car list, and I would spend many hours as his passenger. David inevitably owned the latest Audi Quattro sports car, and while usually driven at high speed it was always a comfortable ride. Indeed, the safety or size of the car was irrelevant: if you were senior enough to be on the list, you were entitled to take your own car. Although destined to become my closest friend and room-mate, Les Taylor and his clapped-out white Morris Marina was without doubt the shortest of short straws.

Finally, the discussion turned to cricket and the aims and targets we would be setting for the coming season. Happily, in 1979, before the days of two divisions, every team was in the position of starting the season with the chance of winning the Championship. Clearly, this was the ultimate ambition – it was the most prestigious and important competition of the summer and carried the most valu-able prize in terms of the winner's cheque.

The discussion focused on the types of pitches the senior players thought our groundsman ought to produce, how the loss of Illingworth's off spin would be a significant factor in Leicestershire's ability to play a balanced team of five bowlers in the coming summer, and how important it was for the whole squad to feel part of the first-team effort. 'Anyone could play at any time,' was the message. It was a galvanizing afternoon and the only time the whole squad was in the same room together during the entire summer, other than for the pre-season drinks evening with the committee, which, for reasons I could never fully understand, would always be a less than comfortable affair.

Yet another new experience lay in store that spring, one that would become a pre-season ritual for the next twelve years: a trip to Duncan Fearnley's warehouse in Worcester to pick up our kit for the season. My mate, Les Taylor, and I always went together and since neither of us could lay any claim to being able to hold a bat our visits never lasted long. Duncan always greeted us warmly, before dragging out a bat for each of us from what appeared to be the reject box that sat forlornly alongside one holding the beautiful, pristine, shiny new bats reserved for Ian Botham, Dennis Amiss and the like. A pair of batting gloves, some trousers, shirts, socks and jockstraps and that was it for another year. Needless to say, while a number of high-profile batsmen were paid well to use the bats made by a number of leading manufacturers, neither Les nor I was ever offered a penny, presumably on the not-unreasonable grounds that our forthcoming season's worth of batting exhibitions would be more damaging to, rather than enhancing of, the bat maker's reputation.

In 1979 the annual meeting of the Professional Cricketers' Association (PCA) at Edgbaston held particular interest because the Packer affair was coming to a head. For a modern cricket-loving audience, perhaps the best way to empathize with the impact of Kerry Packer's Circus, as it became known, is to imagine a breakaway Indian Twenty20 League buying up the best cricketers in the world to play on a rival television network at the same time as Test cricket is being staged, and consequently those players being banned from representing their countries in any form of the game. Incidentally, this is a scenario that could become reality, and is one of the main concerns worrying cricket's administrators today. One crucial difference between this possible course of events and Packer's World Series Cricket (WSC) in 1977 is the amount of money that international cricketers earn these days. Packer was able to utilize the players' widespread and deeply felt financial dissatisfaction to his advantage, and his supporters would claim, with some justice, that all professional cricketers, whether or not they were signed up by him, saw their earnings improve significantly as a result of the rebellion he brought about. A pirate league today would require immense financial backing to entice all the best cricketers in the world away from Test cricket as Packer was able to do.

With the counties threatening to ban England's crop of Packer players – Tony Greig (England's captain at the time and one of Packer's right-hand men), Alan Knott, Derek Underwood, Bob Woolmer, Dennis Amiss and John Snow – this was a critical meeting. John Arlott chaired it magnificently, introducing much-needed calm to the proceedings when the strength of feeling shown by county professionals towards the WSC players reached a head, as illustrated by two of the proposals tabled and recorded by Jack Bannister, secretary of the PCA at the time:

> Members of the Cricketers' Association will only play Test cricket with or against players not contracted to professional cricket outside the jurisdiction of the ICC and the TCCB.
>> Proposed by Mike Hendrick. Seconded by Ian Botham.

> Members of the Cricketers' Association will not play first-class cricket or one-day cricket against any touring side, which includes players contracted to professional cricket outside the jurisdiction of the ICC and the TCCB.
>> Proposed by Bob Taylor. Seconded by Mike Gatting.

Ultimately, the proposals were never put to the vote. The counties backed down and the Australian Cricket Board patched up its differences with Packer a few months later. But with the county game more divided than at any time in its hundred-year history, this was certainly an interesting time to be starting out on life as a professional cricketer. The meeting itself was an amazing experience, catching glimpses of famous faces that I had previously only seen on television. To witness Tony Greig, the iconic captain of England, taking so much flak from the rank and file is something I will never forget. His fellow county professionals all harboured the same career-defining ambition to play cricket for England, and many felt that the position of the England captaincy had been abused. But Greig's response also struck a sympathetic chord, unsurprisingly, when he argued straightforwardly that county cricketers should be paid more. It was true that the honest county pro in those days was receiving less than the average national wage.

But what better way can there be to make a living than playing a sport that you love? Constantly evolving, cricket has changed a great deal through the generations and what has always struck me when I speak to professional players past and present is how much deep, soul-felt pleasure they took throughout the all-too-brief period of fifteen years or so while it was their turn on the stage. It can be easy to forget that cricket is only a game when it is also your livelihood, and your and your family's wellbeing is dependent on it. Until comparatively recently it was a game that paid relatively poorly when compared with other professional sports, and every county player faced and still faces the serious dilemma of finding employment when his playing career is over; the moment when the limelight dims and the applause of the crowd fades to a sepia-coloured memory. This end-of-career existentialist nightmare has been offered as one possible explanation for the higher-than-average suicide rate among retired cricketers – a disturbing state of affairs, which has been the subject of at least one book.

Despite the promising start, it took me five years to become an established first-team player. Leicestershire had a highly rated pace attack, so breaking in was not easy, and just as it seemed that I had earned a settled run in the side, an injury would crop up and back to the second eleven, via the physio's couch, I would go. There was no shortage of talent all waiting for their moment, and keeping motivated was easy: the choice of playing against Warwickshire Second XI – yet again – at Hinckley when compared with a Somerset First XI fixture at Taunton, who would be fielding Ian Botham, Vivian Richards and Joel Garner, was hardly difficult to make. I remember once going for a training run with Peter Booth, who was in danger of being overtaken by the younger crop of fast bowlers at the time, and with every step we pounded around the boundary rope at Grace Road, he chanted rhythmically and determinedly: 'I want to get in the first team . . . I want to get in the first team . . .' In fact, Peter only ever made fleeting appearances in the first team again, but was one of a very rare breed of professional cricketers who always seemed to be genuinely pleased by his intra-team competitors' successes. This was hardly the norm in such a cut-throat, competitive and testosterone-fuelled environment, but Peter was different. No surprise, therefore, that he returned to teaching full time when he finally retired from the professional game.

The real breakthrough for any professional sportsman in a team sport is when you become an automatic selection. You have to earn that right, of course, through proven success on the field of play; with it comes a surge in confidence and the inner knowledge that you now really belong on the county circuit. As a player, you have finally 'made it', if you like. The satisfaction of having played a full season, barring a match or two absent only through injury, is immense; and meant, at Leicestershire at any rate, that you were entitled to your own place in the dressing room. I inherited my old mentor Ken Higgs's spot, tucked away behind the door with a view directly out onto the pitch, making it, on first inspection, the best seat in the house. That was until the ancient electric drying machine, which dried our sweaty clothing and was located in the same area as I now found myself, was pressed into service when play was under way. The unappealing smell of baking jockstraps, socks and batsmen's protective padding was quite overpowering. Still, it was my corner and I was fiercely proud to own it.

It was from my little piece of territory within that first-team dressing room that I was able to observe my colleagues: to watch how they prepared and how they relaxed, and to see how they coped with pressure and with failure, in particular. Although part of the same team, each cricketer is a unique character within the group and goes about his daily routine very differently from the man he is changing alongside. The state of his kit bag is a good place to start. We all had hard, rectangular cases shaped like, and therefore called, coffins. Everything was housed in our coffins: equipment and clothes (both clean and dirty). Some players were meticulous in the way they maintained their changing area, which consisted of little more than a couple of clothes hooks, a place to sit and their coffin. Chris Balderstone, the opening batsman, who was also a professional footballer, fell into that bracket. 'Look smart, play smart,' was his oft-repeated mantra and it was hard to argue with him. He despaired when Phil Whitticase, the wicketkeeper, settled down in alarmingly close proximity because, like all wicketkeepers, Phil's coffin resembled a rat's nest. It did not help that his inner wicketkeeping gloves smelt horrible – sweaty, putrid and nasty – but in my experience there is something about wicketkeepers that makes them untidy and rather unkempt individuals. Obviously, I except the fastidious Alec Stewart from this rule, but I never worked out how Phil managed to close the lid on his coffin with its disarray of clothing, pads, gloves, bats and everything else a professional cricketer needs crammed inside.

Our backgrounds were very different, too. James Whitaker and I had both attended the same public school while Les Taylor, my roomie, was a miner from Bagworth Colliery. Nigel Briers, Russell Cobb and Nick Cook were local Leicestershire products while Peter Willey came to us via Peterlee in County Durham and Northamptonshire and David Gower from Kent – different characters drawn from very different walks of life who for six months every year ate, slept and played cricket together.

It sounds ridiculous to describe playing professional sport as work, let alone hard work, but we spent a lot of time on the road. Sometimes the fixtures would stack up, so we were playing for two weeks nonstop, all over the country. I recall one particularly crazy weekend when we played the opening day of a Championship match against Glamorgan at Grace Road on the Saturday. That evening, the players from both teams had to hit the motorway and travel to Cardiff, where we all played against each other in a Sunday League game, before returning to Leicester again that night to resume the three-day match on the Monday morning. Bonkers! Scarborough to Canterbury on a typical traffic-nightmare Friday evening was another that springs to mind. Essentially, there was far too much travel – and at Leicester we had the advantage of being based in the Midlands, of course – and it meant we were seldom fresh for the start of the next match and, as far as the bowlers were concerned, rarely fully fit either. Little wonder that Simon Hughes chose to call his excellent journal of a county cricketer's lot *A Lot of Hard Yakka*, while my rather irreverent diary of the 1988 season was called *8 Days A Week*, both titles reflecting the relatively hard graft of our professional lives.

The first professional player from an opposing team that I got to know reasonably well was David Steele. I had watched him walk out to bat at the Oval against West Indies in 1976 in a match during which Michael Holding bowled like the wind, taking sixteen wickets, including poor Balderstone, for a pair. From the distance of the boundary edge and, indeed, on television, Steele appeared to be a rather dour and dull individual with more than a passing resemblance to a bespectacled middle-aged bank manager rather than an international sportsman. But when he came as a guest player on Leicestershire's tour of Zimbabwe in 1980 he was a revelation. I have yet to encounter a drier and more laconic wit and we were also quick to discover that his nickname, Crime (as in 'crime doesn't pay'), while affectionately bestowed, was definitely well deserved. Saving a thoroughly chewed piece of gum for the next morning in the field by sticking it to his peg in the dressing room at the end of a day was just one example. Between making us laugh a lot, Steele also demonstrated to the Leicester lads what can be achieved through sheer hard work and dedication. He was not the most talented batsman in the world, but practised relentlessly, pushed himself and was also extremely brave against fast bowling, which was how he earned his reputation. He gave the opposition absolutely nothing. It was not a dissimilar attitude of narrow self-serving concentration to the one I had experienced at Surrey; the difference being that Steele was nice about the way he focused determinedly on his career and bettering himself.

Bowling at Steele in Championship cricket was one of the great challenges in the early 1980s. Planting his front foot down the pitch, but quick to swivel onto his right foot and pull short-pitched deliveries, gave him a solid technique against fast bowling. Like many of the old school he preferred a cap to a helmet and one day I remember delivering a ball that struck him a stinging blow on his unprotected inner thigh, an area that when hit, as any cricketer will tell you, is eye-wateringly painful. 'Thanks, youth,' he shouted up the pitch to me through gritted teeth. 'Just what I needed to wake me up a bit.' Typical Steele.

I suppose he was, in a way, like a rather more humorous version of Geoffrey Boycott. Now there is a man I used to love playing against. To be fair, Geoffrey did have his moments on the field. He enjoyed winding the bowlers up a bit when his eye was in and he felt set, but generally batting was a deadly serious business for Geoffrey. He had a solid, entirely natural technique based on good footwork and, for a bowler of my age, was the man to get out. When you did so – and I did rather more than he is comfortable with – you really knew that you had earned and thus deserved his wicket.

I had first encountered Geoffrey during my stay with Frank Tyson in Melbourne on the Whitbread scholarship. England were touring Australia that winter and I was called upon to bowl at them in the nets. There are no prizes for guessing that Geoffrey, whose life revolved almost exclusively around batting, made the most of me. Hour after hour in the blazing heat I would bowl at the great man in a single net right in the middle of the vast Melbourne Cricket Ground. Just me and him. 'I've got you under my skin,' he would sing, time and time again, his mouth in that lop-sided grin, as another ball thumped into the middle of his bat.

Afterwards, when I was spent, Geoffrey told me to come back with him to the team's hotel as he had got something for me. We went up in the lift with me wondering what this might possibly be. A personally autographed Geoffrey Boycott bat, perhaps? 'Right,' he said, when we reached his room. 'English Breakfast, Darjeeling or Ginseng?' That's right. My reward for all that hard work was a cup of tea.

I never played in the same team as Geoffrey, which might explain why I have such a good relationship with him on the radio today. The charges of selfishness that have been made by many of those who appeared for Yorkshire and England alongside Boycott are too many not to suggest, at least, that there must be some basis in truth. As a batsman Geoffrey was a superb technician who practised day and night to eliminate any faults that might lead to his getting out, and he undoubtedly saw his role as being the one man in the team who had to steadfastly defy the opposition at every turn. He would argue that, with a batsman's occupation of the crease, the bowlers became tired, and the runs would come in their own good time. Others would say that because Boycott only batted at one speed, it was too often left to those who came in after him to pick up the scoring rate, often losing their wickets in the process. Not surprisingly, this led to great resentment and is a good illustration of how difficult it can be to tread the very narrow line between batting for yourself and batting for the team. Cricket is a team game played by eleven individuals, and Boycott is certainly not the only batsman in the professional game to have been called selfish.

Another towering figure on the county circuit at that time was Graham Gooch. His slumped shoulders, shuffling walk, drooping Pancho Villa-style moustache and surprisingly thin legs would not immediately make one think that Gooch was a supremely fit batsman at the very top of his game if you chanced upon him in a Chelmsford supermarket aisle circa 1984. But when in whites and padded up for combat, Gooch was a merciless and ruthless opponent, with an unquenchable appetite for scoring big hundreds – 'Daddies' as he now calls them. Indeed, of all the fine English batsmen playing county cricket at the time – and there were a number – Gooch was the most feared and revered. When he changed his stance to one in which his bat was raised very deliberately behind him when the bowler was running up, and he twitched his shoulders to the left to keep him sideways-on, it was copied up and down the land – but never with his results.

I doubt there has been a cricketer more committed to training and practice than Gooch. When he became captain of England in 1990, this predictably became an unlooked-for issue in that he expected every member of the England squad to have the same attitude to unrelenting hard work when, frankly, that was never going to be the case. Gooch's Ashes tour in 1991–2 included men like David Gower and Wayne Larkins, who were both supremely talented touch players, born with an innate, higher-order level of skill than most mere cricket mortals (Gower in particular, of course). Both players placed little store in nets or running laps of the field. Gooch was aggravated beyond belief by this apparent laziness and insouciance about one of his most firmly held tenets of the game. It amounted to heresy in his opinion, which explained the heavy-handed fine meted out to Gower and John Morris (another who would barely have taken a training run in his career) when they hired two Tiger Moths and buzzed the cricket ground at Carrara in Queensland. Admittedly, England were batting at the time, and having not won a game, the tour up to that point had been written off as a disaster by the accompanying media. But the punishment was excessive and it seriously damaged the relationship between Gower and Gooch.

I always felt intimidated by Gooch when I played against him. I did not know him very well, and rarely bowled well at him, but since our retirements we have become firm friends. Now the England batting coach, Gooch has found his ideal niche, and a mark of his standing in the game is the respect for him shown by the current generation of players. Believe me, that is not always the case.

Gooch, Boycott and others such as Dennis Amiss, Derek Underwood and Alan Knott were all examples of the household names playing professional cricket at the time who were famed for their hard work and dedication as well as their skill. But one of the joys of the county circuit is that there is still room for the less-talented individuals who climb to the top the hard way and work and practise at an exhausting rate simply to stay there. At Leicestershire, Nigel Briers was a good example of a man who earned tremendous respect and admiration, not necessarily for the aesthetic quality of his innings but, generally as the underdog, for relishing the battle every day. John Steele was another. Indeed most counties had at least one professional who fell into this category – I can recall men like Alan Hill at Derbyshire, Grahame Clinton at Surrey and the Sussex captain John Barclay digging in and fighting to the death every time they came to the crease. They were unlikely to take any bowling attack apart, but their courage and the evident pleasure they took in playing cricket for a living always provided a healthy balance in the dressing room, where some of their more talented colleagues could be accused of taking it all for granted.

There is no question in my mind that county cricket was at its strongest in the late 1970s and 1980s. Players of earlier generations will be horrified by that statement, and can make perfectly valid claims for their own eras if they like, but apart from the fact that England's players turned out for their counties between Test matches, the clincher was the presence of so many talented overseas players in those years who returned summer after summer. They really were proper full-time members of their county teams. There is so much coming and going these days, because of increased international commitments, that it is impossible to remember who is playing for which county in any given week or competition. Most counties in my time had two world-class overseas professionals, and with England's cricketers also appearing between Tests, the quality of county cricket can surely never have been higher. Richard Hadlee and Clive Rice at Nottinghamshire, Imran Khan and Garth Le Roux at Sussex, Malcolm Marshall and Gordon Greenidge at Hampshire, Viv Richards and Joel Garner at Somerset – the list goes on and on of the partnerships of top cricketers who were deeply committed to their counties, their colleagues and their supporters.

Some of them were very approachable, too. I remember Hadlee, the calculating and robotically accurate New Zealand fast bowler, once wandering up to me as I marked out my run-up before a championship match at Grace Road. He asked how the season was going, and I said it was OK, but that I had started to have a problem over-stepping the crease and bowling no-balls. I explained how I kept lengthening my run by an inch or two to compensate, but the problem simply would not go away.

'That's exactly what you're doing wrong,' Hadlee replied. 'It sounds illogical, but you must always shorten your run-up by a foot. Your stride will be smaller, you won't stretch and you'll stop bowling no-balls. Works for me every time. Good luck.' And with that Hadlee – a member of the opposing team, let's not forget – walked off, having volunteered an absolutely priceless tip.

A counter-argument to the presence of overseas players is that they prevent opportunities for promising young England cricketers to gain the experience they need to progress to Test cricket. I remember the feeling of utter devastation when it was announced in 1983 that the great West Indian fast bowler Andy Roberts would be joining Leicestershire. I recall sending Mike Turner an angry letter, born out of the frustration of knowing that my appearances in the first team would inevitably be limited by Roberts's guaranteed selection in the side. And they were. But even bowling in the same practice nets as Roberts was an education and although he is a quiet man, who preferred a short stare at the batsman to sledging, Andy was and is still prepared to spend time talking to youngsters who are prepared to listen. My chance came the following summer when I became Andy's regular opening partner. We also travelled together, with the Antiguan relishing the chance to enjoy the smoother road surfaces in this part of the world. Andy certainly drove every bit as fast as he bowled, but considerably less straight. We also roomed together a number of times and such was his influence both on and off the field that within four months I was opening the bowling for England. There is no question in my mind that the right overseas professional will always be good for a county club and that if, as a young Englishman, you are good enough your chance will come.

Andy's fellow Antiguan Viv Richards was one of those rare breed of batsmen who are daunting to bowl at but, because they are so special, also mean pitting yourself against them is an irresistible challenge. Viv would emerge from the pavilion with a wonderful swagger, lazily chewing gum while menacingly thumping the top of his bat handle with the palm of his hand. He is a keen boxing enthusiast, and his entrance would stand comparison with the most elaborate and intimidating of any of the great heavyweight champions as they made their way to the ring. Of course it was always a thrill to bowl at Richards. It might well be a bruising experience but you knew you were rubbing shoulders with greatness, and Viv, whom you could hardly describe as a shrinking violet, revelled in his absolute command over his domain. Sometimes this could manifest itself in raw aggression – a stream of expletives and flashing, angry eyes. On other occasions there was great humour to be enjoyed such as occurred one day at Grace Road in 1981.

Around that time, a law had been introduced limiting bowlers to just one bouncer an over. This was designed to put a brake on the dangerous fast bowling perfected so ruthlessly by the West Indians rather than to emasculate young English quicks. But my Leicestershire colleague Gordon Parsons was very aggressive, and since he routinely bowled at least four bouncers every over, the new regulation had a serious impact on his repertoire. Tearing in down the hill against Somerset, Parsons struck early on when Phil Slocombe edged to slip. Typically, Gordon celebrated wildly, but the rest of us, and the bowlers in particular, were not quite so thrilled because we already knew that Viv, the next man in, was in a foul mood. He had been warming up that morning by hitting balls repeatedly against the fence, when Mike Turner made a public announcement over the Tannoy.

'Will players please refrain from hitting balls into the advertising boards. And that includes you, Mr Richards.' On game day this was not a sensible tactic. Viv's upper lip curled and he stomped back to the dressing room. When he came out to bat, it was the first we had seen of him since then, and even by his standards it was quite an entrance. He was at his arrogant, strutting best, staring the bowler straight in the eye before taking guard.

I was standing at mid-off, and could savour every moment from close range. I knew exactly what Gordon would bowl to Richards first ball. In fact, everyone in the ground knew. Viv looked very deliberately towards the deep-square-leg boundary, where a man was standing in hope of a catch from the hook shot.

When the great man was ready, and not a moment before, he settled slowly over his bat. Gordon came charging in like a wild thing. Barely a second after he released the ball, the ground reverberated to what sounded like both barrels of a shotgun being simultaneously discharged. It was Viv's bat making contact with the ball, which was now sailing high and out of the ground. The next thing we heard was the shattering of the glass roof of a factory some distance along the adjoining street. It was a magnificent shot, and umpire Dickie Bird relished the theatre of it all as he paused before, rather redundantly, turning and raising his arms to signal six to the scorebox. Then Dickie addressed Gordon, sufficiently loudly for Viv to hear.

'That's it, Gordy lad. That's your one bouncer for t'over.' At which point Viv rushed up the pitch, left arm raised, shouting, 'No, no, Dickie man. Tell him he can bowl as many as he wants!'

I note here that Richards was eventually bowled by Agnew for 196. It was the last ball before lunch, and it struck him on his pad, then his thigh, and then his ankle before somehow trickling into his stumps just hard enough to knock one bail to the ground. They all count, I suppose, but Viv could barely drag himself away from the crease.

Yes, county cricket was hard to beat in that generation. There were some seriously world-class players appearing alongside a number of very fine cricketers, which left little room for the rest of us. It was very competitive indeed, and the suggestion that three-day cricket was somehow softer than the four-day game that has now replaced it in the County Championship makes me want to laugh out loud.

It is true that attempting to compare eras in any sport is virtually impossible. I think it is almost certainly true that if you succeeded in one generation, you would most likely succeed in another. Cricket is based on technique, and technique can always be adapted or modified; it is something that is definitely evolving over time. The tiny leg-spinner Alfred 'Tich' Freeman, who took 3,776 first-class wickets for Kent – including 304 in a single season – would have bowled differently now than he did on the uncovered wickets between the First and Second World Wars, but I suggest he would still take a stack of wickets. As good as Shane Warne? Impossible to say, but I would like to have seen Freeman bowl.

The immediate aftermath of the Second World War seems to have been a good time in which to play county cricket. After the horrors of war, and with rationing dominating daily life, sport was put very much in its rightful context. It was entertainment, and played in that spirit. Whether the stories about Denis Compton arriving for a day's play still dressed in his dinner jacket from the previous evening's dinner party, or picking up any random bat that happened to be lying about in the dressing room as he set off to begin an innings, are purely apocryphal is now difficult to ascertain. These things assume legitimacy the more often they are recounted down the years, but there is no doubting that while the cricket itself was taken seriously by the international and county players of the time, it was not seen as the be-all and end-all.

'Pressure?' the great Australian all-rounder and wartime fighter pilot, Keith Miller, famously snorted when asked about his take on a tense match. 'Pressure is having a Messerschmitt up your arse!'

The Edwardian golden age of cricket in England came to an end when war was declared on 4 August 1914. It would take the county game some weeks to abandon its 'business as usual' approach. As the scale of British Expeditionary Force casualties became apparent, W. G. Grace stated in a published letter that, 'It is not fitting at a time like this that able-bodied men should be playing cricket by day and pleasure-seekers look on. I should like to see all first-class cricketers of suitable age set a good example and come to the help of their country without delay in its hour of need.' The remaining games of the season were abandoned 'in deference to public opinion'; first-class cricket would not resume until 1919, although Lord's and the Oval would see a number of matches between sides from the armed services over the next four years and the Lancashire League would play throughout the war.

The battlefields would be no respecter of sporting talent and would claim the lives of 226 men who had played first-class cricket, including England and Kent spin bowler Colin Blythe.

The outbreak of the Second World War brought about a much less dilatory approach to shutting down professional sport. The September 1939 issue of the *Cricketer* magazine published an apposite and mordant metaphor: 'England has now begun the grim Test match against Germany.' The war would end the lives of nine Test match cricketers including the Yorkshire and England bowler Hedley Verity.

In 1953 the Imperial Memorial Gallery (now the MCC Museum) was opened at Lord's and was dedicated to those cricketers who lost their lives in both world wars of the twentieth century. Today you can see a stone set in the wall of the museum entrance with an inscription that reads, 'To the memory of cricketers of all lands who gave their lives in the cause of freedom 1914–1918 * 1939–1945. Secure from change in their high-hearted ways.'

JACK HOBBS
Leo McKinstry

Hobbs shied away from confrontation in a literal sense when the First World War began in 1914. The majority of professional cricketers joined the armed forces in the first two years of the conflict but Hobbs was not one of them. Instead he opted to work at a munitions factory, while also finding work as a cricket coach at the elite public school of Westminster. Given the scale of the carnage that engulfed western Europe, Hobbs later admitted to some embarrassment over his initial avoidance of military service. In his defence he cited both family duties and his failure to realise the seriousness of the war. Yet this was not the most controversial feature of his war years. In May 1915 he signed as a professional in the Bradford League, a decision that sparked an explosive row in Yorkshire at a time when the Second Battle of Ypres was at its height in the blood-soaked trenches of Belgium and the *Lusitania* had just been torpedoed by a German U-boat with the loss of over 1,000 lives. Lord Hawke, the autocratic guiding force of Yorkshire cricket, described the signing of Hobbs as 'scandalous' and 'a most unfortunate state of affairs considering the present crisis', a stance that the Bradford League ferociously rejected, claiming that the local people needed weekend entertainment to distract them from the miseries of war. Hobbs's close involvement in the Bradford League ended when he was conscripted into the Royal Flying Corps in 1916, though the hostility between him and Lord Hawke was to last right up to the 1930s, contradicting the myth that Hobbs had no enemies in the cricket world. 'He was a silly old fool and he never had a kind word to say about me,' Hobbs once wrote privately. More painfully for Hobbs, the bad feeling extended to his own family, for all but one of his five brothers joined up in 1914 and two of them were badly injured. According to Mark Hobbs, one of his descendants, the disparity in service led to some friction. 'I think the animosity in the family, which I picked up, comes from the fact that others were expected to serve and Jack didn't because of his position as a cricketer,' he says.

Hobbs's early war years, the most contentious of his career, represent a fascinating episode yet it has never been covered before in his own books or in any profiles. It should not be allowed, however, to detract from his greatness. Sir Jack Hobbs was, of course, neither saintly nor Christ-like and he would have shuddered at the thought of being considered in such terms. He was a very human figure, with light and shade, flaws and strengths, in his character. Like all great men who spend decades in the limelight, it was inevitable that his story should contain incendiary rows as well as crowning successes. But his significance, not just for cricket but for wider British society, cannot be disputed. Through his outstanding batsmanship and the quiet dignity of his personality, he dramatically raised the status of professional cricketers. When he first played for Surrey, the game still operated in a semi-feudal fashion. Pay was poor, security almost non-existent. 'I am a hired servant on low wages,' Wilfred Rhodes once commented ruefully. The paid players had to lead almost separate existences from the privileged amateurs, who usually had their own dressing rooms, lunches, railway carriages and hotel accommodation. Built on naked snobbery against the professionals, cricket in the Edwardian age was riddled with injustices. Farcically, many amateurs actually had higher earnings from the game than the paid cricketers because of manipulation of expenses or bogus employment as club officials. But by the time Hobbs reached his peak, the structure of cricket had been transformed. The first-class arena was now dominated by professionals, who were respected and well rewarded, much to the anguish of some traditionalist diehards who wailed at the decline of amateur influence. Professionals 'are vastly overpaid for their efforts ... Players of today can and do afford to buy motorcars,' moaned E.H.D. Sewell, who detected a creeping political motivation behind the change. 'The whole crusade against the so-called dividing line between amateur and professional is Communistic, if not Bolshevist in tendency.'

Jack Hobbs was no Bolshevik, but his influence was crucial to the progress of professionalism. The very idea of keeping down this national hero, simply because he was paid for his brilliance, would have repelled most of the British public. Moreover, Hobbs elevated his profession in certain direct ways. In 1924/5 he told the MCC that he would refuse a place on the tour to Australia unless he could bring his wife Ada. Such a demand from a professional would have been treated with disdain in the Edwardian age, but because of Hobbs's importance to the England team, the MCC acceded. Similarly, in 1926, when the England captain Arthur Carr was taken ill during the Old Trafford Test, Hobbs temporarily took charge, becoming the first ever professional to lead England out on home turf. Again this is something that would have been unthinkable when Hobbs began. By the time he retired eight years later, the standing of professionals had risen even further. No longer artisans, their pay was on a par with doctors and bank managers and stockbrokers. 'The county cricketer has become a man of bourgeois profession,' noted Neville Cardus with a twinge of regret.

Hobbs's own journey was symbolic of the change, from the dire poverty of late-Victorian Cambridge to the affluent respectability in mid-1930s suburbia, with his villa in Wimbledon, his membership of the local golf club and his children at private schools. But, even in stratified England, Hobbs could never be defined by a single class. Perhaps more than any other celebrity of his age, he was symbolic of England and its values. In his famous wartime essay 'The Lion and the Unicorn', George Orwell wrote that 'the gentleness of English civilisation is perhaps its most marked characteristic. You notice it the instant you set foot on English soil. It is a land where bus conductors are good-tempered and policemen carry no revolvers.' This was the spirit that Jack Hobbs so perfectly encapsulated. He managed to be both a star and Everyman, another reason he was beloved by a public that recognised one of their own. It was a quality extolled by the Labour politician Harold Laski in an eloquent tribute to Hobbs written in 1931. 'In some ways I think Mr Hobbs is the typical Englishman of legend. You would never suspect from meeting him that he was an extraordinary person. He never boasts about himself. His private convictions are not cast at the public. He gets on with the job quietly, simply, efficiently. You could sit next to him in the Tube and remark nothing save a shrewd kindliness in his face, a certain quiet distinction of bearing. You would remark nothing in what he says until he is aroused. But then you would find whatever he feels he feels deeply; all that he thinks he has deliberated over until, as conviction, it has become a real part of himself.' Hobbs had shown 'as finely as any living man,' concluded Laski, 'what is meant by playing the game.'

From *Jack Hobbs: England's Greatest Cricketer*, 2011

HEDLEY VERITY

Max Davidson

A Very English War Hero

In peace there's nothing so becomes a man
As modest stillness and humility;
But when the blast of war blows in our ears,
Then imitate the action of the tiger,
Stiffen the sinews, summon up the blood;
Disguise fair nature with hard-favor'd rage.

Shakespeare, *Henry V*

By the time war was declared, on 3 September 1939, Hedley Verity was at the peak of his powers. In the very last first-class match he played, against Sussex at Hove, his bowling analysis was 6-1-9-7, which would have been extraordinary in normal circumstances. But nobody was concentrating on the cricket pages. As the Yorkshire coach travelled back up north, there had to be an unscheduled overnight stop at Leicester – a blackout had been ordered across the country and it was thought inadvisable to drive through the darkness.

If the war caught some people on the hop, Verity was ready. That he lost his life in the fighting was happenstance, an accident of war. But that he was *prepared* to lose his life was no accident. He had kept tabs on Hitler almost as closely as he kept tabs on Bradman. And he knew what had to be done to stop him. 'As early as 1937 he was certain that war was coming and said it would last for six years,' remembered his friend Bill Bowes. If only Verity had been employed by the Foreign Office, not Yorkshire County Cricket Club...

At the time of the Munich crisis in 1938, he had a meeting with Lieutenant-Colonel Arnold Shaw of the Green Howards in the pavilion at Headingley. The two men had first met five years earlier, when Shaw had hosted a reception during the England tour of India. Now, with Europe lurching towards war, Verity wanted to know how he could best prepare himself to serve his country, if the need arose. Shaw responded by giving him a collection of military manuals, which Verity, the perpetual student, read from cover to cover. On the 1938–39 England tour of South Africa, he could be seen boning up on army tactics and manoeuvres. Cricket had been a serious business. Now there was even more serious business to be conducted.

By the end of 1939, he had been gazetted in the Green Howards and was attached to the 1st Battalion under the command of Colonel Shaw. Its first posting was to Northern Ireland, on training exercises. There was even time for the odd cricket match. But Verity had no illusions about the seriousness of the challenge ahead. 'This is no chuffing garden party,' he wrote to his sister Grace. 'This fellow Hitler means it, if we don't stop him. We have got to stop him.' To his young sons, Wilfred and Douglas, he issued what sounds, with hindsight, like a personal credo. 'Always remember to do what's right,' he wrote, 'and to fight for what's right, if necessary.'

In training, he was far from a model soldier. The skills of his new profession did not come easily. 'To watch him stripping a Bren gun, you would think he had two right hands, mainly consisting of thumbs,' joked one colleague. Verity had little appetite for square-bashing: he was more interested in the finer points of military tactics. But when it came to the big picture, he knew where he stood. His attitude to the enemy was simply stated. 'They started it, now let them take it,' he told his commanding officer.

The same steely resolve could be seen among many of his Yorkshire team-mates. They had been a formidable fighting machine, the most successful in the history of the county championship. They had shown loyalty to colleagues, resilience under pressure. Now they had to exhibit those qualities in a new arena.

The first Yorkshire player to be called up was Herbert Sutcliffe, who had been a reservist before the war. He joined the Royal Ordnance Corps and attained the rank of major, but did not see service outside Great Britain and was discharged in 1942, at the age of 48, having undergone two operations for sinus trouble. Len Hutton, Sutcliffe's protégé as opening batsman, was called up to the Army Physical Training Corps, promoted to sergeant instructor, but damaged his wrist in a fall in 1941, necessitating a series of operations which left his left arm two inches shorter than his right. Verity's great friend Bill Bowes – appropriately for one of the fast bowlers who had formed the England attack in the Bodyline series – joined the Royal Artillery. He was promoted to lieutenant and served in North Africa, but was captured at Tobruk in 1942 and spent the rest of the war as a POW, losing four-and-a-half stone in the process.

Other Yorkshire cricketers in uniform included Maurice Leyland, Arthur Wood, Norman Yardley and Frank Smailes, the fast bowler. Many of them passed through the Green Howards depot in Richmond, prompting Verity to boast: 'I reckon we can put out a team from this depot to beat any county side in England.' George Macaulay, born in 1897, served his country twice – in the Royal Field Artillery in the First World War and in the Royal Air Force in the Second. He died of pneumonia in 1940, while stationed at Lerwick.

Even the non-combatants did their bit. The Batley-born batsman Edgar Oldroyd – well described by R. C. Robertson-Glasgow as 'one of those small, tough, humorous, militant men... who bounce and argue their way down time's corridors' – was 50 when war was declared but volunteered as an air raid warden. He took his responsibilities so seriously that, when he heard a siren go off in the night in 1947, two years after the end of the war, he immediately got out of bed, dressed and put on his helmet, ready for duty.

At first blush, it seems the most natural thing in the world that young men who had excelled at sport should also have been among the first to serve their country at a time of war. But we should not take that link for granted. In the First World War, Yorkshire, or parts of it, had been a hotbed of conscientious objection. As documented in Cyril Pearce's *Comrades of Conscience*, there was particularly strong opposition to the fighting in Huddersfield, where George Hirst lived. It was not just a few isolated individuals: Quakers and socialists found common cause.

After conscription was introduced in 1916, special tribunals had to be convened to hear the cases of those refusing to go to the front. One of them, Arthur Gardiner, argued his corner so eloquently that he was absolved from service for two months while his case was given further consideration. After the war, far from becoming a pariah – the fate of many conchies – he went on to become Mayor of Huddersfield.

One of Hedley Verity's best-known Yorkshire contemporaries was the actor James Mason, born in Huddersfield in 1909. He was studying architecture at Cambridge when war broke out, and declared himself a conscientious objector. His family found his attitude incomprehensible and severed all contact with him for a long period. Mason was not quite a social outcast, but he paid a price in his professional as well as his private life. Noel Coward refused to cast him in his Second World War classic *In Which We Serve*, arguing that it was wrong for a man who had refused to wear a uniform in real life to wear one in a film.

A united front was presented to the enemy. British propaganda was subtler than the German equivalent, but still seems artless today. There is an old BBC film, shot to raise morale, of three young men from Huddersfield, with ear-to-ear grins, cycling across the moors to the strains of *Ilkley Moor Baht 'At*. It conjures an innocent, wholesome world, pastoral in its unscrubbed charm, under threat from the forces of oppression. But the reality was more complex.

Not all the conscripts who turned up at the Green Howards depot in Richmond were spoiling for a fight with Hitler. Many of them would have been happier staying at home. Going to war might have felt romantic in 1914. It did not feel romantic now. Training could be pretty haphazard. One sergeant major tried to encourage his recruits to take their responsibilities seriously by organising a rifle-shooting competition with a small cash prize. The competition was won by a local gypsy, who absconded with the cash and was never seen again.

Barry Davitt, a furnace-man from Sheffield, was dumb insolence personified, if his account of his experiences at Richmond is any guide: 'Never mind this slop about King and Country. It's a load of old codswallop. You're fighting for yourself... We are herded into a barrack room and the sergeant introduces himself and impresses upon us that, although we are the worst-looking bunch of humanity he has had the misfortune to see, he will make soldiers out of us – that is what *he* thinks.

'Our first day is spent being inspected by doctors. The fashion seems to be nudity, as we are very rarely dressed. Someone wants you to cough, somebody wants you to look at something, somebody wants you to pass urine, and so it goes on...'

After a 6 a.m. parade in teeming rain, a close encounter with the dentist from hell, a brisk cross-country run and a difference of opinion with a butch PT instructor who wants to get rid of his beer belly, Davitt is left to muse: 'Is this the beginning of the end?'

At least Hedley Verity, ever single-minded, knew his priorities.

From the moment war was declared, his focus was on one thing – winning. When his unit was training in Northern Ireland, his wife Kathleen was able to slip across the Irish Sea to spend time with him, leaving her sister in charge of their three children. But the call to arms could not be long delayed. In early 1942, the 1st Battalion of the Green Howards sailed from Liverpool to India, from where it would eventually make its way to Egypt, via Persia and Syria, preparatory to the Sicily landings in the spring of 1943.

While in India, Verity had such a debilitating bout of dysentery that his doctors wanted to send him to a more congenial climate. But he was not to be sidetracked, insisting on rejoining his battalion before being declared fit. When he met up with his men on manoeuvres, he was still looking so weak that he was asked if he had got clearance from his doctor. 'No, but I'm not waiting any longer,' said Verity.

He could no more have cried off sick than he could have asked to be excused playing for Yorkshire because he had a headache.

The Green Howards are no more. The famous foot regiment – with a history dating back for more than 300 years – was amalgamated with other regiments in 2006 and is now part of the drably named Yorkshire Regiment. Administrative efficiency has done for the Howards what it did to the Ridings. It is not only Yorkshire County Cricket Club that has withered in the winds of change.

There is still a regimental museum in Richmond, North Yorkshire, and anyone curious to know more about the Green Howards, and the men who served with them, will get rich pickings there. Faded black-and-white photographs show soldiers slogging their way across the plains of Sicily in punishing heat. How they must have longed to be walking in the Dales or along the beach at Scarborough! But there is a grim determination on their faces. Hedley Verity's fellow Green Howards included Middlesbrough and England footballer Wilf Mannion, known as the Golden Boy, and Miles Smeeton who, along with his wife Beryl, became a celebrated explorer and round-the-world sailor. But it is the unsung heroes of the regiment, their names long forgotten, who bring a lump to the throat; fighting and dying thousands of miles from home.

There have also been some fine memoirs of the Second World War by soldiers of the Green Howards. The most recent is the excellent *Fighting Through – from Dunkirk to Hamburg* by Bill

Cheall, published in 2011. Edited by Cheall's son Paul, it is one of those extraordinary books, typical of the genre, where the most harrowing events imaginable are described in the most soldierly, matter-of-fact prose. 'All my six-and-a-half years in the army did not change my character and principles,' writes Cheall, a grocer from the village of Normanby, near Middlesbrough. 'I always minded my own business, had my pals and got on with the job.' It could be a Yorkshire cricketer speaking. No posturing. Just an honest day's work done, without complaint, for scant reward – two shillings a day (10p) when Cheall joined the Green Howards in 1939.

Cheall was younger than Verity, and their paths did not cross – Verity was in the 1st Battalion, Green Howards, Cheall in the 6th – but they both took part in the invasion of Sicily, crossing from North Africa on the HMT *Orontes* in July 1943. Cheall, who had also fought at Dunkirk, later took part in the D-Day landings as well. He had a crowded war, and the Sicily chapters seem like a pastoral interlude compared to some of the other horrors he saw. There are some beautiful vignettes of Mount Etna, glowing in the moonlight, and of hillsides refulgent with orange and lemon trees. But he captures the human landscape even better: the square-bashing and the sing-songs; the interminable journeys, by boat and train, to destinations unknown; the comradeship and the cups of tea; the larking about and the lurking terror. The book is a homage to the 'good north-country lads' that Cheall served with – many of whom never returned. Just boys when they enlisted, they had a man's job to do and they knew it.

Cheall's account of the preparations for the D-Day landings suggests that, despite a few backsliders, the needs of the regiment were paramount: 'There was to be no slacking or scrounging, and it would be stamped on in no uncertain terms. Nobody was allowed to go sick unless his condition was serious. Some of the lads used to play hell, and there was no shortage of foul language, but that was all part of the rough life we led – we did not pretend to be angels, but they were really grand lads and tough nuts to crack.'

Like Verity, Cheall was a devout Methodist and his religious faith informs his account. Others were not churchgoers, but in the solemnity of war, fell into line: 'I knew many lads who had tough characters, and didn't give a damn for anything or anybody, but they closed their eyes as soon as the Padre said, "Men, let us pray" – there were no objectors.' We think of the stiff-upper-lip generation that won the war as stoical, come rain or shine. We could not be more wrong, if Cheall is to be believed: 'Over the years, I saw some lads who, after being in battle, just gave vent to their feelings, and wept and trembled, out of control. These boys were not discriminated against in any way because we were all aware that lads of a particular nature just could not help showing their feelings in the aftermath. They had endured a very traumatic experience and they were by no means cowardly, because they had fought well and extreme tension had built up within them.'

For some, it all became too much. Poet and novelist Vernon Scannell of Leeds was not lacking in physical courage – he had been an amateur boxer before the war – but was so disgusted by the scale of the slaughter at Wadi Akarit, in the Western Desert, that he just walked away: 'I didn't think. It wasn't something I'd planned. I just turned around and walked like a machine or a ghost or something. It was unreal… I remember all those dead bodies lying out there… and got out and walked. It was like a dream. Why didn't anybody stop me? I just floated down that fucking hill like a ghost or the invisible man.'

Scannell was court-martialled as a deserter, but went on to write some of the most haunting poetry of the war, including 'The Walking Wounded':

> *… A humble brotherhood,*
> *Not one was suffering from a lethal hurt,*
> *They were not magnified by noble wounds,*
> *There was no splendour in that company,*

If there was no splendour, there was certainly solidarity. From every page of Bill Cheall's memoir, one catches the flavour of rough-and-ready friendships, laced with humour: men of few words sharing such extraordinary experiences that the bond between them would last for a lifetime.

While male comradeship was the glue that held everything together, women were not forgotten. Soldiers wrote tear-stained letters to their wives or went to their deaths with photographs of their sweethearts in their pockets. At one point in his memoirs, Cheall asks a friend to type out the words of 'Lili Marlene', so he can commit them to memory. The song had got under his skin – and he was not alone.

Originally a German song, recorded by Lale Andersen in 1939, 'Lili Marlene' became such a hit when it was broadcast on Radio Belgrade that soon soldiers on both sides were getting their nightly fix. 'Husky, sensuous, nostalgic, sugar-sweet, her voice seemed to reach out to you as she lingered over the catchy tune and the sickly, sentimental words,' wrote the diplomat Fitzroy Maclean, who listened spellbound to 'Lili Marlene' while serving in the Western Desert. English translations soon followed. It was more than the catchy tune that transcended national boundaries. The central conceit of the song – a soldier haunted by memories of a woman kissing him under a lamp post outside his barracks – had universal resonance. It spoke to a whole generation of men at war.

Hedley Verity had always been a dreamer, his mind a-wander. It would have been no different in wartime. As Siegfried Sassoon wrote of the soldiers of the Great War:

Soldiers are dreamers; when the guns begin,
They think of firelit homes, clean beds and wives.
I see them in foul dug-outs gnawed by rats,
And in the ruined trenches lashed by rain,
Dreaming of things they did with balls and bats.

But reveries on past glories could not be allowed to deflect from the main objective – the defeat of Nazism. 'Keep going, keep going, keep going...' The last instructions Verity gave to his men in Sicily before he was shot were of a piece with the man.

When you go home,
Tell them of us and say,
For their tomorrow
We gave our today.

The famous words of the Kohima Epitaph were not composed until 1944, a year after Hedley Verity's death, but if they still bring a lump to the throat, it is because of men like Verity and the sacrifices they made in such cruel, capricious circumstances.

The vagaries of cricket pale beside the fortunes of war. Edna Johnston of Sunderland married her husband, 'Shaky' Stewart, a sergeant major in the Green Howards, in 1939 and lost him, in near-farcical circumstances, on the very last day of war. He had survived the carnage at Tobruk and El Alamein, but fell off the top of a truck in Syria while lighting a cigarette. What a contrast with the experience of John Gandah of Durham, who was only four years old at the end of the war, but has never forgotten the homecoming of his elder brother, another Green Howard, who had been captured in Sicily and spent the rest of the war as a POW: 'When my brother came through the door, I remember hiding behind the easy chair in our sitting room, as I was confused at all the excitement and shouting and crying that was going on, and mostly I was a bit scared of this tall, very thin stranger who was my brother George that I had never seen before... Then the serious rejoicing started with my sister's boyfriend playing the accordion and my grandmother, all four foot eleven of her, banging a tambourine and singing "Where did you get that hat? Where did you get that hat?" There was a lot of eating and drinking and laughter that day. I even had a sip of beer out of my brother's glass, but my mother did not say a word. Her precious boy was home and he could do no wrong.'

There was no singing and dancing in the Verity household in Rawdon, not even a coffin draped in a Union Jack, just memories of a good man cut off in his prime. For what kind of tomorrow *did* Verity give his today? Was post-war Britain a better place than pre-war Britain? And, if it was a better place, has it remained a better place?

Hedley Verity would hardly recognise the Rawdon of 2012. The surrounding countryside is unspoiled. There are still bluebells in the woods through which he jogged. There are still some lovely views across the valley. But the town centre is such a shrine to 21st-century life at its most girlishly vacuous that a man of Verity's generation would run screaming down the road to Leeds. A home fit for heroes? More like a home fit for hedonists, fops and popinjays.

There are three hairdressers so close to each other that they resemble a cordon of Yorkshire slip fielders. A beauty salon offers 'lash perming', 'eyebrow sculpture' and 'semi-permanent make-up'. The florists are 'designer florists'. (Have they invented a new brand of gladioli?) Another shop advertises 'custom-made eyewear' – otherwise known as glasses.

Try and buy tea in the delicatessen and you will be offered a choice of three-fennel tea or mint-and-chilli. Try and hire a morning suit for a wedding and, if the mannequin in the window of the menswear shop is any guide, you will have to wear a white waistcoat with grey swirls. Even a traditional-looking butcher has a sign in his window reading 'Male and Female Models Required'. Throw in a French patisserie, where you couldn't get a bacon butty for love nor money, a bar called Nabu, packed with women reading *Hello!* magazine, and a clutch of boutiques with foreign names, selling dresses at prices that would have given Mrs Verity heart seizure, and you have an environment through which Hedley Verity would have walked uncomprehending, stunned by the frivolity of it all.

One of the men sitting at a pavement cafe looks not unlike Verity c. 1936, when he had just turned 30. He is similar in height and build and has an unassuming air: he does not say much and, when he does open his mouth, his girlfriend has to crane forward to hear what he is saying. But what would Verity have made of his matching ear-studs, spiky hair, salmon pink T-shirt and yellow shoes?

Perhaps Verity would have adapted with time. The men who fought in the war were nothing if not versatile. But Verity was a serious man at heart: happier working than idling. What would he have achieved with his life if he had survived the war? Cricket fans have naturally focused on the additional wickets he would have taken for Yorkshire and England. He would have been 40 by the time the war ended and, taking Wilfred Rhodes as a precedent, might still have had a few productive seasons to look forward to. Don Bradman's 1948 Invincibles might never have earned that tag if Verity had been bowling at Headingley when the Don and his men famously chased down 400 on a turning pitch.

But it is what Verity might have accomplished after retiring from the game that is really intriguing. With his tactical acumen, he might have been a superb coach and mentor to younger players, like George Hirst before him. He could have served as an England selector, as Herbert Sutcliffe did. But suppose he had tried to spread his wings and make a mark beyond the cricket field?

His son Douglas reckons he might have wanted to stay on in the Army. He had developed an appetite for leadership and military challenges. As a stalwart of his local Congregationalist church, he might have become a lay preacher, like his father. But there is another possibility. One woman who billeted Verity in Omagh, when he was training with the Green Howards, remembered him saying: 'After the war I would like to go into politics to make this world a better place to live in.'

Just idle chatter? Or evidence of more serious ambitions? Verity did not get actively involved in politics before the war. But he was not a man for idle chatter either. All through his life, he had set himself goals and worked tirelessly to achieve them. One can perhaps see him as a sedulous and effective backbench MP, harrying ministers on behalf of his constituents, the way he had once harried Australian batsmen. His very name on the ballot paper would have brought voters flocking to the polls.

One Yorkshireman of Verity's generation who both fought in the war and went on to have a successful career at Westminster was Denis Healey, one of the most formidable politicians of the post-war era. He was born in 1917, grew up in Keighley and represented his Leeds constituency for more than 40 years.

Intellectually, Healey is a heavyweight, where Verity was no more than a light-middleweight. He went to Bradford Grammar School, then got a double first in Greats at Balliol College, Oxford. He was terrifyingly well-read, not to mention having an extensive knowledge of art, music and the cinema. But in his general studiousness, his hunger to learn and go on learning, he could have been first cousin to the cricketer.

War challenged Healey, the way it challenged Hedley Verity. As a bright academic boy, he had been in his own words, 'an individualist intellectual'. Now he was suddenly faced with the need to be part of a team effort. The account of his wartime service in his autobiography *The Time of My Life* is bracingly free of cant or sentiment: 'Unfashionable though it is to admit it, I enjoyed my five years in the wartime army. It was a life very different from anything I had known, or expected. Long periods of boredom were broken by short bursts of excitement. For the first time I had to learn to do nothing but wait – for me the most difficult lesson of all … A dumb, animal endurance is the sort of courage most men need in war. I was constantly amazed by the ability of the average soldier, and civilian, to exhibit this under stress.'

Healey served in the Royal Engineers and, like Verity, took part in the Allied landings on Sicily in 1943. Later he saw action in Italy, was beachmaster at the Anzio landings, and attained the rank of major. The most valuable legacy of his war service was 'the knowledge that I depended on other people and other people depended on me'. That knowledge, in turn, created 'the sense of comradeship so characteristic of wartime and so lacking in peace'. No military operation, he realised, had any chance of success without concerted planning – a lesson he carried forward into his political career. Certainly there was room for initiative, bravery, individual acts of daring, but those qualities alone would never carry the day. The individual had to subordinate himself to the common cause. If Healey despised the every-man-for-himself rapaciousness of the Thatcher years, it was partly because of lessons he had learnt 40 years earlier on the beach at Anzio.

Hedley Verity, who was both the ultimate autodidact, forever learning, and the ultimate team man, doing his bit for his side, would surely have echoed Healey's sentiments. Yes, it was good to have talent, something that set you apart from the crowd. But that talent was worthless unless it was used in the service of a greater good, whether it was Yorkshire County Cricket Club, a successful Ashes campaign or the defeat of Nazism. There is a touchingly direct link between the young cricketer shuffling hairbrushes around on eiderdowns to work out his field settings and the captain in the Green Howards leading his men into battle after months spent studying military tactics. One belongs to comedy, the other to tragedy. But they share the same intensity of purpose.

Verity probably comes across as a greyer figure than the other cricketers featured in this book. Partly that is because he was so shy; he shunned the limelight whenever possible. Partly it is because he died young. But it also reflects the age he lived in. One of the paradoxes of the men who served in the war is that, for all their courage, they were also extraordinarily similar: they dressed the same, talked the same, had the same general outlook on life. Individual traits were flattened by the need to form a united front against the enemy.

If it had not been for the two great wars, the social conformity which had been one of the hallmarks of the Victorian era would surely have been relaxed faster than it was. Even in the Edwardian era, the discarding of corsets, literal and metaphorical, was well advanced; more individual self-expression was now admissible. But war, and the disciplines of war, retarded that progress. Every man in every regiment knew that he was part of a larger whole. It was no time for personal agendas. You had to march into battle together.

To their children and grandchildren, the men who fought in the war, and were lucky enough to return, were frustratingly opaque. They had lived extraordinary lives, but rarely talked about them. Reticence was second nature to them. As men, they could sometimes seem colourless as a result. There was none of the flamboyance, the jauntiness, the self-assertiveness that in peacetime makes a man the envy of his peers. But the unobtrusiveness of their virtues should not diminish them. Their willingness to function as a unit, putting self aside, was their lasting memorial.

Long before he put on his soldier's uniform, Hedley Verity was a good team man in a great Yorkshire XI. The three most productive periods in the county's history – the years before the Great War, the 1930s and the 1960s – were only possible because there was harmony in the dressing room and a strong team ethic on the pitch. When all that evaporated in the 1970s and 1980s, it resulted in a period of internecine warfare that made Yorkshire a laughing stock throughout the cricket world. There were some good players in the side, and some strong personalities, but they lacked the humility that is the integral aspect of manliness in a team sport.

The coming of war reinforced attitudes and principles that had been instilled in Verity since he first walked through the door of the Yorkshire dressing room. Fitting in was more important than standing out. It was not a time for show ponies.

He rose to the challenge, as if he had been born to face it.

From *We'll Get 'Em in Sequins: Manliness, Yorkshire Cricket and the Century That Changed Everything, 2012*

Fred Trueman held trenchant views to which he stuck remorse-lessly, refusing or unable to move with the times, which is why, in the end, he had to leave *Test Match Special*. It's OK for a while to hark on about the past but it gets to that stage when it loses its relevance, and unfortunately that is where Fred ended up: still telling his stories, still making people laugh, but when he said 'I don't know what's going off out there', he really didn't know what was going off out there. And that was the sign that it was time to let Fred go. That said, I will always regret the way it was done, as was the case with Trevor Bailey. They were never given the send-off they deserved as really important members of the *Test Match Special* team, and they both ended up feeling very bitter about it.

FRED TRUEMAN

John Arlott

Father of the Man

Scotch Springs is such a place as the Industrial Revolution and accidents of geology combine to scatter about the North of England. It is a terrace of twelve brick-built houses, each closely-set pair of front doors capped by a gabled porch. From their backs rich, dark ploughland runs to the village of Stainton, something over half a mile north-west. On the other side of the terrace, above the pocket of coal set in the farmland, is the vast grey whaleback, wrinkled with rain runnels, of the tip; the gaunt shaft and all the harsh surface works of Maltby Main, one of the most important mines in the south Yorkshire coalfield.

Fred Trueman, the fourth of Alan Thomas Trueman's seven children, was born at number five Scotch Springs on 6 February, 1931. The extravagance of the Trueman legend may be said to have begun at birth, when his weight was 14 lbs 1 oz. No record survives of any comment. He was christened Frederick Sewards – the latter his grandmother's surname – in Stainton Church.

By January 1971 the coal tip had pressed up on Scotch Springs: number five, like half the other houses in the row, was derelict, its windows broken and doors boarded. 'The colliery wants the land,' said one of the women who remained. When this appears in print the last of Scotch Springs will be buried under the waste of the pit.

Trueman senior, the son of a stud groom, was one of many grateful to find work in the pits during the slump of the early thirties, and he worked at the coal face in Maltby Main. A keen and useful left-arm bowler and batsman in local club cricket, he taught all his sons the game and encouraged them to play. Fred Trueman spent much spare time of his childhood in Stainton, a typically English village of two or three hundred people, where he went to his first school. It is now being 'in-filled', to use the planners' term, with ambitious residential development between the cottages.

There was plenty of cricket and regular evening practice on the pleasant small ground at Stainton until, when Fred was twelve, the family moved to Maltby on the other side of the colliery. Tennyson Road, Maltby is newer than Scotch Springs and number ten – red brick and tile, just across the road from a well-trodden football ground – is larger than the earlier house. It is part of the concentrated housing within walking distance of the colliery where virtually all the employed males of the district work; and near the centre – a cross roads, the largest pub, called the Queens, the Grand Cinema (also Bingo), a working men's club and some shops – of a town of some 10,000 population. It is a two-storey town, apart from a few ambitious gestures like Millards emporium; and its size and atmosphere are such that everyone knows, or knows about, everyone else; and no one is so far out of the swim as not to know Fred Trueman and to recall clearly some dramatic incident – true or untrue, but firmly believed – of his early life.

The switch from the village school at Stainton to Maltby Modern offered more opportunities for cricket, organised there by two masters, Mr Stubbs and Mr Harrison, who encouraged the young Trueman's ambition to be a fast bowler. He played for the school at football and rugby, too, and in the classroom laid the foundations of quick reading and retentive memory through which he is more deeply versed in cricket history and statistics than many first-class players who had more pretentious educations.

'Ah! Now, I grant you–that is out!'

Playing for the school at Wickersley, near Rotherham – and batting, like many a boy before and since without a protector – he was hit in the groin by a fastish bowler. He was taken to hospital in Sheffield for emergency treatment and for nearly two years – significantly for him two complete cricket seasons – he was virtually immobilised, and under treatment for an injury so serious that at one point dire consequences were feared. Through that depressing period, Messrs Stubbs and Harrison, with admirable sympathy, sustained his enthusiasm for cricket by arranging for him to score or umpire in school matches until, at fourteen and a half, he left to work in the local newsagent's shop.

If at this point he had been less than wholly committed, not merely to cricket but to becoming a fast bowler, the injury and consequent inhibitions, loss of practice and progress must have caused him to give up the game. His conviction, though, was complete; so complete that it carried along with him not only his father, who was predisposed to sympathise, but his brothers, sisters and mother as well. He joined a club called Roche Abbey and in his first four matches took twenty-five wickets at a total cost of thirty-seven runs.

This helped him to bridge the gap – not so wide in Yorkshire as in other parts of England, but still a fact even there – between boys' and men's cricket. His few matches for Roche Abbey brought him an invitation to go on a southern tour with a Yorkshire Federation boys' team that included Brian Close. This was an advance, but he remained impatient. He was now working in the pit as a haulage hand with the tubs, and this helped to harden him physically: but both he and his father realised that if he was to continue to make progress he needed to play in better cricket than he could find in Maltby. Sheffield was the obvious centre for him: he applied to join the Sheffield United club, at the beginning of the 1948 season, only to find the membership closed. Elsewhere this might have proved a long term, if not an insuperable check: but the Yorkshire system worked, as it usually does.

Sheffield has not played the important part in the county's cricket since the First World War that it did in earlier days. In some directions that is no bad thing: it means that no good potential is likely to be overlooked, and there is always someone keen to renew the credit of the district by the production of an outstanding performer. Cyril Turner, a left-hand bat and right-arm medium bowler for Yorkshire between the two wars, became professional to the Sheffield United club after 1945. In response to a carefully argued letter from Trueman senior, he watched Fred bowling, recognised the spark of talent, and persuaded the committee to reopen its membership to let him in.

The youngster's purpose and the excellence of his action made an impression: but he was yet appreciably short of his full height: often when he strove for extra pace his delivery became a sling, and he lost both length and direction. After a few matches for the Sheffield Second XI, and some expert guidance by Cyril Turner on his grip and his follow-through, he was brought into the club's Yorkshire Council team for the last five matches of the season when he took fifteen wickets.

Once more the Yorkshire system proved itself. The seventeen-year-old was erratic and inexperienced; but he had a basically good delivery and the positive merit of speed. That information was transmitted to the county's cricket committee and during the winter he was summoned – expenses paid – to Leeds for the indoor winter coaching classes under Bill Bowes and Arthur – 'Ticker' – Mitchell.

They watched and studied him and were convinced that his delivery swing – which argued his case as a young player more effectively than anyone or anything else, and saved his county career – was so essentially fine that all else had to be built round it. The first need was for control. He had to learn to bowl within himself, to use only as much pace as allowed him to maintain accurate length and line. He tended to over-pitch; and, for years after he should have known better, his response to anything in a batsman which displeased him – an edged stroke, a narrow escape, an effective stroke, above all, a successful hook – was the bouncer, dug in regardless of the state of the pitch or the batsman's ability to hook. It was late in life that he learned to threaten the bumper so convincingly that the batsman moved on to the back foot to deal with it, and then bowl him out with a yorker. Control for him was primarily a matter of temperament. In the nets he could maintain an accuracy which seemed beyond him under the tension of actual play.

He dragged his right foot an inordinate distance, but it was decided that any attempt to cure that fault might destroy much that went before: although subsequent changes in the laws were to make his drag a serious embarrassment, that decision was certainly correct. Some detailed but crucial alterations in the landing of his feet in the three strides of the actual delivery involved changing physical acts that had become automatic, but they were tested and practised until they, in their turn, were assimilated.

Bill Bowes has always said that Fred Trueman was the ideal pupil, not only desperately anxious to learn, but unquestioningly obedient and untiring in practice. So this was a winter of improvement, though at the end of it the decision was still 'Superb action, fairly fast, but....'

Yorkshire have no formal relations with their younger players, whose enthusiasm has generally made it possible for the county committee to be autocratic in its dealings with them. Their telegram summoning the young fast bowler from Maltby to play against Cambridge University on 11, 12 and 13 May, 1949, meant simply what it said, but not what he and his family inferred from it. He was single-mindedly ambitious about his future in cricket; but when the county's invitation arrived – indeed, when he took the field at Fenners – he had never played for the Second XI, nor even seen a first-class match; and he had next to no understanding of cricket politics.

The fact is that, when Yorkshire invited him to play at Cambridge, he had no place in their future plans. For years the county, to the pique of some of its opponents, has contrived three or four 'friendly' matches – against MCC, the Universities and perhaps a touring side – as high quality practice before they engage themselves fully in the graver business of the County Championship. The scores of these 'non-business' matches in *Wisden*, especially over a few years after the last War, contain the names of sometimes a couple of players, generally pace bowlers, who were virtually never heard of again. Yorkshire conscientiously try out cricketers who have reached a certain standard in their nets or in serious – preferably Yorkshire Council – club cricket. These early matches are constantly used to eliminate borderline players.

The new bowler they took to Cambridge could well have been intended for elimination – like six other opening bowlers who appeared in Yorkshire's University fixtures of the next five years. It was all but impossible to see a place for him within the county's current strategy: in respect of pace bowlers they were already, to use a Yorkshire expression, 'suited'.

At the level of first principles, Yorkshire are the last of the counties to be impressed by sheer pace. As historic fact they have had few truly fast bowlers, because they have always made accuracy their first demand and, hence, have generally preferred the medium or fast-medium bowler with his capacity for control, economy and long spells, rather than the man of higher speed who is likely to be less precise, less flexible in technique and capable of fewer overs. At this time their opening bowlers, both fast-medium, were already established: Alec Coxon – who had played for England against Australia in the previous year – and Ron Aspinall, a strong young man of high promise who had made good his place in 1948. They had both loosened their arms in the two preceding matches, against the New Zealanders and the Championship fixture with Somerset and now, since they were likely to have a heavy summer, they were being rested: hence the vacancy for Trueman. Norman Yardley was a capable third seam bowler in a team which would always maintain the traditional balance with at least two spin bowlers. Brian Close, the strongly fancied new all-rounder, could bowl both medium paced outswing and off-spin: he would be the other opening bowler at Fenners. All this was sufficient to remove any need for a new pace bowler. If one should be wanted in the future, Yorkshire already had two actively in mind. Bill Foord, now qualified as a school teacher, and John Whitehead, an undergraduate at London University, had been prevented by their studies from playing regularly: but Whitehead since 1946 and Foord from a year later, had turned out in occasional matches for the county after the end of the summer term. Both in their early twenties and experienced club cricketers, they had attracted interest beyond Yorkshire for pace above medium to an extent impressive in English cricket of the immediate post-war years. Neither was available in mid-May; but the need was not yet urgent. Other young pace bowlers, too, were in mind, such as Brooke, McHugh, George Padgett and Barraclough: but they had all been seen in Second XI or Council matches in the Leeds area. There was too, an awareness of local interests; justice to Sheffield must be seen to be done in Sheffield.

Yorkshire alone among the first-class counties do not maintain a ground staff. Traditionally a Yorkshire cap is hard to win; harder than an England cap, they say in Yorkshire; and certainly Yorkshiremen have played for their country before they were capped by their county. Thus, while contracted young players competing for established places in other counties know one another from regular contact on the ground staff, those of Yorkshire often do not. The rival is also a stranger and usually the more keenly resented for that fact. Competition for caps can be harsh and, even in the case of players of outstanding potential, long drawn-out. Len Hutton fought for his place as opening batsman with Ken Davidson (who subsequently made a high reputation as a badminton player). Bill Bowes disputed his cap with Frank Dennis, later Len Hutton's brother-in-law; Johnnie Wardle was matched with Alan Mason for the place of slow left arm bowler; and in 1970 Neil Smith and David Bairstow competed for the wicket-keeper's place left by the retirement of Jimmy Binks.

The objective captain or county selector can be certain that competing cricketers will not relax and can prevent any complacency in a player by protracting the competition. It may not be comforting to the cricketers but it makes for combative efficiency, and it can be reasonably assumed that Yorkshire have more than once taken that pragmatic view.

Little if any of this was in Fred Trueman's mind on the evening of 10 May, 1949 when he met the rest of the Yorkshire team – all of them except Brian Close complete strangers to him – at the Danum Hotel at Doncaster for the journey to Cambridge.

He has said that when he went on to the field at Fenners next morning he was nervous for the only time in his life. Perhaps that was the beginning of the transformation of the basic Fred Trueman. He – probably only he – sensed that he had ceased to be an ordinary boy.

From *Fred: Portrait of a Fast Bowler, 1972*

20 DECEMBER 1991

ARLOTT'S DELIVERY

SIR – The death of John Arlott (obituary, 16 December) will be a heavy blow to all cricket lovers, because he enriched our lives for nearly 40 years.

My favourite of so many rich items with which he regaled us goes back to a 1947 Test match when K.G. Viljeon had driven the ball out to deep extra cover. John said: 'And Doug Wright's running after it as only Doug can run: variety in every stride'. All who remember the great D.V.P. Wright's 'hop, skip and jump' run-up to the wicket will see the picture immediately. Of course, with John's deliberation and his lovely accent it sounded much better – variety in every syllable.

A.D. Mills
Totnes

From *Not In My Day, Sir: Cricket Letters to the* Daily Telegraph, *2011*

I spent many hours in the *TMS* commentary box with Fred and my favourite story of our time working together happened when we were at Headingley one year. In those days we didn't always have a television monitor in front of us and on this occasion one had been set up at the back of the box. I was talking to Fred on air, during a break in play, and he was chattering away, reminding everyone – as ever – what a great fast bowler he was. Looking over his shoulder at the television, I could see that they were showing a young Fred running in to bowl. I quickly worked out that it was the 1963 Lord's Test, famous for the game-saving appearance of Colin Cowdrey when he was forced to bat with a broken wrist. What is not so well known is that the West Indian opener Conrad Hunte hit the first three balls of the match for four – off Fred. I started to laugh and Fred turned around just in time to see Hunte play admittedly not a great shot, but the ball still flashed away for the third four. By now I was really laughing, but without missing a beat Fred turned back to the microphone and stated in that wonderfully gruff Yorkshire voice, 'Isn't it funny how much slower you look in black and white?'

FRED TRUEMAN

Chris Waters

Bollocks To You, Mate

The telephone rang in the RAF sports store. Fred Trueman answered and was greeted with the words, 'How does it feel to have been picked to play for England?' Not recognising the voice, and sensing a wind-up, Trueman replied, 'Bollocks to you, mate,' and slammed down the phone. His fellow erks were always playing practical jokes.

A few seconds later, the phone rang again. 'Fred, how does it feel to have been picked to play for England?' Again he said 'Bollocks' and slammed down the phone. A few seconds later, the phone rang a third time. 'Fred, it's Bill Bowes. The chap who just called was John Bapty of the *Yorkshire Evening Post* and he's brought me to the phone to convince you it's true. Fred, you *have* been picked to play for England. Congratulations on your marvellous achievement.'

It was Friday 30 May 1952. Trueman had been chosen for the first of a four-match Test series against India at Headingley. He'd just returned from two weeks' leave to play in Yorkshire's opening four home games of the season, taking twenty-five wickets. Now he went back to Group Captain Warfield and asked for more leave, Warfield agreeing on one condition – Trueman arranged some tickets for him and his wife.

Trueman reported to the Prince of Wales Hotel in Harrogate for the traditional pre-match dinner and immediately felt ill at ease. 'The first thing I noticed was that there was a hierarchy in the England team similar to the one that existed in the Yorkshire dressing room. And being the young debutant I was at the bottom of the pecking order. I was made aware of that by the fact that Bill Edrich, Denis Compton and even my club team-mate Len Hutton kept themselves to themselves all evening, only recognising my presence by way of a nod of the head when I was initially introduced to them. I felt as if I had gained entry to a small and elitist club.' Trueman quietly sipped orange juice and looked around for someone to talk to. The experience did little to calm his nerves.

Hutton had his own worries: he'd just been appointed England's first professional captain to celebration in Yorkshire and a mixed response elsewhere. Lord Hawke's famous remark, 'Pray God no professional will ever captain the England side', reverberated loudly in Hutton's ears. As it turned out, Hutton could not have wished for a better series to slip into the role. The Indians were weak, despite having won their first ever Test against England in Madras the previous February, and particularly fragile away from home. India had lost five of their six matches on foreign soil since entering Test cricket in 1932, the other a rain-ruined draw against Australia in Sydney. Their 1952 side was young and inexperienced: Vijay Hazare's men had only fifty-seven caps between them going into the Headingley Test, in which Hutton was making his fifty-seventh appearance, against a combined England aggregate of 234.

On a typically benign Headingley pitch, Hazare won the toss and opted to bat. Alec Bedser opened at Trueman's favoured end, the Kirkstall Lane end, while the newcomer ran up the slope from the Rugby Stand end. When England took the field, Trueman strode up to Bedser, who was playing his thirty-ninth Test and had carried England's pace attack since the war. 'If you keep 'em quiet at one end,' he advised, 'I'll get the bastards out.' Trueman made little impression against openers Pankaj Roy and Datta Gaekwad, so Hutton quickly took him off. He wanted to save him for a crack at Polly Umrigar, a prolific scorer against lesser pace but known to be vulnerable against faster men.

After Bedser bowled Gaekwad, Trueman was recalled for a shot at India's no. 3. Sure enough, Umrigar jabbed unconvincingly at a short ball from Trueman and edged to wicketkeeper Godfrey Evans, handing Trueman his first Test wicket. After slipping to 42 for 3, India recovered through a splendid stand of 222 between Hazare and Vijay Manjrekar, the latter dominating Trueman as he swept to a maiden first-class hundred. But in the final hour of the opening day, England clawed back the initiative when the visitors lost three wickets on 264. Trueman claimed two of them: Manjrekar well caught low at second slip by Allan Watkins for 133 and Coimbatarao Gopinath bowled for a duck. Next morning, overnight rain came to the aid of Jim Laker, who took the last four wickets as India were dismissed for 293. Trueman finished with 3 for 89 from 26 overs – an encouraging but expensive start compared with Bedser's 2 for 38 from 33 overs. England replied with 334, the elegant Tom Graveney top-scoring with 71 and Evans contributing a jaunty 66. Then, at five minutes to three on Saturday 7 June 1952, and with more than 25,000 crammed into Headingley, India began their second innings. What happened next was straight out of *Boy's Own* ...

Trueman – this time given the Kirkstall Lane end – purposefully marked out his twenty-two-yard run. A hush of expectation fell on the ground as he tugged up his sleeve and tore in to bowl. His first ball to Roy was well outside off stump and allowed to pass through harmlessly to Evans. The second was a rank long hop: Roy topedged a hook and was caught at first slip by Denis Compton ...

0 for 1.

India sent in Madhav Mantri, a solid defensive player who'd scored an unbeaten 13 in the first innings at no. 8. Mantri somehow survived the rest of the over – a wicket maiden – as Trueman worked up a fierce head of steam. From the fourth ball of the second over, Bedser got one to lift awkwardly off a length to Gaekwad – the only delivery of the day that behaved unpredictably. It took the splice of the bat and ballooned apologetically to Laker in the gully …

0 for 2.

Umrigar played out the remainder of the over – another wicket maiden – before Trueman eagerly re-entered the fray. Inspired by the growing excitement of the Leeds crowd, which seemed to infuse him with an extra yard of pace, Trueman steamed in to bowl the opening ball of his second over. It was arrow-straight, took Mantri by surprise and sent his middle stump cartwheeling …

0 for 3.

As the stands erupted, a disconsolate Mantri trudged back to the pavilion. To his astonishment, it wasn't Hazare – India's most experienced batsman – who came in next, but Manjrekar, with the captain having opted to drop down the order. Mantri considered it a pusillanimous decision. 'I crossed Manjrekar on my way in and his pale face is still vivid in my memory. He looked at me and muttered in Marathi: *"Mala bakra banaola"* (I've been made the sacrificial goat). Hazare wanted to avoid the intense pressure of going in at nought for three and had asked Manjrekar to bat ahead of him. It was an act of self-preservation that should never have been allowed to happen.' Despite his first-innings century, Manjrekar was a twenty-year-old playing only his third Test. Like most of his colleagues, he'd little experience of dealing with pace, the pitches in his own land discouraging speed. Unsettled by his team's situation, and momentarily frozen, he aimed a loose cover drive at his first ball from Trueman and lost his leg stump …

0 for 4.

In the space of fourteen balls, India's batting was in shreds. Trueman had three wickets in eight balls and English cricket had found a new hero – not to mention a long-awaited answer to Lindwall and Miller.

'There was pandemonium in the stands,' recalled Trueman. 'I couldn't believe what was happening to India, to England, to me. I happened to glance across to Len Hutton. For a brief moment our eyes met. Then Len's head fell, he sighed and shook his head from side to side as if saying, "I don't believe it, Fred." I was having trouble believing it myself … Dad was somewhere in that crowd.

The man who had sacrificed so that I could have the opportunities he was denied. The man who had stuck by me when I had been injured and Yorkshire had not given a thought to my welfare or well-being. I wondered how Dad was feeling.'

As England celebrated Manjrekar's wicket, Hutton pointed to the scoreboard. 'Take a good look at it,' he urged his players. 'You'll never see another like it in a Test.' Such were the feelings of disbelief that attended the most dramatic start to a Test innings, the sports editor of the *Yorkshire Evening Post* telephoned his reporter at the ground to check whether India, in actual fact, were 4 for 0.

Trueman was on a hat-trick. Hutton stationed eight men around the bat as Hazare – having finally appeared at no. 6 – tentatively took guard. Trueman raced in and produced a searing yorker that flew an inch past the outside edge and just missed off stump. The crowd let out a collective gasp. Caught up in the emotion, Trueman followed with an indifferent couple of overs and was rested by Hutton. He took his sweater to intense applause. Gaekwad recalls the mood of the Indians. 'We were shell-shocked. There's no other word for it. To be nought for four in a Test match was incredibly upsetting. We'd been very much in the game until then but Freddie changed all that. He was focusing totally on out-and-out speed. He didn't have the control of later years, but it didn't matter. As the wickets went down he was shouting and swearing because that's how he thought a fast bowler should be. He was making all sorts of elaborate gestures and loving every minute.'

Watching at the Kirkstall Lane end was eleven-year-old Geoffrey Boycott, who'd gone to the game with friends. 'We caught the train at 7.55 a.m. from Fitzwilliam and got the bus to Headingley and queued up there. Then we ran like hell to get behind the bowler's arm to make sure we got the best seats possible. When Fred got his first two wickets, this fella said to us, "If he gets another wicket this over, I'll buy you all an ice-cream." Well, he bloody well did get another wicket, so we all had an ice-cream on Fred.'

After the players trooped off for tea, Trueman sat on his own in a corner of the dressing room. 'I was acting as substitute fielder and I brought Freddie a sandwich and a drink,' said Bryan Stott. 'He was in a state of shock, quite frankly. He was mesmerised the way things had gone. He was temporarily lost for words, which, for

Freddie, was quite amazing.' Stott recalls the fear in the Indians' eyes. 'I could see their batsmen on the balcony when Freddie was on the rampage. There was sheer panic among them. It was quite incredible. Most of them looked a bag of nerves.'

After tea, Hazare and Dattu Phadkar mounted a revival of sorts, lifting their side from 26 for 5 to 131 for 5. But ten minutes from the close, Hutton brought back Trueman, who clean bowled Hazare with another straight ball that effectively settled the contest. Trueman returned England's best figures of 4 for 27 and wasn't needed on day four as Roly Jenkins and Bedser mopped up the tail. Reg Simpson top-scored with 51 as England won by seven wickets. Pankaj Gupta, the India manager, admitted his players had been scared of Trueman. 'It is terrible, terrible,' he told the *Yorkshire Post*. 'I am very distressed. This Trueman has terrified them.'

There was no time for Trueman to bask in his triumph. Directly after the match he joined an RAF cricket tour of Holland and Germany, from which he was released for the second Test at Lord's. Trueman's journey back to England was impossibly laborious. He left Germany at 4 a.m., caught a bus, a train, a ferry, a taxi, followed by another train and taxi, eventually arriving at the team hotel in London at 8.15 p.m. Such a journey would be unthinkable now just two days before a Test. Trueman still managed four wickets in each innings but his performance was patchy. On another good pitch, he conceded 182 runs, which offended Hutton's sense of economy. England won by eight wickets on the back of a splendid 150 from Hutton and 104 by Evans in a first-innings total of 537. Trueman was back in action the following day for Combined Services against the Indians at Gillingham. He tried to bowl too quickly, turned his ankle, and wasn't fit again until the third Test at Old Trafford three weeks later.

Anyone who thought Trueman's display at Headingley a happy accident was emphatically disabused of the notion in Manchester. England batted first and made 347 for 9 declared, their innings extending into Saturday morning after rain delays on the first two days. With the pitch wet through and the light uncertain, India were clearly intimidated by Trueman. Operating from the Stretford end with a stiff wind blowing over his right shoulder, he made the ball spit and soar as Hutton attacked with three slips, three gullies, two short legs and a silly point. After Bedser had Vinoo Mankad caught at short leg, Trueman got to work. He had Roy and Hemu Adhikari caught in the slips as India plunged to 5 for 3.

In came Umrigar, who'd looked as scared and susceptible as any top-order batsman and whose arrival invariably prompted Hutton to call on Trueman. On his way to the middle, Umrigar stammered, 'B-b-bowling's not bad today, F-F-Fred.' Trueman looked him up and down with something approaching contempt and replied, 'It's not meant to be, Polly.' As Umrigar hopped around during his fifteen-ball innings, Tony Lock – fielding at backward square leg – taunted, 'I say, Polly, do you mind going back a bit, I can't see the bowler when you stand there.' Asked by the umpire where he wanted the sightscreen, Umrigar was said to have replied, 'Between me and that mad devil Trueman.' Tom Graveney says the only certainty is that Umrigar was petrified. 'Polly was bloody terrified of Fred. His first movement when Fred came running in was back towards square leg and he wasn't able to deal with his pace. Fred was a dragger, and his front foot pitched two or three feet beyond the popping crease. Apart from being quick anyhow, he was a yard closer than the modern bowler, and poor old Polly just couldn't cope.'

After softening up Umrigar with a salvo of short balls. Trueman shattered his stumps so spectacularly one of the bails broke (it was the bail he gave his brother Arthur). Such was his stranglehold over Umrigar, he dismissed him four times in the series as he scored just 43 runs at 6.14. When he left Test cricket in 1962, Umrigar had made 3631 runs at 42 and become one of India's all-time greats. But his failures in 1952 – and cat-on-a-hot-tin-roof antics at the crease – were largely responsible for propagating the image of Trueman as a bowler so devastating that batsmen bolted for cover behind the square-leg umpire.

Roared on by a packed and partisan crowd, Trueman followed Umrigar's wicket by having Phadkar caught in the gully off a wild slash to leave India 17 for 5. Hazare and Manjrekar added 28 for the sixth wicket – the highest stand of the innings – before Trueman bounced out Manjrekar, who fended to short leg trying to protect his face. Trueman bowled Ramesh Divecha, Bedser bowled Hazare, before Trueman rounded off the innings by having Gulabrai Ramchand and Khokhan Sen caught at the wicket. In 21.4 overs, India had been routed for 58 – their joint-lowest Test total – and Trueman had 8 for 31 from 8.4 overs: the best Test figures by a truly fast bowler. 'I was backed up by magnificent fielding from all my colleagues,' said Trueman. 'It gives you heart when you have people like that fielding to you. You can't do without luck and I certainly had my share. Another time I might have returned none for 131.'

With India on the ropes and his bowlers still fresh, Hutton enforced the follow-on. Trueman soon removed Roy for a duck and followed up by hitting Adhikari so violently in the mouth the batsman was carried off in some distress. But Trueman himself succumbed to injury as he suffered a sudden attack of stitch, managing only eight overs in the innings. Adhikari reappeared to top score with 27 as India staggered to 82, Bedser taking five wickets and Lock four as England won by an innings and 207 runs. Nineteen years later, Adhikari returned as manager of the first Indian team to win a Test series in England. John Hampshire, the former Yorkshire and England batsman and international umpire, recalls the moment Trueman encountered his adversary at Bradford Park Avenue. 'Yorkshire were playing the Indians and I missed the match with a broken thumb. I finished up in the bar with Fred at lunchtime and Fred saw Adhikari coming out the committee room. He said, "Nah then, sunshine. I'm glad to see you've got your colour back." '

No sooner had the Manchester Test finished than Trueman received a telegram from Captain Warfield. He assumed Warfield had taken the trouble to convey his congratulations. Instead, the telegram instructed: 'Report back to unit 8.00am Sunday.' Trueman had done himself out of two days' leave. A fortnight later Trueman was released for the Roses match ahead of the fourth and final Test at the Oval. After Yorkshire scored 200 at Old Trafford, Trueman and Eric Burgin, his old Sheffield United coach, took advantage of a drying pitch to skittle Lancashire for 65, claiming five wickets each.

Yorkshire made 163 for 8 in their second innings to gain a lead of 298, but Trueman lost his head on the final day. He had a set-to with Lancashire captain Nigel Howard and was spoken to by the umpires. 'We were pressing hard for victory and Fred lost his temper when Howard took a few runs off the edge of the bat,' said Burgin. 'He started giving Howard some verbals and it got out of hand. Eventually, the umpire called Norman Yardley over and said, "I can't have this sort of language being directed at the opposing captain." Meanwhile, Fred had gone back to the start of his run-up and was casually sitting on the grass without a care in the world. Norman Yardley went over and said a few gentle words when he should have given him a right old rollicking.'

The game ended with the last pair of Frank Parr and Bob Berry hanging on for dear life as Lancashire closed on 166 for 9. 'Funnily enough, Fred was held up in some quarters as being responsible for us not winning the match,' added Burgin. 'Roy Tattersall came in towards the end and Fred was more about hurting him, I think, than bowling him out. He hit Tattersall on one occasion and he had to have physio. In those days, you didn't play so many overs because of the time factor. We lost about ten minutes while Tattersall was being treated and that made a big difference. Fred could get very upset if things didn't go his way.'

Although he'd matured as a bowler since debuting at Cambridge, Trueman had yet to mature as a thinking cricketer. Against county players he now expected to get out, and certainly against batsmen who played him as timorously as the Indians, he was prone to over-enthusiasm in his lust for speed. Like many a young fast bowler. Trueman didn't always use his loaf; he relished making batsmen jump about as much as he relished taking their wicket. He revelled in the terror and theatre of his pace, even asking the Yorkshire groundsman to water the stump holes so the stumps would go flying through the air when he hit them. But even when striving and straining for extra zip, his action remained a thing of great beauty. As R.C. Robertson-Glasgow wrote of Don Bradman, 'Poetry and murder lived in him together'. So they did in F.S. Trueman.

John Arlott captured the Trueman in motion of 1952. 'There was in his approach that majestic rhythm that emerges as a surprise in the Spanish fighting bull. It steps out of the toril, stands hesitant, cumbersome then, suddenly, sights the peon from the cuadrilla, pulls itself up and sets off towards him in a mounting glory of rhythm, power and majesty. Such was the run-up of the young Trueman as, body thrown forward, he moved first at a steady pad and gradually accelerated, hair flopping, and swept into the delivery process. Again the analogy of the bull holds good, for the peak of its charge is controlled violence, precisely applied in a movement of rippling speed. Trueman's body swung round so completely that the batsman saw his left shoulder blade: the broad left foot was, for an infinitesimal period of time, poised to hammer the ground. He was a cocked trigger, left arm pointed high, head steady, eyes glaring at the batsman as that great stride widened: the arm slashed down and as the ball was fired down the pitch, his body was thrown hungrily after it, the right toe raking the ground closely behind the wicket as he swept on.'

From *Fred Trueman: The Authorised Biography, 2011*

What a fascinating double act Jim Laker and Tony Lock were. Jim always seemed such a gentle person, but there was clearly steel in him as his eventual falling-out with Surrey would prove. Laker was a classic off-spinner who took nineteen wickets in a Test match while left-armer Lock, at the other end, was firing it in flatter and flatter, getting crosser and crosser. There was clearly a very competitive edge to their relationship. How must Lock have felt driving away from Old Trafford that day in 1956? Of course they had just beaten Australia, but he must have felt people were laughing at him. And there was, of course, an issue with his action. As he darted the ball in again and again, his elbow got more and more bent, but what an intriguing combination. As a kid I signed up for the *Cricketer* magazine and my welcome gift was a facsimile front page of the newspaper that reported Laker's amazing achievement. I can still see it now. Nineteen wickets in a Test match! Will anyone ever get twenty? You can't imagine it.

JIM LAKER

Amol Rajan

The Second Flourish

Of the 149 bowlers who have taken more than a hundred wickets at Test level, only six (S. F. Barnes, Colin Blythe, Johnny Briggs, George Lohmann, Bobby Peel and Charlie Turner) have averaged less than [Johnny Wardle's] 20.39. Only three among those 149 have a more miserly economy rate than Wardle's 1.89 runs per over: Trevor Goddard (1.64), Lohmann and Verity (both 1.88).

And yet, for all that, Wardle would be forever in the shadow of another bowler, Tony Lock, somewhat ironic when you recall that Lock himself seemed forever in the shadow of Jim Laker. Lock and Laker's association runs very deep, and goes far beyond the sharing of twenty wickets at Old Trafford in 1956; but perhaps the more illuminating parallel for our purposes is that between Lock and Derek Underwood. Both were left-handed spinners for England, yet the appellation 'slow' when talking about their left arms could hardly be more insulting, so hastily did they come over in both cases.

Lock got fatter rather than flatter with age, but when in his prime during the mid-fifties, two things marked him out: one broadly good, the other broadly bad. The first was his speed. Bowling at slow-medium or medium pace, he was frightfully quick off the wicket, sometimes skidding in with the arm, sometimes fizzing sharply away in the direction of slip.

The second was his crooked arm. Everyone knew that Lock chucked his quicker ball, but there was an influential camp in cricket's fraternity that said he chucked every ball. This led Lock to prolonged bouts of anguish and self-enquiry. He excited little sympathy, despite the known provenance of his technical difficulty, which was the low roof beams at the indoor school in Croydon where this son of Surrey learned his trade. Lock had started out as a flighty slow left arm in the mould of Rhodes or Bedi, but his winter in this indoor school caused his arm to bend, and fundamentally altered his approach to bowling. He pounded his way through the crease with such effort that he needed a steel toecap in his left boot, to stop the sole tearing off. His bent arm was causing consternation, and was the subject of endless gossip. When, after India were beaten in three days in 1952 (including being bowled out twice in one day, both times for under a hundred), Fred Trueman raised the subject with Len Hutton: 'Isn't Tony's new action a bit strange?' Trueman asked his captain, during a drive over the Pennines. Hutton smiled wryly, and added: 'It is, but I think I will beat the Aussies next summer with him.' Sir Len was never one to be distracted from the chance to put one over on the Great Enemy.

In a sign of that perseverance which separates the spinners in these pages from the also-rans of cricket history, Lock remodelled his action not once but twice, having seen film footage of his shortcomings. Still, the remark made to an umpire by Doug Insole, who had just had his stumps rearranged by Lock's 'thunderbolt' delivery, never left him: Insole enquired if he'd been bowled out or run out. Perhaps it was that infamous comment that Bedi was drawing on in his later insults towards Muralitharan. Some claimed this faster ball was genuinely lock-up-your-daughters quick; more likely, it sometimes nudged 80mph.

An obsessive watcher of westerns, which he would frequently scurry off to catch in a local cinema if a new one came out on tour, Lock was an inspirational and successful captain of Surrey during their glory days of the 1950s. He later migrated to Australia where he continued to be an outstanding leader of men. He was one of the first great short-leg fielders, held exceptional catches off his own bowling (Trueman considered him the best catcher he'd ever seen) and appealed as vociferously as some modern-day Pakistanis (well, nearly). But even in his adopted homeland, a sense of controversy lingered around him. In 1964–5, he was sent from the field in a game to wash the Friar's Balsam from his hand. Again, he received little sympathy when pictures were released showing the appalling lacerations on his hand: Lock suffered more, and for longer, than most spinners from raw, bleeding, swollen fingers. Scars from the wounds proved useful weapons in countering the argument that he was a medium-pace bowler rather than a spinner, as did his appearance in the dressing room. As Bailey put it, he was a 'mystifying collection of bandages, elastic stocking supports and various plasters, while his spinning finger was treated by a magic formula which was intended to harden the skin and heal the cuts'.

Friar's Balsam was one thing, and forgivable in the eyes of those who know what spinners suffer for their shilling; but further controversy followed when he was twice accused of assaulting some young girls he was coaching in Australia. He was cleared of both charges, but his reputation never fully recovered.

It's hard to know what makes a man behave in ways that land him in such difficult situations; but it's a consistent thread of Lock's life, sympathetically conveyed in Alan Hill's fine biography, *Tony Lock: Aggressive Master of Spin*, that he seemed insecure at some deep level. He had vulnerabilities, and a sensitive character, and though his anxieties were sometimes the butt of team humour, as when they produced the sleepwalking or vivid nightmares Bailey introduced us to in an earlier chapter, at other times they were more sobering. When he was called for throwing against the West Indies by a square-leg umpire (the uncle of Clyde Walcott, in fact), Bailey reports:

I will never forget the look on Tony's face. He was shattered, as was the team because he was a vital link in our bowling attack. It took quite a time for him to get over that pride-wounding incident and he cut the fast ball out of his repertoire.

But, as Hill argues, it's inevitable that a major cause of Lock's anxiety must have been his association with Laker. It's not widely known that the two didn't speak for about a month after their twenty-wicket extravaganza in 1956, though they were slightly closer friends in later life; and it seems somehow unfair that Lock's fate is to be remembered, in some quarters at least, as simply an append-age to the greatest bowling achievement of all time. Lock said years later that he wished he hadn't denied Laker all twenty, and perhaps from his point of view that would have lessened the focus on his comparative failure in that July Test. It might then have been *all* about Laker, and not just 95 per cent about him, which naturally draws attention to the conspicuous 5 per cent remaining, Lock's solitary wicket (Jim Burke, caught Colin Cowdrey, bowled Lock for twenty-two, first innings). He bowled one more over than Laker in the game, but took eighteen fewer wickets. Peter Richardson, who scored a hundred on the opening day of that Test, recently wrote: 'Lockie would attack; Jim would chip away. It was no secret they didn't get on. They were always competing.'

It's not just what happened at Old Trafford that would have fuelled his inferiority complex: the two were conjoined at Surrey, the alliterative energy of their names forming a music heard down the ages, not least through the immortal lines

Ashes to ashes, Dust to dust
If Laker don't get you, Lock must

(These words were later bastardised and adopted by those fabu-lous but far simpler creatures, Dennis Lillee and Jeff Thomson, the terrifying Australian fast-bowling duo.)

And who couldn't feel inadequate, when bowling at the other end to a man who was essentially unplayable, and in the business of acquiring match figures that, though they may hypothetically be passed, are likely to stand the test of time? As the ever useful Bailey pointed out years later, the tragic thing from Lock's point of view, the thing that must have given him sleepless nights, was that

Laker took nineteen of the twenty wickets despite Lock bowling his heart out:

> The most remarkable thing was not that Laker took nineteen wickets but that Lock took only one and the reason, of course, was temperament. The more wickets that Laker took, the more Lock tried and tried and the faster and faster he bowled. Meanwhile, Jim just carried on putting the ball on the spot and letting the pitch do the work.

There was no question that Lock felt terribly hard done by. Keith Stackpole, the Australian, asked Lock years later why there was only one wicket in his sixty-nine overs. Lock's answer was blunt – and bitter: 'Destiny was against me: catches fell short, batsmen played and missed, appeals were turned down, nothing went right for me.' This was remarkably similar to the popular account of Laker's ten-wicket haul for Surrey earlier in that season, when Lock again struggled in vain, only to be outshone by Laker. William Keegan, the legendary economics writer still penning his brilliant column for the *Observer*, was at the Oval when Laker took all ten. 'No one was in any doubt,' he told me, 'that Lock was absolutely going hell for leather in both innings. There was no suggestion of him trying to send down long-hops for Laker's benefit.' There is a lesson for young spinners in this, but it speaks of something rather sad and iniquitous, namely that Laker made it look easy while Lock toiled from the other end. The pitch *did* do the work, but only for one of them.

'The mere idea of [Laker] showing enthusiasm,' said Peter May, who captained them both at Surrey and at England level, 'is absurd.' The black-and-white footage we have of that magnificent spell testifies to Laker's method: he loped in with that lackadaisical approach of his, lobbed the ball up to the right-hander from around the wicket and watched the Australians tumble one by one. If the first great lesson of this spell, of letting the pitch do the work, is harder to translate into the modern game because we have covered pitches, the second important lesson – that off-spinners going around the wicket to the right-hander can be a devastating form of attack – is not so hard to translate into the modern game, and should be learned urgently.

Of course, Laker did have the advantage of a sticky wicket – rain dampened, but drying out because of the sun. But posterity should know that from the very start of the game the pitch had been the talking point. Treated with red marl (known as 'treacle') earlier in the season, it seemed certain not to hold together. Gubby Allen, chairman of England's selectors, had instructed Bert Flack, the groundsman, to shave the pitch. He duly did so – and covered the pitch to conceal it from the press. The Australians suspected a conspiracy, knowing what great form the English spinners were in (strange to think there was a day when that sentence didn't seem absurd). But England, batting first, amassed 459 at a speedy rate, dampening the disquiet of the Australians temporarily. As for Flack, his infamy was short-lived, but mainly because of events elsewhere. 'Thank God Nasser had taken over the Suez Canal,' he reflected years later. 'Otherwise, I'd have been plastered over every front page like Marilyn Monroe.'

Half an hour after he started bowling in tandem with Lock, Laker switched to the Stretford End, from where he would take all of his wickets. (This trick has worked well much more recently too: Graeme Swann took 5–76 against Bangladesh in June 2010 by switching to this end.) Less than an hour and a half after Laker and Lock began their partnership (including the tea interval), Australia were bowled out for eighty-four, with Laker having taken 9–37. In the Australian dressing room Ian Johnson, the visiting captain, lambasted his players for their shortcomings against spin, but then declared that they could still win the game if they batted their hearts out. As Benaud has subsequently confirmed, Keith Miller then piped up and said '6–4 we don't'. The Australians left the dressing room deflated.

Their spirits were raised, as so often when one team is being battered, by the arrival of rain. When most of play was washed out by rain through Saturday and Monday – all of it thirstily consumed by the wicket – the Australians thought Miller's prophecy, and cheek, might be trumped after all. But when opener Colin McDonald fell to the second ball after tea, Laker's calm annihilation unfolded. Five bowled, three leg-before, ten caught in the slips or leg-trap and one stumped: footage of the nineteen-wicket rampage is deceptive in how straightforward it makes his approach seem. Around the wicket Laker goes, arm coming over at one o'clock, sometimes lower, a big pivot of his braced front foot, plenty of air, the ball dipping violently on to a fullish length outside off-stump, and the

Australians, terrified of coming forward, mostly playing, or failing to play, from the crease. When he took the tenth wicket, John Arlott's commentary came as close to Kenneth Wolstenholme's 'They think it's all over' as cricket can: 'Old Trafford has redeemed itself with a last hour of glorious sunshine. Laker comes in again, hair flopping, bowls to Maddocks, it turns and Laker appeals, and he's out leg-before and Laker's taken all ten!'

The great man responded with the kind of understated emotion you might expect of a chap whose career started in a bank. Throwing his jumper over his left shoulder, and uncrossing his legs from the position they acquired as he made his final appeal, that loping gait of his carried him from the pitch, with what must have felt like a thousand handshakes causing his giant, and now swollen, spinning finger to ache further. That afternoon, a round of interviews finally having been completed, Laker drove away from the ground, heading to London. He stopped off at a pub in Lichfield, Staffordshire, for a pint. Sitting there sipping his beer, not long after producing the greatest of all bowling performances, he wasn't recognised by a single person. And yet all around him the pub was abuzz with chatter about the Test result. When he got home that evening, his wife – who, being Austrian, didn't have a strong cultural affinity with the philosophy of off-spin – said she was perturbed by the dozens of congratulatory phone calls. 'Jim,' she said, 'did you do something good today?' She had her answer when the next morning's *Daily Express* splashed with 'Ten Little Aussie Boys Lakered In A Row'.

That 'something good' would have been more than enough to mark Laker out as a sporting great, but his imprint on the game was strengthened by events after his retirement. He became a dry, witty and perspicacious commentator for the BBC, his voice loved by millions, and his partnership with Benaud made one wonder what they might have done if they could have bowled in tandem as well.

Here, too, was a spinner who, despite the everyman, classless aspect of his character, was not as uncomplicated as that subdued celebration upon his tenth wicket in Old Trafford might have intimated. In the dressing room he was a loner and stubbornly introverted, his favourite companion often the fag in his mouth. Indeed, there seemed an incongruity between his status as a living legend and his boy-next-door lack of glamour. He wrote an angry autobiography which led to his being stripped of honorary membership of Surrey, the club he had served so well as a player. They felt that he had misrepresented them, and were irate at the perceived discourtesy. The MCC felt obliged to show solidarity, stripping Laker of honorary membership with them, too. Both Surrey and the MCC eventually recanted and restored membership, but it left a sour taste. Nor were the game's administrators united in support when he honourably declined the offer to work on Kerry Packer's World Series Cricket in 1977, a decision interpreted as stubborn and old-fashioned.

Born illegitimately in Shipley, near Bradford, in 1922, Jim Laker was the only boy of five children. His father left when he was two, and he was spoilt by a doting mother who was dead by the time he returned from war aged twenty-three. His aunt, a teacher named Ms Ellen Kane, was a cricket nut and introduced him to the game. He had initially wanted to be a batsman or fast bowler, but took up off-spin in time to practise it while serving in the Middle East, partly because even as a child the enormous knuckle on his index finger – that is, his spinning finger – had inspired comment. Some said he was deformed; Laker said he was lucky. It would eventually be the source of his greatest successes in life, though finally it developed arthritis and led to a premature end of his playing days. Before the war he had worked for two years at Barclays in Bradford; later, when billeted at Catford while posted to the War Office, he joined the local club, and soon made it to Surrey, but not before he had enquired as to whether or not he might get into the Yorkshire side. Failure to do so, and the rejection he felt, led to his briefly returning to a career in the bank. In the interim he also missed a trial for Essex because of the lacerations on his spinning finger, and took ten wickets in an innings in a club match, something he would make a habit of.

Laker made his breakthrough relatively late by modern standards – though having seen the case of Grimmett, we can forgive him for so doing. In 1956, aged thirty-four, he had played in only twenty-four Tests, roughly half of those for which he was available. He made that statistic look silly when he took those nineteen wickets, but it wasn't simply that performance that suggested he'd been underused by England. Laker had taken the phenomenal figures of 8-2 in the Test trial at Bradford, his home town, in 1950, a performance he rated as his finest ever. The Australians knew about this reputation before they arrived in 1956, but if there had been any lingering doubts about his skill, they would have been dispelled by that 10-88 he took when they played against Surrey early that very season. He later said he thought this a better performance than his Test 10-fer, given the quality of the pitch (as against the deteriorating track in Manchester). By painful irony, Laker only got the ten Australian wickets narrowly: Miller was dropped at extra cover when the Australians were nine down. The bowler? Step forward, Tony Lock. He seems wronged many, many times over.

Sometimes known by the same epithet as that other great spinner – Tiger – because of his energy in the gully, there should be no doubt that Laker's best attribute as a bowler was ferocious, devilish, air-munching spin. It was said that even in Test matches, with packed crowds, you could hear from the boundary the rip he gave the ball. This spin he allied to unfailing accuracy, and on rain-affected pitches he would go around the wicket to right-handers with sometimes five close fielders on the leg-side. 'A craftsman in a great tradition,' wrote Cardus, 'a classic exponent of off-spin, the most classic of all kinds of bowling.'

Such competence made him probably the finest orthodox off-spinner to play the game, though it's hard to account for the exact benefit he derived from uncovered wickets. He was the best spinner to play for England and on his day the finest bowler, too. Certainly, if Barnes could claim to be the most complete bowler, Laker could claim to have been intermittently the most unplayable. And yet, for all that, the wonderful thing is that he had, at least in the years before that Old Trafford Test, genuine rivals for the status not only of best bowler in the world, but best spinner, too – and the two men who came closest to rivalling him were both bowlers whose stock ball came in from the off.

From *Twirlymen: The History of Cricket's Greatest Spin Bowlers, 2011*

28 JANUARY 1955

STUMPED

SIR – Mr H.H. Thomas might have ended his letter with the cricket conundrum to beat them all: Why it is that wickets are pitched to start the day's play but stumps are drawn to end it?

F.A. Allcott
London W1

29 JANUARY 1955

WICKETS OR STUMPS

SIR – Mr H.H. Thomas seems unable to differentiate between the words 'stump' and 'wicket'. The *Oxford Dictionary* clearly states that a wicket comprises one set of three stumps and two bails.

In the light of this etymology, it is not difficult to understand why a batsman may lose his leg, middle or off stump, but not his leg, middle or off wicket. Similarly, a bowler bowls round or over a wicket because three stumps equal one wicket. Again, 'stumps are drawn' because each stump is plucked out of the ground individually; if three stumps were drawn intact with the bails simultaneously the wicket would be drawn.

G. Bernard Edgeler
London SE25

From *Not In My Day, Sir: Cricket Letters*
to the Daily Telegraph, *2011*

I like Geoffrey Boycott enormously. We have always enjoyed mutual respect since we first played against each other, and I would add that he has always been very kind to me, even when I was a freshly minted professional bowling to him all day in the nets at Melbourne during the winter of 1978–9. We have worked together in the media for years and, as you would expect, he is the most professional of broadcasters who speaks a great deal of sense, even if he does witter on about uncovered pitches. Unlike another erstwhile Yorkshire commentator, Fred Trueman, Geoffrey has moved on with the times and appreciates how the game has changed. He is a strong advocate of day/night Tests, although I am not sure he would have been too keen to bat in one.

Geoffrey has allowed me to poke fun at him ruthlessly for more than twenty years, believing that it helps popularize him. That way he hasn't got to work too hard to make people laugh at his jokes, but he knows I will sometimes make him seem absurd. When I do, he takes everything I say with a smile.

As a batsman he was the epitome of methodical precision based on preparation, a classical player who had all the shots even if he didn't play them very often. Has anyone been more dedicated in honing his talents than Geoffrey Boycott? I suspect not. As he says, 'I can look at myself and know I could do no more.' His self-absorption when at the crease could be difficult in a team situation and it is true that he didn't always press on as others might have liked, but he would argue that once he was set it was the job of those coming in after him to be a bit more expansive. That those players might be trying to nail down their place in the side was not his concern, and it is understandable that this sort of tension could lead to acrimony. But there is always room in a team for an individual, and to Yorkshire and England's benefit that individual was the great Geoffrey Boycott.

GEOFFREY BOYCOTT
On Batting

Self-discipline and a strong, clear mind are vital and those qualities are more important than quantity in terms of practice. It is more productive to work very hard one day and have the next off as a holiday than to turn up on a regular basis and be casual. I have seen Yorkshire and England players mess about for a quarter of an hour in the nets, slogging away unconcerned about what happened to the ball. They claimed to have been practising, but really they were wasting their time, going through the motions. When I batted with John Edrich in the West Indies on Colin Cowdrey's tour of 1968, he said of me: 'Geoff makes you play well because he seems so much in charge at his end.' Composure and determination are by-products of sensible preparation. Too many lose interest during practice because they lack concentration. I concentrated for every minute, whether in the nets or out in the middle, whether taking strike or standing at the bowler's end. I tried to work out how long a particular bowler would stay on, how many overs the best bowlers would get through in a session, which fielders might concede runs under pressure and how the pitch was playing. Also, I counted my runs, which helped me to shut out all distractions. I remember batting with Hampshire's Richard Gilliatt in Malaysia on an England 'A' tour and, as we did not have a scorer with us, the local official, a young girl, did duty for both sides. When we came off she proudly informed me that I had scored 154 not out. 'You're wrong there,' I said. 'I got a hundred and seventy-six. You've given Gilliatt twenty-two of my runs. I'm glad you won't be scoring in the first-class games.'

The scoreboard can be used in other ways as an aid to concentration. To avoid becoming complacent, especially if we were doing reasonably well, I used to add a couple of wickets on to the score and reflect on the situation then. There is a great deal of difference between 120–1 and 120–3 and it is surprising how often when one wicket goes down another follows quickly. Gloucestershire's Jack Russell works on a similar principle to keep himself up to the mark. He keeps an eye on his individual total and continually asks himself: 'Would you really like to get out for that?'

Concentration is the key, and without it a batsman is always likely to throw away his wicket. I remember a day–night match in December 1979, between England and Australia at Sydney. We faced Dennis Lillee, Len Pascoe, Rodney Hogg and Geoff Dymock on a decent pitch, but one which had just that little bit in it for the quicks. Australia was restricted to 194–6, a total which indicated accurately the degree of difficulty for the batsmen. The contest was reduced to forty-seven overs a side, so we had a real fight on our hands. Peter Willey helped me to put on 111 for the second wicket. Across the road in the Sydney showground rehearsals started up for a Rod Stewart concert; this was followed by a speedway meeting and then by a firework display which began with giant rockets whizzing into the night sky. The noise was tremendous, and five wickets went down for 27 runs in no time. In the middle of all this pandemonium Derek Randall marched down the wicket complaining bitterly. 'I can't go on with this banging and crashing. It's impossible to concentrate,' he said. 'Why, what's happening?' I asked. I could, of course, hear the disturbance, but I had shut it out so completely that it represented no more than a hum in the background. 'I'm well established,' I told Randall. 'There's no way I'm going off. We'll win, don't worry – do your best.' He got out for one and gave me a resigned glare as he stalked off with that unmistakable walk of his, but I finished unbeaten on 86 and had Yorkshire wicketkeeper David Bairstow for company as England got home by four wickets with eleven balls to spare.

The secret of concentration is not to let outside factors register. Be aware of them by all means, but keep them outside the mental bubble in which you are operating. Concentration is about channelling your mind into a specific area while directing your energies in one direction. It is not as simple as saying that you will not let your thoughts drift on to what you might be going to do that night or something similar. The mind has to be trained, and there is a lot to be said for building up a regular pattern, starting with homework. This should be done before each day's play and I used to work backwards from the time I wanted to be able to sit down with a nice cup of tea and give myself a short break before the match began. My routine had to account for the possibility that I might be batting straight away, as I would be on the first day 50 per cent of the time. As a matter of habit, I arrived on the ground an hour and a half before the start of play, leaving myself ten minutes to get changed, fifty minutes for exercise and a net and thirty minutes to cool down and think through what the day might have in store.

By always planning ahead I avoided having to rush into a game. It is crazy for a batsman to walk out without giving due thought to the bowlers. Who does what? Which bowlers swing the ball out or in? Is there anyone with a peculiar characteristic? It is possible to be out-witted once – that is human – but anyone falling into the same trap twice is a fool. West Indian Franklyn Stephenson's superb slower ball, which has gained him so many wickets, demands respect. Marshall's bouncer tends to skid through because he is only five foot nine inches, and he has hit a lot of batsmen who did not do their homework. Joel Garner continued to surprise the unwary with his yorker, speared in from something over nine feet. Going back to Mike Procter's lbw hat-trick at Cheltenham, where he bowled round the wicket, it amazed me to see Bill Athey and John Hampshire not offering a stroke, for they should have known that the South African allrounder brought the ball back sharply, forcing batsmen to play at deliveries pitched very much wide of the off stump. Padding up to Procter was asking for trouble.

Being fully prepared was particularly important to me as an opener. I could not enjoy the luxury of sitting in the pavilion watching the early exchanges while I assessed the bowling and the conditions. I had to be ready for anything, as I faced up to the first delivery in nearly every game in which I played. I kept a little black book in which I put notes against the various bowlers who had dismissed me. I thought they would remember how they had got through my defences, and it made sound sense for me to remember as well.

By this simple means I built up a dossier on my leading oppo-nents, and I discovered that some bowlers were easier to score off in certain areas, so a few minutes' homework reading up before a game often paid dividends. I never regarded these notes as being infallible, however, because I had to be flexible and ready to adapt to changing circumstances. Nevertheless, I left as little to chance as possible. It never fails to surprise me when I talk to other cricketers and find that they are not aware of the strengths and weaknesses of other players. They are simply not giving themselves the best chance of doing well. The 1975 men's singles final in the Wimbledon tennis championships stands out as an example of what can be achieved by thoughtful preparation. Arthur Ashe overturned the odds to beat the clear favourite Jimmy Connors because he had devised a plan beforehand. Ashe had lost to Connors often enough to appreciate his power and he knew that the bouncy left-hander liked nothing better than the ball being driven hard at him. Connors used the speed of the ball onto his racket to hammer the ball back, so Ashe countered by gently angling his returns, forcing Connors to stretch across the court and generate his own pace of return.

I had serious trouble in 1978, after I had broken my left thumb in a one-day international against Pakistan at Old Trafford and missed a string of matches. Pressures put on me by the Yorkshire committee forced me to return before I should have done. Because my left hand was not completely healed, I could not grip properly and my right hand began to take over more and more of the work without my realizing it. When I came back from New Zealand that winter I found that I had slipped into something approaching a two-shouldered stance. This was a real shock to me as I had always had a model stance completely sideways on to the bowler, showing nothing of my right shoulder. I could barely recognize myself on the video. I realized that I needed to take immediate action to get back into the correct position, so I contacted Don Wilson, who is in charge of the indoor school at Lord's. He arranged nets for me morning and after-noon; one of the bowlers was a youthful and distinctly pacy Norman Cowans, at that time making his way towards the Middlesex side. I had to force myself to turn around sideways on and it felt awkward, as though my left shoulder was pointing to extra cover, but in reality I had done nothing more than resume my normal stance. I spent the first few weeks of the season uneasily forcing myself to keep my right shoulder back out of the way, but all the effort brought due reward when I finished the 1979 season with an average of 102.53, to enter *Wisden* as the only batsman to top the three-figure mark twice in an English season.

From *Boycott On Cricket, 1990*

I managed to fall out rather badly with Mike Brearley a year or two after the 1981 Ashes series. During a Leicestershire-versus-Middlesex county game at Lord's, I was batting, Middlesex were losing the game, and Mike was at slip, clearly in an unhappy frame of mind. He distinctly asked Middlesex fast bowler Wayne Daniel to 'soften me up', which the big man duly tried to do. Mike and I exchanged a few words when I was finally dismissed, and I was disappointed when he did not open the batting for the second innings. It took a while to resolve the tension between us, but I have always had great admiration and respect for him and it is good to see that he is still very much involved in the game.

ABOUT CAPTAINCY

Mike Brearley

That series also illustrated in a clear-cut way the different approaches adopted by England and Australia to choosing a captain. Traditionally, England have appointed the captain first, and then co-opted him to pick the team, while Australia have selected their best eleven and made one of them captain. In 1978, neither Yallop nor I would have been captain had the methods been reversed.

Historically, the English attitude has been connected with class distinctions. Until well after the Second World War, the view was that a bunch of professionals needed an amateur as captain. (A similar view applied in the West Indies, until 1960.) The Australians valued 'leadership qualities' less; at least on the surface, for I presume that they were not entirely unconcerned whether they had in their eleven a man capable of leading the side. Similarly, for England it was not an entirely irrelevant consideration that the captain should be a decent player.

In an ideal world each system would produce the same result. But it can happen that the best tactician is nowhere near being the best player; and then the relative values of personal performance as against leadership ability have to be weighed up. Such balancing may, naturally, be called for at any level in the game, but the most notorious examples occur in the selection of Test captains.

The difference in Australia's and England's approach to captaincy is well-known. What is not so well-known is that Australia moved closer to our method after their 5–1 defeat under Yallop in 1978–9, when Hughes was named captain for the tour of India in advance of the rest of the party.

In England, too, we oscillate in the emphasis we place on a person's experience or reputation as a captain alone. This oscillation depends on recent successes or failures. For example, in the Australian season following our win there, we were decisively beaten, 3–0, in the three-match series. At the end of that tour, I announced that I would not be available for future tours. The man chosen to replace me for the home series against West Indies had had no previous experience as a captain; there was, further, no question about his being good enough for the side, since he was at that time the best all-rounder in the world. I refer of course to Ian Terence Botham who, incidentally, I too felt should succeed me.

A little more than a year later the selectors were debating another change. England had, not surprisingly, struggled against West Indies and then Australia; Botham himself had had a rough time with bat and ball. Now the cry in the press and elsewhere was for someone at the helm who was without doubt qualified as a captain, whether or not he would be included on playing ability alone. My name and Keith Fletcher's were most widely bandied about as possible choices; but the press mentioned also others even less likely to be selected except as captain, like Roger Knight of Surrey or John Barclay of Sussex. At that time, no one talked of Bob Willis or David Gower or Graham Gooch, though they were firmly established in the team.

Part of this shift in the stress on captaincy *per se* lies in the image of potential captains, and how that image fits in with the mood of the cricketing public of which the selectors form a part. In 1982, for example, when Peter May took over from Alec Bedser as chairman of the selectors, Willis replaced Fletcher for the home series against India and Pakistan. I believe that this choice had much to do with the respective images of these two in May's mind; one extrovert, dominant, prepared to castigate players for lack of will, personally courageous; the other retiring, less intense, more reflective. Two years before, Botham had seemed a perfect antidote to me, as he was charismatic and of heroic stature.

Partly, too, such a shift reflects a genuine conflict. We *do* value tactical shrewdness and the ability to bring the best out of the players: we are also rightly reluctant to 'carry' a Porbandar in any side.

Certainly the *best* player is not necessarily an adequate captain, any more than the best salesman makes a sales manager. Indeed, the outstandingly gifted may well find it difficult to understand the problems of the average performer in their field. The Peter Principle is that people are inevitably promoted beyond their sphere of excellence. Nevertheless, at any level of the game, the captain, as with the sales manager, needs to be at least an adequate performer in the practical, first-order skills, otherwise it will be extremely difficult for him to gain the respect of the team, and to keep his own self-respect. I would go so far as to say that he *should* be worth his place in the side as a player alone, unless he has unequivocally proved his value as a captain. In 1977, just to remind the reader, when I was appointed captain of England in place of Greig, I had been picked as a batsman for the previous six Tests.

So, we have established the not very novel point that our headhunters must take into account both playing skills and leadership ability. But how are they to spot leadership qualities in those who have never had experience of the job? Clearly we constantly do form an impression of someone's potential on the basis of what we know of them (though I recall Tacitus's cautionary *mot* about the Emperor Galba, that he was *capax imperii nisi imperasset* – capable of ruling, if he had not ruled). Each appointment is to some extent a guess, every step in life has an element of uncertainty. But everyone who has ever captained a side once captained for the first time. Someone must have made a favourable judgement about his potential.

I keep flourishing this phrase 'leadership qualities'; what would our headhunters take this to mean? Again, this is a large question, to which much of the book is an attempted answer. Here I should like to discuss one approach to leadership that is sometimes suggested – that the great captains, like others who command respect, have some indefinable quality called 'charisma'.

Charisma originally had a religious meaning. It was a God-given grace of the personality capable of inspiring others by means of love, admiration, affection or a touch of fear. 'I'd follow him anywhere,' someone says. Or, 'They'd do anything for him.' Charisma is an effulgence of personal qualities, innate, or at any rate not capable of being acquired by study. In England, charisma and leadership have traditionally been associated with the upper class; with that social stratum that gives its members what Kingsley Amis called, 'the voice accustomed to command'.

Until 1954, every captain of England was an amateur; that is, he was not paid to play cricket. (The Latin root implies that amateurs played because of love of the game, rather than for anything so base as money.) Before the War, and for some time afterwards, the distinction was secure. Amateurs had different changing-rooms, stayed in better hotels, and emerged on to the playing area through separate gates. They stated when they were able to play, which explains why a cricketer of G. O. Allen's stature played only 146 matches for Middlesex in a career spanning twenty-six seasons. Their names were represented differently on score-cards either as 'Mr' or with 'Esq', or with the initials before rather than after their surnames. In 1950 Fred Titmus played his first game at Lord's. It was a fine Saturday, with a good crowd. An announcement came over the loudspeaker: 'Ladies and gentlemen, a correction to your scorecards: for "F.J. Titmus" read "Titmus, F.J." '

As late as 1960 I played for the Middlesex 2nd XI at Hove. I was still at school; this was only my second game with a mainly professional side. I was told to change in a large room, plush with carpets and sofas, along with our captain R.V.C. Robins (Esq). The other ten – all professionals – were changing in a tiny makeshift room virtually under the showers. Perhaps it was not entirely a coincidence that I was run out twice in the match.

By no means all the amateurs in cricket were High Tories in background or style. They had simply gone on from school to Oxbridge, been good at cricket, and followed a natural route into the first-class game. (Indeed, until 1981 the *Wisden* 'Births and Deaths' list marked out those of us who played for Oxford or Cambridge as 'Mr'.) Trevor Bailey and M.J.K. Smith were among those who took up secretarial jobs with their county sides in order to enable them to afford to play. The post-war amateurs became more like the members of Margaret Thatcher's cabinet than of Harold Macmillan's; more, too, like the latter than like the MCC Committee of the 1950s, when Lord Monckton was alleged to have said that in comparison to it Macmillan's cabinet were a group of 'pinkos'. Being an amateur not only kept one's status honourable amongst one's friends; it also opened up, for the better players, the chance of the ultimate honour – the England captaincy. Wally Hammond, after all, had changed from being a professional with this aim in mind.

Ted Dexter was undoubtedly one with the personality, style, and looks to fit his Radley background. Imperious as a player and, at times, as a man, it was not for nothing that he was widely known as 'Lord Ted'. Dexter scorned run-accumulation as much as he might money-grubbing, and it was typical that he would often get out to fourth-change bowlers who, he thought, ought not to be allowed to bowl.

I have already mentioned the West Indies' attitude to captaincy. For many decades the leader had to be white. It was axiomatic that no black man could be considered. Thus when in 1960 Frank Worrell was appointed captain for the tour of Australia it was a turning-point in West Indian cricket. (His leadership also marked a telling transformation in the performance of the team, whose success has continued almost unbroken until the time of writing.)

In England the abolition of the amateur/professional distinction did not formally arrive until 1962. Now that there is no restriction according to colour or social origin, far more players have become candidates for the captaincy of county or country, and more still see themselves as candidates. Captaincy is no longer a job reserved for members of a certain caste, and one result is that there is more rivalry, envy, and even jostling for position. In common with other members of society cricketers are not as humble as they once were; they no longer compare their own lot only with that of their nearest rivals. They say 'why not me?' about a wider range of possibilities. This fact itself implies alterations in the task of the captain.

However, my main point is that it has long been recognised that the charisma of a leader is not a matter of social origin. I have already used the word to describe Botham, for his power, combativeness, and his ability to transcend the limitations of the ordinary cricketer. He also has a rare generosity to those of less ability; he values the stodgy but resolute contribution of a hardworking batsman, even if his score might only be 15 or 20, and a word of acknowledgement from him means more than fulsome praise from others.

In a quite different way Brian Close had charisma. He of all the captains I have known led from the front. His courage was notorious.

Fielding incredibly close in at short square-leg, the great dome of his head thrust belligerently forward, he was regularly struck by the ball. The story goes that it once rebounded from his forehead to second slip. 'Catch it!' Close shouted. After the catch the Yorkshire players hurried up to him. He assured them he was all right. 'But what if it had hit you an inch lower?' one asked. 'He'd have been caught in t' gully,' Close replied.

Less apocryphal is the episode of his catch to dismiss Gary Sobers for 0 in the match between England and the Rest of the World at the Oval in 1970. The pitch was easy-paced, and Sobers was one of the most powerful hookers the game has known. Few players apart from Close would have stood at short square-leg to Sobers on such a pitch, even before he had scored. The bowler, John Snow, produced a token bouncer, and Sobers, seeing it early, was quickly in position to smash it to the square-leg boundary. I am convinced that any other cricketer with an ounce of sense would, in Close's position, have thrown himself to the ground, protected his head and closed his eyes. But the indomitable Close did not even flinch. As luck would have it, Sobers was too early with his shot, and too high; the ball touched the bottom edge of his bat, was deflected on to his hip, and bounced up for what turned out to be a simple catch. Close, still in position, and still looking, caught him.

In the Lord's Test against West Indies in 1976 we had gained a first-innings lead. West Indies were batting cautiously against Underwood and Pocock in their second innings; but were beginning to fret. Close, in his usual suicidal position, turned to David Steele at backward short-leg and whispered, 'They're getting fed up; they'll have a lap (i.e. a sweep) in a minute. I'll get in t' road, and you catch t' rebound.' This was, of course, in pre-helmet days; I cannot imagine Brian wearing one anyway. He is also alleged to have maintained that a cricket ball can't hurt you as it's only on you a second. Such neglect of personal safety is, if not admirable, certainly awesome.

My last example of a charismatic captain is the reverse of the caricature with which I began. Ian Chappell was an anti-hero, firmly anti-Establishment. In many ways he was an inspiring, tough and shrewd captain; but he also nudged cricket in the direction of gang warfare. I never played against Australia in a Test when he was captain, but in 1979 I did play against South Australia when he was in charge. In that match, which admittedly occurred in the turbulent aftermath of the Packer division, I was struck by the lounging hostility of their fielders and the way remarks would be directed out of the corner of the mouth, half out of earshot of the batsman but not, I felt, particularly complimentary to him.

I had always admired Ian's attitude to umpiring decisions until that match. It was quintessentially Australian – never walk, but never show dissent either. In one Test against England in Australia, the sixth, at Melbourne, in 1974–5, he was given out twice in the match caught at the wicket when the ball had merely touched his pads. He marched off in his usual trenchant way, allowing none of the spectators to know that the umpire had made a mistake. In the 1979 match I was referring to, however, I squeezed a ball into the slips: I thought I played it off the toe of the bat into the ground. On appeal the umpire gave me not out. The fielders made their disappointment very clear; in response to which I said with some heat, 'I played it into the ground.' At the end of the over Ian muttered to me as he crossed, 'You do the batting, we'll do the appealing, and leave the umpiring to the umpire, Mike.' However, he was, in this match, unable to live up to this admirable sentiment. For when it came to his turn to bat, on his first ball (a bouncer which he tried to evade) the umpire (wrongly, in my opinion) refused to allow him to run for a leg-bye; whereupon Chappell threw down his bat and gloves in disgust, remonstrated with the umpire, and caused play to be held up. When the next ball was eventually bowled, Botham had him caught at the wicket for a duck.

Charisma seems to me a most limited asset to a captain. It helps in the early stages: any cricketer would be inclined to give Botham, or Close, or Dexter or Ian Chappell the benefit of any doubt about his decisions. Their mistakes would be tolerated for longer, and with less resentment, than would, say, the Maharaja of Porbandar's (unless the members of the latter's team depended on him for their livelihood. A story of cricket historian David Frith's hints at Porbandar's not being unaware of pecuniary influences – he is said to have been in the habit of presenting diamond-encrusted tie-pins to umpires – *before* the match!).

But honeymoons come to an end, and charisma does not imply steadiness, patience, concentration, or considerateness, all invaluable in a captain. Above all, placing too much emphasis on charisma might well involve ignoring the central requirement of a captain, namely, that he knows his task. Charisma is not the same thing as leadership.

The case of Dexter proves the point. His main failing was that he easily became bored. In all three matches that I played under him in South Africa in 1964–5 there were periods in which he had lost interest and was more concerned with getting his golf-swing right at square-leg than with who should be bowling or with what field. He was an excellent theorist on the game; but when his theories failed to work, or he had no particular bright ideas, he would drift; and the whole team drifted with him. I would guess that Dexter was, in those days, more interested in ideas than in people.

Or take Close. Of course his personal qualities were inseparable from his captaincy, and they unquestionably enhanced it. Physically, he was immensely hard, and no one would risk provoking him. His players also felt affection for him. On top of this, he was a fine attacking captain. He was much happier when his team was 'on the go' in the field, trying anything to get a wicket (when, too, he could caper about at the batsman's feet as happy as a hippo in wet mud), than when they had to fall back on defence or containment. But his strengths as a captain had less to do with his courage than with his shrewdness and competitiveness. Towards the end of his career, his wish to 'make things happen' had an unsettling effect on the team, especially on the bowlers; for Brian found it hard to let things happen of their own accord, or to allow the bowlers to find a rhythm and to force a batsman into error by tying him down first.

Botham too has sufficient tactical sense; his main problem, apart from the loss of his own form, was that he has been too sensitive to criticism. He allowed people to niggle and upset him. Even the England players became cautious about offering advice if they suspected that Ian would not agree with it.

So: birth, breeding, superficial attractiveness are dangerous grounds on which to select a leader. Yet for almost a century England and the counties restricted their choice of captains to a small percentage of those who played first-class cricket. The reverse attitude is equally inappropriate. As Jim Swanton once remarked, 'There is such a thing as *inverted* snobbery.' Either way, to search for the charismatic leader implies ignoring the needs of the task, and (to continue with the helpful categories of John Adair's *Action-Centred Leadership)* is an inadequate substitute for the complicated personal qualities required to motivate individuals and the group.

So far we have established that our captain-seeking company

would not ignore first-order skills (batting, bowling, etc); that they would not restrict themselves to any particular social sub-group (McKinsey's, the management consultants, recently showed that none of ten outstandingly well-managed companies showed any indications of nepotism, class distinction or elitism in their selection or promotion practices) and that charisma, the possession of readily discernible charm or magnetism, is an inadequate basis for choice of leader. Instead, they would want to make their assessment on two grounds: how well does a candidate know the game (and how ready is he to learn)? And, secondly, will he be able to motivate the others?

Captain of the visiting side (to hefty substitute). 'You'd better go out in the deep, then you can move the screen about.'

A few words about the task. The type of knowledge required will be practical, not theoretical. We have all known those who are brilliant at theorising, but who cannot make decisions and have no common sense. This syndrome is not unknown among university graduates. A captain's decisions are practical, and share with others of this type the feature that they often have to be made on imperfect evidence. You move a man from backward short-leg to third slip: you can never know for certain that the next ball will not lob up exactly where your fielder had been. This 'glorious uncertainty' of cricket is one factor in a tendency amongst down-to-earth players to denigrate thought; so often they have heard theories based on assumption rather than on fact. They know from experience the role luck plays in the short-term.

In my first year as captain of Middlesex we played a ten-over game against Glamorgan at Ebbw Vale. As we fetched our bags from the cars (the rain had unexpectedly stopped at about tea-time) I said excitedly, 'We'll have to think about this!' The senior players found this hilarious: *think* about a ten-over match! About a sheer slog! I can see their point; in those days I did have too much confidence in the power of thought in predicting or controlling events.

I can remember in that first season in 1971 referring to *Wisden* to discover which types of bowlers had been most successful the year before against each of the counties we played. I now think this was a pretty fatuous exercise: current conditions are far more relevant than the patterns of a year before. However, I also believe that there are no activities on which thought, properly and appropriately carried out, cannot be a help. A captain and a team *do* need to think about their approach to a ten-over match, and about how it might differ from a forty-over encounter.

Sir Donald Bradman goes so far as to say that any good captain should be an avid reader of the game and know not only its laws but also a fair degree of its history. I find this far-fetched: every captain I have known would have been found lacking in this respect. Awareness of cricket's history would not harm a captain; but I find it hard to see how it could be of much practical help.

So our potential captain should be able to talk sense about tactics; he should value thought, provided that it is down-to-earth: he will be interested in, perhaps even passionate about, this side of the game. He will also be aware that there is no *one* task of captaincy;

there are many different tasks, with varying degrees of immediacy. I shall be discussing this point in the next chapter.

Let us return to the question of motivation. Can we make any remarks that are not entirely predictable about the sorts of qualities that enable a man to bring the best out of others? What will the headhunters look for?

Clearly they will not be satisfied if they find someone who, like a contemporary of G. O. Allen's, was (in Allen's words) 'excellent on tactics, but his word didn't count for sixpence as no one would listen to him.'

I have said that a captain has from time to time to be prepared to take an unpopular line. He must have a measure of independence. He cannot always be 'one of the boys'. He will have to criticise individuals or even the whole group, and say things, or insist on activities, that they do not like. He will have to be able to drop senior players from the team, and give them the news. He must be prepared to recommend that some members of a staff be sacked.

Nevertheless, he must be able to engage with his players, to communicate with them. He cannot keep a glacial distance. I often envied captains who never lost their tempers; but I noticed, too, that this coolness was sometimes bought at the expense of involvement. Nor is it likely that any captain will be able to keep his team enthusiastic if he is positively and widely disliked by them. There was, in the 1960s, a county captain in the West Country whose bowlers tried to hit him with the ball whenever he had a net.

A captain should not crave affection from his players; but nor should he court, or make a virtue of, their disaffection. He should always, too, be available to players, whether to listen to their ideas or to their complaints. In choosing a captain, some such assessment of a man's personality is essential.

What about more humdrum biographical facts about the candidates? Does his age matter? (I presume that it is not sexist to assume, in our present context, that the candidates will be male.) Should he come from the current staff of a side, or from outside? Is he likely to be a batsman or a bowler?

With regard to age, I myself found that dealing with players significantly older than myself was, on the whole, harder than dealing with the rest. Not everyone feels the same, though there must be at least a trace of unease in most people when, in a situation as intimate and domestic as a cricket dressing-room, they are installed in authority over men almost old enough to be their fathers. The 'fathers', too, often resent this reversal. However, other captains find that it is the arrogance or insolence of youth that they find hardest to stomach; and for some it is the rivalry and envy of their peers. The main problem in appointing a very young man as captain of, say, a county side is of course lack of experience. I think our headhunters would be unwilling to lay down any hard-and-fast criteria on this issue.

They would take a similar line on the question of whether to find an insider to take over the ailing team, or an outsider. The more feeble the side has become, and the longer its decline has lasted, the more reason there is to import. For by then some at least of the likely candidates from within will already have been tried. Moreover, the pattern of apathy and expectation of defeat will have become entrenched. For an insider both to see it clearly and to manage to change it will be difficult though not of course impossible. In his unobtrusive and unselfish way Jim Watts gradually steered Northamptonshire from the doldrums in the early '70s to being a team that held their heads high and a force to be reckoned with ten years later. No doubt there are many other such cases.

Nevertheless the more dramatic uplifts have often been caused by the arrival of a captain from outside. I will mention two such examples. First, Tony Lock at Leicester. Lock's achievement was remarkable in that he captained Leicestershire for only two years yet his impact was immediate. Moreover, Leicestershire's brief rise in the county championship did not outlast his presence as captain. The figures are striking. In 1963 and 1964, the county finished sixteenth; in the following year they were fourteenth. In 1966, Lock's first season at Leicester, they rose six places to eighth in the table, and in his second year he lifted them a further five places to third, equal in points with Kent, who finished second. After Lock's departure the side declined again; ninth in 1968 (again under the leadership of Maurice Hallam, who had preceded Lock). And in Illingworth's first two seasons as captain, in 1969 and 1970, the county finished fourteenth and fifteenth. Not that statistics tell the whole story. *Wisden* states in 1967 that:

'The former Surrey and England player was clearly resolved to make a success of his captaincy and infected his team with his own exuberance, which was an important factor in recording eight wins, the most since 1961. Lock's urgent approach to his duties delighted supporters and brought a lively response from the players, evidence for which was often to be seen in the field … The season should prove to have been most useful in rebuilding Leicestershire's morale, and the effects of this ought soon to be seen in 1967.'

Indeed they were. Next year *Wisden* commented on his 'drive and brilliance on the field', and remarked that he 'sustained a belief in the capacity to win'. I never played against a side that Lock captained, but I can imagine his energy, optimism and enthusiasm combined with a shrewd cricketing brain. And if confirmation of these remarks were needed, his achievement in leading Western Australia to their first-ever outright win in the Sheffield Shield in his first season as captain underlines his immense contribution. In the previous four seasons – 1962–3 until 1966–7 – Western Australia had been fourth (out of five), fifth, second and fourth.

My second example is Eddie Barlow's brief period as captain of Derbyshire. The county had been propping up the table during most of the '70s when halfway through 1976 Barlow became their fourth captain in five seasons. In the six seasons between 1971 and 1976 they had finished fifteenth twice, sixteenth once and seventeenth (last) three times. Under Barlow they were seventh in 1977 and, though they dropped to fourteenth in 1978, they reached the final of the Benson and Hedges Cup in that season. These figures may not sound so impressive as Lock's, but I have a vivid impression of the transformation he brought to his team. At last Derbyshire looked and played like a side that believed they could win. Barlow was a fitness fanatic himself and one of the first county captains to insist on intensive training for a county squad. Their improved physical shape no doubt helped them; but far more important was the tremendous improvement in morale which he inspired.

Finally, will the search for a new leader be concentrated mainly on batsmen or bowlers? On openers or middle-order batsmen? And what of wicket-keepers? We might compare this issue with a parallel one in business: is the best managing director most likely to have been an economist or an accountant, a sales manager or a marketing man?

By far the largest proportion of captains, at least at the level of first-class cricket, has been provided by those who are pre-dominantly batsmen. This pattern arises partly from the class distinctions I have spoken of: gentlemen batted, players bowled, a pattern repeated in services cricket. I remember while at school playing a Combined Services team composed mainly of officers; the bowling was opened, however, by Stoker Healey and Private Stead. Since captains came from the ranks of the gentlemen, it is not surprising that few captains were bowlers.

But are there any intrinsic reasons for the bias? Would the head-hunters of the 1980s find any reason for preferring a batsman? Bradman for one, in *The Art of Cricket*, maintained that the captain should, ideally, be a batsman; for it is extremely hard for bowlers to be objective about their own craft. They tend either to over-bowl themselves or not to bowl enough, from conceit, modesty or indeed self-protection. The captain has decisions to make and a job to do while his team is batting, to be sure. But by far the greater part of his work is to be done in the field, changing the bowlers and fielders, keeping everyone alert. There is a strong case, therefore, against giving the job to someone whose primary task is to bowl.

On the other hand, two of the best post-war international cap-tains were Richie Benaud and Illingworth. Indeed, Illingworth argues in his book *Captaincy* (Pelham, 1980) that the all-rounder, and especially the slow-bowling all-rounder, are, all else being equal, in the best position for the job. Unlike fast bowlers, they do not have to inject so much adrenalin and aggression into their bowling; nor is it quite so physically exhausting. Being bowlers and batsmen, they should be able to understand the mentality of both. It is therefore easier for them to criticise both. One of Illingworth's refrains as captain and as manager was that he could not understand seam bowlers who were unable to bowl on one side of the wicket. ('I could do it better blindfold,' he used to say.) Expecting high standards of himself both as batsman and bowler, it was easier to demand them of others. Moreover, a bowling captain is in a position to convince the rest of the team that a declaration is well-timed if he will be relying on himself, among others, to prove it right.

I would agree there is a strong case for having an all-rounder, if he is a slow or medium-paced bowler, as captain. The one argu-ment against is, however, a strong one: is he in the best position for deciding when to bowl himself? In my view, Illingworth's main flaw as a captain was in not bowling himself enough.

I have already implied my opinion about fast bowlers as captains; it takes an exceptional character to know when to bowl, to keep bowling with all his energy screwed up into a ball of aggression, *and* to be sensitive to the needs of the team, both tactically and psychologically. Willis in particular has always shut himself up into a cocoon of concentration and fury for his bowling. Our headhunters should recommend a fast bowler only as a last resort; unless, perhaps, they have a man of Mike Procter's qualities available.

Captains who are batsmen are also liable to display their own short-comings. First, I think, there is a greater risk that he will not understand his bowlers. Richard Hutton once complained to me that I expected the bowlers to perform like automata, and his criticism was probably just. I had never had to charge in twenty-five or thirty yards and hurl the ball as fast as I could at the stumps. More empathy is called for in the batsman-captain. I do not mean that he needs to know a great deal about the mechanics of bowling, though doubtless this would at times be a help. Rather, he needs to enter imaginatively into the mind of his bowlers, young and old, quick and slow, and learn how to get the best out of them.

There is also a minor drawback in being an opening batsman. For any opener starts to feel signs of nerves when the opposition have lost eight or nine wickets, or are likely to declare. For the captain who also opens the batting the transition from concentrating on taking these last wickets (which may require him to spur on tired bowlers and deal with his own and the side's frustration) to the kind of calmness that he needs for his next job is stark. Close used to urge me to give myself more chance as a batsman by going in lower in the order, at least in Tests.

From a purely tactical viewpoint, the man who is in the best position to see what the bowlers are doing, and to judge the nature of the pitch, is the wicket-keeper. He is often the first to know that a bowler is tiring from the way the ball comes into his gloves. What is more, he can often advise the bowler if there is something slightly wrong; for example, if he is running in too fast or not fast enough, if he seems to be straining. It is often the 'keeper who knows whether a slow bowler is bowling a little too fast or too slow, too short or too far up, for a particular pitch or batsman. Titmus, the great Middlesex off-spinner, would constantly check with John Murray behind the stumps on all these aspects of his craft.

Yet remarkably few 'keepers have become captains; and many of those who have have quickly given up the job. One problem is simply logistic. The captain needs to talk to his bowlers. The wicket-keeper may be seventy yards away from his opening bowler when he starts his run-up. And though a similar problem confronts a captain who fields at slip, at least he is not encumbered by pads for his repeated sprints from bowler to fielding position.

The main problem, however, seems to be the degree of concentration that 'keeping entails. Not only do they have to expect to take each delivery, but whenever the ball is struck they have to prepare for a throw-in, which often means dashing up to the stumps. Taylor was one who found, in a few months of captaining his county side, that one role adversely affected the other; he was no longer 'keeping at his best. Wicket-keepers make invaluable advisers to the captain; rarely captains themselves. I would rate Rodney Marsh the exception to this rule. For behind the abrasive front was a thoughtful, astute and humorous man, whose players, when he led Western Australia, were totally committed to him. The Australian Board, however, were not. But their prejudice was not based on technical considerations, such as having a wicket-keeper as captain. For them he was tarred with the same brush as Ian Chappell, the brush of revolution and extremism. Greg Chappell, with his more dignified air, they could stomach as captain; but they refused to swallow Marsh. This was a major mistake; he might well have proved a more imaginative Test captain than Greg.

From *The Art of Captaincy, 1985*

I hardly knew Ian Botham when I turned up at the Oval for my first Test match, against the West Indies, in 1984. Although he wasn't captain, he was the epicentre of the dressing room. Then, as is the case today, you were either in or out: there were and are no shades of grey with Ian. He is very forgiving – you can be out and come back in again – but you do have to be admitted to his inner circle, and as a player I never really felt part of his coterie.

When Ian swung the ball he was devastating, but there were times when he tried to bowl too fast and became rather carried away with the short stuff. He could certainly bowl quickly: in the Oval Test, when he got his 300th Test wicket (Jeff Dujon), I was fielding at mid-on and witnessed some seriously quick balls, but he was a better bowler when he employed that rare gift of being able to swing the ball. Too often, Ian seemed to want to just bowl his bouncers and get batsmen out hooking.

As a media colleague, I hugely enjoy Ian's company and it is clear that he has a deep love for cricket. In fact, I would say that he is one of those commentators who are constantly frustrated that they are not out there still playing for England. Fred Trueman, looking on from the commentary position, would always reckon he could still pick up five wickets before lunch, and Ian is much the same because of his enormous self-belief. Looking back, I can safely say that no one I ever played with had more genuine confidence in their own ability than Ian Botham. Not in a big-headed or unpleasant way, but no opponent or situation ever held any fear for him.

Ian was an intimidating sort of character: strong and lairy, who could be very outspoken and entirely dismissive if he disagreed with you; and yet a very loyal friend. When I fell ill in Mumbai after the 2011 World Cup final, Ian helped me through all the formalities and security at the airport and took me into his executive lounge. Things were looking up until he said, 'Here, drink this, it will sort you out.' It was a very large port and brandy and it most certainly didn't sort me out, but he did get me on the plane and home again.

IAN BOTHAM

Simon Wilde

Playing for England, though, Botham was at his athletic and competitive peak. He was confident, enthusiastic and strong, and indifferent to physical pain or ailment, while lean and lithe enough to swing the ball at pace. There was a ferocious energy in everything he did, a youthful zest that only a man in his early twenties could display. He was a joyous cricketer, playing for love and glory, with no hint of the jaundice that scarred his later cricket. A perfect example came at the Oval in 1979 when England looked a beaten side going into the final hour of a long and exhausting game. India were 366–1 chasing 438 and on course for a historic victory when in twelve overs Botham roused himself to take a catch, three wickets – including India's linchpin Sunil Gavaskar for 221 – and execute a run-out. The match ended in a thrilling draw with India 429–8, and both sides tantalisingly close to victory. He was an exponentially better cricketer for having two strings to his bow: the better he bowled, the better he batted, and vice versa. Mostly he batted in the top six and always opened the bowling or came on first change. This was what he had always wanted to do and he proved it made him most effective.

In a way he was unlucky that this pomp coincided with the Packer split because he would have been a handful for any full-strength side, as he showed when the Packer players returned for England's tour of Australia in 1979–80. In his first Test against the full might of Australia, he took eleven wickets from a gargantuan 80.5 overs and conceded barely two runs an over. In his third match, he dealt calmly with Dennis Lillee's skilful bowling on a slow pitch to score an unbeaten century. He did squander his wicket in the second Test, much to Brearley's wrath, but it was not his fault England lost the series 3–0. These efforts were often forgotten when it was claimed that he never did much against the strongest sides.

If there was one area of his game over which there remained a question mark it was how he played spin. New Zealand's left-armer Stephen Boock caused him problems and he got in a tangle against India's spinners – so much so that Viv Richards, watching the second Test on TV, chided him for losing his nerve. Richards encouraged him to remain bold and Botham was certainly that during a rumbustious century in the next Test, a rain-blighted affair at Leeds, where he took 43 runs off the 34 balls he received from Bishen Bedi and Srini Venkataraghavan. It was an exhilarating display in an otherwise forgettable game: Botham scored ninety-nine during the morning session of the fourth day and in all hit five sixes, then a record for a Test in England.

There were other reasons why England did well at that time, just as there were other reasons besides Botham why Somerset were so effective at one-day cricket. The batting acquired two significant additions in 1978. Graham Gooch was recalled as an opener with a new determination based on a strong fitness ethic. David Gower, like so many, had fallen into county cricket happily, unconcerned at the low wages, his enthusiasm sparked at Leicestershire by Ray Illingworth and his academic career having foundered at University College London. 'I was supposedly there to read law but never actually found the library,' he said. 'I wasn't so much reading law as hearing about it.' Gower was an instant success; a silky stroke-maker and athletic cover fieldsman who – and this was to be significant given his friendship with Botham – required little training to stay fit and in form. John Emburey arrived on the scene the same year, giving Brearley a third spin-bowling option alongside Phil Edmonds and Geoff Miller. The fielding was exceptional, with Gower and Derek Randall in front of the wicket and Taylor, Brearley, Botham and Hendrick behind. Boycott, who had been playing since 1964, said it was the best England fielding side he was involved with.

But it was the fast bowling that gave the side its edge. Bob Willis was the spearhead with a style that complemented Botham's perfectly. Taylor saw the effects at first hand. 'Bob bowled wicket to wicket, relying on pace and a quick bowler's length, which was shorter than Beefy's. If you were going to swing the ball like Beefy, you had to pitch it up. Facing him, batsmen were looking to get on to the front foot. No one in England swung the ball as much as he did but he hit the gloves hard too. But against Bob the batsmen needed to be on the back foot, fending the ball off their bodies. It was a good combination.' The best game they had together was at Lord's in 1978 when New Zealand were all out for sixty-seven and Botham, swinging the ball outrageously, finished with eleven wickets.

They were supported occasionally by Chris Old and John Lever, and more regularly by Hendrick. On the day that Botham claimed Gavaskar as his hundredth Test wicket at Lord's in 1979, Botham and Hendrick went for a drink in a pub near the ground called the Artillery. 'It used to do a good pint of Bass,' Hendrick recalled. 'I said, "Well done, 'Both', on your hundred wickets." And he said, "Well, thanks ... I probably owe thirty of them to you." ' Botham had required just nineteen Tests for his hundred wickets, the fewest by any bowler for nearly fifty years.

England were not the only nation well armed in fast bowling. In the 1970s, a whole host of men capable of unusual speed had come onto the horizon and, encouraged by the confrontational style promoted by Kerry Packer, their intentions were rarely anything but hostile. It became generally understood too that without legislation fast bowlers could pretty much batter opponents into submission. Amnesties for tail-enders were sometimes negotiated but any lower-order batsman who hung around was regarded as fair game. When Iqbal Qasim, used by Pakistan as a night-watchman in the first Test of 1978, was hit in the mouth by Willis after resisting for forty minutes, a heated public debate arose about the morals of targeting batsmen of limited ability, but Brearley and his players were unrepentant. 'Qasim was in a negative mood in what is supposed to be a positive game,' Botham said. 'I saw nothing wrong with bouncing him.' England felt their tactics were vindicated when Qasim failed to score for the rest of the series.

Botham loved this new climate. Even before the Tests against Pakistan he had made excessive use of the bouncer in a one-dayer at the Oval and a few days later got into hot water with umpire Bill Alley in Somerset's derby match with Gloucestershire. Alley warned him for bowling too many bouncers at the prolific Pakistan batsman Zaheer Abbas, missing from Pakistan's tour because of his Packer contract. By the time Botham succeeded in bouncing him out, Zaheer had sped to 140. In the same game, Botham committed a rare breach of on-field etiquette by running out from slip opening batsman Alan Tait who, thinking he had edged a catch, was on his way back to the pavilion.

Botham had the mind and the methods to bully tail-enders into submission. Although primarily regarded as a swing bowler, he possessed a deceptively quick ball, and an awkward bouncer. It was a package that was simply too much for many tail-enders. He was also adept at undoing them with changes of angle, squaring them

Reverend Umpire (to village bowler). 'Now, my friend, how do you bowl? Round, or over the wicket?'
Bowler, 'Well, Zur, zometimes I bowls this way and zometimes t'other but mostly I bowls at their legs!'

up by bowling at their legs from wide of the crease; he got countless wickets this way. Nor was he afraid of roughing up those who
were fast bowlers; the thought that they might retaliate was of no
concern to him. Derek Underwood, a tail-ender who faced Botham
with trepidation in county cricket, appreciated his talent for laying
waste to the tail. 'He would be at you even before you'd reached the
crease. He was very forthright and could unsettle you with just the
odd comment. He would often take two of the top six wickets but
end up with five in the innings.'

Through necessity, batsmen began better arming themselves
and by the end of the decade the use of helmets was widespread.

Even Botham wore one at times, though less often than many (he arguably batted better without one, the greater element of danger seemingly raising his game). Indeed, the predominance of pace at the expense of spin suited him well. The helmet transformed the batting of many, particularly those late-order players who had previously feared for their safety. It certainly cost Botham wickets: up to 1980, one in four of his Test wickets was provided by numbers nine, ten and eleven, but this slipped to below one in five later. Stories such as those of Iqbal Qasim largely disappeared from the game. Richard Hadlee was among those whose batting was dramatically improved by the helmet.

Brearley's England team were winning and happy. Under him, a sense of collective purpose was forged among a diverse band, a process assisted by Packer having laid siege to the traditional cricket in which they were involved. Boycott was tolerated because he was their most dependable batsman and Brearley made sure that Boycott, like everyone else, felt important and wanted.

Botham was at the heart of this common mission. After returning from New Zealand, he scored a century in the first Test of the 1978 summer against Pakistan at Edgbaston, an innings played with England already well on top against weak opponents. Then, in the next game at Lord's, he dazzled with bat and ball in typically serendipitous fashion. After the first day's play had been not so much washed away as drowned, Botham and Old – his erstwhile rival – were given permission by Brearley to have a drink that evening, everyone confident that there would not be a prompt start the next morning. Their night finished at around 2.30am but to their alarm play began at 11.30am. Brearley took pity on them by opting to bat first but by mid-afternoon Botham was at the crease and in belligerent mood despite England's precarious position at 134–5. His second scoring stroke was a six and he had raced to a hundred shortly before stumps, by which time Old had joined him, still shaking his head at Botham's capacity to play so well after their night out. Three days later, Botham ran amok with the ball after Pakistan, thoroughly demoralised, had followed on more than 250 in arrears. Having previously taken only one wicket in the series, Botham claimed a first victim on the Saturday evening when the ball wasn't swinging and then added seven more during a sensational passage of play on the Monday morning. Even though the skies were clear he managed to swing the ball prodigiously from the

Nursery End, where Brearley had originally called on him merely to let Willis change ends. The ball that swung late to take Haroon Rashid's off stump was among the best Botham ever bowled.

Graham Gooch remembered Botham's relish at being the centre of dressing room attention. 'There are characters who have a self-confidence bordering on arrogance. They fancy themselves but they could back it up. Ian was like that. It was good for his cricket. You have got to believe in yourself as a cricketer.'

During this period, Botham was a terrific team man – selfless, popular, mischievous. He got up to any number of pranks inspired by his size and strength. He shoved people into swimming pools (he himself was not, according to some, a keen swimmer), singed their hair with cigarette lighters and, with breathtaking predictability, turned up to Christmas fancy-dress parties as a gorilla. Once, on a coach journey from Newcastle to Sydney, shortly after England had retained the Ashes on the 1978–79 tour of Australia, he was the instigator behind Boycott being stripped of his clothes and his privates covered in shaving foam in a clear re-enactment of the ritual Botham endured on the Lord's groundstaff. When the coach reached the team hotel in Sydney, Botham and the rest of the team disembarked with Boycott's clothes, leaving Boycott threatening to walk into the hotel naked unless his items were returned. In the end, he marched through reception missing his trousers but semi-clothed. Boycott generously did not hold this incident against him, insisting that Botham was one of his three favourite cricketers along with Graham Stevenson and David Bairstow. 'I admired and liked him immensely,' Boycott said. 'He made me laugh and made the game fun to play.'

One of the reasons Botham was held in great affection was because, despite his own enormous personal success, he had the generosity to share in the triumphs of others. 'He was the first guy to go to anyone who did well,' John Lever said. 'When you get to the top level and you're looking after your place, a lot of people have found it hard to be that gracious. OK, his place wasn't in danger, but he showed a lot of others the right way to go.' Derek Underwood noticed that he was particularly good with people who were new to the scene: 'He always noticed and encouraged them.'

A few people, though, felt ill at ease with his high spirits and some were hurt by his teasing. Bob Willis tired of being compared to a wounded camel when he was experiencing injury problems, and

Botham was asked by Brearley to desist. Not many were capable of warning him off. One who did was Peter Willey, a powerfully built batting all-rounder who played a full part in the 1979–80 tour of Australia. Asked if he found Botham intimidating, Willey said: 'No, because I stood up to him. I'd first got to know him well in '76, when I got 220-odd against Somerset. We were both young lads and became good mates. I didn't take his pranks or bullshit. Poor old Boycott … if he [Botham] knew he could dominate them, he made life a misery. I wasn't going to have that. I have never been intimidated by anybody. We had a carry-on in Australia where I was going to hang him [Botham] up on the hooks in the showers because he was messing about.'

The challenge for anyone who captained Botham was harnessing his extraordinary energy and talent. It has been suggested that Brearley received too much credit for Botham's success under him. There is no doubt that Brearley was lucky to have him in his side when Botham was so young, eager and good. Equally, the quasi-magical power of man-management that has been attributed to Brearley owed much to what happened later in 1981. But it is only necessary to survey how things went wrong when Brearley was not around to appreciate that his relationship with Botham must have been something out of the ordinary.

From *Ian Botham: The Power and the Glory*, 2011

I don't think Phil Tufnell ever quite appreciated what a good cricketer he was. These days on the radio you hear all the cheeky, funny asides that have always been part of the man. He is very quick, naturally funny, and doesn't need to prepare any of his stuff – it's all off-the-cuff one-liners. Phil is very sharp and can surprise people when he talks about cricket by his knowledgeable approach and tendency to be right most of the time. As a player he used to drive his captains (Gatting and Gooch) insane with his antics and attitude. At the time, he didn't seem to have a huge amount of self-confidence. Had he had a greater belief in his abilities, coupled with the cricketing wisdom that he shares now so engagingly with others, he might have been an even better cricketer.

PHIL TUFNELL

Four Blondes

I was in the clear – or so I thought. Not wanted for the limited-overs stuff at that stage, I was about seventeenth man out of seventeen for the game, so I had no worries about another big night. As things turned out, it might easily have been my last on that tour.

It began at one of the many excellent bars the beautiful city of Adelaide has to offer. I had been with a load of the boys, but one by one they had drifted away, leaving me on my own with a couple of lovelies. I had had rather too much to drink, but the chat was in full steam and seemed to be working when they asked me if I would like to pop back to their place. Unable to think of a single good reason why not, I agreed and we bundled into their car. Knowing that, even though I was not required to play, I was still expected to show up at around nine the next morning for the trip to the ground, I wanted to make sure we wouldn't be driving to Ayers Rock, but they insisted that they lived a mere ten minutes away. Three-quarters of an hour and a couple of beers in the back of the motor later we arrived, with me now past caring.

A couple more drinks and a bop and the next thing I knew we were all hopping into bed. It was more playfulness than anything Swedish, but there was some wrestling along with the boozing and it was all fairly good exercise. After half an hour or so, the door opened. I ducked under the sheets, thinking 'boyfriend, husband, father, shotgun, horrible death', and was therefore more than pleasantly surprised to find that we had been joined by two more of Adelaide's finest. Helleuuw. These were the flatmates of the two girls I had arrived with, and within seconds they were down to their briefs and in the bed as well. So there we all were, me and these four delicious darlings, all strawberry blonde and all with legs like stairways to heaven, enjoying a little roll around and a few more drinks. Cramped, yes. Cosy, certainly. Glory, glory, hallelujah. The time was flying and I didn't have a care in the world. Cricket? I'm not sure cricket figured too prominently in our discussions.

Once everything had calmed down a bit, I identified the girl whose bed we were actually in and tried to sort out arrangements for the morning. I established that, according to her at any rate, we were about fifteen minutes' drive from the hotel, and told her that on pain of death I had to be there at 8 a.m.

'No worries,' she said. 'I'll set the alarm for 7.30.' Only about a couple of hours' kip as it happens, but better than trying to get back there and then.

I don't know what woke me up, but it was definitely not the alarm clock. A little groggily I came to and checked the time. It was half past eight. Oh shit. I went cold. I felt the blood draining out of me. 'Oh my God. Oh my God. Wake up. I am in so much trouble,' I said, uprooting my sleeping companion.

'Zzzzzzzzz,' was her response.

'Oi!' I said. 'What happened to your f***ing alarm clock?'

'Huh,' she said. 'Oh well, you see. I don't know why exactly but sometimes it just doesn't work.'

I grabbed all my gear and threw most of it on as we dived into the car and flew down the highway towards the city. Meanwhile, back at the hotel and unbeknown to me, one or two of the boys, having realized I was not where I should have been, started to think of a covering story. What they were thinking of when they came up with this one, I will never know. 'Where's Tuffers?' asked Micky Stewart as they were preparing to leave. 'Well,' said Robin Smith, 'sometimes he likes to jog down to the ground early.'

Brilliant.

We finally arrived at about ten past nine, by which time a hundred potential excuses were rushing around my brain. None of them sounded particularly plausible, but I was in a blind brown-trousered panic so I plumped for the least stupid, i.e. I had been in my bedroom all the time but the automatic wake-up call facility hadn't worked. Now time was of the essence. I was for the high jump, come what may, but if I could just get to the ground within about half an hour of the others and in some kind of shape, they might turn half a blind eye. So I came sprinting through the double doors of the hotel, picked up my key and made straight for the lifts, running very fast. The floor covering between the reception desk and lifts being polished marble, and the new shoes being slightly too big, the result of this manoeuvre was like a scene from *Carry On Cricketer*.

First, I slipped and went arse-over-tit, taking out a couple of rubber plants, the information board listing 'Today's Events' and a rather nice vase. Next, coming to a sliding halt right in front of the lift, I heard 'ding' as the doors opened. And then I saw them: three pairs of rather-too-familiar-looking training shoes. Inside them were Peter Lush, Micky Stewart and Graham Gooch. It turned out later that they were on their way to the ground after having attended to some team matter or other. Now Gooch was attending to me.

'Don't say a word,' he started. 'Get your arse upstairs. Have a shower. Sort yourself out and get yourself down to the ground. I will talk to you later.' I feared the worst. They knew. How could they not have known? I was still in my clubbing gear, stubbled up and looking like something the cat wouldn't dare drag in. I'm dead, I thought to myself. They'll send me home and I'll never play for England again.

By the time I arrived at the ground the story was out among the lads, who were biting their own hands to stop laughing in front of the management. In due course, I was pulled by Gooch and Stewart.

They fined me £500, I think, which I was a bit pissed off about. Looking back, I probably got off lightly, but at the time I couldn't quite get my head round it. If I'd had half a brain, I would probably have realized that with a little cleverness, I could have enjoyed the best of both worlds. But I was twenty-something, footloose and fancy free, and it just seemed that a lot of doors were being opened for me. Granted I was late at the ground and I might not have prepared myself for the match in the ideal fashion. But all I had been doing was enjoying myself. I didn't seem to be doing too much different from some of the more senior guys. The management knew they couldn't lock me up in a box. In fact they did say that there was nothing wrong in going out and having a good time. It was just that I never quite got the timing right. I was simply having too much fun, I suppose. Perhaps my biggest problem was my naivety. That and dodgy alarm clocks.

~

Debut against the West Indies

The fact is that had Richard Illingworth – a bloke for whom, incidentally, I have always had a lot of time – taken the opportunity to establish himself in the England side, that might have well been time, Tufnell, please. As it was, however, defeat at Trent Bridge and then in Birmingham meant England were 2–1 down going to The Oval. Gooch was desperate to win the final Test and square the series, particularly after having come so close to a similar result in the Caribbean during their previous encounter. Desperate men sometimes employ desperate measures.

Strange things began to happen. Just prior to the selection meeting, I heard and read suggestions that I might have been growing more mature in my approach. Was I? According to whom? Or was this information being put about by the selectors to explain their impending U-turn in policy over yours truly? The fact that I had been bowling well and with a fair degree of success in county cricket might also have had something to do with my return to the colours. Not wishing to be ungracious about this, or ungrateful for the second chance, chaps, but in years to come it often struck me that some people's perception of a player's 'attitude' and 'character' seemed to depend on how many runs or wickets that player was taking at the time. Or was this merely a case of Gooch becoming a little less rigid in his thinking?

It's fair to say that my private life was somewhat less hectic than it had been in Australia. Jane and I were now an item and we were having a lot of laughs. She had a bit of fire and spirit in her and the raving exploits of the previous summer were again pursued with some vigour. Acid House parties were still in vogue, we liked going to them, and the lifestyle clearly wasn't affecting the cricket. No harm done.

So when I turned up at The Oval, I had mixed feelings. I did want to succeed – desperately. But I went there determined to be myself, to prove to Gooch and the others that I could be an England bowler on my terms. At this time of my life my attitude was that off the field my life was nobody's business but mine. All I ever wanted and expected anyone to do, and all anyone was actually entitled to do as far as I was concerned, was to judge me on what I did with a cricket ball in my hand.

And then into the dressing room, for the first time in two years, exploded Ian Botham. *This* was what I had signed up for.

It is hard to describe the wave of relief that washed over me when I heard the noise with which Botham announced his entrance. The sound itself is hard enough to describe, emanating as it appeared to do from a deep underground cavern, then booming from his mouth like the horn of an ocean-going liner announcing its imminent departure. Incorrectly aimed, the vibrations from one of Botham's belches might be capable of laying waste to a small market town. To me, though, it sounded like the music of the gods. As I sat in the corner of the changing room at The Oval, not quite knowing how to react to having been given a second chance, watching this living cricketing icon completely grip the attention of every single person just by being there, I offered up a silent prayer.

'Thank God,' I thought. 'Thank God there is someone here who will stop everyone looking at *me*. Thank God there is someone here who is not blindly going to obey the regime if he doesn't think it is right. Thank God Beefy has come to save me.'

'Come on, lads,' said one of the hierarchy. 'Let's do a couple of laps.'

'Yeah, right. In a minute,' said Beef.

And I thanked God again.

With all that was going on between Gooch, Gower, myself and others, the atmosphere inside the England dressing room during those last two Ashes Tests had been extremely tense. No one quite knew if it was okay to talk to X or be seen with Y. It was office politics gone mad. And now this. This bloke came in and single-handedly threw all that nonsense out of the window, lifted the mood and took all the worry and the tension out of proceedings. His message was simple: do your thing, take no shit, enjoy yourself. For me it was as if someone had ripped down the curtains that had been blocking out the sunlight. And it was the same on the field.

Whereas in Australia the blokes in the slips were so petrified of missing a chance that they looked as though they had pineapples stuck up their arses, Beefy was actually standing there in the slips with his hands on his knees making stupid faces.

At last I was playing in a Test match where people were not going around frightened of their own shadows, caught up in the nerve-racking fear of doing something wrong and letting the side down. At last it was all right to have a laugh on the cricket field when playing for England.

Beefy's sense of fun was infectious. Although we were determined to win, the experience just wasn't so deadly headbanging serious as it had been before. Instead of me thinking, 'Don't let the ball come to me in case I bog it up,' I was thinking how bloody marvellous it was and how lucky I was to be out there.

On and off the field his presence had an effect. Robin Smith, who had worshipped Beefy from the first time he came in contact with him, made a sparkling hundred. Botham himself made 31 before failing to 'get his leg over', as Jonathan Agnew and Brian Johnston fell apart trying to tell the nation, and we made a highly useful 419 – including a well-crafted two by me, prior to having the living crap scared out of me by Patrick Patterson.

They had moved quite happily to 158 for three when I came on for my first bowl on the Saturday. Desmond Haynes, my Middlesex buddy, was cruising. Clayton Lambert, the left-hander renowned as a fierce walloper of the ball and who felt all spinners were put on the earth for his own personal gratification, was equally well set. And as I prepared to deliver my first ball, I noticed with some trepidation Clayton actually laughing out loud as he swung his arms and rehearsed a huge mow towards deep mid wicket. Deep as in halfway down the Harleyford Road. Here was a good test of my new-found *joie de vivre*. Sod it, I thought, if he wants to have a go, let him. I popped one up just outside off stump, nice pace, little bit of turn. He launched himself at it and sent it about 150 yards almost perpendicularly straight up in the air. Ramps was never going to drop it: 158 for four.

Viv Richards was suffering with piles, so Jeff Dujon came in next, to be cleaned up by David 'Syd' Lawrence at 160 for five. But after I had Malcolm Marshall caught by Botham in the slips for nought at 161 for six, the moment could be delayed no longer.

I have to say that there are very few batsmen whose mere

presence actually struck fear into my heart. Plenty of bowlers, yes, but very few batsmen. And Richards was the scariest of them all. The way he strode to the wicket, with that incredible swagger of his, carrying his bat like a club – he made time stop. Spectators and players alike went deathly quiet in his presence, out of sheer respect. And there he was at the other end from me. My boyhood hero, the bloke I had watched on my television smashing very good bowlers to all parts, getting ready to bat against little me. He looked absolutely gigantic. Inside me a tiny voice was crying 'he-e-elp'.

Searching for a crumb of comfort or even encouragement, I sought out Beefy. Surely to God, if anyone knew what I should do next it would be him. The two men were soul mates, blood brothers. From their years playing together with Somerset and against each other in Test cricket, they each knew instinctively what was going through the other guy's mind. Somewhat unhelpfully, Beefy was pissing himself.

There was nothing for it. I simply had to bowl the ball. I did. I gave him my best looping, spinning, ball-on-a-string. It was cleverly flighted and dropping on a perfect length … and Viv played it with his dark eyes closed. Then he looked at me from under that peaked West Indies cap, a strange, piercing look of contempt. 'Is that the best you have, Philip?' said the look. 'Is that it? Is that what I walked all the way out here to bat against?' And I thought to myself: 'Jesus Christ almighty. This bloke is going to whack me f***ing everywhere.'

I tried to walk back to my mark but my legs were like jelly. For a split second I actually thought I was going to faint. Then, somehow, I pulled myself together. What's the worst thing that's going to happen here? I asked, but left the question unanswered. Come on, *come on*, I urged myself. If he's going to come gunning for me, there's nothing I or anyone else can do about it. So I bowled the next ball, held it back a fraction and saw him coming at me full pelt.

Now when Viv came at you, he used to do it with a leap. He used to cross his legs in mid air so high that you could almost see the sole of his leading boot coming straight for you. And in that moment I was convinced that he was going to hit this ball harder than anyone had ever hit a ball in the whole history of cricket. So I did what I had to do. I made myself as small a target as possible. Down on my haunches and turning sideways, I assumed the cricketing equivalent of the crash position. When he started the huge heaving motion from the top of his backswing, the gust it created nearly blew the hair out of my head.

I knew. There wasn't any doubt in my mind whatsoever. It was a certainty that if Richards hit the ball the way he looked as though he was going to hit it, I was a dead man. But he didn't hit it the way he looked as though he was going to hit it. Out of the corner of my half-turned-away head, I saw it pitch, turn and bounce – and then I saw and heard him just get a little nick on it as it passed through to Alec.

My first reaction was shock. I was numb. 'What do I do now?' I thought to myself. 'Appeal, you idiot, appeal.'

Now there was utter confusion. In the same action as taking the catch, Alec had whipped the bails off to stump him as well. And now the umpire at my end, Merv Kitchen, was looking across to the square-leg umpire John Holder. Holder looked nonplussed, certainly not as if he was about to give Richards out stumped. 'Don't look over there, Merv,' I said. 'He nicked it; he nicked it.'

'That's out,' said Merv.

What? What do you mean, 'That's out'?

Wake up. Think. Think quickly. How to celebrate? Big running, whooping stuff, perhaps? No. No. Don't be a ponce. This is Viv Richards, here. The King. The masterblaster. Something more befitting the occasion. I had it. I strolled down to the other end and quietly shook hands with Alec as though this was the kind of thing I did every day of my life. Mind you, when I spotted my brother and his mates celebrating his stag day in one of the boxes, leaping and jumping and punching the air, I very nearly did forget my sense of decorum.

After that the fun continued: Curtly Ambrose, caught Botham again for nought, 172 for eight; Courtney Walsh, caught Gooch for nought, 172 for nine; and finally Patterson, caught Botham once more for two, 176 all out. All bowled by Tufnell, who finished with six for 25, including a spell of six wickets for four runs in 33 deliveries.

There you go. I was back.

From *The Autobiography: What Now?* 1999

I always found Simon Hughes a bit left-field. He is a fine analyst and quite brilliant at isolating something within the game, but that sort of intelligence doesn't always fit well within the dressing room on the county circuit. People like him can be considered too acerbic or, worse, looked upon as 'boffins'.

Simon's first book, *A Lot of Hard Yakka*, was one of the first and best modern warts-and-all insiders' reports on the less than glamorous life of a professional cricketer. I too produced a county diary, *8 Days a Week*, around the same time after a publisher suggested I model it on Eamon Dunphy's seminal book, *Only a Game?: The Diary of a Professional Footballer*. Simon's and Eamon's books are classics and still stand the test of time. I hope mine does too.

SIMON HUGHES

Bouncers

Saturday 11 June, Surrey v Middlesex, The Oval

The season took ages to get going because of an exceptionally wet spring. Once the wickets hardened up, everything seemed to revolve around the new sport of cranium-clattering, inadvertently pioneered by the West Indies. Nothing gave me a clearer indication of the gravity of this business than facing Sylvester Clarke at The Oval. He was an immense man, so strong he could lift dumb-bells I couldn't even roll. He had a reputation for taking it easy with the new ball, then terrorising the lower order later in the day. So my sanity was seriously questioned when I made to leave the dressing room without a helmet, thinking the wicket wasn't all that quick. When I reached the door Barlow plonked one on my head. 'Don't be an arsehole all your life,' he said touchingly.

I was eternally grateful. The strapping West Indian came pounding in to bowl, looking more menacing with every stride. The

spectators were egging him on and I was hemmed in by close fielders. Some people might think this sounds exhilarating. It's not the
word I would use. Fear is closer to the mark, less of the physical variety, more the potential mortification of being made to look
totally incapable, flailing arms and legs around like a demented
punk.

'Step back and across, back and across,' I repeated to myself as
the ogre approached. 'Keep low and watch for the bouncer.' The
first two balls were relatively straightforward and I played them
OK. Well, they hit the bat, anyway. 'Let's polish 'em off, Silvers,'
several fielders beckoned. 'D'you hear what he called you, Syl?'
another player called out. 'A *fat black git!*' Christ, it's coming this
time, I thought. Back and across, back and acr— I saw the third ball
pitch short. Then it vanished from view. I was vaguely conscious
of flailing my arms skywards and jerking my head sideways – just
like a demented punk, in fact. Then there was a terrible clanging
sound and the ball ballooned upwards and was caught at slip. It
had crashed into my temple, and but for the helmet it would have
scrambled my brain. Instead it left a menacing red autograph on
the perspex side piece, a gory reminder of the time I had been 2mm
of man-made fibre from death.

'HOWZAAAAT!' yelled Clarke jubilantly.

'That's not aaart,' said umpire Arthur Jepson, a charismatic
Midlander, if that's not an oxymoron. He had a dome-shaped head
and protruding ears that made him look like a human FA Cup, 'and
that's enoof of that short stoof.'

'What is this, a ladies' game?' Clarke snorted. He stormed back
to his mark and sent down another bouncer. I felt the wind dis-
placement as it sailed 2 inches over the nape of my neck. Then we
declared.

You could say I was shaken and stirred. With a bit of whiplash
thrown in. Was the ancient game sacrificing its old-fashioned image
of fair play and breaking out into trench warfare? I asked myself.
Were the umpires losing the plot? Was I a hopeless batsman? The
answer to all these questions was yes, and that was somewhat disturbing. Cricket's soul was being trampled on by a growing obsession
with success, mirroring the rise of Thatcherism. Get rich quick and
sod how you achieve it. No one was apparently strong enough to
buck the trend. Asset-owners were all-powerful.

This was the subject of constant debate. In one corner we had the once dominant establishment – the old landlords, if you like – demanding respectability and a curb on short-pitched bowling. It was unethical and boring, they said, and sooner or later someone was going to get killed. In the other corner were the gazumpers, the ambitious county captains and nouveau team managers determined to use any malicious means to win their prize. 'Stick it up 'im,' they ordered. 'You can see he doesn't fancy it.' They didn't care one iota for the fast-bowling lackeys caught in the middle who did as they were told and were then pilloried by sections of the crowd and the media for unseemly conduct. The mind of the young fast bowler was being twisted first one way, then the other, tangling the conscience into knots. It was better to be stupid. Fortunately, a lot of them were. I acted as if I was.

Why hide under a duvet, anyway? There's something quite addictive about setting off your own ammunition, especially on an explosive site. Uxbridge was the fastest, bounciest wicket in the country in 1983. We were there for the next match and I tried out most bits of the pitch against Hampshire, taking a few wickets and clonking Robin Smith on the head first ball with a hasty bumper. He sank to his knees in a combination of shock and annoyance.

Having played with the demon Daniel for three years, I'd learned that after nobbling someone with a bouncer the fast bowler has several options:

1. Pitch up the next ball – an old-fashioned ploy with the aim of nipping through the batsman's defences while he's still groggy.

2. Bowl another short one despite the ostentatious bluff of reinforcing the slip cordon, giving the impression you're going to try the tempting out-swinger.

3. The double bluff: another short one, telegraphed by putting men out for the attempted hook. The batsman thinks you've laid the bouncer trap so transparently that you're bound to try something else (i.e., a yorker), so, theoretically, another bouncer *is* a surprise.

Confused? So was I. I bowled another short one anyway, unsure whether it was intended to be the bluff or the double bluff. Maybe I thought I was Sylvester Clarke. Smith gave a pretty vigorous response in any event, as you might expect of a guy who'd just returned from a stint of South African army training and did 200 press-ups a day. He catapulted the ball off his nose end into a bush. The shot made a sound like a 12-bore rifle crack and there was quite a commotion as several crows rapidly exited the distant undergrowth. After a moment's stunned silence, all the fielders collapsed in hysterics, which wasn't very reassuring. But I suppose it taught me another salutary lesson. Never trust men with bulky physiques and bushy moustaches. And, if in doubt, pitch it up.

From *A Lot of Hard Yakka,* 1997

Matthew Hayden and Justin Langer are two very different characters: Hayden has an enormous physical presence, while Langer is a small, busy, fidgety man. In cricket there cannot be a closer relationship than that of the opening batsmen. They are forced routinely to face the music – such as enduring the last twenty minutes of play together – with the quicks tearing in, and I can think of no other cricketing partnership that reaches such intensity. To walk out together to open the innings time after time, studying your partner from 22 yards, you must get to know each other inside out – what sort of mood your partner is in, how he is playing, and, I suspect, whether he is going to get any runs or not. You are laid bare to your partner. These two are genuinely close mates; in fact judging by a conversation we had on-air in Adelaide, I think their relationship can be said to consist of love and respect, and they would clearly do anything for each other.

MATTHEW HAYDEN

Alfie and Me

It was a moment frozen in time for me. Late October, 2009: I was driving home from a break on Stradbroke Island when my old mate Justin Langer rang from Perth. 'Dus,' he said to me, 'I will never play another game in my life.' After 360 first-class games spanning 19 years, it was all over. Alfie had arrived home from his final stint of county cricket and packed his whites away for the last time.

I was speechless, though I probably shouldn't have been. Initially I'd been surprised that Alfie had batted on after his Test match retirement, playing three more seasons of county cricket with Somerset, yet I was still stunned that the man who once seemed like he could have batted forever had suddenly stopped for good. He sounded at peace with his decision, though, and I was happy for him. He was finally ready to move on, which is the way it should be.

How different to the first time we met, the day before a Shield game at the Gabba in 1991. When I walked past Alfie in what he falsely claims was a gym shirt with a hearty, 'G'day, mate!' he took me for a groundsman. I think he called me mate as well, which isn't surprising. 'Mate' is a very useful word early in your career, when you're not really sure who you're playing against. It certainly ensures you won't embarrass yourself. The next morning, Alfie couldn't believe it when I came out to bat.

We didn't have a decent chat until meeting at the Cricket Academy a few years later, when I gave a presentation at a coaching course. I was asked what it felt like to be out of form, and replied that, at those times, holding the bat was like holding another man's old fella in your hands. Everyone seemed aghast, but it grabbed their attention. Certainly Alfie liked the line. Almost two decades later, he's still sending the story around at guest speaking nights, but unlike a lot of his stories, this one needs no embellishment. In fact, it's a bit of a rarity among his after-dinner tales because it actually happened!

By 2001 I felt I was reasonably established in the Test team. But when Alfie joined me later that year at the top of the order, things really clicked. Of all the things I achieved in cricket, few gave me greater pleasure than my long-standing union at the top of the order with Alfie. We were united in our passion by our work ethic, but diametrically opposed in other areas. I was always in trouble if I over-thought things. I needed to have a great structure in place, then let my instincts take over. Alfie, however, was really comfortable in 'think mode'. In his shower at home he had for many years a laminated sheet with a checklist of four words: physical, technical, mental and spiritual. He'd give himself a tick or a cross against each one, depending on how he'd measured up for the day.

That would have done my head in. Shower time is chill-out time for me. The thought of Alfie standing starkers in the shower after a double century and giving himself top marks for the day was too much information, I'm afraid. I'd say to him, 'Mate, what're you on about? It's life, it's not meant to be that hard.' In our on-field communication he'd think a lot about what he said and was very focused, while I was just running on gut feeling. But I could tap into what he was saying because it made sense, and he'd tap into the way I just let go of everything, which he found hard to do.

Our body language was also very different. We were the original good cop, bad cop. He'd be as smiling and happy as I was cold.

My philosophy was 'Give 'em nothing'. I'd occasionally leave my bunker, exchange a bit of fire with an opponent, then immediately retreat into my mental cave. But we were in the zone together. We were having fun. Ask any athlete about their purple patch, and I'll bet they'd say the same.

Alfie and I spent a lot of time together off the field, too. Even when he wasn't actually with me, he never seemed too far away. In my gym on Stradbroke Island, he wrote a message (now plastered on the front of one of my exercise machines) that read, *The pain of discipline is not as bad as the pain of disappointment*. The night before my 380 against Zimbabwe in Perth, in 2003, I went around to Justin and Sue's place and sat on his front lawn, and we had a big cigar together to mark the start of the summer. He started with a toast to absent friends, then we puffed on the cigar and looked at the stars. Even now I will occasionally get a text from him simply saying 'absent friends', which means he is having a good time, normally with his family. We started the absent friends toast about the time the Waugh brothers retired.

Connections are hard to contrive. They either happen or they don't. But from our very first partnership, Alfie and I just clicked, and I felt amazingly lucky to have found such a connection with someone who also happened to be my opening partner for Australia. And as with any best mate, it's not always about talking. When we were having that cigar under the stars we didn't need to talk much.

We were more compatible technically than most people realise. Before we arrived, people used to talk about the benefits of a left- and right-handed combination, because bowlers had to constantly adjust their lines when the strike was rotated. The assumption was that it was easier bowling to two lefties, because you could use the same plan. Not true – at least not with us.

You couldn't bowl outside off stump to Alfie because he'd just nick you down to third man for fun. In fact, I always felt that's when he was in supreme form, when he was playing those cheeky little nudges through slips that looked half-accidental, but were actually the result of beautifully late, soft hands.

In contrast, that wide ball was not my favourite delivery. For much of my career I didn't enjoy the cut shot, and my footwork was programmed to let dangerous balls go, not defuse and deflect them as Alfie so deftly did. My wrists were trained to turn to steel, his to rubber.

We were products of our cricketing education. Because I learnt on seaming decks at the Gabba, balls that were pitched around off stump and moving away set off warning bells for me. But Alfie, like Damien Martyn, had learnt on the high, true-bouncing decks of Perth, where you can use the pace of the ball with soft hands to glide it to the third-man boundary. Our partnership was a great argument for having different wickets in Australia, because you develop batsmen with different strengths. And it's another reason why I will always argue against 'drop in' pitches, which are more docile and lack character.

There's a certain kind of cricket boffin who likes to visit cricketers' backyards and look for the little things that helped to shape their game, such as the sloping backyard at the Waugh family house that drew the ball towards the legs of the Waugh twins and made both dynamite off their pads. They might well conclude that my reservations about the cut shot were formed by the endless hours of indoor play in our poolroom on the farm – you can still see the white stumps we drew on the wall. A couple of metres away, at point, was our 'no-go zone' – the glass doors. So the cut shot was out, and – as Mum still boasts – the glass doors were never broken.

Alfie's great strength was my soft spot. If I hit the ball behind point it was often a mistake. If we'd been rock groups, I was Hunters and Collectors and he was Nudgers and Deflectors. Bowlers would try and cut off Alfie's strength by bowling at him. When they did that to me, there were runs straight and through the leg side. I loved to murder the straight line. We also transformed our techniques in ways that made it harder for bowlers to formulate plans. Late in Alfie's career, bowlers felt more confident about getting him so they bowled straighter to him, and he developed an excellent cover drive. And bowlers realised that one way to keep me quiet was to bowl wider of off stump, so I developed my cut shot.

Alfie's greatest skill was using the pace of the ball. Mine was being up and at the ball. Alfie could work the ball in a way I struggled to do, and I could vary where I took guard or bat out of my crease to dominate an attack in a way he couldn't quite manage. Quite wrongly, Alfie was accused of being the sluggish one in our partnership. It bugged him a bit, which is why he has a photo up in his poolroom in Perth of a Test scoreboard that reads 'Langer 51,

Hayden 1' – photographic evidence that he was never the barnacle. Often he outscored me early and would beat me to 50, because his method – the off-side glides in particular – were more useful than my driving against the new ball. Quite often, I'd catch him when the spinners came on. He was a rotator against spin, whereas I tried to get hold of them.

People often think that because we were so close we shared absolutely everything. We didn't. I was always a little superstitious about my batting cues, key words such as 'Fight!' or 'Full!' or 'Now!' that went off inside my head and triggered me to do something. They were spoken internally when the ball was just about to be delivered, when I'd tell myself to fasten the bayonet and get down the wicket to a spinner. I didn't explain them to anyone, not even Alfie. I have a theory that once you talk about something like that, its power is somehow diminished.

And as great as our connection was, I just couldn't talk much cricket to Alfie because he was so intense. When we did talk about cricket, it was mainly about his game. If I'd talked to him about my game, it would have sent me bonkers. Ricky Ponting was different. I could talk to him because we were agreed on the right way to go about it.

Ponting is one of the greatest readers of batting technique I've ever seen. He knew my game so well that he could tell what I was thinking by how I picked up the bat in my backswing. Sometimes he'd say to me, 'I know what you're thinking but, mate, let's just refocus.' And I would say the same to him. If he played a sweep shot I'd say, 'Mate, why would you play that shot? You hit the ball better than anyone down the ground on the leg side. If you want to play a sweep I'll throw you 500 balls in the nets.'

We didn't often talk technique, but when we did it was all business, along the lines of, 'This is how we're going to do it.' Meanwhile, Alfie was always looking for new entries to the gospel of batting, and in his hands it was a very thick book indeed. I'd say, 'Mate, just watch the ball,' and did my best to talk him out of any new-fangled trends.

One of those trends – I'll never forget it – was this exotic late twist of the head to face up. I suspect the intention was to get your head straight and eyes as square on to the ball as possible at the point of delivery. It made no sense at all to me but Alfie gave it a go, and because he was a legend of district cricket in Perth, the practice spread faster than a new David Beckham hairstyle. When I saw Mike Hussey do it, I decided it was time to save the cricket world from this dangerous new fad. I said to Huss, 'Mate, what the hell are you doing? Just worry a lot less about it, right?' But then when Ryan Campbell started doing it, I knew West Australian cricket was on the verge of producing its own version of the *Star Wars* classic, *Attack of the Clones*. There was nothing I could do.

In retrospect, it's probably no wonder Alfie thought a lot about the position of his head, because during his career it took a fearful drubbing. The worst of all was in his 100th Test match in Johannesburg, when he was knocked down first ball by Makhaya Ntini. 'Mate, we know you've copped one, now get up,' I said, sauntering down the wicket. But my attitude changed instantly when I saw his eyes. They were gone, and so was he.

There was no question at the time – he had to retire hurt. But should he bat in the second innings? As we were closing in on victory, it became clear it could come down to the last wicket. I was simply in my element that day as a scheming, dressing-room double agent winding up my two great mates Ponting and Langer. Back and forth I went, playing one off against the other, deftly probing their sensitivities. You could argue that such a delicate issue should be beyond any form of gee-up, but I have always reckoned if the Anzacs could poke fun at the Turks by hoisting up cans of bully beef in the trenches for them to shoot at, then we shouldn't stress too much about what happens in a cricket dressing-room.

I knew Punter didn't want Alfie to bat, so I went up to Ricky and said, 'What are you talking about? We're going to lose a Test here. You have to let him bat!' But Punter wouldn't budge and was saying things like, 'Mate, he's gonna die, he's been hit on the head so many times.'

Deep down I also knew Alfie shouldn't be batting, because he still couldn't see properly and was off balance. It actually took him several months to fully recover from the blow. But I couldn't help myself, because I knew what it meant to Alfie to place the team before himself. So I said to him, 'Mate, he's going to declare on you,' and he snapped back, 'Dus, Dus … I'm gonna walk out there and bat. I don't care. He can declare but I am going to let the world know he's pulling me off because I'm not going down in history as a weak prick. If he declares, I am declaring our friendship over!'

So I rushed back to Punter with the most earnest face I could muster and said, 'Mate, you're going to kill him anyway by not letting him bat, so you may as well do it with a cricket ball. It's his 100th Test – this could be the greatest thing he ever does.' By that stage Punter, whose natural inclination is to get punchy when cornered, had had quite enough of me. I've never seen him so vulnerable. I knew he couldn't get too angry with me because of one simple fact – if he was the man who'd taken the head-blow, he'd have batted.

Eventually we won with two wickets to spare, and the question of whether Alfie should bat or not was successfully avoided. Alfie showed his true colours in the rooms after the match, walking around saying, 'Helluva Test, that one,' and enjoying the celebrations as much as anyone, even though he'd faced just one ball.

Wouldn't you miss that spirit? I know I did. After Alfie retired from Test cricket in January 2007, I never felt quite the same. It had absolutely nothing to do with the calibre of his replacements, Phil Jaques and Simon Katich, who are terrific blokes and fine players. But when you have a partnership that's right, everything just flows. It's like driving from Brisbane to Cairns at your own pace, just floating along. Having a new partner is like making the same trip with a police car on your tail. You're instantly aware of every little detail. Should I be indicating? Am I going too fast? Alfie and I never tried to analyse our connection too much. It was what it was. When Jaquesey came in, I wanted him to do well and build a solid start to his career, and I wanted to be a part of that process. But it takes energy to start a new partnership in any form of life – especially when the old partnership has been so fulfilling.

The bond between Alfie and me was cemented each Christmas Eve, when our two families, the Buchanans and anyone else who wanted to come shared mass together in Melbourne. Father Pat Maroney, who married Kell and I, had moved to Melbourne and gave us a special service at Mazenod College in Mulgrave. We had a few beers and a bit of a get-together afterwards.

When we were playing together, Alfie and I developed a custom where he would mark centre as he faced the first ball of a Test, then I would cross it with a line when we changed strike to form the sign of the cross. When I was at the bowler's end while he was preparing to face the first ball I would mark centre and he would cross it when we changed ends. It was another anchor in our relationship.

When we marked the sign of the cross at the crease I would always say a silent prayer: *Whatever happens today is in your hands.*

From *Standing My Ground, 2011*

GENTLEMEN
AND PLAYERS

Few things are more deeply rooted in
the collective imagination of the
English than the village cricket match.
It stirs a romantic illusion about the
rustic way of life, it suggests a tranquil
and unchanging order in an age of
bewildering flux.

Geoffrey Moorhouse

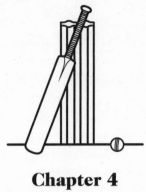

Chapter 4

'His clarity of mind enabled him to pierce the woolly romanticism and anachronistic feudalism which so long obscured the truth of cricket.'

John Arlott pays tribute to Mike Brearley's modernism.

O nly fifty years ago, spectators at a county match would be familiar with the image of members of the same team taking the field from two different dressing rooms and through two different gates – one for professionals, the other for amateurs. Such hierarchical divisions were part of the history of cricket for some 250 years, but society has moved on and such divisions would be unthinkable today – and downright confusing to a new follower of the game.

One definition of the word 'amateur' is 'a person who engages in an activity, especially a sport, as a pastime, rather than professionally or for gain'. However, the word 'amateur' also has connotations of ineptitude and lack of skill, and I can think of any number of professional cricketers in the early days of the game who would agree wholeheartedly with such a description of the amateurs who turned up to play when they chose, one of whom was invariably the captain of the team. The hard-nosed old pros, whose second-class status in the team reflected that of their everyday lives, would have watched the gentlemen in their brightly coloured, stripy blazers and caps heading for the amateurs' dressing room on match day with a measure of wry amusement and some social contempt. The pros were usually miners or farm workers out of season, but as cricketers they were generally the more talented and worked hard at their sport every day. They were pragmatic and, on the post-war county circuit, often dour batsmen who placed great importance on safety first. Yet tradition dictated that the amateurs – largely upper-class characters from the entirely different world of public school and, usually, university-educated – should be paid the utmost respect on the field and called 'sir'. The amateurs were often more free-spirited than the professionals because their jobs, and thus the welfare of their families, were not on the line if they played a rash shot.

The distinction between the two dressing rooms was made perfectly clear on the match scorecard: the amateur players would be listed as Mr D. R. Jardine, for example, or D. R. Jardine Esq., while a professional appeared as Larwood, H. An amateur would address a professional by his surname only. Although not always the case, most amateurs were batsmen while the pros were more likely to be the hard-working bowlers, who provided the practice material for their superiors in the nets. It makes you wonder how on earth a healthy team spirit, as we understand the concept today, was ever engendered back then – although, in fact, I'm not talking about that long ago. It was, after all, only in 1962 that the distinction between amateur and professional cricketers was finally dropped. At that point, every county player became a professional, at least supposedly, thus ending the traditional segregation in cricket teams between those who were paid to play and those who were not.

With amateurism abolished, 1962 also saw the last of the traditional matches between the Gentlemen and the Players – a fixture that was first played in 1806 at Lord's and was usually scheduled twice every season. It says everything about the lofty manner in which the amateurs perceived their status in society that they should form the Gentlemen's team, while the pros were the Players. The Gentlemen generally dominated the early years, but when the Players defeated the Gentlemen by seven wickets at Scarborough in September 1962 it completed a run of eighteen consecutive matches without a single victory for the Gentlemen. Trueman, F. S.'s typically forthright opinion of the fixture was that it was 'a ludicrous business', and this view would definitely have been echoed by his fellow professionals.

While the main condition of a cricketer's amateur status was that he did not receive any payment for participating – the MCC's guideline was that a 'gentleman ought not to make any profit from playing cricket' – this has always been of varying definition and a matter of some controversy. Even the most famous amateur of them all, Dr W. G. Grace, was the subject of an enquiry into the expenses that he and his brother, E. M. Grace, claimed from Surrey when they played for Gloucestershire at the Oval in 1878. The Graces survived that particular embarrassment, despite it being widely known that WG probably made more money from playing cricket than any professional of the time. However, being a doctor, he would have had to provide locum cover for his patients whenever he was playing cricket. He was also the biggest draw in the game, easily doubling a crowd – and gate receipts – if word got out that he was playing. He might have revelled in his popularity to the extent that he regularly indulged in gamesmanship to overturn umpires' decisions against him, but Grace was definitely philanthropic and generous.

The First World War played a significant part in the start of the breakdown of the rigid class structure in Great Britain, in which you lived either upstairs or below them, and the Representation of the People Act 1928 gave women equal voting rights to men. Society was changing fast, but on the cricket field, at least, the distinction between the amateurs and professionals remained intact.

The infamous Bodyline tour of 1932–3 is an excellent example of the influence that the amateur commanded over his professionals, and also of the way in which the establishment ultimately protected one of its own. The captain of MCC (under whose flag England toured until 1977) was Douglas Robert Jardine, of Oxford University and Surrey. Born in British India, Jardine was a talented and courageous batsman who had toured Australia successfully in 1928–9, but his mannerisms appear to have been those of the quintessential amateur. He preferred the bright stripes of the Harlequin cap to the traditional MCC touring cap with St George slaying the dragon, and often fielded (clumsily) in a cravat. Under his command for what promised to be a very challenging tour were Harold Larwood and Bill Voce, two fast bowlers from the Nottingham coal mines, whom Jardine had identified to carry out his controversial tactic of bowling deliberately short and at the ribs of the Australian batsmen – and Don Bradman's in particular.

It is worth remembering that although unsporting, and not in the best interests of the game, bodyline was technically legitimate at the time. It seems inconceivable, therefore, that Larwood or Voce would have been able to talk their overbearing captain out of his plan, even if they had wanted to – let alone refuse to take part in it. However, Jardine's third pace bowler on the tour was George 'Gubby' Allen, an amateur, who was able to use his status as Jardine's social equal to voice his disapproval. Ultimately, Allen refused Jardine's instruction to bowl bodyline. Such clear dissent would have been unthinkable for a professional. However, it was Larwood who was later held accountable by the authorities, the MCC. In the aftermath of the tour, which England won, Larwood was reprimanded for the manner in which he had bowled and asked to sign a letter of apology to the Australian Board of Control and its players. No action was taken against either Jardine or Pelham Warner, who had been an entirely ineffectual manager of the tour and who would be knighted for services to cricket some five years later. Unsurprisingly, Larwood's refusal to be a scapegoat meant he never played for England again.

Among the ranks on the Bodyline tour was one of the finest batsmen ever to play for England. Wally Hammond was a stylish right-hander, renowned for a classical cover drive, who began his career with Gloucestershire in 1920 as a professional. He enjoyed a prolific tour of Australia in 1928–9, scoring 905 runs at an average of 113.12, a record beaten only by Don Bradman. Although the lack of television and rapid communication made proper comparisons difficult in those days, Hammond found it frustrating forever living in Bradman's shadow when, in virtually any other generation, Hammond would in all likelihood have been regarded as the best batsman in the world. Another natural source of discontent was that, being a professional, Hammond could never captain England – that distinction still being solely reserved for amateurs. In 1937, Hammond not only scored heavily against the visiting New Zealanders but also overtook Frank Woolley's record sixty-four Test appearances and became England's highest ever run scorer, making the question of the captaincy a frequent talking point. Everything changed, however, when, at the end of the season, it was announced that he had accepted a job outside cricket: he would now play as an amateur, and that changed everything. Not only was Hammond named as England captain for the 1938 Ashes series and elected to life membership of Gloucestershire, he was also elected a member of MCC, which still barred professionals. When Hammond captained the Gentlemen against the Players at Lord's that summer, he became the only cricketer ever to have led both teams. Hammond's decision played a large part in blurring the lines between amateur and professional status: should it really be necessary for one of cricket's greatest players to take a job outside the game in order for him to captain England? As the country went to war for the second time in twenty years, with Hammond serving an administrative role in the Royal Air Force, the class-dominated constitution of English cricket was looking increasingly outdated, unjustifiable and ultimately unsustainable.

It was the Second World War that did for the amateur cricketer in the professional game. Six years of suffering and hardship that had been felt and endured on an equal basis for the most part had broken down the social barriers that until then had divided every aspect of British life. It simply was not going to be possible to return to things the way they were. The National Health Service Act of 1946, which led to the creation of the NHS two years later and guaranteed free medical care for everyone, reflected the mood of a nation needing to rebuild itself from the very foundations. There simply was no mood for a two-tier society.

Britain was also broke. Rationing was every bit as strict after the war as during it, only ending completely in 1954, and the money needed to rebuild the country had to come from somewhere. With eye-watering taxation on annual incomes exceeding two thousand pounds, the days of the leisured class swanning around playing cricket were well and truly over. The wealthy amateur simply could not afford it any longer, adding further to the crisis now felt by cricket's administrators. After a boom immediately following the war, crowds were now falling away dramatically at county matches and gate receipts were down. An indication of how desperately counties struggled to find an amateur captain is the case of Major Nigel Harvie Bennett, a former public-school boy with no experience of first-class cricket who turned up at the Oval and asked for some second-eleven cricket (Bennett had played three times for the Surrey second eleven in 1936). To say he was surprised to find himself offered the captaincy of the Surrey first team is an understatement, but he accepted the offer and captained the side during the 1946 season, taking them to their worst ever finishing position of eleventh. It is widely believed that on his arrival at the gates he was mistaken by the Surrey committee members for the notable cricketer Major Leo Bennett, who would go on to play for Northamptonshire.

Change and progression take time, and that is definitely the case with cricket. Yorkshire soldiered on with their amateur captains, winning the Championship under Ronnie Burnet's leadership in 1959. However, Burnet's personal contribution that year was an average of 11 with the bat, 6 catches and 1 wicket. 'Nice men,' Brian Close wrote of Burnet and his predecessor Billy Sutcliffe, 'but they should have had neither the captaincy nor a place in the side.'

The established system limped on for a while but, with amateurs feeling the pinch and still unable to earn anything from playing cricket, there is no question that, in some cases, ways were found to bolster expenses or award 'bonuses'. Others took up nominal administrative positions at county clubs. This became known as the age of the 'shamateur' and in 1952, as a reflection of the prevailing situation, MCC appointed Len Hutton as the first professional player to captain England since 1888.

It still took another ten years for the MCC Advisory County Cricket Committee to meet and decide by a clear majority to abolish amateur and professional status. All players, the committee declared, should be called 'cricketers' – quite a radical departure. This was approved by the MCC Committee and came into effect in 1963, bringing to an end the recognized manner in which cricket had been played in Britain for 250 years.

Elsewhere in the cricketing world the distinction between amateur and professional players was less clearly defined than it was in England. Australian first-class and Test cricketers had to juggle between their careers and their cricketing commitments – Don Bradman, for example, worked in real estate before moving to a sports goods retailer. With fewer teams competing in the Sheffield Shield than in England's County Championship, there was more time between games, but even so you needed a sympathetic employer because although cricketers were paid an appearance fee for first-class and Test cricket, it was nowhere near enough to be called a living wage.

New Zealand cricket was run along very much the same lines as Australian cricket, but elsewhere in the Empire cricket was established along strict racial and religious lines, rather than skill or wealth, with the white elite naturally assuming superiority over their coloured subjects. In both India and the Caribbean, playing cricket became an indicator of superior social and racial status.

The Afro-Caribbean population of the West Indies was discouraged from forming organized club cricket, and it was not until the end of the nineteenth century that the first non-white club was formed, and this was for players of mixed race. Afro-Caribbeans continued to be considered inferior to the extent that it was not until 1960 that a black cricketer – Frank Worrell – was appointed captain of West Indies. This was ten years after West Indies had won their first Test series against England, a series win that was of great political significance in the West Indies, proving that they were capable of beating Englishmen. However, while their captain, John Goddard, was born in Barbados, he was white.

Worrell's appointment coincided with the emergence of truly talented West Indian players who firmly placed their region on the cricketing map. With limited scope for advancement in the Caribbean, many of the first West Indian professional players plied their trade on the often cold, wet and windswept cricket fields of northwest England, in the Lancashire League, a valuable source of experience and income. Prior to the Second World War, Learie Constantine – later Lord Constantine – had spent nine lucrative seasons as Nelson's professional. Postwar, the 'three Ws' – Worrell, Everton Weekes and Clyde Walcott – and Garfield Sobers were just a few of the world-class West Indian cricketers who spent their summers in the mill towns of Lancashire. What a life-changing experience it must have been for them. Now, because of the declining quality of cricket in the Caribbean, club professionals are more likely to be South Africans or Australians. However, the legacy of those early West Indian pioneers was the passion for cricket they inspired in the Caribbean. Young boys suddenly discovered heroes whose triumphs they could dream of emulating one day. Cricket became a means of bettering oneself; of becoming rich and famous. The next wave of West Indian cricketers, including Viv Richards, Andy Roberts, Clive Lloyd and Michael Holding, fired by the experiences and the success of their predecessors, formed arguably the finest Test team there has ever been.

The evolution of Indian cricket, from the strict religious and racial segregation that formed the late 1930s Bombay Pentangular cricket tournament to today's secular Ranji Trophy, coincided with the country's independence in 1947. In the run-up to the Second World War, there was growing hostility towards the tournament in which five sporting clubs, known locally as gymkhanas, competed. The Bombay Gymkhana was a whites-only club, and the other teams were formed individually by Parsis, Hindus, Muslims and the Rest, which included Buddhists, Indian Christians and Jews. The Pentangular, or Presidency Match, as it was also known, enjoyed a tradition dating back to 1877 and was a much-anticipated annual sporting event and social occasion in British India. When the Parsis defeated the Europeans of the Bombay Gymkhana in 1889, the victory had the same seismic political impact as Goddard's win over England in 1950, but by the 1930s India as a whole was impatient for more than just occasional victories on a cricket field. Time was running out for the British Empire, and when Mahatma Gandhi condemned the structure of the Pentangular, arguing that its divisions illustrated those created by British rule in everyday life, it was clear that the winds of political change sweeping the subcontinent would blow through the Bombay Maidan. In 1946 the Board of Control for Cricket in India (BCCI) announced that the Pentangular tournament would be replaced by a new zonal competition. As was the case in Australia, the top-class cricketers in India and (from 1947) Pakistan were effectively amateurs, being nominally employed by large companies like Indian Railways or, in Imran Khan's case, Pakistan International Airlines. This gave them a steady income and enabled them to play as much cricket as they wanted.

While the decolonization of European empires continued for the next fifty years, producing scores of newly independent countries, the regulation of cricket was still the responsibility of the Imperial Cricket Conference (ICC). This was founded at Lord's in 1909 by England, Australia and South Africa, with membership being confined to countries within the British Empire where Test cricket was played – in other words, England, Australia and South Africa. In 1926 West Indies, New Zealand and India were elected and in 1952 Pakistan was granted Test status. South Africa left the Commonwealth in 1961, thereby losing its membership of the ICC, but when the Imperial Cricket Conference was renamed the International Cricket Conference in 1965, new rules permitted the inclusion of countries from outside the Commonwealth. As well as admitting non-Test-playing countries, called associate members, this enabled England and Australia – who, as founding members, retained the right of veto – to continue contact with South Africa, despite external pressure growing on its apartheid regime. Political persuasion through the 1971 Singapore Declaration of Commonwealth Principles, which led to the 1977 Gleneagles Agreement, finally forced South Africa into sporting isolation. When the governing body was rebranded a third time, becoming in 1985 the International Cricket Council, the full Test-playing members all received equal status and in a symbolic gesture – as well as a tax-saving ploy – the ICC moved from Lord's to Dubai in 2005. From definitely amateur status in 1909, the ICC is now a fully professional organization employing more than 120 staff around the world and running three global tournaments.

So far, we have charted the progress of the high-profile amateur cricketer – someone fortunate enough to have sufficient wealth and social standing to enable him to play cricket, in some cases, at the very highest level. He was a capable cricketer, and almost certainly a batsman, but in many cases it was his background that gained him selection rather than his talent. Changing attitudes towards the class structure following the Second World War, as well as the dwindling number of men who could afford to play for nothing, saw off the amateur in England, while the injection of money from television – kick-started by World Series Cricket in Australia in 1977 – enabled the best cricketers elsewhere around the world to turn professional some twenty years later.

What cannot be disputed is that the amateur injected boundless enthusiasm and passion into top-class cricket. After all, it was his hobby, whereas the professional cricketer, while loving the sport and the way of life it provided, is nonetheless working for a living, and that can introduce complacency and staleness, along with the pressure to perform and retain your place. The amateur did not have to worry unduly about that – he simply played cricket with all the gusto of a fan who suddenly finds himself propelled into a county first eleven. It is a shame that the only way to savour that experience these days is while daydreaming in a deckchair on the boundary edge. Yet the enthusiasm for and obsession with the game lives on within every ardent cricket lover just as it always did, now forming what we recognize as today's amateur game.

And what a diverse and colourful world it is. Players, umpires, scorers, coaches, groundsmen, fixtures secretaries and the hardy, loyal souls who turn out to support their teams every week whatever the weather – is there anybody more committed to their sport than cricket fans? They form a disparate group of individuals with a heartfelt love of the game and an unwavering desire to take part in arguably the greatest team game ever invented – despite, sometimes, lacking any discernible talent or mastery of the requisite skills! Actually that is a bit unfair: many non-professional cricketers have a considerable amount of skill and are keen and ready to pass on their expertise to a younger generation.

We all started in the same place by playing some form of cricket at school. For many of us fortunate to play outside on hot summer days on grounds that smelt of freshly mown grass with like-minded eager contemporaries, this was an idyllic time of our lives. However, increasingly these days, it is not the proper version of the game that our children play, but a plastic variety. One of the great crimes of the last century was the selling off, by successive governments, of school playing fields, reducing them to building sites. The impact on all school sport as a result of this short-sighted policy has been devastating: cricket has suffered particularly badly because it needs more space than most. The huge sums of money raised might have been welcomed by successive governments, but at what price? It is young people who have to foot the bill by becoming a generation of unhealthy individuals who are denied the basic right to routinely play and enjoy sport.

The only option was to cram a condensed form of cricket into a tarmacked playground or school hall and hope that the opportunity to hit a ball and enjoy the thrill of chasing a score to win would light a spark of enthusiasm for the real thing. Kwik Cricket, as it is known in the United Kingdom, has many of the 'proper' game's rules but is played with a bright plastic bat and ball. It can be adapted to be played in virtually any space and has proved to be an inspirational but necessary replacement for 12,000 primary school cricket fields, as well as 4,500 clubs. For the majority of young children, Kwik Cricket is their first introduction to the great game. Inter Cricket, another softball adaptation, is aimed at 12- to 14-year-olds, bridging the gap between Kwik Cricket and the real thing. Various charities and initiatives have been set up to assist schoolchildren to play cricket, the best known probably being Chance to Shine, the president of which is Sir Mervyn King, Governor of the Bank of England. This targets inner-city schoolchildren and connects them with local clubs that have the facilities and the coaches to introduce their charges to the game and, hopefully, to initiate a link to that club that can be pursued into adulthood, thus protecting the future of club and league cricket. Other schemes in rural Britain, such as the Belvoir Bees in Nottinghamshire, transport children from far-flung schools to one central point with the same purpose in mind. Through necessity there has been a dramatic change in the way children forge an interest in cricket, but the numbers suggest that it seems to be working. This should enable the sport to flourish despite the decline in the number of school playing fields and, indeed, the lack of live cricket broadcast on terrestrial television.

A spark is all that is needed to ignite a passion for the game of cricket that can last a lifetime, and playing the game is only one option. Many armchair followers have never held a bat in their lives, while those driven by statistics find a fascination in scoring and the seemingly boundless opportunities to explore the game through the immeasurable depths of cricketing data. There really is something for everybody.

But it is through actually playing the game that the most fun and, indeed, frustration is derived. Whether it is representing a club in one of the county premier leagues, or turning out for a village team, the same challenges remain for every cricketer, whatever his or her ability. Village cricket still provides a social backbone to our country, just as it did when the ever-present huge-armed blacksmith rolled up the sleeves of his shirt and tore in to bowl from the boundary edge while the squire opened the batting in his multicoloured striped cap. Village cricket brings communities together. Local rivalries are often steeped in folklore and deep history, with the annual contest against the neighbouring village eagerly anticipated all season. The game will be played every bit as keenly as a Test match and, due to the complicated laws and usual absence of fully qualified umpires, there are often disputes over dismissals and even over the result itself. These are often discussed and arbitrated upon in our 'Ask the Umpire' slot on *Test Match Special* (when in doubt, calling 'Dead ball' seems to be the best solution), giving rise to much unintended humour as we unravel Byzantine by-laws and sub-clauses. But when it is all over as the evening descends along with the dew, a pint or two in the local pub remains as essential to the fixture as the cricket itself.

My own experience of village cricket was at Ufford Park, located in the farming community between Peterborough and Stamford. Based at a tiny pretty ground surrounded by woodland and cattle grazing on the edge of the ground, Ufford Park remains a classic example of what village cricket is all about. The same man religiously mows the outfield every week, and meticulously prepares the pitch. Another, the club secretary, would be a familiar figure in every club up and down the country. A slave to his administrative duties, this fellow is a superb organizer of people, a tireless chivvying focal point of the club.

For those of you familiar with the great era of BBC television comedy, picture one of Britain's finest actors, the late Richard Briers, in his masterful comic creation, the eternal worrier, ever-put-upon Martin Bryce in the brilliant comedy *Ever Decreasing Circles*, and you have the man. Clipboard in hand and with a spare bedroom stacked with ring binders, this is the chap responsible for the smooth running of every aspect of the club, from team selection to organizing the tea rota, from scouring the land for fixtures to collecting the club subscriptions. This is not a job for the faint-hearted and, truth be told, most of us would run a mile rather than be saddled with such a burden. But every club needs a Martin Bryce, because it simply could not function otherwise.

To turn out for Ufford Park at the tender age of 14 was a wonderful experience, and an important part in my progression as a cricketer. Playing amongst men – farmers, predominantly – definitely expanded my vocabulary and also taught me invaluable lifelong lessons about playing cricket the right way. The matches were keenly contested, but batsmen were politely applauded to the crease, and walked when they were dismissed. No one sledged and a member of the batting team would almost certainly be required to umpire at one end, and be prepared to give his team-mates out when necessary.

The standard of cricket played was probably most kindly described as 'mixed'. It seemed that every team had a star player who had been around for years and was talked of in hushed, reverential tones. There was always a promising youngster making his way through the ranks and someone who was completely hopeless but picked every week simply to make up the numbers. Much of the bowling was pretty friendly, and if you bowled straight for long enough, you would invariably pick up wickets. Fielding was enthusiastic but less than agile and some of the batting lower down the order would be defined as positively agricultural. But it was a great learning experience, and I still love popping into the club whenever I can.

Terry Rawlings, my Ufford Park captain back in the mid-1970s, is still playing for the club in his late sixties, having first played for the club when he turned 12. Village cricket is more than just a game to people like him: it is a passion, a tradition and a way of life – a way of life that must be nurtured and protected. In a curious way, the decline of cricket in schools might well help to keep clubs like Ufford Park going.

A casual flick through *From the Boundary's Edge* by the photographer Laurence Griffiths reveals another irresistible appeal of club and village cricket, and that is the beauty of the playing fields themselves. Many have characteristic and challenging features such as a steep bank that makes the ball speed away into a bed of nettles, or an awkwardly placed, one-hundred-year-old oak tree standing proudly at third man, but these simply add further charm to an already idyllic scene. The emerald green of the grass against the stark white of the players' clothing combine perfectly with the unmistakable sound of bat hitting ball and the polite ripple of respectful applause welcoming a new batsman to the wicket. To describe anything as quintessentially English these days is to mire it in cliché, but how much more English can this possibly be?

This charming village scene is replicated all over the world, but tailored to local circumstances. In the Caribbean, beach cricket might be in decline, but there is usually a game to be found somewhere with fielders standing up to their waists in the azure water and barefooted bowlers hurling down tennis balls. In India, the vast maidans in Mumbai and Kolkata play host to myriad games of cricket, often played impossibly close to each other. The grass might be scruffy, and there is always the likelihood of a cow or two sauntering through, but despite the heat of the subcontinent, the game goes on. The popularity of the Indian Premier League – locally, at least – has prompted a tremendous increase in impromptu cricket in that part of the world, particularly among young boys.

There are no coaches to guide them, and the rules are adapted to suit, so there is a certain amount of unorthodoxy as a result. One very good example of this unfettered unorthodoxy crossing over into the professional game is Lasith Malinga, the Sri Lankan fast bowler with an almost impossibly low arm and slingshot action. His ability to bowl so straight and so fast defies every coaching manual, and he is the product of genuinely unstructured and liberated cricket. I wonder if Malinga would have made it to the top had he been playing in any other country? Sri Lanka has a tradition of producing unusual, highly talented cricketers who would probably have been written off and discarded by the certificate-wielding coaches anywhere else. One also wonders what might have become of Muttiah Muralitharan had he appeared at one of England's many cricket academies, rather than simply being encouraged to bowl with his highly unusual action at the Tamil Union Cricket Club in Colombo.

Cricket can be played and enjoyed almost anywhere. I have played the game on a green mat laid on the frozen lake at St Moritz in Switzerland, and great fun it was, too. In 2007, a group of enthusiasts including the Essex all-rounder Graham Napier played a six-a-side match at the Mount Everest base camp. Two years later a second match was staged on Everest – this time it was a full eleven-a-side affair – on a plateau called Gorak Shep, 17,000 feet above sea level. In 2012, on the 100th anniversary of Captain Scott's expedition, a game was staged at the South Pole at minus 35°C. And on it goes, example after example of man's desire to take cricket to weird, wonderful and unlikely locations around the world, and to play the game as close to the real thing as it is possible to do.

Geoffrey Moorhouse, journalist and writer, was in many ways a natural successor to the great Neville Cardus: both were from north-west England, Cardus from Manchester, Moorhouse from Bolton; both were distinguished writers for the *Manchester Guardian*; and both had a deep abiding love of cricket.

The year 1978 was a potentially cataclysmic one for cricket. With the arrival of Kerry Packer's World Series Cricket, the game was thought to be on the point of irreversible, and not entirely welcome, change. Moorhouse set out to record the season he felt might be the last traditional one seen in England. He would write about fourteen fixtures ranging from a Test match to a county game, a minor-county fixture to a village-green championship. The resulting book, published a year later, magnificently caught a moment in time, and is as readable today as it was when first published.

THE OLDEST FIXTURE

Geoffrey Moorhouse

July 15 Lord's – Eton v Harrow

The schoolboys picked a perfect day for the start of the annual ceremony at Lord's. Cricket was meant to be enjoyed under just such a cloudless sky, with players, watchers and everything about the ground glowing with midsummer warmth. This, at any rate, is how imagination persists in idealising the game, misinforming us that rain never stopped play in the traditional past. And here, at the Eton and Harrow match, we are at the deep end of cricketing tradition, for this fixture has a longer history than any other cricket match still being played. The schools probably met in 1804, certainly in the following year, when lame young Lord Byron scored 7 and 2 for Harrow with the assistance of a runner, and afterwards conceded that they had been "most confoundedly beat" by Eton. Early records of the rivalry are incomplete, but from 1822 onwards the two sides have turned out at Lord's each year almost without a break apart from the interruptions of war. The University match didn't get under way until 1827, organised county and international cricket were even further behind. A man comes to the Eton and Harrow, therefore, with a healthy regard for seniority, even if he has no commitment to any of these downy lads.

He should also, of course, bring a taste for social history if he is to savour the day to the full. When the Eton openers begin to bat this morning, and the zebra caps of Harrow stripe the infield grass, there will be nobody on this ground unconscious of the fact that he is attending an occasion for which the cricket itself is not much more than the excuse. To some extent this is true of all cricket matches, where wider loyalties are invariably at stake, but the Eton and Harrow crowd make this a particularly arresting example of tribal display. Devotion to the schools has brought them here, as well as pride in siblings and sons, but the majority, I think, are attracted to Lord's for these two days in every year to exhibit a more substantial *esprit de corps*. During the first half hour's play, when Compton-Burnett and Morris are struggling to master some steady bowling from the Harrow attack, there is much more clapping out on the pitch, from players who have been drilled in the politenesses of this game, than there is from the spectators, who are still settling down to their own performances of the day. Nine-tenths of them are congregated by the Tavern, or in immediately adjacent seats, and this will not just be because the wicket for this match is closer to that side. It is as much an expression of solidarity as any gathering of strikers outside a factory gate. This is, for the most part, the assembly of an elite whom history has been overhauling this past forty years. There is comfort in whatever numbers remain.

Neither the numbers nor anything else about this fixture are what they were when George du Maurier caricatured the spectators as a languid lot with impedimented speech. At the end of the nineteenth century, and for many years after, stagecoaches were driven to Lord's and encircled the field this day, so that ladies and gentlemen could watch the affair from some height and in much elegance. Today, a solitary vehicle in yellow and brown has been parked by the covers at the Nursery end, lonely memorial to a gracious past, with five people sitting on tubular deckchairs in its lee. Grey toppers and morning suits are still just holding their own, propped up, here and there, by an ivory-handled stick. The

'Now, sir, your father don't pay £300 a year in school fees
to have you flicking at balls just outside the off stump.'

Harrovian quota is distinguishable by that suburban annual in the
lapel, and the proportion of cornflowers at Lord's today suggests
that Eton face overwhelming odds in support. "This is supposed to
be the strongest Eton batting side for years, isn't it?" enquires one
such gentleman of another on a Tavern bench. It doesn't look like
it, when Feather and Murray replace the opening bowlers and Eton
wickets begin to go down. By the time Feather takes Benthall's off-
stump out of the ground, the Etonians have mustered only 37 for 3.

At this point, sheets of pale Cambridge blue are hung in front of two boxes on the Tavern stand, to match the colour of the Eton caps. They look like frayed washing but they are meant to rally a cause.

And in those boxes above the Tavern bar, the quintessential spectators of the Eton and Harrow match are themselves to be seen. There are similar boxes on the Grandstand side of the ground, similarly filled with people who must be straining their eyes to observe details of the play; though, as I say, they have posted themselves there for reasons other than that. These boxes have been hired for princely sums by Mr E. W. Swanton, Mr C. Martin-Jenkins, Brigadier Gordon Lennox and their peers for the purpose of entertaining guests, which they appear to do handsomely and well, judging by the parade of Bloody Marys and other intoxicants visible through the rails. Blander visions carefully stay within view, decked in fashions scarcely seen nowadays outside Ascot and garden parties at the Palace. A woman poises herself at one balcony above the Tavern, exquisitely modelled in white; dress flowing from chin to floor, hat brimming widely beyond her head, ribbons fluttering down her back, the whiteness relieved only by a small cameo in china at her throat. When Dudley Carew wrote his short story about the Eton and Harrow match some time after the Great War, he portrayed a Gainsborough lady who intently followed every incident of play, motionless on a bench down there on the grass. Her counterpart today leans conversationally on the rail above, toying with a gin and tonic, early Anna Neagle in a production by Herbert Wilcox.

Wickets continue to fall in quick time, until Eton have descended to 42 for 6 and Harrow's slip fielders are crouched behind the batsman as tight-strung as any arc of professionals scenting victory in a Test. Batsmen come out with determination in their walk, to return shortly afterwards more slowly, with cap shoved back and a puzzled expression on the face. There will be some very old Etonians who must already be bracing themselves on the memory of Fowler's match in 1910, whose outcome sensationally reversed the general pattern of play. Eton followed-on 165 behind that year, and were only 4 runs ahead when the ninth wicket of their second innings fell. They won by 9 runs largely because R. St L. Fowler, who had made Eton's top score twice, bowled ten overs of off-breaks that took 8 Harrovians for only 23. For the moment, the people wearing cornflowers are enjoying much the better of things, and this corner of Lord's becomes raucous with a peculiar cry of triumph and joy. It is a prolonged version of the school's name, rendered full-throated as "Harr-oho! Harr-oho!" Gentlemen in top hats are shouting it, as well as Harrow boys, necks straining upwards to throw the cry out, so that it looks as well as sounds like the baying of hounds. But it would be misleading to imply that these are the only origins of the Harrow cry. There are two strangers in that Tavern crowd, standing by the benches that border the fence. They flourish no cornflowers, are not smartly dressed, men of indeterminate age whose eyes never leave the cricket except when one or other of them goes to fetch pints for them both. One has a silk scarf tucked into his shirt, and a bushy moustache, image of a Spitfire pilot during the war. The other's face is keen and tanned, suggesting regimental duty in some burnished land. They mutter to each other, words that do not always properly form, and the Spitfire pilot giggles mirthlessly whenever an Eton player misses his shot. The other catches my eye and grins with a friendly nod. "Oh, they're doin' very well today, aren't they? Very well indeed!" Then he joins his companion in the Harrow cry, to which they add embellishments of their own. "Let's 'ave another one, Harr-ohoho! Give 'em the 'ammer, Harr-ohoho!" They do not bay like hounds, those two. They croon the words gently, as parents lull infants to sleep.

Davies and Speke mount a rearguard action, which quietens some of the Harrow noise and brings Eton to lunch with 64 runs and no further loss. Large hampers are opened here and there around the Tavern seats, revealing contents that would satisfy appetites and thirsts at Glyndebourne just as well. Up in the boxes even greater gastronomic feats have been prepared while, down at the stagecoach, the boot below the whip's seat has been opened to disclose a cocktail cabinet as well stocked as any that ever fortified a boardroom. Yet, although a decade or more has passed since every Eton schoolboy was obliged to turn up at this match, there are still enough youths without parents on the ground to make inroads into the heaps of sausage rolls and meat pies that are forever the standby at Lord's. The lads are having a terrible time trying to extract beer from the bar, though, with the caterers insisting on proof that dubious customers are over eighteen. I suspect that some of the top hats were not, in their day, so bound to abide by the law. One lunch-time habit has certainly suffered a change. It was a tradition of the Eton and Harrow match that all its elegance, all this finery of toppers and tulle, should take to the field at the break and stroll for mutual admiration on pretext of examining the pitch. Today the field stays empty until a dozen people set off for the middle just before the umpires reappear, and five of them are children in jeans.

Many of the schoolboys watching this game are similarly clad; not one Eton collar is anywhere in sight. But the most extraordinary thing about these supporting youths, a highly conversational group, is that their talk does not refer to this or to any other cricket match. As Eton begin to bat again, judgment is delivered on an absent competitor in another field. "He finally got an exhibition to Cambridge – sickening creep!" Speke drives Lloyd-Jones through the covers for 4, inspiring a young spectator to turn to a friend with a sudden thought. "What profits did your father's firm make last year?" he asks. A very new old boy is hailed by some fellows with incredulity bordering on surprise. "Don't say you work at Coutts as well?" and there are moments, listening to the babble along the Tavern seats, when one forms the impression that without Harrow the merchant banking system might be distinctly different in tone. When they do address themselves to their team, the young Harrovians are not always kind. Sealey flings himself sideways to catch Davies marvellously in the slips, and mid-wicket, standing very deep, looks pleased that this obstruction has been removed. "Don't smile, Edward," calls one of his chums from the crowd, "It spoils the makeup." Surnames evidently went out of public school life along with flogging and fags.

The two strangers are still rapt, still crooning their allegiance to Winston Churchill's old school. "Get 'em on the run again, Harr-ohoho! Let's 'ave another wicket, Harr-ohoho!" They are missing nothing out there as Eton go into final collapse. Someone else watches steadily from the crowd in front of the Tavern bar, a tall and heavy man, red-faced these days, with much grey in his thickly swept hair and fine veins running along a predator's nose. Cardus once wrote of this spectator that "his attitude to cricket is almost as obsolete as chivalry": after his last match here, with ten wickets under his belt, he tossed the bails into the MCC members' seats, a gesture as lordly as any man could make. But that was twenty-two years ago, and I see no hint that anyone by the Tavern has recognised Keith Miller today. There is first-class cricket at the Oval this afternoon but the incomparable Miller, of Melbourne, New South Wales and Australia, has chosen to be at Lord's, to watch a bunch of schoolboys play. Perhaps, like the besotted racegoer he has always been, he wishes to spot promising youngsters before they are entered for major events. In this case it will be a hopeful quest more than a reasonable bet, for the plain fact is that neither Eton nor Harrow has produced an England cricketer for even longer than Miller has been out of the game, not since F. G. Mann (of Eton) captained the side against New Zealand in 1949. These boys play with great style, though their coaching now seems to permit certain departures from the classical rules; young Morris this morning faced the bowling like Mike Brearley, standing upright with bat hanging a foot off the ground. This may or may not be one reason why the Eton and Harrow match no longer deserves the reputation it once had, when it fostered great cricketing talents like those of F. S. Jackson and the ineffable Lord Hawke. It is not merely the trappings that have been reduced over the years. Wisden still logs the match attentively, because of its place in the history of the game, but the *Telegraph* newspapers are now the only ones that give the scores in full. Keith Miller is an accolade of which these boys should be proud, and it would be nice to record that some of them rush up to him with scorecards to be signed as he stands there with his pint, old devil-may-care himself, giant in a sloppy cardigan with its buttons undone. But nobody does.

Speke is still there when Eton struggle to 100 for 9, still not out when they are dismissed for 112. Without his 30 runs they would have made a very sorry show and, though they quickly take Sealey's wicket when Harrow come to bat, it is not long before they are thrust on the defensive again. For that exuberant moment when Harrow are 1 for 1, the outnumbered Etonians in the crowd raise a lusty counter-cheer, and it is the first time today they have really made their presence heard. Presently their noise subsides, as Wiggin gets the measure of the attack and starts to collect runs. Even more so does Haggas, a self-possessed young man who struts round his wicket like a turkey cock when he is not cutting deliciously and driving balls to the off with wristy strokes. This pair take Harrow up to 69 by tea and, as the fieldsmen of Eton clap them off, their ears ring to the triumphant baying of their crowd. The Harrovian din, indeed, has been unabated since they began to score, and only the ladies seem to have exempted themselves from contributing to the noise. Among these is a formidable matron, gloved to the elbows and cultured with pearl, whose conversation since that wicket fell has steadily perambulated through her acquaintance with Sir John Betjeman, Virginia Wade and a gentleman who owns a flamingo park. The decorum of Lord's, so much extolled by historians of the game and to be expected, perhaps, at this fixture above all, only descends when the gladiators are out of sight. Two grey toppers pause conspiratorially in the alley behind the stands, one watching closely the other's face, which scrutinises the asphalt and the ferrule of an ebony stick, and otherwise offers advice full of portent through rather tight lips. There may be a killing on Monday, when the City gets going.

There is no stopping Harrow after tea, as Wiggin and Haggas belabour the bowling again, exceeding Eton's total by themselves before another wicket falls. Then Harrow's captain, James, comes out and continues where Wiggin left off, and it is clear that unless Eton can produce another Fowler from the back of their hand, they are not going to win the 143rd contest between the sides. In the golden light of midsummer, as an evening sun still burns warmly above the pavilion at Lord's, all this is a remembrancer of cricket's Golden Age. Young men, mere boys with sharp and eager limbs, are bending themselves to the game as though nothing in the world mattered but this, then wandering across the field slowly, having been taught that it is well to be casual about even the most momentous things. Some of the watchers have been nurtured to treat the whole of life like that, while others are still acquiring the habit, for it is not a thing that can be instantly bought. Thus the Eton and Harrow is balanced betwixt and between, with graceful combat on the cricket field, with the pandemonium of conquest coming from its edge. And with those two strangers, who have been watchful all day, still murmuring their chant in a long lost undertone. "Let's 'ave some more, Harr-ohoho! Keep the pot boilin', Harr-ohoho! Give 'em the 'ammer, Harrohoho!"

From *The Best Loved Game, 1979*

If village cricket sits at the bottom of the ability pile, club cricket is the next rung up, and Northern League cricket several rungs above that. Having written entertainingly about football in the north-eastern outposts in *The Far Corner*, Harry Pearson turns his attentions to cricket and takes a slow turn around the Yorkshire and Lancashire Leagues, revisiting the famous clubs where some of the great home-grown and overseas Test cricketers learned their trade. In these extracts, he talks about the anachronistic charm of invitation XIs, the legendary three Ws and perhaps the greatest League player of them all, the incomparable Sir Learie Constantine.

SLIPLESS IN SETTLE

Harry Pearson

The pavilion has half-timbered eaves, mullioned windows and a general air of the stockbroker belt about it. A sign on the gate that leads into the enclosure in front of it reads, 'No access to the ski slope', which must be unique. The pavilion was built in 1892, the year the field was bought by the club from the Duke of Devonshire. Cricket had been played in the Great Border City since the 1820s when the local paper was called the *Patriot*, just in case anybody thought Jacobitism might still be lurking in the city. Carlisle CC had begun life in the Border League, switching to the North Lancashire League in 1949.

In the clubhouse a big screen TV was showing *SpongeBob Square Pants*. There are rows of photos on the wall, including one of a game played at Edenside Park in 1926 between the touring Australians and G. Palmer's XI. It was the final match of what was something of a marathon visit for H. L. Collins's side. They arrived in Carlisle on 16 September, having played their opening game on 28 April. As well as playing five test matches and all of the first class counties they also took on: Minor Counties, the MCC, the South, the North, Cambridge University, Oxford University, Public Schools,

an England XI (at Folkestone), the Civil Service, C. I. Thornton's XI
and an England XI (Blackpool). If the Aussies were sick of cricket
by this stage you could hardly blame them, but the public plainly
couldn't get enough of it because five thousand turned up to watch
the game at Carlisle.

G. Palmer's XI included some of England's finest players – Percy
Holmes, Herbert Sutcliffe, Patsy Hendren, Roy Kilner, George
Gunn – and one local man, Cumberland wicket-keeper Roland
Saint, but the visitors were too strong for them, winning a one-
innings match by six wickets thanks mainly to a century from
Charlie Macartney.

I have a particular fondness for teams like G. Palmer's XI because
every August during my boyhood my father and I would go to
Marine Road, Scarborough, to see T. N. Pearce's XI play the tourists. My father had been going to watch this highlight of the premier
cricket festival in Yorkshire (and therefore, by extension, clearly
the entire world) since he was a youth. Back in those hazy days of
ration books and the wireless, however, the responsibility of selecting a side to play in what was dubbed by Yorkies 'the sixth test
match' fell to H. D. G. Leveson-Gower (Leveson-Gower had himself
taken on the mantle from the aforementioned C. I. Thornton). How
the succession was arranged I am not certain, but a cursory inspection of the respective careers of H. D. G. Leveson-Gower (known
to his chums as 'Shrimp') and T. N. Pearce (perhaps best remembered for being the facing batsman when Jehangir Khan's delivery
killed a sparrow) uncovers two things the pair had in common –
neither of them played for Yorkshire and neither of them came
from Yorkshire. (When asked why Leveson-Gower organised a
team to play at Scarborough my father replied that he believed him
to be 'some sort of a relation of the Duke of Sutherland' – the exact
relevance of which to the matter at hand I am uncertain.)

Whatever his qualifications for picking a team to play at
Scarborough, these days I find T. N. Pearce both a comfort and
an inspiration. There are few cricket fans who have not spent idle
moments selecting a World XI to take on and thrash visitors from
some weird, alien civilisation (or Australia, as it is more com-
monly known). T. N. got to do it for real, though admittedly by the
time I saw the results the pool of players available to him seemed
to consist entirely of Yorkshire seconds, a couple of unknown
Barbadians who happened to have a weekend off from playing in

the leagues and Robin Hobbs of Essex, a leg-spinner whose appearance at Scarborough was compulsory under local by-laws.

T. N. was not the only one to get to make his mark in this way, of course. A. E. R. Gilligan, whose XI traditionally played the tourists at Hastings, was another. In fact, dozens of 'special selects' have been and gone, writing their names across Wisden for posterity and the puzzlement of future generations. What, for example, of Sir Julien Cahn's XI that played Glamorgan in 1936, or J. G. W. Davis's XI, which took on Cambridge University in the J. C. Stevens Memorial Match (not first class) at the Saffrons in 1969, or L. Robinson's XI that lined up at Attleborough to do battle with the Australian Imperial Forces in 1919? And then, of course there were the International Cavaliers, who mysteriously got to play a first class match against Barbados. At Scarborough.

D. H. Robins had a first class cricketing career that stretched from 1947, when he played two games for Warwickshire, to 1971 when, at the tender age of fifty-seven, he turned out against the Indian tourists, and encompassed a grand total of five matches. For a decade he picked a team that played the tourists in a three-day game, took on various counties and universities and made sporadic forays to South Africa (Robins displayed a frankly international cavalier attitude to decent opinion. As well as offering succour to the apartheid regime he also, while chairman of Coventry City, appointed Jimmy Hill as manager.) The team were based at Eastbourne. I imagine their HQ was a stucco-and-glass penthouse apartment complete with tubular steel furniture, zebra-skin wall hangings and a Scandinavian PA played by Julie Ege in a terry-towelling bikini. Though no doubt the truth was far more glamorous than that.

Graham Gooch, David Gower, Mushtaq Mohammad, Tony Greig, Barry Richards, Gordon Greenidge and Clive Rice all turned out for D. H. Robins's XI over the years. Occasionally he captained the side, selflessly batting at number eleven and, with a restraint that is nothing short of saintly, steadfastly refusing to bring himself on to bowl even when conditions were entirely favourable.

In 1969 D. H. Robins's XI played Wilfred Isaac's South Africans shortly after that redoubtable team of visitors had thrashed Cambridge Quidnuncs at Chislehurst. In my view, this sentence alone entirely justifies the existence of humankind.

∿

In the clubhouse, between the ladies' and gents' toilet doors, there's a big picture of the great West Indian batsman Everton Weekes, side parting, pearly-toothed grin, standing in front of the old pavilion at Lanehead.

Weekes spent seven seasons at Bacup in the fifties, scoring 9069 runs for them at an average of 91.61, and including twenty-five centuries. He wore an Army and Navy greatcoat even on what the locals considered the hottest summer days and lodged in Gordon Street, where the landlady, Mrs Sharrold, fed him up on meat-and-potato pies. Weekes got his Christian name because his father supported Everton. When the West Indian told Shipley-born Jim Laker this, the off-spinner replied that it was just as well his dad hadn't been a fan of West Bromwich Albion.

The Barbadian was a brilliant batsman who could produce his effervescent best on any surface. His style was so special, precise yet exuberant, that dozens of cricket lovers turned up at Lanehead on weekday nights just to watch him in the nets. Like Constantine, Weekes knew the value of a bit of showmanship. One day when a young medium pacer was bowling to him, the Bajan waited until the ball had left the bowler's hand, dropped his bat, reached back, uprooted the middle stump and cover drove the delivery perfectly with that instead. The applause from the spectators went on for several minutes. This might be apocryphal, but it has become part of history.

Weekes, along with Frank Worrell and Clyde Walcott, was part of the famous trio of West Indian middle order batsmen nicknamed the Three Ws. Frank Worrell was the professional at Radcliffe. An elegant stroke-maker, the Jamaican was a man of quiet dignity who studied for an economics degree at Manchester University during the week and impressed everyone who met him. At Radcliffe there was a bronze sculpture of Worrell in the bar and a plaque on the terraced house where he and his family had lived. The old fellow who as a boy had watched George Francis bowl at The Racecourse had lived next door. 'Our daughters were born at the same time,' he recalled, 'and every afternoon when it was coming up to visiting time Frank would knock and we'd get the bus to the maternity hospital. I can still picture the two of us sitting together on that bus, him with a little jar of homemade jam in his hand as a gift for his wife. He was a great cricketer, a smashing fellow, and everyone in Radcliffe loved him.'

While Weekes was at Bacup and Worrell at Radcliffe, Clyde Walcott was playing for Enfield, where he became the first batsman in league history to finish the season with an average of over one hundred (Weekes shattered the record the following year, averaging a staggering 158.25). On Saturday nights the three of them would meet up at a chip shop in Clayton-le-Moors, which belonged to Lancashire stalwart Jack Simmons's Aunty Bertha, for a fish supper. It's the sort of scene, combining the fabulous with the homespun, that was the hallmark of league cricket in the North.

As Catherine and I ate our Bakewell tart and wondered about having a scone or two, a couple of old men standing nearby started talking.

'Are you going to Rammy tomorrow?'

'I am.'

'Have you got a lift?'

'I have.'

'Who's taking you?'

'Me.'

There's a similar comical air to nearly everything we overheard. It's something about the Lancashire accent. Although Bacup doubled for Royston Vasey, the style of humour is less grim, more gentle. At one point a ball crossed the boundary and a man standing nearby made a fumbling attempt to pick it up, mis-fielding the ball several times and then chasing after it trying to pick it up. Watching the display his mate yelled, 'He's not practised, you know. It's pure reflex, is that.'

∼

On the street outside cars *ka-bumped* over the traffic-calming hummocks as Windhill's players went through their catching drills. I wandered round the ground and looked for somewhere to sit down. None of the benches on the boundary had backs on them. It used to be the same on the Western terrace at Headingley, as if everybody involved with Yorkshire cricket was trying to stamp out slouching.

The Windhill Clubhouse is a squat brick building with an aspect that seems designed to warn off potential intruders. The Cross of St George, the Union Flag and the Yorkshire Rose banner flapped from the flagpoles. A large scoreboard stands at square leg, the scorers' heads visible through a slit to one side. The umpires' room is a small larch-lap shed of a type in which you'd normally expect to find a Flymo, a paraffin heater and some bags of potting compost.

It wasn't particularly pretty, but I didn't find that at all surprising. When it comes to playing cricket most people tend to come over all misty-eyed and start burbling fondly of tree-fringed parks, long shadows on the greensward and strawberries and cream for tea. The reality though is that most club cricket – in the North and the South – is actually played on council pitches in grim suburbs where the sound of willow on leather is drowned out by the over-flying 747s and the barking of gigantic dogs, and third slip is what happens when you step in yet another Rottweiler turd. The teas are nothing to write home about either, unless your parents happen to be health inspectors.

Windhill played in the second division of the Bradford League. Despite its august history I have to admit to a slight prejudice against this league. It was just a bit too West Riding for me. It had that I've-done-very-well-for-myself Masonic regalia and golf club ties aura about it. If it had spoken it would have sounded like a radio broadcast by J. B. Priestley in which he quoted himself and chuckled. A friend of mine who also came from the North Riding called this self-congratulatory attitude Duxburyness. 'I'm not fond of Betty's Tea Rooms,' he'd say. 'There's a bit too much Duxbury-ness about them'.

My friend had coined this expression in honour of Councillor Duxbury, the pompous, self-made West Yorkshireman from Keith Waterhouse's novel *Billy Liar*. He felt that the Bradford League was rank with Duxburyness, and he didn't like it. Where we come from in the North Riding, the worst thing you could be accused of was showing off, of having ideas above your station. 'I've took again him,' people would say. 'He's a bit over proud of himself.'

The Bradford League is very proud of itself. Not, I hasten to add, that it doesn't have plenty to be proud about. The Bradford League is the beating heart of Yorkshire cricket, make no mistake about that. It was founded in 1903. Every club that plays in it is located within a ten-mile radius of Bradford town hall, and just about every great player the county has ever produced was either raised in it or played in it at some point. Len Hutton started out as a school-boy at Pudsey St Lawrence, so did Herbert Sutcliffe. Percy Holmes had played at Great Horton, Jim Laker at Saltaire, Ray Illingworth at Farsley, the undemonstrative Arthur Mitchell at Baildon. As its reputation grew nationally, the Bradford League had sucked in other greats from all over the place. Jack Hobbs played for Idle, S. F. Barnes for Saltaire, Charlie Llewellyn and George Gunn at Undercliffe, Frank Woolley and Bill Hearne at Keighley. Windhill had Les Ames, mainstay of a legendary Kent batting order that tripped off the tongue like the shipping forecast: Todd, Fagg, Crapp and Ames. And, as it happens, Jack Crapp played at Eccleshill and Arthur Fagg at Saltaire.

Part of the reason I'd chosen to come to Windhill was because Learie Constantine had captained the side in the 1940s. The Trinidadian had left Nelson as a player in 1937 – he continued to live in the town for another twelve years – and gone to play for Rochdale in the Central Lancashire League. He spent the 1939 season with the West Indian team that was touring England and during that summer signed to play at Windhill the following year. The contract was by all accounts the largest of his career, though in typically canny West Riding style it included various clauses that reduced its value in the event of war. Still, it was worth twenty-five pounds a game – three times what first-division footballers were earning in 1939.

His old West Indies bowling partner and fellow Lancashire League stalwart Manny Martindale joined Constantine at Windhill. A fearsome five foot eight Barbadian paceman, Martindale had split Walter Hammond's chin open with a bouncer at Old Trafford in 1933, a ball that was said to have finally convinced the MCC to outlaw leg theory. He played all over the north, settled in Lancashire and was still turning out in the Bolton Association when well into his sixties. Such longevity was not unusual. S. F. Barnes was still formidable in his seventh decade and Sonny Ramadhin, who like Martindale had made his home in Lancashire, was still twirling his spinners well enough aged fifty-six to take 9–12 playing for Delph and Dobcross in a Saddleworth and District match in 1985.

When I met up with Cec Wright he'd just celebrated his seventy-fourth birthday but that hadn't stopped him bowling twelve overs for Uppermill seconds. I asked Cec if he ever considered retirement, 'At the end of every season,' he said, 'but then the spring comes and I think, well maybe one more.' Cec had come over to England from Jamaica to play as a professional for Crompton in 1959 and stayed, turning out for Colne, Walsden, Astley Bridge and a handful of other teams. 'Everything I have,' he said, 'my house, my wife, everything, is because of cricket.'

From *Slipless in Settle: A Slow Turn Around Northern Cricket*, 2012

This is, perhaps, the quintessence of amateurism. The Captain Scott XI was formed by Harry Thompson and Marcus Berkmann when they were both up at Oxford together. Neither had played any form of competitive cricket before but had mysteriously fallen under its spell. Barred from playing for any other team, they decided to form their own and named it in honour of the failed polar explorer, who was synonymous with coming second. Thompson, a radio and television producer and comedy writer whose credits included *Have I Got News for You* and *Da Ali G Show*, went on to play 640 consecutive games for the 'Scotties' with an astonishing 100 per cent attendance record. He stood in for a colleague who was late arriving for his 641st game, even though he was suffering from terminal lung cancer. He retired undefeated and died soon after the season ended; *Penguins Stopped Play* was published posthumously the following year. In this extract, Thompson describes playing cricket in the snowy wastes of Antarctica on the ultimate cricket tour.

ANTARCTICA

Harry Thompson

I am in Antarctica. I am standing at Cape Evans, a promontory on the western side of Ross Island, a rugged, solitary slab of rock that thrusts through the clean lines of the Ross Ice Shelf. Or, to be more precise, I am standing nine miles out to sea from Cape Evans, on the iced-over surface of the ocean. My weight is supported only by a membrane of frozen sea water. It is a gorgeous, windless day, the sky an impossibly perfect cornflower blue. Or, to be more precise, it is a gorgeous, windless night, for, despite the sunshine, the time is half past three in the morning.

The scene that presents itself is one that instinctively commands hushed respect. Behind me tower the massive, smoking bulk of Mount Erebus, a 13,000-foot active volcano smothered from top

to toe in creamy snow, and the harder black wedge of its lieutenant, Mount Terror. Ahead, the Olympus range of the Transantarctic
Mountains stretches to the northern horizon, the serried peaks
riven only by gigantic frozen waterfalls of ice: the Wilson Glacier,
the Oates-Piedmont Glacier, the Nordenskjöld Ice Tongue. This is
an almost entirely white world. Even through my sunglasses. the
brilliant glare of sun on snow lances effortlessly into my streaming
pupils. The silence is absolute.

In the distance, a man in a bright vermilion cagoule is running
towards me, picking up pace as his thermal boots grip the ice. He
is a teacher from New Zealand, and his name is Craig. I blink my
eyes dry and try to focus intently on the tightly gripped fingers of
his right hand. When he arrives at a spot approximately twenty-
two yards away from me, he leaps high into the air and releases
the object in his hand at speed in my direction. It is a cricket ball.
I am holding a bat. I am doing what any right-thinking Englishman
should be doing at times of hardship and adversity: I am playing
cricket. The silence is absolute because, of course, it is rank bad
manners to carry on chattering once the bowler has begun his
run-up.

Well, of course, it wasn't a real cricket bat. It was an oar. And the
wicket was really a purple rucksack. But the ball was real enough
– trust a Kiwi to pack a cricket ball in his luggage on a trip to
Antarctica. The match was New Zealand v. The Rest of the World,
and I was opening the batting for The Rest of the World – the only
time in my life that's ever going to happen. Craig's first ball kept
low and skidded harmlessly past the purple nylon of my off stump.
Cricket balls don't actually bounce a great deal on ice, in case you're
interested. No? Oh, very well then. Back to the match. His second
ball did much the same; but the third was on target. I jabbed hastily
down on it, and it squirted down to long leg for what looked like
an easy two. As I turned for the second run, however, I beheld an
extraordinary sight: the long-leg fielder was being attacked by a
gigantic seabird. It was an enormous skua, all beak and talons, and
it had evidently arrived at the erroneous conclusion that the ball
was a big, succulent red egg. Fielder and ball were locked in a whirl-
ing dance of brown feathers and Day-Glo nylon.

Now, there are those who would argue that sport should always
follow a clear-cut moral code. In the late eighties, for instance,
the football team I support, Everton, was banned from European

competition because of the violent activities of certain Liverpool supporters. Nick Hornby, a better man than I, delivered a well-argued homily in *Fever Pitch* to the effect that any decent, upstanding member of the human race could only concur with the decision. I, on the other hand, couldn't help feeling that it was a monstrous injustice. And so it is with no little embarrassment that I must confess, here and now, that whereas others saw a man being attacked by a giant bird – a fellow human being in distress, let's face it – I saw only the opportunity to steal a third run. And what's more, what was even better, to turn a streaky inside edge into an all-run four.

By the time the bird had finally been driven away using various nautical-looking pieces of wood, and I was several runs to the good, it was clear that our hushed and deserted white world was about to undergo a profound change. Some fifty yards away was the ice edge, where our tour vessel, a robust little Russian scientific ship that had been tossed about like a cork on the way down, now lay moored. Behind was the deep, cerulean mirror of the Ross Sea itself. Suddenly the surface was broken, the light scattered like stars, by a pod of killer whales which porpoised the length of the jagged ice edge. Next, rearing out of the water, a glistening humpback whale followed suit. Thunderstruck with excitement, we stopped to watch. Then, when the whales looked as if they would porpoise off into the distance, they all performed an about-turn, and back they came, bounding in and out of the water as they passed by a second time. The humpback, I swear, even cocked its head to one side, to get a better view of us. They were watching us watching them. It was quite incredible. Never before had I seen this many spectators at an amateur cricket match.

It wasn't just the whales. A leopard seal, perhaps the most fearsome predator of the southern ocean, hauled itself up on an ice floe to take a gander. Ignore the 'seal' bit – think 'leopard' here. These creatures are twelve feet long, with evil little heads and wicked jaws. Imagine the head of Ridley Scott's Alien atop the body of Mike Gatting after a particularly hefty tea. One of them recently killed and ate a wetsuited British research scientist who was swimming in the Ross Sea. Luckily for us, the leopard seal has a top speed of about 2 m.p.h. on dry land (the Mike Gatting comparison becomes ever more relevant). If it was indeed eyeing us up with a view to a tasty snack, it was clearly out of luck. That is, as long as the ice beneath our feet held firm.

Clearly, our thundering footsteps on the ice sheet had echoed into the very depths of the Ross Sea below, and had brought a whole David Attenborough-documentary's worth of wildlife up to take a look. It was not long before the first penguin hopped out of the water, wandered across, and stood there on a length, facing me down as I brandished my oar. The game halted. We gazed at each other, our eyes locked. Hell, I wasn't scared. He was eighteen inches high. I knew everything there was to know about his breeding habits, gestation period, feeding habits and moulting timetable. The fact was, I knew a hell of a lot about penguins. He, on the other hand, was a relative novice when it came to cricket. I had the advantage, both physical and intellectual, and I think he could sense that.

I should explain at this juncture that if you choose to holiday in the Antarctic you have to spend five days on a boat, being battered by gales for the first two of them, then grinding slowly and agonizingly through hundreds of miles of pack ice for the remainder of the trip. The daylight being constant, you soon stop going to bed, and resort to catnaps instead. You are up for nearly twenty-four hours a day, with nothing to do but eat, read, play cards or listen to music on headphones. To fill your time, the expedition naturalists lecture you constantly about penguins. By the time you get within spitting distance of the South Pole, you have learned more about penguins than the entire staff of London Zoo. I knew everything there was to know about the king penguin (the one on the biscuit wrapper – coloured chest), the gentoo (red feet), the rockhopper (Denis Healey eyebrows), the emperor (fat bastard), the royal (looks like Michael Winner after a few drinks) and many, many more. So I knew by its black face and white staring eyes that the penguin now before me was an Adélie, named by the early French explorer Dumont d'Urville after his wife. As to what had prompted that romantic gesture – whether his wife had an especially beak-shaped nose, or had smelt of fish – history sheds no light. Suffice to say that the Adélie, being named after a French *girl*, is one of the more effeminate penguin species. So, in strict defiance of the Antarctic convention that prohibits the disturbing of wildlife, I hustled the little fellow away.

The game lurched on. The next ball was fast, short and wide – the bowler was a Kiwi, not an Aussie – so I had a speculative welly at it. For once, I connected. As so often when I've hit a ball as hard as I can, the ball didn't actually go anywhere, as all the power seemed to flow backwards from the impact, into the bat. In this case the oar actually shattered, into a trillion pieces. It had spent the night out on deck, and was frozen solid: wicketkeeper and slips alike were showered with tiny, glassy shards of frozen wood. Again the game had to be halted, while another oar was fetched.

The delay was an open invitation to the penguins. They came in waves, hundreds of them, crowding across the outfield, mingling with the slips, poking around at silly mid-off, blocking the bowlers' run-up, and invading the wicket itself. Antarctica is famous for its immense penguin colonies, million-strong bird cities that reassemble every spring in the same spot, year after year. Here it appeared that we were about to found a brand-new colony. Naturalists would one day be confounded as to its origin. One penguin on its own I could bully, but against wave after wave of inquisitive little monochrome invaders we were all helpless. Before long there was a vast crowd of them, filling the space between myself and the bowler, peering up in confusion. Waving the splintered handle of the oar to keep back the dinner-jacketed hordes, I felt like the conductor of the LSO at a particularly drunken staff party. Already, many of the outfielders had run back to the ship to grab their cameras. There was only one option open to us. For the first time – surely – in history, a cricket match would have to be cancelled because penguins had stopped play.

So what the hell was I doing there, in Antarctica, facing up to two hundred untamed Adélie penguins with only the handle of a frozen oar to defend myself? Why had I travelled fourteen thousand miles to play this game? Why had I braved the heaving seas of the Roaring Forties, the Furious Fifties and Screaming Sixties? (I didn't name the latitudes in question – that really is what they're called – but, believe me, there's nothing camp about a forty-foot wave.) Well, it was all the fault of Captain Robert Falcon Scott, RN, leader of the failed Antarctic expedition of 1911–12. Cape Evans was his base, and Shackleton's before him. A long, long time ago – more than a quarter of a century ago, in fact – I and a few friends had begun a cricket team, which we named after Captain Scott, that most splendid of runners-up. Inevitably, books and videos about the Captain had followed, presents from well-meaning relatives. I had stored up a modicum of useless knowledge about polar exploration as a result. Many years later, when I developed an enjoyable sideline as an occasional travel writer, it seemed entirely logical for a national newspaper to suggest that I travel a mere fourteen thousand miles to see a hut – the hut where Scott, Oates, Evans, Bowers, Wilson and Co. had overwintered before their last, fatal journey.

We'd already stopped at Shackleton's hut on the way down: it was an incredible place, freeze-dried by the Antarctic cold at the exact moment that Shackleton and his men had abandoned it, running down to the shore to board their relief ship. Here was a veritable polar *Marie Celeste*: Shackleton's own filth-encrusted socks hung rigid above his reindeer-skin sleeping bag; his boots stood to attention on the floor below. A half-read copy of the *Gentleman's Magazine*, offering discounted Eton collars, lay unfurled on a half-made bunk; uneaten hams hung from roof-hooks; the shelves groaned with tins of tripe and onions, Bird's egg powder and Heinz India Relish. Scott's hut promised more of the same on a grander scale, tinged with the desperately sad knowledge that – unlike Shackleton, who was to survive a series of remarkable escapades – Scott and his men had walked out of there to their deaths, beaten to the Pole by Amundsen and caught by ill chance in one of the worst blizzards in Antarctic history on the return journey.

As our little vessel headed south in glorious sunshine, nosing optimistically around Cape Evans, we were met with an unpleasant sight: sea ice, nine miles of it, thick and unseasonal, clogging the shore. Our ship was not an icebreaker. It seemed we had reached the end of the road: 13,991 miles was to be our limit. There was nothing we could do to force a passage. I was utterly downcast: after all those years of being bombarded with polar literature, Scott's hut had taken on an almost spiritual significance. It had become the Kaaba at the heart of my own personal Mecca. (That, and the awkward fact that I was being paid to write an article about it.) Refusing to be beaten, I bearded Rodney Russ, the expedition leader, in his den. Russ was a genial Kiwi who put me in mind of Sir Les Paterson, if Sir Les had gone three years without cutting or combing his hair. Such setbacks were part and parcel of Antarctic life for an experienced old campaigner like Rodney, but, incredibly, moved by my predicament, he agreed to my suggestion that we mount a ground assault. Why, it was only an eighteen-mile round trip. We could actually see Scott's hut in the distance, taunting us, a little wooden rectangle on the tip of Cape Evans: it didn't look that far away.

We set out across the sea ice in the small hours – not that the Antarctic summer makes any distinction between the small hours and the middle of the afternoon. The slippery surface and the extraordinary glare aside, it was easy going. Bravely, Rodney decided that he should forge ahead, ten yards out in front of everyone else. We fell in behind. After five miles of pleasant Sunday stroll, reality kicked in when Rodney suddenly disappeared. A small dark hole in the ice marked the spot where he had last been seen. Milliseconds of utter panic followed, then waves of relief as he spluttered to the surface, shivering fit to burst but otherwise all right. Thankfully, it appeared that there had been no leopard seals in the vicinity. He was fished out, and items of dry clothing were donated. Ruefully – and very gingerly – we made our way back to the ship.

A pall of disappointment hung over our little camp. The whole day had been set aside for the visit to Scott's hut. There was nothing else on the menu, nothing to do.

'I've got a cricket ball in my bag,' said Craig the teacher.

A score of faces – Australian, New Zealand and English – lit up.

From *Penguins Stopped Play*, 2006

Marcus Berkmann, co-founder of the Captain Scott XI, broke away to form Rain Men after the inclusion of a few too many overseas ringers – people who could actually play the game rather than the usual collection of useless layabouts who typically populated the team. In his first book, described by the *Daily Telegraph* reviewer as 'the *Fever Pitch* of cricket', he describes the traditional beginning of the season in April.

THE NEW SEASON

Marcus Berkmann

April

Sheets of torrential rain crash to the ground. Indistinct figures in waterproofs battle through the gales as a swirling river of rainwater washes away small cars, children, anything that hasn't been bolted down against the fearsome winds. You hear your slates peeling away from your roof. The telephone lines are down. There are reports of avalanches in the West Midlands. A huge glacier is said to be about to overwhelm Dorset. Welcome to April.

In the depths of winter, cricket fans pay little attention to the weather. We know it is still out there, doing whatever weather does, but we show no interest. Rain is as nothing to us. Snow is white and fluffy and appealing. None of it matters at all, as we are indoors with the central heating on, watching tapes of old one-day internationals. As long as the fridge is full, we are happy.

But as soon as April arrives, and with it the prospect of a new cricket season (this will be the one, I'll score more runs, take more wickets, won't drop a thing etc. etc.), meteorology suddenly becomes our favourite branch of science. From now until late September, we will check the weather at least a dozen times a day, referring to at least two different newspapers as well as Ceefax and Ian McCaskill on an almost hourly basis. By midsummer we won't even need to read the summaries – we'll just look straight at the isobars. Everything has to be right for the next game. It has to.

April's particular revenge is to foist upon us the most intemperate weather patterns seen this side of Saturn. Men with beards explain this away as a consequence of global warming, but I think the Grim Inevitability of Fate has a hand in it somewhere. April showers we could live with, but we don't get April showers any more. We get April gales interspersed with April snowstorms ('... and there's a cold northerly wind sweeping down from the Arctic ...') and, unforgivably, a two-day April heatwave to destroy our resolve once and for all. It all counts, because as the first weekend of the season grows ever closer, every last hailstorm has a bearing on whether or not the early games will take place. Once again, the strong religious undercurrent in cricket bubbles to the surface. Please, God, please stop this rain. I'll do anything. Please stop it. Please.

But weather-forecasting is an inexact science, dealing in probabilities rather than certainties, and it relies on the interpretative skills of its practitioners. This is a polite way of saying that you can easily get it wrong, and as all those sad figures who read tealeaves and seaweed routinely demonstrate, with only one screw loose you can be wrong about most things most of the time. As for the Met. Office, their prognostications have been tainted by doubt ever since Michael Fish told us there definitely wouldn't be a hurricane, stop being so silly. For the troubled cricketer, who only wants to know whether he is going to play at the weekend and how many sweaters he should pack, this lack of certainty leaves rather too much room for manoeuvre. Denied the consolation of scientific rigour, he tends to lay his own interpretation over the vaguer prophecies of Messrs Fish, Giles and Kettley. Thus, for cricketing meteorologists, weather-forecasting becomes a matter of temperament rather than measurement. People will see in a weather forecast only what they wish to see, or what they fear to see. Show two cricketers the same forecast, and the chances are that they will interpret it completely differently.

If you're like me, the eternal optimist, you always assume things will clear up. 'Oh don't worry, it'll be fine,' I tell everyone as the tropical thunderstorm rages. The waves are lapping against my bedroom window, but I'm still convinced that the game will go ahead. 'Those Suffolk pitches drain very quickly,' I hear myself assuring people on the phone, even though at the moment you would be unable to reach mid-off without scuba gear.

The pessimists' cricket club wins the toss.

Harry, by contrast, sees only disaster and misery ahead. For Harry, no weather can ever be clement enough. If the sun is shining from here to Siberia, he is remembering the freak downpour at Finchingfield that once washed out a game in the midst of a heat-wave. Should Suzanne Charlton even hint that there may be a spot of rain around the end of the week, Harry is out there in his galoshes and sou'wester battening down the hatches for the expected flood warning. Animals wander two by two into his West London flat.

And so, on Mondays and Tuesdays, as we are trying to sort out the teams for the weekend ahead, Harry and I bicker on the telephone about the long-range weather forecast. Both of us know that weather can only be forecast to any degree of accuracy four days into the future. We know that after that the variables make prediction too haphazard, and the probabilities are undermined to such an extent that even the most detailed prediction becomes little more than a wild guess. We know all this. But while we both know we are talking nonsense, we both feel in our livers and kidneys that the following weekend will witness magnificent Mediterranean sunshine (palm trees sighted in the Home Counties) or vicious Arctic squalls (huskies become Britain's best-selling dog). As ever, rational thought is no match for mindless prejudice. These ridiculous conversations continue long into the night.

Fortunately, we do have other things to talk about. Whatever the weather, the preparations for a new Captain Scott season must continue. Fixture lists have been sent out, Richard has bought some new kit through someone he knows somewhere who can sort out these things (ask no questions etc.), most members have paid their annual fees, and the general air of anticipation is almost edible. To take advantage of this brief interval of good cheer, Harry and I arrange a pre-season jolly in which members can chat, have a few drinks and enjoy each other's company in the sort of relaxed atmosphere that the start of the season proper will render impossible. Just as memories of last season's personal failures have been numbed by five months' intellectual hibernation, so have the collected grudges and arguments that form the backbone of a summer's cricket. Experience has shown that it takes a few weeks of a new season for bitter personal hatreds to flare up into fully fledged international incidents, so any last fragments of goodwill have to be lovingly nurtured while they survive. Like mayflies, however, their life expectancy is brief.

One disadvantage we immediately encounter is the relative shortage of funds. First-class counties can arrange relaxing tours to Portugal and the Bahamas for their young charges, allowing them to ease gently into the pressures of another hectic season. We go to a wine bar off Leicester Square, and ease gently into about fifteen bottles of red wine. Initially, everyone seems delighted to see each other. Backs are slapped, and as the wine is consumed, drunken sentimentality softens people's harder edges. It is wonderful to see them all in such high spirits. Six months ago, several of these players swore they would never speak to each other again. Fingers were prodded in chests. Now all thoughts of vengeance have been abandoned. The slate is clean. X's black eye has long since healed, and Y has nearly forgotten that Z reported him anonymously to the Inland Revenue. The new season is the only season that counts.

The evening meanders along, and the wine continues to flow. The humorous stories about last season's exploits begin, concentrating on those foolish individuals who have neglected to turn up. Poor saps! They should have known better. You don't want to be out of the room when this lot start. Occasional satirical gibes about hairlines and waistlines are made, but all in a spirit of the most generous bonhomie. For God's sake, these are the people with whom you've got to spend every weekend for the next five months. (Another three bottles of house claret? Can I pay by credit card?) Bloody hell, if you can't get on with them for a single evening in a wine bar, you've got no bloody chance. Whoops, sorry, got to go to the loo again.

By 10.30, the mood has subtly altered. Jokes about other players are becoming more pointed, and a fire lights up in the eyes of Tim, our perennially angry fast bowler. This is the time to leave. I am just walking out of the door when I hear the first barbed comment about the notorious run out at Bradenham. The alcove falls silent. One or two other people whisper something about getting their coats. Someone else orders some mineral water. But it is too late. There is no stopping it now. The accusations fly, and all those half-forgotten antipathies burst excitingly to life. Harry's captaincy is torn apart. Before I am five yards down the road, mine will be as well. Selfish batsmanship, lazy fielding, incompetent wicketkeeping, vengeful umpiring, greedy bowling – these are the stuff of conversation now. The cricket season has begun.

~

The first match looms, and you are still going to nets. By net three, you are occasionally getting to the pitch of the ball. By net four, your bowling is passable. You are beginning to enjoy yourself. MCC has played the champion county; the match has ended in a draw. Leicestershire are playing Oxford University at The Parks. Leicestershire declared on 515 for 2. Oxford are 17 for 8 in reply. You have caught your first sight of Tony Lewis on the television. His eyebrows are even bushier than they were last year. What do they do with Tony Lewis in the winter? You trust he is well looked after. The season is gearing up. After half a dozen nets, and a little patient coaching from a kind colleague, your confidence has slowly improved. Perhaps you're not so bad after all. Perhaps this will be the season.

And then you go out and play a proper game and remember again why you don't usually come to nets. For four or five weeks you have been playing in regulated conditions: indoors, in the warmth, on a reliable, entirely predictable surface. Controlled temperatures have allowed bowlers to warm up gradually. Batsmen have grown used to the regular bounce and the way the ball comes sweetly on to the bat.

It is laughable to think that this is supposed to prepare you in some way for the first game of the season, which is played in a howling gale on a typical April pudding with optional cowpats. Bowlers bowl as they have done in the nets and tear twenty-three muscles. No cricket for them until July. For batsmen, the ball is suddenly behaving in ways that nets could never begin to help you predict. The bowler bowls, the ball pitches, and about three days later it arrives at your bat, long after you've played the shot, trudged back to the pavilion, had a shower and gone home. Pride may come before a fall, but nets come before a nought.

And each year, so lulled are we into a warm, indoor, utterly fallacious sense of security that it all comes as a surprise. We stride out to the crease oozing confidence, and wander back a minute or two later utterly dejected. Never, in sixteen years of Scott service, have I begun the season with anything other than a 0. Sometimes they have been long, attritional 0s, full of character and spunk. Mostly they have been brief, risible 0s, with me playing far too early and the ball bobbling hopelessly up to short mid-off.

The simple explanation is that it is still winter. All those nets prepare you for summer, but although cricket is historically 'the summer game', the season begins long before anything remotely resembling summer has arrived. Every April, when the early-season tourists arrive, the ones who have never toured here before cannot believe how cold it is, or that anyone would want to play cricket in such weather. Nor can we – and we have been playing here all our lives.

Back in 1985 our first game of the season was against Sidney Sussex College, Cambridge – a plum fixture for us, because we were used to playing Oxford second teams and Cambridge colleges are generally too snobby to have second teams. This was the full might of the First XI, rangy, firm-jawed bastards one and all. Our best hope was for a draw, and we got it, but not in the way we expected. For this was April, and an unusually cold and forbidding April at that. We lost the toss and fielded first, and our fast-bowling ringer took a couple of wickets before the home side's blatant superiority began to tell. But it was getting colder and colder, and after an hour it started to snow. We were so cold that for a couple of minutes we just stood there, unable to move. Not that all of us wanted to leave the field. Bob Jones, our well-upholstered leg-spinner, wanted to stay on to see if the ball would turn off the snow. But by this time the outfield had changed colour, so we shuffled gratefully towards the pavilion. A log fire blazed invitingly within. We took an early tea, just in case the snow stopped. By 4.30 three inches of snow had settled on a good length. Only then, as body temperatures returned to normal, did Neal, who had been standing in as wicketkeeper, realise that two of his fingers were broken.

A more consistently Arctic fixture has been Marsh Gibbon in Buckinghamshire, the only known tundra wicket in the south-east of England. The pitch sits on a lofty and isolated plateau, vulnerable to every meteorological whim. Polar bears wander freely in the surrounding fields. Captain Scott players never go anywhere unprepared, and one particularly chilly fielding session saw a spontaneous outbreak of woolly scarves, at least one overcoat and, from Terence at deep third man, a balaclava. By the time a bowler had put on all his layers after finishing an over, it was time to take them off again for his next over. Only my friend Stephen had come unprepared, but with admirable resourcefulness he found a dirty old blue plastic bin-liner which, after tearing the end open, he put on over his head. It looked like a prototype for an all-over body condom. He couldn't move his arms, but then he wasn't exactly the most skilled fielder on the side anyway, so it didn't reduce his effectiveness by much. At least he fell on top of the ball a couple of times.

These days we kick off at Englefield Green in Surrey, another beautiful venue so open to the elements that even when it's sunny, you are a fool not to wear at least three sweaters and a full set of thermals. Here, it would seem, is the perfect opportunity for us to emulate the high standards set by our mentor, the Captain. Not for nothing do we wear caps inscribed with our team motto *'Modo Egredior'* ('I am just going outside'). But the wetness of the thirtysomething middle-class English male is deeply entrenched. For each year, in the first game of the season, we remember something else we have forgotten during the wasted winter months: that in April the ball is remarkably hard. When it hits your hands, you drop it. Every year at Englefield Green, we drop cartloads. So you have played only one game, your batting has collapsed, your bowling is a pale imitation of itself, and your fielding has gone to pot. Nothing like a good start to the season.

From *Rain Men: The Madness of Cricket, 1996*

In his follow-up book, *Zimmer Men*, written some ten years later as he and his fellow cricketers advanced into middle age and beyond, Berkmann imagines himself as a cricketing agony aunt, answering questions pompously on a whole range of tactical subjects. Here he muses on the subject of leadership.

ZIMMER MEN

Marcus Berkmann

Dear Dr Berkmann,
First, the big ones. Heads or tails? Bat or bowl?
Name and address withheld

Dr B writes: Is it not bizarre that, as you walk out to the centre of the pitch with the opposition captain at the start of the match, so much of your brain should be concentrating on which side of the coin you should nominate? For years I fretted about this, until someone told me that heads comes up not 50 per cent of the time, as previously assumed, but 50.0000423 per cent of the time, owing to the greater wind resistance of the Queen's head. This turned out to be rubbish, but it gave me the excuse always to call heads, despite knowing that in August the greater heat and thinner air make tails come up approximately 100 per cent of the time. I still stick doggedly to heads, like the last child in the class to realise that they are the butt of a cruel joke.

As for the batting/bowling question, this has history. In Captain Scott, Harry, when captaining, would always insert the opposition. This was partly an aggressive, partly a defensive strategy. If he had the better bowlers and the pitch looked promising, he obviously wanted to have first use of it. And if the other team was palpably stronger, he wanted the chance to hold out for the draw batting second. Add the many occasions when the other team won the toss and chose to bat on a belter, and we seemed to spend whole seasons bowling first. This became a little dull. So rampagingly, deadeningly tedious, in fact, that we all decided when we started Rain Men that we would *always* bat first, however green the pitch, however overcast the sky. This may seem a little self-defeating. Indeed, it has proved completely self-defeating on several occasions, but only recently have players begun to question the policy. Finally, I think, we have got it out of our systems, and can now start choosing to bat or bowl first as conditions demand it. Assuming, of course, that we have the slightest idea of how to interpret those conditions, which is what Dermot Reeve would call 'a big ask'.

Some reasons to bat first: It's a beautiful day. The pitch looks flat. Our bowlers look fat. Three of our team are lost on the motorway. It looks like raining heavily, and chances are we won't finish the game, and nearly everybody prefers batting to bowling if they are only going to do one of them. We are grievously outclassed, and want the game to be over as quickly as possible. We are sick of bowling first.

Some reasons to bowl first: It's cold and wet and the pitch hasn't been mowed so much as gently trimmed. Our bowlers are fit and raring to go. Steve Harmison has wandered up and asked if he can get a game. Half the team want to leave at six o'clock to go to parties and so would rather bat after tea and then drive off after they are out. We are grievously outclassed, but think we will be able to hang on for the draw. We are sick of batting first.

Dear Dr Berkmann,

Field placings. As a village captain myself I am always struggling to get people in the right places. Half of them don't go where they are put and the rest stonedrift blatantly between balls. What do you suggest?

Name and address withheld

Dr B writes: This is an unsolvable problem: experiments have shown that, asked to go to cover point, 47 per cent of fielders will go to extra cover, 32 per cent will go to backward point or gully, and 1 per cent will go to square leg. Many fielders regard it as your responsibility to remember where the field placings are, not theirs. As for stonedrift, I have come to the sad conclusion that there is no cure for it, other than death. Stonedrifters cannot stop themselves moving from the field placing to which they have been assigned; indeed, they are probably not even aware that they are doing it. And when a catch goes straight to where they should be, but anything between ten and eighty yards from where they have ended up, they look at you with a shrug as though it is your fault. You can always spot a captain on the field of play: if he is not shouting, he is the one with the vein pulsing dangerously in his temple.

Some bowlers like to set their own fields, which is fine, as everything that goes wrong afterwards is therefore their own fault. On occasion I have had to resist some of the more forceful requests of bowlers. Once, when asked if there was anything he wanted, Francis the sharp-toothed stockbroker replied, 'Yes, change the fucking wicketkeeper.' The Human Sieve hadn't missed that many, and I owed him money, so obviously I had to quell that little revolt. Other bowlers set 7-2 fields and then bowl everything down the leg side: they deserve everything they get, which includes being taken off after the second over.

Otherwise, though, I have a few rules of thumb that, so far, have helped me stave off that life-threatening cerebral haemorrhage. One, place the field so that as few people have to move between overs as possible. Mid-off becomes long leg and so on. We bowl our overs slowly enough as it is, so we have to find some way of speeding things up. And no one in the world walks more slowly than someone compelled to field at long-on both ends. Two, make your field roughly symmetrical, to ensure that only a bare minimum of fielders have to move when a left-handed batsman comes in. Identify which of your fielders have it within them to memorise four fielding positions – this is a rare talent, given only to a few – and entrust them to move around between balls and overs. Let everyone else take root, bud in the spring and bear fruit towards the end of August.

Three is, expect no one to field at short leg. Bowler will bowl slow long-hop, batsman will hit ball straight at short leg and you will henceforth only have ten fielders. Or nine if you only had ten before. Or eight if you only had nine before.

(But if twelve players have shown up, and one of them is sleeping with your wife, this could be the solution to all your problems.)

Four is, don't follow the ball: in other words, don't put a fielder where the ball has just gone. Following the ball is the classic signal of captainly weakness. The temptation can be overwhelming. Indeed it may actually be the sensible thing to put a fielder there. But by doing so you show everyone that you made a horrendous cock-up by not putting a fielder there earlier. Instead do it quietly at the end of the over, after the ball has been hit there another three or four times.

Five is, you can run but you can't hide, and your weakest fielders can't do either. If you are playing on a slope, put them uphill. Otherwise, first slip is always safe as no one is ever going to catch anything there. Square leg by the umpire isn't bad: there is always someone else running around behind to cut off the boundaries, and any catches taken there are instinctive, and therefore possible. And resist the bowler's desire to move a fielder who has just ballsed things up, because if you do, over half of all remaining balls in the match will go to that fielder and through that fielder's legs. Unlucky fielders are magnetic. But remember the most important rule: if in doubt, do a lot of shouting. It will distract everyone's attention, even if it doesn't solve anything.

Dear Dr Berkmann,

I think my captaincy is perfectly adequate, in sometimes difficult circumstances. But I am constantly being criticised for it. Why can't people be more understanding?

BCL, Trinidad

Dr B writes: Have you made the mistake of being the best player in a moderate team? As virtually all village teams are extremely moderate, everyone knows the perils of entrusting executive office to the highly skilled. For one thing they throw their weight around, scoring all those runs and taking all those wickets, catching everything and generally getting people's backs up. People don't turn up to cricket matches just to watch someone else do everything. They want the chance to fail, and they want it every week. Remember, in village cricket, when someone drops the first catch of the day everyone else on the field breathes a sigh of relief because it wasn't them. A captain has to understand such responses, and he is more likely to understand them if he feels them himself.

Most teams benefit by choosing a completely mediocre player as their captain. After all, what's so great about being captain? Whatever happens, it's just worry, worry, worry. Who to put in at number eleven who won't drive home in a huff? Who can score, or umpire, or field behind square on the leg side? Then the bowlers tell you they all want to bowl from the end without the sightscreen.

It's a nightmare. How are you supposed to go out and concentrate on your own game with all that going on? So pass on the responsibility to someone who doesn't have a game of his own. Free yourself from worry. You know it makes sense.

> *Dear Dr Berkmann,*
>
> People think I'm eccentric because I always soak my Weetabix in gold-top milk for precisely forty-three minutes and fourteen seconds, and eat nothing but baked beans and golden syrup when I travel abroad. Would I be considered such a bare-faced loon in village cricket?
>
> *RC'J'R, address withheld*

Dr B writes: Not at all. Village cricket is, some say, the final refuge for what mental-health professionals call 'distinctive behaviour'. My friend Maxie, who runs a team like mine, is well known for his unfortunate tendency to wail like a banshee whenever his younger brother is out for less than 50. His younger brother is the team's best batsman and tends to carry their hopes on his shoulders. But, whatever the circumstances, it can't be good for team morale to see your captain weeping publicly. And the opposition can only ever be encouraged by cries of 'Now we're *really* fucked!' ringing around the ground. Compared to this, your unusual dietary requirements and unconfirmed tendency to blindfold anyone you drive to your home seem to me very small beer. Have you thought of coming to play for us?

> *Dear Dr Berkmann,*
>
> I used to love captaincy, and I think I was pretty good at it. But with all the pressures of the job, I noticed that my own form began to suffer. What should I have done?
>
> *NH, Chelmsford*

Dr B writes: Well, as I said before, first thing you should do is hand over the captaincy to someone worse. Although, if the captaincy has made you worse, it's possible that there is no one worse than you to hand it over to. In which case, you're stuck with it, matey. Someone has to butter the sliced bread and put out the boundary flags while all his teammates are in the pub before the game, and that someone is you.

As for the batting, there are several ways you can try and end a lean spell, not all of which involve threats to umpires. As no one has the time or the inclination to practise properly during the season, you may not have held a bat between last week's embarrassing dismissal and approximately eight minutes before you have to bat this week, when you have just strapped on your pads and you ask, in a desultory fashion, whether anyone could bung a few balls at you. Someone will then bowl you an equally desultory leg-spin which you will fail to lay a bat on, thus not preparing you even slightly for the hostile fast bowling you are about to face in the middle. This 'practice' will therefore have made you less confident about batting than you were before, which is quite an achievement. So why do it? Here are some alternatives. 1. Very large drink of something. 2. Don't practise against a real bowler. Practise against an imaginary bowler. Play elegant drives and savage cuts without having to fetch the ball afterwards. Looks silly but so what? 3. Another large drink of something. 4. Nip behind the pavilion. Ring someone on your mobile and get them to call you back straight away. Take the call in full view. Gasp several times. Tell the rest of your team that your house is burning down. Run to car and drive away. No need to think about batting for another seven days.

Dear Dr Berkmann,

Were captains so much better in the past, as everyone always says? For various reasons I'd prefer to think that they weren't.

MPV, by email

Dr B writes: One of the masters of the captaincy art died in 2004. According to cricketing legend, Keith Miller tended to set his field by telling his players, 'Scatter'. On another occasion he omitted to nominate a twelfth man. Finding himself with twelve players on the field, he said, 'Well, one of you had better fuck off.' In four years as captain of New South Wales, his side won the Sheffield Shield three times.

Dear Dr Berkmann,

OK then, so tell me: what attributes does a modern cricket captain need?

MPV, by email

Dr B writes: I asked my team-mates this in the pub after a game and we compiled a list. Cheerleader. Man-manager. Tactical mastermind. Warrior. Player of mind games. Psychotherapist. Head boy. School bully. Brilliant fielder (because if you drop a catch, it's incredibly hard to take off the bowler at the end of that over). Collector of match fees. Negotiator. Salesman. Opportunist. Sneak.

My team-mates told me I am without equal when it comes to collecting match fees.

Alternatively, consider what the 1952 MCC Coaching Manual has to say on the subject:

> Captaincy wins matches and can lose them but it should do more than that; it can make or mar a season, not only in terms of wins and losses but also in the general satisfaction and happiness which playing cricket can bring ...
>
> A captain must be an optimist and inspire optimism in his side: he must show confidence in them in order that they may feel confidence in him. By personality and example he can set and keep his team alight ...
>
> Encouragement is everything ... criticism should always be constructive: slackness and conceit alone merit and should get the rough side of the captain's tongue ...

There's much to think about there, as I'm sure you'll agree. But I'll tell you one thing: I'm not giving anyone the rough side of my tongue.

From *Zimmer Men: The Trials and Tribulations*
of the Ageing Cricketer, 2005

Michael Simkins is another literary cricketing thespian. His memoir is subtitled '*How Cricket Saved My Life (Then Ruined It)*', which aptly describes the transformation from youthful enjoyment to middle-age obsession. In the 'first innings' devoted to his childhood, he describes learning the rudiments of the game in his father's sweet shop in Brighton and getting his first proper bat on his eleventh birthday.

FATTY BATTER

Michael Simkins

Stumped

We have other interruptions to deal with of course, pitch invasions being the commonest. A customer we call Chimney-pot Charlie because he spends his days on the opposite pavement talking to an imaginary character up on our roof disrupts play for about ten minutes each evening for half of Old Holborn and a Mint Cracknell, and on one occasion Ernie Black, who owns the dirty book shop in Gardner Street, causes an entire session of play to be cancelled with reminiscences of his recent caravan holiday to Porthcawl. But there are other, glorious evenings as well, evenings when not a single customer comes in for the entire twenty overs in the last hour. Slowly, week by week as the nights draw in, my eye gets keener, my hitting cleaner, my stats neater and the sweet spot sweeter.

The rules of shop cricket are complex. A nudge into the crisp boxes at third man counts as a single; a clip past the soft-drinks dispenser next to them at backward point counts as two, as does a hit into the loose toffees at cover. A lofted drive over their heads into the Raspberry Ruffles at deep extra is a boundary, as are the ciggie shelves at long on and long off, although I avoid them as there's always the chance of Dad intercepting and taking a smart return catch.

I soon learn to work the ball squarer, using lots of bottom hand, round towards the ice-cream fridge at midwicket. In fact, the cross-batted smear soon becomes my most productive shot. Dad does all he can to encourage it as the fridge hasn't been defrosted for nearly three years and the lid won't close properly, so any scuffs or dents only strengthen his pleas to Walls for delivery of a new model. Through square leg into the revolving ladies' stockings display is three, and fine leg offers a single down to hairnets and sleepnets, or a couple if it reaches gift wrap. Anything hit into the window and demolishing Dad's seasonal displays is automatically Out without Dad having to give any reason.

Yet by November, shop cricket is beginning to pall. I'm painfully aware that a half-size beach cricket set is a long way from the real thing, and however much I try to imagine myself batting at Lord's I can't escape the reality that backward point is corn plasters, fly slip is Andrews Liver Salts and my wicket is merely a greetings-card stand, with slip and gulley 'Good Luck In Your New Home' and the wicketkeeper 'Sorry You're Leaving'.

I'm desperate for something more in which to lose myself, something which will allow my imagination to roam free, something which will make me feel more like my heroes on the screen.

Shot

The great Albert Trott of Middlesex once hit a cricket ball over the roof of the pavilion at Lord's. The sensation of hitting a perfectly timed cricket stroke with a piece of sprung willow ruined him for ever, as he spent the rest of his life trying, and failing, to repeat the shot and relive the exquisite sensation. His game went to pieces, and he finally blew his brains out with a service revolver in lodging houses in north London.

It's 3 February 1967, the eve of my eleventh birthday. Tomorrow morning I'm receiving my first genuine cricket bat. By 'genuine' I mean it will be made from willow, will have a V-shaped splice at the top of the blade, will be properly sprung so that it doesn't feel like you're playing with a coffin lid when you hit the ball, and will have a proper rubber handle with dimples to provide consistent grip during the long hours at the crease.

And there's something else. Above all, it'll have a label full of instructions for proper care stuck on the back. No more 'Do not put bat in mouth' warnings, but mysterious rituals involving linseed, lint cloth, brown-paper covers and fine high-grade glass paper, and procedures of which all cricketers speak but which are rarely witnessed in public. Sanding. Oiling. Knocking in.

Dad hasn't mentioned it, of course. He's tried to put me off the scent by talking about Action Men and Scalextric. But I know. I *know*. No more kiddie bats from Taiwan, items purchased from toy shops and packaged in cheap plastic mesh, shaped from compressed sawdust with childish logos emblazoned on the face, props for beach cricketers. This will be the real thing. I even know which one I'm going to get. They're all hanging up in the window of our local sporting goods emporium, Kilroy Sports and Games in Grand Parade.

Mr Kilroy is a typical Irishman, garrulous, charming, ever ready with a saucy compliment for Mum or a friendly tweak of my ear. He's also rumoured to be in terrible financial difficulties after weeks of backing donkeys at the bookies. That old nag doddering past the post three hours after the others is the direct reason for my imminent delivery of a top-of-the-line willow wand from his shop window display. I used to hate horseracing almost as much as speedway, but I've got a lot to thank it for now.

One of the problems you face if you run a newsagent's is the number of customers who are behind with their bills. Dad tries to play the tough guy, but the fact is he's just too soft. A few weasel words from his creditors about cash-flow problems or personal difficulties and he'll soon cave in, allowing them to do what they always do and settle the bills by offering him some item from their own stock in lieu of payment.

Eva's Continental Delicatessen in Sydney Street recently settled up for six months' worth of unpaid-for motorcycle magazines by persuading him to accept a crate of baby pears in Calvados from Uruguay. The Home Brewing Centre in Gloucester Road gave him three yards of rubber tubing and some demijohns, while the Kensington Wool Shop offered 250 wire coat hangers in recompense for six weeks' worth of unpaid *Daily Expresses*. We've had sets of chimney-sweeping brushes, a stuffed moose head, and a full-size xylophone that collapsed at 3am, persuading Mum that a jazz combo was trying to break into the shop.

'If he's in form he's got a very powerful snick over first slip's head.'

And now Liam Kilroy of Kilroy Sports and Games is apparently on the verge of bankruptcy and eight months behind with payments for the *Racing Post, Sporting Life* and the *Angling Times*. And Dad wants me to have a cricket bat.

Five different bats. Five different dreams. I've spent weeks gazing in at them as they hang there in his window: pristine rectangles of biscuit-coloured willow, each with the signature of some cricketing hero burnt across the top of the blade in skimming black lines. The

Ken Barrington, for instance: his name massive, impregnable, safe as the Bank of England; or the Gray Nicholls Ted Dexter Autograph, with the batsman's name slashed carelessly across the splice as if he'd been in a hurry to catch a private jet to some fashionable party in Cannes. Or what about the one next to it, the Tom Graveney County Pro? Or the Lillywhite's Colin Cowdrey Truespot? Or even the Gary Sobers Crusader short handle at the end? With that I'll be driving on the up past point or lofting sixes against the spin, the sort of strokes to send crusty old brigadiers spluttering into their coaching manuals.

It proves a difficult night. My dreams are crammed with jumbled cricket visions juxtaposed absurdly with unlikely characters from my domestic environment and the world of popular entertainment. In one troubled scenario, Mrs Brooks, one of our regular customers, a woman in her sixties with no teeth and a penchant for stuffing handfuls of Victory V lozenges into her holdall when our backs are turned, is helping me to erect a cricket net in our upstairs toilet with my invented Pakistani Owzthat star Abdul Hashish-Orandi.

In real life I've never seen Mrs Brooks display the slightest sign of interest in anything, apart from once making the startling observation that most of the residents of central Brighton are 'only on earth to make up the numbers'. But at 3am she's issuing imperious orders to one of the most dashing batsmen ever seen on the subcontinent as to how twenty-two yards of netting and scaffolding might be successfully erected in a first-floor lavatory by wedging the poles down inside the toilet bowl.

By the time I've clambered free they've been joined by Michael Miles, genial host and Quiz Inquisitor of ITV's popular game show *Take Your Pick*, and I now find myself a contestant in a nightmare version of the celebrated Yes–No Interlude. Except that he and Mum seem to be coalescing into the same person. The prize for successfully answering his barrage of quickfire questions without using those two dreaded words is a cricket bat from Kilroy Sports and Games.

'So you like cricket, do you?'

'I do like cricket, Michael—'

'You didn't nod your head then, did you?'

'I did not nod my head, Michael.'

'Are you looking forward to your doings in the morning?'

'I am looking forward to my doings, Michael.'

'So which bat would you prefer: the Tom Graveney, the Gary Sobers? I suppose Dexter is your favourite, isn't it?'

'I don't have a preference, Michael.'

'No preference?'

'That's right, Michael.'

'So who's your favourite cricketer, do you wear a box, have you ever been to Lord's?'

'My favourite cricketer is Colin Milburn, I do not wear a box, no, I've not been to Lord's—'

BONG!!!

I wake with a start. My ordeal is over. I swing out of bed, ferret for my slippers and pull on my dressing gown. Outside it's still dark, the only illumination the pallid yellow sodium glow of a street light. And it's raining. As I reach the ground floor a voice on BBC Radio Brighton is already issuing a severe weather warning for all the county's roads. Dad is lugging the morning papers in from the porch, while from the basement kitchen the aroma of Mum's attempts at a special birthday breakfast pervades the house, burning bacon and stewing plum tomatoes.

Dad too has obviously had a bad night. He's dressed in an acrylic zip-up cardigan over a flannelette pyjama top and an old pair of tuxedo trousers. A strand of crinkled Sellotape clinging to his knuckles suggests an early and presumably bad-tempered encounter with wrapping paper. Somebody has urinated on the morning papers while they've been sitting in the porch so he's now got to dry out a hundredweight of assorted newsprint in front of our Magicoal flame-effect fire and then persuade his customers to part with good money for them.

The presents have been heaped hastily in the corner of the rear parlour, a pile of oddly shaped packages and parcels, the biggest and most impressive an object resembling a full-size short-handle cricket bat. Dad would normally like to be there while I unwrap my presents but already the rush hour is building up, so I'm left by myself. I'm happy with that. At least I won't have to go through the charade of pretending to be interested in reading the messages in all the cards.

And my campaign of heavy hints has hit the bulls-eye. Our assistant Vi Hacker has bought me a proper junior pro cricket box, made of tough pre-moulded plastic, shaped like a tiny bicycle saddle and in the same garish pink as the candy shrimps we sell in the shop.

Fred and Ida Wackett have bought me a proper cricket ball, Uncle Jim and Auntie Joyce have sent me a set of stumps, and Uncle Percy has given me a pair of batting gloves with green rubber spikes attached to the fingers.

Brother Geoff has bought me a magnificent maroon cricket cap with a prodigious peak and an adjustable headband, while Pete, who's obviously earning good money, has left me a set of magnificent buckskin pads with proper leather straps and buckles. Even Auntie Gladys has tried her best. Hers may only be a copy of Palgrave's *Treasury of Inspirational Verse For Children*, but even she has had the decency to insert a little note inside pointing the way to page 24, a poem with a cricketing theme called 'Vitae Lampada' by Sir Henry Newbolt ...

There's a breathless hush in the Close tonight –
Ten to make and the match to win ...

Auntie Lena has bought me a jigsaw.

I can't wait any longer. Turning to the star prize I tear greedily at the paper. I wonder how they see me? Will it be with the dashing hauteur of Dexter, the graceful elegance of Graveney, or the dazzling informality of Sobers? The brown dimpled handle is even now poking through. Any moment now I'll be both taking the money and opening the box ...

From *Fatty Batter: How Cricket*
Saved My Life (Then Ruined It), 2008

Touring India as a broadcaster has always been a delight, but at times it demands a considerable personal reservoir of patience. Everything works in the end, but you have to accept that there will be daily encounters with unbending officialdom that are going to be exasperating. It is said that when the Brits withdrew from the subcontinent, India inherited two great colonial vestiges – the railways and the civil service. Reading the marvellous *The Goat, the Sofa and Mr Swami* by economist and first-time novelist R. Chandrasekar, one is immediately immersed in the world and the mindset of an archetypical Indian bureaucrat, who is forced to deal with the exigencies of Pakistan's prime minister's sudden decision to invite himself to a cricket series to be played in India.

JOINT SECRETARY SWAMI

R. Chandrasekar

The PM had made it clear that he was to be woken up only in the event of war.

There was no war, so I did not wake him up when the Pakistani PM called. There was no war, so he woke up at his usual time of nine or so. There was no war, so he had his bath, his morning prayers and his breakfast (aloo parathas with ghee, hot jalebis and a glass of sweet lassi) undisturbed. He then settled down to watch the Tom and Jerry show, something he enjoyed and appreciated immensely. Half an hour of this and I felt that he was ready to face the newspapers. It was past eleven in the morning.

He disliked reading and it was my job to read him the news I considered important. I must admit that I did not look forward to this on that particular morning. I suppose I could have skipped the bit about the cricket match, but he would have learned about it at some point and then it would have been up shit creek for me. He can be a formidable old SOB when he chooses and I've yet to figure out how best to handle him. I took a deep breath and plunged into the news.

Indo-Pak Relations Hit a New Low

By Our Correspondent

Relations between India and Pakistan, touchy in the best of times, spiralled to a new low over something as mundane as a cricket match. It will be recalled that the Pakistan team is due to play three tests in India in a month's time. At a hastily called press conference last night, the Prime Minister of Pakistan, Mr Hafez Ali Shah, announced that he had accepted an invitation from the Prime Minister of India, Mr Keshavchand Motwani, to witness the test match in Delhi.

Mr Shah went on to express his desire to watch the other two tests as well, to be held in Itanagar, Arunachal Pradesh, and Tirunelveli in Tamil Nadu.

Contacted by the press, the Indian ambassador here, Mr Vikram Kapoor, denied that any invitation had been extended by the Indians. 'There has been no invitation to the Prime Minister of Pakistan to visit India nor is there any invitation planned,' he said.

He went on to accuse the Pakistan government of violating the spirit of the Shimla Agreement of 1972. Asked to elaborate, he stated that Mr Shah's statement was 'a cheap stunt aimed at embarrassing the Indian government'. He added that a visit 'could only come about after elaborate consultations on both sides' and that 'there were no plans to hold such consultations now or in the future'.

A spokesman for the foreign ministry in New Delhi elaborated on the consultative mechanism set up as part of the Shimla Agreement and stated that Pakistan had violated it.

Mr Shah expressed dismay when told of the Indian reaction:

'All I want to do is watch the cricket match. Sports can help ease the tensions between our countries and I was hoping to cheer both sides on the field. The Prime Minister of India was very positive in welcoming me. It appears that he has changed his mind. Doubtless there are hardliners in the Indian government who want to discourage any move towards peace. I am sorry that Mr Motwani has given in to them. This will not help the cause of peace. I have no intention of going to India under the current circumstances.'

While the sequence of events remains unclear, with each side accusing the other of falsehoods and duplicity, what is clear is that relations between the traditional enemies have touched a new low.

I cleared my throat and waited for the explosion. It came.

'What is this nonsense? What is this rubbish? What is that idiot Kapoor talking about? I have invited Shah. I am the Prime Minister of India. I will transfer him to Jhumritalayya.'

It was not the moment to remind him that IFS officers cannot be transferred to Jhumritalayya. It was not the moment to speak or comment. It was a moment to stand silently.

I stood silently.

'Well, what are you waiting for? Call up Kapoor and tell him to pack up his bags.'

I couldn't very well do that. These IFS chaps can be oversensitive; their dealings with us are prickly even at the best of times.

'Sir, the service rules of the Government of India...'

'You think I am a fool? Mujhe ulloo samajhte ho?'

'Certainly not, sir. You are like a respected grandfather to me.'

'I am like your grandfather? What was your grandfather?'

'Which one, sir?'

'You idiot! Talking back to me like this? Any grandfather. All grandfathers.'

'Sir, one was an assistant station-master and the other worked in a mental asylum.'

'You are calling me a mad station-master? I am a freedom fighter, you understand, a freedom fighter. I get a freedom fighter's pension from the government. While your bloody grandfather was working for the British, I was fighting for India's independence.'

Taking abuse from politicians is part of the job, but having one's ancestors insulted is not. It was a difficult moment for me, but I knew deep within that I had to do what I had to do.

'My grandfathers were honourable gentlemen, sir, unlike some assistant village munsifs serving under the British that I know of who were caught stealing dhotis and put into prison. I shall be resigning from the IAS, sir, in view of the gratuitous insults I have had to put up with, and once relieved from service, shall hold a press conference explaining in detail the reasons for the extreme step I have been forced to take.'

'How do you know about all that?' His face was suddenly ashen.

'All what, sir?' Time to string the bastard along.

'What you were just saying. Just saying, you know what.'

'You know what what, sir?'

'Arre, surely you are understanding, that what, you know what?'

'What what, sir?'

He wrung his hands. 'The assistant munsif bit, that's what.'

'My grandfathers were honest gentlemen, sir.'

'Just a joke, you are understanding, just a joke.'

'A very poor joke, sir.'

'Yes, yes, a very poor joke indeed. But how come we are talking about these very honourable gentlemen, your grandfathers?'

'Conversations sometimes meander, sir, like the river Ganga.'

'Yamuna as well. As also the Narmada, Godavari, et cetera, et cetera. All meandering.'

'Yes, sir.'

'Tell me, is this Leander also meandering?'

'I don't understand, sir.'

'This tennis player, Leander. Why is he called Leander?'

'I have an idea sir.'

'You know why Leander is called Leander?'

'I have no idea, sir.'

'But you just said that you have an idea. You are confusing me now.'

'An idea, sir, but not about Leander. You see, the Pakistanis might beat us in cricket. Not good if Mr Shah is watching. So why don't we challenge them to a tennis match? That way, if Leander is playing, we will beat them.'

'A tennis match, eh? What a good idea! I will invite Shah myself.'

'Sir...'

'What is it now?'

'About that cricket match...'

'Oh yes. The cricket match. What will that Shah think?'

'He called last night, sir. Perhaps you should return the call.'

'I know he called last night. I spoke to him.'

'Sir, he called once again. After Kapoor spoke to the press.'

'Why wasn't I told?'

'You had given instructions not to be disturbed unless there was a war. There was no war. However, if you feel that I erred, I will not hesitate to resign, sir.'

'No, no, no. Don't resign. I've already told you, your grandfathers were very honourable. Good patriots. No need to resign. No. Now get me Shah on the phone.'

~

Chaos

1

The start of the test match was nigh and I made myself comfortable. It had taken a while, but I was now able to appreciate the situation in which I found myself. Full salary plus benefits, meals from the Taj, a comfortable air-conditioned room, no work to do and all the time in the world to take in the test match.

Not bad at all.

I switched channels.

There was trouble at Kotla. The civil engineering professor had suggested demolishing a part of the stadium to let the sofa in. This had not gone down too well with the stadium authorities and he had stormed off in a huff. The mechanical engineering professor was hard at work on a Computer Aided Design program to try and figure out a way to manoeuvre in the sofa. The computer had knotted itself into an infinite loop and was refusing to respond to the good professor. He sat there, in full view of the TV cameras, looking as though he wished he was someplace else.

One of the commentators thought this was all very funny; most of the rest failed to appreciate the humour in the situation.

In the meanwhile, the start of the match had been postponed. Knots of officials stood and argued. Off to one side, I could see Kapoor shouting and gesticulating with the rest. The two teams practised desultorily and the crowd grew restive. The VVVIPs were still at their respective residences, waiting for the word to move. The minutes ticked by.

One of the commentators had a bright idea: a phone-in competition for suggestions on how to get a move on.

Get rid of the politicians, said one. Let them watch the match on television, said another. Why can't they sit on plastic chairs like

'Our new bowler doesn't seem to be coming off, Skipper?'
'Doesn't he? You watch him at the end of this over.'

everyone else? asked a third. All well and nice, but what was needed
was a constructive suggestion. I called in, as Purushottaman.

'Why don't they saw the sofa into shorter lengths?' I asked. 'Then
they can use Araldite or something similar to glue the pieces back
together.'

An hour or so later, the reconstituted sofa was in place. I have to
say that it made for a grand sight – impressive, resplendent even,
as it sat on the grass in the pale, watery sunshine. I had created
a problem for myself, though: I had won a refrigerator along with
tickets for the match as a reward for my efforts. The refrigerator would be presented along with the Man of the Match awards.
Problem was that as a public servant, I was expected to maintain
the highest standards of probity and accepting rewards was just not
on. I have always prided myself on my ethics and was not about to
be tripped up by some two-bit phone-in contest. The easiest thing
would have been to give them a false telephone number along with

the false name. This I had neglected to do and was dreading the prospect of telephone calls asking for Purushottaman.

2

The delay had caused other problems. The roads to Kotla had been sanitized in accordance with security procedures. The procedures called for traffic to be held up for a maximum of twenty minutes. An hour-and-a-half had now gone by. The traffic cops had not been told of the delays and had not let any traffic through. The result: gridlock throughout New Delhi – the paralysis had spread as far as Azadpur in the north and the Rajasthan border in the south. Uttar Pradesh was effectively cut off as was Haryana. Connaught Place, sorry, Rajiv Gandhi Chowk, was a giant parking lot as were the sidewalks and any other bit of available space. Frantic calls by delayed office-goers on their mobiles had jammed the airwaves. Frantic attempts at freeing up some bandwidth had caused further communications breakdowns and all air traffic was being diverted away from Delhi. I heaved a sigh of relief; the dreaded telephone call was unlikely to come any time soon.

I had further cause for satisfaction as well: Vikram Kapoor was making a royal mess of things. I sat back, sipped a glass of nimbu pani and gratefully surveyed the situation.

Things got worse.

A lot stranded near Parliament got restive and started shouting slogans against politicians, who, they assumed, were responsible for this and various other grievances. Their proposition found many takers. A helicopter-based TV crew got good shots of a mob storming Parliament. The gridlock meant that no reinforcements were forthcoming, so the security staff quickly locked themselves into the Central Hall of Parliament.

One could see that the mob was enjoying this unfettered access to the realm of the rulers.

3

At some point, a decision was made to bring the VVVIPs to the match by helicopter. The sanitized route was desanitized and the gridlocked traffic filled it instantly, causing another gridlock. It was a good thing Shah was in Delhi – this would have been an ideal opportunity for a Pakistani attack.

There were any number of heartrending tales filling the airwaves – people stranded en route to airports and stations, people unable to make it to hospitals, children lost in the general confusion, and so on. Unfortunate, certainly, but also increasingly monotonous. I switched back to cricket.

The helicopters (separate ones for Shah and the Old Man, I was glad to see. Kapoor had learned one lesson at least) had landed. The overnight rains meant that dust was not kicked up and I could see the haggard look on Kapoor's face as he helped the Old Man down the steps. The Old Man looked grim and barely acknowledged Kapoor. I couldn't help but be pleased. My known experience in handling crises had been overlooked not once, but twice, in favour of Dixit's and Kapoor's slick and superficial ways and I was entitled to a modicum of personal satisfaction even if there had been a serious breach of national security.

Shah looked preoccupied as well. He must have been following developments on TV and was perhaps rueing the missed opportunities. Either that or he was worried about what the generals would say about the limousine caper. Another missed opportunity: he could have kidnapped the Old Man and there was nothing we could have done short of war if he had decided to drive on to Wagah.

In any event, joy at the prospect of the test match was absent.

An MI 24 brought in the first lot of ministers, but the two PMs did not wait for them. The players' introductions were brief and grim and the two made for the sofa. I had made charts detailing where the ministers were to sit and I was glad to see that Kapoor had the good sense to use these. But wait – something odd was going on. Naturally enough, the cameras were trained on the two PMs, so at first, they did not pick up what was going on offstage.

One of the ministers had jumped the gun and seated himself next to the Old Man. Kapoor had been busy assigning ministers to seats and, along with the real assignee, was startled to find this prime spot occupied. The man seated there, a tobacco magnate from Warangal, refused to move. The real assignee, Hukum Singh Rathore from Jaipur, refused to accept anything less. Hot words were exchanged. Kapoor attempted some diplomatic mediation. It was soon clear that he had never attempted mediation between politicians. Dealing with Somali warlords was one thing; dealing with ministers from the GNC was something else again. The Old Man refused to intervene – it was evident from his expression that the matter was beneath him. Shah looked on eagerly: Indian democracy clearly had features of interest.

Kapoor pleaded and cajoled – in vain. Hukum Singh Rathore was a Rajput and Rajputs did not take things like this lying down. Or standing up, as was the case here. He slapped Subbarama Reddy from Warangal who, in his dealings with the Naxalites in his district, had learnt a thing or two about firmness. He pulled out a revolver.

I should point out that ever since jumbo cabinets had become the order of the day, I had insisted on ministers being frisked before being allowed near the Old Man to prevent just this sort of eventuality. Indian democracy, in the course of its meanderings, had bred many deviants and one could never be too sure. Kapoor had not learnt his lesson – too many years attending posh cocktail parties had dulled what edge he had.

But even he must have realized what two stray shots could do to Indo-Pak relations. He flung himself on Reddy with admirable alacrity and the gun fell down. Some SPG types materialized. One went for the gun and the others were soon wrestling with the ministers. Rathore, spying a vacant spot on the sofa, made for it, dragging three SPG jawans along with him. They fell with a thud onto the sofa. The sofa began to sink into the ground, which was sodden from the overnight rain. It tilted over. Shah got up as did the handful of pre-geriatric ministers. The geriatrics, the Old Man included, keeled over helplessly with the sofa.

From *The Goat, the Sofa and Mr Swami, 2010*

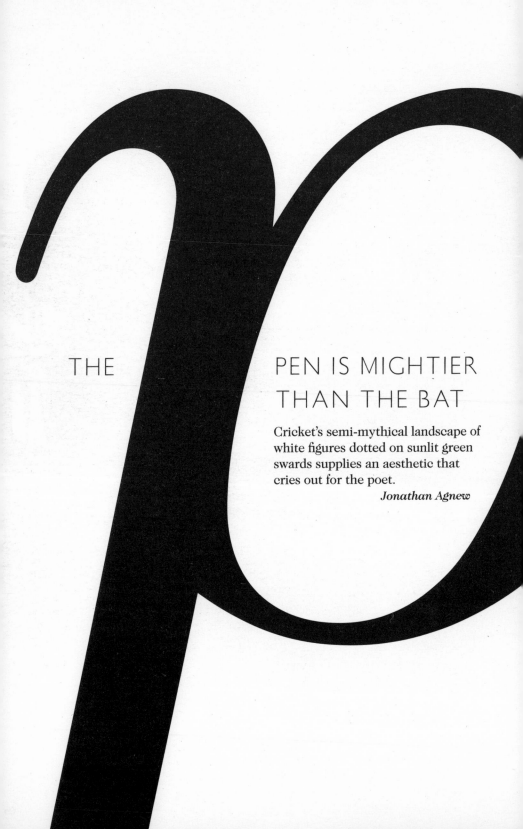

THE

PEN IS MIGHTIER
THAN THE BAT

Cricket's semi-mythical landscape of
white figures dotted on sunlit green
swards supplies an aesthetic that
cries out for the poet.

Jonathan Agnew

Spoiling Sport.
[Most of our prominent Cricketers are now engaged
as expert reporters by various journals.]

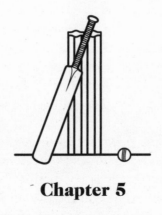

Chapter 5

*Interviewer: 'Do you feel that the selectors and
yourself have been vindicated by the result?'*

*Mike Gatting: 'I don't think the press are vindictive.
They can write what they want.'*

Cricket has become synonymous with powerful, poetic and colourful writing of a type and intensity that rarely exists in other sports. A match can be multifaceted, ebbing and flowing over many days, with periods of quietude, even languor, interrupted by moments of great athletic brilliance. It can reach summits of considerable dramatic tension that are the equivalent of any in sport (or in works of stage and screen for that matter) and have a cast of characters ranging from the humble spear carriers to the sublime *tour de force* of gifted individuals whose talents, skill and application lift the game to new heights, often transforming the outcome of matches in the process. All this is set in a cultural and historical landscape that encompasses two hundred years or more of history of the game, colonialism, post-colonialism, classism and the vast changes witnessed in social circumstances on several continents. And its actual physical, semi-mythical landscape of white figures dotted on sunlit green swards (or dusty tracks in far-off countries) supplies an aesthetic that cries out for the poet – somehow cricket has become symbolically important. It is no wonder that the breadth of canvas that cricket offers to writers has resulted in a canon of such literary distinction.

There is so much inherent complexity and variability in cricket, beyond its time-occupying nature, that offers the writer and commentator a unique and profound opportunity to flourish. It is founded on solid principles of a strict moral code that demands courtesy and sportsmanship, and conservatively insists on players respecting a higher authority without dissension in that the umpire's decision is always final (DRS notwithstanding). Cricket teaches every youngster to take the rough with the smooth and, crucially for the writer, luck plays a significant part in determining success or failure on the pitch – whether a player leaves the outfield as a hero or villain. The sights and the sounds of cricket – the white against green and leather striking willow – are soothing and evocative (to an Englishman at least) while nothing, for me, can beat the contented murmur of thirty thousand spectators enjoying their day out at Lord's. To me as a radio commentator, they form the orchestra to which I set the pitch and volume of my 'aria'.

Turning to the game itself, the contrasts in the passages of play are both dramatic and captivating. From one end a fast bowler charges in from a thirty-yard approach to hurl a hostile bouncer at a batsman who chooses either to rise to the challenge and hook the ball to the boundary or, in the interests of self-preservation, to sway his head from the ball's path. At the other end, a spinner tosses the ball into the air towards a batsman surrounded by predatory close fielders to create an entirely different contest within the main event. A draw can be an excruciatingly tense and dramatic affair – surely more so than in any other sport – and, after five days' hard work, can also be a well-deserved and satisfactory outcome.

We see the players in all manner of contrasting situations during the course of a match – batting, bowling and fielding – each of which presents the individual in a very different way. A player such as England and Sussex's Monty Panesar is a gift in this respect.

A serious left-arm spin bowler, always deep in concentration and with an infectious, explosive celebration whenever he takes a wicket, Panesar is a determined, would-be-stubborn, somewhat hopeless lower-order batsman of whom little is expected and whose usually brief innings end in visibly crushing disappointment. All of which would explain the legendary status granted to his heroic innings of 7 not out, made in thirty-seven minutes against Australia at Cardiff in 2009 – a brave and defiant performance from the worst batsman in the England team that ultimately saved the Test. It was a fine example of cricket's ability to throw up the most unlikely of heroes in, quite literally, testing circumstances – the sort of delightful narrative that allows writers of skill to present the time-old story of the reluctant hero battling the odds in the context of an actual and vital sports outcome. An outcome that matters to a lot of people, but who like to have their anxiety and satisfaction about such a result leavened with a story of humility and unintended humour. In the right hands, it is what great storytelling is all about. In Shakespearean terms, Panesar can be cast as the Fool. In the field, he shines as an unwitting and reluctant comedian, whose howlers and dropped catches inevitably bring forth sublime moments of commentary, particularly when none of his team-mates on the field are remotely amused. The response of Andrew Strauss to Panesar dropping two simple chances in Colombo in 2012 was to dispatch him from one side of the field to the other in order to keep him as far from the ball and his irate colleagues as possible. Any correspondent with an eye for humour was supplied in spades. Thus Panesar's contributions to a cricket match offer three very distinct areas for a correspondent to savour – and he is just one of twenty-two players.

What other sport is so rich in plot, character and circumstance? For tragedy, perhaps boxing, and in sheer gladiatorial combat, then perhaps tennis, but none other, I think. Cricket writers and broadcasters are fortunate, indeed.

The very earliest reports of cricket matches started to appear in newspapers after 1720. These were not the comprehensive, detailed accounts that we have come to expect and were usually little more than an advertisement for a forthcoming match. The *London Evening Post*, which was founded in 1726, became a reliable source of cricket information until it closed in 1797. On 27 August 1726 the *Post* promoted a single-wicket competition between Perry of

London and Piper of Middlesex. This is the earliest report of a single-wicket competition, and also the first time that players were named in the press. Cricket was a burgeoning sport and newspapers were also gaining in popularity, so both parties benefited from the growth of interest in cricket. More newspapers appeared on the scene – some did not last long – and the reports they contained became increasingly detailed. There was, for example, a lively conclusion to a match on 23 August 1731 between Mr Chambers's XI and the Duke of Richmond's XI, with 200 guineas riding on the result. Although universally accepted laws of cricket would not be adopted until later in the century, articles of agreement determined the basics of a cricket match, such as the timing of the close of play. This was the issue at Richmond Green that day when the game ended at the appointed hour, despite the start of play having been delayed by the late arrival of the Duke. With Mr Chambers's team clearly on top, needing to score only a further 8 to 10 notches with four or five batsmen still to come in, the decision to leave the field caused outrage among the spectators and a number of the Sussex (Richmond) players had 'their shirts torn from their backs' in the ensuing fracas. Later reports suggest that the Duke finally conceded defeat. Cricket was already attracting headlines for the wrong reasons.

Nearly two hundred years later the arrival of John Frederick Neville Cardus in the cricket press box shortly after the Great War changed cricket writing forever. Cardus was born in Rusholme, Manchester, in 1888. Leaving school at the age of 13, Fred – as he was known at the time – spent eight years as a marine insurance clerk before becoming assistant cricket coach at Shrewsbury School, then secretary to the headmaster. The largely self-taught young man had developed a passion for literature, music and the theatre, and in 1916 he successfully applied – as Neville – for a post at the *Manchester Guardian*, becoming its cricket correspondent in 1919. He demonstrated his devotion to the game two years later, when, having watched the opening overs of the 1921 Roses match between Lancashire and Yorkshire, he travelled to Chorlton to get married. He then returned to Old Trafford for the pre-lunch overs, and reported that, while he was away, Lancashire had scored 17 runs.

After the unprecedented industrialized slaughter of the First World War, the 1920s and the 1930s saw a period of extraordinary social change including economic decline, the threats of emerging fascism and communism, the weakening of colonial ties and the erosion of a deeply embedded class system; it meant that cricket, somehow symbolically tethered to the national identity, was imbued with the legacy of a lost world's certainty. New tensions in a post-war world would be the context in which Neville Cardus would write about the game, and in time become the heart of cricket literature – cricket's own Shakespeare.

John Arlott, himself a wonderful wordsmith and poet, best described the manner in which Cardus transformed the art of cricket writing.

'Before him, cricket was reported,' Arlott wrote. 'With him it was for the first time appreciated, felt and imaginatively described.'

Cardus's vivid and colourful portrayal of the players turned them into legendary figures – characters that the readers could both identify with and get to know and follow. As he said: 'The men on the cricket field were mixed up with the heroes of books and plays.' Cardus personalized the game of cricket. He, too, would have loved writing about Panesar, and he would, of course, have done so quite beautifully. Cardus wrote critically about music in the same instantly identifiable style, and became greatly respected by the leading cricketers and musicians of his time. At a memorial service held for Sir Neville in 1975, the cricket writer Alan Gibson paid this tribute to him:

'All cricket writers of the last half-century have been influenced by Cardus, whether they admit it or not, whether they have wished to be or not, whether they have tried to copy him or tried to avoid copying him. He was not a model, any more than Macaulay, say, was a model for the aspiring historian. But just as Thomas Macaulay changed the course of the writing of history, Cardus changed the course of the writing of cricket. He showed what could be done. He dignified and illuminated the craft.'

Gibson revealed the problem that every cricket writer of the time must have experienced. How to write expansively, romantically and creatively about the game without being accused of attempting – however unsuccessfully – to copy the great man? It says a great deal for Arlott, who was twenty-five years younger than Cardus and shared his passion for poetry, that he was able to flourish despite the overpowering presence of Cardus.

Arlott loved cricket from an early age, but a future as one of the game's finest writers and broadcasters seemed most unlikely when he worked, first, as a records clerk in a mental hospital and then took up a career as a policeman, progressing to the rank of sergeant. However, he was also a published poet, with broad interests, and in his early thirties he was offered the position of talks producer for the BBC's Eastern Service. In the summer of 1946 he was asked to submit reports on the first two games of India's tour of England, which went down so well in India that he was asked to cover the whole tour; thus began a commentating career that would include every single home Test match through to the end of the 1980 season.

Arlott had a wonderful, smooth and distinctive voice, and his gentle, calm Hampshire burr became the sound of summer; his style was poetic, highly descriptive and not without humour. He also used silence to great effect – sometimes for the whole time that it took a bowler to walk back to his mark. That was one of the most striking aspects of his delivery, one that I discovered when I bought some cassette recordings to play in my car – you would never be able to leave such a pause these days. For a start the summarizer sitting next to you would jump in with something to say, thinking that you had dried up. Arlott, on the other hand, was never interrupted.

Arlott's beautifully written account of that 1946 India tour of England, *Indian Summer*, revealed a deep love and understanding of the game of cricket and an affinity with the people who play it. It also set the cricket in its broader context, that of post-war Britain, with its bomb damage, its rationing and the sense of joy and relief that the war was over. It marked the beginning of a prolific writing career that would cover cricket in all its aspects, and a good deal more. In 1950 Arlott started writing for the *London Evening News* on cricket, football and wine; he moved on to the *News Chronicle*; and in 1968 succeeded his hero Cardus as cricket correspondent of *The Guardian*, which restricted his appearances on *Test Match Special*. Arlott would commentate on the radio only before lunch before heading to the press box with a couple of bottles of fine claret tucked inside his briefcase (he was also *The Guardian*'s wine correspondent) to help him compose his thoughts for his match report. When Arlott delivered his final commentary during the Centenary Test between England and Australia at Lord's in 1980, the crowd rose to applaud him. It was significant that the players too, including Geoffrey Boycott who was batting at the time, paused, turned to the box, and joined in with the applause – Arlott had been elected president of the Cricketers' Association in 1968, which he regarded as the greatest honour he had received in the game.

These were the days in which cricket correspondents sold newspapers, their readers eager to know what Cardus, Arlott or E. W. 'Jim' Swanton, the broadcaster and hugely influential cricket correspondent of the *Daily Telegraph*, had to say about the previous day's play. Another authoritative voice was John Woodcock, cricket correspondent of *The Times* from 1954 to 1988 and editor of *Wisden* from 1981 to 1986. Dubbed by Alan Gibson 'the sage of Longparish', he still appears occasionally in *The Times*, providing historical context to events in the cricketing world. When Christopher Martin-Jenkins moved from the *Daily Telegraph* to *The Times*, he took a large readership with him. Michael Atherton has since built very successfully on that platform and contributed significantly to his newspaper's coverage.

The best cricket correspondents have the necessary gravitas to become trusted by their readers, and the same applies to radio commentators, too. We are the listeners' and the readers' eyes and ears. However, there has been a marked shift away from this style of reporting, even in the broadsheets, with more weight and importance being placed on what the players involved in the matches have to say, rather than what the correspondents' dispassionate opinion from the boundary might be. If the player can offer genuine insight, that's fine, but too often readers are exposed to a variety of facile and banal quotes – often trawled from Twitter – that lack meaningful analysis or insight and tell us absolutely nothing we do not already know. It would be a great pity if match reports by fine writers like Atherton and *The Guardian*'s Mike Selvey were compromised by the requirement to include a current player's assessment of bowling 'in the right areas'.

The appointment of both Selvey and Atherton as cricket correspondents is a reflection of how the role of the former player in the press box has evolved over the last twenty years. There is a strong tradition of former Test cricketers writing newspaper columns or comment pieces (as opposed to match reports) going back to the Surrey and England all-rounder Percy Fender – the colourful amateur was often outspoken in print. But until I joined the tabloid *Today* newspaper as its cricket correspondent in 1990, former players did not hold such positions. My appointment was not popular with fellow correspondents – trained journalists who immediately recognized the precedent that had been set and the inevitable consequences that would surely follow. Selvey, who had written for *The Guardian* for several years as the newspaper's number two, duly succeeded Matthew Engel as correspondent. Derek Pringle and Angus Fraser joined the *Daily Telegraph* and *The Independent* respectively, and when Christopher Martin-Jenkins retired from *The Times* – after many years as correspondent first for the BBC then the *Daily Telegraph* – Atherton became the chief correspondent for *The Times*. I am not convinced that the resentment from the career journalists has disappeared completely, and I do not entirely blame them.

It would be a great shame if cricket writing became exclusively the domain of former first-class cricketers. While we bring the insight, knowledge and experience of the game that can only be gained from actually having been out there and done it at the highest level, there is much more to cricket writing than that. In addition to which retired cricketers can and often are understandably jaded and perhaps a little cynical about a game that has also been their job for many years. Immersed in the hard realities of professional cricket day in, day out will make you view the game from a different, more world-weary perspective, while cricket writers usually remain fans of the sport – retaining their enthusiastic optimism at the start of each new series or match.

Television has advanced so rapidly that I really think it is almost impossible to commentate now without the specialist knowledge that a player brings to the microphone. There are notable exceptions such as Tony Cozier and Harsha Bhogle, both of whom began their broadcasting careers on the radio and fall back on that experience to bring description and humour to their television commentary. Nowadays, though, television audiences expect to be coached via the wonderful ultra-slow-motion cameras and long lenses that take them right into the heart of the action. Doosras and reverse-swinging mystery balls are detected, analysed and explained, followed by advice on how to bat against them. This is very much the world of the player, and I cannot see that changing.

It is different on the radio, where you don't need to commentate with that level of detail. We are sitting some distance from the action and describe the scene as a spectator might see it from the stands. Often we have to wait for the action replay on our television monitor before establishing exactly what has just taken place, and this is analysed by the 'expert' – a former Test player – who sits beside the commentator. The commentator needs to be able to communicate what is happening in the game to an attentive audience, enjoy and promote banter with their on-air colleagues and have an eye for, and a willingness to paint, the general picture. And a distinct on-air personality helps of course. Clearly, a radio commentator needs to understand the game and, I believe, to have played it to a reasonable club level, but first-class or international experience is definitely not the essential requirement that it is fast becoming on television.

While writing is an individual discipline, broadcasting is very much a team game. Contrast is needed between the commentators' characters and voices in order to maintain the listeners' interest. In the interest of integrity and balance, it is also important to have representatives of both participating teams. As with newspaper reporting, the style of commentating has altered over the years. Long gone are the periods of reflective silence in a television broadcast that were the hallmark of Richie Benaud's commentary for the BBC. Nowadays, because of commercials, commentators have to do their talking between balls, rather than between overs. Benaud was the master at knowing when to speak or when to let the picture do the talking for him. 'Never say anything that does not add to the picture,' was his maxim and he was brilliant at choosing the precise and concise phrase that fitted the moment. Just as Cardus was the example to every budding cricket writer, Benaud was the model for all television commentators. But, as with Cardus, no one ever quite managed to match Benaud's exacting standards.

Arlott and Brian Johnston were poles apart in just about every way in their radio commentaries, but they combined to form an outstanding team. Arlott was quiet and thoughtful, a political animal who twice stood as the Liberal candidate for Epping. While he had a great sense of humour, he could never be accused of being frivolous. Johnston was an old Etonian whose views on forcing South Africa into sporting isolation until apartheid was dismantled were the polar opposite of those of Arlott, who favoured the boycott. The atmosphere in the commentary box in the summer of 1968, when the Basil D'Oliveira affair brought the South African issue to a head, must have been interesting, to put it mildly.

Johnston was the great communicator who came to cricket commentary from a broadcasting background featuring live Saturday evening entertainment; he brought the same sense of fun and enjoyment to brighten up the radio commentary of the time. It was thanks to Arlott and Johnston that *Test Match Special* became so renowned. Its intelligent conversational approach, with room for digression, humour and reflection, meant that as a broadcasting phenomenon it managed to attract an audience that was, in part at least, made up of listeners who were by no means cricket fans (at least not initially). Their legacy is still enjoyed by those of us who work on *Test Match Special* today. Henry Blofeld has been a tireless freelance writer and commentator for many years. His vivid description and ability to make the most trivial incident on the field, especially if it involves pigeons or distant red buses, sound like the most exciting thing that could possibly happen has become one of summer's great joys; it was in rich contrast to the measured tone and gravitas that Christopher Martin-Jenkins brought to the microphone. The role of the scorer was refined and expanded by the master statistician Bill Frindall, and the expert summarizers have always been larger-than-life characters. Freddie Brown and Norman Yardley were regular fixtures in the early days, sitting alongside commentators Arlott, Swanton, Rex Alston, Robert Hudson and Alan Gibson. England stalwarts Trevor Bailey and Fred Trueman became the next regular pairing and a third guest Test player, usually from the opposing Test nation, would join the team for a home series. With the combination of Arlott, Johnston, Blofeld, Martin-Jenkins and Don Mosey at the helm, *Test Match Special* made its name and forged its reputation. Listeners enjoy continuity, hence the need for a small team which now includes Michael Vaughan, Geoff Boycott, Vic Marks and Phil Tufnell. The personnel changes with the passage of time, but the core disciplines of the programme remain – that the summarizer should stop talking when the bowler starts his approach, and that we do not miss a ball. The rest of it just happens. And of course, the essentials of *TMS* – expert commentary, analysis, humour and lively conversation – are now replicated by other broadcasters around the world wherever Test cricket is played.

Criticism of players has always been a thorny issue and there are certain times when, in the immortal words of Fred Trueman, you wonder, 'What is going off out there?' As a broadcaster, correspondent or reporter, how critical should you be of skilled professional cricketers attempting to ply their trade in exacting circumstances? As a player, I always found it easier to accept criticism – and praise for that matter – from former players, who would base their observations on their own brushes with success and failure. It seems that even previous international experience on the part of the commentator who has the temerity to strike a negative note is now regarded as having insufficient kudos for some modern players. In May 2012 Kevin Pietersen resorted to Twitter to question Nick Knight's credentials to commentate on Sky television. The fact that Knight represented England 117 times in international matches appeared to matter not. The implication is that the right to commentate – which includes offering constructive criticism – now depends on the relative average of the commentator and the player concerned. A month later, Andrew Flintoff had an extraordinary rant against Michael Atherton, comparing Atherton's marginally inferior average to that of Alastair Cook but ignoring Atherton's experience and, more relevantly, respected views and reading of the game. If current players really feel prickly about the well-founded opinions of men like Atherton, who led England in fifty-four Tests, then heaven help the hack whose cricket career never progressed beyond his village team.

The essential requirement is that criticism is fair. Any honest sportsman can accept that, and it matters not whether it comes from an observer with a hundred Tests to his or her name, or none whatsoever. There is always the temptation to look back misty-eyed at periods in the history of cricket – in the case of players, this will unquestionably be the peak moments in their careers – and instinctively take the view that the game was somehow better then than it is now. There is hardly a former cricketer I have met who doesn't think like that, with truly great players like Fred Trueman, Ray Illingworth and Denis Compton broadcasting that unarguable belief for many years. Sir Ian Botham enjoyed a fractious relationship with the media during his career, largely because he attracted some unfavourable headlines alongside the well-deserved praise, but he now sits happily in the media centre (I wonder what Cardus or Arlott would make of that title for their places of work) believing that if the players do not like what he has to say, that is their problem – which is probably exactly what those members of the press thought when they wrote about him.

There have been occasions when a meeting between a player and a member of the fourth estate is necessary in order to clear the air. In the not-so-distant past, this would have been conducted at the corner of a bar over a pint and ended in a handshake. These days, such get-togethers are instigated by the media relations officer at the England and Wales Cricket Board, who is usually present as both sides present their cases – and it will not take place in a bar: more likely on the outfield before play, or after net practice. The cricket family is a small one, and functions much more smoothly when everyone within it tolerates each other, at the very least.

Finally in this section, it is worth pointing out that cricket was undoubtedly used as a civilizing force during the colonial expansionist period of British history. Its inherent code of conduct was used to transform the outlook of cultures of British subjects and later, as the Empire shrank, would be one of the means by which the still subjugated or recently independent nations could demonstrate their vigorous sense of self-worth by taking on (and beating) their colonial (or former colonial) masters. This found expression in the emergence of politically informed international cricket writing, and today can also be discovered in both fiction and great travel writing like that of Geoffrey Moorhouse.

To finish, I would like to quote the late Benny Green: 'Not only does cricket, more than any other game, inspire the urge to literary expression; it is almost as though the game itself would not exist at all until written about.'

I have had the pleasure of interviewing Sir John Major on *Test Match Special* on several occasions and can testify to his deep love and profound knowledge of the great game. In this masterful, painstakingly researched and beautifully written book, the earliest roots of cricket are examined and brought to life through the miscellany of quirky and imposing characters that laid the foundation of the modern game. As a former county cricketer, I am fascinated by this description of the emergence of the county scene as we know it today.

CRICKET'S EARLY COUNTY MATCHES

Sir John Major

More confidence, more leisure and more disposable income were contributory factors to the further growth of cricket. The game had long since moved beyond its earlier days as a plaything of wealthy individuals, but the Victorian eye for business would enable it to develop a commercial aspect of its own. The combination of wider interest, more spectators and ease of travel were essential preconditions for the next phase of cricket, the birth of a County Championship. But it would be a long time coming.

The county system of cricket in England is now so embedded that it is easy to assume that it was always there. But it wasn't, and, appropriately for a game whose birth date is unknown, the gestation of county cricket was prolonged and messy. Teams designated as a 'county' had contested games since the eighteenth century, but the names were fakes, mere 'cover-alls' for groups of scratch players brought together for a particular contest. When the *Postman* newspaper of June 1709 advertised a game between 'Kent' and 'Surrey', no such clubs existed. Nor did the members of the two teams play together on a regular basis. The names were concoctions, the players mercenaries, mere vehicles for a wager between men of wealth and influence. And yet, these early *ad hoc* contests were to influence the later structure of cricket.

The fallacious naming of 'county' clubs was an ancient tradition that became entrenched when teams masquerading as county sides began to dominate their eras. In the early nineteenth century 'Kent' were in the ascendancy, later 'Sussex' with the influence of the round-arm bowling of Lillywhite and Broadbridge, followed by the great 'Kent' teams built around Mynn, Pilch, Felix, Wenman and Hillyer; but in each case no such county club had been formed. The cricket historian Peter Wynne-Thomas brought together research on cricket between the 1820s and the 1860s to suggest nominal 'county champions' during that period: Sussex, Kent and Surrey are the only counties to feature up to 1852, when Nottinghamshire began to upset the early dominance of the south-eastern counties.*

By 1860 four county clubs – Sussex (1839), Nottinghamshire (1841), Surrey (1845) and Kent (1859) – had been established. They were private clubs. They did not distribute profit. They were owned by their members. Their ethos was that of the amateur, and they were fiercely independent. The MCC, by right of history, was *primus inter pares* and the accepted lawmaker for cricket, but it had no legitimate authority over the county clubs, which had their own priorities, employed their own staffs, arranged their own fixtures and were often unbiddable. The question of a formal County Championship was not even a gleam in a visionary's eye.

Other clubs joined the four pioneers, but only in a leisurely fashion. Yorkshire and Hampshire were founded in 1863, followed by Middlesex and Lancashire (1864) and Worcestershire (1865). Derbyshire (1870), Gloucestershire (1871), Somerset (1875), Essex (1876) and Leicestershire (1879) appeared in the next decade with Warwickshire (1882) and Glamorgan (1888) bringing up the rear. There are three oddities in this progression: an Essex Club existed in 1790, but faded away; Northamptonshire founded a club in 1820, but did not enter the County Championship until 1905; and Glamorgan did not do so until 1921. The seventeen counties would become eighteen in 1992, with the addition of Durham.

As county clubs formed, inter-county fixtures rose in number, although by 1870, when eight clubs – Surrey, Lancashire, Gloucestershire, Nottinghamshire, Middlesex, Sussex, Yorkshire and Kent – were in existence, only Surrey played all seven other counties, and even by 1880 only forty-six inter-county games were played. To a later generation, familiar with the county game, it seems odd that its advantages were not seized more swiftly. But it did not seem odd in 1860, or for the following quarter of a century. The paucity of clubs and the difficulties of travel argued against it. So did their parochialism. None favoured ceding their power to the central control that would be necessary. Nor was there any mechanism to thrash out such objections to see if they could be overcome. A County Championship was simply not on the agenda. Moreover, the amateur touring sides, I Zingari ('The Gypsies') first among them, and the professional mercenary teams had captured the public imagination. All this would change only slowly.

Meanwhile the All-England Eleven and its many imitators – up to twenty at one time – carried cricket around the country. Games were predominantly in the north of England, although Scotland and Ireland were additions to this itinerary. Games in London or the south, where there was more competition and less demand for them, were a rarity. The allure of the travelling elevens remained huge, and the cream of contemporary talent – Richard Daft, Bob Carpenter, George Parr, Tom Hayward, George Tarrant, John Jackson and Jemmy Shaw – turned out for them regularly. These players' commitments reduced their availability to the counties, and cut down the number of inter-county fixtures.

Cricket in the 1860s was played against a background of turbulence and ill-feeling. As we have seen pay, and William Clarke's imperious style, had caused unseemly rows within, and between, the travelling mercenary teams, but other professionals were worried about money too, fearful of the future as they neared the end of their cricketing years. This concern manifested itself in resentment by the (largely professional) north of the (much more amateur) south, and between individual professionals and amateurs. Many petty disputes, accompanied by much petulant behaviour, soured the game. Jealousy erupted in the north when H.H. Stephenson of Surrey was appointed captain of the England side to tour Australia in 1861–62.[†] Central to the unpleasantness were disputes between northern and southern players, in particular the counties of Surrey and Nottingham.

This was given a focus in 1862 following a match between Surrey and England at The Oval. For over ten years, round-arm bowlers had raised their arm above shoulder height, and although still illegal, this had been tacitly accepted by umpires. But flouting of the law was unsatisfactory, and was about to come to a head. England's Ned Willsher, whose action was 'high', was warned for throwing by his close friend, umpire John Lillywhite, and then no-balled for six successive deliveries. Willsher stalked off, followed by his professional colleagues, who believed, or affected to believe, that the umpire was acting upon the instruction of the Surrey Club. Some northern professionals, notably Nottinghamshire's often queer-tempered George Parr, reacted very badly, and refused to play either against Surrey or in the two most important representative fixtures of the year, North vs South and Gentlemen vs Players. For a while Surrey and Nottinghamshire refused to play one another.

The atmosphere worsened two years later when the United South of England Eleven was formed, largely at the instigation of Surrey professionals led by Julius Caesar. Its formation was a direct result of the schism between northern and southern players, and did nothing to heal it. The new eleven drew players from the All-England Eleven and the United All-England Eleven, and further infuriated professionals who feared, with cause, that their livelihood was at risk.

One problem was soon resolved. John Lillywhite's no-balling of Willsher brought common practice and cricket law into collision, and overarm bowling was legalised, with the arm permitted to be extended as high as the bowler wished. Willsher's action became legitimate. It is an irony that it was Lillywhite who brought the matter to a head, for it was his father William, forty years earlier, who had been one of the foremost advocates of legalising round-arm bowling. Times had changed, but the Lillywhites were consistent in their gift for revolution.

To add to all this pent-up frustration there was significant agitation in 1864, fuelled by anonymous letters to the *Sporting Life* which advocated a cricket 'Parliament' to replace the authority of the MCC. No doubt the letters were mischievous, but they did reflect concern that the MCC's control over cricket was feeble. The club had sanction over the game's laws, but not over the conduct of its players. The commercially inspired professional elevens were their own masters, and their behaviour could be anarchic. More happily, that year the *Wisden Cricketer's Almanack* was born, and the sixteen-year-old W.G. Grace entered top-class cricket.

The instinct for reform that had dominated the politics of the first half of the eighteenth century was also alive in cricket. Indeed, so active was it that the moneyed and patrician Henry Hyndman, a Sussex cricketer from 1863 to 1868, would become an intimate of Marx and a leading advocate of socialism. Radical passion was not excluded from the dressing rooms of cricket.

In the midst of squabbles, new players were emerging to enrich the game. The quality of batting was improving. University and schools cricket was thriving. On the field, professional players comfortably outperformed amateurs. In the Gentlemen vs Players fixture, which had begun in 1806, the Players had won thirty-nine victories to only fourteen by the Gentlemen, and some of the latter's successes had only been won with teams of more than eleven players. W.G. Grace would soon balance the scales.

As cricket moved at pedestrian pace towards the structure we know today, games between counties remained occasional, although they began to increase towards the end of the 1860s. The shortage of fixtures make comparisons odious, but Nottinghamshire, Yorkshire and Surrey appear to have been the strongest sides. The game remained very Victorian in its attitudes. The distinction between 'amateurs' – respectfully addressed as 'Mr' – and paid professionals – known only by their surnames – remained stark, especially in the south. In the north the situation was less clear-cut: Tom Emmett, a professional, captained Yorkshire, but even he offered to stand down as soon as the amateur Lord Hawke became available. Hawke declined, not out of modesty, but to learn the trade under Emmett so that he could replace him. It was a feudal arrangement, and Yorkshire were fortunate that the sharp eye of Mrs Gaskell was not around. Nottinghamshire were more democratic. For more than fifty years, from 1838 to 1889, the county was successively captained by William Clarke, George Parr, Richard Daft, William Oscroft, Alfred Shaw and Mordecai Sherwin – all professionals.

Amateurs changed in separate dressing rooms, entered the playing area through separate gates, and ate apart from the professionals. The great Lancashire openers Hornby (a dashing amateur bat) and Barlow (a stonewalling professional but a deadly bowler) would only meet on the pitch at the start of their innings. If Barlow resented this, there were consolations: if Hornby ran him out, as he did the first time they batted together, he would present Barlow with a sovereign. The distinctions were absurd and insulting, but in Victorian England they were commonplace. Irritation flared up from time to time. There was an especially serious outbreak of discontent when the Australian tourists of 1878 were treated with the social courtesies due to amateurs, and paid more generously than the English professionals. Half a century later, even after the egalitarian impact of the First World War, the old prejudice lingered on. When Percy Fender led his Surrey team, amateurs and professionals alike, onto the field at Lord's together, he was summoned by an irate Lord Harris and informed curtly 'we don't want that sort of thing at Lord's, Fender'. By 'that sort of thing' he meant that Fender should not flout convention, and amongst the class conscious in post-war England convention ruled that birth, blood and wealth bestowed natural advantages that a wise society should not challenge. To those who thought in this way, it was evident that only amateurs were 'gentlemen'. This attitude was reinforced when professionals deferred to amateurs even when their cricketing skills were inferior. The preference for amateurs as captain remained ingrained in some counties until all distinctions between amateurs and professionals were abolished in 1963. Some genuine cricket-lovers believe in it still, however. Fashions sometimes move faster than instincts.

The pay of professionals did not compensate them for their inferior status. They had cause to be aggrieved. In the 1860s, Surrey professionals – and Surrey was among the richer clubs – were paid £3 a game, with a win bonus of a further £1. Ten years later they only commanded £5 a game, with the win bonus unchanged. Moreover, out of this modest income professionals had to pay their travel costs and hotel bills, which swallowed part, and occasionally all, of their match fees. In 'great' games the pay rose: £10 was the fee for Players in the annual match against the Gentlemen, and £6 for representing the North against the South. Over a full season of six months – April to September – an average county professional might earn around £80, although the very best of them might double that sum.

It was a modest salary for a high skill when compared to the £85 per annum of an unskilled labourer, although those professional cricketers fortunate enough to find winter employment were able to add to their income. The modesty of cricketers' resources was illustrated by Charles Alcock, Honorary Secretary of Surrey, when he observed that professional Surrey players in the early 1880s had one pair of flannels each for the entire season. By 1890 the basic professional salary had risen to about £275 per annum (far exceeding unskilled wages of £95 per annum), made up of match fees supplemented in many cases by coaching and ground staff positions. But even after this increase the average professional's pay only matched Alfred Mynn's income in the 1840s – and Mynn once, and possibly twice, went bankrupt without enjoying a lavish lifestyle.

The Cricket Statistician, December 1980.

†This was unlikely to have been a protest against Stephenson personally, who was an easy-natured, popular professional. It was probably caused more by frustration that the opportunity had gone to the south.

From *More Than A Game: The Story of
Cricket's Early Years*, 2008

Raymond Charles 'Crusoe' Robertson-Glasgow was born in the summer of 1901 in, confusingly, Edinburgh. A right-arm, faster-than-medium pace bowler, he would take 464 first-class wickets playing for Oxford University and Somerset in the 1920s and 30s. He later established himself as a widely read writer on cricket, whose work appeared in the *Daily Telegraph* and the *Sunday Times* as well as countless books. Wit and humour – the characteristics that made him so popular both as a man and as a cricketer – infuse his written word. Here he is describing his experiences in the press box (or media centre, as we are obliged to call it nowadays).

PRESS BOX

R. C. Robertson-Glasgow

Cricket reporting used to be a solemn affair, and the Press Box, anyhow at Lord's, recalled the Silence Room of a Carnegie Library in Scotland. Small wonder, then, that the reports emanating from these precincts were as severe as a written judgement from Chancery. Humour was almost unknown, and cricket was conveyed to the reading public with a gentility which seemed to imply a rebuke to hastier and more vulgar pastimes.

The champions and exemplars of this method were the Pardons, of whom Sydney Pardon was the ablest and most illustrious. The Pardon Reporting Agency began, and still carries on, the business of serving to the newspapers reports of the principal cricket matches. The Agency achieves a remarkable standard of accuracy and impartiality. The firm have also for long been responsible for collecting and editing *Wisden's Almanack*, probably the most reliable sporting handbook in the country. Sydney Pardon was editor of *Wisden* for thirty-five seasons, from 1891 to 1925. His writings were distinguished by integrity and lucidity, and his opinion, though he himself had no practical experience of first-class cricket, was much sought by high authority. But the psychology, as we should now call it, of the cricketer was wholly unexplored. Off the field he had no relevant existence. A dry objectivity was achieved, and decorum, at all costs, was preserved. In the hands of a master, for such Sydney Pardon undoubtedly was, this method justified itself. But, when debased by clichés and rank "journalese" it had little to commend it but its lack of impropriety. There were a few rebels. Of these, Freddy (F. B.) Wilson was the wittiest and most notable. He had strong natural ability at ball games, playing cricket for Cambridge against Oxford in 1902–3–4 and being captain in his last year. He also excelled at tennis and rackets. He played with a sort of casual brilliance which was later to be reflected in his writings, where he invented technical terms of his own, and delightfully explored the limbo between fact and fancy.

The pendulum has swung full distance. Dullness is feared and avoided. So, unfortunately, is fact. The News Room has invaded Sport, and, on the occasion of Test matches, the cricket correspondent is often reinforced by a columnist or news-hawk, who, with furrowed brow, scours hotels and pavilions on his dark and dubious assignments. The technique of the game now ranks far below the "story", and you will often hear reporters, at the end of a full day's cricket, lamenting that "nothing has happened". No one has fallen dead while taking guard, or been arrested while placing the field.

In my own reports of cricket matches, I tried for naturalism. Flippancy was never far absent, because cricketers, especially bowlers, need flippancy to live and to avoid going a little queer. I was doomed, therefore, to affront those to whom cricket is a quasi-religion. As old Podmore would have said, "the Admirals and Generals won't stand it". Well, I cannot answer for the higher ranks, but some of the Colonels were very angry, and wrote complaining about "inane asides and abominations" and demanding the immediate return of Sir Pelham Warner and his articles.

In the Press Box, I have always been attracted to the unknown. Who, for instance, was that devotee, silent as the Sahara and methodical as the ant, who attended matches for the sole purpose of keeping the score? Was he the cricket editor of "Vital Statistics"? And to what mysterious end did sit, melancholy and on the backmost bench, a drooping red moustache on a mottled face and enormous ears? Some said that he was a telephonist, but I don't think so. That moustache would have entangled itself in the instrument. I think he had stepped from the pages of Lewis Carroll; he was the illustration for "the wild man went his weary way to a strange and lonely pump". Perhaps "Old Ebor" might have solved such problems; but he was never one to give knowledge away.

I am glad I overlapped "Old Ebor", whose legal name was Mr A. W. Pullin; an able critic of the old and tawny school. It was he who should have had a famous Scoop at Lord's. The Australians were here; 1926. On the first day of the second Test Australia had scored 338 for 8 wickets. Early on the Monday morning it was discovered that someone had been careless about a hose-pipe, which had over-watered a large area of grass, including a segment of the pitch. "Old Ebor", who rose early, was first of the journalists on the scene, and he at once sent off a Press telegram to his Yorkshire Evening paper, describing the untoward incident; the Scoop Complete. Then he sat back in comfortable silence. Some hours later, a messenger-boy came into the Press Box and asked if a Mr Pullin or Bullin was present. "Well," said the boy after introduction, "I was to tell you that the telegraphist is very sorry but he can't read the writing in your message early this morning, and would you very kindly do it for him again?" It was then that "Old Ebor" broke silence.

H. J. (Bertie) Henley was the cricket correspondent of the *Daily Mail*, and also a member of the Kitchen Committee of the Surrey County Cricket Club at the Oval. Heavy, tall, even Falstaffian of aspect, Bertie loved controversy. Somewhere, I doubt not, he is still rapping his stick on the floor, and saying, "I don't agree". He had strong powers of exposition and a strange gift of being able to sketch with both hands at once. He said it was something to do with the hemispheres of his brain. He did not believe in watching all the cricket all the time. "The world is too much with us," he would say, "and too many facts clog the judgement." But he had a sixth sense for knowing what mattered, whether he saw it or not. Bertie was a defender of defensive play and of matches heroically saved, and he belaboured the Brighter Cricket School. "All sixes and sevens", he called them. He wrote his reports on paper that looked to be intended for less literary purposes, and scattered his notes round and round the free spaces on the score-card. When this was full, he would sometimes be seen gazing in a predatory sort of way at the white stiff collar of a colleague in front. He was never quite happy away from the Oval, where he knew the very gasometers by name. Ernie Hayes was his hero, and, when they met, the cricket could look after itself. For matches in distant parts he travelled with a

'Gerald darling, are you all right? The man at the
gate told me you'd just been caught in the gullet.'

bag of very small size and professional aspect. He loathed luxurious
hotels, preferring inns of unfashionable address but satisfactory
cellar. Bertie Henley cannot be replaced.

The Oval for H. J. Henley; for Major "Beau" Vincent of *The Times*,
Lord's. Not that there is anything pompous or conventional about
R.B.V. Far otherwise. He has a reverence, well concealed, for tradi-
tion; a belief in oligarchy; but he is no respecter of persons; nor of his
dentures, which sometimes live in his overcoat pocket. He goes to
Lord's in summer as he goes to Richmond Rugby ground in winter,

to meet his friends. These are his clubs, where he pursues leisure and his profession. Both are admirably done. His writing reflects the soul of cricket; its dignity and humour; its old age and perpetual youth; and he has a unique gift of transferring to print, without loss to either side, the inconsequent wisdom of conversation.

He is an authority on the inner life of Rye, and can tell you, better than books, about Henry James and E. F. Benson. His father was a memorable and loved law to himself as Secretary of the Rye Golf Club. Dacre Vincent had his own ideas, coincident with most of his members, as to what visitors should play golf at Rye, and he was not to be won over by important motor-cars and expensive golf-bags. His best friends were not safe from criticism. "You can always tell," he remarked one day, "when the Eton masters have been here; the wash-basins are left full of dirty water." To which the most famous of golfers among Eton masters, stung beyond bearing, replied, "I would have you know, Vincent, that, if seven people died, I should be a Viscount." I asked "Beau" what was his father's answer to that. "Oh," said "Beau", "he walked off into his office and addressed a few envelopes."

I know no stronger partisan than "Beau" for places and teams. He is not wholly answerable when Cambridge, for whom he played golf in the late Edwardian years, are pitted against Oxford. For many years too, he was unfavourable to Manchester as a venue for Test matches. Restlessness would seize him soon after the train left Euston, and he would prophesy a choice between sunstroke and death by drowning. It was in that citadel of Free Trade that we were ambling disjointedly one day when we saw two newspaper-posters, placed side by side. One said, "Read R. C. Robertson-Glasgow in the *Morning Post*"; the other, "Read *The Times* and see what really happened".

The turf at Manchester's Old Trafford, unlike the neighbourhood, is a thing of beauty, and has broken the hearts and loosened the tongues of many bowlers. The present groundsman, however, promised and, to some degree, performed a reformation. But the Press Box was surely designed by Einstein, after a Reunion Banquet of Mathematicians. From its rear-most seats, on the right, only a castrated version of the match is visible. One umpire, one batsman, and three or four fielders, according to the length and flexibility of the critic's neck. Hardly a quorum. The front row gives a more total view. Here sat Neville Cardus, of the *Manchester*

Guardian, slim, grey, contained; master of the rhapsodical style, cutting his sharp epigrams from the most amorphous material.

Like Bernard Darwin with golf, Cardus has made cricket-readers of many who would not walk across the road to see a stump fly or a ball driven against the sight-screen. Also like Darwin, he has the gift of fluency. "Page 48", he once said to me half way between the lunch and tea interval, "and I'll soon be off the Sports page and round to the Agony Column in front." But, amid his copiousness, he is eclectic. He scorns the common phrase, just as, in daily inter-course, he eludes the common man. I know a worthy fellow, a good cricketer, who, spotting Cardus in a crowd waiting for a train on the platform, went up to him and said, "Mr Cardus, I presume." This is not the right approach to Cardus. It did not succeed. On the great moments and the great cricketers, he has no equal. He is made for the mountain top, and he ranks among the English essayists.

Harry Carson, of the *Evening News*, was like a Bishop who had absentmindedly strayed into journalism. Tall, debonair, with white hair and ruddy complexion, he gave the Press Box a strong social uplift. Writing on cricket was one of his hobbies. He also dealt in Acrostics and Chess Problems. He was something of the same cut as Philip Trevor, C.B.E., formerly of the *Daily Telegraph*, an able and abundant writer, who once showed a startling contempt for the sensational at Manchester. This was in the match between Australia and South Africa during the Triangular Tournament of 1912. T. J. Matthews of Australia had done the "hat-trick" in the first South African innings. Near the close of play, with numbers 6, 7, and 8 of the second innings, he did it again. Trevor merely reported the second event as if it were some change of bowling. Neither Matthews' nor Trevor's feat is likely to be repeated. Harry Carson was a wise and witty talker, if a little hard to hear. Sometimes, too, the general sense was difficult to pick out of the volleys of "doncher knows" which punctuated his information. In compari-son, his writing lacked ornament, possibly because he under-rated the scope and desires of his readers. A man of great charm and kindliness, he was the author of much silent charity. In 1936 he went to Australia to report the Test matches; but the work and heat and travelling were too much for his advancing years, and, to the sorrow of his friends, he was struck down by illness.

Bill Pollock, of the *Daily Express*, like Bertie Henley, had dropped into cricket reporting from dramatic criticism. Bill was a benevolent, witty, leisurely man. He disliked hurry, disputes, and over-rapid drinking. For nearly all of which reasons he was oddly cast for his journalistic part. By nature gentle and reflective, he was called upon constantly to be writing something telling and brief. So, incapable of being lurid or unkind, he turned to light comedy; experimenting in puns and such-like quirkeries. But he was not afraid to criticize, and he once offended Herbert Sutcliffe by referring to the great man's over-lordly fielding at the Oval. Some days later, Sutcliffe and Pollock met at the latter's club, the Savage, where members of the Yorkshire team have been frequent and welcome guests. An introduction was, as they say, effected. After some rather sticky preliminaries Pollock remarked, "I did not know that cricketers were as touchy as actors." To which Sutcliffe answered, "Believe me, Mr Pollock, infinitely more so."

Bill Pollock's last illness was difficult and painful. He took it, as he had taken a switch-back life, with a wry smile. I connect him most with Brighton, and Maurice Tate bending vastly at short-leg, and The Old Ship Hotel; just as I connect Frank Thorogood with an inn in Gravesend, where we danced some solemn steps, which, he said, were a saraband, to mechanical music. Frank wrote for the *News Chronicle*, keeping notes of the cricket in a sort of Chinese shorthand of his own, and tucking away quarter-smoked cigarettes for some benevolent but undisclosed purpose. Each year he produced a handbook on first-class cricket, presenting a copy with up-to-date alterations and an air of proprietary apology.

Of Australian correspondents, Arthur Mailey is the most familiar on English grounds. He appears, like a parachutist, from nowhere, picks up the latest about our cricket, renews friendships, and withdraws without demonstration.

There was a blighted atmosphere about English cricket in summer 1934. The "Body-line" volcano had erupted, and, having been told not to do it again, had subsided into unintelligible mutterings. Nothing had been explained to the public. How, for instance, did Jardine stand with the oligarchy of control at Lord's? Was he to be vindicated as a hero, forgiven as a prodigal son, or cast away with gnashing and wailing? The England captain, then on tour with a Marylebone team in India, kindly solved one knot by announcing that he had no intention of playing in our forthcoming Tests against Australia. About the same time, a newspaper article appeared under Larwood's name in which he expressed the same decision as Jardine, only in more ample and rhetorical terms. Certain mandarins condemned the newspaper and Larwood for his outburst. But newspapers can hardly be blamed for interesting themselves and their readers in a matter of fervent public interest, nor Larwood for expressing himself in unequivocal terms after sustaining some five months of personal abuse.

In this imbroglio, the most hopeful sign was the presence of W. M. Woodfull as captain of the visiting Australian team. Bill Woodfull, in an office where character counts for even more than skill, stands as one of the greatest Test captains of all time. It is easy to be tactful for merely utilitarian reasons, but Woodfull's tact sprang from kindness and a true interest in others. As a slight instance, in 1930, on his first captaincy in England, when we were playing the Australians in the Folkestone Festival, he threw out a generous reference to a short spell of my bowling. I had taken no wicket and earned no praise. Cricketers remember little things like that. Not that Woodfull's name for benevolence depends from such insignificant hooks. He had the greatness to rise above quarrel and clamour. He could keep together pride and the personal touch. He rode the worst storm in the story of international cricket, and his stature grows with time.

We spent many hours of those 1934 Tests wondering under what new law or infringement of law Bradman and Ponsford might be removed from the wicket. Within the framework of Australian victory, these two champions were playing out a private match of their own. In bald arithmetic, Ponsford won by a short whisker, averaging 94.83 to Bradman's 94.75. It is the joy of the critics, when appraising a great player, to say why he is not quite to be compared with this or that hero of the past. When all else fails, they bring up the question of style. "Wonderful," they cry, "yes, very wonderful, but not so *beautiful* as so-and-so." So-and-so, in his day, of course had the same thing said about him. Thus, elusive perfection is chased ever back. Maybe Adam had an off-drive that made the Serpent weep for very delight.

Since the days when the other Sussex batsmen watched Ranji and C. B. Fry, I doubt if any cricket team has produced such a duet as Bradman and Ponsford; the lightning of Sydney and the thunder of Melbourne. In modern times, Hobbs and Sutcliffe, or Hobbs and Hammond, or Hammond and Woolley, or, we hope,

Compton and Edrich, might stand technical comparison with the Australian pair, but there is no evidence that any one of these had envy for each other, whereas Bradman and Ponsford, we have seen, pursued the individual championship without comment or relaxation. At the wicket, Bradman saw what needed to be done sooner than the others, and did it with more precision. He may or may not have equalled Trumper, Ranji, Macartney, Hobbs, Woolley, in sheer artistry. Such things are arguable. He was not Jovian, like Doctor Grace. He had not the splendour, the mien, of Hammond, who came from the pavilion like the *Victory* sailing to destroy Napoleon. But Bradman went on. He had one eye, as it were, on the heavens and the other on the ledger-book. In the whole game, he was the greatest capitalist of skill. Poetry and murder lived in him together. He would slice the bowling to ribbons, then dance without pity on the corpse. It has been objected that Bradman was fallible on a damaged pitch. He was. This is like saying that a man may slip when walking on ice. But the critics condemn him on one act of rashness against Verity. Verity himself knew better, and told me how Bradman, for over after over at Sheffield in 1938, played his sharpest spinners on a sticky pitch in the middle of the bat.

Bradman's pads and gloves seemed incidental, just a concession to custom; but Ponsford always suggested the old advertisement for Michelin tyres. His pads would have made a summer cottage for little Willie Quaife, and his square and muscular frame further bulged with indefinable shock-absorbers. Ponsford was a wonderful driver; like the earlier Hammond, he played most of his scoring strokes off the front foot. His bat looked horribly broad, and it weighed only four ounces under 3 lb. Against fast and rising bowling, he favoured the turn-about method when he feared a catch to the short-legs, tympanizing his ample back and buttocks. Against slow spin bowling he was near to infallibility, and seemed to sight the bias from the start of flight. His foot-work, for a heavyish man, was dainty and precise, and I recall a lesson he gave me, as I stood at short slip, on the playing of "Tich" Freeman. Freeman was bowling beautifully, with accurate length, clever flight, and acute spin; but Ponsford, with his crustacean sidle, kept playing the leg-breaks firmly off the middle to the covers. You needed to be near Ponsford to understand his full art. You could catch Bradman's mastery with half an eye, while guarding a pint of bitter from predatory hands. The talk is always of Bradman, but I doubt if the bowlers fancied themselves more against Ponsford. Either end was a headache and a marvel.

There were also Woodfull himself, ripening for retirement, but still a great stayer; Stanley McCabe, that gay genius who across the years and the miles had caught the sense of great English batsmen in times untrammelled and unperplexed; the classical W. A. Brown; the busy and competent A. G. Chipperfield. And all the bowling that mattered was done by the magician Grimmett and the unconquerable O'Reilly. Grimmett we thought we knew; but it was one thing to know, another to answer. No bowler of his kind has so accurately controlled the amount of spin imparted; English batsmen used to say that his top-spinner was born in hell.

Bill O'Reilly was new to England. At first, the critics were happy to find much to blame. He was vast and awkward. They searched about for metaphor and simile. There was mention of camels and windmills, of carpenter's rules unfolding. He came up to the wicket like a perambulating pump-handle. He ducked at delivery. But, soon, we had to confess his greatness or go out of business. O'Reilly was faster than is thought decent or practicable in leg-spin and googly bowlers. The size and strength of his hand could make the spin live with the pace. His variety was most difficult to detect. The post-mortem was monotonous and inconclusive. Off the field, he was a friend; as a bowler, he showed with all of him that batsmen are objects of loathing, forts to be stormed, enemies to be confounded by violence or ruse, erosion or subtlety. He wasted nothing. A ball let past by the batsmen was not a ball at all. He would attack Hammond's leg stump by the over and the hour. At Nottingham, in that first Test of 1934, he took 11 for 129, and put Australia's hand firmly on the urn of Ashes. He took 28 wickets at less than 25 each in the Test series, and he and Grimmett together took 53 of the 71 England wickets that fell. But he stands clearest in my memory and admiration at the Oval in the Australian disaster of 1938. For many hours he was the whole Australian attack. Fleetwood-Smith twiddled himself away into vanity. The opening bowlers opened nothing but the scoring; but on and on O'Reilly went, with no help but hope and no prop but the indomitable heart.

In 1934, only Maurice Leyland wholly answered O'Reilly and Grimmett. Leyland scored three centuries in these Tests. His was a broad-bottomed administration, body and mind. For strength of character and purpose and arm he comes second to none in his generation of cricket. "Jannock" was not enough for him. True, he excelled at heavy rescue; but, he was never dour just because dourness was a native tradition, an inescapable inheritance. I fancy he found relief and fullest expression in his own left-arm bowling. Jauntily, with a kick-up of the heels, he experimented with oriental spins, and accepted their frequent success with an air of modest pleasure and candid surprise.

Leyland was never finer than in his 110 that summer at the Oval. Australia had topped 700. Half of the England side went for about 150. Leyland refused to understand reasons, and batted as if only three hours were left to win a victory depending on him alone.

Frank Woolley was brought out for that match. As a player of strokes in County games he was still incomparable; hero of Canterbury; on every ground that he visited, a perpetual expectation and a frequent fulfilment of delight. At forty-seven, he made ten centuries in the Championship. Numerically, he had played himself into the Test. But it didn't do. The years can be cajoled, but not mocked. Ames, while helping Leyland with the batting, was suddenly bent double by a strain; and there was Woolley, keeping wicket with merely formal grace. We were hoping that fate would allow him, now if ever, an innings with stuff in it to remember; little enough, perhaps, if set against the inexorable quantity of the Australian masters; not an oratorio, only a melody sweetly played in tune. But Woolley just swished and was gone. He waved the wand, and the magic didn't work.

"Beau" Vincent and I drove back to Fleet Street to write, somehow, a column each; for readers who would already know the horrid truth. We were silent; except for interjections.

From *46 Not Out, 1948*

THE PRESENT DISCONTENTS

Neville Cardus

July 1923

When we went on with cricket again in 1919, after the war, bowling was so poor that batsmen were under little compulsion to learn the difficult art of scoring from a good attack. To get a decent number of runs a batsmen needed simply to stop the occasional dangerous ball that came his way; he could fatten his score from the long-hops and half-volleys. As he could depend on a constant supply of indifferent-length stuff, he required to take no risks with the occasional good bowling sent him, and it is no difficult matter for a batsman on a first-class wicket to stop an average good ball so long as he is not compelled to try to score from it. How different it was from this in the 1904–1912 period! (I purposely hark back no farther because I do not wish readers to imagine I am one of the old fogies who are continually declaring that things are not as good as they used to be. I wish readers simply to compare the impressions they get from cricket to-day with those they got from cricket a dozen years ago.) Suppose in, say, 1910 a batsman had never tried to score save when a rank bad ball was wheeled up to him: would he not have starved for runs from bright May till misty August? How many definitely loose balls could a batsman in those times look forward to in an afternoon from W. C. Smith, Blythe, Hirst, Dean, Tarrant, Mead of Essex, Rhodes, Arnold, Brearley, F. R. Foster, Haigh, to name a few? As everybody knows who knows cricket history at all, these bowlers did not give runs away to batsmen. And yet batsmen did contrive to hit these bowlers—and hit them harder than bowlers of this era are hit day by day.

It is true that the cricketers who got runs from these fine bowlers, and got them more quickly than runs are usually scored now, were such as P. F. Warner, K. L. Hutchings, H. K. Foster, Spooner, A. O. Jones, Jessop, Sharp, Woolley. Amongst batsmen of to-day it is difficult to think of any save Hobbs, Woolley, Hendren and Mead who have command of the wide range of strokes possessed by all those cricketers of 1910 just mentioned. Who in our cricket besides Woolley, Hobbs, Mead and Hendren may be said to be master of a full range of hits? The truth, as I have already suggested, is that it is not necessary for a batsman of the moment to learn *all* the strokes: the bowling he has to face does not challenge an extensive range of strokes. One or two simple hits, like the pull and the push "round the corner" to leg, will serve to get a man a century from average modern bowling. (Consider the century, for example, by Stevens against the Players at Lord's last summer.) The good balls that put in an appearance from time to time may, as we have seen, be carefully and negatively treated.

The low condition of English batsmanship in 1919 and 1920 was noted by many an old judge of the game, but their warnings were unheeded. "Jeremiahs!" said the batsmen, who then turned again to their half-volleys. But their fool's paradise was about to crash down and dusty disillusion rise up from the wreckage on our cricket fields. The Australians came in 1921 and forthwith smote our bowling hip and thigh, hitting runs with a fury that had never before been excelled by Australians in this country. Even Hill, Trumper, Darling, S. E. Gregory and Noble could not score as quickly and as prolifically as in 1921 the Australians scored against modern English bowling. And how did the English batsmen—who had been "brought up" on this bowling which the Australians flogged— how did they fare against the good-length stuff of Armstrong? I do not mention the routs of English batsmen before Gregory and Macdonald because I wish simply to show what happened to our batsmen as soon as they were tackled again on good wickets by a slow bowler, without much spin, but one who rarely bowled the bad length to which English cricketers had for a while been largely accustomed.

Armstrong in 1921 was, on his own confession, not half the bowler he was before the war: how could he have been, seeing that he was not only older but less mobile and also had lost a lot of his spin? Yet in 1921 Armstrong bowled over our county XI's whenever he felt urged to get wickets. Our batsmen could not score heavily from Armstrong in his declining years simply because, taking them in the lump, they had not for years been under the necessity of learning to hit good-length bowling. This is no fanciful theory; it is proved a point further by the success of Rhodes, who even in his veteran period can, without the superb spin of his young days, get wickets as cheaply as ever he did. Moreover, this theory is proved up to the hilt by the work in these days of the Yorkshire bowlers, who rarely meet a batsman with the power to hit them. The Yorkshire bowlers, under the strategical eye of Rhodes, jumped to the situation, and they have gone steadily to work with this philosophy in mind: "Batsmen have not for seasons past been forced to study the science of scoring off good-length stuff; they are merely content to stop it. Well, no mystery bowling for us; no 'googlies' and 'leg-spinners' in our team. We'll concentrate on length, length, length. Batsmen will not get any loose ones from us, and they will sooner or later be compelled to try to score from our good-length stuff. They will get out as soon as they try—because modern batsmanship has lost the knack of forcing runs for good bowling."

And throughout last summer we saw this philosophy beautifully put into action and justified. Cricketers tell you Yorkshire bowling cannot safely be hit. "Batsmen who try to drive Kilner will get out." What they ought to say is that the modern batsman will get out. And that is because he has few scoring strokes and because his foot-work is crude compared with the footwork of the average batsman of ten years ago. If any reader considers that this is an extravagant statement, and if he cannot from his own memories of pre-war cricket confirm it, let him consult any cricketer in the land who has played both pre-war and post-war cricket. Why *should* the batsman who attempts to drive Kilner inevitably be dooming himself to destruction? Is Kilner a better left-handed bowler than Blythe was? Yet Blythe on a good wicket was constantly getting driven to the boundary. Last summer, at one period, Kilner had bowled some 270 maidens in some 720 overs; in 1910 Blythe could bowl only 274 maidens in 1941 overs.

Study the footwork of the average modern batsman and you ought not to be long before finding out why he cannot score freely from a good-length bowler. As soon as an average batsman to-day sees the beginning of the bowler's run—before he even knows what kind of ball he is about to get—his right foot instinctively goes over the wicket to the off-side—a movement which places his legs in front of the stumps and sends his left shoulder swinging away towards the on-side. Now this position is admirably contrived to bring into play "the second line of defence"—that is, the pads; and without the use of the pads, seemingly, batsmen nowadays are not confident of their ability to cope with good-length balls. But plainly this position prevents a batsman from exploiting most of the remunerative hits. If your right foot is across the wicket to the offside as the ball pitches and your left shoulder is pointing rather towards square-leg, with your chest full to the bowler—well, then, you cannot possibly cut, or off-drive, or drive straight, or drive powerfully to the on. All that you can do now is to turn the ball round to the leg-side, or, if you possess wonderful fore-arm strength, push the ball for mild runs to the off-side. The modern batsman, of course, does not get into this foot-tied position for every ball he comes across; if he did we should never see a good hit in cricket to-day—and of course we do. If he finds a bowler against him who is not too accurate, our batsman gains the confidence to "open out" whatever of style he owns. My point is that as soon as our modern average batsman knows that a good-length attack will be directed at him unfailingly, he then falls into a position which roots him more or less helplessly to the earth. He is not possessed of an elaborate foot-play that works instinctively and that is because (to repeat and to clinch!) he has not been compelled by continuous acquaintance with length bowling to master that extensive foot-play without which good-length bowling cannot safely be scored from. Yorkshire bowlers to-day are masters of the length ball as no other bowlers in the country are, and they are harder to hit than were such men as Hirst, Peel, Jackson, Haigh and Booth! "O tempora, O mores!" as Smee declaims in *Peter Pan*.

From *Days in the Sun, 1948*

DONALD BRADMAN

Richie Benaud

I doubt that there has ever been a batsman of more value to any side than Bradman, even up to the moment of his retirement in 1948. As an old bowler it makes my fingers itch to think of bowling at the opposition with 500 and 600 run totals at my back, and the knowledge that once in every three times he went to bat Bradman made a hundred. Over the years there have been comparisons made with Trumper, Hobbs, Hammond and Macartney. Remarkably only twice did Australia win Test matches in which Bradman did not score a century and I can only say that it must have been a joy to be in the same side as him, even if some of the glory that would normally go to the other ten players would find its way on to Bradman's shoulders. The story goes the rounds that in the timeless Test in 1938 at the Oval England had made 903 for seven by tea on the third day. But the only reason the closure was applied was that Bradman broke his ankle and had declared himself unfit to bat—simply because 903 might not have been sufficient for victory had he been able to get on the field. The authority for that—*Wisden*—and, whilst believing that the writers of this great cricket journal have a good sense of humour, I am prepared to believe that on this occasion they are deadly serious.

I first saw Bradman in that already mentioned match of 1940 when he batted late in the day and then was dismissed by O'Reilly the following day. I should think I was too young then really to be able to define genius whether with bat or ball and it is true that Grimmett impressed me more in that match than did Bradman. I little thought then that when I grew older I would come under his eagle eye as a selector and critic and eventually be sitting over the dinner table with him discussing the merits of a 1963 Henscke claret. I really know very little about him as a cricketer for his greatest days were over when I began watching Test matches in 1946 and he retired from the game when the 1948 side came back from England in the same season as, possessed of a keen eye and high backlift, I made my own debut in first-class cricket. More's the pity! I'd have given a lot to play in a side under Bradman and to be able to watch the master at work, whether with bat or in the field of captaincy, but I have managed the next best thing and picked up a lot about the game from him off the field.

I find him a remarkable man. I have heard a number of stories from not disinterested parties that indicate when young he was of cold and uncompromising disposition but, as one who generally likes to make up his own mind about things, I balanced this with conversations with people who knew him just as well as the anti-brigade. I have no doubt that in his young days he was at times most uncommunicative and I am sure that he must have been under tremendous pressure from the time he came into the game to the start of the Second War. He was *the* batsman, in fact *the* cricketer in the world, and everyone wanted to know him, write about him and be associated with him in some way. Some of the players of his own early era leave no doubt that their feelings for him are less than lukewarm and I can imagine that his emergence as the one great cricketer of his time, with the rest slightly behind, would scarcely have endeared him to any lacking the backbone to accept this situation. No doubt some of the acid had a basis in fact for I can't imagine a young Bradman, or a young anyone for that matter, doing all the right things all the time. He could well have been a difficult man but I scarcely think that anyone could be as difficult as he has been credited with being and still make as many friends as he has done.

There are very few cricketers who have ever played the game who have had a particular method of attack devised purely to keep them in check. Only one, Bradman, has ever had an attack such as Bodyline devised—an attack that was to have repercussions throughout the empire in all fields, not just on the cricket field. I never saw Bodyline but I have read a number of accounts of it and I should think it is the most unfair method of playing the game ever produced by any cricket team. I have read the brilliant book by J. H. Fingleton written in 1946 wherein he leaves little doubt that he considered Bradman's methods of countering Bodyline well divorced from those that should have been used by any tenacious Australian batsmen. *Wisden* at the same time said of Bodyline "a method of bowling was evolved—mainly with the idea of curbing the scoring propensities of Bradman—which met with almost general condemnation among Australian cricketers and spectators, and which when something of the real truth was ultimately known in this country, caused people at home—and many of them famous in the game—to wonder if the winning of the rubber was, after all, worth this strife". Bradman in that Test series made 0, 103 not out, 8, 66, 76, 24, 48 and 71 and, if he had made them in 1968 as a normal batsman, would no doubt have been congratulated on having a great series. He averaged over 50 which is the norm these days but, by his own standards, he had failed. I know of Bodyline only what I have been told and I am delighted never to have seen it in modern day cricket.

All this was pre-war stuff and, apart from that one Sheffield Shield match in 1940, I didn't see Bradman play until the England–Australia Test series in Australia in 1946. He had been dogged by ill-health and it was very doubtful if he would turn out for Australia in that series—eventually he did so, as usual with tremendous success. I would think his decision to play cricket in 1946 was probably one of the hardest he ever had to make in his career. He had tremendous offers from newspapers all over the world to cover the Test series but in the end it became a question of duty to him and Australian cricket got the benefit of his decision. I can remember reading stories of that 1946–7 tour, and reading the accounts of the play from journalists and ex internationals, and wondering at the "edge" to some of the comments made about this man I had never met but had always thought of as the greatest player in the world.

His career ended in 1948 just as mine was beginning and I first met him in the 1949 season. That he should have gone to England in 1948 at all was in itself a rather remarkable thing. Johnny Moyes tells how, when the team was to be chosen at the end of the Fifth Test match in Melbourne, he and Bill Jeanes were with Bradman in his room when he produced from his pocket a statement indicating that he was available for the English tour but that on his return he would retire from cricket of all grades.

The 1948–9 season then was to be the first since 1928 that had got under way without Bradman's playing influence. There was no real reason for him to go to England but, in conversation with him, I am certain that he felt he owed something to the game in both Australia and England and that his form was probably good enough to get through the tour. I am equally certain he had no real desire to spend six months playing cricket six days a week and that he could have commanded a tremendous fee just for sitting in the Press box writing about the players he had instead decided to lead. He did write on the 1953 and 1956 tours after he had led that 1948 team on an unbeaten tour where Australia easily retained the Ashes. That would have been a most important thing for Bradman simply because he was keen on winning and he believed that the game should always be played hard and fairly. But he must have also derived great satisfaction from the tremendous boost to the game in England and could satisfactorily retire at the end of that tour knowing the job he had set out to do had been completed successfully in every way.

There must have been great pressure on him as a player throughout his career, never more so, I would imagine, than when he made his comeback in 1946. At 28 in the Brisbane Test match the Englishmen thought he was caught at gully by Ikin off Voce. There was enormous publicity given to this incident where apparently the umpire said immediately "not out" to the appeals for a catch. Reading back on the incident, it seems very similar to the day Kline caught Cowdrey in Brisbane when those who wrote of the incident were in the new Press box. This is in a much better position than the old Press box which was in the old stand, a long way from the actual play. In the 1958 Cowdrey incident Cowdrey didn't believe he had been caught at short backward square leg off Meckiff but, on appeal, and after McInnes had consulted square leg umpire Hoy, he was given out. Hoy was standing a few yards from where Kline took the catch. We were playing five on the on side to Meckiff at this stage and I was at deep mid on with another player at short mid wicket covering the single. From where I was I had no chance of seeing whether or not Kline had taken the catch and, with Cowdrey dragging his bat and looking over his shoulder, I moved in quickly to ask Kline and Grout if it had been a fair catch. Kline confirmed he had caught the ball and Grout said it had been deflected directly into the fieldsman's hands—but there were still a large number of those watching from the Press box who would have it that the ball had hit the ground, and they were twice as far away as I was at mid on.

But this was only a minor incident compared to anything concerning Bradman and his 1946 comeback was made even bigger news, with a variety of people insisting that it had not been a bump ball caught at gully by Ikin. In fact, everything Bradman did was big news from the time he stepped on to a cricket field to make his first first-class century. Nowadays he lives in a pleasant home in Adelaide where he is President of the South Australian Cricket Association. He plays golf off a handicap of three, frequently being under the card and taking golf balls off hapless interstate visitors almost at will. He is a director of a number of companies but no longer has a seat on the Stock Exchange where he was in business for a number of years. At weekends occasionally he goes to a small farm in the Mount Lofty hills where he will clear scrub and trees, partly for the obvious purpose of clearing them but also to retain the fitness that he never seems quite to have lost. I commented to him one day recently about the length of his drives on the golf course and he put this down largely to the physical work he had been doing. He is a sound judge of good wine, occasionally producing a special bottle of some obscure claret for dinner guests, but much of his time now is taken up in the business of helping run Australian and South Australian cricket. He was always something of a perfectionist as a batsman, even in an unorthodox way, and he strives for perfection in administration as well.

Some 20 years ago a writer with some foresight suggested that once Bradman retired from the game there would be an inevitable slump. Perhaps this accounts in some measure for the desperate search since his retirement for "another Bradman". Harvey never filled the bill because he was a left-hander, they talked of Craig, who may have been another Jackson but never in a million years would be another Bradman, and they grasped O'Neill as the one most likely to follow the great man. Since then Walters and Sheahan have come on the scene and borne the same comparisons, particularly after Walters made a century in each of his first two Tests against England.

All the talk of who was the greatest player the world has ever seen seems to centre round players like Bradman, Trumper, Hobbs, Macartney and Hammond, but it is interesting that young players are rarely described as, say, another Hobbs or another Macartney, or even another Trumper. The thing the public and publicity mediums desperately want is only another Bradman and not another anyone else. I think probably over the years feelings have changed greatly towards players who are star turns in the game. If Bradman were playing now I have a feeling that he would be far more welcome in any team than when he was in his own hey-day. Modern day players may or may not be as good as those who have gone before and I am not prepared to argue that now or with any of the good players of the past. But, from what I have heard and from what I have read, the fact that Bradman was pre-eminent in his era did not necessarily make him the most popular man in the side.

I have a feeling that in modern days there is more effort made to make sure a team runs smoothly and team members themselves are treated as a godsend that they should have one great player in a side able to make more runs than anyone else, and therefore get the team more publicity and win them more matches. I know one young cricketer in Australia, a potentially great player, who in recent years has got more than his share of publicity, sometimes deservedly and sometimes not. I also know that his team treats him as a valuable commodity and that team mates and others have been eager to help in making sure that his future in the game is secure. I mark this down as good teamwork and correct appreciation of a player's skill.

I am always amused by criticisms of the better players and often have a quiet chuckle when anti-Bradman hour begins. The ones who produce the remarks and tell the tales could be thought nothing but paragons of virtue themselves from the way the stories go. I have never heard a Bradman critic, for instance, tell much of a story against himself so I can only assume that those who like to produce the information and story that blasts the Don have themselves led nothing more nor less than blameless cricket lives. It is not so, of course, and I suppose the fact that even 20 years after his retirement there are those willing to have a dash at him indicates that he is still a large-sized figure in the cricket world. On figures anyway, he is the most remarkable player there has ever been and I doubt very much that anyone will ever approach him. But, in the time I have known him, he is a very human person who has never objected to adverse criticism if it is factual. If it is personal and impinges on his private life then he does as I would, or, as his critics would, and rightly resents it.

They say he has made a lot of money out of cricket and I have no doubt that he has made more money out of the game than most other individuals who have played. He has also put back in ten times as much money in gate receipts and, at the same time, has sacrificed a great deal for the game. I suppose he could have got £12,000 sterling to cover the 1948 series for a paper and could have done the same in 1946–7 when M.C.C. visited Australia. The same applied in 1961 but he had other things to do for each tour, all of them connected with the welfare of Australian cricket and, in the case of the 1948 team, the welfare of English cricket as well. He has a remarkably analytical mind with regard to cricket and I presume he was the same in business otherwise he would hardly have been successful on the Stock Exchange.

One of the most important things I find with him is that he is not dogmatic either with regard to players or situations in the game. None of this business I hear so often of "so and so's not much good" or "Bill Smith will never make a really good player". He is always prepared to look for the best from every player and to look at him in the light of his value to a team rather than whether or not he is a star. It is the same with situations, in that there is no dogmatic statement of right or wrong, but he is prepared to approach both sides of a question and then give an opinion, instead of coming out with a blunt one sentence verdict that brooks no argument. Lesser lights in the administration world in Australia will condemn a young cricketer to oblivion in a few short words, whether it be for a lack of technique or purpose. They would listen to Bradman occasionally giving a run-down on the player's ability in each department of the game and then drawing a line on his lack of skill in others. The latter is always accompanied by the provision that he might well improve "if we can concentrate on helping him in some particular way".

A remarkable man—I have no doubt he has always been a remarkable man—but, in the time I have known him, he has added much to my knowledge of cricket and to my enjoyment of the game.

From *Willow Patterns, 1969*

5 AUGUST 1961

RICHIE BENAUD

SIR – A friend of mine sent a copy of Richie Benaud's book *Way of Cricket* to Old Trafford during the fourth Test match, explaining it was for a sick friend in hospital and requesting Benaud's autograph. The book was received back by return of post, duly autographed by the entire touring side, together with a 'Get-Well' card bearing the message: 'Wishing you a speedy recovery to Health and Happiness – Richie Benaud'.

Great cricketer and captain the man undoubtedly is. By such a simple personal gesture amid the worries of leading Australia in the crucial match of the Test series does he also show himself to be a gentleman in the truest sense.

N.A. Thompson
London SE19

From *Not In My Day, Sir: Cricket Letters
to the* Daily Telegraph, *2011*

The voice is always stage one of commentary (there is no stage two if the voice offends) and John Arlott had the perfect voice for cricket commentary. His slow thoughtful delivery, Hampshire burr and beautiful choice of words, punctuated by surprisingly long pauses (to the modern ear) with just the susurrus of the crowd drifting through the open window of the commentary box, was timeless and sublime. The poet in him supplied a descriptive power replete with wry humour that painted a picture of what was before him probably better than anyone before or since.

INDIAN SUMMER

John Arlott

Record Days: The Oval: Banerjee and Sarwate

Surrey v India
At Kennington Oval, May 11, 13 and 14.
India won by 9 wickets.

What an ugly place the Oval is! Love it if you will for the sake of Richardson or Hayward, Hobbs or Fender, Fishlock or Gover, find it, as I do, dignified by the cricket of D. J. Knight, but man may not love the Oval for itself alone. When I was a little boy the tepid lemonade at the Oval was nearer warm than any other tepid lemonade in England: and the bookstall sells books which are not cricket books. I don't mind their not being cricket books so much as their being non-cricket books which I don't like. I always experience at the Oval the feeling of unease at my back that I used to experience when a neighbour (who knew I stole his apples) was watching me from his window as I went down the road. Perhaps the ghost of Craig the Surrey poet does not approve of cricket commentators.

India batted first on Saturday with Hazare promoted to number two and Modi to number three. Bedser dismissed them both for 0.

Then Gul Mahomed, with a stride longer than his legs would seem likely to achieve, joined Merchant. While Merchant inspected the Oval wicket, the bowling of Gover and Bedser and the general state of cricket in his usual fashion, Gul enjoyed himself. Flashing an impudent left-hander's bat outside his off stump he sent the ball careering through every angle between cover and slip to bring the fieldsmen to their toes but no catch to hand. He made a crowd-delighting 89, and Merchant an irreproachable 53 but, despite the retirement of Gover with an injury after bowling only seven overs, at two minutes past four the India total was 205 for nine wickets and junior Surrey supporters were discussing in high voices the possibility of a century by Fishlock. At three minutes past four Banerjee joined Sarwate: authentically numbers ten and eleven, both their scores stood at 0. Three minutes before half-past twelve on Monday, when Parker bowled Banerjee, the India total was 454, Banerjee 121, Sarwate 124 not out. Their last-wicket partnership had yielded 249 runs. This was a record for English cricket, the highest partnership ever recorded by numbers ten and eleven, the first time that numbers ten and eleven had both made centuries and a record for a touring side. Even more impressively, the stand was chanceless; Sarwate sent one streaky shot through slips but no catch went to hand. The two men batted capably and correctly, defending well against Bedser who bowled industriously, and scoring, chiefly in front of the wicket, by strokes made out of confidence and with no trace of last-wicket anxiety.

The effect of this stand was at once apparent when Surrey commenced their innings. Despite a strong innings by Fishlock each of the five bowlers used took wickets, Nayudu performed the hat-trick and, for the first time, the fielding was uniformly eager: Surrey totalled 135. Following on, Surrey made a brave fight with a first-wicket stand between Fishlock and Gregory (100) of 144 but Sarwate, who had not bowled in the first innings, took five wickets for 54 and India needed only 20 to win. It was a little sad that, when Merchant took Sarwate in with him to open the second innings, the little Maharastrian should have been out for 1. India won their first victory by nine wickets and emerged from the match a confident team. The last-wicket stand of Banerjee and Sarwate changed the team's outlook from that of sixteen newcomers, to that of a team playing the game at which they excelled in their own country.

∼

S. Banerjee

Banerjee was the commentator's joy: in a uniformly capped and sweatered team, he, apart from being its largest member, was most likely to be hatless, or executing a little dance or talking to his neighbour and punctuating his speech with grins.

Banerjee was twenty-three when he came to England with the 1936 Indian team as second-string to that massively hostile fast bowler, Nissar. He was young and strong and willing to bowl for long spells: a useful fast-medium bowler. Ten years of life in India, with cricket a week-end matter and often with war-work to prevent him from training, had done little to make him a more effective bowler. He had put on weight and he tired more easily; it seemed that back and stomach muscles were not in sufficiently good trim to stand up to prolonged spells of bowling which had to forge pace out of slow wickets. So Banerjee played in none of the 1946 Test Matches, but he had a magnificent spell of bowling against Middlesex in August and he shared in a last-wicket partnership at the Oval which may well stand as a record for many years. As a batsman he was often more than useful in a crisis, defending with an honest straight bat and hitting hard in front of the wicket. In the field lack of pace and tiredness betrayed him too often. On his good days he was good to watch, on his great day at the Oval it was impossible not to rejoice with him: I think he enjoyed his trip.

C. T. Sarwate

In Indian cricket it is a custom to use opening batsmen merely to see the shine off the ball, saving the best batsmen for number four or five (thus Merchant rarely opens for Bombay nor Mushtaq Ali for Indore). Sarwate opens the innings for Holkar but his legitimate place in this India team's order was in the last four. Slight, with large brown eyes and an engagingly boyish smile, Sarwate won his place as a spin bowler. He delivers the ball with a good sideways action, the ball looking large in his small hand. His stock ball is the leg-break, which he turns sharply and at fair speed. He does not bowl the googly, relying for variety on a straightforward off-break which is not always so easily detectable as one would expect. Sarwate does

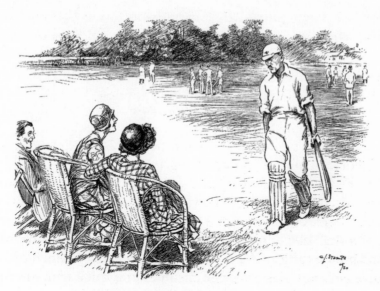

Fond wife (first ball, first wicket). 'That is nice, darling;
now you'll be able to enjoy the cricket with us.'

not vary his flight to any marked degree but his trajectory is usually
low enough to prevent all but the quickest-footed batsmen from
coming down the wicket to him. He rarely defeated class batsmen
during the tour, though he could compel them to some degree of
defence, but against batsmen of the calibre of the last five in most
county teams, he could be, and often was, absolutely deadly. More
variety, greater development of tactical knowledge and some greater
degree of control may make him—he is only twenty-six—a dangerous spin bowler.

For one of his slight stature he batted powerfully, hitting hard
between mid-on and mid-off and to square leg. In the field he was too
often caught on his heels; he started slowly and lacked confidence in
catching, particularly when placed near the wicket. The Oval match
was his great game, when he scored a sensational hundred and took
five wickets for 54 runs in the only innings in which he bowled.

From *Indian Summer, 1947*

Cricket has been played in Afghanistan since the nineteenth century, when it was introduced by British soldiers during the Anglo-Afghan Wars. It would be another one hundred years before the game would reassert itself as Afghan refugees redis-covered the game in neighbouring Pakistan. On their return home the game remained popular until banned – along with all other sports – by the Taliban. However, in 2000 the Taliban, in a bizarre move, successfully applied to the ICC to become an affiliate member.

Timeri N. Murari, who is an award-winning writer, film-maker and playwright, sets his novel in war-torn Kabul as the Taliban make their propaganda-minded application to join the ICC; thereafter he explores the awful ramifications of living under the Taliban's perverse rule through the eyes of a spirited cricket-mad young woman who sees the opportunity to escape the horrors of her oppressed life by coaching her brother's cricket team to win the first and only Taliban-sponsored Afghan tournament.

The novel's heroine, Rukhsana, tells her team that violence has no place in cricket. If that's so, someone replies, then 'cricket will never become popular here'.

CRICKET AND THE TALIBAN

Timeri N. Murari

The Stadium

They were in the front hall and I immediately noticed the despair-ing hunch of their shoulders as they paced in the narrow space.

"Hoshang knows the guard at the stadium," Parwaaze burst out. "He told Hoshang there is an official state team in the tournament. We won't have a chance to win against it."

"I went to the stadium just to check," Hoshang said. "They're practicing there. The team has a Pakistani cricketer named Imran teaching them."

"It's not Imran Khan, is it?" I asked in apprehension. He was one of Pakistan's best cricketers. "A tall man, well built …"

"No. This Imran's small and quite round."

"What difference does that make?" Jahan cut in. "They'll win."

"Why should they just because they have a professional coach?" I wasn't in the mood for their pessimism. "He still has to teach them how to play, just as I'm teaching you. You have to beat them, that's your only chance. We'll watch them tomorrow before we panic."

I reached over and straightened each one's shoulders, forcing them to stand straight.

"That's not our main worry," Parwaaze said with anxiety. "They will fix it so their team wins."

"How can they, with an ICC observer? They have to stick by the rules, and you have to believe in yourselves and win the match."

He looked at me with pity. "It's the Talib, Rukhsana," he said as they went out.

Ghazi Stadium was the venue for our cricket matches and the eleven of us squeezed into an old Toyota taxi to get there. I sat on Jahan's lap, holding the passenger door closed, my *lungee* crammed down on my head and my *hijab* up to my eyes, as an added precaution, to protect me from the driver. It was cheaper than the bus.

I shivered with fear when I saw the stadium again. The Talib regularly executed people during the intervals of the football matches.

The main entrance rose like a cooling cliff of ice, and was striped with red pillars. Only Talib officials entered through the wide entrance. The huge Olympic sign of five rings was framed high on the cliff, mocking us with the pretense that we were a sporting nation.

This time the road into the stadium was deserted except for a lone guard, a young man with a cane, who stood at the gate. Hoshang and he greeted each other warmly—they played on the same football team.

"It's good to see you all," the guard said cheerfully. "It gets lonely here. But you must leave before night comes."

"Why?" Royan asked, though we had no intention of remaining that long.

The guard lowered his voice. "The spirits of the dead executed here sit in the stands and call out to each other when the sun sets."

"You've seen these s-spirits?" Qubad asked nervously.

"I have heard them. I hide out here and pray they never see me."

"What do they say?" Atash asked, also uneasy.

"They don't speak in Dari or Pashtu. They talk in the language of the dead."

"I don't believe that," Parwaaze said as we climbed the narrow steps into the stadium.

"Why not?" I said and shivered, along with the others. "Where else can they go?"

Apart from the covered stand by the main entrance, the stadium was open to the sky. It was oval shaped, a shallow saucer, and above the rim rose Paghman to the west and Maranjan to the east. A baleful sun, hazy with dust, watched over us. A neglected dirt track, with faded lane markings, surrounded the football pitch.

Five months ago, Parwaaze had come as my *mahram* for an execution in this stadium. Mother refused to allow Jahan to accompany us. Normally, women were not permitted at public gatherings, but the government made an exception for the execution of the murderer Zarmina.

The buses were packed—even the women's section behind the drab, dusty curtain—and all along the road, crowds moved steadily toward the stadium. We had to get out of the bus and walk the last stretch to the stadium entrance. On both sides of the road were carts selling fresh fruit, smoky kebabs, naan, and children's cheap toys. I tried to judge the mood of the crowd. Some were excited, with expectation, talking and laughing; many more were silent and solemn, even fearful.

The Taliban herded us along to the gate, wanting us to hurry and not miss even a moment of their grand spectacle.

The crowd was funneled to other entrances, and Parwaaze protected me, pushing his way through the mass of people going up the narrow steps leading to the terraced seating area. There was barely a seat to spare, and we pushed our way down to the front and squeezed into a space next to a woman. I looked toward the covered stand, filled with important Talib officials, enjoying a convivial afternoon of entertainment, and then across the football field. Three Land Cruisers were parked at different positions and Talib fighters stood beside them facing the crowd, holding their guns. At either end of the football pitch were the goalposts, sagging in the center from the weight of the many men who'd been hanged there, kicking and struggling. Dark patches spotted the grass, blood being no substitute for water.

Taliban Execute
Mother Of Five Children

Today, a crowd of around 25,000 people has gathered, many coerced by the police, to watch the Talib execute Zarmina, the mother of five children. She was accused of murdering her husband by beating him to death with a hammer. Her husband, Alauddin Khwazak, a policeman, had also owned a shop in north Kabul. Their marriage was arranged when she was sixteen and it had grown into love. She had one-year-old twins, Silsila, a female, and a male, Jawad; another son, Hawad, age eleven; and two other daughters, Shaista, fourteen, and Najeba, sixteen.

The government told everyone that the strain of the violent events in the country had affected Alauddin Khwazak, and by participating in the continued brutality, his mood had grown darker and threatening. He started to beat Zarmina frequently in front of the children. The elder girls, no longer able to bear to see their mother abused and mistreated, decided to kill their father. Najeba mixed a sleeping potion into his night meal, and when he slept, she killed him with a hammer. Zarmina claimed a robber had broken into the house and killed him.

The Taliban judge did not believe her story. To protect her beautiful daughters, Zarmina confessed to the crime when she was tortured in prison, beaten continuously with cable wire, the normal method of torturing women who could have broken a Taliban law. Although the government claimed the murder took place a few months ago, my sources informed me that Zarmina had been in prison for the last few years, tortured and starved. Her daughters had taken her food daily, until the day they vanished.

According to custom, the two elder girls and the boy were left in the custody of Khwazak's brother, a Talib supporter. Two months ago, he told Zarmina that he had sold her beautiful daughters Shaista and Najeba for around 300,000 Pakistani rupees each to a brothel in Khost, on the Pakistan border. Zarmina had cried in despair, knowing she would never see her beloved daughters again, and beat her head against the prison walls.

On this cold November day in 1999, an open jeep entered the stadium. Zarmina, in her blue burka, stood in the back, supported by two Talibs. The crowd remained silent as the jeep circled the stadium. Then we heard the thin cries of her twin children coming from somewhere in the crowd, calling out to her, "Maadar, Maadar ..." Her head turned, searching for her children in the crowd. "Silsila ... Jawad," she said, trying to comfort them, but she was silenced by her captors. As if this was a sporting event, an announcer broke the silence. "Zarmina, daughter of Ghulam Hasnet, is to be executed for killing her husband with a hammer." The jeep stopped. The guards carried Zarmina down from it and escorted her to the goalposts. They forced her to sit, but she struggled to crawl away. She could see little through her burka.

The crowd now awakened. "Spare her ... spare her ..." they called out, but the Talib ignored the chants. The crowd fell silent. Zarmina tried to crawl away again, a moving blue bundle. A tall Talib came to stand behind her with his rifle. His hand was unsteady. His first shot missed her, though he was only a few feet away. As she could not sit or kneel without falling over, Zarmina cried out, "Someone, please take my arms." No one moved to help her.

The Talib took a step forward, aimed more carefully, and fired a 7.62-millimeter bullet into her head. It was a flat sound and we could barely hear it. The executioner was Zarmina's brother-in-law, the one who had sold her daughters into prostitution. (SENT BY LBW)

The crowd was silent, only the shuffle of feet was heard as we flowed out of the stadium, each cocooned in his own thoughts, and we avoided all eye contact with strangers. Even those who had come for the "entertainment" remained quiet.

We waited until we were some distance from the stadium.

"I feel sick," I whispered as a huge wave of nausea surged up into my mouth. I bent over and, hurriedly lifting my burka, puked on the street. It had been waiting from the moment I heard the children cry out for their mother. I was vomiting out my uncontrollable rage at what I had witnessed. My throat and stomach hurt as nothing heaved out. I remained bent like an old crone and waited until the wave receded. I felt Parwaaze's sympathetic hand resting on my back and finally straightened and returned to my faceless anonymity under the burka.

Parwaaze looked around before he burst out, "There were thousands of us, only a few Talibs, and we could have rushed down and saved her. Rukhsana, you must not write anything."

"I have to. I can't have her death on my hands or in my mind."

We remained silent on the bus going home and parted at my gate without speaking anymore, burdened by melancholy. I told Mother and Jahan every detail.

"Does conscience exist anymore?" I asked Mother.

"Not as far as I can see. In Dostoevsky's novel *Crime and Punishment*, Raskolnikov's punishment, at first, is not the state's punishment for his crime of killing the moneylender but is his own conscience. His conscience haunts him through his life until, no longer able to live with it, he surrenders to the police and confesses his crime …"

"But that's in a novel," I protested. "The brother-in-law will not even think anymore of the woman's life he's taken. He will sleep peacefully, even as other murderers sleep like innocents."

"Conscience controls our impulses to do harm," she said, taking hold of my hand to comfort me. "Our religions are meant to instruct us in what is right and what is wrong, but they can be misinterpreted, words twisted in their meanings, by those who wish to justify their killings in the name of their religion and in the name of God. Conscience does and must exist among us, as otherwise the whole world would go up in flames. You must believe in it, as I know you possess it. Never lose it."

That night, in the secrecy of my bedroom, I wrote the story, and spent half the night trying to fax it from Father's office to my contact in Delhi, the telephone sullenly unresponsive until nearly dawn, when it came to life. I disconnected, hid the modem and computer, and took to my bed. I was sick for two days after witnessing Zarmina's murder and cried for her lost daughters.

Now, I watched three men lethargically cut the grass for the wicket in the center of the football field.

It would be an uneven pitch with a variable bounce, it would take spin because of the surface and runs would be hard to get. Remembering Zarmina, I wondered whether the dead would awaken to watch the match. Would they recognize the particular black patch of grass on which a ball landed, and think that is where they had died?

From an entrance at the opposite side we saw five men drift in and take their places in the stands. I thought I recognized Azlam as one of them, and paid no further attention. There was another group of six men also watching the government's team practicing their game in the nets. Jahan, Parwaaze, Qubad, and I sat together, the others of our team scattered around as if we were just idlers, passing the time of the day, with little else to do but watch a new sport. But we weren't idle. I had coached them to study every batsman and bowler, watch for their strengths and weaknesses, and to remember everything they saw. I jotted down notes in my book.

Parwaaze pulled out a scrap of newspaper, torn out of the *Kabul Daily*. "See ... the preliminary cricket matches will take place on Saturday and ..."

I took the brief report. "... the final match will be played on Sunday the twenty-third and the winning team will be sent abroad for further training."

"It doesn't say Pakistan."

"Abroad can only be Pakistan," Parwaaze insisted. "Where else is abroad?" He looked across the stadium.

He turned his attention to the team practicing. "What do you think? Are we as good?"

There were thirteen on the state team, young men around the same ages as my cousins, dressed in green tracksuits. Only one man was immaculate in white trousers and a cream shirt, with a cap pulled low over his face to protect him from the sun. The coach. He was portly, bearded too, and he strode busily among his team. From the size of his paunch, he must have been a spin bowler. Pakistan had great spinners, and fast bowlers too, but this one in particular didn't have the build for speed.

They also had professional equipment—a few real cricket bats, many cricket balls, pads, and gloves. They had laid and rolled half a pitch, and had nets erected on either side and behind the stumps. They had chairs on which to sit and straps on their pads. The scene reminded me of our practice pitch in Delhi where we met in the late afternoons, when the sun wasn't so brutal, to hone our batting and bowling skills.

I watched the young men bowl and bat; despite their equipment, they were as new to the game as my team. The bowlers were erratic, and we could hear the coach shouting at them and pointing to the spot where they should bounce the ball. The batsmen swung clumsily or their feet got tangled up when they tried to defend. But one bowler drew my attention. He was fairly tall, a shade or two darker and older than the others. He ran up to the wicket smoothly, had a high action, and the ball whipped down the wicket to hit the stumps.

"Well? What do you think?"

"They don't look better than us," I said truthfully. "Except one of them. Now watch that bowler. See how he runs up and bowls. It's a coached action, he's played cricket before. He's the one we must watch out for. But the others are all on our level."

The tall pace bowler worried me the most. He could run through the other teams like an AK-47. The match was fixed already, with the ringer on their side. I didn't confide my fear to Parwaaze and the others when we rose to leave the stadium after a half hour. The other young men remained watching, hoping to learn the game. On the way to the university, we stayed silent in the taxi. When we reached the grounds, we sat in a circle and I waited for one of them to start the discussion. If they believed they could be beaten now, I had wasted my time. I hoped that all the training and talking I had done would influence their thinking and attitude.

They had keen eyes and had learned enough of the game to read the nuances and, without my telling them, knew the pace bowler would cause them problems. I wanted them to work out how they would play him.

"We'll have to be d-defensive when he's bowling," Qubad said. "Play him on the back foot, as the bounce could be high on that wicket."

"Wait for the change bowler and hit him then," Namdar said, smiling.

"We should also try to hit him," Royan suggested. "He won't be accurate with every bowl, and if we hit him around, he could start bowling badly."

"He looks too cocky," Parwaaze said, also starting to smile. "We'll deal with him, so we must not worry now. We must only think of winning."

"He looks like a P-Pakistani too," Qubad said dourly. "Who's going to lead us?"

"Parwaaze should be the captain," I said.

Parwaaze grinned. "Yes, I'm the captain." He straightened and threw me a glance of gratitude for electing him as their leader.

"Why can't he be a general?" Qubad mocked. "A c-captain is very low down in an army. Generals are the ones in charge, leading from b-behind."

"Do any of you want to be captain?" I said, stopping the discussion. They hesitated and remained silent. "Then Parwaaze must be the captain." I nudged Jahan.

"I think he should," he said quickly when he caught my eye.

"What does a captain do?" Parwaaze asked, pulling me aside when we started to practice.

"He goes out with the opposing captain for the coin toss. If you call right, then you decide whether to bat or field first. That depends on the pitch. On the stadium pitch, you should bat first as it will break up after a few balls and hopefully be harder to play on in the second innings. And the captain leads the team out onto the field for a start."

"I'll never remember all this," he wailed.

I smiled in sympathy at his dilemma. A captain who knew nothing, leading his men, who knew less, into battle and off the cliff. Yet, I felt he would have an instinct for the role. "Don't worry. I'll write it all down."

We joined the others at practice and I saw how excited and motivated they had become after having seen how vulnerable the state team was. They cheered themselves when they hit a good shot and when they took a wicket. Each one had acquired different skills that rose out of their personalities. Once more, they were individuals, even in the way they walked, the swagger of their steps, turbans at an angle, the grins on their faces. As the hills melted into the arms of the sky at dusk, we practiced our fielding and catching. Where once they had been lethargic, they now ran like hares to the ball, scooping it up and throwing it back.

"We're going to win," they shouted to each other until it grew too dark to practice.

On our street corner, Jahan and I heard the motorbike behind us and kept walking, expecting Azlam to pass. Instead, he switched off his engine and, as he drew parallel, stopped.

We exchanged *salaam aleikums*, my greeting only a whisper, and waited for him to talk.

"I want you to bring the book and teach my team to play cricket," he announced, looking at me. "How much is Parwaaze paying? I'll double it."

"He's not paying us anything," Jahan said. "He's our cousin."

"You should be paid, cousin or not." Azlam hooked a leg over the petrol tank, preparing for a long bargaining session. "I'll give you ten thousand. It's a lot of money."

"I just told you, we're not doing it for money," Jahan said testily. "We love the game, and our cousins wanted to learn it, and that's enough for us."

"Twenty then, and no more."

"No."

"Can't he answer?" Azlam stared at me intently.

"He has a very sore throat and a fever," Jahan said, ending the negotiations and nudging me toward our gate.

"Twenty-five, and that's the last offer," Azlam called out.

"We're going to win the match," Jahan called back.

"We'll see," Azlam shouted and started his bike. He roared up the road, gunning it as he passed us.

"What's he going to do now?" I said, looking after him.

"What can he do? Just lose to us."

Abdul had opened the gate to see who was shouting.

"Have you seen that motorbike before?" I asked.

He shrugged. "Once or twice. It could be the same one, but I can't tell the difference."

"Any letters, packages?" I asked.

"No. Don't worry, they will come."

When we went in, Dr. Hanifa heard us and came out of Mother's room. Even in the gloom, we could read her face.

"She's sleeping, and I gave her dinner. I've increased the dosage of morphine. You'll have to give her another injection if she wakes." She touched my face, and then Jahan's, and we understood the message: death was speeding toward our mother and we would be orphaned very soon.

Jahan went out to walk Dr. Hanifa home. I cooked dinner, kebabs, rice, and a salad, a simple meal for both of us and for Abdul to eat in his quarters. When Jahan returned, we ate, and midway through we heard the telephone, crying out like a lost child. Jahan hurried to answer it and I listened to someone call "Hello" again and again until he gave up.

"Who was it?"

"Sounded like a man, but all I could hear was his hellos. Stupid phone."

"Shaheen?" I asked hopefully.

"No, I'd know his voice, even in a hello."

"Was it Uncle?"

"No, I'd recognize his hellos. It was a stranger's voice."

"Long distance?"

"There was such a buzzing on the line, it was hard to tell."

As we rose from the floor, Abdul knocked on the door and, without thinking, I ran down the stairs and waited in the well, poised to sprint into the secret room.

From *The Taliban Cricket Club, 2012*

CRICKET AND THE MEDIA

Gideon Haigh

The Pantomime Horse

Cricket and the media ... the topic has haunted me since Boria Majumdar suggested it, for all sorts of reasons, but chiefly this— that it's often hard to think of one without the other. Unless we happen to play cricket at the very highest level, the bulk of the cricket we experience will be mediated, accompanied with a ready-made expert narrative; we will recollect it in terms of the voices of the commentators, the words of the writers, the immediate explications of the replays, the lasting imagery of photography, and more recently the competing, clamouring voices of the chat room, the blog and Twitter, each informing and influencing the other. Our conversations about the game are composites of abiding views, received opinions, instant impressions, borrowed prejudices—all of which, nonetheless, have a capacity to endure.

The best example of that endurance is on show this English summer of 2009, the Ashes originating in a jeu d'esprit of the *Sporting Times* 127 years ago. Technology has played its part from the first, too. The first great five-Test series, 1894–95, was partly so because of the *Pall Mall Gazette*'s decision to take advantage of the new telegraphic cable from Australia, allowing the English public to partake of events within a day of their occurring—an extraordinary novelty. Of course, it was originally words that had power. It was on the basis of words that Englishmen dug in to defend Bodyline seventy-seven years ago, on the basis of words that Australians complained of their team being dudded at Old Trafford in 1956. Now it is images that matter, and television's economics have become cricket's—cricket must be sold in order to be played.

That changing relationship between cricket and the media, indeed, now puts me in mind of two theatrical images. Once the relationship was that between a ham and his dresser, cricket being costumed and made up for the stage by a media that maintained fairly obsequious and deferential relations in return for a privileged acquaintance. Now cricket and the media seem more like the front and back halves of a pantomime horse—one, furthermore, where the actual division of responsibilities is unclear: that is, which of cricket and the media is the half that gets to stand up straight and peer out, and which half has to spend its time bent over with its nose in its partner's backside. Whatever the case, it's a relationship of some delicacy and mutual dependence.

The relationships between the different parts of the media are also evolving. When I began writing about cricket about twenty years ago, I recall the very decided demarcation between the print and electronic spheres. Ink-stained wretches were crammed together like steerage passengers on the *Titanic*; the radio and television boys, meanwhile, dressed for dinner in the first-class saloon. There's now a bloody great tear along the waterline, and everyone is flooding into one another's areas. Cricket can be watched on free-to-air television, cable, the internet, the phone. Newspaper and agency websites are running video; cable has invested in the Web. Television entrepreneurs have taken to promoting their own independent cricket enterprises; national cricket boards are producing their own online content. Bloggers link to YouTube;

intellectual property lawyers run after everyone with a big litigation stick. There's an air of excitement, leavened with *Titanic*-style panic, because of a feeling, particularly among my print colleagues, that there may not be quite enough lifeboats.

Media, moreover, spends only part of the time with its eye on the cricket. Much of its exertion is expended reporting on what has already been reported, which way the journalistic herd is stampeding, whether it is to a press conference announcing a sudden outbreak of unity in the Indian team, or to decrypting the enciphered utterances of *Fake IPL Player*. Lately, too, the commentary box has been swept up directly in the sales and marketing tsunami, with DLF Maximums and Citi Moments of Success bound to lead on to the Google googly, the PlayStation Play-and-Miss, the Dillards Dilscoop and the Three 3.

I could discuss many aspects of this, but it's this increasing coalescence of cricket and media that intrigues me—the sense that, as Eric Morecambe used to say of Ernie Wise's toupee, 'You can't see the join'. That is, the tendency over time for those involved in the description and interpretation of the game to become simply the handmaidens of corporate interests.

This is not, of course, a new challenge. Perhaps you can date it to 1977, when Kerry Packer launched his World Series Cricket venture. At the time of Packer's irruption, of course, the coverage of cricket was generally the preserve of public broadcasters—the BBC, ABC, Doordarshan and others—watching cricket from a suitably discreet distance and stationary aspect. Packer's broadcasting package was unprecedentedly lavish and spectacular: it involved both the *coverage* of the game *and* its promotion. It made ordinary players into stars, and stars into gods, so the limelight they reflected might also impart a shimmer to the goods and services being advertised between overs.

Commentators went from being impartial imparters of cricket's eternal verities to commercial courtiers of an entrepreneur promoting the game as a media property. But the key figure in that change was the one who belied that there was a change taking place at all. Richie Benaud was the face of cricket at the BBC, *primus inter pares* among public broadcasters; to what might at Channel Nine have been a crass and raucous affair, he brought a deft and discriminating touch, an air of rectitude, a sense of being above it all.

Historians have been apt to celebrate the contributions to Packer's progress of Ian Chappell and Tony Greig, or Austin Robertson and John Cornell, but Richie Benaud is the man who *really* made it credible. You bought what he was selling almost before you knew it was for sale; and, as with the best salesmen, the transaction left you feeling enriched.

Benaud had played cricket, we all of us knew, yet his commentary seldom betrayed this directly. The general but unspecific cognisance of his playing career acted instead as a form of quality certification: his was a warming but weightless past. Instead of banging on about how things were better in his day, he endorsed the present and blessed the future; he was the Pangloss of the pitch, who assured us, over and over again, that all was for the best in this best of possible cricket worlds.

Over time, of course, cricket lurched from disaster to disaster: rebel tours, illegal actions, ball tampering, match-fixing, racial squabbles, aggression that trembled on the brink of cheating, commercial chicanery that skirted the bounds of legality. Yet nothing threatened the serene majesty of Benaud's commentary, as interested and engaged by his hundredth one-day international as by his first. Over the years, one waited for Benaud to take a firm position on any of the game's major issues, while knowing also that nothing would ever endanger that stance of magisterial disinterest, and that unstated but unswerving commitment to the product.

Benaud still commentates—what purports to be his last summer lies ahead in Australia later this year. But we're starting to see the strains underlying his position that Benaud's silky skills so successfully disguised—strains laid entirely bare during the IPL in South Africa, where commentary was reduced to the level of infomercial.

The subtle thrall exerted by the commentary voice, in fact, has been integral to the diffusion of Twenty20. Because so much money rides on its success, there has been a competition in who can praise it and its participants more lavishly—every game is thrilling, every player a star, the whole concept the most exciting innovation since the incandescent lightbulb, and, of course, Lalit Modi a modern-day Moses, to the extent that the commentators have almost drowned themselves out, becoming indistinguishable from the advertisements between overs. But great rewards and honours await those who can endear themselves to the right people.

One of my most vivid recollections of the Twenty20 revolution is the game in Melbourne in February 2008 between Australia and India—quite possibly the worst international cricket match I have ever seen, over in two hours and twenty-eight overs, India capitulating for 74. Yet afterwards, Channel Nine's finest prowled the outfield for almost as long as Australia batted, interviewing players about the non-stop excitement that nobody had just seen. It was as credible as a Chinese government press release that the tanks in Tiananmen Square were simply participating in a segment of *Top Gear*. Who did these commentators think they were fooling?

The print media has always occupied a subtly different niche to the electronic. The television is there because cricket is entertainment on the basis of money spent on acquiring rights; newspapers are there because cricket is regarded as news, and enjoy access on a grace and favour basis, while the roles of those who straddle both forms are confused and confusing, like Ian Botham, an aura-for-hire, whether by Sky, the *Mirror* or Allen Stanford. But, as I said earlier, the fissuring boundaries between technologies are further collapsing news into entertainment and vice versa, with inevitable implications for what we say in the print media and how freely we can say it.

My trade has always been a mixture of the superficially sensational and squalid and the thoroughly tame and incurious. 'We do not need censorship *of* the press', noted Chesterton. 'We have censorship *by* the press.' Yet how is it that, in a period of such convulsive change, change that will define the direction of the game for decades to come, there is such limited interest in the relevant institutions: the BCCI, ICC, ECB, Cricket Australia, Sony, ESPN? How was it, for example, that Stanford had to go broke before anyone sussed that he was a fraud? Why the rapt fascination with the prices paid for players at the IPL auction, and such indifference to whom else cricket is making hugely wealthier?

I wonder *now* if we are not, consciously and unconsciously, avoiding evidences of corruption in cricket, as indeed we did in the 1990s, so heavily implicated have we become in this sports–industrial complex. I'm not sure I can offer a definitive answer to that, and there will certainly always be exceptions. But I do know that a lot of the toughest, cleverest, funniest and best informed writing about cricket these days is to be found in the blogosphere, where the writers are without fear or favour, and also, of course, money. Avid viewers, curious readers, discriminating consumers— they are out there in vast numbers, and it is up to cricket *and* the media to deserve them.

ICC History Conference, July 2009

From *Sphere of Influence: Writings on
Cricket and its Discontents, 2011*

Shortly after *Test Match Special* went on air one morning Peter Baxter, the erstwhile producer of the programme, received a call on his mobile phone:

'Hello, Peter? CMJ here. I've a horrible feeling I've gone to the wrong ground. Is the Test at the Oval today?'

'Yes!'

'Fishcakes! I'm at Lord's.'

An occasional listener to *Test Match Special* might be surprised by that agitated exchange, but anyone with more than a passing interest in the programme would recognize this as merely another of Christopher's little 'moments'. A man whose life might have been lifted from a scene from *Clockwise* – and whose tall, thin and long-limbed frame offered more than a passing resemblance to the tortured character played by John Cleese in that chaotic film – CMJ was capable of creating a crisis out of almost anything. And only very rarely was he ever on time.

Peter simply shrugged his shoulders, replaced the phone in his trouser pocket and looked at his watch. Even by CMJ's standards, this was a good effort – for if the match *were* being staged at Lord's, he would still have missed the start of play.

Whenever Christopher finally made his entrance to the commentary box, you could hear the hurried steps along the corridor some seconds before the door burst open. He would be clutching an old A4 hard-backed diary – no surprise that this was always some years behind the current season – in which he would scribble spidery notes, which were often indecipherable to him, let alone to everyone else. His precious binoculars would swing from a cord around his neck, and these would invariably become hopelessly entangled with the trailing cable from the headphones that he tugged over his ears.

What followed was a transformation. Clear, precise, carefully selected words with the most perfectly rounded vowels were delivered very deliberately, helping to make him such a brilliant mimic of Trevor Bailey, in particular. Christopher's description of play was unfailingly accurate and measured, and he delighted in lingering over a batsman's perfect footwork.

Authority and trust are a top commentator's prerequisites, both earned only through years in front of a microphone, and I believe that of all those through the generations who did not play cricket at the highest level, Christopher is in a league of his own. Sadly, such is the developing trend, it is quite possible he will be the last in a line of respected broadsheet cricket correspondents and broadcasters who did not play county cricket, at the very least. If that is so, it will be cricket's loss.

More evident than anything from his commentary was CMJ's absolute love for the game, his admiration for those who played it, and his joy merely at being present at a cricket match. This was the case whether the game in question was a Test against Australia at Lord's, a Championship match somewhere in his beloved Sussex or, during a winter tour, a game between the respective media groups. This would offer the opportunity for CMJ to roll back the years and bowl a few off breaks, which although increasingly creaky, were always delivered tenaciously and in the firm belief that every ball would claim a wicket. In fact, so competitively did CMJ play all his sport that his language would have been surprisingly colourful, were it not for his carefully chosen substitutes for the f-word. 'Fishcakes' was generally self-admonishment delivered through clenched teeth, while a bellowed 'Fotherington Thomas' was reserved for moments when the world was against him – like finding the water with his approach shot to the green, or when failing for the umpteenth time to send his match report from his laptop.

Wonderful stories of CMJ's mishaps abound, with the hapless victim always happy to join in with the laughter that was generated at his own expense. Running late as usual one day in Barbados, Christopher hurriedly threw his golf clubs into the back of his open-top Mini Moke, and drove at breakneck speed from the course, through Bridgetown, before screeching on two wheels into his hotel car park. There, to his horror, he discovered that the entire contents of the bag had been lost en route. The expensive set of clubs he had been loaned by a local Barbados cricket administrator lay strewn somewhere in his wake. His commentary on Voice of Barbados the following day included an urgent appeal for the return of any golf clubs found in the roadside. None was recovered.

His meticulously organized end-of-tour dinner a short stroll from our hotel in Bombay ended calamitously when, departing late, CMJ opted for a taxi – the driver of which failed to find the restaurant. Three hours later, and just as the rest of us were paying the bill, a flustered Christopher arrived and quickly wolfed down what food remained. The devastating bout of poisoning set in almost immediately, delayed his return home and he took weeks to recover. Most famously, of course, was his attempt somewhere on the road between Montego Bay and Kingston to telephone the office on his hotel's television remote control. However, just a couple of days later and following the controversial abandonment of the Test at Sabina Park after only ten overs, CMJ was in the press box and right up against his newspaper deadline. Front page, back page – he had written thousands of words when, fatally, he pressed the wrong button on his laptop and lost the lot. There was nothing else for it but to pick up the phone and dictate to the copytaker every word off the top of his head. It was a masterful, controlled performance under the most intense pressure.

Christopher would say that he has enjoyed the perfect life. With Judy's patience, love and support, what could be better for such an enthusiast to have spent his days watching, writing and broadcasting about his favourite pastime amongst colleagues who share the same obsession? I will miss dreadfully the moment in the commentary box late every afternoon when CMJ reached for his laptop. Through my headphones, the eager tap, tap, tapping of his fingers on the keyboard in the background sounded like falling drops of rain. And how prolifically those words flowed. Considering the years he worked as editor of *The Cricketer* magazine, as correspondent for the BBC, the *Daily Telegraph* and *The Times*, forty years commentating on *Test Match Special* and the many books that he wrote, it's doubtful that anyone has contributed more in a lifetime to the overall coverage of cricket than Christopher Martin-Jenkins.

JOINING *TEST MATCH SPECIAL*

Christopher Martin-Jenkins

My performance at Old Trafford apparently met with general satisfaction. To my great good fortune I have been part of the commentary team in every season since. The pleasures are twofold: the actual business of cricket commentary, a delight in itself; and the interaction with those who listen. They include some very interesting and important people, as guests on our Saturday lunchtime programme, *Beyond the Boundary*, regularly prove. But it was still a pleasant surprise when, as *TMS* producer and cricket correspondent Peter Baxter, and I were summoned to lunch at Westminster a few years ago.

Sir John Major was 'only' the First Secretary to the Treasury then but, like many MPs, he was concerned about a threat to the future of *TMS*. Cricket commentaries had not until then struck me as being the sort of issue that might be debated in the House of Commons. Bodyline, the 1970 South Africa tour, and more recently cricketing relations with Zimbabwe, have all been legitimate political issues, but was the question of whether or not cricket commentaries might be interrupted by football really a matter of national importance?

To the future Prime Minister there was no question that it was. Over a convivial lunch round the corner from Parliament, the amiable future president of Surrey and MCC committee member, and his Lancastrian political ally Robert Atkins, also now knighted, left us in no doubt about how strongly they felt the need to preserve the programme's individual identity.

The interplay between commentators and listeners both then and now suggests that he was right. People of all ages and types love the combination of cricketing know-how and friendly chat in an atmosphere of relaxed enjoyment. The threat that was worrying followers of *TMS* then was that ball-by-ball commentary on Radio Three was destined to take its chance with other sport on a wavelength carrying a burgeoning news and sports service called Radio Five Live. The Government had decreed that in 1990 the BBC would lose two of its eight wavelengths and the plan was for Radio Five to take the Test match commentaries under its wing the following year, or as soon as the old Radio Three medium wave disappeared.

In 1989 no fewer than 140 MPs signed a motion deploring the proposed changes. Gillian Reynolds supported them in the *Daily Telegraph*, calling *TMS* 'a piece of radio which is very British yet which transcends class, age and gender'. *The Times* reported a spectator at Headingley, Denis Read from Ramsbottom in Lancashire, as saying of *Test Match Special*: 'It's cricket and it's England and it's marvellous. It wouldn't be the same without it. It just makes me feel good and it always has done.'

Happily, and thanks largely to the public outcry, a solution was found, namely to reposition *TMS* on Radio Four long wave. Now we also transmit to a growing audience on Radio Five Live *Sports Extra*, in the crystal clear digital quality of DAB.

From Howard Marshall through John Arlott and Brian Johnston to Jonathan Agnew and Henry Blofeld; from Norman Yardley and Freddie Brown through Trevor Bailey and Fred Trueman to Mike Selvey, Vic Marks, Geoffrey Boycott and a wide choice of overseas summarisers, the programme has carefully mixed its characters, never ignoring the cake and champagne but, touch wood, never taking its eye off the ball. All of us are forever reliant on the wonderful variety and unpredictability of cricket to keep a devoted audience interested; sometimes even enthralled.

It may seem just the same as it was in the Arlott/Johnston era, when 'Blowers' and myself were cutting our teeth and Frindall was already established as the statistical pillar of the programme. In truth, however, the approach has gently and subtly changed, maintaining its light-hearted, civilised, authoritative approach to a day's cricket, with no holds barred on any topic thrown up by events in the middle and on the fringes, but gradually developing a sharper journalistic edge without ever abandoning its core role: to tell the listener what is happening in the match and why.

Listeners to *Test Match Special* of a certain age – and there are many still about – look back with nostalgia to the days of the 1960s and 1970s when Johnston, the jester, and Arlott, the poet, jointly built the programme's reputation. John became a treasured companion in the commentary box and Brian a personal friend, despite our difference in age.

A mix of voices and personalities has always been part of the attraction of *TMS*. The two most famous and fondly remembered commentators proved it. In voice and character alike they were poles apart; but as a professional act (although in both cases they were natural broadcasters who never needed to act) they were as complementary as cornflakes and milk.

They were linked by their talent, their love of cricket, the freedom offered them by the burgeoning OB department in the years after the war and the affection and admiration in which they were held by grateful listeners.

They were separated by much more. Where Arlott was often sombre and serious, Johnston was skittish and comical; where Arlott paced himself like an Oriental spinner, Johnston rushed in like an Aussie fast bowler; where Arlott treasured words like the poet he was and mulled them over as if he were testing the nose of a vintage Château Lafite, Johnston used them with gay abandon, without art or pretension. One was the student of the game who became a professor; the other the eternal schoolboy who believed that every day's cricket might, at its dawn, become the greatest and most exciting he had ever witnessed. One was sometimes maudlin, heavy as a brooding cloud, the other invariably light as a soufflé. One carried and dwelt upon the burdens of life; the other cast them aside as quickly as he could.

Both were original, completely true to themselves. If Arlott was more troubled by self-doubt and insecurity, deep down he knew that he was a man worthy of his calling. Johnston never doubted it: he could not believe his good fortune at finding a medium that suited him so well. If Arlott's performances as a cricket commentator were less even than Johnston's he was capable of truly virtuoso performances of inspired description. The occasion I remember best was the one when the BBC's managing director, Ian Trethowan, came into the box during the World Cup final in 1975. Clive Lloyd was batting majestically and John knew that there was an influential audience. Besides that, like all of us at Lord's on that glorious day, he was enjoying himself.

'The stroke of a man knocking the top off a thistle with a walking stick' was his description of one majestic Lloyd pull into the Grandstand. Equally graphic was his portrayal of little white-capped Dickie Bird, with his hunched back, catching the excitement like everyone. 'And Umpire Bird is having a wonderful time, signalling everything from six to "stop" to traffic coming on from behind.'

Brian was not capable of such imagery but in their contrasting way both were consummate broadcasting professionals. To listen to them was a delight and to work with them an extraordinary privilege for me, in John's case from 1972 until he retired to a quieter, contemplative life on Alderney in 1980, and in Brian's until he had a fatal heart attack while still working hard at the age of eighty-one in 1993.

It was not possible to be their colleague for so long without becoming immensely fond of them both. I knew Brian longer and better; often during Lord's Test matches staying with him and Pauline, his pretty, forceful, sometimes impetuous but always staunchly supportive wife. Exactly ten years younger than her beloved spouse, she still lives in the house at Boundary Road in St. John's Wood that succeeded the family home a few hundred yards away, at Hamilton Terrace, one of the most elegant streets in London.

'B.J.' was wonderful company, as funny in private conversation as he was on his feet after dinner on a public occasion. He loved to pun, and gossip, not least, of course, about people in cricket. All his huge fund of stories became familiar in time but it was his flair for entertainment, both in private and in public, that made them genuinely funny every time. Barry Johnston, his eldest son, recalled in his biography of his father how, sometimes, his reaction to something that had amused him on television – a bad piece of acting, perhaps or the way that someone had said something, would start Brian giggling and soon have the whole family overcome by tears of laughter too, sometimes without even knowing what had started it.

The famous 'leg-over' incident with Jonathan Agnew, a classic example of why live broadcasting is so often more interesting or amusing than recorded, was a case in point. What created the uncontrollable mirth, of course, was the very professionalism of them both: the desperate attempt to keep going. Aggers soon became speechless but the old trouper did his best to carry on.

Everyone listening loved it and of course the giggles were utterly infectious. I wish there had also been a recording of the day that Brian and I simultaneously collapsed into similarly uncontrollable laughter during a meaningless World Cup match between England and Canada to which practically no one can have been listening. On that occasion there was simply a long silence as Brian, unable to believe the name of the Canadian player that I had just identified for him, Showkhat Bash, retreated from the microphone to try to regain his power of speech. The hiatus seemed to us interminable. In the studio in London the engineers thought the line must have gone down. I have got the giggles on air only once since, in 2008 when, commentating as Stuart Broad bowled to New Zealand's captain, Daniel Vettori, I said:

'Broad runs in, he bowls, and this time Vettori lets it go outside the off stump. It was a good length, inviting him to fish, but Vettori, so to speak, stayed on the bank and kept his rod up.'

Jeremy Coney, my summariser, offered no assistance as I realised the double entendre. According to a report in the *Evening Standard*, 'seconds later listeners could hear the veteran commentator … struggling to keep his composure. His voice got steadily higher as he said: "I don't know if he's a fisherman, is he?" '

From *CMJ: A Cricketing Life, 2012*

Acknowledgements

This book has been a sizeable undertaking and has relied upon the enthusiasm and expertise of many colleagues and friends, a genuine team effort.

My grateful thanks first and foremost must go to the writers who have contributed to this anthology. Their insights into the great game, eloquence, wit and willingness to put my desire to include their work ahead of the demands of the wallet has ultimately led to a wide, varying and fascinating collection of extracts.

This book could never have been undertaken without the tremendous resource that is the MCC Library at Lord's. Neil Robinson and his team of Andrew Trigg, Zoe English and Linda Gordon, along with archivists Robert Curphey and Alan Rees, have made the days of research a pleasure, and their expertise, advice and direction has ensured that the book is significantly better than it might otherwise have been.

Rick Mayston and his team at Getty Images have thrown themselves into the picture research with skill and enthusiasm. Andre Gailani at *Punch* deserves a special mention for locating and supplying the wonderful cartoons dotted throughout the book, aided by the consummate research and archiving of all cricket-related *Punch* material by David Rayvern Allen.

The book you hold in your hands has been designed by Marcus Nichols with inspiration by typographer Tim Lewis at Unreal.

Tim Jollands has done an excellent job of taming my own words; any mistakes, of course, remain entirely my responsibility.

Finally, I am immensely grateful to my publisher Patrick Janson-Smith, who has had enormous faith in the idea all along, and my agents Michael Doggart and Jonathan Hayden, who have kept the project on the rails even when I have had to disappear on overseas tours.

We are grateful for permission to include the following extracts:

John Arlott: *Fred: Portrait of a Fast Bowler* and *Indian Summer* (Eyre Methuen, 1972, and Longmans, 1947) reprinted with the permission of Tim Arlott for the Estate of John Arlott.

Richie Benaud: *A Tale of Two Tests: With Some Thoughts on Captaincy* and *Willow Patterns* (Sportsman's Book Club, 1962, and Hodder, 1969) both reprinted with the permission of the author.

Marcus Berkmann: *Rain Men: The Madness of Cricket* and *Zimmer Men: The Trials and Tribulations of the Ageing Cricketer* (Little, Brown Book Group, 1996, and 2005) reprinted with the permission of the publisher.

Sir Derek Birley: *A Social History of English Cricket* (Aurum, 1999) reprinted with the permission of the publisher.

Geoffrey Boycott: *Boycott On Cricket* (Partridge Press, 1990) reprinted with the permission of the author.

Mike Brearley: *The Art of Captaincy* (Hodder, 1985) reprinted with the permission of the author.

R. Chandrasekar: *The Goat, the Sofa and Mr Swami* (Hachette India, 2010) reprinted with the permission of the publisher.

Max Davidson: *We'll Get 'Em in Sequins: Manliness, Yorkshire Cricket and the Century That Changed Everything* (John Wisden & Co Ltd, 2012) reprinted with the permission of the publisher.

Basil D'Oliveira: *The Basil D'Oliveira Affair* (Collins, 1969) reprinted with the permission of Damian D'Oliveira for the estate of Basil D'Oliveira.

Christopher Douglas: *Jardine, A Spartan Cricketer* (Allen and Unwin, 1984) reprinted with the permission of the author.

Gideon Haigh: *Sphere of Influence: Writings on Cricket and its Discontents* (Melbourne University Press, 2011) reprinted with the permission of the publisher.

Duncan Hamilton: *Harold Larwood* (Quercus, 2009) reprinted with the permission of the publisher.

Ed Hawkins: *Bookie Gambler Fixer Spy: A Journey to the Heart of Cricket's Underworld* (Bloomsbury, 2012) reprinted with the permission of the publisher.

Matthew Hayden: *Standing My Ground* (Aurum, 2011) reprinted with the permission of the publisher.

Simon Hughes: *A Lot of Hard Yakka* (Headline, 1997) reprinted with the permission of the author.

Steve James: *The Plan* (Bantam Press, 2012) reprinted with the permission of Random House.

Martin Johnson: *Can't Bat, Can't Bowl, Can't Field* (Collins Willow, 1997) reprinted with the permission of the author.

Sir John Major: *More Than A Game: The Story of Cricket's Early Years* (HarperPress, 2007) reprinted with the permission of the author.

Christopher Martin-Jenkins: *CMJ: A Cricketing Life* (Simon and Schuster, 2012) reprinted with the permission of Peters Fraser & Dunlop.

Leo McKinstry: *Jack Hobbs: England's Greatest Cricketer* (Yellow Jersey Press, 2011) reprinted with the permission of Random House.

Geoffrey Moorhouse: *The Best Loved Game* (Hodder and Stoughton, 1979) reprinted with the permission of Aitken Alexander Associates.

Timeri N. Murari: *The Taliban Cricket Club* (Allen & Unwin, 2012) reprinted with the permission of the publisher.

Paul Nixon: *Keeping Quiet: The Autobiography* (The History Press, 2012) reprinted with the permission of the publisher.

Harry Pearson: *Slipless in Settle: A Slow Turn Around Northern Cricket* (Little, Brown Book Group, 2012) reprinted with the permission of the publisher.

Vaibhav Purandare: *Sachin Tendulkar: The Definitive Biography* (Roli Books/The History Press, 2008) reprinted with the permission of Roli Books.

Amol Rajan: *Twirlymen: The History of Cricket's Greatest Spin Bowlers* (Yellow Jersey Press, 2011) reprinted with the permission of David Higham Associates.

Michael Simkins: *Fatty Batter: How Cricket Saved My Life (Then Ruined It)* (Ebury Press, 2008) reprinted with the permission of Random House.

Martin Smith (Ed.): *Not in My Day, Sir: Cricket Letters to the Daily Telegraph* (Aurum, 2011) reprinted with the permission of the publisher.

Rob Steen: *500–1: The Miracle of Headingley '81* (John Wisden & Co. Ltd, 2007) reprinted with the permission of the publisher.

Harry Thompson: *Penguins Stopped Play* (John Murray, 2006) reprinted with the permission of the publisher.

David Tossell: *Grovel! The Story and Legacy of the Summer of 1976* (Pitch Publishing, 2007) reprinted with the permission of the author.

Phil Tufnell: *The Autobiography: What Now?* (Collins Willow, 1999) reprinted with the permission of the author.

Chris Waters: *Fred Trueman: The Authorised Biography* (Aurum, 2011) reprinted with the permission of the publisher.

Simon Wilde: *Ian Botham: The Power and the Glory* (Simon & Schuster, 2011) reprinted with the permission of the publisher.

Wisden Cricketers' Almanack 1934: *The Bowling Controversy – Text of the Cables* and *Sydney J. Southerton's Analysis*.

Wisden Cricketers' Almanack 2012: *The Obituary of Basil D'Oliveira*

Articles from Wisden Cricketers' Almanack are reproduced by kind permission of John Wisden & Co Ltd.

We have tried to trace and contact copyright holders in the case of all extracts; sometimes this has been to no avail. If we are notified, the publisher will be pleased to correct any errors or omissions as soon as is practical.

Denzil Batchelor: *Games of a Lifetime* (Laurie, 1953)

Sir Donald Bradman: *Farewell to Cricket* (Hodder, 1950)

Neville Cardus: *Days in the Sun* (Rupert Hart-Davis, 1948)

R.C. Robertson-Glasgow: *46 Not Out* (Hollis and Carter, 1948)

Ray Robinson: *The Wildest Tests* (Pelham, 1972)

Index

Page numbers in **bold** refer to main references

Abbas, Zaheer 100, 333
ABC Television 198
Abid Ali 242
Adair, John 321
Adams, Jimmy 168
Adhikari, Hemu 295, 296
Advisory County Cricket Committee 49, 365
Afghanistan **476–86**
African National Congress (ANC) 40
Agnew, Jonathan 122, 123, 262, 343, 496, 498
Aird, R. 85
Akram, Wasim 35–6, 114
Alam, Intikhab 244
Alcock, Charles 447
Alderman, Terry 226, 235
Alexander, Gerry 178, 181, 182
All-England Eleven 444, 445
Allan, Norman 198
Allen, David 159
Allen, G.O. 'Gubby' 21, 22, 72, 205–6,
    205–18, 304, 317, 324, 363
Alley, Bill 107, 333
Alston, Rex 439
Amarnath, Mohinder 167
amateur players **360–73**
    abolition of distinction with professionals
        318, 361–2, 365, 447
    at St Moritz, Mount Everest and the South Pole 373
    background and style 317–18
    and the captaincy 314, 317
    country differences 365–8
    definition 360–1
    dressing-room distinction 360–1, 446
    effect of Second World War on 364–5
    enthusiasm and obsession of 368–9
    influence on Bodyline 362–4
    and payment 362
    and school sports 369–70
    and village cricket 370–3
    see also professional players
Ambrose, Curtly 164, 345
Ames, Les 55, 208, 210, 388
Amir, Mohammad 38, 144
Amiss, Dennis 32, 99, 102, 251, 252
    summer 1976 at the Oval 104–11
Andersen, Lale 275
Antarctica 373, **390–6**
Antigua 6
apartheid 7, 24, 25, 28, 83–8, 92
Arlott, John 24, 33, 81, 82, 85–6, 91, 102, 288,
    297, 305, 434–6, 439, 472, 496, 497
Armstrong, Warwick 14, 43, 461
Arnold, Geoff 242, 244, 460
Aronstam, Marlon 37
Ashe, Arthur 312–13
Asif, Mohammad 38–9, 144
Ata-ur-Rehman 35
Atherton, Mike 37, 440
    dirt-in-the-pocket affair **120–6**
Athey, Bill 312
Atkins, Robert 495
Australia 5, 6, 12, 315, 336
    amateur-professional distinction 365–6
    and Bodyline controversy 13, 19–24,
        48–51, 54–72, 80, 185
    bouncers and beercans at Sydney
        Test (1971) **184–204**
    corruption and scandal 35
    great Test matches 157, 158, 159–65, 166–8, 171–3

Headingley Test match (1981)
    169–71, **219–28, 229–36**
Old Trafford Test match (1956) 299, 302–7
tied Test in Brisbane (1960) **175–84**
and WSC 28–33
Australian Board of Control 20, 22, 23, 54,
    57–9, 62–8, 69, 102, 103, 199–200, 363
Australian Broadcasting Corporation (ABC) 28, 99
Australian Cricket Board (ACB) 29–33, 35, 252
Australian newspaper 35
Azharuddin, Mohammad 34, 36, 141,
    167
Azlam 484, 485

Badcock, Jack 210, 214, 216, 217
Bailey, Trevor 281, 301, 317, 439, 496
Bairstow, David 224, 287, 311, 336
Balderstone, Chris 105, 112, 246, 254
Baloo, Palwankar 10–11
Banerjee, S. 473
Bangladesh 5, 8
Bangladesh Liberation War (1971) 8
Bannister, Alex 107
Bannister, Jack 37, 252
Bansda, Benny 82, 83, 91
Bapty, John 290
Barbados 6, 245, 493–4
Barbour, E.P. 48
Barclay, John 259, 315
Bardsley, Warren 79
Barlow, Eddie 326, 446
Barnes, Alan 197
Barnes, Sydney 216–17, 299, 307, 388
Barnett (1936) 209, 213, 215
Barraclough, Eric 287
Bash, Showkhat 498
Baxter, Peter 116, 492, 495
Beckham, David 355
Bedi, Bishen 98, 332
Bedser, Alec 27, 111, 194, 291, 294, 296, 315, 472, 473
Benaud, Richie 189, 304, 327, 471
    betting on matches 197, 224
    as commentator 107, 111, 174,
        242, 305, 438, 488–9
    tied Test in Brisbane (1960) 17, 165–6, **175–84**
    and WSC 29, 100
Benjamin, Kenny 164
Bennett, Harvie 364–5
Bennett, Leo 365
Benson, Charles 222
Berkmann, Marcus 390, 397, **404–10**
Berry, Les 243
Betfair 134–5, 136
bets, betting 197, **219–28**
Bettington, R.H. 206
Bevan, Richard 147
Bhogle, Harsha 437
Binks, Jimmy 287
Bird, Dickie 104, 107, 108, 261, 262, 497
Bishop, Ian 164
Bisseker, E.G. 80
Blackham, Jack 160
Blofeld, Henry 222, 439, 496
Blythe, Colin 264, 299, 460, 462
Board of Control 49
Board of Control for Cricket in India
    (BCCI) 141, 367, 490
Bodyline series (1932-3) 13, 19–24, 41,
    42–73, 80, 362–4, 455–6, 487

at Adelaide 21–2, **54–61**, 69
attempted counter-measures 51–2
and the Australians 48–51
cables between MCC and Australian
    Board of Control 62–8
editor of *Wisden's* comments on 68–72
effects of 52–3
mastering 50–2
nature of bowling 42–3
origins and development of 43–6
reports on 46–8
Bolton Association 388
Bombay Gymkhana 10
Bombay Presidency Match (1877) 10
Boon, David 164–5, 166
Booth, Peter 253, 463
Border, Allan 160, 161, 166, 167, 222, 234
Botham, Ian 251, 253, 345
    captaincy 169, 229, 315, 316
    character and description 37, 318, 320,
        321, 330, 336–7, 342–3, 490
    cricketing skills **330–7**
    Headingley Test (1981) 170–1, **229–36**
    and the media 440
    Melbourne Test (1982) 161
Bowes, Bill 20, 43, 45, 209, 268, 269–70, 284, 285, 290
Boyce, Keith 223
Boycott, Geoffrey 224, 293, 335, 435
    character 256–7, 258, 309, 335
    as commentator 439, 496
    Headingley Test (1981) 170
    injuries and illness 189, 195, 204, 242
    and racial intimidation 6
    skills at cricket 242, 256–7, 258, **309–13**
    and WSC 101–3
Bradford League 265, 386–9
Bradman, Donald 157, 277, 297, 323, 327,
        363, 365, 456, 457, **464–70**
    1946 comeback 467–8
    at tied Test in Brisbane (1960) 178
    Bodyline series 20–2, 42–53, 70
    comment on Jardine 15
    comment on rigging the game 143
    cricketing career 17–18
    Melbourne Match (1936) 208, 210, 214, 215, 217
Brearley, Mike 224, 460
    captaincy 33, 101, 103, 121, 169–70, **229–36**,
        314, 331, 332, 333, 335–6, 337
    Headingley Test (1981) 170, 171
Bridgeman, Viscount 60
Briers, Nigel 255, 258
Briers, Richard 371
Briggs, Johnny 160, 299
Bright, Ray 167, 171, 222, 234, 235, 236
Brind, Harry 107
British Empire 4–9, 367
British Expeditionary Force (BEF) 73, 74, 264
Broad, Stuart 499
Bromley, E.H. 47
Brooke, R. 287
Brooks, Tom 193, 194, 201
Brown, Freddie 439, 496
Brown, W.A. 458
Budd, Zola 117
Buggy, Hugh 23
Burge, Peter 121, 123, 124, 125, 126
Burgin, Eric 296, 297
Burke, Jim 302
Burnet, Ronnie 365
Butt, Salman 38–9, 144

Cahn, Sir Julien 384
Calcutta Cricket and Football Club 9–10
Campbell, Alistair 147
Campbell, Ryan 355
Cape Times 47
Captain Scott XI **390–6**, 397, 399–400, 403, 404
captaincy 15, 20, **314–29**, 365, **404–10**
Cardus, Neville 267, 307, 374, 433–4, 453–4
Carew, Dudley 377

Caribbean 5–6
Carpenter, Bob 444
Carr, Arthur 19, 45, 266
Carson, Harry 454
Cartwright, Tom 27, 93
CBI 141, 142
Central Lancashire League 24–5, 84
Chandresekar, R. 418
Channel Nine TV 28, 30, 33
Chapman, (1930) 208, 212
Chappell, Greg 33, 98, 151, 189, 190, 192, 202, 203, 329
Chappell, Ian 29, 185, 186, 189, 190, 191,
        197, 198, 201, 319–20, 329, 489
Chappell, Trevor 171, 232, 233
Chawla, Sanjay 36
Cheall, Bill 272–4
Chifley, Ben 79
Chipperfield, A.G. 210, 213, 216, 217, 458
Clark, David 199
Clarke, Michael 163
Clarke, Sylvester 346, 347
Clarke, William 444, 446
Clinton, Graham 259
Clive, Robert 9
Close, Brian 243, 284, 287, 318–19, 321, 365
club cricket **383–9**, **390–6**, 397, 399–400, 403
Cobb, Russell 255
Cobham, Lord 25
Coltart, David 147, 150
Commonwealth countries 367–8
Compton, Denis 196, 225, 262, 457
Coney, Jeremy 499
Conn, Malcolm 35
Connors, Jimmy 312–13
Constantine, Leary 44, 49, 52, 71, 366, 388
Cook, Alastair 440
Cook, Geoff 247
Cook, Nick 255
Corbett, Ted 222, 226, 227
Cornell, John 489
Corrican, Dr A.B. 199
County Championship 34, 49, 250,
        255, 256, 262, 442, 443, 459
county cricket **442–8**
Courier Mail newspaper 175
Cowans, Norman 160–1, 313
Coward, Noel 271
Cowdrey, Colin 26, 27, 159, 186, 188,
        199, 289, 302, 310, 467
Coxon, Alex 286
Cozier, Tony 110, 437
Crapp, Jack 388
Crawley, John 228
cricket
    and age of the 'shamateur' 365
    at St Moritz, Mount Everest and
        at the South Pole 373
    bats and batting 242, **253–6**, **309–13**,
        404–5, 414–15, **460–3**
    beach 372
    bowling **346–9**, **460–3**, 483
    and British colonialism 4–13
    and children 369–70
    comparing and analysing players
        and matches **156–73**
    controversies 13–28, 41–2, 301, 362, 489
    field placings 405–7
    formation of WSC 28–33
    gambling, match-fixing and corruption 34–9,
        116–19, **127–38**, 141–2, **143–4**, **219–28**
    as gentlemen's game 12
    innovations in 11
    local circumstances 372–3
    musings on leadership **404–10**
    new season **397–403**
    origins 33–4
    and politics 39–40, **145–53**
    rivalries and tensions 12–28
    shop **411–17**
    spin-bowling 299–307

village 370–3
wickets and stumps 308
see also amateur players; professional players
Cricket Academy 227
Cricket Australia 490
Cricket Council 98, 200
Cricket World Cup 7
    match-fixing between India and
        Pakistan (2011) **127–38**
    Zimbabwe 2003 series **145–53**
The Cricketer 494
Cricketers' Association 101, 102, 103
Croft, Colin 247
Crompton, Alan 35
Cronje, Ewie 5, 116
Cronje, Hansie 5, 34, 35–6, 37, 38, **116–19**, 144
Crook, Frank 225, 226
Cummins, Anderson 168

Daft, Richard 444, 446
Daily Express 222, 305, 454
Daily Mail 46, 107
Daily Mirror 91
Daily Telegraph 73, 77, 437, 449, 454, 494, 496
The Daily Worker Cricket Handbook (1949) 76
Daniel, Wayne 104, 109, 314
Darling, Joe 461
Darwin, Bernard 454
Davidson, Alan 165–6, 178, 179, 180–1, 203–4
Davidson, Ken 287
Davis, J.G.W. 384
Davis, Winston 159
Davison, Brian 246, 249
Davitt, Barry 271
Dean, Geoff 150, 151, 460
DeFreitas, Phillip 125–6
Dell, Tony 189, 201
Dempster, S. 207
Denness, Mike 97
Dennis, Frank 287
Dev, Kapil 140, 141–2, 167
Dexter, Ted 224, 318, 321
Dilley, Graham 171, 225, 226, 229, 230–1, 232, 234
Divecha, Ramesh 295
D'Oliveira, Basil 7, 39, 438
    and anti-apartheid movement 27–8, **81–9**
    at the Sydney Test match (1971) 189, 201, 202,
        203
    early career 24–7
    obituary of **89–95**
D'Oliveira, Brett 94
D'Oliveira, Damian 91, 94
D'Oliveira, Lewis 90
D'Oliveira, Naomi 81, 82, 88–9, 90, 91, 94
Doshi, Dilip 247
Douglas-Home, Sir Alec 93
Dravid, Rahul 140, 142, 172
Drum, Chris 143
Duckworth, George 47, 49
Dujon, Jeff 343
Dunell, Owen 90
Dunphy, Eamon 346
Dwyer, Edmund 194
Dymock, Geoff 311
Dyson, John 222, 232, 233, 234

East India Company 8–9
Eastwood, Ken 191, 201, 202
Edmonds, Phil 332
Edrich, John 97, 98, 189, 201, 242, 244, 310, 457
Egar, Colin 193, 197–8
Elliott, Charlie 92
Emburey, John 232, 332
Emmett, Tom 446
Engel, Matthew 437
England and Wales Cricket Board
    (ECB) 34, 146, 441, 490
Eton v Harrow **374–81**
Evans, David 234
Evans, Godfrey 220, 224, 291

Evening News 454
Evening Standard 499
Ezeike (reggae artist) 107

Fagg, Arthur 211, 212, 217, 388
Farnes, Ken 211
Favell, Les 178
Fearnley, Duncan 251
Fender, Percy 15, 19, 45, 75, 447
Ferguson, W.H. 45–6
Figgis, Bob 187
Fingleton, F.H. 465
Fingleton, Jack 16, 21, 51–2, 79, 210, 214, 215, 216
Finn, Steven 136
First World War 13, 60, 262, 264, 270, 362
Fishlock, L.B. 473
Fletcher, Duncan 147
Fletcher, Keith 189, 201, 315
Flintoff, Andrew 163, 440
Flower, Andy **145–53**
Foord, Bill 286–7
Foster, F.R. 45, 46, 460
Foster, H.K. 460
Fowler, Graeme 160
Fowler, R. St L. 377
France 5
Francis, George 385
Fraser, Angus 437
Fredericks, Roy 104, 106, 110, 112, 113
Freeman, Alfred 'Tich' 75, 262, 457
Frindall, Bill 439, 496
Frith, David 320
Fry, C.B. 456

Gaekwad, Datta 291, 292, 293
Gandah, John 276
Gandhi, Mahatma 11
Ganguly, Sourav 172
Gardiner, Arthur 270
Garner, Joel 253, 259, 312
Gatting, Mike 40, 171, 223, 224, 230
Gavaskar, Sunil 140, 166, 167, 331, 333
Gentlemen vs Players 103, 361–2,
    364, 445, 446, 447, 461
Gibbs, Herschel 36
Gibson, Alan 434, 439
Giffen, George 159, 160
Gilani, Yousuf Raza 127
Gilchrist, Adam 172
Giles, Ashley 162
Gillespie, Jason 172
Gilliatt, Richard 100, 310
Gilligan, A.E.R. 384
Gleneagles Agreement (1977) 39, 97, 368
Goddard, John 366
Goddard, Trevor 299
Gooch, Graham 157, 170, 230, 257–8, 315,
    332, 336, 340, 341, 342, 384
Gopinath, Coimbatarao 291
Gover, Alf 91, 243, 244, 473
Gower, David 223, 225, 250, 258, 315, 332, 342, 384
Grace, E.M. 362
Grace, W.G. 71, 157, 264, 362, 445, 446, 457
Graveney, Tom 91, 291, 295
Green, Benny 441
Greenidge, Gordon 108–12, 259, 384
Gregory, Syd 159, 461, 473
Greig, J.G. 10
Greig, Tony 29, 30, 32, 33, 197, 242, 316, 384, 489
    concerns over his captaincy 97–8
    summer of 1976 at the Oval 95, 96–8,
        106–7, 110, 112, 114–15
    and WSC 99–103, 252
Griffith, Billy 26
Griffith, Charlie 193
Griffith, S.C. 85
Griffiths, Laurence 372
Grimmett, Clarrie 190, 208, 209,
    210, 212, 306, 458, 464
Grout, Wally 166, 178, 180–3, 467

The Guardian 100, 148–9, 435, 437
Gunn, George 383, 388
Gupta, Pankaj 294
Guyana 6

Hadlee, Richard 140, 247, 259–60, 335
Haigh, S. 460, 463
Hain, Peter 28
Hair, Darrell 164
Hall, Wes 82, 159, 165, 166, 175, 177,
    178, 180, 182, 193, 196
Hallam, Maurice 241, 243, 325
Hammond, Walter 'Wally' 16, 71, 209, 210, 212,
    214, 215, 318, 363, 388, 456, 458, 464
    and Bodyline series 45, 47, 49, 51
Hampshire, John 201, 312
Hardstaff, Joe 74, 209, 213, 214
Harford, Noel 194
Harmison, Steve 163
Harris, Chris 153
Harris, Lord 77
Hartigan, Roger 49, 63
Harvey, Neil 176, 196, 468
Harwood, George 87
Hassett, Lindsay 187
Hawke, Lord 60, 77, 265, 290, 446
Hawkins, Ed 127
Hayden, Matthew 162, 172, **350–7**
Hayes, Ernie 451
Haynes, Desmond 343
Hayward, Tom 444
Hazare, Vijay 290–1, 294, 295, 472
Healey, Denis 278–9
Hearne, Bill 388
Hedges, L.P. 206
Hendren, Patsy 71, 75, 383, 460
Hendrick, Mike 332, 333
Hendriks, Jackie 182
Henley, H.J. 'Bertie' 451–2
Higgs, Ken 28, 92, 249–50, 254
Hill, Alan 259, 301–2, 461
Hirst, George 270, 277, 460, 463
Hobbs, Jack 15, 16, 49, **265–7**, 388,
    456, 457, 460, 464, 468
Hogg, Rodney 161, 229, 311
Hogg, Vince 151
Hoggard, Matthew 162, 163
Holder, John 106, 109, 112, 113, 345
Holding, Michael 31, 32, 157, 366
    summer 1976 at the Oval **104–15**
Holmes, Percy 383
Hookes, David 30–1, 109, 160
Hopwood, (1929) 207
Hornby, A.N. 446
Hoshang Amroliwala 476
Hotson, J.H. 47
Hough, Nigel 147, 148, 152
Howard, Nigel 296
Hudson, Andrew 168
Hudson, Robert 439
Hughes, Kim 160, 170, 219, 221, 226, 234
Hughes, Simon **346–9**
Hunt, Albert 103
Hunt, Bill 191
Hunte, Conrad 159, 166, 183, 289
Hussain, Nasser 36, 147, 228
Hutchings, K.L. 460
Hutton, Len 161, 194, 199, 287, 290–6, 300, 365
Hutton, Richard 328
Hyndman, Henry 446

Iddon, Jack 207
Ikin, Jack 467
Illingworth, Ray
    and Atherton affair 124, 126
    captaincy 97, 126, 185, 187, 188, 190, 194, 195,
        196, 197, 199, 202, 203, 325, 327, 332
    as chairman of selectors 120–1, 123
    League cricket 388
    professionalism of 242–6, 249

Illingworth, Richard 341
Imperial Cricket Conferences 50, 367–8
The Independent 437
India 5, 6, 98
    1946 Test match at the Oval **472–5**
    1952 Test match at Headingley **290–4**
    Bombay Quadrangular tournaments (1912-1919) 11
    British in 8–10
    earliest record of cricket in 9–10
    evolution of cricket in 367
    granted test status 12
    great Test matches 158, 166–8, 171–3
    Hindu Gymkhana Club 11
    Indian Premier League 372
    Pakistan prime minister's attendance at
        Indo-Pakistan match **418–26**
    Presidency Matches (1906 & 1907) 11
    Pune Cricket Club 10
    Tendulkar as player for 139–43
    World Cup match-fixing (2011) **127–38**
Innes, Gerald 83
Insole, Doug 26, 27, 93, 103, 300
International Cricket Conference 96, 99, 368
International Cricket Council (ICC) 29, 30, 37, 38,
    42, 102, 121, 123, 124, 125, 151, 157, 490
Inverarity, John 26
Inzamam-ul-Haq 36
Iqbal, Asif 100
Iredale, Frank 159
Isaac, Wilfred 384

Jackman, Robin 244
Jackson, Archie 45, 71, 463
Jackson, John 444
Jackson, Stanley 60
Jacques, A. 70
Jacques, Phil 356
Jadeja, Ajay 141, 142
Jahan 484, 485
Jardine, Douglas Robert 41, 209, 361, 455–6
    as all-round sportsman 14
    and Bodyline series 18–19, 20, 21, 23, 42, 44,
        45–7, 54–5, 56, 57, 60–1, 69, 70, 362–3
    business interests 75, 78–9
    cricketing career 14–17
    disliked by Australians 16
    education 13–14
    emigrates to Australia 79
    illness and death 79–80
    as journalist and radio commentator 73, 77
    marriage, family and social life 73, 77–8
    post-War career 75–7
    wartime experiences 73–5
Jardine, Euan 78
Jardine, Fianach 78
Jardine, Malcolm 13, 76
Jardine, Margaret 75, 78
Jardine, Marion 78, 79
Jarman, Barry 26
Jeanes, Bill 466
Jenkins, Roly 294
Jenner, Terry 190, 193, 194, 195, 199, 200
Jepson, Arthur 347
Jessop, Gilbert 460
Johnson, Ian 304
Johnston, Brian 187, 242, 343, 438–9, 496–8
Johnston, Edna 275
Jones, A.O. 460
Jones, Dean 166–7
Jones, Geraint 146, 162, 163
Jones, Simon 163

Kabul Daily 482
Kalachowki, Shobhan 131
Kane, Ellen 306
Kaneria, Danish 39
Kanhai, Rohan 179, 183
Kashmir 8
Kasprowicz, Michael 161–2, 163, 172
Katich, Simon 356

Kay, John 82, 85, 86, 87, 91
Keegan, William 303
Kenyon, Don 27
Khan, Imran 100, 102, 259, 367
Khan, Jehangir 383
Khwazak, Alauddin 479
Khwazak, Zarmina 479–82
Kilner, Roy 383, 462
King, Collis 106, 108, 112
King Commission of Inquiry 36, 116
King, Judge 34
King, Sir Mervyn 370
Kippax, Alan 42–3
Kirsten, Peter 168
Kitchen, Merv 345
Kline, Lindsay 165, 166, 178, 183–4, 467
Knight, Barry 28
Knight, Roger 139, 315
Knott, Alan 32, 97, 99, 191, 192, 200, 202, 203,252
    summer 1976 at the Oval 108, 109, 112, 113
Kortright, Charles 70
Krishnan, Murali 128
Kumble, Anil 142
Kwik Cricket 369–70

Labrooy, Graeme 5
Ladbrokes 220–1, 223, 224, 225, 227
Laker, Jim 242, 291, 292, **299–307**, 385, 388
Lamb, Allan 126, 159, 160, 247
Lamb, Christina 148
Lamb, Clive 247
Lamb, Tim 146
Lambert, Clayton 343
Lancashire League 388
Langer, Justin 164, **350–7**
Lara, Brian 168
Larkins, Wayne 258
Larwood, Frank 248–9
Larwood, Harold 18, 19, 20, 21, 23, 41,
    72, 79, 209, 363, 456
    and Bodyline series 44–8, 50, **54–61**, 70, 71
Lawrence, David 'Syd' 343
Lawry, Bill 187, 191, 197
Laws of Cricket 12, 41–2, 50, 52, 64,
    100, 123, 187, 433, 456
Lawson, Geoff 222, 234
Laxman, V.V.S. 172
Le Roux, Garth 259
Lee, Brett 163
leg theory *see* Bodyline series
Leicestershire County Cricket Club 241
Lennox, Gordon 377
Lever, John 98, 332, 336
Lever, Peter 190, 191, 192, 194, 198, 201, 202
Leveson-Gower, H.D.G. 383
Lewisham, Viscount 60
Leyland, Maurice 209, 210, 213–17, 270, 458–9
Liberation Tigers of Tamil Eelam (LTTE) 8
Lillee, Dennis 95, 97, 114, 170, 171, 189, 194,
    196, 200, 201, 202, **219–28**, 302, 311, 331
Lillywhite, John 445
Lindwall, Ray 76, 194, 196
Llewellyn, Charlie 388
Lloyd, Clive 24, 31, 32, 98, 246, 366, 497
    summer 1976 at the Oval 107, 109, 110, 112,
    113, 114
Lock, Tony 194, 295, **299–307**, 325–6
Lockwood, Bill 70
Lohman, George 299
London Evening News 435
London Evening Post 432–3
Lord, Mr and Mrs 87–8
Loxton, Sam 196
Luckhurst, Brian 188, 200–1
Lush, Peter 340
Lynch, Ernest 198
Lynch, Monte 244
Lyon, N.H. 206
Lyons, Joseph 23

Macartney, Charlie 383, 457, 464, 468
Macaulay, George 270
McCabe, Stanley 20, 51, 209, 210, 214, 215, 217, 458
McCormick, Ernie 210, 211–12
McDermott, Craig 164
McDonald, Colin 176, 177, 193, 304
McErlane, David 194
McGilvray, Alan 165
McGrath, Glenn 162, 172
McHugh, F. 287
McInnes, Mel 467
McIntyre, Arthur 244
Mackay (1960) 178
McKenzie, Garth 193
Maclean, Fitzroy 275
McMahon, John 243
Maddocks, Len 305
Madhavan, K. 141
Mahomed, Gul 473
Mailey, Arthur 79, 455
Majeed, Mazhar 38–9
Major, John 442, 495
Malad, Jayanti (*real name* Jayanti Shah) 131–2
Malik, Salim 35
Malinga, Lasith 373
Manchester Evening News 82
Manchester Guardian 374, 453–4
Mandela, Nelson 40
Manjrekar, Vijay 291, 292, 293, 295
Mankad, Vinoo 294–5
Mannion, Wilf 272
Mantri, Madhav 291–2
Marks, Vic 439, 496
Marsh, Geoff 151
Marsh, Rodney 160, 161, 170, 171,
    191–2, 203, **219–28**, 234, 329
Marshall, Howard 496
Marshall, Malcolm 259, 343
Martin-Jenkins, Christopher 377, 437, 439, **492–9**
Martindale, Manny 49, 71, 388
Mason, Alan 287
Mason, James 270–1
Mathews, Angelo 5
Matthews, Greg 167–8
Matthews, T.J. 454
Maxwell, Jim 163, 173
May, Norman 198
May, Peter 27, 303, 315
May, Tim 164, 165
MCC (Marylebone Cricket Club) 19, 22, 24,
    25, 26, 28, 41, 42, 43, 48, 49, 50, 57–60,
    62–72, 77, 93, 100, 169, 205, 266, 286,
    306, 317, 362, 364, 401, 443, 445, 470
Mead (of Essex) 460
Meckiff, Ian 34, 166, 178, 180, 182–4, 467
media coverage 28–9, 32, 33, 99, 103, 125, 139,
    159, 165, 175, 193, 198, 241–2, **486–91**
    newspapers and journals 20, 27, 35, 38, 43,
    46, 47, 73, 76, 77, 91, 100, 102, 103,
    107, 148–9, 175, 195, 211, 219, 221,
    222, 225, 226, 303, 305, 374, 432–3, 435,
    437, 449, 453–4, 482, 487, 494, 499
    radio 116, 139, 159, 163, 165, 173, 437–8, 495, 496
    television 28–9, 32, 99, 103, 125, 159,
    193, 198, 241–2, 437, 487, 488
    see also Test Match Special
Meman, Babu 151
Menzies, Robert 79
Merchant, V.M. 208, 473, 474
Metropolitan Police 34
Middleton Cricket Club 24, 82, 91
Milburn, Colin 26, 93
Miller, Geoff 108, 109, 113, 160, 161, 332
Miller, Keith 76, 186, 196, 263, 304, 307, 409
Mitchell, Arthur 'Ticker' 284, 388
Mitchell, Tommy 61
Monckton, Lord 317–18
Mongia, Nayan 141
Moorhouse, Geoffrey 374, 441
More, Kiran 167

Morgan, David 146–7
Morning Post 43
Morris, John 258
Mosey, Don 439
Mossop, Brian 225, 226
Motwani, Keshavehand **418–26**
Moyes, Johnny 466
Mudge, Harold 210
Mugabe, Robert 40, 149
Muralitharan, Muttiah 373
Murari, Timeri N. 476
Murphy, Pat 90
Murray, David 106, 111, 113, 164
Murray, John 328
Mushtaq Ahmed 36
Mushtaq Ali 74, 474
Mushtaq Mohammad 384
Mynn, Alfred 448

Napier, Graham 373
Nawaz, Sarfraz 247
Nayudu, C.S. 473
Neale, Phil 94
Nelson, Trevor 107
New Society journal 103
New Zealand 5, 12, 30, 140–3, 194, 242
    amateur-professional distinction 366
    great Test matches 158
    match played at Antarctica 391–4
News Chronicle 435, 455
News of the World 27, 38
Nissar, Mohammad 474
Noble, M.A. 49, 63, 461
Ntini, Makhaya 355

Oborne, Peter 93
The Observer 73, 303
O'Connell, Max 187, 188
Odendaal, André 90
offorth, Fred 157
O'Keeffe, Kerry 189, 193, 201
Old, Chris 171, 232, 233, 235, 332, 335
Oldfield, Bert 22, 54–7, 62, 79, 212, 217
Oldroyd, Edgar 270
Olonga, Henry **145–53**
One State Cricket Association 49
O'Neill, Norm 165, 176, 177, 468
O'Reilly, Bill 56, 190, 194, 209, 210,
    212, 213, 215, 216, 458, 464
Orwell, George 267
Oscroft, William 446
Oxford University 14, 15
Oxford University Cricket Club 77

Packer, Kerry 28–33, 99–103, 251–2,
    306, 331, 333, 335, 488–9
Padgett, George 287
Pai, M.D. 11
Pakistan 5, 6, 8, 35, 38–9, 91, 99, 333, 335
    amateur-professional distinctions 367
    great Test matches 158
    prime minister's attendance at Indo-
        Pakistan match **418–26**
    World Cup match-fixing (2011) **127–38**
Pakistan Board of Control 101–2
Pakistan Cricket Board 35
Pall Mall Gazette 487
Palmer, G. 383
Pandit, Chandra 167
Panesar, Monty 431–2
Pardon Reporting Agency 449
Pardon, Sydney 449–50
Parr, Frank 297
Parr, George 444, 445, 446
Parsons, Gordon 116, 117, 261, 261–2
Parwaaze 476, 477, 478, 480–1, 484, 485
Pascoe, Len 311
Patel, Parthiv 136
Patterson, Patrick 343, 345
Paynter, Eddie 209

Pearce, Cyril 270
Pearce, T.N. 383–4
Peat, Sir Harry 78
Peebles, Ian 78
Peel, Bobby 160, 299, 463
Perry, Bob 297
Phadkar, Dattu 294
Philpott, Peter 222
Pietersen, Kevin 145, 162, 440
Pocock, Pat 319
Pollard, Ron 220–1, 224
Pollock, Bill 454–5
Pollock, Peter 194
Ponsford, Bill 22, 209, 214, 456, 457, 458
Ponting, Ricky 162, 354, 355
Porbandar, Maharaja of 320
Postman 442
Pothecary, Jim 83
Prabhakar, Manoj 141
press-box **449–59**, 467
Preston, Norman 111
Prideaux, Roger 26, 92
Pringle, Derek 437
Procter, Mike 30, 40, 100, 186, 312, 328
Professional Cricketers' Association (PCA) 33, 251, 252
professional players **240–63**
    breakthroughs 253–4
    and the car list 250
    coaching young players 243–6
    discussions on aims and targets 250–1
    disparate background and character of 255–62
    dressing room distinctions 361
    each player as unique 254
    early appearances 246–8
    family backgrounds 255
    lucky breaks 240–1
    and the Packer Circus 251–2
    and picking up kit 251
    and Players' meetings 249–51
    and pre-season training 249
    as role models and heroes 241–3
    role of opening batsmen 242
    salary 447–8
    sponsorship 248–9
    and winter employment 248
    see also amateur players
Pullin, A.W. 'Old Ebor' 451

Qasim, Iqbal 333, 335
Qayyum, Justice Malik 35, 36
Quaife, Willie 457
Qubad 477, 483, 484

Radcliffe, Robert 91
Rain Men 390, 405
Ramadhin, Sonny 178, 388
Ramchand, Gulabrai 295
Randall, Derek 247, 311, 332
Ranjitsinhji, Kumar Shri 11–12, 456, 457
Rashid, Haroon 336
Rawlings, Terry 372
Read, Denis 496
Reddick, Tom 84, 85
Redpath, Ian 187, 190, 192, 201, 203
Reynolds, Gillian 496
Rhodes, Wilfred 277, 460, 461
Rhodesia 7, 91
Rice, Clive 247, 259, 384
Richards, Barry 384
Richards, Viv 168, 253, 259, 260, 261, 262, 331–2, 366
    summer 1976 at the Oval 106, 112, 113
    Tufnell's reaction to 343–5
    World Series Cricket 31, 32
Richardson, Peter 302
Richardson, Richie 168, 169
Richardson, Tom 159
Richardson, Victor 20, 49, 51, 63, 70, 191
Roberts, Andy 260, 366
    summer 1976 at the Oval 105–9, 111, 113–15
    and World Series Cricket 31, 32

Roberts, Ron 91
Robertson, Austin 489
Robertson-Glasgow, R.C. 270, 297, 449, 453
Robins, D.H. 384
Robins, R.V.C. 317
Robins, R.W.V. 210, 215
Robins, Walter 211, 213, 214
Robinson, L. 384
Robinson, Ray 210
Roope, Graham 244
Root, Fred 43, 70
Roux, Pieter le 25
Rowan, Lou 187, 188, 194, 195, 197, 198, 200
Rowe, Lawrence 110, 111
Roy, Pankaj 291, 295, 296
Royan 477, 483
Russ, Rodney 395, 396
Russell, Jack 310
Ryder, David 220
Ryder, Jack 15

Salisbury, Ian 124
Sandham, Andy 75
Sarwate, Chandu 473, 474–5
Sassoon, Siegfried 275
Scannell, Vernon 274
Scott, Captain R.F. 373, 394–5
Second World War 243, 262, 264,
    268–76, 278–9, 364, 368
Selvey, Mike 108, 109, 110, 112, 114, 496
Sen, Khokhan 295
Shah, Hafez Ali **418–26**
Sharma, Chetan 167
Shastri, Ravi 167
Shaw, Alfred 446
Shaw, Arnold 268–9
Shaw, Douglas 269
Shaw, Jemmy 444
Shaw, Wilfred 269
Sheppard, David 27
Sherwin, Mordecai 446
shop cricket **411–17**
Shuttleworth, Ken 246, 247
Sievers, Morris 213, 216
Sillitoe, Warren 107
Simkins, Michael **411–17**
Simmons, Phil 116
Simpson, Bobby 31–2, 32, 175, 193
Simpson, Reg 294
Singh, Harbhajan 172
Singh, Maninder 167–8
Singh, Manmohan 127
Skinner, Lonsdale 246
Slade, Justice 30
Slater, Michael 172
slave trade 5–6
Slocombe, Phil 261
Smailes, Frank 270
Smith, Ian 7
Smith, M.J.K. 317
Smith, Neil 287
Smith, Robin 339, 343, 348
Smith, W.C. 460
Snow, John 30, 32, 99, 100, 242, 252
    Sydney Test (1971) **184–204**
Sobers, Garfield 6, 91, 165, 176, 179, 180, 193, 319, 366
Solkar, Eknath 242
Solomon, Joe 165, 166, 179, 180–1, 184
South Africa 269, 368
    apartheid in 7, 24, 40, 92–3
    British in 6–7
    corruption and scandal 35–7
    and D'Oliveira 25–6, 27, 83–8, 92–4
    Dutch connection 5, 6–7
    great Test matches 158, 168–9
    sporting isolation 28
South African Cricket Association (SACA) 7
South African Cricket Union 40
Sparling, John 194
Spofforth, Fred 70

Sporting Life 445
Sporting Times 487
Springboks 28
Sri Lanka 35, 373
    and the British Empire 7–8
    Burgher people 5
    Dutch connection 5
    great Test matches 158
    Test Cricketers in 5
Srikkanth, Kris 167
Stackpole, Keith 185, 187, 190, 191, 201, 202–3, 303
Stanford, Allen 490
Star newspaper 77
Steele, David 97, 98, 104, 112, 113, 247, 255, 256, 319
Steele, John 259
Stephenson, Franklyn 312
Stephenson, H.H. 444
Stevens, G.T.S. 206
Stevenson, Graham 336
Stewart, Alec 254
Stewart, Micky 339, 340
Stewart, 'Shaky' 275–6
Stoddart, Andrew 160
Stott, Brian 293–4
Strauss, Andrew 162, 432
Sun newspaper (Australia) 225
Sun newspaper (London) 219, 221, 225
Sunday Express 195
Sunday League 34
Sunday Times 449
Surrey County Cricket Club 451
Sutcliffe, Herbert 16, 75, 77, 209,
    269, 277, 365, 383, 455
Swann, Graeme 304
Swanton, E.W. 'Jim' 321, 377, 439
Sydney Morning Herald 211, 225, 226
Sydney Sun 20, 102

Tait, Alan 333
Taliban **476–86**
Tamil Union Cricket Club (Colombo) 373
Tarrant, George 71, 444, 460
Tasmania 16
Tate, Maurice 75, 455
Tattersall, Roy 297
Tavaré, Chris 160, 161
Taylor, Bob 160, 223, 224, 231, 232, 233, 332
Taylor, Ken 242–3
Taylor, Les 249, 250, 251
Tendulkar, Sachin **139–43**, 172
Terry, Paul 159
Test and County Cricket Board (TCCB) 30,
    33, 34, 97, 98, 100, 101, 102, 123
Test Match Special (radio programme) 116, 139, 159,
    163, 173, 222, 289, 370–1, 435, 439, **492–9**
Test Matches 7, 11, 320
    1928–9 series 15–17
    1930 series 18, 44
    1932–3 Bodyline series 18–24, **42–72**
    1934 series 23–4
    1936 in Melbourne **209–18**
    1938 (Oval) 464
    1946 (Oval) **472–5**
    1948–9 series 466–7
    1952 (Headingley and Lord's) **290–8**
    1956 (Old Trafford) 299, 302–7
    1960 (tied Test in Brisbane) **175–84**
    1960 (West Indies) 366
    1963 (Lord's) 289
    1968 series 26–8
    1971 (Sydney) **184–204**
    1975 series 96–7
    1976 series 95, 96–8, **104–15**, 255, 319
    1978 series 333, 335
    1979 series 331, 333
    1980 Centenary match 435–6
    1981 (Headingley '81) 169–71, **219–28**, **229–36**
    1991 (Oval) **341–5**
    1994 series **120–6**
    1998–9 series 35

2005 series 173
2010 series 38
2011 series 171–3
Centenary match 98–9
classic matches **156–73**
media coverage 487
and WSC 28–33, 99–103
Thomas, Bernard 202, 223, 231
Thomas, David 244
Thomas, J.H. 23
Thompson, Harry 390
Thomson, Alan 186, 187, 188
Thomson, Jeff 32, 95, 97, 114, 161, 302
Thornton, C.I. 383
Thorogood, Frank 455
tied Test (Brisbane, 1960) 17, 165–6, **175–84**
tied Test (Madras, 1986) 166–8
The Times 98, 103, 150, 437, 452
Titmus, Fred 245, 317, 328
Tobago 6
Topley, Don 34
Trescothick, Marcus 162
Trevor, Philip 454
Triangular Tournament (1912) 454
Tribe, Peter 222–3, 225
Trinidad 6
Trott, Albert 412
Trueman, Fred 159, 194, 243, **281–8**,
301, 362, 439, 496
1952 season **289–98**
Trumper, 457, 461, 464, 468
Tufnell, Phil **338–45**, 439
Turner, Charlie 299
Turner, Cyril 284
Turner, Mike 241, 245, 247, 260, 261
'TV: Make it Australian' campaign 28
Twenty20 489–90
Tyson, Frank 198, 248, 256

Umpires Association 77
Umrigar, Polly 291, 292, 295
Underwood, Derek 26, 32, 99, 107, 108, 113,
192, 193, 194, 203, 252, 319, 334
United South of England Eleven 445

Valentine, Alf 179, 182
Van der Merwe, Peter 83
Vandort, Michael 5
Vaughan, Michael 439
Venkataraghavan, Srini 332
Verity, Hedley 47, 77, 209, 214, 215,
217, 264, **268–80**, 299, 457
Vettori, Daniel 499
Viljeon, K.G. 288
Villiers, Fanie de 126
Vinay (Indian bookmaker) **127–38**
Vincent, Dacre 453
Vincent, R.B. 'Beau' 452–3, 459
Voce, Bill 19, 23, 24, 45, 57, 209, 211,
214, 215, 217, 218, 363, 467
Vockins, Mike 94
Vorster, John 26, 27, 83, 92–4

Wadekar, Ajit 141
Walcott, Clyde 110, 366, 385, 396
Wall, Tim 209
Walsh, Courtney 164, 345
Walters, Doug 188, 192, 468
Ward, Alan 195, 246, 248
Ward, Albert 160, 210
Ward, Frank 213, 215
Wardle, Johnny 287, 299
Warfield, Captain 296

Warne, Shane 35, 163, 165, 262
Warner, Pelham 'Plum' 14, 20, 22,
43, 50, 61, 363, 450, 460
Washbrook, Cyril 91
Watkins, Allan 291
Waugh, Mark 35
Waugh, Steve 143, 172
Weekes, Everton 6, 196, 208, 366, 385, 396
Weigall, Mr 72
Wellham, Dirk 221, 226
Wessels, Kepler 168
West Australian newspaper 227
West Indies 5, 6, 15, 25, 31, 71, 92, 93,
206, 207, 255, 315, 388
1991 at the Oval **341–5**
amateur-professional distinction 366–7
attitude to captaincy 318
great Test matches 158, 159, 164–5, 168–9
Summer 1976 at the Oval **105–15**
tied Test in Brisbane (1960) **175–84**
West, Peter 114
Westcott, Dick 83
Westfield, Mervyn 39
Wheatley, Ossie 123
Whitaker, James 255
Whitehead, John 286–7
Whiting, Steve 225
Whitticase, Phil 254
Willey, Peter 106, 171, 255, 311, 337
Williams, Henry 36
Willis, Bob 98, 109, 110, 113, 161, 170–1,
186, 191, 192, 193, 194, 197, 198, 200,
201, **229–36**, 315, 328, 332, 336–7
Willsher, Ned 445
Wilson, Don 313
Wilson, F.B. 'Freddy' 450
Winchester College 13–14
Wisden 15, 23, 25, 49, 52, 59, 75, 90, 93, 98, 101,
111, 205, 286, 313, 326, 445, 449, 464, 465
Wood, Arthur 270
Wood, Graeme 226, 231
Woodcock, John 98, 103
Woodfull, W.M. 'Bill' 20, 21–2, 23–4, 49,
54, 56, 62, 63, 70, 209, 456
Woolley, Frank 75, 363, 388, 456, 459, 460
Woolmer, Bob 32, 37, 99, 104, 111, 252
Worcestershire County Cricket Club 25
World Series Cricket (WSC) 28–33, 39–40,
99–103, 251–2, 306, 368, 488–9
World Sports Magazine 82
Worrell, Frank 6, 90, 164, 178, 179–80,
208, 318, 366, 385
Worthington, (1936) 212, 214
Wran, Neville 33
Wright, Cec 388–9
Wright, Doug 288
writing about cricket **430–41**
Wyatt, Bob 20, 23, 209
Wynne-Thomas, Peter 443

Yadav, Shivlal 167
Yallop, Graham 32, 33, 226, 234, 314, 315
Yardley, Bruce 161
Yardley, Norman 270, 286, 297, 439, 496
Yorkshire County Cricket Club 272, 279
Yorkshire Evening Post 290, 293, 294
Younis, Waqar 36, 114

Zimbabwe 5, 7, 40, 143, **145–53**, 255
great Test matches 158
MDC (Movement for Democratic Change) 147
Zimbabwe Cricket Union 151
Zoroastrian Cricket Club 10